593396

D1327664

THE WORLDWIDE HISTORY OF DRESS

PATRICIA RIEFF ANAWALT

THE WORLDWIDE HISTORY OF DRESS

WITH OVER 1,000 ILLUSTRATIONS, 900 IN COLOUR

Thames & Hudson

CONTENTS

To my late husband Richard Anawalt,
who so enthusiastically launched me on this adventurous journey

p. 1 Woman's boots, Bhutan: see p. 260.
p. 2 Dress, Ramallah: see detail on p. 59.
p. 3 *Ghaghara* skirts, Kutch: see p. 241.
p. 8 Child's dress, Kutch: see p. 245.
p. 9 (above) Gold-embroidered robe, China: see p. 172.
p. 9 (below) Moche ear ornament, Peru: see p. 452.

Design and maps: Ben Cracknell Studios

First published in the United Kingdom in 2007 by
Thames & Hudson Ltd, 181A High Holborn,
London WC1V 7QX

thamesandhudson.com

Reprinted 2009

© 2007 Patricia Rieff Anawalt

All Rights Reserved. No part of this publication may be
reproduced or transmitted in any form or by any means,
electronic or mechanical, including photocopy, recording or
any other information storage and retrieval system, without
prior permission in writing from the publisher.

British Library Cataloguing-in-Publication Data

A catalogue record for this book is available from the
British Library

ISBN 978-0-500-51363-7

Printed and bound in China by C&C Offset Printing Co., Ltd.

PREFACE

THIS HISTORY OF NON-WESTERN CLOTHING grows out of a lifelong fascination with the world's myriad array of traditional societies. As a youngster, my idea of heaven was God granting that one could live for all of eternity in a series of exotic cultures scattered throughout time and space. As I grew older and realized that I might never be offered that option, I concluded that anthropology was the next best alternative.

As an anthropologist I made the fortuitous decision to become an Aztec ethnohistorian and—to understand better the Aztecs' descendants—an ethnologist working in the back-country of central Mexico. The focus of my investigation was the continuity of prehispanic dress. After reconstructing the Aztec costume repertory, it was revealing to discover how many of those garment styles have continued into the present. This was particularly impressive considering that those survivals weathered Mexico's traumatic 16th-century Spanish Conquest, history's true War of the Worlds: I have learned at first hand that traditional clothing can have a tenacious longevity.

My Mexican years served me well when I set off in search of similarities and differences in the dress of thirty-two global regions. This enquiry into the world's diverse clothing has proven to be as fascinating an undertaking as ever I anticipated in my youth.

INTRODUCTION

I N THE UPPER PALEOLITHIC ERA, some 30,000 to 40,000 years ago, prehistoric man discovered that by manipulating plant stems, he was able to make long, sturdy string. Those cords were used to create crude aprons and hats, the earliest recognizable forms of fiber-based clothing. Since that time, people in all corners of the world, from the Middle East to Eastern Europe, from North America to North Africa, have been using plant fibers and animal materials—bark, cotton, silk, flax, raffia, wool, fur, hide, feathers—to create remarkable garments and body decorations. This book tells the story of the ethnographic clothing that indigenous peoples have been pounding, curing, felting, weaving, sewing, embroidering, appliquéing, beading and dyeing for millennia—and in many areas of our globe those vibrant clothing traditions continue to this day.

Since the history of the world is one of constant migration and exchange, it is no surprise that influences can be traced from culture to culture. This book provides historical backgrounds for each region, including the mix of population, often noting the ways in which invaders, settlers and traders have left their mark on dress and various forms of decoration. To elucidate the historical progression, every chapter is prefaced by a schematic map that documents the population spread into a geographic area. Additional maps appear for each region, showing the various places and peoples mentioned in that particular section.

Details are also given for each region's terrain and climate to facilitate an understanding of the development of that area's clothing customs. From the dusty arid conditions of the Arabian Peninsula, through the grasslands of the Mongolian steppes and American plains, from the frozen wastes of the Arctic to the tropical rainforests of Amazonia, humans have found ingenious ways of fabricating clothing to suit the demands of their environment.

Religious, spiritual and cultural customs—whether Islamic veiling, the donning of shamanic ritual dress replete with animal symbolism, or the wearing of items appropriate to a given life-stage—are also covered, showing how apparel has long been intrinsic to each particular way of life.

Whether Ancient Egyptian linen shifts, Roman woolen togas, Japanese silk kimonos, colorful Indian saris, embroidered European dirndls, African ceremonial cloths or Middle Eastern burqas, a vast and truly astonishing array of clothing has been envisioned, created and worn, all reflected in the varied traditions encompassed in the worldwide history of dress.

ARCTIC

NORTHWEST
COAST

PLAINS

WOODLANDS

SOUTHWEST

MESOAMERICA

AMAZONIA

ANCIENT AND
PRESENT ANDES

PATAGONIA

Map of the world, showing
the areas covered in this book.

EUROPEAN FOLK TRADITION

PREHISTORIC
EUROPE

CLASSICAL
EUROPE

MONGOLIA

EASTERN
MEDITERRANEAN

IRANIAN
PLATEAU

SILK ROAD

KOREA

JAPAN

NORTH AFRICA

ANCIENT
NEAR
EAST

CHINA

ARABIAN
PENINSULA

HIMALAYAN
KINGDOMS

INDIA

WEST AFRICA

MAINLAND
SOUTHEAST
ASIA

EAST
AFRICA

CENTRAL
AFRICA

ISLAND
SOUTHEAST
ASIA

SOUTH
AFRICA

OCEANIA

1

THE MIDDLE EAST

SEVERAL OF MANKIND'S most far-reaching innovations have originated in the Middle East. Some 2,000,000 years ago, the archaic hominid *Homo erectus*—the immediate ancestor of our own species, *Homo sapiens*—first wandered out of Africa along the earth's mightiest geological cleft, the Rift Valley system, which extends through modern-day Egypt, Israel, Jordan, Syria and Lebanon. Some 75,000 years ago modern humans also journeyed from Africa into the Middle East, where, over the millennia, those early hunters and gatherers slowly brought about the domestication of plants and animals. As a result, the population grew, settled down, accumulated surpluses and, ca. 3000 B.C., the world's earliest civilizations began. A millennium later the Old Testament patriarch Abraham conceived a simple but profound idea: the existence of a single, almighty God. Out of that powerful concept have grown three great monotheistic religions—Judaism, Christianity and Islam—all born in the dry, harsh, transforming lands of the Middle East.

THE ANCIENT NEAR EAST

1 It is now believed that only six primary "hearths of civilization"—areas in which combinations of sophisticated technological innovations and social institutions flourished—have occurred relatively independently on our planet. Two of these were in the Ancient Near East, in Mesopotamia and Egypt; two further to the east, in the Indus Valley and China; and two in the Americas, Mesoamerica and the Andes. For the subsequent cultures of the Western European world, the Ancient Near East represents a direct heritage, just as descendants of the other four hearths reflect aspects of their own earliest beginnings, each of which will be examined in turn in this book.

The Ancient Near East has long played a pivotal role in mankind's development. When *Homo erectus* first moved out of Africa and through the Middle East, he probably followed the Israel–Jordan Valley that runs inland from the eastern Mediterranean seaboard. This so-called Levantine Corridor was one of the great highways of human prehistory.[1]

The African hominids may have been following big game; their larger bodies would have needed a ready supply of meat. In addition to knowledge of hunting and the production of rudimentary Oldowan chipped stone tools, by 500,000 B.C. these early wanderers may well have known how to use fire.[2] If so, when a sub-species of *Homo erectus* began to evolve into the archaic *Homo sapiens*—with a slightly larger and more complex brain than its forebear—this new hominid did so with an enormous achievement already in its grasp. Modern *Homo sapiens* appeared around 100,000 B.C. and subsisted in the Middle East for millennia as hunters and gatherers before developing new patterns of subsistence.

By 9000 B.C., the Neolithic—New Stone Age—had evolved in the Fertile Crescent, a particularly productive region extending from Palestine through Syria (an area known as the Levant) and into Mesopotamia [Map 1]. Greater Mesopotamia—the latter the Greek word for "between the rivers"—was bounded by the Tigris and Euphrates rivers, and their drainages, and extended some 700 miles (1,125 km) north from the Gulf. During the Neolithic, technological innovations developed in this region that were to bring about fundamental change: the invention of stone tools with ground rather than chipped edges; the start of permanent open-air villages instead of seasonal caves and camps; and the discovery of how to domesticate plants and animals for a readier supply of food and fibers. Accordingly, the population steadily grew.

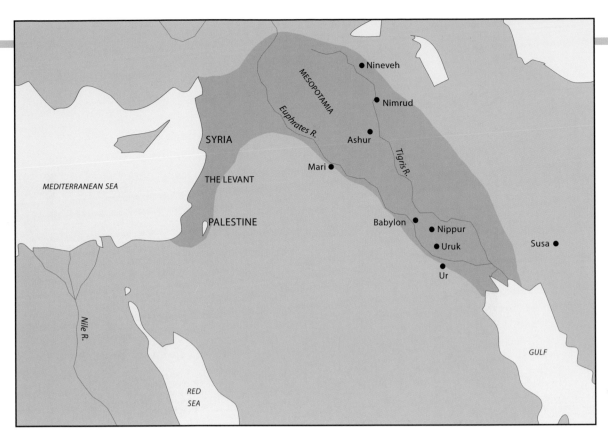

Map 1 The Fertile Crescent and Ancient Mesopotamia. The earliest civilizations appeared more than 5,000 years ago in this region, a succession of rich, arable plains that extended in a broad arc from Palestine in the west to the Tigris and Euphrates rivers in the east.

By the 3rd millennium B.C. the rise of competing city-states had occurred in lower Mesopotamia. This southern end of the Fertile Crescent had been increasingly studded with farming villages during the Neolithic. The development of irrigation and the reclamation of marshy delta lands where the two rivers merge and empty into the Gulf indicate an increasingly complex social organization that led to true urbanization in the kingdom of Sumer, the ancient name for southern Mesopotamia. It was in this heartland of cities that the first Near Eastern civilization emerged, ca. 3000 B.C.

One of the greatest achievements of Sumerian civilization was the invention of writing, an innovation that began with the use of impressions made on clay to record receipts and memoranda for lists of goods. Although the initial purpose was economic, this system slowly evolved into cuneiform writing, which could represent sounds rather than just objects. Now it was possible to store legal records, historical accounts and literary compositions. Two of the most important of Sumer's city-states are associated with this written cultural repository: Uruk, home of the legendary Gilgamesh Epic—the world's oldest story, which has survived more than 5,000 years—and Ur, the traditional home of the biblical patriarch Abraham.[3]

In the flat, flood-prone plains of Sumer, the gods dwelt in "high places"—man-made, elevated temples—and each city's populace envisioned itself as created to labor for its pantheon of deities, who personified the elements and natural forces. Even the rulers were considered servants of the gods. These deities were organized into a hierarchy that both affected and reflected the Mesopotamians' view of human society. This was the backbone of Mesopotamian religion and the beginning of recorded human theology.[4] Among the by-products of Sumerian religion were its attendant artistic expressions, which produced the first true likenesses of humans depicted in ritual acts, martial activities and genre scenes—all useful sources of clothing information.

Mesopotamia was not, however, the only great river valley to cradle an early civilization. Ancient Egypt—although developing slightly later—was its rival or superior, both in terms of staying power and as the source of the world's greatest visible inheritance from Antiquity. Because Sumerian civilization appeared first, Egypt benefited from its example, including the acquisition of writing. Hieroglyphics, the life-like picture writing of Egypt, may owe its origins to early Mesopotamian script.

Egypt itself is a narrow, river-fed oasis some 600 miles (965 km) in length and never—except in the

Map 2 Ancient Egypt, ca. 1380 B.C. The apparent reversal of "Upper" and "Lower" Egypt is caused by the terminology's derivation from the flow of the Nile—from East Africa (upstream) to the Mediterranean (downstream).

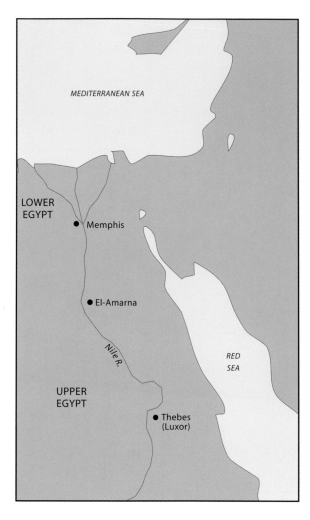

Egyptian historical tradition maintained that in 3100 B.C.—during the predynastic period—Menes, a king of Upper Egypt, conquered the north and unified the country. This was the beginning of a civilization that was to survive into the age of Classical Greece and Rome. For nearly 2,000 years, Ancient Egypt remained a distinct entity with a history that Egyptologists have divided into five phases: the Old, Middle and New Kingdoms, each a period of success or consolidated government, and the intervening First and Second Intermediate periods, interludes of weakness and disruption from external and internal causes.[6]

It was under the Old Kingdom—ca. 2685–2186 B.C.—that the pharaoh came to be viewed as the absolute lord of the land. Visual proof of pharaonic power and self-confidence still exists in the great pyramids at Giza, testaments to an unsurpassed social and administrative concentration of human labor, including slavery. It was also during this period that the artistic canon first developed that was to serve as the model for subsequent Ancient Egyptian art.

By 3000 B.C., both Egypt and Mesopotamia were experiencing a vast increase in trade and travel as the result of a major development that marked the start of the Early Bronze Age: knowledge of how to harden copper into bronze by adding tin. A search to obtain the necessary minerals from ore deposits—often found in mountains located far from urban production centers—was now on. This was true not only in the Ancient Near East but throughout the Eastern Mediterranean and Southeast Europe. The high price of tin restricted its use mainly to weapons: when supplies of tin dried up, sturdy bronze weapons gave way to those made of softer, unalloyed copper.

Egypt's second period of stability was the Middle Kingdom, ca. 2040–1780 B.C. It was during this era that the belief was established that all Egyptians, not just the pharaoh, could anticipate an additional, happy existence after death, a concept quite unlike the Sumerians' gloomy view of the afterlife. The entire Egyptian culture now was given over to the real purpose of living: proper preparation for death.

delta region—more than a few miles in width on either side of the great river that sustains it [Map 2]. The Nile's annual flood was the basic mechanism of the ancient economy, setting the rhythm of life.

Early Egypt was composed of two kingdoms, Upper and Lower Egypt, but—unlike Sumer—neither contained walled city-states. The population lived in the countryside, using little towns and temples as service centers and dwelling places. Although there were a few large cult areas, for the most part the country contained scattered villages and markets.[5]

Memphis and Thebes were the principal religious centers and palace complexes, but they never evolved into true urbanism. Further, the kings never emerged—like the leaders at Sumer—to rule over a city-state that deputized them to act for it. When Egyptian kingship appeared, it was unrivaled: the pharaohs were gods, not servants of the gods.

In about 2000 B.C., a decisive struggle took place in Mesopotamia's Fertile Crescent, one that may have centered on control of the Iranian trade routes which guaranteed access to the highlands, a source of much needed minerals, particularly tin. Sumerian civilization ended with the fall of Ur to the Elamites, a people located east of the lower Tigris River. In other regions of the Near East new groups began migrating into Mesopotamia, hence new lineages began to appear. The Amorites established themselves in Ashur—the first Assyrian stronghold—as well as in other Mesopotamian cities. The Akkadians became part of the new power that now appeared in the land between the rivers: Babylon, the greatest state yet to rise in Mesopotamia. The fall of this empire, ca. 1700 B.C., coincided with another wave of migrants coming into the Ancient Near East, intrusions that resulted in confusing tumult.

During this disruptive period, Egypt also experienced outside intrusions, disorder that led to innovation. In the New Kingdom, 1570–1070 B.C., a transformation in warfaring tactics came about through the adoption—from the Syrian Mitanni—of such military improvements as horse-drawn chariots and long-bow archers. In addition, a huge consolidation of royal pharaonic power now took place. There was also a new richness of artistic achievement. This was particularly true at El-Amarna, the center established in ca. 1350 B.C. by the Pharaoh Amenhotep IV—who soon took the name Akhenaton. He attempted a religious revolution through the substitution of a henotheistic cult of the sun god Aton for the pantheon of Ancient Egyptian deities. The art of the Amarna period conveys a new, relaxed sense of intimacy, particularly within the Pharaoh's family—a quality seldom found elsewhere in the Ancient Near East. However, Akhenaton's innovations were short-lived; following his death the attempted changes quickly faded. Indeed, the whole world that had been the setting for Egypt's prior glories was passing away; Ancient Egypt's greatest days were over by 1000 B.C.

The destructive migrations into the Near East during the 13th and 12th centuries B.C. came from the West—from the so-called Sea People—and created the background for the rise of Assyria, located in northern Mesopotamia. By the 9th century B.C., the Assyrians come fully into view, ushering in a new, important phase of Near Eastern history. This aggressive empire reached its apogee in the 8th century when Nineveh, its capital located high on the Tigris, became the focus of Mesopotamian history, just as Babylon once had been. Assyrian civilization systematically conquered the communities of the Fertile Crescent, as is recorded on many carved wall panels that once decorated palaces in the Assyrian heartland. Despite such displays of power, in about 612 B.C. the Assyrian Empire was finally defeated by a coalition of Babylonians and a new Iranian power, the Medes, whose sack of Nineveh caused Assyria to pass into history.

Babylon—which had been the most important city in southern Mesopotamia in the first two centuries of the 2nd millennium—then had a second moment of splendor. The neo-Babylonian King Nebuchadnezzar gave Mesopotamian civilization an Indian summer of decadent grandeur that has captured the imagination of posterity. The city's "hanging gardens" were also to be remembered as one of the Seven Wonders of the Ancient World.

This was the last flowering of the Mesopotamian tradition. In 539 B.C. Babylon fell, following an invasion by a new power from the east. This incursion was led by a minor Iranian dynasty called the Achaemenids, who would establish the greatest of all early Middle Eastern empires, that of 6th-century Persia (see "The Iranian Plateau," p. 66).

CLOTHING FIBERS AND CONSTRUCTION TECHNIQUES

The origin of fiber use—and of constructed fiber garments—began some twenty to thirty thousand years ago when humans first learned how to create long, strong string from short, weak plant stems. The eminent textile historian Elizabeth W. Barber refers to this landmark event as the String Revolution:[7] once humans had learned how to make sturdy cord they were equipped to catch, to hold and to carry. They could also produce some of the world's earliest garments, which included string skirts (see "Prehistoric Europe," p. 84).

All of the archaeological finds of Upper Paleolithic string and thread have been made of twisted plant fiber. Thread, in turn, was a prerequisite for the construction of woven cloth—that is, the interlacing of two sets of threads, the warp and weft, in which the vertical warp is held taut under tension by some form of loom so that the horizontal weft can be threaded through it.

A wide range of plant fibers have been used throughout the world to produce cloth. In the Middle East, the principal fiber was flax, a plant that likes a hot climate. Domestic flax (*Linum usitatissimum*), which provides the cloth we know as linen, was one of the earliest and most important of the bast fibers—woody plant fibers—used for textiles. Flax may originally have been domesticated for its oil-bearing seeds instead of, or as well as, for its fibrous stems. The most likely of the progenitors of domestic flax is *Linum bienne*, which occurs as a perennial along the Mediterranean and Atlantic coastal areas, and as a winter annual in the foothills of Iran and Iraq-Kurdistan. The earliest definite evidence yet located for the domestication of flax comes from sites in eastern Iraq, ca. 5500 B.C., and in northwestern Iraq, ca. 5000 B.C.,[8] although people had been using flax since at least 6500 B.C., possibly collecting it wild.

To the north—in the cooler climes beyond the Near East—hemp was the more commonly utilized plant fiber, particularly for ropes and nautical gear, because it is impervious to salt water. Cotton was domesticated in northern India before 3000 B.C. but did not move out into the Mediterranean areas until nearly 700 B.C., and only then as a curiosity, hence cotton played no role in Ancient Near Eastern clothing.[9]

The earliest plant-fiber clothing seems to have had nothing to do with either warmth or modesty. Apparently humans first began wearing such garments to indicate a stage of life, particularly the onset of fertility and/or marital status. Not all of these early clothes, however, draw attention to the body's reproductive parts. The earliest evidence for a plant-fiber garment—fragments of which were found in Nahal Hemar Cave, Israel[10]—dates from ca. 6500 B.C. and points to the construction of a non-woven, needle-netted linen bag with stone buttons, thought to have been used as a ceremonial hat. Indeed, hats appear to have been among the first fiber-craft items to be worn (see "Prehistoric Europe," p. 83). Again, the advertising of one's age stage or status appears to have been the purpose.

The first clear proof of woven cloth from Mesopotamia, ca. 7000 B.C., comes from the Neolithic village of Jarmo—located in northeastern Iraq—in the form of two little clay balls that bear textile impressions. This evidence indicates that the original cloths were fine and neatly woven, and in not one but two different weaves. Clearly, the people of Jarmo had been weaving long enough to be highly skilled at it. An actual garment of plain-weave textile, also ca. 7000 B.C., has been found at Çayönü Tepesi in southeast Turkey.[11] (The earliest clear evidence for a vertical, warp-weighted loom—the warp threads held taut by heavy clay weights—dates to the mid-6th millennium B.C. and was found in Hungary.[12])

The arrival of sheep in Mesopotamia around 4000 B.C. heralded the appearance of another fiber vital to the history of clothing in the Near East. The earliest sheep, however, looked not at all like today's fleecy creatures. Sheep were first domesticated in Iran, in an arc extending through the Zagros-Taurus mountains, a region where there was sufficient rainfall to provide sustenance for these grazing animals but their hides were very much like those of present-day deer; there was nothing on their backs that could be spun into thread. Obviously a long breeding process was necessary to arrive at woolly-coated sheep.

To determine the evolution of domesticated woolly sheep, Elizabeth W. Barber studied the archaeological remains of sheep bones to determine the kill patterns of ancient flocks for human use.[13] When sheep were only valued for meat, it was yearlings that were slaughtered; when attaining milk was the object, the bones of older female sheep were found. However, by 4000 B.C. both

2 A statue (front and back), ca. 3000 B.C., of a Sumerian male, Ebih-il, superintendent of the Ishtar temple at Mari, the wealthy city-state located on the Middle Euphrates River in present-day Syria. The steward wears a calf-length skirt composed of multiple tiers of fleecy material. This garment—called a *kaunakés*—is decorated with a tassel at the back, perhaps a reference to the tails of animals whose fur was used for such garments in former periods.

sexes were being sustained until old age; clearly, the owners were now keeping these animals for their wool. This shift in the maintenance of flocks in order to shear their wool repeatedly was a major breakthrough in the development of cloth and clothing, in part because wool can be dyed into rich and glowing colors. Prior to 4000 B.C. in the Ancient Near East only plant fiber had been used to construct garments, and flax is not so easily dyed.

Whether considering clothing made from wool or plant fiber, it should be noted that, just as our understanding of the earliest Upper-Palaeolithic garments comes from that period's art, so too can we only comprehend the details of the clothing of the ancient people of the Near East from their graphic depictions. Because these kingdoms were all so highly stratified, usually only the privileged classes were recorded; as a result, any interpretation of their clothing repertories is unavoidably skewed.[14]

An additional caveat is needed in the case of the Ancient Egyptians. All of their human likenesses conformed to the dictates of the abiding Old Kingdom artistic canon, which governed an individual's size, proportions, age, posture, and also the choice of his/her clothing. Because representations painted on tomb walls and depicted on tomb sculptures affected an individual's subsequent fate in the afterlife, artists were reluctant to change established details for fear of jeopardizing the well-being of those entombed. The overarching concern was always to present an ideal: women were young, slim and beautiful, men youthfully vigorous or corpulently successful. This long-lived artistic conservatism is borne out in renderings of Egyptian dress: even in later times old-fashioned tight-fitting white linen garments are usually shown, despite the fact that linen tends to sag rather than cling.

MEN'S BASIC DRESS

The Ancient Sumerians recorded two categories of clothing. The first appears to be ritual attire [2], which may commemorate the earliest types of garment worn by these people: animal skins, particularly long-haired sheep skins or goat pelts that were wrapped around the lower torso.[15] The term *kaunakés*—which originally referred to a sheep's fleece or a goatskin with long tufts of hair—was later applied to the garment itself. The costume historian François Boucher suggests that from

3 A stone plaque found in Nippur, ca. 2500 B.C., depicting Ur-Nanshe—king of the city-state of Lagash—who carries a basket of bricks on his head, commemorating his role in the maintenance of the main deity's temple. Facing the ruler stands his wife, who also wears a fleecy garment. The couple's four sons, their hands reverently clasped, wear plain skirts, each bearing cuneiform script.

4 (opposite left) An early 13th-century statue of St. John the Baptist wearing a *kaunakés*-cloth cloak. Church of Saint Urbain, Troyes, France.

5 (opposite right) A ca. 2500 B.C. statue of a dignitary—Ishtup-il—found in the Sumerian city-state of Mari. This black stone sculpture, 4¹/₂ feet (1.4 m) high, was excavated in the early 1900s. The bearded figure wears basic Sumerian attire. He also wears a Mesopotamian-style headcovering—an encompassing skullcap surrounded by a broad, halo-like band.

about 2700 B.C. until the 4th century B.C., the animal pelts originally used to make this clothing were replaced by *kaunakés* cloth, a textile that imitated fleecy goat or sheep skin.[16] On such cloth the woolly faux tufts were arranged far more regularly than would be the case on actual animal pelts, giving the effect of regularly overlapping flounces. Whatever the nature of those early garments, both elite males and females are shown wearing them [3]. Depictions of this type of cloth continued in Europe into the Middle Ages to represent people from distant, little-known lands. *Kaunakés* cloth also served as a symbol in religious iconography, as in the fleecy cloak of St. John the Baptist [4].[17]

The second category of Sumerian attire constituted the basic apparel: a long rectangle of fringed woolen cloth wrapped around the torso like a skirt—its two edges overlapping—with the cloth's end placed over the left shoulder, leaving the right arm free [5]. More sumptuous cloth and more complicated ways of draping it gradually evolved in Mesopotamia, as did embroidery and tasseled fringes.

The prevailing fashion for thick, elaborately decorated, predominantly woolen garments continued into the subsequent Babylonian and Assyrian periods. Increasingly, important Mesopotamian men began to wear long, short-sleeved tunics over which a fringed

rectangle of cloth was draped in the Sumerian manner [6]. Long robes denoted high status; Assyrian wall reliefs show common soldiers wearing short kilts in battle.[18] Richly ornamented garments were reserved for kings, queens, courtiers and depictions of gods; high court officials folded their fringed rectangular cloths into a band worn over the tunic. The length of the increasingly important fringes reflected social status.

Sumerian-style draped attire remained the standard in Mesopotamia over a long period; it was the color and patterning of cloth that became increasingly lavish [7]. All of this clothing was woven on a horizontal ground loom using thread spun from sheep's wool, goat's hair or—to a lesser extent—flax. Goat's hair seems to have served for such utility items as ropes, blankets and beds; linen was used for covers or curtains in the temples, priests' attire, bed sheets, depictions of deities' garments, and in medical rites or other rituals.[19]

Ancient Egyptian clothing was also produced on the frameless horizontal ground loom, but far more usually out of flax than wool, which Herodotus erroneously claimed the Egyptians considered unclean.[20] In sharp contrast to Mesopotamia, almost all Egyptian garments were made of linen, mainly in white. The cloth of the upper classes was finely spun, beautifully woven and intricately pleated [8].[21]

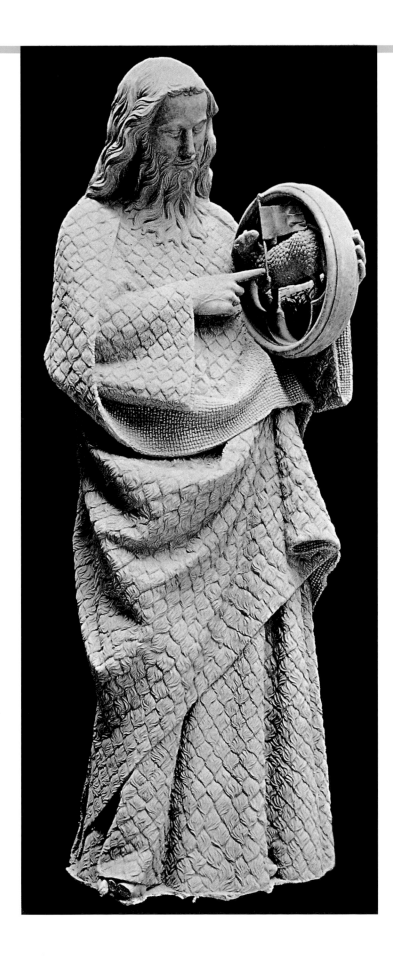

6 (above) Depicted on one register of the Assyrian monument known as the Black Obelisk of Salmanazar is Jehu, King of Israel (842–814 B.C.), shown prostrated before the Assyrian King Salmanazar III. The dominant ruler wears the official Assyrian crown—a fez-like headpiece supporting a pointed finial—as well as a fringed cloth wrapped around his tunic and then draped over one shoulder. The king's attendants also wear sleeved tunics, together with draped, fringed cloths. All wear sandals that lace at the ankle and hold the big toe in a ring. Only the two kings are bearded; the three clean-shaven attendants may be eunuchs. King Jehu wears a stocking cap-type headgear that is probably from the Levant.

7 (right) A guardsman— depicted on a reconstruction from a building in the ancient city of Susa, 7th–6th centuries B.C.—wears short hair and a neatly trimmed beard, as well as shoe-like footwear. The regularly spaced, richly patterned, repeating designs on his garments appear to have been woven in a tapestry technique.

8 (below) One of the world's oldest preserved garments: the upper portion of a linen dress with pleated sleeves from the Egyptian 1st Dynasty, Tarkhan, ca. 3000 B.C. The dress is composed of a woven rectangle sewn up into a tube to create the garment's body to which were added two wide, intricately pleated straps secured over the shoulders, pulled down and seamed so as to create sleeves. The pleats were not stitched down but rather pressed in, probably using an application of gum resin.

As established by the first pharaohs, the exclusive use of draped linen garments and the wearing of similar styles by men and women remained almost unaltered as the main features of Ancient Egyptian costume. The characteristic male garment was the white linen kilt, a rectangular piece of cloth wrapped around the lower body and tied in front; beneath was worn a triangular loincloth, or *shente*, whose ends were sometimes fastened with cord ties. The length, fullness and method of adjustment of the kilt varied with the social position of the wearer and the period in which he lived. In the Old Kingdom, the kilt was usually short, pleated and draped smoothly around the hips [9].

By the Middle Kingdom there was a fashion for longer kilts—almost like skirts—reaching from waist to ankles, sometimes even hanging from the armpits [see 30]. During the New Kingdom, the man's kilt panel—seen earlier in the opening of the skirt—emerged to be worn outside [10]. This pleated-kilt adornment progressively developed into a wide, triangular, front panel [11]. On Egyptian clothing, fullness was always concentrated in front, and all garments—both male and female—were adjusted so as to fit the figure smoothly behind.[22]

WOMEN'S BASIC DRESS

The characteristic female garment of the Egyptian Old Kingdom was a long, tight sheath held up by wide straps over the shoulders. In the 16th century B.C., a new type of costume appeared, the short-sleeved tunic [see 11]. Although it was the artistic convention to portray such costumes as molded tightly over the body, these depictions are deceptive: actual surviving clothing is loose and flowing for ease of movement.[23] During the more luxurious New Kingdom, the tunic became fuller and was worn as an outer garment; this clothing was made of particularly fine, diaphanous pleated linen [12]. Throughout Ancient Egypt's long history, all women—as well as men and children—wore a triangular loincloth secured to the body with cord ties.

The variety of ways in which Egyptian female costumes could be draped was enormous. Suffice it to say that—as with men's clothing—female garments consistently remained simple, accentuating the squareness of the shoulders, the narrowness of the waist and hips, and the elongation of the figure.

Among the Sumerians, there was little distinction between the sexes in their draped costumes. Males and

9 (right) An Old Kingdom Egyptian sculpture—ca. 2600 B.C.—of King Mycerinus with the goddess Hathor on his right and the personification of a province on his left. The two male figures are clad in sharply pleated white linen kilts. Wigs are worn by both the smaller figure and the goddess, who is clad in a sleeved tunic and wears the horned solar disk. The towering white crown of Upper Egypt adorns the king.

10 (far right) A limestone slab, ca. 1353 B.C., shows two men and a boy, perhaps a family group, or possibly the same male at three stages of life (Ancient Egyptian art often depicted male pectorals almost like female breasts). The kilt on the left displays the New Kingdom style—a triangular pleated panel worn at the front of the garment. White linen pleated clothing continued to be depicted in the New Kingdom just as it had been in the Old Kingdom over a millennium earlier.

11 (right) A statue from the New Kingdom tomb of Meryt and her husband Maya, treasurer under pharaohs Tutankhamen and Horemheb, ca. 1319–1292 B.C. The couple both wear carefully arranged wigs and white sleeved tunics; the large triangular section of Maya's pleated kilt is clearly featured. This depiction of the dignitary and his wife—who gaze into the beyond in a static manner reminiscent of over a thousand years before— reflects the return of Egyptian art to the classic Old Kingdom mode following the failed religious reforms of the pharaoh Akhenaton.

12 (above) A scene from the 18th Dynasty at Thebes, 1539–1292 B.C., shows slaves—wearing only belts, wigs and jewels—dancing at a banquet. The guests wear transparent, pleated tunics and jeweled pectorals typical of the New Kingdom. Balanced on their heads are oily cones of spikenard, a scent derived from an East Indian aromatic plant (*Nardostachys jatamansi*). The female musicians at lower left also wear these perfumed devices. As the cones melted, their yellow oil dripped down onto the participants' garments. The musicians' tunics are particularly stained: no doubt they had performed at many such functions.

14 The Assyrian monarch
Ashurbanipal and his queen
depicted at a ceremonial
banquet in a garden, ca. 7th
century B.C. Note the rich,
decorative detail of repeating
rosettes on the queen's
sleeved tunic, as well as the
intricate, tapestry-woven
designs on her fringed shawl.
The attendants of both the
king and queen wear draped
garments reminiscent of
Sumer almost two thousand
years before.

15 The 7th-century B.C.
Assyrian king Ashurbanipal
wears a protective boot/shin-
guard while engaged in a lion
hunt (an activity reserved for
royalty). The king's horse is
richly caparisoned with
tassels and saddle cloths
woven in geometric patterns,
trappings that served as
protective padding. Note
that the ruler's feet hang
free; stirrups had not yet
been invented.

13 (opposite) A plaster
statuette, ca. 2500 B.C.,
depicting a Sumerian couple
in an affectionate pose. The
woman wears a simple tunic
wrapped so that her right
arm and shoulder are bare.
Her hair is parted in the
middle and pulled back to
frame her face. The man's hair
is similarly parted; his long
curls reach to his chest, as
does his rectangular, carefully
crimped beard.

16 A pair of sandals from the New Kingdom carved in the finest "sunk relief" style of Amarna, ca. 1353–1335 B.C. Depiction of all five toes on the foot nearest the viewer was an innovative anatomical detail reserved exclusively for the Pharaoh Akhenaton and his family: the subject is a royal woman, probably Queen Nefertiti.

females both wore their long woolen cloths wound around the body in order to leave the right shoulder free [13]. This Sumerian style of draping a piece of cloth over/around the body continued over the millennia, as is evidenced in the fringed cloths worn over Assyrian men's sleeved tunics [see 7]. The richly decorated Assyrian female attire had a similar evolution [14].

FOOTWEAR

Prior to the 9th century B.C., there is little evidence of footwear being worn in the Fertile Crescent by either kings or priests, nor in depictions of deities. However, by 814 B.C., sandals—laced at the ankle and holding the big toe in a ring—appear on the Assyrians depicted on the Black Obelisk of Salmanazar [see 6]. In the 7th century B.C., the mounted King Ashurbanipal is shown with his leg encased in a protective boot/shin-guard [15]. By the 7th–6th century B.C., all-encasing, shoe-like footwear is also visible on a Neo-Babylonian guardsman [see 7].

In Egypt, footwear did not vary according to sex. Most ancient sandals were made in a coiled technique using grass and clean palm leaves or sedges (papyrus); many are still extant. Leather sandals were worn infrequently. Elegant sandals are shown on figures

depicted during the Amarna period [16]. In Tutankhamen's tomb nearly one hundred items of footwear were found, ranging from the everyday to the extraordinary [17].

OUTERWEAR

Although Egyptian summer temperatures were high, winters could be cold. Accordingly, shirts and dresses were made up in both light summer weight and heavy winter weight. Also, both men and women wore cloaks for warmth; some of these garments were made of wool.[24]

HAIRSTYLES

Sumerian men attired in fleecy garments are sometimes clean-shaven and bald-headed [see 2, 3], whereas other Sumerian males have a great deal of hair, worn with a middle part and falling to the chest in thick curls [see 13]. In addition, the latter men have heavy, rectangular beards that appear to be crimped. This same type of stylized beard also occurs on depictions of Assyrian kings almost two millennia later. A king's beard is always larger and more ornate than those of his attendants; beardless Assyrian courtiers are believed to have been eunuchs [see 6, 14].[25] The Assyrians spent a great deal of time oiling and dressing

17 This remarkable pair of sandals from King Tutankhamen's tomb were never worn. Wood with bark, green leather and gold foil were used to create depictions of bound Asiatic and Nubian prisoners, as well as the eight bows that symbolized Egypt's traditional enemies. The choice of decoration made it possible for the king to tread continually on his foes.

18 This tomb sculpture of a New Kingdom woman displays a large tiered wig composed of a series of closely arranged braids set in place with beeswax. Elegant Egyptian ladies of the period were typically attired in fringed linen tunics with diaphanous pleated shawls.

19 An ivory head of an Assyrian woman—ca. 9th–8th century B.C.—with her hair parted in the middle, pulled taut to frame her face, and then arranged in long curls on either side of her head. She wears an elegant headband consisting of flowers and linked disks. This piece was found in the Burnt Palace at Nimrud.

their beards, using tongs or curling irons to create elaborate ringlets and crisp curls worn in a tiered effect.[26] However, in the following centuries that style changed: the Babylonian guard's shorter, squared haircut—secured with a kind of net—was now in fashion, as was his short, carefully groomed beard [see 7].

The earliest records indicate that Egyptian men grew hair on their chins. They frizzed, dyed, or hennaed this beard and sometimes plaited it with interwoven gold thread. Later, a ritual beard of painted wood or metal was worn by the rulers on state occasions as a sign of sovereignty [see 20]. This royal chin device was held in place by a ribbon tied over the head and attached to a gold chin strap, a fashion existing from about 3000 B.C. to 1580 B.C.[27]

As for the Egyptian upper class, from an early period both men and women wore heavy wigs or padding of false hair. This headgear served not only as an adornment but also to protect the wearer's head from the burning rays of the sun, hence in a way wigs served as hats. Wigs were dressed in many different ways, each characteristic of a given period; generally speaking, as time went on wigs became longer [see 11] and the arrangement of curls and braids—set with beeswax—more complicated [18].

Sumerian women appear to have worn their hair parted and framing the face [see 13]. Almost two millennia later, Assyrian court ladies were still wearing a similar hairstyle, albeit adorned far more lavishly by a fashionable diadem [19]. It was not until long after Sumerian times that Mesopotamian law began to emphasize the importance of virginity and to impose the veil on respectable women, both signs of a more constraining role for females.[28]

HEADGEAR

The most famous of Ancient Egyptian headgear, however, were the pharaohs' crowns [20], including the red crown of Lower Egypt, the towering white crown of Upper Egypt [see 9], the double crown of united Egypt (i.e. the combined red and white crowns), and the blue crown of battle [see 33].

The cloth headdress of King Menes was also worn by the Egyptian pharaohs [21]. This garment was made of a square of material which was folded so that two fillets hung down over the shoulders; at the back of the head, the excess material was tied together into a pigtail. A gold headband held the headdress in place and supported the attached *uraeus*, the symbol of sovereignty depicted by the sacred asp (*Naja haje*, a small poisonous cobra).

Another type of Egyptian headdress was the *khat*, a semi-circular piece of material allowed to hang over the nape of the neck and held in place by a headband that went across the forehead, as well as by ties that fastened to the head.

Skullcaps apparently were also sometimes worn—one was found in Tutankhamen's tomb—although they are not depicted in the art. Skullcaps are not a surprising form of headcovering in a land where men and women regularly shaved their heads and wore wigs.[29]

In Mesopotamia, a type of male headcovering that was repeatedly depicted in the late 3rd millennium B.C.—and even ca. 3000 B.C.—was a tight skullcap surrounded by a broad, thick band forming a halo about the face; the hair was completely covered [22; see also 5]. This headgear—although worn by kings—was not necessarily a sign of rank because it is also depicted, ca. 2000 B.C., on a musician who appears on a plaque strumming his harp [23]. Over a millennium later, 7th-century Assyrian kings appear on wall reliefs wearing their insignia of royalty: a high, fez-like hat that supports a spike-like finial [see 6].

Mesopotamian women appear to have particularly favored headgear, some that towered [24], others composed of multiple layers [25]. A surviving inventory lists a dowry consisting of 24 separate outfits, each with two hats.[30]

As for the most striking of Ancient Near Eastern headgear, certainly there are no more beautiful examples than the elegantly simple crown of Queen Nefertiti of Egypt [26] or the elaborate creation belonging to Queen Puabi of Ur [27].[31]

Early Dynastic Period, ca. 3000–2625 B.C.

Djoser
ca. 2630–2611 B.C.

Old Kingdom, ca. 2685–2130 B.C.

Cheops (Khufu)
ca. 2585–2560 B.C.

Cephren (Khafre)
ca. 2555–2532 B.C.

Mycerinus (Menkaure)
ca. 2532–2510 B.C.

New Kingdom, ca. 1539–1075 B.C.

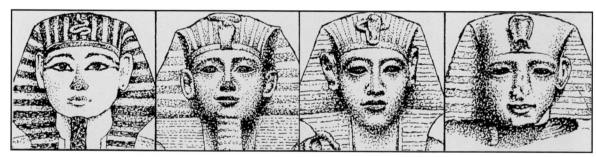

Ahmose I
ca. 1539–1514 B.C.

Tuthmosis III (Thutmose)
ca. 1479–1425 B.C.

Amenhotep IV (Akhenaton)
ca. 1353–1336 B.C.

Ramses II
ca. 1279–1213 B.C.

20 Various Egyptian dynasties represented by the pharaohs' official headcoverings, particularly the headdress first associated with King Menes. This distinctive headgear, which covered the hair but exposed the ears, displayed the *uraeus*, the symbol of sovereignty. Here, two rulers wear the towering white crown of Upper Egypt, depicted in truncated form [see also 9]. Note, too, that almost all the pharaohs wear the ritual false beard, although in at least two cases this royal symbol has broken off.

21 A sculpture of the New Kingdom pharaoh Akhenaton wearing a Menes headdress adorned with an *uraeus*, the emblem of sovereignty. He also holds the two symbols of Ancient Egyptian rulership, the flail and crook, originally related to agriculture and stock-raising. This depiction of the ruler typifies the Amarna art style introduced during Akhenaton's religious revolution: elongated face, spindly arms and a flaccid stomach; scholars ponder whether these distortions have symbolic or medical significance.

22 A diorite bust from Susa showing the broad-banded, skullcap type of hat typical of those worn by Mesopotamian males in the late 3rd millennium B.C.

23 The broad-banded skullcap is shown here worn by the so-called blind musician depicted on a clay plaque, one of many such artifacts showing various aspects of Mesopotamian life almost 4,000 years ago.

24 The head of a clay Sumerian female figurine wearing the towering *polos*

headdress, ca. 2600 B.C., excavated from the Ishtar temple at Mari.

25 The head of a Sumerian female figurine—from Tell Agrad in the Diyala region, first half of the 3rd millennium B.C.—wearing a multi-layered headdress consisting of five individual pieces of cloth. From cuneiform texts we know that such headdresses were constructed of multiple pieces of separately woven linen strips.

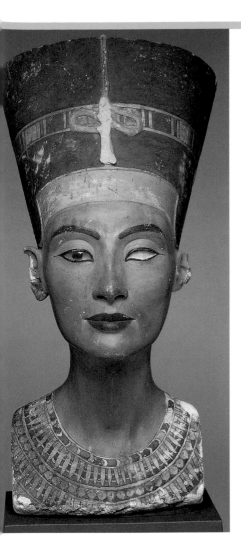

27 The headdress of Queen Puabi, buried in the Royal Cemetery at Ur, ca. 2500 B.C. This complex creation—apparently supported by a coiffure incorporating false hair—was composed of many individual pieces. For example, a gold ribbon was wound repeatedly around the head; a frontlet of lapis lazuli and carnelian beads supported gold ring pendants; golden poplar and willow leaves were each tipped with a carnelian bead; a gold hair ornament adorned with seven rosettes rose to tower over the back of the head. The splendor of this headgear was augmented by a pair of huge golden earrings supported by four gold wire spirals set in at the hairline. The Sumerian queen was buried with 74 servants, many of whom also wore elaborate headdresses, but none to equal that of the queen.

26 Queen Nefertiti—principal wife of the controversial New Kingdom pharaoh Akhenaton—wears a towering crown of elegant simplicity that serves to enhance her beautifully symmetrical features. This ancient bust of the queen, ca. 1379 B.C., was found in an Egyptian sculptor's workshop at El-Amarna by a German archaeologist in 1912.

28 A 10th-century B.C. Mesopotamian soldier—discovered in Tell Halaf, Syria—prepares to whirl a sling above his head before dispatching a sharpened-stone missile. These so-called "whirlers" were formidable fighters who could hit a mark at up to 650 feet (200 m). Even after the development of metallurgy, the sling was one of the most lethal weapons in an infantry's armory.

ACCESSORIES

In Mesopotamian art, one sees few accessories other than weapons—sling shots [28], metal axes and sickle swords, as well as staffs, arrow quivers [see 7] and metal maces. In Egyptian art, one of the most often reoccurring sets of accessories are the pharaonic staffs of office: the flail and shepherd's crook [see 21]. Also included among the treasures found in King Tutankhamen's tomb were a pair of magnificent, tapestry-woven gloves.[32]

JEWELRY

Among the most impressive treasures from the Royal Tomb of Ur, ca. 2500 B.C., was Queen Puabi's elaborate cloak of beads, together with an array of her necklaces, bracelets, rings, earrings, and pins [29]. This magnificent set of jewelry was fashioned principally from lapis lazuli, gold and carnelian, creating a striking combination of blue, gold and red. These same precious metals and semi-precious stones also appear in Egyptian jewelry, but assembled in quite a different manner [30]. The simple white pleated clothing of the Egyptians was often richly enhanced with wide, collar-like pectorals but these decorative pieces were only a sample of the range of jewelry available to the pharaohs.

The British archaeologist Howard Carter's sensational discovery in 1922 of the tomb of Tutankhamen revealed the mastery attained by Egyptian goldsmiths. In addition to the Pharaoh's innermost coffin being made entirely of pure gold, the mummy was also covered with a huge quantity of jewels. Yet more were found in cases and boxes in the tomb's adjacent rooms: pectorals, diadems, amulets, pendants, bracelets, earrings and rings. Some authorities think the superb quality and refinement of these exquisite pieces have rarely been surpassed—or even equaled—in the history of

jewelry.[33] However, a 1998 discovery in Mesopotamia revealed 8th-century B.C. Assyrian pieces which may challenge that claim.

The Assyrians had an affinity for gold jewelry. In addition to armlets with animal-head terminals and bracelets featuring a single large rosette at the wrist, they wore heavy rings, earrings, diadems, beads, pendants, necklaces, clothing plaques and even fibulas—safety pins—made of solid gold.[34] An excavation at Nimrud,[35] however, reveals that the Assyrians could also produce delicately crafted gold pieces created in an impressive array of sophisticated techniques [31].

29 The beaded cape and assorted jewelry of Queen Puabi, found in the Royal Tomb of Ur, ca. 2500 B.C. The unusual, heavy cape was made of carnelian, agate, lapis lazuli, silver and gold beads. These same precious and semi-precious materials were also used in various combinations to create an impressive array of jewelry.

30 This scene appears on the back of a throne belonging to Tutankhamen, who reigned from ca. 1332 to 1322 B.C. The pharaoh wears a long, full, double kilt, with the upper garment doubled and gathered in front. The queen, who is anointing her consort, wears sheer, pleated attire tied at the breast and draped over the arms. Both wear richly bejeweled pectorals as well as tapered sashes woven so that the ends are rather wider than the middle—a real weaving feat. To the right of the queen is a stand displaying additional collar-like pectorals.

ARMOR

Depictions on the Standard of Ur, ca. 2500 B.C., show a Sumerian military procession in which Mesopotamian soldiers wear protective capes and helmets [32]. The Sumerians also used chariots as part of their martial gear. By the time of the New Kingdom, the Egyptians were using chariots in battle, too, but—in keeping with the idealized nature of Egyptian art—scenes of such engagements are highly stylized [33]. Over a thousand years later the formidable Assyrians—going into battle in more sophisticated chariots—were protected by conical iron helmets and waist-length chain mail [34, 35].

As for infantrymen, on a polychrome wooden tomb sculpture a group of Nubian mercenaries armed with bows and arrows march into battle in orderly array [36].

SPECIAL COSTUMES

Egyptian priests who represented the pharaoh in certain religious rites wore—in addition to their white pleated tunics—a leopard skin thrown over the right shoulder: the animal's head rested at the waist and its tail hung down the back. Apparently the pharaohs, when serving as priests, also wore such skins.[36] At Memphis, on the remains of the Colossus of Ramses II—arguably the most important of Ancient Egypt's rulers—just such an animal tail can be detected.

31 Assyrian gold jewelry from the 8th century B.C. These pieces were among the spectacular discovery made in 1998 at Nimrud.

Below left: A delicately crafted gold crown.

Below right: A golden necklace whose closure is created with entwined snake heads.

Bottom left: An ornamental headband of woven gold.

Bottom right: An articulated bracelet incorporating stylized snake heads into its design.

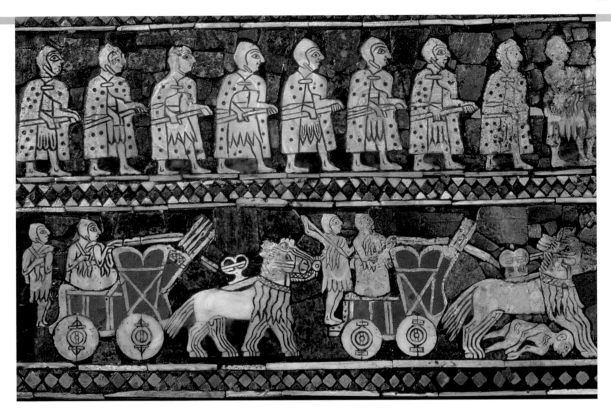

32 (left) Sumerian soldiers taking part in a martial procession appear on The Standard of Ur—a mosaic constructed of shell, lapis lazuli and red limestone — that was excavated from the Royal Cemetery of Ur, ca. 2500 B.C. These two scenes represent aspects of a battle and its aftermath. In the top register march a row of identically clad soldiers, each wearing a calf-length scalloped skirt and a cloak that may have been made of leather covered with metal studs, as well as tightly fitting headgear, probably either a leather cap or copper helmet.

33 (below) A battle scene on one side of a small wooden "hunting" coffer shows King Tutankhamen—wearing the blue battle crown decorated with the royal *uraeus*—fearlessly leading his orderly force against a confused and disheveled group of enemies, the North Syrian Mitanni. In keeping with the idealizing nature of Egyptian art, all is calm and control around the magnificently attired pharaoh and his richly caparisoned horse.

35 A scene on an Assyrian wall plaque depicts a war chariot carrying Assyrian warriors into battle. They wear pointed iron helmets and brandish round shields; one valiant pulls his bow taut to propel an arrow.

34 An extant Assyrian conical helmet hammered out of a single piece of iron. The helmet is decorated with bronze inlays that form parallel lines. Around the base of the helmet are a series of holes, probably for the attachment of a lining. This helmet, ca. 8th century B.C., was restored from fragments found at the Assyrian capital of Nimrud.

36 On a polychrome wooden tomb sculpture, a group of Nubian mercenaries— probably dating from the 12th Dynasty, 1938–1759 B.C.—march dutifully forward in orderly file.

GARMENT DECORATION

By 2200 B.C., multicolored wool tapestry weaving was already established in the Near East, having developed particularly at Ebla (Syria).[37] In the 9th century B.C. Assyrian court, lavishly worked textiles were *de rigueur* in royal circles. Two centuries later King Ashurbanipal's consort wore a tunic beautifully patterned with repeating rosettes, a textile pattern that also appears on the king's lion-hunting attire [see 14, 15]. This same traditional rosette motif appears again on the later, impressive attire of the Neo-Babylonian guard, ca. 6th century B.C [see 7].

FACE AND BODY MODIFICATION

The Ancient Egyptians placed a high value on cosmetics. In particular, women enhanced their eyes, painting the underside green with ground-up malachite—a basic carbonate of copper ore—that served as an antibacterial to protect the eyes from a swamp fly whose bite was capable of blinding.[38] The eyelids, lashes and eyebrows were painted black using kohl—made from antimony sulphide—and applied with an ivory or wooden stick [37]. In addition to eye make-up, henna was used for dyeing the fingernails, palms of the hands and soles of the feet.[39]

TRANSITIONAL DRESS

By the middle of the 1st millennium B.C., the world of the Ancient Near East was in dramatic transition. The glory days of Egypt were in the past and the successive line of aggressive Mesopotamian empires had finally played out; the area's power base was shifting. New players were about to step front and center on the Middle Eastern stage, bringing with them new demands for the roles their clothing would play.

The garment tradition inherited from the receding world of the Ancient Near East featured long, loosely draped clothing for both sexes, as well as a pronounced focus on headcoverings. In the case of Middle Eastern females, this emphasis would increasingly entail veiling,[40] a practice strengthened and solidified with the eventual arrival of Islam.

37 "The Weepers," a depiction of mourners painted on the wall of the Tomb of Ramose in the Valley of the Nobles. Although kohl was regularly used to enhance the eyes of Egyptian women, this cosmetic was obviously not guaranteed waterproof.

THE ARABIAN PENINSULA

38 A black-clad Saudi woman, completely covered by an enveloping outer cloak, the *abaya*, and a double-veil (an optional piece of black gauze can be pulled down so as to obscure even the eyes) moves anonymously through a group of Saudi men, all identically clad in the Kingdom's standard attire.

The Arabian Peninsula—that almost bone-dry, often searingly hot region that lies between the Red Sea and the Gulf [1]—was the original Arab homeland.[2] This area has been a crossroads since earliest times, a junction where migrants coming out of Africa and other pockets of human development met, mingled and merged into the Semitic peoples. By the Neolithic, waves of these Semites had moved north and west, away from the barren Peninsula. Others, however, stayed; as early as the 9th century B.C., Assyrian records contain references to the Arabians.[3]

The aridity of the majority of the Peninsula cannot be exaggerated: modern-day Saudi Arabia is the largest country in the world with no major river and very few year-round streams. Much of this stark terrain of sand, gravel fields and lava beds was almost impenetrable before the domestication of the camel sometime between the 13th and 11th centuries B.C.

Thriving on harsh vegetation that would starve other beasts, the camel provided milk, meat, wool and leather as well as transport for the region's nomadic people, the Bedouins, "desert dwellers" [39].

The need for water and pasturage shaped every aspect of Bedouin life. Much of the Peninsula was divided into tribal ranges within which were located the vital wells belonging to the various groups; nothing in life was more important than tribal allegiance. Today the term "Bedouin" refers to the nomadic people involved in the rearing of camels, sheep and goats, and the migratory search for pasture. The Peninsula's other inhabitants are referred to as Arabs.

In the distant past, the desert tribes controlled the overland transport of the Peninsula's most valued commodity: incense. Ranked among the most precious items of the ancient world were frankincense and myrrh, aromatics that moved overland via camel

Map 3 The Arabian Peninsula.　39 An ageless Arabian scene: two Bedouin men, wearing loose robes and protective headgear, guide camels over the Peninsula's harsh terrain.

caravans that navigated their hazardous way through shifting sands, warring kingdoms and contentious tribesmen. No one, however, interrupted so lucrative an enterprise—the attendant tolls and levies enriched their cities—and no one was indifferent to the cultural advantages such trade provided.[4] The caravan routes passed through the town of Mecca (Makkah), a rest stop on the edge of Arabia's dry western mountains. This trading center had long contained a religious sanctuary, a small, cube-like structure, the Ka'ba (Kaaba), which housed some 360 idols, a pantheon of ancient tribal gods.

In A.D. 570, Muhammad ibn Abdulla was born in Mecca. His Revelations, later set down in the holy Koran (Qur'an), became the foundation for the Middle East's third monotheistic religion, Islam.[5] However, his teachings were not well received in polytheistic Mecca and in 622 Muhammad and his followers were forced to leave their homes and travel some 250 miles (400 km) north to a small date-palm oasis/caravan town, Medina; it was there that Islam first took root. From Medina, the Prophet and his followers subsequently returned to Mecca to conquer the city for Islam and purify the Ka'ba of the idols.

The present-day rulers of Saudi Arabia pride themselves on being caretakers of two of Islam's holiest shrines: the mosque at Mecca that houses an enlarged Ka'ba—the spiritual center of the Islamic universe and focal point of the annual *hajj*, the prescribed pilgrimage for all Muslims—and the Prophet's mosque at Medina, the destination of an additional, optional holy journey.

Today the diverse Arab countries of the Peninsula [Map 3] are united in Islam, but each reflects its unique ecological zone and historical past. At the southeastern corner is the Sultanate of Oman, an ancient incense source and entrepot. At the Peninsula's southwestern extremity lies Yemen, a country containing 12,000-foot-high (3,700 m) mountains where the summer monsoons annually provide 25 to 30 inches (65–75 cm) of rain, enough to sustain agriculture that in biblical times supported a wealthy kingdom.[6]

Lying along the southwestern shore of the Gulf— an increasingly pivotal waterway, occupying a geological basin containing half of the world's oil supply[7]—are the Arabian countries of the United Arab Emirates, Qatar, Bahrain, Kuwait and Iraq, petroleum exporters all. The Gulf has long been strategic: it is depicted on Sumerian clay tablets, the world's first maps. Indeed, this maritime passage was a focus of trade—and of contention—long before the present-day scramble for oil.

The northern portion of the Arabian Peninsula is occupied by the region's largest country, the modern kingdom of Saudi Arabia, a particularly oil-rich nation that in recent years has undergone one of the most remarkable financial and physical transformations ever recorded in historical times.

Saudi Arabia takes its name from the powerful Al Saud family that presently rules it. In 1902, Abdul Aziz Al Saud, the twenty-one-year-old son of an exiled tribal leader, captured the oasis town of Riyadh from a competing family. Thus began a series of conquests that were to unite the warring tribes of the Arabian Peninsula into one nation. In 1932 Abdul Aziz—known to the West as Ibn Saud—declared himself King of Saudi Arabia [see 63]. At his death in 1953 he was succeeded by 34 surviving sons and uncounted daughters. Today there are at least 8,000 royal Saudi princes, and no doubt as many princesses.

Possessors of the Prophet's homeland, the Saudis see themselves as having a certain birthright as defenders of the faith, and hence endeavor to conduct themselves in as pious a manner as possible. When the oil boom of the 1970s caused a massive transfer of wealth from the industrialized nations to those who actually owned the oil, no Gulf country felt the impact more than Saudi Arabia. Suddenly an impoverished, mainly uneducated, tribal society became a phenomenally wealthy nation located in a neighborhood of paupers. Soon there was a pressing need for a completely new infrastructure. As a result, 21st-century technology was imported into a feudal kingdom, bringing with it Western ideas, modern buildings and urban layouts. Today, the country combines Islamic beliefs with advanced technology, an improbable amalgam that has had almost no effect on the way the Saudis and their conservative neighbors dress.

Although the present Arabian costume of loose, simple, kaftan-like garments and protective headgear existed in the Middle East prior to the Prophet's Revelation, it is the interpretation of the strictures of Islam that is responsible for maintaining this modest attire. Practices and traditions set by the Prophet stipulate that clothing be suitable for the movements and positions necessary for the prescribed five daily prayers. These supplications—in the Saudi's interpretation of Islam—involve a series of obeisances made first from a standing position and then from a kneeling one, where the forehead and nose touch the ground. Proper garments must never cling to the body and should conceal while conforming to every movement.[8] A further tenet of Islam is the belief that all men are equal in the sight of God. As a result, every Saudi male—regardless of social rank—dresses in the same simple, unadorned manner [see 38]. Although the cloth in a Saudi prince's garment is far finer than that of a lowly commoner, both are constructed and worn in the same manner.

To understand female dress one must realize that the values of the culture are based on the exalted position of the male, a belief rooted in nomadic warfare, as well as in the teachings of Islam. There is a verse in the Koran that states: "And say to the believing women that they should lower their gaze and guard their modesty; that they should not display their beauty and ornaments except what must ordinarily appear thereof; that they should draw their veils over their bosoms…" Sura 24: 31.[9]

Although headgear is often considered the most distinctive element of women's dress, in the more fundamentalist Islamic countries such as Saudi Arabia the concealing of the entire body appears to be the essential point. To understand fully the underlying rationale, one must realize that the chastity of all females under a man's care (i.e. his mother, sisters and daughters) reflects directly on his personal and family honor. As a result, all relations between unmarried men and women are highly sensitive. Also, social practices in public are strictly observed in Saudi Arabia due to the proximity of the holy site of Mecca.

40 (far left) The *thobe*, a long, slim, kaftan-like garment that allows for free circulation of air. Length 58¼ in. (148 cm), width 63 in. (160 cm).

41 (left) The long, cotton *sirwaal* are worn under the *thobe*, together with a white cotton T-shirt and a pair of boxer shorts made without a Western-style fly. All of these garments are manufactured in Syria. *Sirwaal*: length 37¾ in. (96 cm), width 27½ in. (70 cm).

MEN'S BASIC DRESS

The Saudi male's standard dress exemplifies the basic formula for Arabian clothing: total coverage to avoid strong sunlight and layered garments to conserve body moisture. A long, slim, undecorated shirtdress-like garment known as a *thobe* is usually worn. This is made of white cotton but, in winter months, is also constructed of light wool or polyester [40]. Under the *thobe* is worn the *sirwaal*, long underpants with elastic at the waist [41]. In addition to the *thobe*, a headdress is worn as protection against the relentless sun and wind-blown sand [see 38, 39]. In contrast, Yemenis living at the southwestern end of the Peninsula wear a calf-length, wraparound skirt, the *futah*, together with a cotton top and loosely wound turban. In many places in Yemen, men wear woolen jackets of Western manu-facture both in winter and summer [42]. In the nearby mountains of Saudi Arabia's Asir Province, sheep and goat herders also wear kilt-like skirts but their hair is uncovered and decorated with garlands of fragrant flowers and greenery, earning them the sobriquet "Flowered Men" [43].[10]

42 A highland Yemeni, his beard dyed red with henna, wears the regional wraparound skirt, a loose top and a woolen jacket of Western manufacture. He also has a white carrying cloth thrown over his shoulder. Prayer beads hang from his curved silver dagger and a silver-capped, 4-foot (120 cm) pipe dangles from his left hand. Common local items of footwear include square-toed sandals cut from discarded tires.

43 A group of Qahtani sheep and goat herders who live in the remote mountainous Tihamah region of Saudi Arabia's southern Asir Province. The ending of inter-tribal feuding in this area has provided more time for attending to masculine beauty: the shadowing of eyes, the styling of hair, and the wearing of multicolored woolen headbands resplendent with fragrant flowers, fresh leaves and aromatic plants.

WOMEN'S BASIC DRESS

Long before Islam, it was customary in the Middle East to wear an enveloping outer garment when traveling beyond the home. This millennia-long tradition has prevailed in the Arabian Peninsula up to modern times. In cities, women's all-enveloping, black *abaya* [44, 45] and impenetrable veils render their faces and bodies virtually invisible to anyone they casually pass on the street. Whatever the style of an Arabian woman's dress, in public her hair is customarily covered and her face usually veiled [46; see also 38]. Most exceptions to this rule are found in the Peninsula's far south [47].

Of all Islamic practices, it is the veiling of women that is least understood in the West. Assumed to be a dictate of

Islam, the veil, or *burqa*, is actually a product of culture. Although the Prophet did state that a woman should guard her modesty, it is the hair and bosom that are mentioned, not the face. The exact origin of the veil is unknown, but the practice is recorded by the Assyrians as far back as 1100 B.C.;[11] then it was not a religious matter but rather was intended to protect upper-class women of child-bearing age from lascivious male glances, and also to set them apart from "slaves, servants and harlots," all of whom were unveiled by decree.

Today, particularly among the northern Peninsula's older women, a veil in some form is almost as ubiquitous as the male headdress. Veil styles range from the heavy, mask-like face-coverings of Bedouin women [48, 49],

44 Today's *abaya* cloaks are invariably black, perhaps a harkening back to the premier, costly textiles of the past that were thrice-dyed in indigo. The voluminous modern cloaks have slits at the top of the side seams for the hands—the garment is held closed with one hand—and can be shortened at the hip. Dammon, Eastern Province, Saudi Arabia, 2001. Length 73⅝ in. (187 cm), width 72¾ in. (184 cm).

45 This encasing gauze *abaya* is worn over the head; the only openings are at the hem and sleeve ends. The red underarm gussets are made of the same gauze weave as the body of the cloak. As a design element, underarm gussets are the most predominant feature of central Arabian women's garments. Hofuf, Eastern Province, Saudi Arabia, 1975. Length 65⅞ in. (167 cm), width 85 in. (216 cm).

46 Omani Bedouin women—such as this tribeswoman from the Salalah region, who is painting an incense burner—wear clothes as colorful as any seen in Arabia. Although the woman's dress and headscarf are commercially printed—the latter somewhat resembles a tablecloth—her ornate, mask-like veil is no doubt of her own creation.

47 Two young Rabíah girls—faces unveiled and straight bangs revealed—wear the traditional straw hats and indigo-dyed headcloths of their tribe. In this isolated region of Saudi Arabia's mountainous Asir Province, there is little of the subdued demeanor that usually characterizes Arabian female behavior.

49 A Bedouin mask incorporating silver coins together with silver decorations. Purchased in Jeddah, Saudi Arabia, 2001. Length 7⁷⁄₈ in. (20 cm), width 8¹⁄₄ in. (21 cm).

48 A Bedouin mask displaying coins as a central design motif. Purchased in Jeddah, Saudi Arabia, 2001. Length 13³⁄₄ in. (35 cm), width 9³⁄₈ in. (24 cm).

usually made of a stiff fabric ornamented with embroidery, beads and/or rows of coins, through to urban women's plain veils made of heavy black silk that reveal only the wearer's eyes and have attached at the top an optional piece of black gauze that can be pulled down so as to completely obscure the entire face [50, 51; see also 38], and to silk headscarves decorated with metallic embroidery [52, 53].

Beneath their *abaya*, urban women wear modest, commercially made Western dresses. In contrast, the traditional dresses of Bedouin women [54–56]— similar in cut to the male *thobe* and also worn over the *sirwaal* [57]—are often colorfully decorated with ornate embroidery and metallic thread. An established canon determines the placement of this decoration: the prescribed boundaries include the neckline yoke and the sleeve cuffs, the only sections of a dress visible when worn under an *abaya*.

In stark contrast to the modest outerwear is the up-to-date, Western-style underwear on view in Saudi Arabia's ultra-modern malls. This indicates that some interpret Saudi clothing strictures as applying only to public apparel.[12]

50 (left) A present-day urban woman's black silk veil that ties behind the head so as to reveal only the eyes. This face-covering also has an optional veil attached, a sheer piece that can be pulled down so that the wearer's face is entirely obscured. Dammon, Northern Province, Saudi Arabia, 2001. Length 27⁷⁄₈ in. (71 cm), width 19⁵⁄₈ in. (50 cm).

51 (above) A Bedouin veil from Oman—almost a mask—that has been dyed in indigo and then burnished to attain a sheen. Such face-coverings present a beak-like appearance when a stiffened rib is inserted in the opening between the eyes; this ridge extends for the length of the mask [see 46]. Saudi Arabia, ca. 1975. Length 6¹⁄₄ in. (15.9 cm), width 9 in. (22.8 cm).

52 A headscarf composed of black silk and sheer tulle net. The machine-embroidered decorations are done in metallic silver thread. Hofuf, Eastern Province, Saudi Arabia, 1975. Length 47³⁄₈ in. (120.5 cm), width 34 in. (86.3 cm).

53 A black silk headscarf with machine-embroidered metallic gold thread decorations. This garment covered the hair; the wearer's face would have been veiled. Saudi Arabia, 1986. Length 53 in. (134.6 cm), width 26¹⁄₄ in. (66.7 cm).

54 The blue satin cloth of this dress provides an excellent background for displaying the embroidery of metallic gold thread around the neck yoke, down the sleeves and on the cuffs. Hofuf, Eastern Province, Saudi Arabia, ca. 1975. Length 51 in. (129.5 cm), width 57 in. (144.8 cm).

55 This Asir-style black velvet dress makes a special feature of its red satin underarm gussets from which the side-gore panels radiate down to the hemline. Tayif, Asir Province, Saudi Arabia, ca. 1975. Length 52¼ in. (132.7 cm), width 51 in. (129.5 cm).

56 The embroidery on this red velvet Asir-style dress appears in the same designated design areas as 55, but in a more elaborated fashion. The garment also employs the Asir region's diagnostic palette: red, green, yellow and silver rendered in embroidery thread. Tayif, Asir Province, Saudi Arabia, ca. 1975. Length 56 in. (142.2 cm), width 51 in. (129.5 cm).

57 In a society where reclining and squatting are favored ways of relaxing—and such workaday Bedouin activities as gathering, carrying and weaving are strenuous—underclothes must provide both ease of movement and decorum. The women's *sirwaal* combines these qualities, thanks to an ample crotch gusset set into the "drawers" so as to create a roomy seat. Tayif, Asir Province, Saudi Arabia, 2001. Length 35⅜ in. (90 cm), width 33⅜ in. (85 cm).

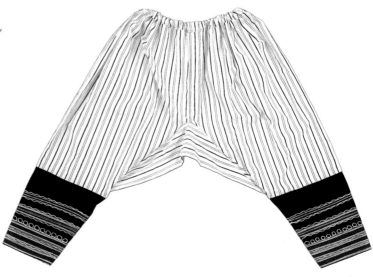

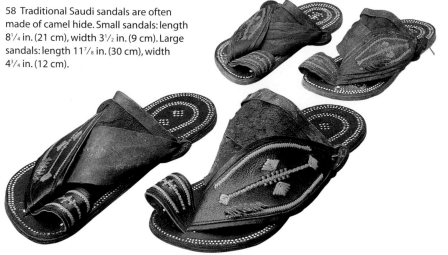

58 Traditional Saudi sandals are often made of camel hide. Small sandals: length 8¼ in. (21 cm), width 3½ in. (9 cm). Large sandals: length 11⅞ in. (30 cm), width 4¾ in. (12 cm).

FOOTWEAR

At the present time the traditional items of male footwear most often seen are the so-called Bedouin sandals with their distinctive big-toe piece and flat leather soles [58]. In the hot and humid coastal areas, simple sandals woven of palm fronds are sometimes still worn; they are not as durable as those made of animal hide but are no doubt more comfortable.

OUTERWEAR

Traditional male outerwear consists of a huge, square-cut cloak, the *bisht*, made of finely woven camel hair or imported British wool. *Bishts* are trimmed with black cord or gold braid [59]. The latter style is particularly associated with important political or religious leaders [60].

Some women, in addition to their plain black *abayas*, also have special ornate overgarments for festive occasions [see 52, 53]. These elegant pieces are often richly decorated with beads and intricate embroidery of colored and metallic threads.

HAIRSTYLES

Almost all Arabian men display some form of facial hair, either a beard or mustache [see 38], and wear their hair fairly short. As for women's hair, only family members and other women—at special celebrations—ever see it. Such an occasion might be a woman's wedding party where folk dances are performed, entertainments put on strictly by women for women. At such an event, one regional dance is the *al-na'ish*, "hair toss," where the dancers loosen their waist-length hair and swing it in spectacular arcs around their heads, to the rhythm of the drumming. The guests also sometimes uncover their own hair and swing it back and forth in time to the music.[13]

59 These floor-length cloaks are made of finely woven camel hair or British wool and are worn over the shoulders like a cape. Small slits in the seams allow the hands to extend when desired. The cloaks are made in natural wool colors of black or brown, more rarely in tan or cream. Black: length 60⅝ in. (154 cm), width 58¼ in. (148 cm). Brown: length 60¼ in. (153 cm), width 67⅜ in. (171 cm).

60 The Omani Council of State, set up in 1920 as a four-man "cabinet" to administer the country during the absence of the Sultan, consisted in 1928 of Rashid bin 'Uzayyiz al-Khusaibi, for religious affairs; Sayyid Muhammad bin Ahmad, the Wali of Muttrah; Wazir Bertram Thomas, for financial affairs (the British had a long and fruitful relationship with Oman); and Shaikh Zubair Ali, for justice and the courts. Note the prestigious gold-trimmed *bishts* of the Omani council members.

HEADGEAR

Headscarves are an important element of men's costume. The designs—and particularly the way of wearing one's headgear—give clues to the wearer's origin. The Saudi style combines three elements: 1) the *kutiyah*, a white skullcap; 2) the *ghutra*, a triangular-folded square cloth that is placed over the skullcap; 3) the *agal*—a ring of black rope or cord that holds the *ghutra* in place [61, 62]. When worn by important dignitaries, the *agal* often consists of several cords covered with gold thread [63]. The alternate style of headcovering—worn in most of the Peninsula's southern countries—is a turban created by wrapping a long headscarf several times around the skullcap before securing the scarf in place. Both men and boys sometimes wear only the skullcap; Muslim males also use this to cover their heads when at prayer.

63 Ibn Saud, the first king of Saudi Arabia, shown wearing a distinctive double *agal* wrapped in gold thread, an ornate variation of the usual double-black-band accessory that holds the headcloth in place. In the background is the ancient walled oasis stronghold of Diraiyah, the first capital of the Al Saud clan.

61 (far left) The *kutiyah*, a small white skullcap. Above: height 2⁷/₈ in. (7.3 cm), diameter 5¹/₂ in. (14 cm). Center: height 2¹/₂ in. (6.3 cm), diameter 6 in. (15.2 cm). Below: height 3¹/₄ in. (8.2 cm), diameter 7³/₄ in. (19.6 cm).

62 (left) The *ghutra*, the triangular-folded cotton headdress, is placed over the skullcap. Black/white: length 44¹/₂ in. (113 cm), width 43⁷/₈ in. (111.7 cm). Red/white: length 44¹/₂ in. (113 cm), width 40 in. (101.5 cm).
The *agal*, usually two black rings, holds the headdress in place; more ornate versions are worn by important officials. Black: height ¹/₂ in. (1.2 cm), diameter 13⁵/₈ in. (34.7 cm). Silver: height 2¹/₄ in. (5.7 cm), diameter 9 in. (22.8 cm).

64 An Al Wahibi tribesman wears an ornate curved dagger tucked into the decorated belt that wraps around his *dishdashah*—the Omanis' fuller version of the Saudi *thobe*. He also carries a rather ancient rifle, a common accessory of Bedouin male attire.

65 A veiled Al Wahibi tribeswoman wearing a portion of her jewelry collection. Her cucumber-shaped pendant may hold a fragment of the Koran. Her large, hollow, silver bracelets are particularly popular in Oman; they are often worn with matching anklets which also have small stones sealed within so that they rattle when worn.

ACCESSORIES

Although men sometimes carry prayer beads, their principal accessory is the *khanjar* (known as a *jambiya* in Yemen), a curved, highly decorated silver dagger worn tucked into an elaborate belt [64; see also 42, 60]. Another favored accessory is a cartridge belt; rifles and pistols are also popular additions to Bedouin male attire. Indeed, it is a common sight at any Bedouin gathering—fairs, markets, or camel races—to find the assembled crowd armed as though the desert were on the brink of war.[14]

JEWELRY

Most jewelry found in the markets of the Arabian Peninsula is made of either silver or gold. Before the oil boom, brides were adorned with heavy, low-grade silver jewelry [65], sold throughout the Peninsula by Jewish silver/goldsmiths from Yemen and surrounding areas. Today it is primarily Western expatriates who collect this Bedouin jewelry, which the Saudis and many of their neighbors have rejected.

Arabian brides receive agreed-upon, expensive gifts of gold jewelry from the groom, jewelry which then becomes a woman's exclusive property and is, in essence, her alimony if she is divorced. In the Saudi gold bazaars, showcases hold stacks of 18-, 21-, and 24-karat gold jewelry. Today's brides receive 21-karat breastplates, known as *kirdans*, made of gold ceremonial objects—that often look like actual coins—strung together so as to reach from shoulder to shoulder and down to the navel [66]. These impressive pieces are accompanied by a matching ring, bracelet, and large earrings.[15] The workmanship on such mass-produced items is said to have no bearing on their price, value being determined strictly by weight and the current cost of gold, which varies daily depending on the international market. However, the cost of workmanship on custom-made jewelry does play a role in the pricing of more detailed, finely crafted pieces.

66 A small sample of the variety of jewelry on display in the gold bazaar of Jeddah, Saudi Arabia, January, 2001. All such mass-produced jewelry is sold by weight, the price tied to the international cost of gold.

SPECIAL COSTUMES

One of the most impressive of the Saudi's logistical feats is the organization of the *hajj*, the annual pilgrimage to Mecca. Each year between 2 to 4 million pilgrims fly into Jeddah airport on planes that arrive at the rate of one per minute. Upon entering into the sacred rites of the four holy days, males wear the two simple, seamless garments that constitute *ihram* clothing [67], now often made of white, terry cloth-like cotton. One piece is wound skirt-like around the lower half of the body; the other is thrown loosely over one shoulder. Today, women wear modest, loose clothing that varies by country and go through the entire four holy days with their hair covered but their faces unveiled. Wearing *ihram* garments makes it impossible to distinguish rich from poor: all pilgrims are equal in the eyes of God.

GARMENT DECORATION

Male clothing tends to be simple and unadorned. In contrast, Bedouin dresses and female festive attire are richly decorated with colored and metallic embroidery [see 52–56].

FACE AND BODY MODIFICATION

Many Arabs, including tribesmen, wear kohl—powdered antimony sulphide—around their eyes as a deterrent to insects, eye disease and the sun's glare, and also for the enhancement of beauty. Bedouin women sometimes tattoo their chins with simple geometric patterns and use henna to dye their nails, skin and hair. For special occasions, henna is also sometimes applied in intricate patterns to female arms, legs and hands. Like many Middle Eastern women, Arabian females remove their pubic hair. Bedouins accomplish this using a thick depilatory paste made of sugar/honey and water; upper-class women shave with razors.[16]

TRANSITIONAL DRESS

In the last century, the diverse traditional garments worn by men in various parts of Arabia have become increasingly uniform throughout most of the Peninsula. The present standard seems to have been set by the Saudis when, in the early 1950s, new government officials chose to wear a slimmer kaftan with narrower, more serviceable sleeves. Changes in men's attire have also taken place in outerwear and foot coverings: in lieu of cloaks, men sometimes wear sweaters and Western-style tailored jackets; in place of sandals, men increasingly wear Western-style shoes.

67 A 19th-century painting of *hajj* pilgrims' *ihram* clothing. Today male clothing remains essentially the same, though the type of cloth varies, and females still wear enveloping cloaks that cover both hair and body; now, however, women's faces are unveiled.

THE EASTERN MEDITERRANEAN

68 Charles Robertson, *Arrival of the Caravan, Khan Asad Pasha, Damascus*, 19th century. A richly laden caravan arriving at a *caravanserai* in Damascus, the world's oldest continually occupied city and an Eastern Mediterranean trading center known for its outstanding handicrafts, including textiles: damask, a beautifully self-patterned cloth, takes its name from its place of origin.

The Eastern Mediterranean—since Antiquity the commercial and cultural crossroads linking Africa, Asia and Europe—has been swept for more than 4,000 years by recurring waves of conquerors ranging from Assyrians to Romans, from Ottomans to the British and French. None of these conquests, however, had as profound or long-lasting an effect as the 7th-century Islamic expansion.

When Islam's founder, the Prophet Muhammad, died in A.D. 632, the members of his new faith were clustered around the oasis communities of Mecca and Medina. These early Muslims, spurred on by their new religious creed, quickly began their long campaigns of

conquest. Between 634 and 650 they had already taken control of the Levant—present-day Syria, Jordan, Israel, the occupied territories and parts of Lebanon—as well as Egypt and Iraq. By 655 Muslim armies were victorious from Samarkand in the east to Tripoli in the west.

After the Muslims had defeated Sassanid Persia, they were prevented from expanding into eastern Europe by a Byzantine offensive mounted in Anatolia. The Byzantine Empire had come into being in A.D. 330 when the Roman emperor Constantine—the first of the Caesars to convert to Christianity—moved the capital of the eastern half of the Roman Empire to the site of the old Greek colony of Byzantium, located at the entrance to the Black Sea. The emperor renamed his new capital Constantinople. The subsequent Christian-Byzantine Empire—heartland of the Greek Orthodox church—developed into an opulent oriental monarchy whose holdings encompassed a sizable portion of the Eastern Mediterranean.

The initial thrust of Arab conquest came to an end in the middle of the 8th century by which time the banners of Islam spanned three continents, from China's borders to Europe's Pyrenees. This contiguous geography served as one of the first great corridors of cross-cultural fertilization. Among the Muslims, a lust for conquest gave way to a thirst for knowledge. In the 9th century, learning in Arabic flowered at the Abbasid court, drawing inspiration from Ancient Greece and India. At a time when Baghdad, Damascus and Alexandria were centers of research into mathematics, chemistry, navigation and medicine—as well as a revived interest in ancient classical literature—it has been noted that European contemporaries at Charlemagne's court were still "dabbling in the art of writing their names."[1] Indeed, it was discoveries of Islamic scholars that sparked the enlightenment, helping to end medieval Europe's Dark Ages.

By the 10th century a new source of power was becoming evident in the Euro-Asiatic region. Central Asian Turkic tribes—nomadic horsemen who had evolved on the grassland steppes and whose way of life was based on animal husbandry, rudimentary trade and the sacking of cities—were launched on an ever-expanding series of conquests. By 1453, the Ottomans—one of the Turkic groups already converted to Islam—had seized Constantinople, making it the capital of the Ottoman Empire.

The Turkic peoples brought a new type of clothing to the Eastern Mediterranean. Instead of the area's traditional ankle-length, body-encasing tunic, the conquerors wore loose-fitting, baggy pants together with a separate top that wrapped around the upper torso, with the right side folded over the left. These horsemen also introduced stirrups and boots, specifically red boots [69].

The Eastern Mediterranean remained part of the Ottoman Empire for well over 400 years. It was the events and trends of the late 19th and early 20th centuries that finally brought about the political and geographic changes evident today. The empire itself was abolished due to nationalism and the dividing-up of its lands as a result of the mandate system following World War I, divisions that resulted in today's nation-state configurations. Historically, the countries of the Levant had once been a part of the Roman province of Syria, whose extensive southern portion was known as Syria-Palaestine.[2] It is from this Greater Palestinian region [Map 4] that the best-documented, late 19th-/

69 A 13th-century portrait of a seated Turkic prince and his attendants wearing the baggy pants and red boots of the nomadic horsemen of the Central Asian steppes. Since this lord is a non-Arab, the weapon he holds is not the Arabs' sword but rather the Turkic bow and arrow, symbol of power in the eastern grasslands from whence the Turkic tribes came.

71 A 1924 painting of an
Ottoman princess dressed
in voluminous Turkish-style
decorated pantaloons as well
as an elegant sash, richly
embroidered jacket and pair
of golden slippers.

70 Frederick A. Bridgeman,
The Favorite, 1882. This
romantic painting depicts
a harem woman looking
wistfully out over a Cairo-like
cityscape. Her lustrous baggy
pantaloons, elaborate sash,
richly decorated outer coat
and elegant slippers reflect
the Turkish influence of the
Ottoman Empire on the dress
of the Egyptian upper class.

72 A kaftan once worn
by the famous Ottoman
ruler Sultan Suliman the
Magnificent, whose reign
extended from A.D. 1520 to
1566. The majority of the
fine silks produced by the
court weavers must have
been designated for imperial
wear. Such garments—which
served as outer robes—had
slits at the shoulders through
which the arms passed; the
long sleeves rested at the
back. Because the kaftan
hung open, elegant inner
robes were also displayed.
Length 15⅛ in. (135 cm).

73 In the Eastern Mediterranean, baggy pants were
and are worn by both men and women. Varying
greatly in size and cut, some extend clear to the ankle,
others only to the knee; some have close-fitting legs,
others are shaped into wide, voluminous pantaloons.
All types of baggy pants are gathered into folds at the
waist by a drawstring that is sometimes decorated.
Length 60 in. (152.4 cm), width 34 in. (86.4 cm).

early 20th-century regional clothing comes, garments that often reflect the area's 400 years of Ottoman rule.

In the late 19th and early 20th centuries painters and photographers began to chronicle the clothing worn in what was then the Ottoman Empire [70, 71]. During those early decades, no area of the world except Europe was so thoroughly photographed as the Middle East, particularly Egypt and Palestine, the Holy Land held sacred by Jews, Christians and Muslims alike. In the early 20th century, Christian missionaries worked in the Palestinian area and it is to them that we owe the survival of many of the finest Eastern Mediterranean garments currently found in costume collections.

Elite historical garments and textiles are also still extant thanks to the later Ottoman sultans' practice of cataloging the wardrobes and furnishings of their predecessors. These magnificent pieces [72] were all carefully preserved in the Topkapi palace, the imperial court located at the heart of the Muslims' Istanbul, formerly the Romans' Constantinople, formerly the Greeks' Byzantium.

Up to the time of the British Mandate (i.e. prior to the 1920s), the population of the Eastern Mediterranean divided into three distinct groups: village peasants, urban townsfolk and the nomadic Bedouin. To the latter group national borders were meaningless; for them the Middle East's dry and arid regions constituted a single cultural area wherein all dressed in essentially the same manner (see "The Arabian Peninsula," p. 44). For that reason, the following discussion focuses only on the garment styles worn in the Palestinian and Egyptian villages and urban centers, populated mainly by Muslims, although the Christian and Jewish minorities led similar traditional lives.

MEN'S BASIC DRESS

Men's clothing was essentially uniform not only throughout most of the Palestinian area but, indeed, throughout most of the Middle East: rich and poor wore more or less the same articles of clothing, differing only in quality of material, degree of embellishment and manner of wearing. The basic male wardrobe

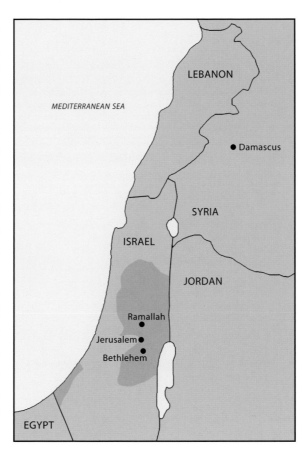

Map 4 The Greater Palestine region, ca. mid-20th century.

consisted of baggy pants, a long tunic, an overgarment with a belt, and perhaps a vest or shoulder mantle.

It was in the Palestinian area, at the end of the 19th century, that village men first began wearing baggy pants, probably in imitation of Turkish officials; these ample garments were not common throughout the entire area until the late 1920s [73; see also 76]. The waistline of the earlier pants was gathered by a woven, ornamented drawstring but later a simple cord or plain elastic were used.

Throughout the Palestinian and Egyptian areas, the basic garment for the average man—or woman— was an ankle-length, long-sleeved, loose shirt. The cut and name for this garment varied by region; in Egypt it is called a *galabiya* and is a full garment [74], whereas among the Palestinians it is known as a *thob* and is of a narrower cut [75].

On a man's head there was always a skullcap, over which was placed a larger red felt cap—a fez, or *tarbush*—around which was wrapped a head cloth to create a turban [76].[3]

75 A Palestinian couple picking figs. Over the man's simple white *thob* is worn a Western-style sweater. His headscarf is held in place by two black head ropes secured over his skullcap. The woman wears the Palestinian version of the Middle Eastern *thob*: a full, ankle-length tunic—girdled at the waist—with an embroidered yoke. Because the woman's hair is covered by a flowing white headcloth, she is considered to be "veiled."

74 An early 20th-century photograph of an Egyptian farming family. The woman, who is balancing a water jug on her head, wears the traditional Egyptian garment also worn by men, the fully cut *galabiya*. The boys wear white Muslim skullcaps.

76 A late 19th-century tinted photograph of Palestinian stone-cutters. Their turbans consist of a red felt fez, or *tarbush*, around which is wound a long length of patterned cloth. The men wear the Turkish-influenced baggy pants. The man to the far right wears a sheepskin jacket with the fur side turned in.

77 A Jerusalem dress of black cotton with geometric designs embroidered in bright pink silk. Length 54¾ in. (139 cm), width 57⅞ in. (147 cm).

78 A Bethlehem dress of brown velvet used for ceremonial occasions. The pointed sleeves, bodice and sides of the dress are elaborately embroidered with colorful silk thread. Length 58¼ in. (148 cm), width 56⅝ in. (144 cm).

WOMEN'S BASIC DRESS

In Palestinian Arabic, the word *thob* referred to a woman's dress in general, usually a loose, ankle-length, collarless garment intricately embroidered at the yoke and sides and bound at the waist with a woven-cloth girdle [see 75]. These impressive garments are among the most famous of the Eastern Mediterranean's regional clothing [77–80]. Until the introduction of machine stitching, all Palestinian embroidery was executed in cross stitch, half and double cross stitch, using silk thread from Damascus. During the 20th century, however, synthetic fibers replaced silk thread.[4] In some areas, dominant red embroidery is implicitly associated both with menstrual blood and the blood of defloration.[5]

In public, Palestinian women always wore a long, flowing headscarf [see 88]: their hair thus covered, they were considered to be "veiled."

79 Detail of a Ramallah dress of natural-colored linen used for summer wear and festive occasions (see also p. 2). These dresses are distinguished primarily by their striking red embroidery, which here includes a sprinkling of black, blue and pink. The embroidered chest panel is executed on a separate piece of cloth and then stitched to the dress without cutting out the garment's backing. Length 59⅜ in. (151 cm), width 52¾ in. (134 cm).

80 Detail of a Syrian wedding dress featuring intricately executed red embroidery on a black cotton groundcloth. Length 49⅝ in. (126 cm), width 53⅝ in. (136 cm). This type of lavish work in vibrant colors was fundamentally associated with marital status and prime womanhood. It was considered shameful to wear heavily embroidered dresses before marriage, and inappropriate after menopause, when dresses with sparse, muted embellishments were favored.

81 Typical brown leather village footwear, and a red leather boot reminiscent of those introduced into the Eastern Mediterranean region in the 13th century by the Ottoman Turkic tribesmen.

FOOTWEAR

Before European footwear was introduced, village men went barefoot or wore simple shoes. Horsemen—well into the 20th century—wore short red boots reminiscent of those introduced by the 13th-century Turkic tribesmen who originally founded the Ottoman Empire [81]. Palestinian red boots were made in cities by specialists, whereas brown leather shoes were produced locally. The shoe trade boomed at harvest time, in part because farmers needed protection when walking over stubble in the fields, but also probably because then people had money to buy footwear.

Palestinians thought it odd that European men removed their hats when entering a house but kept on their shoes. To Muslims it is exactly the opposite; shoes are considered unclean and hence are removed at the threshold of a house or mosque, whereas headwear is always kept on in deference to the Almighty. In certain ritual situations, shoes are also believed to be instruments of harm, especially if their soles are exposed.[6]

Until the 1920s most village women went barefoot; shoes were only worn by those who considered themselves urban. As a result, putting on shoes was synonymous with upward mobility, and shoes and stockings were status symbols because of their association with European fashions.

OUTERWEAR

Middle Easterners took a layered approach to dressing and used several types of outerwear. In winter, a sheepskin jacket with the wool turned inward was sometimes worn [see 76]. Another garment used for warmth was the *abayeh*, a simple mantle that could serve as cape, coat, shoulder cover, blanket or—when pulled over the head—a giant veil. In the 19th century, the *thob* and *abayeh* were the main garments of both villagers and Bedouin (see also "The Arabian Peninsula," pp. 45–46), but by the end of the century Palestinian village men increasingly wore—over their *thob*—a calf or ankle-length coat usually called a *qumbaz*, an outer garment also worn by women [82]. The *qumbaz* was made of a variety of fabrics, the most common for a man being striped cotton or silk. The garment was slit on the sides from the hem upward, a short slit or none at all for males, and a long slit for women whose full pantaloons shielded their legs, thus preserving their modesty.

The word *jillayeh* is used in many parts of Palestine to designate a wedding costume—either a dress or coat, depending on the region—displaying fancy embroidery. A similar outer garment for women, the *yelek*, is a more tightly fitted coat [83],[7] whereas the Middle Eastern kaftan is an ample, full-length robe worn by both sexes [see 72].[8]

A variety of jackets or waistcoats were worn, some unisex [84].[9] These garments were first copied from the Turkish ruling elite, then from Europeans including the British. The European jacket became increasingly popular at all levels of Palestinian society during the Mandate period (1920–1948), largely replacing the older cloaks and overgarments discussed above. In the urban centers, the jacket was worn with European-style trousers but in the villages it was worn over both the long shirts (*thobs*) and the coats (*qumbaz*) [see 85]. Thus Palestinian village men were often clothed in three historical layers: a "traditional" *thob* shirt, a Turkish-style coat, and a European-style jacket.[10]

The *jubbeh*, a unisex Middle Eastern long coat, open in front, had sleeves that could be either narrow or wide and extend anywhere from elbow to wrist [85].

82 The *qumbaz*, an ankle-length, unisex outer garment, opens all the way down the front with the right side brought over the left, under the arm, and then fastened. On this example both side seams have pocket openings and the garment has a short slit up the sides from the hem, indicating that it is for a man. Length 57⅞ in. (147 cm), width 63⅜ in. (161 cm).

83 The word *yelek* is Turkic, as is the origin of this female coat which may have been introduced into Syria-Palestine during Ibrahim Pasha's occupation, between 1831 and 1841. The *yelek* is slit on each side of the skirt's hemline so as to show the dress and baggy pants beneath, which might have been of a matching fabric and embroidery. Length 49⅝ in. (126 cm), width 54¾ in. (139 cm).

85 A tinted photograph of five Palestinian village men and a boy, all draped in *abayeh* cloaks—each in his own manner—worn over their layered outer garments, the coat-like *qumbaz*, *jubbeh* and a waistcoat. Note that only at puberty will the youngster begin to wear the turban.

84 Palestinian women often wore short embroidered jackets over their dresses. There are several styles of these garments, and a great many names for them throughout the Muslim world. The example shown here is a classic Bethlehem jacket made of blue wool felt decorated with fine Bethlehem couching of multicolored silk, mostly orange and magenta thread used to create flowing floral and arabesque motifs. Length 18¾ in. (47.6 cm), width 32 in. (81.3 cm).

86 A 19th-century Palestinian girl displaying her lavish headgear, an ornately decorated cap to which were attached rows of gold and silver coins. A silver chain holds her headpiece in place. When in public, these ornate caps were hidden from view by a headscarf, sometimes beautifully embroidered.

87 The distinctive conical hat was worn only by married women. It was made of cotton or linen, padded or quilted until it was hard; other examples were constructed of stiff cardboard covered with red felt and lined with cotton. The hat was worn balanced atop the head, with no pretext of fitting. So as to hold it in place, a silver chin chain hooked into the two side flaps, one above each ear. In order to protect the expensive hat from being soiled by oiled hair or sweat, a little cap was first placed beneath it. Height 6 in. (15.2 cm), width 4½ in. (11.4 cm).

88 Headcoverings for both sexes are ubiquitous throughout the Middle East. In the Palestinian region, women use long, flowing, sometimes richly embroidered scarves to hide their hair completely. Beneath their headcloths some women wore a unique, richly decorated hat [see 86, 87]. Length 82½ in. (209.5 cm), width 42½ in. (107.9 cm).

HAIRSTYLES AND HEADGEAR

In the Eastern Mediterranean, with the exception of village women on their wedding day, women did not hide their faces. However, modesty did dictate that in public women's heads, like those of men, should always be covered. Female headgear usually consisted of a tight-fitting cap or bonnet covered by a headscarf—the "veil"—that completely hid it. Head-coverings varied regionally and indicated marital status—they were first worn to show readiness for marriage—while also displaying wealth through the incorporation of precious metals and actual coins. In Palestine an ornate headpiece was worn, which was often a 6- to 7-inch-high (15–18 cm) conical cap [86, 87].[11] Women embellished these padded caps with rows of gold and silver coins from their bridewealth money—the more coins, the greater the prestige—and draped an often beautifully embroidered head-scarf on top [88].

Men of the Eastern Mediterranean wore their hair short—their heads were usually covered—and most had facial hair, a short, trimmed beard and/or a mustache. The Jewish men of Palestine, however, usually wore full beards and sometimes also displayed the long Orthodox sidelocks under their traditional, wide-brimmed, black hats and wrapped turbans [89].

The male headgear of the Arab villagers consisted of several layers. First there was a white cotton skull-cap, over which was placed a white or grey felt cap, over which was then placed a red felt hat, the *tarbush* or fez [see 85]. The fez worn by Ottoman officials, Turkish soldiers and urban Palestinians was tall, stiff and shaped like an upturned flowerpot, whereas the village *tarbush* was softer, smaller and more rounded. Around the *tarbush*/fez was wrapped a length of cloth to form a turban. Sometimes little articles, such as cigarette papers, tax documents, small bottles of scent or a wooden comb for grooming one's beard, were stored between the layers of the caps or in the folds of the turban.[12]

As Shelagh Weir notes, the head was the locus of a man's honor and reputation, hence it was proper and

89 There are parallels between headcovering practices in Islam and Judaism, both of which originated in the Middle East. These 19th-century Jewish men living in Palestine wore long, bushy beards and traditional, wide-brimmed, black hats as well as wrapped turbans. The remainder of Jewish male clothing was similar to that of their Muslim neighbors: the long, loose, Middle Eastern tunic covered by layered outer garments.

90 A Palestinian jewelry shop whose main wares were silver or metal wire for the use of silversmiths, plus evil-eye beads (top left) and Hebron-made glass bracelets. The turbaned proprietor—clad in his white *thob*—is absorbed in his book, perhaps a copy of the Koran.

dignified that it should be covered.[13] By association, the headwear itself took on connotations of honor. Men swore oaths on their turbans, and the removal of a man's headgear in anger was a slur and provocation, and could necessitate material compensation.

JEWELRY

Silversmiths based in all the main towns produced a variety of silver bracelets, necklaces, chokers, hair ornaments and rings worn by Palestinian villagers and Bedouin [90]. Silversmiths could easily travel with their craft and many migrated to Palestine from parts of Arabia during periods of Levantine prosperity, or hardship in their own countries. As a result, Eastern Mediterranean jewelry styles and techniques have diverse origins, as did the Levantine clothing which also was subject to continual foreign influence.

Certain jewelry was important for its beneficial physical effects, as well as decoration. Blue beads, and glass beads with "eyes," were considered particularly effective against the "evil eye"—the jealous glance of malevolent persons—which was believed to cause disaster, illness or death. Children were considered to be especially vulnerable to the "evil eye" and were kept scruffy and unwashed to avoid attracting dangerous attention; their caps were also often covered with amulets, beads and charms, as was their clothing.[14]

91 A circumcision waistcoat, possibly from the Hebron Hills during the British Mandate period, or earlier. The groundcloth is Atlas satin, a luxury fabric woven with a silk warp and a cotton weft. The front of the waistcoat is thickly covered with a variety of coins, the better to express the high social value of the boy wearing it. Length 11⁷⁄₈ in. (30 cm).

SPECIAL COSTUMES

There were no special Islamic priestly vestments because Islam has no priests. There were, however, two particular classes of special-event clothing that marked important stages in the Islamic life-cycle. Circumcision was a mandatory occasion that could be carried out at various ages, though most boys were circumcised under the age of six. It was shameful for an adult not to have been circumcised as it was necessary both for marriage and entry into paradise. The circumcision ceremony was one of the main events in a male's life, not only for the celebration itself but also as a display of his social value. A boy's position in society was expressed by adorning him with precious coins and jewelry [91]. Also, a highly decorated *tarbush*/fez was worn following the ceremony [92], as though in anticipation of the circumcised boy's manhood; the *tarbush* was associated with sexual and social maturity.[15]

At the other end of the Islamic life-cycle, grave clothes also qualify as special-event garments. If the man had gone on the *hajj*—the annual pilgrimage to Mecca—his prestigious *ihram* clothes would serve as his shroud (see "The Arabian Peninsula," p. 53). Otherwise, shrouds were made of newly purchased material and sewn only by a "praying woman:" a ritually pure female past menopause. The grave clothes for a man consisted of two long robes, one white, the other green, plus a girdle, white cap, white turban, the loincloth worn during the body's washing, trousers and a winding sheet. Grave clothes for a woman included the same two robes, plus several additions: her headdress was sewn with coins, and a full face-veil was added, as well as trousers. Although face-veils and trousers were not ordinarily worn by Palestinian Arab women, they were considered essential for protection of female modesty, even in the grave.[16]

92 A Palestinian father and his sons in Ramallah, 1905. The ornamental *tarbushes* worn by the boys suggest they are Muslims dressed up to celebrate their circumcision ceremony.

93 Palestinian women in a Ramallah market in 1987. The two center figures wear traditional Palestinian embroidered dresses, whereas the woman to the left has adopted a transitional, undecorated, "Islamic" dress.

TRANSITIONAL DRESS

Many women of village origin—including those living in West Bank communities and refugee camps as well as in the Gaza Strip and Jordan—still wear the traditional embroidered dresses and flowing white headcloths, either as everyday wear or for special occasions [93]. This attire is not only donned by older women, who might be expected to be more conservative in dress, but also by some younger ones, many of whom have not lived in a village since childhood, or perhaps have never done so. At a period when alternative clothing styles are readily available— Western attire and "Islamic" dress of varying degrees of modesty and concealment—it is interesting that the "traditional" Palestinian embroidered costumes continue to be worn.[17]

THE IRANIAN PLATEAU

94 A 17th-century Persian miniature features preparations for a coronation. Traditional crafts that will contribute to this celebration are under-way in a garden. From upper right, artisans are involved in spinning, weaving, engraving, forging and metal-working.

A series of massive, heavily eroded mountain chains surround Iran's 1,500-foot-high (455 m) interior basin. The great spine of the Zagros range slants 1,300 miles (2,100 km) southeastward; the Elburz range walls off the north. These massifs encircle the great central plateau, a fertile but discouragingly dry land. The country that we know today as Iran—three times the size of France, with approximately half its population—stretches across arid mountains and deserts from present-day Iraq to the Afghanistan/Pakistan borders, from the rainy, landlocked Caspian Sea to the torrid, dry coast of the Gulf [Map 5].

The heartland of this region has been known throughout history as Persia but in 1935 its name was officially changed to Iran[1] to honor the ancient Aryans who first built a mighty empire there. These tribesmen were Caucasoid Indo-European speakers who, in the 1st millennium B.C., rode down from the Asian heartland into the central basin that lay between their own Eurasian steppes and the civilized world of Western Asia. They settled in the southwest of the plateau, a region known as Pars,[2] the Greek Persis, the English Persia. The first Persians, leather-helmeted warriors mounted on bronze-bedecked horses, were but one of the tribal groups to come out of Central Asia and settle in Iran.

Another group of Indo-European migrants were the Medes who established themselves northwest of the Persians, near the present-day Iraqi border. It was the remarkable Persian ruler Cyrus the Great of the Achaemenid dynasty who first united the Iranians by conquering the Medes; by 539 B.C. the Persian Empire was the largest the world had yet known. In less than a hundred years the Persians had evolved a government that encompassed a diversity of ethnic groups living in what historians regard as a period of peace and religious tolerance under a single, just rule, albeit an autocratic one.

The now-eroded, barren Iranian plateau, uninviting as it appears, is a strategic land bridge between three continents and, as such, has drawn down upon itself the fiercest of fighters and the most ambitious of princes from surrounding lands. For the better part of 2,500 years foreigners have been covetous of Persia's possessions. Although besieged in sequence by Greeks, Romans, Arabs, Turks and Mongols, in each case the invasion, destruction and formation of a new culture reflected abiding Persian precepts: artistic sensibility, political survival and cultural endurance. It was the Arabs who introduced Islam, ca. A.D. 642. In the 16th century the Muslim Persians adopted Shiism,[3] a belief as distinct from Sunni Islam as Catholicism is from Protestantism.

By the 20th century, the reigning powers of the Western world were attracted to Persia by the same magnets that had drawn the ancient invaders: its strategic location and its resources—once gold, now oil, life-blood of the industrial world. As Western arms and bribes posed an obvious threat to Iran's national sovereignty, so Western manufactured goods posed a threat to Iran's cultural integrity. Much of this Westernization occurred under the Pahlavi Dynasty, 1925–1979. For 54 years the Pahlavis worked to modernize Iran, breaking up many of the large estates, giving women the vote, spreading literacy, winning high prices for Iranian oil in world markets and decreeing nationwide Western dress (Parliament outlawed ethnic dress in 1928 and banned veiling in 1936). In bringing about these changes Iran increasingly became allied with the West and, inevitably, its secular ways. This secularization outraged the Shiite religious establishment and stringent pressure was increasingly brought to bear on the Crown by the fundamentalist mullahs.

In 1979 the reigning ruler, Mohammad Reza Shah Pahlavi, was forced to abandon his throne. After the Ayatollah Ruhollah Khomeini became the supreme Shiite religious authority, he declared Iran an Islamic republic. The Ayatollah then proceeded to enforce on the entire country what were termed Islamic codes of behavior and dress. Women were forced to appear in public completely covered, often by the black *chador*— a long, loose, all-enveloping outer wrap[4]—and although not forced to veil their faces, women did have to cover their hair completely [95].

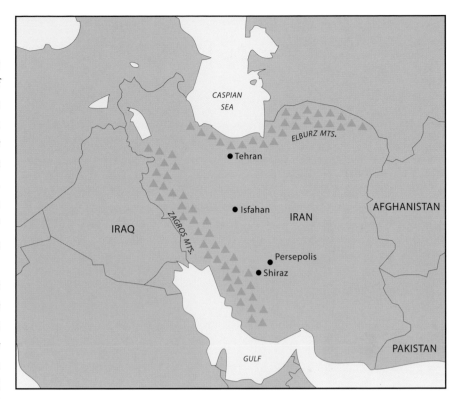

Map 5 The Iranian Plateau. In addition to Iran's modern-day cities, the ancient site of Persepolis is indicated.

95 At a grave in an Iranian cemetery, *chador*-clad women—their hair completely covered— mourn their dead with offerings of fruit and flowers. The *chador* of the region is similar to Saudi Arabia's *abaya* (see "The Arabian Peninsula," pp. 46–47).

Today it is only among tribal groups that Iranian ethnic clothing is still being worn. As of 1975, Iran contained some 2,000,000 nomadic and semi-nomadic people from 25 major tribes, many still herdsmen who migrated twice-yearly to fresh pastures. These Iranian nomads, whether of Aryan, Mongol, or Turkic stock, had brought with them from Central Asia a pattern of social organization quite distinct from that of the egalitarian Semites of the Arabian Peninsula. The Iranian nomads live in a highly stratified world, in which wealth and its benefits are not shared throughout the tribe. Whereas in theory anyone can attain rulership among the Arabs, in Iran the tribes are organized on the Genghis Khan model whereby one hereditary leader—whose superior power must be acknowledged—is solidly established at the top.

The clothing of two of these Iranian tribal groups—the Kurds and the Qashqai—will be examined here. The Kurds of northwest Iran are part of a much larger, widely dispersed Kurdish group that has been separated by the modern boundaries of Turkey, Iran, Iraq, Syria and the former USSR. Despite these artificial barriers, the Kurds consider themselves very much a distinct and recognizable "nation," pointing out that they have occupied their larger, politically splintered region for some 6,000 years. The Iranian Kurds, although Sunni Muslims, identify with their present homeland because they speak an Indo-European language related to Persian. In addition, they are probably descended from the Indo-European Medes who captured Nineveh from the Assyrians in 612 B.C., and then were defeated in turn by the Persian ruler Cyrus the Great in 530 B.C.[5]

By 1981, the Iranian Kurds were concentrated in the northwest province of Kurdistan and in parts of Azerbaijan. Traditionally these people have been nomadic, migrating up and down the Zagros range from winter to summer pastures. Today most are settled in villages where their lifestyle is still mainly pastoral, combining the grazing of sheep and goats with the cultivation of wheat and fruit crops.

The second nomadic group is the Qashqai, one of the most important and colorful of Iran's tribal confederations. An Islamic, Turkic-speaking people, the Qashqai have been living in the southern province of Fars (i.e. Pars) since at least the 16th century and continue to inhabit territories in the southwest Zagros range. They have maintained their migratory way of life despite the efforts by Reza Shah Pahlavi to disarm them, force them into Western dress and permanently settle them. The Qashqai, however, view the survival of their traditional way of life as being dependent on the successful grazing of their livestock. The annual Qashqai migration route conveniently allows them to stop in the city of Shiraz, which serves as their principal market town and also provides an urban outlet where the women can sell their rugs.[6]

MEN'S BASIC DRESS

In contrast to men of other Iranian tribal groups, who now mainly wear European-style shirts and trousers, the Kurds have managed to retain many aspects of their

96 Two Kurds involved in the ancient Persian card game of *ahs*. Each of the men wears the large Kurdish turban with "fly-whisk" fringes. Their yard-long shirt cuffs reportedly reflect lessons learned in the past when Kurd warriors—anticipating wounds—carried their own bandages into battle.

mass-produced in China together with tiny commercially made beads, printed rayons and other synthetics assembled for their turbans.[8]

The traditional wrapover robes of the Qashqai men were far less frequently seen after Reza Shah's clothing edicts but some were still being worn as late as the early 1950s [97]. These long coats were sometimes brightly colored [see 100] but more often grey or blue, with slashed sleeves. Around the waist the Qashqai wrapped a voluminous sash. In more recent decades, their men's costume has largely been replaced by European clothing: ready-made trousers, shirts and jackets bought in the Shiraz bazaar. It is only the man's felt hat with its rounded top and turn-up flaps that continues to serve as the Qashqai tribal marker [98].[9]

97 A young nomad, ca. 1950, wearing traditional Qashqai attire: the loose blue/grey-striped wrapover robe, the voluminous sash, cloth shoes and rounded felt hat. The camels—tribal moving vans—wear tasseled scarves for decoration.

98 The Qashqai rounded felt hat may be worn in several ways. Here an elder prefers to have both flaps up but the hat can also be turned around so that one flap is used as a snap-brim visor. In winter, both flaps may be pulled down to protect the ears.

male costume as a symbol of their ethnic identity [96]. The traditional Kurd suit used to be made of narrow strips of handwoven wool which were carefully seamed together. Today certain concessions have been made for practical convenience, and the older techniques of weaving and tailoring are fast being replaced by factory-woven cloth in broad-loom widths. A substitute for the traditional neat, close-fitting Kurd jacket [see 99] is a loose blouson top resembling the jacket of a European soldier's battle dress, a garment often acquired from army surplus supplies bought in the bazaars of Kurdistan and worn with the traditional voluminous Kurdish trousers, tightly fitted at waist and ankles, which one observer noted sometimes makes these nomads look as though they have just stepped out of a combat tank.[7]

Today the Kurds' elegant white shirts with their long, full cuffs are frequently replaced by European-style, commercially made shirts from the local bazaar. The unique "fly-whisk" Kurdish headdress [see 96] is also made up of purchased items: crocheted skull caps

99 Mahabad Kurdish man's traditional costume. Northwest Iran, 1974. A patterned "fly-whisk" turban is wrapped around and over a small cap; a short tailored wool jacket is worn over a white shirt with long sleeve cuffs; voluminous black wool trousers are tightly fitted at the waist and ankle; and the outfit is completed with a velvet sash.

100 Qashqai man's costume. Southwest Iran, 1974. A colorful wrapover robe with slashed sleeves is worn, along with the tribe's signature rounded felt hat with side flaps. A Western shirt, neck scarf, dark pants, wide sash and cloth shoes are also worn.

101 Sanandaj Kurdish married woman's costume. Western Iran, 1977. A long-sleeved dress is worn, with a colored sash around the waist, over voluminous trousers. Over the dress is worn a long, narrow coat, combined with a short velvet jacket. The married woman's black/brown turban is further decorated with a piece of braid and colored sequins.

102 Mahabad Kurdish unmarried woman's costume. Northwest Iran, 1974. This costume consists of a full-skirted dress with a wide sash, short jacket, voluminous pants and elaborate pillbox hat covered by a patterned gauze scarf.

103 Qashqai woman's costume. Southwest Iran, 1974. A long, loose dress is worn over three petticoats. A short tight jacket is worn on top. To cover the head a white gauze veil is worn over a small cap and fastened under the chin with a gold brooch. The headdress is held in place with a silk headscarf, whose ends hang down the wearer's back.

WOMEN'S BASIC DRESS

The principal feature of nomadic women's clothing is its emphasis on layering, the number of layers depending on the whim of the wearer and the season of the year. But regardless of seasonal dictates, for all of these multi-layered garments there is a consistent use of lavish, brilliantly colored and ornately patterned fabrics, materials now often locally manufactured but formerly imported from India, Constantinople or Japan. An interesting aspect of the flamboyant nomadic finery is its pattern of use: it is worn every day—in towns, villages and during migrations [104]—as women go about their domestic chores. Obviously, this attire is not saved for special events but rather is daily wear symbolic of a group's ethnic identity.

A Kurdish married woman's ensemble consists of the Middle East's ubiquitous baggy trousers, a wide sash encircling the waist, a long, combined coat/short jacket and a black turban made of a fringed scarf decorated with gold and colored sequins and black braid [see 101]. The clothing of an unmarried Kurdish woman [see 102] differs from that of the matron by featuring a full, gathered skirt; the headdress is a festively decorated pillbox cap over which is worn a large triangular veil of patterned white gauze. The ends of this scarf are loosely tied and thrown back over each shoulder.[10]

The Qashqai women's lavish costume [see 103] also consists of multiple layers, which produce a remarkably full skirt made up of several petticoats over which is placed an elaborate skirt. On top of this is worn a long-sleeved, loose-fitting dress with deep side slits, the better to display the layers beneath. A short, tight jacket, often of some flamboyantly glittering material such as Lurex, completes the outfit [see 104]. The female headdress consists of a cap covered by a gauze scarf.

FOOTWEAR

The cloth shoe is a Persian tradition dating back to at least the 12th century. The oldest type consisted of a home-made, white cotton upper section sewn in a button-hole stitch with strong cotton thread to a sole—produced by a professional solemaker—formerly made of cloth strips sized, folded and beaten into shape and then reinforced by strips of tanned leather. A shoemaker added a welt—a double-edged strip—when sewing the two parts of the shoe together on a last.[11] Shoes of better quality have a cloth lining and reinforced heels, although today either leather soles are used or those made of

104 Qashqai females wear their colorful clothing as daily attire, even during hot and dusty migrations. They dress in a series of full layers with their outer garments slit or worn open to reveal the prodigious number of petticoats beneath. This bride has covered her face for protection from dust. Zagros Mountains, Southwest Iran, Spring, 1970.

105 Old Kurdish men wear unique felt vests together with their tribe's "fly-whisk" turbans and the traditional voluminous pants tightly gathered at waist and ankle.

worn-out car tires. Cloth shoes are not foot-specific hence can be worn on either foot [see 97, 106].

Women's shoes are either locally manufactured plastic sandals or inexpensive, commercially made, international-style footwear. Stockings are not usually worn except in cold weather.

OUTERWEAR

Being water-repellent and providing insulation in extremes of both heat and cold, felt is the fabric traditionally used by Central Asian nomads for their clothing and colorful horse/camel trappings, as well as for their mobile huts—the round, wind-resistant yurts. Distinctive examples of felt outerwear include the unique vests worn by men in one Kurdish sub-tribe located in Kurdistan [105].

Perhaps the most ancient example of Persian outerwear is the shepherd's cape constructed of handmade felt [106]. This cape is worn by both the Persian Qashqai and the Iranian and Iraqi Kurds. Garments of this cut have had a wide distribution in the past, ranging from West Turkestan to the Balkans, where the shepherd's cape is regarded as a

106 A Qashqai shepherd's felt cape—note its long, narrow, closed sleeves— provides the wearer with an insulating, waterproof covering during the long hours spent watching over a flock.

Turkic fashion.[12] Coats with similar long, narrow, closed sleeves, dating from the 5th to 4th centuries B.C., have been found in the Central Asian barrow-burials of Katanda and Pazyryk. These have been compared to the long coats of the Achaemenid-period Persian aristocracy, who wore their narrow sleeves hanging empty. According to the Greek historian Xenophon, ca. 352 B.C., this fashion was adopted from the Medes.[13]

That two of the Iranian nomads' traditional garments—the Kurd/Qashqai shepherd's cape and the Qashqai hat—are constructed of hand-made felt is of particular interest, as these pieces probably represent ancient survivals from the Eurasian steppes.

HEADGEAR

Today the Qashqai felt hat—commercially made and bazaar marketed—serves as the men's sole remaining ethnic garment [see 97, 98, 100, 106]. There is speculation that this hat's ancestry can be traced to the rounded helmets worn by the Medean soldiers displayed on the reliefs at Persepolis [107].[14]

HAIRSTYLES

As do all Iranian females, Kurdish women cover their heads. However, their long hair is not completely confined but rather is allowed to fall over their shoulders. Among the Qashqai, styles of hairdressing distinguish married from unmarried

107 A sculptured relief from the great Achaemenid palace and ceremonial center of Persepolis, ca. 521 B.C., showing alternating figures of Persians and Medes. Note that the Medes' conical helmets are reminiscent of modern-day Qashqai felt hats.

women: both have their long hair dressed in many fine plaits at the back but married women tuck their hair inside their veil, whereas unmarried women frame their faces with their locks.[15]

ACCESSORIES

For Iranian tribesmen, as for other Middle Eastern nomadic groups (see "The Arabian Peninsula," p. 52), a gun is a man's proudest, most important accessory. Almost every adult carries some form of firearm, new or old: shotguns, AK57 or Kalashnikov rifles, G-3 machine guns, Uzi submachine guns. This abundance of weapons was not lost on Reza Shah Pahlavi when he was trying to control the all-too-independent nomads; the ruler's clothing edict included a directive to disarm the tribes.

JEWELRY

Much Iranian tribal jewelry includes styles of silver pieces common throughout the Islamic world: prayer containers and necklaces with inscriptions from the Koran or hung with pendant coins (see "The Arabian Peninsula," p. 52). There are, however, two specific types of jewelry particularly important in Iran: 1) open-ended bracelets with their finials in the form of an animal or serpent head associated with the Achaemenid period, although similar pieces are also found in the Aegean area; 2) an impressive collection of gemstones amassed over the centuries by conquering Persian rulers.

The Iranian crown jewels and their tumultuous lineage hold a unique place in the annals of Persian history. This spectacular collection—now housed in

108 On the stone cliffs of Naqsh-i-Rustum—a site located near the older Achaemenid center of Persepolis—are great carved rectangular tableaux of 3rd-century A.D. Sassanian rulers. Here the warrior king Shapur I, ca. A.D. 226, confronts his prisoner, the Roman emperor Valerian. Shapur wears the distinctive Sassanian crown, above which balloons a snood that contains the king's virilely abundant hair.

the vaults of Tehran's Central Bank of the Islamic Republic of Iran—is understandably famous. Indeed, in 1975 the jewels' collective worth served as backing for 75% of all Iranian currency.[16] One of the most intriguing and instructive pieces in the entire collection is the crown made for the coronation of the first Pahlavi ruler. Reza Shah chose not to use the crown traditionally worn by his Qajar-dynasty predecessors but instead had a new royal insignia designed, one fashioned on the headgear worn by the powerful Sassanian rulers of the 3rd century A.D. [108]. The similarity between these headpieces [109] is unmistakable and speaks to Reza Shah's determination to symbolize both the continuity of Persia's 2,500-year monarchial tradition and his break with the immediate past so as to force Iran into a new, modern era.[17]

TRANSITIONAL DRESS

Although today Iranian tribal women, when seen on the city streets of Kurdistan, Shiraz or Tehran, are prudently clad in the cover-up black *chador*, the items they purchase in their own special section of the bazaar—the nomad market—make it clear that the daily clothing worn in their own milieu is still colorful and very much a part of the on-going nomadic tradition. Despite all of the political pressures brought to bear in the 20th century, some fraction of Iranian indigenous dress has stubbornly continued into the new millennium.

109 The new crown designed for Reza Shah Pahlavi at the time of his 1925 coronation was modeled on that of the ancient Sassanian kings.

EUROPE

THE SUBCONTINENT known today as Europe is a huge promontory that juts out from the western edge of the Eurasian landmass. The period of initial European peopling by *Homo sapiens* is generally accepted as ca. 50,000 B.C., though waves of hominid migration occurred much earlier—starting, according to some anthropologists, as long ago as 1,000,000 B.C. Except in the east, none of Europe's inland areas is located far from the sea. When humans finally learned how to manage long-distance water travel, the Europeans found themselves favorably placed at the edge of major wind systems and air currents, which later enabled them to set forth to colonize the world. For internal communication, Europe's river valleys initially provided the main north–south routes. East–west movement took place along the great plain that extends across the northern European heartland where modern-day France, the Low Countries, Germany, Poland, the Baltic lands and Russia are now located, a great two-way corridor along which Central Asian migrants moved west and subsequent Europeans trekked east. This broad plain—an entity roughly the same size as the United States, with a similarly diverse ethnicity—plays out in the foothills of the Ural and Caucasus mountains, the arbitrary eastern end of Europe. What Europeans chiefly share is their diversity, the factor that may have made them both energetic and combative. Successive waves of invasions, mainly from the east, followed by centuries of rivalry and conflict both within Europe and overseas, have repeatedly proven Europeans to be enterprising and aggressive.[1]

PREHISTORIC EUROPE

110 Upper Paleolithic women wearing fur skirts. Detail from a mural painted in a rock shelter at Cogul, Lérida, Spain, ca. 8000 B.C. The colors here have been artificially enhanced to show details.

Recent genetic data indicate that anatomically modern humans—*Homo sapiens*, ancestors of us all—migrated into Europe from the Near East as early as 50,000 years ago.[1] Until that time the early hominid *Homo neander-thalensis*, who apparently evolved as a distinct species some 130,000 years ago, had Europe all to himself. However, over a period of a few thousand years after the arrival of modern man, *H. neanderthalensis* had disappeared.[2] Subsequently, the number of early Europeans diminished drastically during the last Ice Age, but then began slowly to rebuild.

The period of human activity at the end of the last major Pleistocene glaciation is termed the Paleolithic (Old Stone Age); that portion of it from 35,000 to

8000 B.C. is known as the Upper Paleolithic, a time span that occupies only approximately one-tenth of the entire period. Early man made his greatest cultural breakthroughs during the Upper Paleolithic, innovations that included the development of the earliest-known garments, clothing for which we have only inferential evidence.

FUR/SKIN GARMENTS

The advance and retreat of the ice sheets with their accompanying glacial environments had significant impact on human activity. A necessary solution to the problem of surviving under extremely cold conditions was the creation of warm clothing fashioned to encase the limbs, follow the lines of the body, and protect the head [111]. These fur/skin garments were probably similar to those still being worn by the Alaskan Inuit in the early decades of the 20th century (see "The Arctic," pp. 335–339). This analogy is strengthened by European archaeological finds—eyed needles made of antler, bone or ivory that were apparently used for sewing fur garments—and also by clothing data deduced from burial remains.

Although few Upper Paleolithic burials have been found, the extant evidence indicates that both males and females were buried fully dressed. The archaeologists Olga Soffer, James M. Adovasio and David C. Hyland state that "reconstructions of clothes worn by the deceased in three of the most complete burials from Sungir [Russia]…25,000 B.C.…use the placement of beads and deformation in the bead strands to posit sewn, hooded top garments, pants with attached footwear, capes and caps or hats."[3] The three individuals found in one of the burials—an older male, an adolescent female and a 7- to 9-year-old boy—all wore a plethora of bracelets, necklaces and rings.

The scholar Carl Schuster, studying social symbolism in Paleolithic iconography, focused on the practice of extended families illustrating their genealogical relationships by painting their particular "statements" on their clothes, bodies and tools. As a result, each kin group proclaimed its lineage whenever it set forth. Schuster maintained that the same genealogical rules that had originated in the Upper Paleolithic—as well as their underlying rationale—were everywhere the same throughout the world [112].[4] He contended that this ancient phenomenon, while surviving in the tribal arts of certain ethnic groups removed from the modern mainstream (see also "Island Southeast Asia," p. 300), fell into disfavor with the rise of city-states and the invention of writing.

The appearance of art was a major innovation in the history of mankind. The earliest examples in Europe date from the Upper Paleolithic [see 110]. The most spectacular of these artworks are the paintings and incised images found on the walls of ancient caves located mainly in France and Spain [Map 6]. These dramatic scenes are dominated by large animals such as mammoths, horses, bison, rhinoceroses, bears and lions.[5] Although depictions of human figures are rare, there are repeating abstract symbols such as dots and negative handprints. Modern scholars have interpreted prehistoric cave paintings in various ways: shamanic visions, hunting magic, and even as signs of social divisions, with

111 This human figure, apparently seated and wearing a parka, was discovered at Le Gabillou, Sourzac, Dordogne, France. Because the image appears at the very center of the cave's major compositions—where females tend to be depicted—it may in fact be a woman.

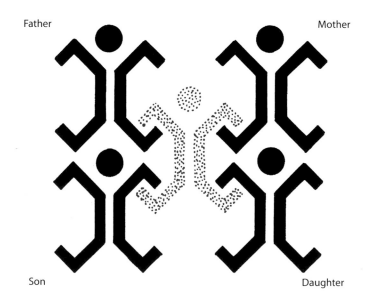

Father

Mother

Son

Daughter

112 Abstracted human figures may have been the basic building blocks used to illustrate genealogical lineages, a phenomenon that possibly originated in the Upper Paleolithic and has remained extant in a few tribal arts created by isolated present-day ethnic groups.

certain animals interpreted as representing men and others as women.[6]

PLANT-FIBER GARMENTS

On a par with the first appearance of art—and occurring within that same time span—was the life-altering discovery of how to create string from plant fiber (see also "The Ancient Near East," pp. 17–18). Because plant fibers are highly perishable, archaeologists have had to seek out indirect evidence of a fiber technology. It was recently determined that a "mature" textile and basketry tradition was already established in early Upper Paleolithic times. This data comes from two Paleolithic sites, ca. 26,000 B.C., in the Moravian region of the Czech Republic. At the site of Pavlov I,[7] the evidence was obtained from imprints of woven material—interlaced basketry and textiles—found on four specimens of fired clay. The archaeologists' use of the term "textile," defined as a fully flexible fabric or cloth, implies that some sort of stationary hanging or horizontal non-heddle frame or loom was employed in the manufacturing process during the Upper Paleolithic. This is much longer ago than had been previously imagined.[8] Indeed, one of the principal Pavlov I investigators, James M. Adovasio, believes that European textile manufacture probably predates the 26,000 B.C. readings for the Czech sites, appearing "as early as 40,000 B.C., at a minimum, and possibly much further back in time."[9]

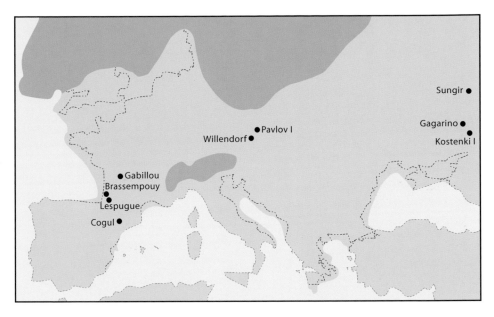

Insight into Upper Paleolithic cloth and clothing comes not only from archaeological excavations but also from iconographic evidence. Depictions of enigmatic prehistoric garments appear on some examples of Upper Paleolithic portable art: small female figurines made of finely carved stone, ivory or fired clay created during the Gravettian/Pavlov Period, 27,000 to 20,000 years ago. These so-called Venus figures show a marked similarity all across Europe, from the Iberian peninsula to the Russian plain. All of the hand-sized statuettes display emotionally charged primary and secondary sexual characteristics: vulvae, breasts, stomachs and buttocks [113]. There are somewhere between 70 to 200 of these figures, depending on whether one includes all of the torso and head fragments.[10] Soffer et al state: "There have been varying explanations of these provocative figurines [ranging from] 'fertility symbols,' 'mother goddess,' paleoerotica, gynecological primers and self-portraiture to suggestions that they were signifiers of widespread social ties."[11] In marked contrast to the Venus statuettes, there is a scarcity of male Paleolithic figurines.

Inasmuch as the daily wear of Ice Age peoples would have been made of such animal by-products as furs and hides, it is particularly noteworthy that the scanty clothing depicted on some of the Venus figures appears to be made of plant-based textiles. There are three categories of these fiber garments: 1) headgear; 2) bandeaux; 3) belts and skirts.

HEADGEAR

The headgear worn by the Venus of Willendorf [see 113] is not an elaborate hairdo but rather a hat or cap constructed of one or two flexible plant-fiber cords worked into a "spirally or radially handwoven item which may be initiated by a knotted center in the manner of some kinds of coiled basketry."[12] Such a complex construction probably could not have been produced simply by manipulating the hair on an individual's head.

It is of interest that when such hats/caps are depicted on Venus figurines, all facial details are quite

often absent. This could perhaps point to the social as opposed to the individual importance of headgear in Paleolithic ideology.[13] On the other hand, the makers of the Venus figures could have been drawing attention to the hair on the head as an analogue to the pubic hair that indicates the attainment of puberty/fertility.[14]

Map 6 Map showing locations of Upper Paleolithic cave sites and Venus figurine sites.

▨ Upper Paleolithic glaciations

------ Present-day coastlines

113 The Venus of Willendorf, a 25,000-year-old limestone statuette originally colored with red ochre, was discovered in Austria in 1908. The figurine is depicted wearing a plant-fiber hat made of one or two cords worked in a spiral manner from a knotted center, a technique also seen in coiled basketry. Venus figurines wearing such hats often lack facial features.

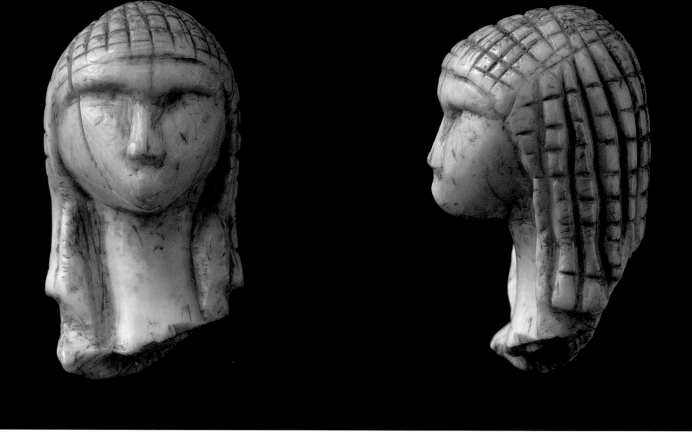

114 Two views of a fragmentary head of a Venus figurine from the Aurignacian-Gravettian period (ca. 22,000 B.C.) found in the Grotte du Pape, Brassempouy, Landes, France. Height 1³/₈ in. (3.5 cm). This ivory head is depicted wearing a plant-fiber hairnet.

There is a further category of Venus headgear to be noted: nets or snoods [114]. These headcoverings appear to be made of some form of flexible, open, perhaps twined construction to create a net or netted snood that was fitted over the head.[15] Similar netted headgear has been found in Danish bogs on female bodies recovered from prehistoric interments made during the Iron Age, ca. 1200 B.C.[16]

BANDEAUX

The second group of fiber-based textiles etched on Venus figurines are a series of woven bands worn above and below a figure's breasts and across the upper back, a device that resembles a cupless brassiere [115]. Soffer et al identify the construction of these textiles as being reminiscent of open twining with running-loop, continuous-weft selvedges.[17] Whatever the specific weaves may have been, these engravings of garments indicate woven fabrics. Also, what clearly looks like sewing is carefully depicted at the points where the supporting straps are joined to the body of the bandeau.

BELTS AND SKIRTS

The third set of fiber-plant textiles includes belts worn around the waist or low on the hips. These bands sometimes support string skirts, some worn only across the front [116], others only at the back [117]. The skirt on the Lespugne Venus displays remarkable attention to detail when depicting the twisted fiber strings; the tightness and angle of each individual twist of the fiber is clearly depicted [see also 176].[18]

The question arises as to when, where and why such plant-fiber clothing was used. Given the frigid weather, it was probably not daily wear but more likely ritual attire, real or imagined. Views differ as to why the garments were worn. Some suggest that the clothing served as a signifier of a distinct class of prestigious female—those wearing the fiber garments—and posit that these women were also likely the actual inventors and producers of the figurines.[19] It has also been suggested that the skirts served as particularly provocative announcements of arrival at puberty and thus female fertility, and hence would have been worn at the time and place most auspicious for displaying that all-important declaration.[20]

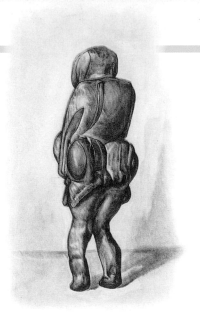

115 (above) The Russian Venus of Kostenki displays a plant-fiber garment worn above and below her breasts and across her upper back. The detailed depictions of these carefully joined textiles clearly indicate woven fabrics.

116 (above right) A drawing of a Venus figure apparently wearing a short string skirt only across the front of her body. The figurine was found on Russia's upper Don River, at the Paleolithic site of Gagarino.

117 (above) A small Upper Paleolithic Venus figure, found at Lespugue, France, carved of bone ca. 20,000 B.C.+ (Gravettian culture). The figure wears a skirt made of plant fiber twisted into strings and suspended from a hip band. Such string skirts apparently signified that a female had reached childbearing age.

TRANSITIONAL DRESS

By the end of the Upper Paleolithic, the crucial genetic changes in *Homo sapiens* had already occurred: geographic and climatic divisions had produced specializations in skin pigment, hair characteristics, skull shape and facial structure. The distribution of the world's major racial divisions had taken place; those in Europe were already light-skinned and physiologically distinctive from darker-skinned humans living in other parts of the world. Henceforth human evolution involved social and cultural developments.

The continuity of Upper Paleolithic cave art stretched over a period of some 15,000 years, "a startlingly long time for the maintenance of so consistent a style and content."[21] This impressive duration not only reflects the slowness with which prehistoric traditions evolved but also their attendant imperviousness to change due to geographic isolation.

As for clothing, certain scholars contend that the fundamental forms of future European garments were established during the Upper Paleolithic—a simple tunic, skirt, divided coverings for the legs, capes and moccasins/boots[22]—and hardly changed in essentials until the middle of the 14th century A.D.

Although the European way of life, including clothing, may have remained static for millennia, the waning of the last Ice Age allowed for a series of momentous events to take place elsewhere, changes that led to the last and greatest breakthroughs in prehistory: the domestication of animals and the invention of agriculture (see "The Ancient Near East," pp. 14–15).

CLASSICAL EUROPE

118 Toga-clad dignitaries at the textile-adorned forum in Léon Jaussely's *Restauratio du Forum de Pompéi*, 1910.

With the receding of the great ice sheets, the developments that would shape Europe's future shifted to the Mediterranean, an inland sea bordered by narrow coastal plains that rise to lofty mountain ranges. As a result of this topography, when European civilization developed it spread predominantly along the Mediterranean's shoreline, influenced strongly by cultural influences from the Middle East.[1]

By the end of the Upper Paleolithic, the Europeans were altering their environment. A conjunction of favorable circumstances—a mild temperature, adequate rainfall and the fortuitous proximity of most of the world's domesticable plants and animals at roughly the same latitude[2]—provided an ideal foundation for the rapid spread of agriculture.[3] Indeed, agriculture would be the key to population growth, just as the ability to produce and store food was a precondition of civilization.

MINOAN DRESS

In the Eastern Mediterranean, between ca. 5000 and 1500 B.C., a new world—different from that of the Ancient Near East and Egypt's Old Kingdom—was taking shape among the multiple islands of the Aegean from which short sea crossings allowed regular access to the earliest civilizations [Map 7]. The nearest Aegean

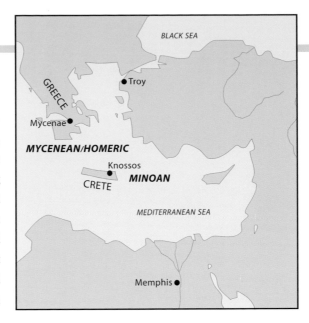

Map 7 The Early Bronze Age Minoan sphere and subsequent Mycenean/ Homeric world.

island to Egypt was Crete and by 2200 B.C. the entrepreneurial Cretans had built a trading network which, in due course, developed into a true civilization complete with a complex social organization, writing systems and monumental buildings. These island people also had a costume repertory that was an intriguing departure from both the spirally wrapped woolen cloths that were standard attire in ancient Mesopotamia (see "The Ancient Near East," p. 20) and the sheer, sleeved linen tunics worn in Old Kingdom Egypt (see "The Ancient Near East," p. 24).

Crete's Early Bronze Age Minoan civilization was named for the legendary King Minos who lived—with his great beast, the Minotaur—in the palace at Knossos. Extant Minoan art, together with archaeological data, provides evidence of the Cretans' way of life. Theirs was a matrilineal society—the sea-faring men spent much time away—where women owned and controlled not only their homes but their textile production as well:[4] the differences between male and female clothing reflect this social structure. The long-haired, bare-chested Minoan men were most often depicted wearing short, wrapped loincloths/kilts—often with decorated borders—secured at the waist by tight, cinched belts [119]. In contrast, female attire was far more elaborate.

119 A bare-chested Minoan dignitary wearing a cinch belt to which was attached a loincloth/kilt with a carefully detailed border, perhaps embroidered. These garments were often woven with distinctive and ornate designs that are sometimes found on the walls of Egyptian tombs; the Cretans' colorful clothing obviously made an impression on their trading partners. This restored image of a Minoan male is reconstructed from two sections of the same Minoan fresco, but not from the same individual. As a result, the figure is somewhat distorted.

120 This polychrome faience statuette was discovered on Crete in the ruins of the palace of Knossos. The impressive bare-breasted female, who holds a snake in each hand and balances a cat on her head, may be a Minoan priestess, or perhaps a fertility goddess. Her elaborate, bell-shaped, flounced skirt, and her sleeved, fitted jacket—as well as her curved apron—reflect a tailored approach to clothing construction.

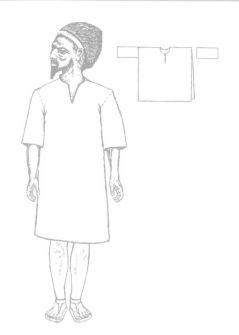

121 A coat of armor made of bronze and a boar's tusk helmet with metal ear plates were found on the Greek mainland at Mycenae (ca. 1400 B.C.), the fortified acropolis of King Agamemnon, one of the most powerful of the Homeric heroes. As the *Iliad* makes clear, these early Greek warriors tended to be all but invincible against enemies who did not have the advantage of such metallic protection.

122 The central section of the Myceneans' tunic pulled over the head to hang from the shoulders, encasing the torso; the attached sleeves appear almost to be an afterthought.

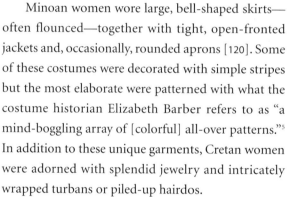

123 The Greeks' sleeveless tunic consisted of a flat linen cloth folded in half vertically and then suspended equally from both shoulders.

Minoan women wore large, bell-shaped skirts—often flounced—together with tight, open-fronted jackets and, occasionally, rounded aprons [120]. Some of these costumes were decorated with simple stripes but the most elaborate were patterned with what the costume historian Elizabeth Barber refers to as "a mind-boggling array of [colorful] all-over patterns."[5] In addition to these unique garments, Cretan women were adorned with splendid jewelry and intricately wrapped turbans or piled-up hairdos.

The distinctive costume of the Minoan women necessitated the cutting and sewing of their cloth. This tailored approach to clothing construction[6] did not continue into the Greco-Roman classical world, but a bell-skirted costume does reappear here and there in certain Bronze and Iron Age Balkan cultures, notably in Bulgaria and Serbia (see "The European Folk Tradition," p. 101).[7]

CLASSICAL GREEK DRESS

When high Minoan civilization fell sometime between 1500 and 1400 B.C., the cultural dynamic shifted to the mainland. As early as the 18th century B.C., Indo-Europeans out of Western Eurasia had begun to conquer and settle areas in the eastern half of Greece. These patriarchal Greek-speakers, the early Hellenes, became aristocratic landowners with horses, war chariots and fortified acropoleis, the most famous of which was King Agamemnon's Mycenae. The early

Greeks' militaristic way of life was immortalized in two oral poems extolling the siege of Troy, the *Iliad* and the *Odyssey*, said to have been composed in the 8th century B.C. by the poet Homer. These heroic epics depict an aristocracy of tribal war chiefs preoccupied with combat and courage [121] and they had a lasting impact, setting forth the fundamental values for the subsequent Greco-Roman world.

The clothing of King Agamemnon's Myceneans had an ancient lineage. Their simple, sleeved, T-shaped garments were constructed of three seamed tubes of cloth [122], a style that apparently originated in the Semitic Near East[8] and then moved into Southeast Europe where it was adopted by the Myceneans, along with the Semitic-based word *khiton*. The long, sleeved *khiton*—also referred to as a *chiton*, tunic or chemise—subsequently became a basic garment for much of European folk dress, particularly that of the Balkans, Central Europe, the steppelands and the Caucasus.[9] But for the Greece of later times a quite different manner of dress evolved, one that was probably introduced at the end of the Bronze Age, ca. 1100 B.C., by Indo-European tribes—sometimes referred to as "the Dorians"—who came down from the north. This untailored, draped approach to clothing construction was not to change for nearly a millennium.

We know a great deal about the Greeks of the Classical Age (500–323 B.C.) thanks both to their literary heritage and to archaeology. With their magnificent monumental architecture and exquisite depictions of the nude—both in statuary and fine-line drawing—the Greeks were cultural exporters, setting standards that included a manner of dressing where the sleeveless, draped tunic was basic attire [123]. This version of the *chiton* was a single piece of cloth, folded in half vertically and suspended from both shoulders,[10] creating a garment particularly suited to the warm Mediterranean climate. The earliest archaeological find of complete Greek clothing—dating to about 1000 B.C.—is a white linen tunic with a pattern-woven sash.[11]

When in battle, the hoplite warriors—the heavily armed infantry who were the backbone of Greek armies—wore short body armor [124] and distinctive crested helmets [125].

All civilian Greek clothing reflected various ways of draping rectangles of linen or wool that, after wearing, could be smoothed, folded and efficiently stored flat.[12] The simple linen *chiton*—usually worn belted—was the primary garment for Greek men and women of all periods [126]. An additional garment was the *chlamys*, the male civic/military cloak worn over the shoulders and fastened with a brooch or stick pin [127]. A longer mantle, the *himation*—a large cloak for men of roughly 6½ × 9 feet (2 × 2.75 m)—wrapped around the body and draped over one shoulder in such a way that no fastener was required [128].

The beautifully draped clothing of Classical Greece emphasized the contours of the human body [129], which the Greeks held in high esteem. It must be noted, however, that the ideal of heroic nudity regularly depicted in Greek art—most often the toned and muscular body of a youthful athlete—does not mean that in real life Greek men had to suffer from the cold by walking about naked at all times.[13]

For some Greek women, the main outer attire—worn over the soft linen *chiton*—was the *peplos* [130, 131], a rather heavy woolen rectangle folded vertically and then wrapped around the body with an overfold at the top that allowed for adjusting the length of the garment to fit the wearer. In addition to the *chiton* and *peplos*, Greek women also sometimes wore a short cape

124 A Greek painting, found on a Corinthian ceramic vase, depicts the movement and formation of the hoplites, who here advance into battle to the sound of the flute. These warriors wore protective helmets with body armor and carried large shields; their main weapon was the spear, used to thrust and stab rather than to throw. Each man, to protect his right-hand side, relied on the shield of his neighbor. As a result it was crucial to maintain an orderly line in combat.

over the shoulders, "a small mantle that usually fastened at or near the throat, opening wide at the front and often stopping short of the breasts."[14]

Both Greek men and women wore sandals; the leather soles were attached to leather thongs that crossed in various ways and were bound around the

125 Two identical Greek warriors appear on a Chalcidian vase of the Corinthian type, ca. 580–510 B.C. Their helmets cover the entire head, the cheeks, the bridge of the nose and the back of the neck; each warrior's hair emerges from beneath his helmet.

126 A Greek charioteer from Delphi wearing a long *chiton*: artisans, warriors and slaves wore shorter versions, often with the right shoulder left bare. The wearer's waist is encircled with a belt, creating a bloused effect. What appears to be sleeves is simply material that has sagged over the shoulders on either side.

128 The Greek man's *himation* was a large woolen cloak that wrapped about the body and draped over one shoulder. This statue depicts the Athenian orator and statesman Demosthenes, carved by the Greek sculptor Polyclitus.

127 The *chlamys* was worn over the shoulders and secured by a stick pin. This sculpture is a Roman copy of a Greek original from the 1st century B.C., an example of how Rome's reverence for Greek cultural objects has preserved ancient treasures that otherwise would have been lost.

129 (top) A fragment of the Athenian Parthenon frieze illustrates the variety of ways in which the Greeks wore simple pieces of cloth draped on the body. The event depicted is the great civic celebration held every four years to honor the goddess Athena. The entire community participated in a solemn procession to the Acropolis, bearing a new robe—made of complex, "story-telling" cloth—for the ancient wooden statue of Athena.

130 (above) A diagram illustrating the folding of the *peplos*, the ancient Greek garment made by draping a flat woolen cloth around the body with an overfold at the top that allowed for adjusting the length to fit the wearer.

131 (right) Figure shown wearing the *peplos*, the rectangular woolen cloth folded vertically and wrapped around the body, leaving an overfold at the top. This esteemed garment was also the traditional dress of Greek goddesses.

Map 8 The Hellenistic world—so-called because Greek language and culture were its unifying components—came into being as the result of the many victories of Alexander the Great, conquests that reached from Greece in the west to the Indian Ocean in the east.

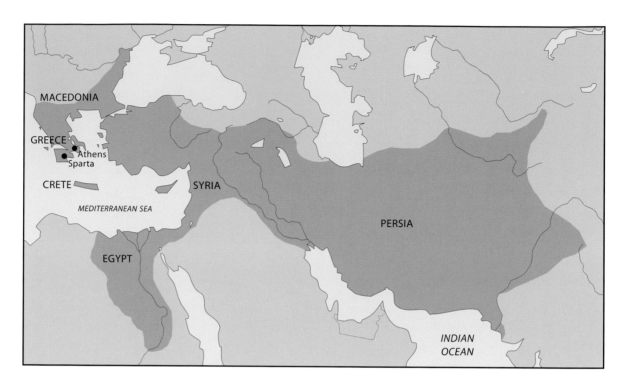

ankle. For travel or warfare, men also sometimes wore fitted shoes—ankle-high or mid-calf length—or leather boots that laced up the front.[15]

Influencing the evolution of Classical Greek clothing were the all-consuming Greco-Persian wars that raged between 490 and 480 B.C., the humiliating year that Athens was entered and sacked. Even before this defeat, the Greeks had considered all things Persian anathema. Because the ornately clad, richly decorated victors from Asia Minor followed the oriental custom of almost completely covering the body, it may have become a political statement for the Greeks to simplify their own garments in order to contrast the "rugged" Greeks with the "effeminate" Persians.[16]

Although the Greek city-states—the institutions that had sustained and sheltered Greek civilization—managed to rebuild after the Persian wars, they increasingly fought amongst themselves. By 404 B.C.—the termination of the embittering 27-year Peloponnesian War between Athens, Sparta and their respective allies—the best days of Classical Greece were waning. History's focus now moved from the original heartland to Macedonia, at the northern edge of Greek culture. This was the region

that produced Alexander the Great, who, by the second half of the 4th century B.C., had conquered not only mighty Persia but also many additional kingdoms stretching from Greece and Egypt in the west to the shores of the Indian Ocean in the east. This impressive series of victories had a profound influence on the clothing of the subsequent Hellenistic Age.

As a result of Alexander's victorious campaigns, the Greeks now became the overlords rather than the besieged; the conquerors' clothing and adornments increasingly reflected their new-found wealth and power. In the extensive Hellenistic world [Map 8] a rich array of exotic textiles was now available: the famous, colorful, beautifully detailed wool tapestries from Syria; the cool, lightweight, easily dyed cotton clothes from India and Egypt; the shimmering, pattern-woven silks from China, heavy brocades carried west in the baggage of Central Asian nomads who received these bright, colorful fabrics as bribes to stay out of the Celestial Kingdom.[17]

Under the reign of Alexander the Great, a magnificent jewelry era began. In the 3rd and 2nd centuries B.C. the technical ability of Hellenistic goldsmiths and jewelers reached the highest level yet attained. Their virtuosity in working with miniatures was reflected in the creation of the first cameos. On a different scale, the wearing of magnificent diadems came into wide use as a result of the Persian conquests. Bracelets in the shape of snakes began to be created in the 3rd century B.C. and remained popular throughout the Roman period, as did snake-motif rings.[18]

ETRUSCAN DRESS

Far to the west of the prosperous Hellenistic sphere another vital world existed. In central Italy lay the Early Iron Age civilization of the Etruscans, who, from their emergence in the 9th century B.C. to their absorption by Rome in the 1st century A.D., played a central role in receiving and adopting the clothing styles of Ancient Greece and transmitting this tradition to Rome. There was, however, one important garment that was original to Etruria, the rounded *tebenna* cloak which was the forerunner of the Roman citizens' toga.

From the Greeks, the Etruscans adopted the use of flat cloth for clothing, as well as the way in which they wore these woven rectangles.[19] An example of this practice is a Greek-inspired Etruscan mantle [132] diagonally draped in the manner of the Greek man's *himation* [see 128]. Despite such similarities, it must be noted that there was a striking and very basic difference between the Greek and Etruscan approach to covering the body. The Etruscans tended to express their respect for an individual or his/her depiction by fully dressing the figure,[20] a marked departure from the Greeks' clothing philosophy of "less is more."

ROMAN DRESS

The historian J. M. Roberts has suggested that the Roman Empire was the last of the successor states of the Alexandrian world and as such was responsible for the transmission of much of Greek classical heritage to future European civilizations.[21] Viewing the matter from another perspective, one Roman wryly noted that Greek culture once again took her captors captive to Hellenize yet another set of barbarians.[22]

Indeed, the Roman world adopted many facets of Greek culture. Just as the Greek gods and goddesses were worshipped under Latin names, so too the same manner of dressing passed from one civilization to the other, via the Etruscans. The Romans made a distinction between garments that were "put on" (*indutus*) and garments that were "wrapped around" (*amictus*). The latter referred to outerwear, whereas *induti* were worn underneath, closest to the skin.[23] Because the Romans did not inherit the Greek attitude toward nudity, there is a high degree of modesty displayed

132 An Etruscan noble attired in a draped garment worn in a manner very similar to the Greeks' *himation*. However, the Greeks would not have been likely to wear an encasing tunic beneath a fully draped cloak.

133 (top) Over the diaper-shaped loincloth, which tied underneath, was worn a short linen tunic fastened so as to leave the right shoulder bare. Such skimpy tunics were the typical garment of the Roman lower classes.

134 (above) Two young Roman women depicted on a mosaic from an excavated villa in Sicily, ca. 3rd or 4th century, wear bikini-like underpants—actually a feminine version of the Roman diaper-shaped loincloth that tied beneath—together with flattening breast binders.

when representing a human body, be it male or female.[24] As a result, there is limited visual evidence for Roman undergarments; only athletes or gladiators were ever depicted wearing merely a loincloth, a shaped, diaper-like garment that tied underneath. Even lowly workmen wore a simple short tunic over their loincloth [133]. As for women's underwear, they wore a "dainty version of the man's loincloth,"[25] resulting in depictions showing females in surprisingly modern-looking bikini-like briefs. The accompanying garment was the breast band, which does not seem to have provided any shaping to cup the breasts; it either flattened or merely held them in place [134].[26]

Another example of distinctively female attire was the special costume worn for a young woman's wedding, the most significant rite of passage for a Roman girl. The most important elements of a bride's attire centered on her head: a special way of arranging the hair into six braids, all covered by a diaphanous, flame-colored veil. Yellow was claimed by Pliny the Elder to be the earliest color to be highly esteemed,[27] while the costume historian Elizabeth Barber notes the Ancient Minoans' practice of collecting the stamens of the saffron lily to obtain a yellow dye, as well as to use in making a medicine for menstrual cramps.[28] Covering the head of sexually mature females was very important to the Romans, who adhered to a practice that may have derived from the age-old belief that a woman's sexual powers are concentrated in her hair (see "The Arabian Peninsula," p. 46). The Romans' bridal veil therefore symbolized constancy and lifelong fidelity to one man.[29]

Roman outer attire differed little from that of the preceding Greek world and was draped in the Greek/Etruscan manner. Males, females and children all dressed in the same basic garment, the tunic, worn to mid-calf by men, to full- or ankle-length by women. These *chitons* were attached at the shoulder by brooches, by buttons or by sewing, and were usually belted; Roman women sometimes created a double-bloused effect by belting their tunics twice, once just below the breast and again around the hips. The Roman matrons' wide tunics—which were often pleated into tiny folds—were sometimes held together at the shoulder by a series of buttons along a sleeve. As for the Roman women's *peplos*, it was an adaptation of the Greek garment of the same name [see 130, 131]. The everyday, wraparound mantles worn by both men and women—the male *pallium* and the female *palla*—were made of varying sizes of wool rectangles; the more enveloping of these warm Roman cloaks were created from elliptical, rectangular, circular or half-circular woolen pieces.

In spite of marked socioeconomic differences, the primary distinction made in Roman society was between citizen and non-citizen, a practice clearly reflected in the society's dress, which was sharply stratified. The Roman citizens' most important mantle was the toga, a draped, elliptically shaped garment that was descended from the Etruscan *tebenna*. The original garment evolved from a multi-purpose wrap for small Latin communities of herders and farmers to become the voluminous, imperial Roman toga [135] that required two or three slaves for its proper draping [136]. Only male citizens were entitled to don the toga; slaves, foreigners and the lower classes were prohibited from wearing it.[30]

Throughout the history of the Empire the toga remained the official dress of successive emperors and high officials. The garment's overall color and border type were rigidly prescribed for most wearers—only the emperor, for example, could wear a solid purple toga—as was the manner in which the toga was draped, which became increasingly complicated. The basic unwieldiness of the toga has been well documented. A man's left arm had to be held firmly against his side in order to hold the cloth in place on the left shoulder since the toga was nowhere pinned; only the weight of the cloth maintained the proper draping.[31] Rich men had special slaves whose chief duty was handling these wide and cumbersome garments. Although the toga obviously had its problems, as the historian Shelley Stone notes, "[the fact that the] imperial toga was a stately and impressive garment…together with its traditional associations, ensured its survival as ceremonial clothing …for formal or festive occasions."[32]

135 The Emperor Augustus Caesar—1st century B.C.—clad in the official imperial robe, the voluminous toga. For dignitaries, these prestigious garments were bordered with stripes of royal purple, an expensive color to attain because it was derived from the murex sea snail.

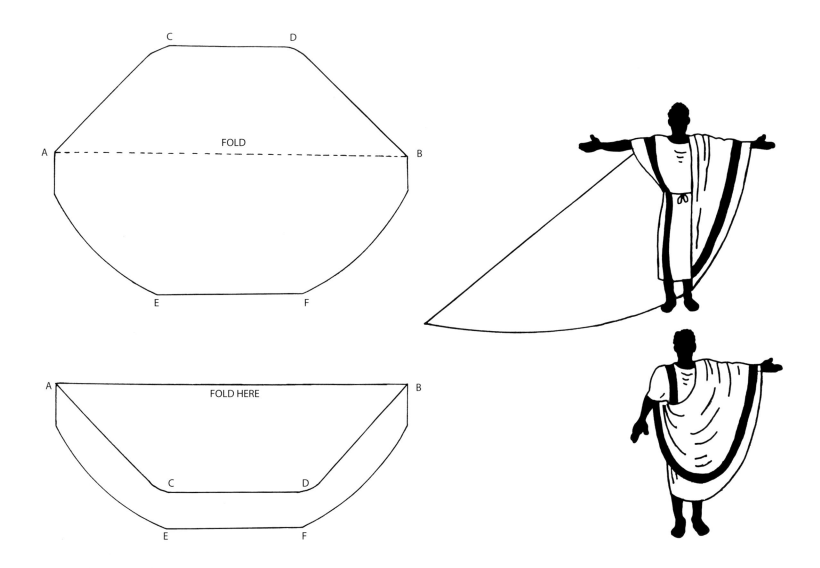

136 A diagram demonstrating the complexities of draping a toga. Once attired in this important garment—and only Roman citizens were allowed to wear it—a man had to hold his left arm close to his side so as to maintain the obligatory series of carefully arranged, draped folds; no fastener was used to secure the toga in place.

Among the Romans, footwear was differentiated by class and produced by specialists—shoemakers, bootmakers, sandalmakers, slipper makers and ladies' shoemakers. Among both the Greeks and Romans, footwear displayed a marked difference between left and right feet. Women wore closed shoes in varying colors; men wore sandals whose colors and straps denoted certain classes. Like Greek soldiers, the Romans wore sturdy, thick-soled boots that tied over the ankles but left the toes bare.[33]

Military power was the ultimate basis of the extensive Roman Empire [Map 9], which was maintained through constant expansion from approximately 27 B.C. to A.D. 400. It was the army that made possible the enlarging of the Roman world. The training, order and discipline of the famous Roman legions set a standard of military effectiveness never before attained.

Legionnaires dressed in distinctive battle array [137]. Nearest to the body was worn a short-sleeved linen tunic which fell to just above the knees. Over this inner garment was worn a protective vest-like jacket made of quilted wool or leather. From the lower edge of the vest a single row of long leather straps fell over the upper legs; shorter leather straps trimmed the vest's armholes.

Roman officers also donned a metal cuirass made in two main sections, the front breastplate and back dorsal plate were joined by a hinge along the right side of the torso with a system of hooks and pins [138]. Over the cuirass was customarily worn a large, rectangular military cloak.[34]

Map 9 The extent of the Roman Empire during its finest period, the Pax Romana—the approximately 200 years of peace between 27 B.C. and A.D. 180—when a traveler could safely traverse the Empire on a system of well-tended roads. This transportation network united the Roman world to such an extent that the Empire's clothing became increasingly homogenized.

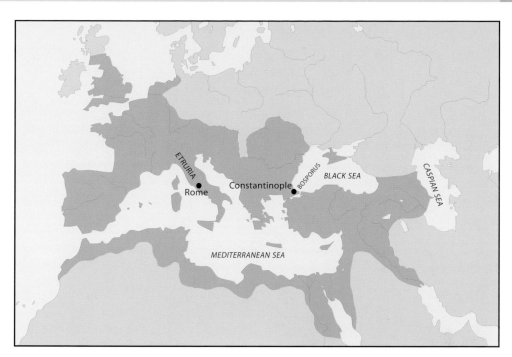

137 A group of Rome's Praetorian guard— ca. 2nd century A.D.— whose role was to protect the emperor, maintain public order and enforce the law. In addition to their protective military garb, the soldiers wear thick-soled, open-toed boots.

138 Roman muscle cuirasses have their origin in Greek hoplite armor. This example is made of bronze. Such heavy, solid pieces were worn only by high-ranking soldiers. They afforded excellent chest and back protection, but for flexibility of movement the garment grew progressively shorter over time until it covered only the ribs as opposed to the whole of the waist.

139 The south frieze of the Ara Pacis Augustae altar, dedicated to the peace established by the Roman Emperor Augustus, depicts a 13 B.C. procession of the imperial family. Note the posture of the toga-clad dignitaries: each man's arm is held crooked in order to hold the garment's heavy fabric secure on his left shoulder. Clearly, the commodious toga of the imperial age was ill-suited to much movement or the maintenance of the garment's complicated draping. Nonetheless, this stately and impressive attire survived as ceremonial clothing for the duration of the Roman Empire.

Ultimately, the Roman Empire's greatest triumph was the Pax Romana, approximately 200 years of prosperity and peace, from the reign of Augustus (27 B.C.–A.D. 14) through that of Marcus Aurelius (A.D. 161–180), which insured a traveler could move safely throughout the Roman world [see Map 9] on well-maintained roads, a communication system that tended to homogenize the garments of the Empire from Britain in the west to the Bosporus and on to the Caspian Sea in the east. As for Roman culture, it was an impressive derivative of Hellenistic Greece; Roman clothing reflected that legacy, though in a more modest and far fuller, more enveloping manner [139].

With the fall of Rome—ca. A.D. 400—a new power came to the fore, Christianity, a religion that had the advantage of emerging in an era of disillusionment and deep spiritual longing among the citizens of the Classical world, an age decreasing in vigor. Despite repeated attempts to stamp out Christianity, the number of converts throughout the Empire grew steadily.

BYZANTINE DRESS

In A.D. 330, Constantine, the first Christian emperor, built an imperial center on the site of Byzantium, an old Greek trading colony. The construction of this eastern capital, Constantinople, signaled the decline of the Western Empire. The new city quickly came to rival Rome, as well as to provide a focal point for the expansion of eastern Christian influence that steadily grew into the rich and powerful Byzantine Empire.

Early Byzantine and Late Roman clothing was virtually indistinguishable but, as time passed, the more ornate oriental mode prevailed, with the garments of the Byzantine wealthy becoming elaborately

patterned with embroidery, appliqué, precious stones and woven designs. The basic Byzantine garment also reverted to the ancient, eastern T-shaped sleeved tunic [see 122], worn either short or long. The latter type was cut with sleeves fitted to the wrist; over this was worn an outer tunic with fuller sleeves, the dalmatic, an ancient garment (a prototype of a sleeved "dalmatic," ca. 1350 B.C., was found in the tomb of the Egyptian ruler Tutankhamen[35]).

For women, the wide, long-sleeved dalmatic was increasingly worn over an under-tunic with closely fitted sleeves [140].[36] By the 2nd century A.D., the dalmatic—with its signature long, flowing sleeves—had also appeared in Western Europe where it subsequently became a liturgical vestment that is still in use today, placing the garment among the most authentic examples of ancient apparel inherited from Classical times.[37]

TRANSITIONAL DRESS

By the 4th century A.D., Europe's balance began to shift away from its original Mediterranean heritage. As the Classical Age faded and the Latin-speaking West grew ever-more distinct from the Greek-speaking East, the clothing traditions of the two areas fared quite differently. In the West—where the barbarian invasions of the 4th and 5th centuries transformed the cultural map of Europe and dealt the decadent Western Empire its death blow—hardly an echo of the Greco-Roman draped-clothing tradition remained. Even the Greeks' basic garment, the sleeveless *chiton* [see 123] disappeared completely; perhaps it was not modest enough for Christianity's new standards of dress.

Quite a different pattern emerged in the Greek-speaking East. The T-shaped linen tunic [see 122] not only survived the collapse of the Classical period but subsequently spread throughout medieval Europe. Indeed, this tunic has continued to be worn as the basic inner garment in rural sections of southeastern Europe. To this day, women are still sometimes seen wearing elaborately embroidered folk dresses over soft linen chemises; some of this woolen outer attire includes such intriguing, ancient elements as double aprons, one worn in front, the other in back.[38]

In sum, it is only examples of Europe's eastern tradition that have continued from Classical times into modern-day folk dress, particularly among the Slavic-speaking peoples of southern Russia, the Ukraine and the Balkans, where a rich tradition of rural clothing is only now, most sadly, disappearing (see "The European Folk Tradition," pp. 110–117).

140 The early Christian dalmatic had an ancient prototype found in the tomb of the Egyptian ruler Tutankhamen (ca. 1350 B.C.). The much later Byzantine version was a long cloak with wide, flowing sleeves that became popular in the eastern Empire and subsequently also appeared in Western Europe.

THE EUROPEAN FOLK TRADITION

141 Local Slovakian women, wearing their colorful regional dress, carry an image of the ancient, traditionally featureless fertility goddess Kisele through the fields at harvest time.

Although European folk dress as we know it fully crystallized only from the mid-18th through the 19th centuries,[1] it is possible to trace specific elements of it far back into pre-history. These ancient antecedents were very potent designs that had continued over the millennia because of their mythic, quasi-religious connotations. How these symbols survived is poorly documented but enough evidence exists to suggest that they appeared on ritual cloths, stone carvings and ceramic vessels used for ceremonial purposes, as well as on articles for household altars and in connection with nature worship, shamanistic practices and sacred clan rites.

During the Middle Ages, European peasant clothing tended to be somewhat uniform: unstructured in cut, muted in tone. The unrelenting pressure of strict sumptuary laws—imposed to govern the materials, styles and colors permitted to common people in a largely feudal society—served to stifle display or change. This was particularly true in Russia where the feudal system was not abolished until 1861, finally permitting the emancipation of the serfs. Once legislation controlling dress codes was lifted, the elaboration of rural clothing began—including the incorporation of ancient symbols—and geographic differences became increasingly pronounced, not only between localities but even between adjacent villages. Thereafter this distinctive attire served to mark affiliation to one's group.

The 19th-century tradition of localized folk dress reflected the conservative nature of the pre-industrial, rural world in which it evolved. Within those isolated, self-sufficient peasant villages there were rigid codes that controlled the communities' moral and ethical standards, detailing a fixed way to do everything from daily tasks to the arranging of marriages. So, too, there was prescribed, age-appropriate attire for every man, woman and child at each stage of their lives. In addition to garments for everyday wear, there was special, more elaborate clothing to be worn for church attendance, feast days and weddings.

Although this particular overview of Europe's folk tradition contains several illustrations of men's special clothing, there is less discussion here of male attire than of female because it was men who tended to mingle in the larger world, hence their apparel was more susceptible to influence from outside "modern" styles. Also, although many examples of male attire certainly display unique attributes [see 143–147], and some items, including the famous Alpine *lederhosen*, continue to be worn to this day, men almost always abandoned their village dress as regular wear long before women did. Even when village-bound, males were more apt to

have adopted the accepted, homogenous garb of their profession: farmer, carpenter, blacksmith, and so on. In contrast, women's lives were centered on the home, hence they were apt to be somewhat isolated; their clothing was also usually perceived to be a particularly important aspect of a community's cultural tradition.

The basic garments that made up the 18th-/19th-century peasant ensembles were fairly uniform: essentially a chemise, skirt and apron(s) for women; trousers of varying shapes, a belt or sash, and a T-shaped shirt for men. Cloaks and jackets might be worn as extra outerwear by both sexes. Although these simple pieces did evolve to a degree, the most intriguing aspect of this distinctive attire resides in its antiquity and the survival of certain of its decorative elements and magico-religious motifs [142]. It is these aspects of European folk costume that are discussed below.[2]

Folk dress is sometimes referred to as being non-Western because it developed outside the dictates of Western European fashion. In peasant villages, change coming from the larger world was judged by local rather than international standards, if it was accepted at all. Indeed, these "non-fashionable" garments—richly colored, painstakingly crafted and often densely embroidered—corresponded to each community's own internal sense of what could properly be elaborated. Even forced migrations were often not enough

142 On the left is a drawing of a Bronze Age clay figurine of a woman, found in a cremation urn at Cirna, southern Romania (mid- to late 2nd millennium B.C.). On the right is a typical Bulgarian folk costume of the 19th and early 20th centuries A.D. Note the similarities of cut and decor to the Cirna figurine of 3,500 years earlier.

143 A man's wool costume, Belgrade, Serbia.

Jacket (*gunj*) of a dark blue, finely woven felt called *coha*, with black couched trim down the front and around the sleeve cuffs; front wrap closure, side slits; white cotton lining; 1930–1940: length 26 in. (66 cm), width 64½ in. (164 cm).

Dark blue *coha* cloth waistcoat (*ferman*), with elaborate black couched trim on front and back; lining of red felt with green trim inside pockets; 1930–1940: length 21¼ in. (54 cm), width 17⅜ in. (44 cm).

Long-sleeved, damask-striped, white cotton shirt (*kosulja*), with 2-button front and stitched-down pleated front placket; 1930–1940: length 38⅝ in. (98 cm), width 64¾ in. (164.4 cm).

Dark blue *coha* cloth pants (*caksire*), with black trim outlining the center front, left and right side pockets, inseam and cuffs; red lining in pockets; drawstring waistband made of black, green, white and grey striped cotton; 1960–1970: length 39 in. (99 cm), width 21¼ in. (54 cm).

144 A man's costume from Mariovo, Macedonia, early to mid-20th century.

White plant-fiber (possibly cotton), collarless, short-sleeved shirt, with decorative white embroidery around the neck opening: length 31½ in. (80 cm), width 38⅝ in. (98 cm).

Black woven felt woolen waistcoat, with narrow decorative couched black trim and silver buttons: length 16⅛ in. (41 cm), width 19⅜ in. (49 cm).

White plant-fiber (possibly cotton), pleated kilt (*vustan*), with drawstring at waist: length 17⅜ in. (44 cm), width 35⅜ in. (90 cm).

White plant-fiber (possibly cotton) pants, with button closure in front and cotton ties at the calf: length 36⅝ in. (93 cm), width 25⅛ in. (64 cm).

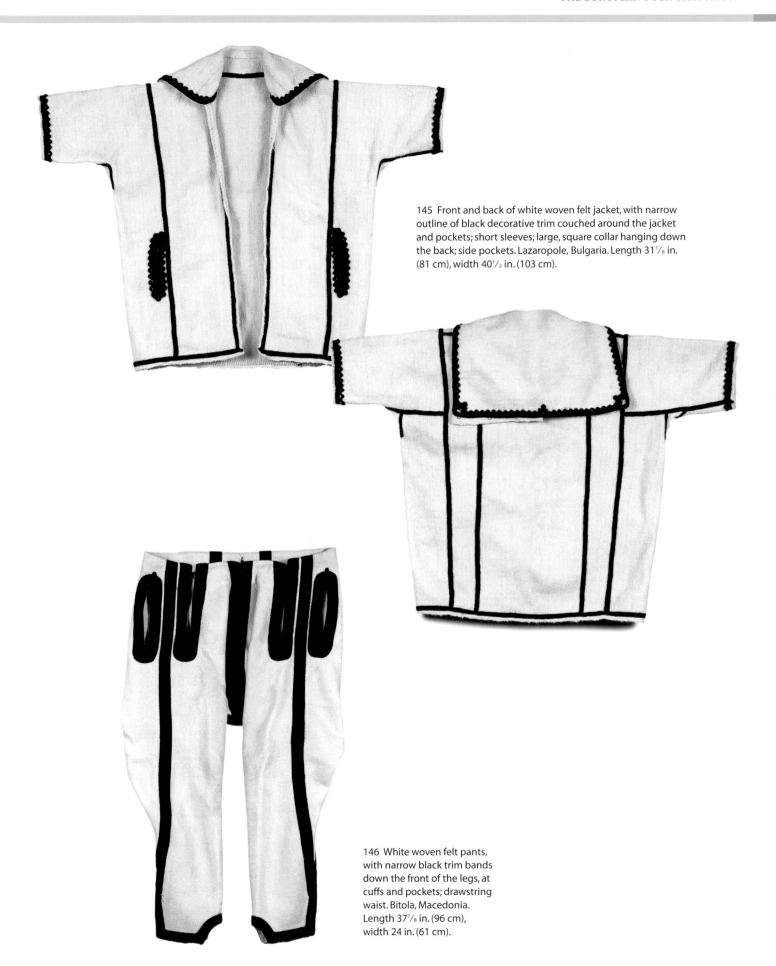

145 Front and back of white woven felt jacket, with narrow outline of black decorative trim couched around the jacket and pockets; short sleeves; large, square collar hanging down the back; side pockets. Lazaropole, Bulgaria. Length 31⁷⁄₈ in. (81 cm), width 40¹⁄₂ in. (103 cm).

146 White woven felt pants, with narrow black trim bands down the front of the legs, at cuffs and pockets; drawstring waist. Bitola, Macedonia. Length 37⁷⁄₈ in. (96 cm), width 24 in. (61 cm).

147 The attire of a bridegroom from Mezőkövesd in the Matyó region of Hungary, late 19th century. Only the embroidered apron is original: the shirt, pants and waistcoat are copies, based on illustrations in Max Tilke's *National Costumes from East Europe, Africa and Asia*, reproduced to complete the ensemble.

White cotton shirt, with long wide sleeves; decorative red embroidery at shoulders, collar and center front; sleeve edges bordered with commercial scalloped trim: length 33³⁄₈ in. (85 cm), width 74³⁄₈ in. (189 cm).

Black wool vest, with narrow black band of trim outlining waistcoat and collar; decorative black buttons and trim on front of waistcoat and collar: length 20³⁄₈ in. (52 cm), width 16⁷⁄₈ in. (43 cm).

Fully cut white cotton pants (*gatya*), with drawstring waist and fringed hem edges: length 37⁷⁄₈ in. (96 cm), width 63 in. (160 cm).

Black cotton apron, with large and small horizontal bands of multicolored floral satin-stitch embroidery; black knotted fringe at bottom; multicolored floral embroidered ribbon ties with knotted fringed ends: length 41³⁄₈ in. (105 cm), width 25⁵⁄₈ in. (65 cm).

to destroy local traditions; there are many examples of alien minorities retaining their original village dress, along with local dialects and customs.

The emergence of differentiated regional dress styles—which included the coalescing of ancient decorative elements into new garment forms—coincided with the 19th-century Romantic age. It was during this period that urban writers and painters first began to pay attention to the common man in the belief that his/her "simple life" contained a beneficent lesson for the larger society. The word "folk" was coined in the first half of the 19th century when European intellectuals began to see in all matters folkloric (i.e. the myth of an idyllic peasant past) a rationale for defining a country's "national character," complete with the glorification of its rural clothing. As the costume historian James Snowden points out, "The flattering attention of [urban] artists and scholars was not lost on the villagers themselves; a synergy was set up that led to the increasing elaboration of 'our dress,' an enterprise that became embedded in the very organization of the rural communities."[3]

Folk dress survived longer in certain countries because the urban promoters themselves began wearing peasant clothing, a practice that served to erase both class and ethnic distinctions. It was against this background that folklore and dancing groups came into being in Germany and Austria, a movement that spread—between the two World Wars—to many European countries, sometimes with state support. Within these groups, strict attention was paid to the authenticity of costume details augmented, however, by some exaggerations.

The rise of European folk dress to its apogee and subsequent decline was swift. Due to today's homogenizing international style, mass-produced, store-bought clothing has become ever cheaper while, ironically, traditional dress has become increasingly expensive. For the younger generation who wish to continue creating and wearing their native dress, the need for traditional folk materials and special sewing skills makes doing so difficult. And none of those earlier skills was more highly prized than embroidery.

THE ROLE OF EMBROIDERY IN EUROPEAN FOLK DRESS

The basic principle underlying the ancient art of embroidery involves a decorative design being added to cloth and clothing in order to enhance them. The basic elements required for embroidery are quite simple: 1) an already-existing ground material (e.g. woven fabric, felt, animal skin, tree bark); 2) a piercing tool (e.g. thorns, sharp bone or stone fragments, metal needles); 3) thread (e.g. long strands of wool, silk, cotton, bast fiber, animal hair).[4]

The esoteric designs that appear on certain European folk costumes often embody multiple layers of meaning, particularly those motifs found on garments from the more remote agrarian communities where ancient, magico-religious beliefs are still deeply rooted. Such embroidered clothing not only dresses the body but also guards it against danger and harm through the use of protective designs.[5] Every nuance of these protective designs is important, including their positioning on a garment.

The correct placement of a motif was important because evil spirits were prone to attack the body at clothing's every opening and edge. As a result, embroidery is commonly found encircling the neck of a garment, along its hem, sleeves, cuffs, pockets and even outlining its buttonholes [148–152]. Particularly vulnerable regions of the body warrant heavy embroidery: the front of the bodice, the shoulders and sleeves, the sexual areas, above the heart, and the center back. It must be noted, moreover, that when related motifs cover extensive areas there is nothing random in the positioning of these embroideries; specific design sets seldom intermingle.

Embroideries deemed particularly effective against evil spirits are often geometrics whose origins lie far back in ancient mythology: triangles, zigzags, rhomboids, labyrinths, crescents, circles, stars and crosses. Motifs from the animal world—birds, fish, horns, eyes and hands[6]—were also thought to have tremendous power.

Color symbolism in folk dress is a complex subject but Sheila Paine, an authority on worldwide embroidery, points out that three colors are basic to the human condition: red, white and black.[7] Although the latter two are used symbolically in costume, they do not usually play a similar role in embroidery; the same cannot be said of red. "Red is the most powerful, the most vibrant, the most exhilarating of colors: it is the blood of life and of death. As such it is also ambiguous: life, fire, the sun and power are counterbalanced by sacrifice and death. Red threads and fabrics are associated with spirit worship and demons, with youth and marriage, with talismanic charms and secret powers. It is the predominant color in all tribal and peasant embroidery…."[8]

Textiles have always played an important role in life-cycle rituals, and never more so than during those most crucial rites of passage: birth, puberty, marriage, death. In almost every society, embroidery reaches its richest and heaviest elaboration on garments for the young—most particularly for marriage [see 147]—only to become more subdued as life continues, ending as a simple neck border in old age. As Paine notes, "In most parts of the world people were buried in their marriage shirt or entire costume, ostensibly so that their partner could recognize them in the next world, but on a magico-religious plane to identify them as a human being."[9]

148 A woman's embroidered jacket (*klasenik*), with atavistic sleeves. Lazaropole, Bulgaria, early to mid-20th century. White felt garment with elaborate velvet chest panel couched with metallic thread; round filigree metal buttons at the edge of the front opening; narrow orange and black felt trim at armhole and pockets; wide orange and black couched band across bottom hem with decorative embroidered accents. The metallic embroidery on red velvet is a technique and color scheme borrowed from the Turks. The unusable, atavistic sleeves hark back at least 2,500 years. Length 39³/₄ in. (101 cm), width 26³/₄ in. (68 cm).

149 A woman's heavily embroidered white chemise worn under a black woven felt overdress couched with white cords in a typical scroll pattern. Lazaropole, Bulgaria, early 20th century. Chemise: length 49¹/₈ in. (125 cm), width 52³/₈ in. (133 cm). Overdress: length 38⁵/₈ in. (98 cm), width 33³/₈ in. (85 cm).

150 (detail) The embroidered patterns on the sleeves of the chemise contain variations of "hooked lozenge" and "sown field" motifs, protective fertility symbols.

151 (detail) The hem of the chemise is decorated with a repeating motif of a highly stylized fertility goddess/Tree of Life image, flanked by two guardian birds.

152 A fur-lined, tassel-fastened man's waistcoat from Romania, with multicolored embroidered floral trim.

THE ANCIENT ORIGIN OF FOLK ICONOGRAPHY

From Paleolithic times onward an iconographic system of folk symbols has existed, a form of "language" that carried the thoughts and concerns of early peoples in some remote areas from the time of their ancestors down to the present. The most basic and central of those symbolic systems involved motifs reflecting ancient ideas about descent and relationships. Early peoples used to paint these genealogical symbols on their bodies and clothing, as well as on their tools, and carry these statements about with them wherever they went. For thousands of years this iconography was directly transmitted from mother-to-daughter, from father-to-son (see "Prehistoric Europe," p. 81).[10]

Other ancient themes have survived in decorative motifs. One example comes from the cult of The Hunt, for Paleolithic man was, first and foremost, a hunter, deriving his food, clothing and in some cases even his shelter from the great herds that roamed the shifting land masses between eras of glaciation and warming. This vast hunting terrain extended from the Iberian Peninsula to northern Asia and even beyond, to the Americas. After 30,000 years, an echo of some of those hunting rituals are still to be observed in embroideries from Spain to Siberia. One example is the motif of

153 A design on a felt saddle-lining from the 4th-century B.C. *kurgan* burial at Pazyryk, located in the Altai mountains of southern Siberia.

154 A design depicting a camel being attacked by a lion embroidered on the coronation mantle of the Holy Roman Emperors. This example is thought to have been made in Palermo in A.D. 1133–34 for Roger II of Sicily.

155 The relatively realistic Upper Paleolithic Venus of Willendorf, carved from limestone, ca. 23,000 B.C.

156 An abstract depiction of a Neolithic Mother Goddess, ca. 5800–5500 B.C. Note the horns that adorn her head.

157 A 20th-century embroidery design from Eastern Europe of the Mother Goddess with arms raised in invocation.

158 A 20th-century embroidery design from Eastern Europe of the Mother Goddess with arms lowered in blessing.

159 In the Carpathian mountains, as well as in Russia, women still embroider the powerful figure of the pre-Christian Great Goddess called Berehinia on clothing to serve both as protectress and provider of fertility. The goddess holds her attendant birds in either hand. As is typical of these abstracted deity depictions, no facial features are shown.

predator and prey [153, 154]. The sun was yet another source of ancient designs. The pictographs that conventionally denote the sun are found in embroidery over most of the world, and these motifs already appeared in Paleolithic art.[11]

EASTERN EUROPE

A design category with deep, mythologically derived roots that appears repeatedly in Eastern Europe is that of an earth mother, who is depicted in a variety of modes. These images of females are not of a generic woman but rather represent an ancient fertility goddess, who is often accompanied by such mythological symbols as birds, deer, horses, plants and/or worshipping figures. This major decorative symbol has an ancient trajectory and is a motif frequently found in isolated or ethnically differentiated areas of Eastern Europe, such as the northern wastes of Russia and isolated regions of the Carpathian Basin. Here depictions of females are often encountered in both realistic and abstract form.

The goddess is almost always shown with a blank face; it is her attendant attributes that convey her sacredness and power. The earliest hunting cultures were of necessity interested in conveying the realism of the here-and-now, hence their women—as well as their depictions of the animals they hunted—were rendered in quite realistic terms [155]. Much later, after

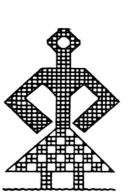

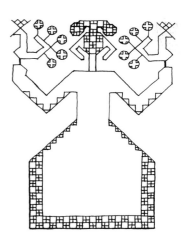

the development of agriculture, cultural needs became more conceptual, focusing on the fertility of seeds and soil; accordingly, the female principle was rendered in more abstract form [156].[12]

Mary Kelly—an authority on mother-goddess embroideries—contends that in the most easily read depictions of the goddess she appears as a single, erect image presented frontally with her full skirt and feet firmly attached at the base and her arms either raised in invocation [157; see also 156] or lowered in blessing [158]. The genesis of these embroidered goddesses may well hark back to mankind's earliest sculptures, the so-called Venus figures who are believed to represent the earliest depictions of this same principle: earth mother, life source, fertility symbol.

The archaeologist Marija Gimbutas wrote about the Great Goddess in connection with the highly stylized female figurines she excavated in Moldavia, the Eastern European region located east of the Carpathian mountains.[13] Gimbutas believed that reverence for the powerful fertility deity never ceased, continuing down from the Paleolithic to the Neolithic and Bronze Ages among the matrilineal societies of Old Europe, even after their culture was overlaid by that of the aggressive, patrilineal Indo-Europeans who, as mounted warriors, literally rode roughshod over their conquests. Gimbutas contended that though the belief systems of the two cultures were substantially different, the sacred images and symbols of Old Europe were never totally uprooted, thanks to their continued use by indigenous craftswomen. For example, she identified female images on Neolithic pottery and 20th-century Russian and Ukrainian ritual clothes as both being representations of the European goddess. To this day, village women living high in the Carpathian mountains embroider the powerful figure of a pre-Christian goddess called Berehinia, "Protectress," [159] on their clothing to serve both as guardian and provider of fertility [see also 141].

The oldest surviving textile carrying an image of what Sheila Paine identifies as the goddess[14] appears on a great felt cover found in a nomadic ruler's frozen tomb at Pazyryk. Repeated across the width of the felt is the realistic motif of a seated woman holding a sacred branch [160], perhaps an aspect of the goddess-associated Tree of Life discussed below. This female is believed to represent a hearth deity worshipped in Russia in pre-Scythian times. In later embroidered depictions from a variety of countries, the goddess is frequently associated with mounted horsemen.

The fertility goddess motif sometimes metamorphosed into the Tree of Life, one of the most common and potent of embroidery designs [161, 162; see also 151]. In Ancient Sumerian art, the tree was sometimes replaced by plants emerging from an

160 On the great felt of Pazyryk—ca. 4th century B.C.—appears the repeated image of a seated female figure, perhaps the Mother Goddess, holding a sacred branch. On the textile she is approached by a rider, perhaps a worshipper.

161 As depicted on a Ukrainian ritual towel used as a sacred item in all important ceremonies connected with life, marriage and death, this stylized Tree of Life grows from the earth, which is represented as a kind of cloud form.

162 This design, also from a Ukrainian ritual towel, is both a figural form of the Tree of Life and an abstraction of the goddess: note the prominent central "head" and upraised "arms."

163 Cloth embroidery design from Moravia, ca. 1780. It was in Ancient Sumerian art that the Tree of Life was replaced by a female-like vase from which goddess-associated flowers connected with fertility emerge: here tulips and a pomegranate are depicted.

anthropomorphosed vase. Worshippers or guardians often flanked this version of the Tree of Life, a favorite motif of European folk art [163]. Significantly, the flowers in the vase are often those associated with the fertility of the goddess—the carnation, tulip and rose; pomegranates are sometimes added.

In the embroideries of certain countries, the tree is replaced by motifs from local iconography. An example is the eagle—with one or two heads—which is an ancient solar symbol representing the power of the sky gods [164]. The two-headed eagle later became a European heraldic emblem for the Hapsburgs and as such sometimes replaces the tree in the embroideries of Spain and Russia, as does the heart in the embroideries of Central and Eastern Europe.

WESTERN EUROPE

Whereas Eastern European embroidery designs such as the Goddess were deeply rooted in ancient beliefs and social customs, the clothing of the West was more decorative than traditional, emerging as it did from a different background, an ecclesiastical and urban tradition that drew from both fashion and trade [165]. As a result of the commercial availability of affordable sewing materials in the West—plus the continual publication, beginning in 1523, of widely circulated pattern books depicting a range of design motifs— a certain sameness of folk embroidery existed from Scandinavia to Spain.

For the peasants of Western Europe, who for centuries had been subjected to sumptuary laws forbidding the decorating of their clothing, it was the French Revolution that brought both freedom and prosperity.[15] Soon Western folk costumes began to incorporate certain elements of urban fashion interpreted using relatively inexpensive commercial cloth and adornments [166]. Outer clothing was mainly decorative with ribbons and trimmings, whereas handwork was usually restricted to headcoverings, aprons and red cross-stitch embroidery on linen garments. Only in such isolated regions as mountain valleys did embroidery motifs still serve to affirm affiliation to a group. This was true in Brittany and in the more remote regions of the Iberian peninsula.

THE CONTRASTING CUTS AND STYLES OF EAST/WEST FOLK DRESS

Although examples of folk dress occurred in almost every European country—Belgium and England were exceptions[16]—the cut and styling of those garments varied markedly depending on whether they evolved in Eastern or Western Europe. To understand better the underlying principles governing the development of these contrasting clothing types, their diagnostic traits are discussed below.

EASTERN EUROPEAN FOLK DRESS

Traces of the most ancient elements of European folk dress are still to be found in certain isolated

164 The embroideries of some countries adopted motifs from local iconography. On the left is a realistic design featuring a two-headed eagle, and on the right an abstracted version from 19th-century Ukraine.

165 A Central European dirndl-style ensemble from Hungary, early 20th century.

White blouse with short ruffled sleeves (possibly added later) and a drawstring neck: length 17³/₈ in. (44 cm), width 26³/₈ in. (67 cm).

Orange velvet bodice with laced front opening, squared tabs at the waist and gold couched trim outlining the bodice at its edges and creating geometric designs in front and back: length 20³/₈ in. (52 cm), width 16⁷/₈ in. (43 cm).

Full black skirt with tiny brocade flowers, black lace and floral brocaded ribbon bands at bottom: length 28³/₈ in. (72 cm), width 69³/₈ in. (176 cm).

Multicolored apron made from multicolored brocade ribbons and trims assembled on red silk fabric, with knotted and fringed edges: length 23⁵/₈ in. (60 cm), width 27⁷/₈ in. (71 cm).

166 A dirndl-style ensemble from Portugal, early 20th century.

White long-sleeved round-neck chemise, with blue floral embroidery at shoulders and cuffs; lace at neck and cuffs: length 24⁷/₈ in. (63 cm), width 23⁵/₈ in. (60 cm).

Short laced bodice of red felt and black velvet with multicolored embroidery; pink and blue trim at edges: length 12¹/₂ in. (31.7 cm), width 13⁷/₈ in. (35.5 cm).

Gathered skirt of red wool with multicolored vertical stripes and horizontal band of red felt with multicolored floral machine-made trim at hem: length 27 in. (68.6 cm), width 25 in. (63.5 cm).

Red wool apron with multicolored vertical stripes and multicolored decorative weft looping, shirred at the top: length 20 in. (50.8 cm), width 23 in. (58.4 cm).

Red felt pocket pouch with multicolored floral embroidery: length 8³/₄ in. (22.2 cm), width 5³/₄ in. (14.6 cm).

Black and red wool skullcap with point at top in shape of pig's tail: height 5¹/₂ in. (14 cm), width 10⁵/₈ in. (27 cm).

White leather boots with red leather cuff: height 9 in. (23 cm), length 10¹/₄ in. (26 cm).

regions of Eastern Europe, where—in such remote areas as the Carpathian mountains—women still practice the full range of the textile arts: planting, harvesting, shearing, spinning, carding, dyeing and weaving flax and wool on home looms. Mothers not only teach their children how to make cloth but also how to embroider it in prescribed locations using motifs customary to their village. This textile production includes weaving the long white chemises that serve as the region's basic garment. These T-shaped linen shifts originally came into Eastern Europe from the Middle East around 2000 B.C. and then were adopted into Western Europe by way of the Byzantine Empire, ca. A.D. 300 (see "Classical Europe," p. 88).[17] Indeed, the shifts served as the basic undergarment for all of Europe's subsequent peasant clothing. It is noteworthy that the most archaic design motifs sometimes do not appear on these shifts—perhaps because they are usually covered by additional clothing—but rather on the region's outerwear.

Over the chemise was worn richly decorated woolen clothing. A principal item of female attire was a long, sleeveless dress held up by two straps. This distinctive pinafore-like garment originated as the classic Russian *sarafan* [167], but it was also found in certain parts of Western Europe, for example in 19th-century Norway, Switzerland and the Spanish Pyrenees. The *sarafan* may represent the survival of a simple garment type still extant among later, more Westernized styles.[18]

Over the *sarafan* a woolen apron was worn; in fact, often two. If the principal garment, the back-apron, was narrow a woman would wear a second of approximately the same size in front [168]. These ubiquitous Eastern European aprons were not intended to protect the clothing beneath but rather to shield the body's sexual areas from evil spirits. Although aprons were mainly female attire, they were also sometimes worn by unmarried men, particularly by bridegrooms [see 147].

The back-apron/skirt, known as the *panjóva*, apparently evolved in the Neolithic and was still being worn well into the 20th century by brides and married women in Russia and Ukraine.[19] In its oldest, simplest form this garment—whose essential purpose was to

167 (right) The Russian *sarafan*, an unfitted, pinafore-like, sleeveless dress that hangs from under the arms straight down to the ankles.

168 Narrow double *panjóva*, one worn in front, the other in back.

169 The wide, squared back-apron, the archetypical *panjóva*, worn with or without a smaller front-apron.

170 The patterned, marital apron evolved into a sewn-up skirt with a contrasting panel—often of black material—producing a tubular garment in such a way that the patterned section of the skirt still gives the visual impression of being a back-apron.

171 The most elaborate embellishments on the *panjóva* back-apron were found in the Russian province of Oryol, as this drawing shows.

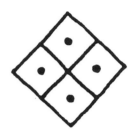

172 (top) A lozenge surrounded by rays and hooks, believed by some scholars to represent the female vulva.

173 (above) A lozenge quadrisected with a dot in the middle of each quadrant: the "fertile" or "sown field" motif.

174 (above left) A bride draped in a ritual cloth embroidered with large "fertile field" motifs that serve both protective and fertility purposes. Kryvorivnia, Ukraine, 1992.

declare the fertility of its wearer—was an uncut, unsewn rectangle of cloth, patterned into small squares, that was belted on at the waist so as to hang down behind as a back-apron [169]. Indeed, the *panjóva* is still worn in this manner in the present-day Ukrainian national costume. In several South Great Russian provinces, the apron(s) evolved into a sewn-up skirt with a contrasting panel in the front that still gave the visual impression of being a back-apron [170].

Sometimes the *panjóvas* were elaborately embellished [171]. Typically, two types of fertility design were embroidered onto the patterned squares of these aprons: a lozenge surrounded by rays and hooks [172] and a lozenge quadrisected with a dot in the middle of each quadrant [173; see also 150]. This latter design is referred to as the "fertile" or "sown field" motif [174]. Both lozenge-shaped symbols are traceable back to Eastern Europe's Neolithic.[20]

175 The final evolution of the Eastern European twin aprons may be the Russian *sarafan*.

188 French regional costume is astonishingly varied. Here a woman from Normandy displays the elaborately patterned apron straps and tall headdress characteristic of her region.

189 *Tracht*—men and women's traditional local costume, most widespread in southern Germany and Austria—is characterized by the use of linen, embroidery and loden, a type of felt originally worn in the Alpine regions. This German woman's outfit is also remarkable for its costly, elaborate hat.

190 This young woman from Hardanger, Norway, wears an intricately decorated bodice trimmed with beads, along with a linen headdress known as a *skaut*. Such folk costume was sometimes worn also by bourgeois urban women who wished to register national identity.

191 The typical loose sleeves, tightly laced bodice and full skirt of a woman's costume from the canton of Berne in Switzerland.

192 The 19th-century tall
hats and enveloping cloaks
of certain of the Welsh
peasantry were markedly
behind the times. These
garments bear a decided
resemblance to the popular
image of a witch precisely
because they were the
characteristic wear of
the time of witchcraft
persecutions of the 1630s.

"INVENTED TRADITIONS" OF EUROPEAN FOLK DRESS

Certain of Europe's folk costume traditions that appear to reflect great time depth were actually invented comparatively recently. This was the case in Wales, where 19th-century scholars and patriots of the Romantic period, concerned that their culture had become lackluster, set about rediscovering their country's past. In so doing, when they felt the historical, linguistic, literary or clothing traditions inadequate, they recreated a new past.

The actual clothing of much of the 19th-century Welsh peasantry was markedly out of date. For example, a style that had been the characteristic dress of English countrywomen in the 1630s—tweed capes and tall black hats—was still being worn by the poor in some remote Welsh mountain areas in the 1760s, and even later. Although these garments [192] were not systematically worn throughout Wales, they were deliberately incorporated into the national costume in the 1830s. The resulting outfit [193] was dubbed "Dame Wales" by contemporary writers.[25] It is particularly ironic that this supposedly authentic dress of the agrarian Welsh peasantry should have become the national costume of a country that subsequently became one of the world's most industrialized.

A second example of invented folk costume occurred in Scotland, where the present-day Highland tradition includes what is regarded as the country's national dress: a short tartan kilt whose plaid indicates the wearer's "clan." This apparel, to which great antiquity is ascribed, is actually relatively modern, although there is an ancient connection between Celts and plaid clothing (see "The Silk Road," p. 139). For our purposes, however, the story begins in the Scottish highlands of the 17th century.[26]

The kilt of 300 years ago was a long piece of woolen cloth woven in a variety of plaids, depending

13692   The Inmates of the Bede Houses, Castle Rising. Endowed in 1610.

on what natural dyes were available locally. At that time there was no association between a particular clan and a particular tartan; men living in the same area might wear any of several regional plaids depending on their own personal fancy. The long kilt, which was wrapped around the body once or twice and then thrown over the shoulder, had a practical advantage. When a highland shepherd was caught far from home at dusk he could wrap up in all of that woolen cloth and sleep warmly. Thanks to a 17th-century drawing, we know what the plaid clothing of that period looked like [194].

Following the decisive Battle of Culloden in 1746, the victorious British appropriated Scottish lands, forbade Scotsmen to carry arms and prohibited them from wearing their plaid kilts.[27] Following this blow to Scottish ethnic identity, some years later the English army, ironically, began recruiting men from the Highlands. The Scots who joined

these newly formed regiments were issued a new and far skimpier version of their traditional apparel: a standard "government" tartan that had nothing to do with either region or clan [195].

The Scottish kilt then went through a further evolution when the officers of the newly formed Scottish regiments—Scottish/British nobility—began to affect a more ample version of the Highlanders' original plaid kilt [196].

The final stage in the evolution of this increasingly fashionable garment took place when the aristocracy adopted the kilt for social events and country wear [197]. As for the differentiated "clan tartans," according to the historian Hugh Trevor-Roper "they were designed as part of a pageant devised by Sir Walter Scott in honor of a Hanoverian king."[28] The lowly, multi-task kilt of the 17th-century Highland shepherds had now fully evolved into stylish attire for the middle and upper classes.

193 Welsh scholars and patriots of the 19th-century Romantic period conceived a "national costume" for Wales composed of disparate elements from the country's past.

194 (above) A German broadsheet of 1631 showing Highlanders who were often mistakenly described as "Irrländer oder Irren," i.e. Irish. Note that the Scots—here probably Mackay's Regiment serving under Gustavus Adolphus— wear traditional Celtic plaids.

195 (above right) A Highlander recruited to serve in the British army was issued a "government" kilt whose plaid had neither regional nor clan significance.

196 (right) Hugh, 12th Earl of Eglinton (1739–1819), an officer commanding a Scottish regiment, wears an enhanced version of the common soldier's kilt.

197 (far right) In this detail from Carl Haag's 1854 *Evening at Balmoral*, a Victorian gentleman wears a finely pleated Scottish kilt in a "clan" tartan.

A final example of the deliberate invention of a national costume comes from Lithuania where reinvented folk dress served several times as a protest statement, first against Russian occupation—both in the late 19th century and again in the 20th—and more recently in the developing of a completely revisionist "ancient" costume. The ideal of an agreed-upon national costume to unify Lithuania as a nation had been constantly in flux. Finally, thanks to knowledgeable ethnographers and historians, costume design was changed from a series of free-form artistic fantasies to accurate copies of the folk clothing now largely held in museums.[29] As a result, a more authentic "national costume" came into being [198].

Within recent decades, some Lithuanians have again reinvented a version of their folk costume in a desire to find a more appropriate symbol of national identity by returning to the "authentic Lithuania" that existed before the Middle Ages, when invading powers introduced Christianity. Unfortunately, this attempt to get in touch with a more "archaic truth" resulted in a somewhat nondescript ensemble, the so-called "neo-pagan" attire based on scant archaeological evidence of what was actually worn in pre-Christian Lithuania.

TRANSITIONAL DRESS
The Golden Age of European folk dress [199] generally declined in the early 20th century because of urbanization, the growth of industry and the beginning of universal education. The conditions in which folk costume could thrive thus came to an end and the tradition of regional dress lost one of its purposes: to display affiliation with a group. Nonetheless, examples of regional folk dress are still to be found in nationalistic ceremonies, performances for tourists and in extremely remote areas (for example, authentic attire is still worn in Albania, outside of the capital). Such apparel, as well as "invented" folk costumes, became rallying points that could serve to lift a country's sagging spirits, as in Wales, or infuse a sense of national pride, as in Scotland, or make a protest statement, as in Lithuania's sequential national costumes.

As for the anciently derived Mother Goddess embroideries, as the 20th century developed increasingly effective technology, the urgent need to invigorate the fields or guarantee fertility by evoking the deity was replaced by modern science and revised ideas about the desirability of profuse female fertility. As new inventions came increasingly to the fore, life could continue without the ministrations of the goddess, whose once-awesome influence had been co-opted by modernity. And yet, beginning in the last quarter of the 20th century a belief in the Great Goddess has revived with fervor among certain feminist groups in several Western countries. Perhaps the empowering capabilities of the Goddess are not to be dismissed quite so quickly after all.

198 The reinvented Lithuanian folk costume, a reflection of actual garments preserved in museums rather than the preceding free-form artistic fantasies that had been promulgated.

199 Charles C. Coleman, *Capri: Scene with Figure,* 1898. A 19th-century romantic view of Western European folk costume.

3

CENTRAL ASIA

CENTRAL ASIA, located at the heart of the great Eurasian landmass, is transversed by a 5,000-mile (8,000 km) belt of grassland that runs from eastern Europe to northern China. The Ukrainian steppe zone of this broad corridor has produced the earliest evidence for the domestication of the horse, ca. 4000 B.C. The control of ever larger herds of domesticated cattle and sheep was eventually made possible by herding from horseback, resulting in a completely new lifestyle: pastoral nomadism. These self-sufficient, mostly Altaic-speaking horsemen—including Mongol and various Turkic peoples—knew neither boundaries nor borders but were vulnerable to drought; their periodic push toward new pastures caused domino-like population pressures throughout Eurasia. The nomads also bettered their lives through recurring raids on settled communities, and none were more tempting than those to the east. China's fertile river valleys were rich sources of grain and women, as well as silk, the alluring textile whose production techniques China kept secret for some 2,000 years. Other ethnic components in the Central Asian story were the Indo-European speakers who migrated from the west: graves dating to 1200 B.C. of tall, fair-haired, blue-eyed Caucasians wearing Celtic-like plaids have been found in abandoned oases communities along the Silk Road, that most famous of all caravan routes. Beginning around 100 B.C., when Chinese goods became involved, the ancient pathways across the steppes and desert lands of Central Asia greatly increased in importance. Throughout this long, difficult journey, trade and religion often traveled in tandem, moving not only luxury goods and exotic art but also ideas, technology and fundamental religious and philosophical world views, among them Buddhism, Hinduism, Judaism and Islam, as well as shamanistic concepts for contacting the spirit world.

MONGOLIA

200 Balduugiin Sharav, *One Day in Mongolia*, ca. 1920s (detail). Each household traditionally produced its own felt in the autumn. One or two pieces of old felt, known as "mother felt," were laid out on the ground and dampened with water. Three layers of new wool were put on top of the mother felt, each layer in turn sprinkled with water. Finally the top layer was covered with grass to stop the wool sticking. All the layers of felt were tightly rolled up, wrapped in a well-soaked ox hide, and bound using leather straps. The felt roll was then dragged by a horse in order to "knead" the fabric.

Central Asia's nomadic world is dominated by a single fabric: woolen felt.[1] The vast territory, stretching across Eurasia from Hungary to Beijing [Map 11], and traversed by the pastoralists for millennia, was described by the Chinese in the 4th century B.C. as the "Land of Felt," acknowledging the fundamental role it played in the nomads' way of life—providing tent covers,[2] warm rugs, animal trappings and protective clothing.[3] Genghis Khan's collective designation for the unified Turko-Mongolian tribes of Asia was "the generations that live in felt tents."[4]

Although for centuries that most notorious of the Central Asian tribes, the fearsome Mongols, only recorded their history orally, their settled, literate neighbors had a great deal to say about them and did so, repeatedly, over a long period of time. Because of the Mongols' ceaseless raids, China's dynastic histories, stretching back some 4,000 years, often describe them and their predecessors as ravenous barbarians greedy for Chinese goods (see "The Silk Road," p. 139). The horsemen were referred to as the Xiongnu, "The State Holding the Bows Beyond the Great Wall." (Descendants of the Xiongnu, the Huns, were united under Attila and terrorized central Europe in the last days of the Roman Empire.)

Until the end of the 12th century, the Mongols were little more than a loose confederation of rival clans. Then, in A.D. 1162, a most unusual child was born among them, with—so legend has it—a blood clot the size of a knucklebone clenched in his fist, auguring for great bloodshed. However apocryphal that tale, the promise of rampant bloodshed was more than fulfilled.

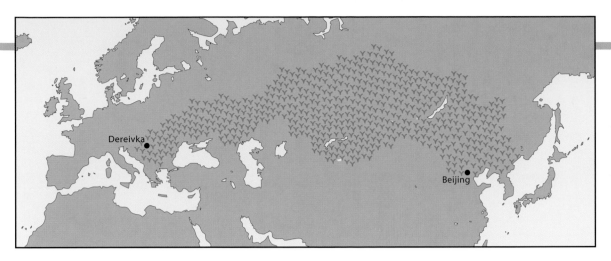

Map 11 The Eurasian steppe zone (indicated area), a belt of grasslands running from eastern Europe to northern China. The earliest evidence for the domestication of the horse comes from Dereivka, located on the Ukrainian steppe. The domestication of the horse is linked to the invention of trousers.

By the age of twenty, the young man had emerged from a power struggle to unite most of the Mongol tribes, prompting the honorary title of "Universal Ruler"— Chinggis Khaan, better known in the West by his Persianized name, Genghis Khan. By 1206, Genghis had created a confederation of all the Mongol tribes, assembled a loyal army of up to 200,000 men and begun his series of bloody conquests reaching from Beijing to the Caspian Sea. In August of 1227, the 66-year-old conqueror died from injuries sustained— most improbably—from falling off a horse while campaigning in northwest China. To the chagrin of both historians and treasure seekers, the site of the great conqueror's grave has never been found.[5]

With the death of Genghis Khan, the empire was divided among his four principal sons.[6] Central Mongolian power passed into the hands of Genghis's favorite, Ogedei, who continued the Mongols' terrorizing expansion into central Europe, right up to Hungary and Bohemia. All of eastern Europe began to pray for a miracle, which indeed did occur. In 1241 the Mongols stopped their advance, turned east and headed back to Mongolia. Two of Genghis's principal sons had died and Mongol custom dictated that all the great conqueror's noble descendants had to return to Mongolia to elect a new leader democratically. This same pattern was repeated in 1259 when the Mongols were poised to take Egypt but suddenly stopped, turned east and returned, yet again, to their homeland. Whatever impressive gains the Mongols may have made in battle, they never conquered their greatest weakness: succession.

The most noteworthy of the subsequent Mongol rulers was Kublai Khan (ca. 1216–1294), Genghis's grandson, who finally subjugated China, ending the Song dynasty. Kublai became emperor of China's Yuan dynasty (1271–1368), establishing his winter capital in today's Beijing, where he is said to have met and hired the young Marco Polo.[7] Kublai's summer camp was further north, at Shangdu, later immortalized as Xanadu by the Romantic poet Samuel Taylor Coleridge. Under Kublai Khan, Mongol holdings reached their zenith, stretching from Hungary to Korea to create the largest empire the world had ever known [Map 12].

Because the Mongol khans relied on subjects and foreigners to administer their empire, over time power shifted from rulers to bureaucrats. This, added to continual feuding among the different khanates, led to the empire's decline and the Mongols' subsequent

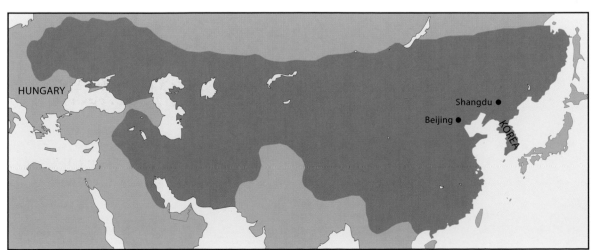

Map 12 The greatest extent of the Mongol Empire, A.D. 1280, under Kublai Khan.

203 (opposite left) Front view of a shaman's regalia from the Buryat tribe, located in Mongolia's far north. The shaman wears a wide, collarless tunic of red cotton whose front panel is adorned with attached metal pieces that symbolize a human skeleton; the rings represent the joints. Sewn all over the garment are rattle rings as well as small bows and arrows. A polished brass mirror hangs around the neck to ward off evil spirits. The shaman's crown consists of a copper band to which copper antlers are attached. His mask is made of chased copper with openings for the eyes and mouth, a nose with nostrils, a beard of fur, and metal bells that hang over the forehead and both temples.

204 (opposite right) Rear view of the shaman's regalia. From between the antlers on the shaman's copper headpiece hang 24 silken snakes, whose bodies extend down the curer's back, familiars who help the shaman to reach the other world successfully.

pulling back to their heartland. During the 15th and 16th centuries, supremacy passed from one quarreling tribe to another. The Manchus finally conquered the factious Mongolians in two stages, which ended tribal warfare but led to the division of the area into two political units: Inner and Outer Mongolia. Cultural differences began to develop between the two regions, with Inner Mongolia becoming increasingly Chinese in character and population. By the 20th century there was widespread dissatisfaction in both Mongolias, compounded by Russian and Japanese intrigue in the region. In 1921 the Russians captured Ulaanbaatar, in Outer Mongolia, and soon after founded the Mongolian People's Republic. In 1992, following the collapse of the Soviet Union, Mongolia declared itself an independent democracy.

Despite past political domination,[8] Mongolia has emerged as a country where an irrepressively nomadic people still retain an intimate knowledge of animals— both wild and domestic—as well as of their vast land,

201 A Mongolian shaman's costume: this fringed cotton and deerskin tunic is decorated with sewn-on metal objects—bells, sleigh-bells, flat copper plates, square metal plates. The iron ornaments and plates are believed to imitate the bones of an animal's skeleton. Octagonal plates with a hole in the middle represent the earth; flat figures represent human beings and animals; long iron bars represent the bones of the body.

202 The streamers hanging down the back of the garment help the shaman to manoeuver on his or her flight to the other world. The metal objects attached to a costume can also be interpreted as a manifestation of the shaman's familiar, or spirit companion, as can the costume itself.

which is almost twice the size of Texas but with a population density of only about 2.5 people per square mile,[9] with approximately one horse per person. The country is made up of three diverse environments: the vast Eurasian steppes, the semi-arid Gobi desert— covered by enough vegetation to support some livestock and herding activity—and the northern Siberian forests where snow-capped mountains and sparkling lakes meet. Mongolia, vulnerably bordered by Russia on the north and China to the south, is one of the highest countries in the world, with an average altitude of 5,183 feet (1,580 m), and is the fifth largest nation in Asia, a part of the world where Buddhism has long served as a major faith. In 1557, this religion entered Mongolia in the form of Tibetan or Lamaist Buddhism. Prior to that introduction, Central Asian mysticism centered on the millennia-old method of accessing the spirit world through a shaman.

SHAMANIC DRESS

Based on archaeological and comparative ethnological evidence, shamanism—the trance-like perception and treatment of the spiritual side of illness—is believed by many scholars to be at least 30,000 years old, and quite probably even older. Mircea Eliade, the authority on comparative religions, proposed that shamanism was the progenitor of all other spiritual systems and religions, although he made it clear that shamanism itself was a methodology, not a religion.[10]

During the shaman's call for spiritual help and entry into the spirit realm, he or she is assisted not only by the rhythmic beating of a drum or the shaking of a rattle but often also by the use of certain esoteric regalia.[11] The intriguing decorations displayed on shaman costumes are often aimed at imitating a special animal, usually a deer, a bear or a bird. Such costumes—often referred to as "armor"—are believed to protect shamans on their journeys into the beyond [201–204].

TSAM RITUAL DRESS

Echoes of ancient shamanism mixed with Buddhist beliefs and Mongolian folklore are combined in the

205 In Mongolia, Buddhism dominates the arts, including traditional dance. The best known of these performances are the Tsam masked dances whose purpose is to exorcise evil spirits. The dancers' magnificent masks are made of papier-mâché. Probably the most famous mask is worn by the White Old Man (second from right), revered as guardian of both human and animal fertility, who also wears the white robes of Genghis Khan's shamans.

highly ritualized Tsam masked dances. The performers wear magnificent costumes [205] while presenting their theatrical dances, whose purpose is to exorcise evil. Prior to the Stalinist religious purges of the mid-20th century, Tsam dances took place every summer in over 500 Mongolian monasteries; today they are held as tourist entertainment.

MONGOLIAN SECULAR DRESS

As early as A.D. 1500 Mongolian tribes regularly began to approach China's frontier in a more conciliatory manner in order to obtain coveted goods produced by the settled Chinese: tea, grains, iron objects and, particularly, textiles. Cloth was especially important because weaving was practically unknown in Mongolia. Naturally, with the import of Chinese textiles came the influence of Chinese clothing.

When analyzing Central Asian garments it quickly becomes apparent that one must set aside the Western idea of a separate mode of dress for males and females. Up to the mid-20th century, Central and Eastern Asian men and women were dressed practically alike, their clothing differing only in details. Indeed, earlier scholars have commented that it was often difficult, based solely on garments, to tell the sexes apart.[12] Further, the Central Asian approach to traditional clothing construction is non-Western; there is no attempt to follow the lines of the body. In Mongolian garments only two dimensions are important: height and breadth. All clothing is made—with as little waste as possible—according to a conventional measure. As a result, nomadic garments can easily be folded up and stored in a box or saddlebag, with no need for Western-style hangers.

As for the types of garment involved, long pants now enter the picture. Just as the horse was first domesticated in Central Asia so, too, does this area seem to be where trousers first evolved.[13] All of the components were in place to bring about a transformation from the wearing of a felt or leather tunic-like garment with tube-like sleeves—perhaps precursors or "stepping stones" to the idea of tube-like trousers—to the donning of limb-encasing pants. As a result of taming the horse, herders slowly began riding astride, thus exposing their legs to chafing and the elements; long trousers provided the needed protection.

A rider's upper body also had to be protected but in a manner sufficiently unrestricted to accommodate being on horseback.[14] The original nomadic upper-body garment may well have been a long, loose coat with a central opening such as the one the 3,000-year-old, trouser-clad Cherchen Man wore (see "The Silk

Road," p. 139). But the upper-body garment that evolved in Mongolia was different: a long, loose-fitting coat that crossed over the chest to fasten on the right. This transformation from central opening to right-side closure is believed by the Danish ethnographer Henny Harald Hansen to reflect the influence of Mongolia's 15th-century Manchurian conquerors.[15] Archaeological evidence, however, testifies that coats with right-side closures were already being worn in Inner Mongolia in the 13/14th centuries [206]. Wherever the right-side closure may have originated, the style obviously came out of eastern Asia and served as the prototype for the present-day Mongolian *del*, the coat worn by traditional men and women alike.

MEN'S AND WOMEN'S BASIC DRESS

Dels, as well as Mongolian waistcoats and jackets, all fasten by means of a strap-and-button combination. These are not, however, Western-style buttons sewn directly onto a garment to be secured by passing through a button-hole. On Asian clothing, button-holes are unknown because buttons are secured to a garment by means of a short strap, or "frog;" a second frog serves as the securing "button-hole."

Both Mongolian men [207] and women [208] wear the *del*. Its seams are not sewn all the way down to the hem in order to create a series of slits or vents which allow the garment to be worn comfortably while on horseback [209]. Beneath the *del* trousers are tucked into sturdy boots.

206 This silk robe, dating to the 13th/14th century—the era of the Mongol Yuan dynasty in China—was excavated from an Ongut tomb unearthed in 1978 in Inner Mongolia. The robe is made of gold brocade patterned with rosettes within rhomboid lozenges; the lining has a repeating design of back-to-back rearing lions with human faces. Note that this early tunic closes to the right in front. Length 55⅞ in. (142 cm), width from cuff to cuff 96⅞ in. (246 cm).

207 A Dariganga tribesman from the southeast of Mongolia wears a green cotton *del* edged with embroidered ribbon. His black felt hat is decorated with brocade appliqué; the ear and forehead flaps are edged with sable fur and a sable tail adorns the crown. His black leather boots are decorated with leather appliqués. Hanging from his belt—and attached with silver fittings—are a knife in a decorated wooden and leather scabbard and, on the left, a firelighter. Mongolian nobles dressed in far more ornate clothing than did commoners; this simple but elegant outfit reflects an earlier era.

208 This Mongolian Uuld tribeswoman wears a traditional *del*. Both its stand-up collar and turned-up cuffs—whose shape resembles horses' hooves— are trimmed in blue. Attached to the belt is a small pouch which contains sewing equipment— thimble, needle, thread. Below the girl's right arm can be seen the tassels that decorate her hair, which is plaited into 24 braids. The girl wears her tribe's round hat topped with the pattern of a crescent moon: all Uuld people, regardless of sex or age, wear this same kind of hat.

209 A 1941 painting by C. Davaachuu of the Feast of Foal-drafting, held at the beginning of summer. Beneath their *dels* the riders wear trousers tucked into sturdy boots. Note also women wearing the "sheephorn" hairdo [see 221, 222].

FOOTWEAR

The Mongolian term for high leather boots is *gutul*. In formal styles, the toes curl up, which may have derived from Buddhist religious concerns: the upturned end touches less earth and hence kills fewer insects.[16] Today the almost indestructible Russian army boots, or copies thereof, are what are most commonly worn [see 209]. In the days of the Mongol hordes, the nomadic warriors wore very specialized boots, with tiny pieces of overlapping metal inserted between the outer leather surface and the inner lining, in order to reinforce and strengthen them [210, 211].

OUTERWEAR

Various styles of sheepskin-lined overcoat were worn in winter. Women's coats from the Mongolian Zakhchin tribe were traditionally reinforced with a thin mat of woven willow or a thin piece of cast iron placed over the breast and stomach in order to protect the vulnerable wearer [212]. As one commentator has stated: "The reason…is that Manchu soldiers shot pregnant women from the right side and the offspring perished in the womb. It was a policy of genocide.…"[17]

HEADGEAR

No aspect of Mongolian attire is more impressive than the imaginative hats collected in the 1930s. These vary widely in style: conical and pointed, skullcap and helmet; covered with brocade, satin, fine velvet, or felt; trimmed in fur, feathers, or gold ornamental braid; with beads or stones placed on top [213–220]. Indeed, of all the evocative aspects of Mongolian dress, it is the pageantry reflected in these hats that most powerfully evokes the exotic world described by Marco Polo.

HAIRSTYLES

Probably the most memorable of Mongolian hairstyles is the "sheephorn" headdress worn by 19th-century noblewomen [221, 222], an amazing sculpture of hair stiffened with congealed mutton fat (mutton still has a ubiquitous presence in Mongolia) and held in place with clips, amulets and tassels. These valued hair ornaments were treasured heirlooms. Henny Harald Hansen, however, quotes a colleague working in the 1940s as saying that "the women of frontier provinces…exchange their old inherited hair ornaments of silver and coral for sewing machines, radios and gramophones."[18]

ACCESSORIES

Because traditional Mongolian garments had no pockets, life's everyday necessities had to be carried on one's person, attached to a belt [see 207, 208]. Wealthy Mongolian men traditionally wore a flint and a knife-chopstick-toothpick set on a silver chain attached to their belt. Under their *del* they carried an ornate snuff bottle, a silver bowl and sometimes an amulet. Women wore a small pouch containing their sewing kit.

210 (left) A modern-day Mongolian horseman rides at high speed while standing up in the stirrups; sturdy boots serve to stabilize this posture.

211 (above) This boot dates back to the 12th/13th century, the time of Genghis Khan. It has had a section cut away to expose tiny overlapping pieces of metal. These were inserted to reinforce the boot when the mounted warrior stood up in his stirrups to gain the extra stability needed to make maximum use of his weapons.

212 The type of sheepskin coat worn by Zakhchin tribeswomen, the upper section traditionally lined with a protective material.

213 (above left) The armature of this hat is made of braided bamboo which has been covered in white silk gauze and lined with red gauze. The hat's upper portion is adorned with glued-on red paper, and its chin-straps are made of blue cotton. The white button at the hat's crown sits atop a holder for a peacock feather. Height 6⅝ in. (17 cm), diameter 12⅝ in. (32 cm).

214 (above right) This sable hat was worn on ceremonial occasions by noble Minggad ladies. Even in winter, the hat's flaps remained in the flared position. Two patterned, red ribbons hang down from the back and the hat is topped by a tall, slender, silver device that holds aloft a piece of worked coral.

215 (below left) This domed hat, decorated in colorful brocade, was worn by Chalka tribesmen. The hat's four flaps are trimmed with sable, and a squirrel's tail is attached at the top.

216 (below right) This colorful round hat was worn by Bayad tribeswomen. One of the hat's most distinguishing features is the large knot of hitches at the top. Red and pink tassels hang down the back.

217 (above left) Uriankhai tribeswomen wore this domed, hexagonal-sided hat for year-round ceremonial occasions. The flaps over the ears and at the back are all lined with fur.

218 (above right) This hat was worn by a bride of the Barun Buryat tribe. The crown is covered with reddish-lilac satin, the inside trim is blue satin, and the outside brim is embroidered with two four-clawed dragons. At the top of the crown, red silk fringe is attached to a decorative metal button. Two long ribbons hang down the back. Height 4 in. (10 cm), diameter 9⁷⁄₈ in. (25 cm).

219 (below left) This round hat was worn by Torguud tribeswomen. The crown is a conical shape—said to make one look taller—and is decorated with coral, as is the knot at the top of the hat, from which cords hang down. The border of the hat is decorated with the "Grass Dragon" pattern.

220 (below right) This fur-trimmed winter hat was worn by both men and women. Its pointed crown is covered with blue and violet satin, the latter fashioned into horn motifs. At the center of the crown is a button made of red silk thread. The two chin-bands are made of pale green satin. Height 5¹⁄₈ in. (13 cm), diameter 11⁷⁄₈ in. (30 cm).

222 The "sheephorn" headdress is created by stiffening and shaping the hair with congealed mutton fat, then holding it in place with silver, turquoise and coral clips. The hair at the front disappears into two richly decorated containers of gilt silver. Two embroidered ribbons hang down the back of the head from a hat that is surmounted by a high silver point.

221 Above her richly patterned sleeveless coat, worn over an ornate red silk dress with high shoulder pads, a stand-up collar and blue turned-up cuffs—an outstanding example of the festive dress of 19th-century Mongolian nobility—this Chalka tribeswoman models the "sheephorn headdress."

SPECIAL COSTUMES

Only two generations after Genghis Khan, the imperial court of Kublai Khan accepted Tibetan Lamaist Buddhism, perhaps because it was the religion that most closely resembled their ancient belief in shamanism. Apparently the conquerors' warrior spirits were tamed by Tibetan lamas when the Mongolian empire was at its height and the khans were coming to grips with the complexities of controlling a multicultural populace. Even today, every devoted Buddhist Mongol tries—once in a lifetime—to make a pilgrimage to the Tibetan holy city of Lhasa, despite the hardship and distance involved. Buddhist monks are easily recognized, dressed as they all are in wine-dark robes worn over a yellow undergarment [223].

TRANSITIONAL DRESS

Today the *del* continues to be worn by many Mongolians [224]. Although the sturdy fabric of a working man's garment may now be pan-global denim, his hat Western and his boots Russian, a traditional yellow sash still encircles his waist and his long coat still closes to the right, in the ancient Asian manner.

223 (above left) A young lama monk wearing the dark red robe of his order over a sleeveless yellow undertunic.

224 (above) A horseman photographed in a *ger* camp at Lake Hovsgol wears the age-old costume of Central Asia: trousers, coat and boots. His *del* is made of simple, strong, woven cloth suitable for hard work; in cut and styling it resembles garments that have been worn in Mongolia for millennia.

THE SILK ROAD

225 Jonathan Kenworthy, *The Afghan Tea House*, 1995. Northern Afghanistan was a part of the old Silk Road, a land where turban-swathed men often took their leisure lounging in comfortable tea houses.

Millennia before the great Silk Road came into being to connect Europe with the Far East, an ancient trade network of camel caravans spanned the rugged terrain of Central Asia.[1] This landlocked Eurasian heartland is an enormous shallow bowl, crisscrossed by mountain ranges that stretch from the outer boundary of Europe—the Ural and Caucasus mountains—east to the border of China, south to include parts of Afghanistan and Pakistan, and north to Siberia's taiga forests. Located within southern Central Asia is the Tarim Basin, an area some 400 by 800 miles in dimension (645 × 1,290 km), at one point more than 500 feet (150 m) below sea level, and bordered by four towering ranges: the Tien Shan to the north, the Pamirs to the West and the Hindu Kush and Kunlun to the south [Map 13]. At the center of the Tarim depression lies the exceedingly dry Taklamakan

desert surrounded by rocky salt flats interspersed with scattered oases. This desiccated environment has preserved some remarkable—and remarkably clothed—human remains.

A series of mummies dating between 2000 and 700 B.C. have been discovered within the past hundred years in such long-abandoned oases as Cherchen bordering the Tarim Basin.[2] These bodies were a surprise to the archaeological world because ethnically they were related neither to the nomadic, Altaic-speaking horsemen to the north nor the settled, agrarian Chinese to the east, but rather were Caucasians and almost certainly Indo-European-speaking. In prehistoric times these semi-pastoral nomads had migrated into Chinese Turkistan from the Indo-European heartland to the west.[3]

The best known of these Tarim Basin discoveries are the 3,000-year-old mummies now displayed in Ürümchi.[4] Some of these brown-haired males, who date ca. 1200–700 B.C., were over 6 feet (1.8 m) tall and wore woven woolen clothing with surprisingly colorful bands of plaited wool [226].

Northeast of the Tarim Basin, near the oasis town of Hami, another group of light-haired Caucasian mummies were found who also wore colorful woven garments. Their diagonal-twill clothing is particularly intriguing. These woolen textiles display broad and narrow stripes—some in as many as six colors—arranged in Celtic-like plaids [227] reminiscent of contemporaneous diagonal-twill plaids, ca. 1200–400 B.C. [228], from the Bronze Age Celtic salt mines located in Central Europe, at Hallstatt and Hallein in the Austrian Alps.

The world of the early Caucasian mummies lies along the ancient caravan routes that much later evolved into the fabled Silk Road [Map 14], the international artery of long-distance trade that began in Roman times, concurrent with the decision of China's Han Dynasty to begin exporting silk. Despite entering into this commercial enterprise, the Chinese always regarded silk as their own closely guarded monopoly.

The origin of silk production and weaving is ancient and clouded in myth but the industry undoubtedly began in China where, according to native legends, it already existed sometime in the 3rd millennium B.C.[5] Silk was one of China's most valuable and sought-after treasures, a commodity whose appeal was universal, transcending levels of cultural refinement or degrees of sophistication. Certainly it was appreciated by the rapacious horsemen of the northern steppes (see "Mongolia," p. 126), who regularly raided north China's rich and fertile river valleys to obtain it.

The trauma of repeated nomadic incursions forced China to begin paying the raiders quantities of silk to keep them at bay. Chinese annals record these payments as "gifts;" the horsemen considered them "tribute." Bribes were regularly given to maintain peaceful relations with the mounted tribes on China's

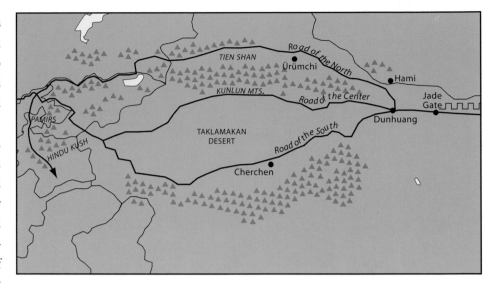

Map 13 Map of Central Asia's low-lying Tarim Basin, showing the three principal routes making up the Silk Road in early times, starting from the Jade Gate at the defensive Chinese wall, then west to Dunhuang. The sites of Cherchen and Hami have produced many mummified remains dating from ca. 1200–700 B.C.

226 A 3,000-year-old mummy, ca. 1000 B.C., from Tomb 2 at Cherchen. Cherchen Man—a tall, 55-year-old Caucasian with light brown hair—was dressed in white deerskin boots and brightly colored wool garments: shirt, pants and felt leggings.

227 A fragment of a woolen plaid twill (ca. 1200–700 B.C.) found in a burial near the oasis town of Hami.

228 A fragment of a woolen, bicolor-plaid twill (ca. 1200–400 B.C.) from Hallstatt, Austria. The similarity between the Hallstatt twills and those from the Tarim Basin suggests a common origin in weaving traditions.

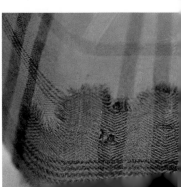

Map 14 The transcontinental Silk Road connecting China with Rome, ca. 300 A.D. From the European West, the Chinese sought woolens, gold, silver, glass, and exotic foods and plants, including the grape; from the Central Asian West, horses, servants, dancers, acrobats and various forms of dress. In return, China exported silks, lacquers, gems and spices. Early on the influence was mainly from West to East, with China absorbing many foreign features, including vessel shapes and decorations of all kinds that transformed Chinese applied arts. In later periods, however, the influence went the other way, with Chinese scientific and technological innovations changing the entire face of the world: printing made possible widespread literacy, the magnet made possible the compass/navigation, and gunpowder made possible ever more lethal warfare.

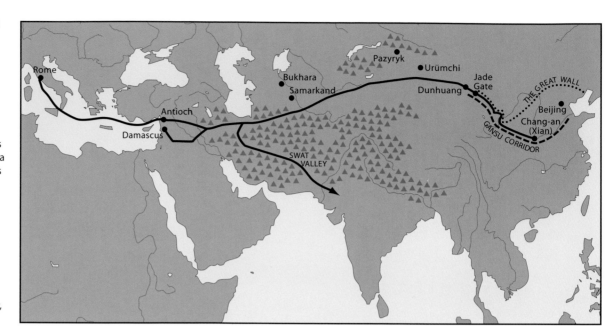

northern border, perhaps in the hope that one day other accommodations might be made.

The Chinese classics taught that eventually all people—no matter how untutored or uncouth—would succumb to the appeal of culture and become civilized. Along China's northern frontier, however, the Central Asian nomads showed no interest in assimilating Chinese civilization. Certainly they wanted the riches that resulted from that settled way of life but the disciplined, restricting organization needed to produce such tempting wares had no appeal to the free-roaming horsemen.

When even huge bribes of silk were not enough to gain protection from the voracious nomads, a series of defensive, tamped-earth walls were built over a period of many centuries, the so-called Great Wall of China. Actually, the wall was never a single, connected unity. Indeed, Northern China is crisscrossed by many different earthen walls built by many different dynasties, but all shared a single purpose: protection from nomadic raids.[6] It was through an opening in one section of the defensive Wall, the so-called Jade Gate, that Chinese caravans began to pass regularly into Central Asia after 100 B.C.

The Silk Road entered a Golden Age in the second century B.C. when the goods and ideas of the world's two supreme civilizations—Imperial Rome

(31 B.C.–A.D. 235) and Han Dynasty China (202 B.C.–A.D. 220)—tentatively touched one another via their various exports. The arduous journey of 4,000 miles (6,435 km) took approximately 8 months from China to the eastern coast of the Mediterranean [see Map 14]; from there the Chinese goods were transported by sea to the markets of Rome.[7] The fortunes of the Silk Road fluctuated: paths were sometimes blocked by wars, brigands or zealots, at other times secured beneath the protection of conquering empires. Probably very few travelers ever made the entire journey from end to end because this trade involved a staggered progression of middlemen: goods passing from merchant to merchant, oasis to oasis, increasing in price all along the way and finally emerging mysteriously at the other end as if the exotic wares had come from another world, as indeed they had.[8]

Just as there is a general misconception as to the unbroken unity of the Great Wall, so too is the Silk Road sometimes envisioned as one single, well-defined passage across the heart of inner Asia. In actuality, by A.D. 300 the Road had become a braided cable of dusty and evanescent trails. All west-bound caravans began in China's silk metropolis, the northern city of Chang-an, modern-day Xian. Leaving Xian, the merchants passed along the Gansu Corridor to the Jade

229 A woman's silk dress, or *kurta*, made of one of the most celebrated Central Asian textiles, *ikat*. This dress was produced in a textile factory, probably in the 20th century. Although the cloth itself is not handwoven, the design—an abstracted version of the Tree of Life pattern—is an ancient one (see "The European Folk Tradition," pp. 109–110).

230 A section of tie-dyed and handwoven silk *ikat*, ca. 19th century.

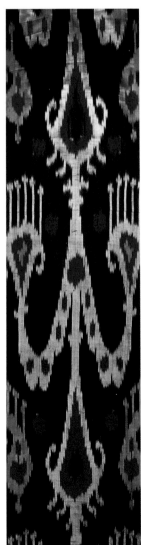

Gate and west to Dunhuang. The caravans then had three choices [see Map 13]: the Roads of the South and of the Center skirted either side of the dreaded Taklamakan desert, passing through dry, stony plains before climbing over the soaring mountain peaks of the lofty Pamir or Tien Shan ranges to continue either west to the Mediterranean or south into India over the formidable Hindu Kush. The third choice of routes, the Road of the North, although geographically less taxing, was the most vulnerable to attacks from raiding nomads swooping down from the steppes. This northern route, after making its way over high mountain passes, continued on toward the Mediterranean coast through the western oases, Central Asia's textile production center.

In the first half of the 7th century A.D., however, a profound change swept through Central Asia with the rise of Islam resulting from the Arab conquests of North Africa and Asia following the death of the Prophet Muhammad in A.D. 632. This Islamic expansion united the worlds of the Mediterranean and Indian Ocean, making Central Asia an integral part of the vast Muslim trading zone wherein textile production was the major industry. The material culture of both the Bedouin Arabs and the Central Asian Turks had always been textile-based, a tradition that was further strengthened by the essentially utilitarian nature of cloth. Fabrics make ideal trade goods: packable, durable and universally usable.

The Islamic conquest was but the first of many. In the early 13th century, the Mongol leader Genghis Khan's invasion of Central Asia—and much of the rest of the Muslim world—began a new and traumatic chapter in the history of the region (see "Mongolia," p. 127). In the 14th century, the Turko-Mongol conqueror Timur, or Tamerlane/Tamburlaine, succeeded to the Mongol Ilkhanid rule, and the oasis cities and towns of southern Central Asia—often referred to as Turkistan—began a renaissance in architecture and painting. Unfortunately, through the next two hundred years the repeated pattern of local wars and political instability continually eroded the

area's trade-based economy, and the busy caravan trade slowed to a crawl. By the 16th century the glory days of the Silk Road had long passed.

The manufacture of textiles in local workshops, however, remained Turkistan's chief industry until the end of the 19th century. The western oasis cities derived much of their fame from the production of outstanding fabrics, particularly those of silk. This cloth and clothing served the needs of prosperous urban dwellers as well as those of such nomadic groups as the Kazakh, Kirghiz, Tadjik, Turkmen, Uyghur and Uzbek. Though silk production was a tightly guarded Chinese monopoly, silkworm eggs and mulberry seeds had been smuggled out of the country as early as the 6th century A.D.[9]

Probably the greatest period of Central Asian textiles was the 19th century and of all the magnificent fabrics produced at that time it was the multicolored *ikat* silks[10] that still remain unrivaled, to the point of now being mass-produced [229, 230]. Although this type of resist dyeing had existed earlier, its re-invention represents the last of the great urban arts of Turkistan, a *sui generis* phenomenon distinct from the *ikat* produced in such neighboring regions as Iran, Iraq, India and Turkey. The Central Asian word for the

231 Two girls dressed in industrially produced *ikat* bind—and subsequently release and rebind—the silk warps for repeated immersions in a series of dye baths.

232 After the silk warp threads have undergone the necessary multiple dye baths, they are threaded onto a manually operated loom. Note that the future cloth's design is clearly visible before the fabric is ever woven, using a white cotton weft.

multi-stage *ikat* tie-and-dye technique [231, 232], *abr-brandi*, derives from the Persian term *abr*, "cloudlike:" the resulting abstract designs have soft-edged, floating borders.

One of the glories of the Central Asian *ikat* silks was the range of vibrant colors achieved through the use of such natural dyes as cochineal, madder, *isparak* and indigo.[11] However, as the rulership of the Uzbek khanates came to an end following Russian annexation in 1865 [233], a dramatic change took place in the dyeing craft, which had varied little since medieval times. As imported synthetic dyes became available in late 19th-century bazaars, the use of ancient dyes decreased. This was unfortunate because the synthetics were color-fast to neither sunlight nor washing. The types of new dye available depended on the political alignment of a particular area, whether to Germany, Russia or England.[12] As time passed, the cloth of khans continued to remain popular as dress fabric with the women of Turkistan [234], but increasingly the cloth was mass-produced in textile factories.

Because Central Asia had no tradition of preserving old cloth or clothing, few fabrics predate the 19th century. Fortunately, some beautiful garments and wall hangings from that period are still extant, many produced in the Uzbekistan oasis cities of Bukhara and Samarkand, as well as in towns of the Ferghana Valley. Throughout these areas, most farm families grew mulberry trees around their wheat or cotton fields for feeding the silkworms. This was women's work; men boiled the cocoons in order to extract the silk thread. Before being woven, this thread was given to the dyers, who were often Jews. After going through the multi-stage, tie-and-dye process, the *ikat* thread was woven using a plain cotton weft. According to Islamic precepts, it was preferable to have cotton in contact with the skin rather than silk, which was considered too sensual.[13]

But of all the Central Asian *ikat* fabrics, the type that gained worldwide renown was the silk-velvet *baghmal*—as dazzling wall hangings [235] and shimmering robes [236, 237].

A great deal of the *ikat* was made up into resplendent clothing—robes, dresses and distinctive headcoverings for the wealthy urban upper class, as well as colorful garments created for some tribesmen. Such apparel played an important social function in Turkistan society: all along the old Silk Road it had always been cloth that made the man.

233 (below left) A 19th-century reception of Russian officers at the Bukhara court. The emir and high court officials all wear magnificent silk robes and broad belts with silver fittings; only members of the urban upper class were allowed to wear such belts. The Turkistan dress code was strictly defined by rank. The ruler and highest court officials wore silk-velvet robes, some with gold embroidery. The robes of the next rank down were of valuable cloth imported from Kashmir. Wealthy merchants and scholars were allowed to wear silk *ikat*. Peasants and nomads usually wore clothes of rather coarse wool. However, gifts of light silk-*ikat* robes were often distributed by the rulers to various tribesmen across the length and breadth of Turkistan.

234 (below) A Tadjik family all wearing versions of the *kurta* and drawstring trousers, typical present-day attire in Turkistan villages and towns. The *ikat* cloth from which these garments were made is mass-produced today in textile factories.

236 (left) A man's 19th-century silk-velvet robe made of *ikat* from Bukhara, lined with Russian printed cotton. The inner flap is made of silk *ikat*—probably a prestigious older piece—that has acquired a shiny gloss as the result of being treated with beaten egg whites and applied pressure. The robe's polychrome trim and embroidered cuffs are probably done in silk cross-stitch embroidery. Length 49 1/8 in. (125 cm), width 74 7/8 in. (190 cm).

235 (left) A fragment of silk-velvet *ikat*—*baghmal*—surrounded by a meticulously embroidered border. The finest of these fabrics displayed up to seven different colors, each reflecting a separate dye bath.

237 (left and below; detail shown right) Front and back views of a woman's 19th-century silk-velvet coat, which displays a repeating design of the Great Goddess motif (see "The European Folk Tradition," pp. 108–109). The garment is lined with a similarly patterned silk *ikat*; the flap displays a glossy silk *ikat* of another design. To attain the fullness needed in women's robes, narrow *ikat* pieces were inserted as tapering panels, often arranged somewhat nonchalantly with the pile lying in opposite directions on adjacent gores or gussets. Women wore such finery at ladies-only events; men's festivities were similarly segregated. Length 47¼ in. (120 cm), width 59⅞ in. (152 cm).

MEN'S BASIC DRESS

The basic apparel of Central Asia—trousers, tunic and robe—represents an ancient legacy from the horsemen of the steppes (see "Mongolia," pp. 130–131). As Kate Fitz Gibbon and Andrew Hale note: "…you cannot ride a horse in a toga. Trousers were among the many gifts brought from the east by the nomadic hordes."[14] An early example of such apparel was also worn by Cherchen Man, ca. 1000 B.C [see 226]. These same basic garment types have continued to be worn throughout the millennia by people at every level of society: nomadic men, women and children as well as aristocratic urban dwellers, the wealthy descendants of earlier conquering warriors. The difference in the clothing of the various classes was only reflected in richness of fabric and complexity of trim.

Men wore drawstring trousers, cut very wide and straight, with tapering legs. Over such trousers went a long, straight-cut, cotton shirt/tunic and a coat, the *khalat*, made of a light material in summer,

padded and quilted for winter. A subtly graded system governed the use of different valuable materials for wealthy urban men's coats: a man's social status could quickly be judged by the elegance of his robe. Clothing was a tool of the social and political system throughout the Islamic world. In 19th-century Turkistan, robes were a kind of social currency, less a matter of personal taste than an indicator of social rank and geographic origin. Social status was further bestowed and confirmed through an emir's gift of robes of honor, social recognition of outstanding service in battle or sport, or as a payment or bribe. The rich dressed in layers, wearing as many as ten robes, one atop another. Elaborated belts were an essential part of this type of male dress, particularly for court officials [see 233].[15]

Silk *ikat* was restricted to the aristocracy. Wearing a robe unsuitable to one's station was cause for corporal punishment and the imposing of a severe fine. It was not until the annexation of Central Asia by the Russians, and the subsequent overthrow of the Uzbek khans, that silk fabrics came into more general use. It was this new demand for *ikat*-patterned cloth that was met largely by machine-printed *ikat* produced in textile mills and colored with synthetic dyes.[16]

WOMEN'S BASIC DRESS

There was a marked similarity between the clothing of both sexes: the only specifically female garment was a long dress with a closed front seam, the *kurta* [see 229, 234]. A woman's total ensemble consisted of a pair of drawstring trousers [238]—like those of men but sometimes with a decorative border at the cuff [see

238 Woman's drawstring underpants, Bukhara, early 20th century. These garments consisted of two types of fabric: cotton above and the best cloth one could afford below. The very wide trousers were drawn together with a woven cotton string. Length 36⅛ in. (92 cm), width 31⅛ in. (79 cm).

239 When an affluent urban woman stepped outside her home, she donned a ground-length garment, the *paranja*, draped over her head so as to envelop the body completely; a horsehair veil was worn over her face. Turkistan, ca. 1900.

234]—along with a dress and a coat, both collarless. As in all parts of the Muslim world, Turkistan women covered their hair; some also veiled their faces. An affluent urban woman, when out and about, enveloped herself from head to toe in a *paranja*—an ankle-length garment with mock sleeves hanging down the back— and covered her face with an impenetrable horsehair veil [239, 240]. A poor woman simply borrowed a male relative's robe and wore that over her head.

As for nomadic women, whose faces were almost never veiled, various styles of headcovering were worn over the *kurta*, the most notable being the Turkoman *chyrpy* [241]. As with the urban *paranja*, these shorter cloaks were placed over the head; the garments' long, vestigial sleeves hung down the back [242]. False-sleeved robes for both sexes have a long history in Central Asia.

The traditional attire of Turkistan tends to be bright and bold, juxtaposing colors and patterns in a manner sometimes jarring to Western sensibilities. The concept of garments that matched never found favor

240 A 19th-century horsehair veil from Khiva is decorated with a jeweled diadem. Such ornate pieces are sometimes described as head jewelry. The items on either side of the veil are hair decorations for the two plaits that hung down a woman's back. The jeweled ornaments are made of silver, fire-gilded silver, turquoise, coral and cotton. Width of diadem 16⁵/₈ in. (42 cm). Length of hair ornaments 14⁷/₈ in. and 11⁷/₈ in. (38 and 30 cm). Length of veil 22³/₈ in. (57 cm).

241 A Turkoman
tribeswoman, adorned in
elaborate jewelry, wears a
chyrpy, a false-sleeved cloak
that completely covers her
hair, shoulders and back.

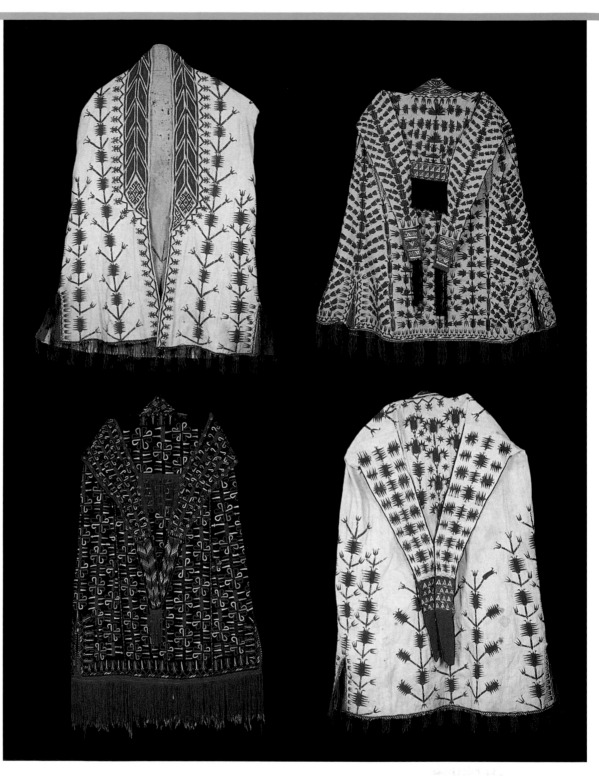

242 The *chyrpy*, the richly
embroidered outer garment
typically worn by Turkoman
females, was placed over the
head in such a way as to hide
the hair. Tribeswomen wore
chyrpys of different colors
depending on their age: dark
blue for the youngest, yellow
for the middle-aged and, as
a sign of respect, white for
the oldest. These cloak-like
garments had false sleeves,
joined by a short ribbon,
hanging down the back.

in women's clothing; fabrics that contrasted were far
more pleasing to local tastes. The varied trims and
lining materials were aimed at mimicking the appearance of multi-layered, luxurious costumes.

FOOTWEAR

Boots of various heights were the most common
Turkistan footwear [243]; some had heels shod with

243 A 19th-century Samarkand man wearing boots, under which soft leather stockings would have been worn. This man is involved in a game of *buzkashi*, a popular sport in northern Afghanistan and Turkistan, in which riders tried to seize a dead sheep or calf from their opponents; the first to carry the carcass past a goal post received valuable presents, including robes of honor. The player pictured here is also attired in a rakishly wrapped turban.

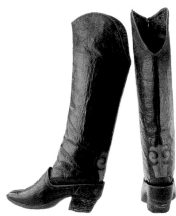

244 Low leather shoes with comparatively high heels worn with leather stockings decorated with appliquéd designs. Length 17³/₈ in. (44 cm).

246 A cotton turban made of elegant cloth, Bukhara, 1891. Length 196⁷/₈ in. (500 cm), width 34⁵/₈ in. (88 cm).

245 In the Muslim world, small, round caps are worn by men when at home or work. The three illustrated here reflect a typical range of Turkistan decorations. When a man went out for business or pleasure, his cap was hidden beneath a wrapped turban.

iron. Inside low boots, leather stockings were worn, some elegantly decorated [244]. For court-connected clients, high-heeled footwear with richly embroidered velvet uppers was custom-made.[17]

HEADGEAR

The most noticeable difference between such nomadic groups as the Turkoman and town-dwellers was their headgear. The large sheepskin hats of the Turkoman were a mark of male tribal dress, whereas town-dwellers wore small, round, often richly embroidered caps at home or at work [245], their quality indicating the status of the wearer. The fact that cap-sellers' shops were situated at the center of the bazaar indicates the importance attached to this headgear.[18] When urban men went out in public, however, their skull caps were enfolded in a turban. Some turbans were huge, made up of as many as 280 yards (840 ft/255 m) of material [see 225, 233, 243]. The quality and color of the turban material also differed according to status [246].

As for marriageable urban girls and young married women of wealthy families [248], they wore so much rich jewelry—silver with carnelian, turquoise, glass stones, coral, fire-gilded silver—that, when fully adorned, they could walk only with difficulty: the full array of bridal jewelry could weigh as much as 36 pounds (16.4 kg).[19]

SPECIAL COSTUMES

A particularly intriguing garment, an ornamental wedding shirt, was made in a remote section of the old Silk Road [249]. This short, full-skirted, multi-gored tunic combines an amalgam of old and new elements, including ancient and exquisite silk cross-stitch embroidery together with sections of zipper, various small metal pieces, and imaginatively positioned plastic and mother-of-pearl buttons.

TRANSITIONAL DRESS

By the end of the 19th century, the style and cut of Turkistan clothing began to reflect the influence of Western "foreign" fashions. As Fitz Gibbon and Hale note, initially pockets, collars, buttons and bits of trim were added to traditional Central Asian garments.[20] The adoption of complete Western dress occurred first in areas with the largest Russian population, particularly among urban men, who quickly started

247 Late 19th-century embroidered pouches from various regions of Turkistan.

248 A young married woman adorned in the complete, ornate wedding jewelry typical of a wealthy city dweller. She and the child both wear richly patterned silk-*ikat* garments: the sleeve of the woman's dress is visible beneath her robe.

ACCESSORIES

Central Asian clothing—whether drawstring trousers, tunic or robe—had no pockets, hence small bags or pouches were a necessity of life. These often richly decorated accessories were attached to a wearer's belt [247].

JEWELRY

Nomad women made lavish use of jewelry and, since they went about unveiled, their adornments did not go unnoticed [see 241]. Such a woman's combined jewelry could weigh as much as 17 pounds (7.7 kg).

249 (opposite, below right) A woman's cotton wedding tunic, or *jumlo*, decorated with silk cross-stitch embroidery, glass beads, plastic buttons, mother-of-pearl buttons, coins, parts of zippers and various metal "findings." The full, gored skirt—length 35³⁄₈ in. (90 cm), width 57³⁄₈ in. (146 cm)—has several hundred inserted triangles. This unusual garment comes from the valley of the Swat River—a tributary of the Indus River—located on a side branch of the old Silk Road that passed over the Hindu Kush range in an area that today is northwestern Pakistan.

wearing Russian styles after the Revolution. Traditional dress of all kinds held on much longer in the women's realm, as has been true the world over.

At the turn of the century, the arrival of sewing machines coincided with the introduction of modern dress styles. By the 1930s a simple calf-length shift and full pantaloons became the standard dress of the rural population [see 231, 234]. Western styles are now worn by Uzbek professional women and the urban working class, though many still prefer the colorful, factory-made *ikat* silks for home and festive wear.

But not all clothing change marches irrevocably forward toward Western fashion. In some fundamentalist Islamic cultures, women have moved back in time, shrouding themselves in such enveloping garments as the Afghan *chadri*: a long, pleated, body-encasing veil [250] with only a small, netted eye-hole for a woman to look out on a man's world [251].

250 (above) In Taliban-controlled Afghanistan, ca. 2001, women—when outside their homes—were obliged to wear a *chadri*, a completely body-encasing outer garment with a netted "window" in front of the eyes.

251 A woman enshrouded in a *chadri*: the confined carrying the caged.

4

EAST ASIA

THERE WERE MIGRATIONS of proto-humans into the Far East as early as 350,000 years ago when Peking Man—a hominid of the species *Homo erectus*—arrived in the Middle Pleistocene with well-developed hunting practices, fire use and a common culture. The arrival of modern man, *Homo sapiens*, reaches back as far as 100,000 B.C. and has been traced through genealogical markers in human DNA: because males pass along a Y chromosome virtually intact, one branch of Africa's early human wanderers can be traced through the Asian population to the Central Asian steppes and then on into East Asia. After millennia of isolation, the dominant culture that gave rise to China's civilization began in the north, along the banks of the Yellow River, around the start of the Late Pleistocene, ca. 30,000 B.C. To the south, the Korean peninsula was also peopled ca. 30,000 B.C. by an amalgam of migrants out of central and northern Asia. Japan received an influx of Koreans, ca. 400 B.C., who merged with the resident population to push the aboriginal Ainu into the northern reaches of the Japanese archipelago. But overall the East Asian sphere has been unquestionably dominated by China, thanks to that country's huge land mass, its enormous population and the antiquity of its high civilization. Both Korea and Japan repeatedly drew on the Chinese example, as is reflected in their shared discipline, capacity for constructive social effort, disregard for the individual, and respect for authority and hierarchy. Collectively these ancient, entrenched Far Eastern civilizations reflect the most deeply rooted, staunchly conservative cultural traditions on earth.[1]

260 This 18th-century embroidered silk satin Twelve Symbol robe appropriately displays the Qing empire's imperial color, yellow. Such semiformal Qing-dynasty robes, inspired by the conquering horsemen's original riding coats, display the Manchu's diagnostic right closure with a curved overlap, as well as the nomads' horsehoof cuffs. Length 54³⁄₈ in. (138 cm).

261 (far left) A 19th-century court winter hat—the Manchu's traditional winter headgear. This example is made of silk satin, sable, silk cord, glass, gilt metal, jadite, and a feather. Height 6³⁄₈ in. (16 cm), diameter 10¹⁄₄ in. (26 cm).

262 (left) A late 19th-century court summer hat, inspired by the peasants' conical sunshades. This example is made of bamboo, silk gauze, floss silk, glass, gilt metal, cotton and a feather. Height 9³⁄₈ in. (24 cm), diameter 13³⁄₈ in. (34 cm).

HAIRSTYLES

The nomadic conquerors made their dominant position visible by decreeing that Chinese officials had to wear their hair in the Manchu manner: shave the front of the head and braid the remaining hair into a long pigtail that hung down the back. Ironically, in later years it was this Manchu *queue* that became a sign of "Chineseness" in countless cartoons in the Western press.[11]

HEADGEAR

Shortly after the conquest, the Qing decreed two types of headgear, both known as the *chaoquan*, to be an indispensable part of ceremonial court dress. For winter, the original Manchu fur-trimmed hat was worn, complete with upturned brim and crown covered with red-dyed yak or horse hair [261]. In summer, a conical sunshade was used; it was woven of bamboo that was completely covered with silk gauze [262]. Both court styles had jeweled finials, easily visible indicators of rank and status.[12] Manchu court hats also indicated rank by the shape of the finial, the type of fur, color, and added accessories such as peacock-feather plumes, or *lingzhi* [see 256]. These hats are reminiscent of those worn by the Mongols (see "Mongolia," pp. 134–135).

WOMEN'S BASIC DRESS

The formal court attire of Han Chinese women was much like that of the men: long-sleeved, full-length robes under which a series of layered garments were worn that added bulk to the ceremonial outfits used on important occasions. In actuality, the difference between formal and informal clothing—the *chaofu* and the *changfu*—was largely a matter of icon-ography: in the Chinese decorative system, almost every motif conveyed a special, auspicious meaning [263; see also 273–278].

As for Manchu female dress, at the time of the conquest trousers and/or leggings, the *ku*, were worn under the robes of all Chinese, regardless of class or gender—a heritage from former nomadic conquerors such as the Mongols of the Yuan dynasty. During the subsequent Qing period, Manchu women's trousers were concealed by a skirt-like pair of joined aprons, the *qun* [264], also borrowed from an earlier nomadic tradition.

263 A nine-dragon robe in the yellow-brown color known as "tawny incense" (*qiuxiangse*). Length 56 1/8 in. (142.5 cm), width 77 7/8 in. (198 cm). The ninth dragon was always placed out of sight, under the Manchu-style garment's overlap (see below).
    Since yellow was the official color of the Qing dynasty, many imperial robes were harmonized with yellow. The exquisite workmanship and attention to detail on this garment suggests that it may have been worn at court by a prince or other noble.

264 Manchu-style paired aprons concealed trousers or leggings. These full garments also created the desirable impressive bulk associated with formality. Only the skirt-like aprons' lower sections had to be decorated (see detail, left) because these garments were always worn under a three-quarter-length coat. Length 44¹/₂ in. (113 cm), width 48¹/₂ in. (123.2 cm).

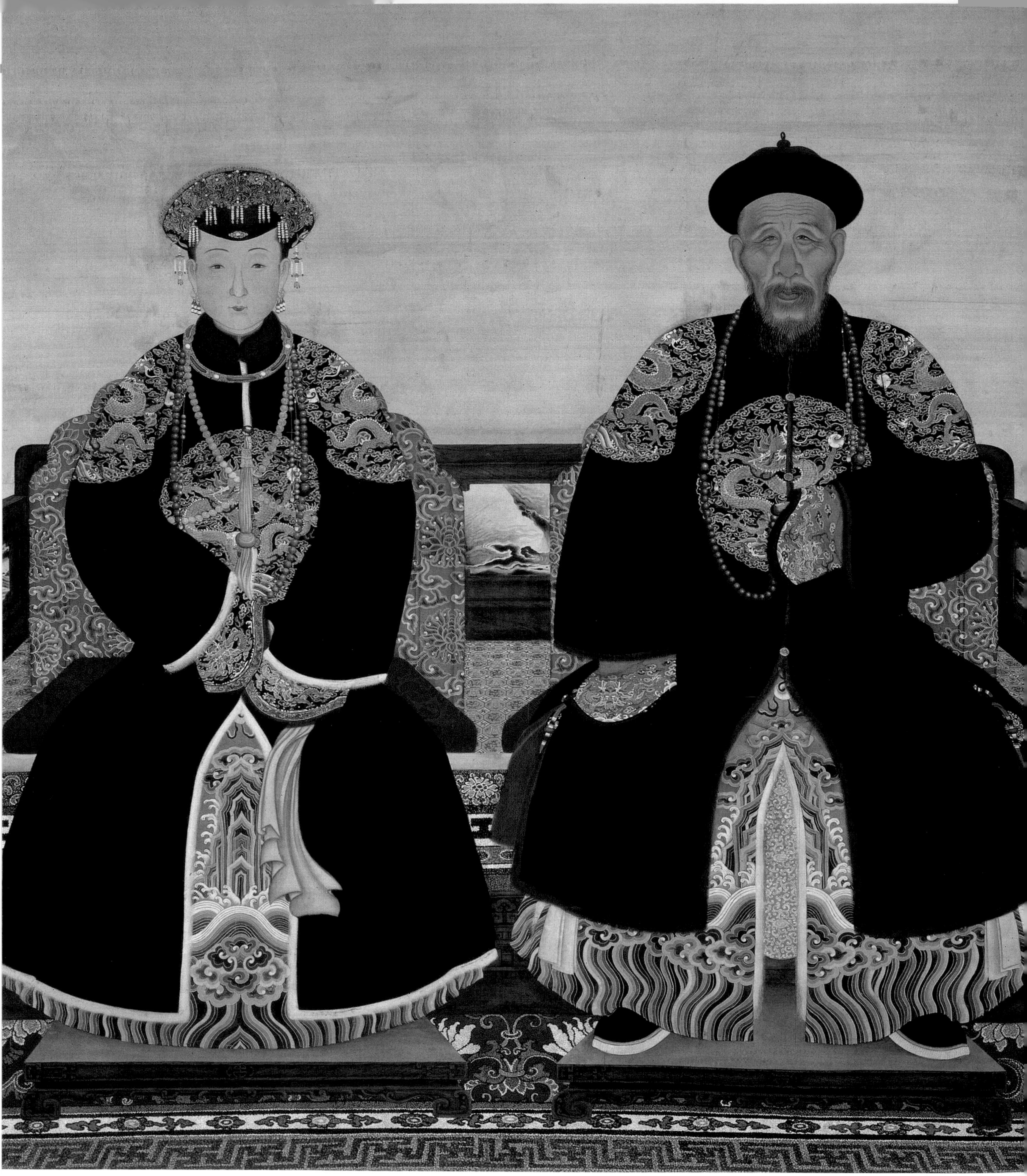

ARMOR

In battle, the pre-conquest Manchu wore their usual riding coats, sometimes quilted and sometimes covered by a coat of protective chain mail; Qing parade armor [271] did not appear until after the conquest. At that time, the Manchu adopted Chinese-style brigandine armor constructed of overlapping metal plates covered with padded textiles.

JEWELRY

Just as Qing clothing and accessories harked back to the warrior horsemen's past, so too did their jewelry.

One example is an archer's ring made of jade or other semiprecious stone that was worn on one thumb. Originally this ring served a functional need: to hold the bowstring while the archer's index and middle fingers steadied his arrow.[15] Manchu court dress also included a distinctive necklace, the *chaozhu*, based on a Buddhist rosary [272]. The nomadic Mongols wore such necklaces and may have introduced them to their Manchu neighbors before the conquest.[16]

270 (opposite) This 18th-century portrait of Yanti, fourteenth son of the Manchu emperor Kanqxi, and his wife show the pair wearing black surcoats displaying imperial dragon imagery embroidered within roundels. Note the surcoats' horsehoof cuffs as well as the pair's imperial necklaces.

272 The Manchu court necklace—composed of amber, jadeite and rose quartz—was based on a Buddhist rosary. The long pendant hanging down the back acted as a counterweight; the three smaller pendants were originally used to keep a tally of prayers [see 256, 270]. This example probably dates from the 19th century. Length ca. 25$\frac{1}{2}$ in. (65 cm).

271 A suit of early 18th-century Manchu ceremonial armor made of metal plates covered with padded luxury textiles and gilt brass fittings. The prototype for this type of armor had been in use since the 3rd century B.C [see 254].

Jacket: length 27$\frac{1}{8}$ in. (69 cm), width across shoulders 14$\frac{7}{8}$ in. (38 cm).

Chaps: length 31$\frac{1}{8}$ in. (79 cm).

273 A Han Chinese style of robe that opens down the center and has full, kimono-style sleeves. Although the garment displays eight embroidered dragons, the crucial ninth dragon is absent. This robe probably dates from the late Manchu imperial period and was perhaps created as bridalwear.

GARMENT DECORATION

Of all the motifs that appear on Manchu imperial robes, the dragon holds pride of place. Dragon motifs appear early on, at the end of the Bronze Age. Han literature links the dragon to the emperor, but putting dragons on robes can only be traced to the Tang court regulations of the 9th century. The earliest surviving dragon robes come from the Liao dynasty of the 10th–11th century. During the Mongols' Yuan dynasty, the 5-clawed or *long* dragon became emblematic of the emperor himself. Indeed, in 1636 the Ming decreed that only the emperor and his family could wear yellow robes with the five-clawed dragon; lesser nobles were relegated to the four-clawed or *mang* dragon. During

the first century of Manchu rule, the Qing court was vigilant regarding this law. Indeed, some museums and private collections contain early Qing robes that have had one claw picked out from each *long* dragon, de-clawed to reduce it to a *mang*.[17]

The dragon motif appears in various configur-ations—front-facing, profile, standing, walking—and could be embroidered or woven on a garment at several locations. In the case of the nine-dragon robe, the *longpao*, which was the signature garment of the Chinese court, three dragons appear on the robe's front, three in the back, and one on each shoulder; the ninth dragon is hidden from sight, embroidered on the front of the robe's inside panel [see 263, 274].

274 A nine-dragon robe displaying the typical Manchu overlapping closure and horsehoof cuffs. Although this finely crafted garment displays all nine of the requisite dragons—complete with the final example hidden under the robe's overlap (see left)—it lacks the elaborate detailing that appears on the yellow-brown imperial robe illustrated on p. 164. This blue garment probably dates to the late Qing period and may have been created as bridalwear. Length 57³/₈ in. (145.7 cm), width 91³/₄ in. (233 cm).

275 A gold-embroidered robe with sea creatures emerging from the ocean around the garment's hem (see detail below), a lively scene creating a completely different mood than its prototype, the imperial court's stately nine-dragon robe. Flamboyant, richly detailed costumes like this were created for the Chinese opera. Length 51⁷⁄₈ in. (132 cm), width 78³⁄₄ in. (200 cm).

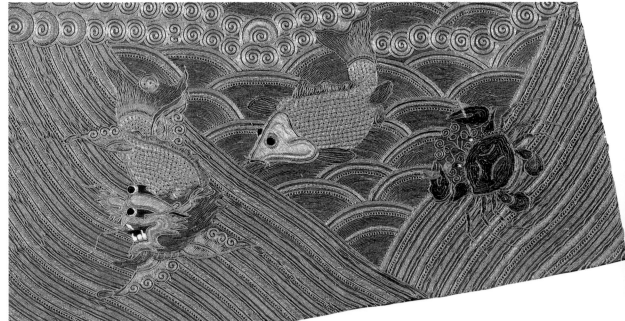

Early in the 16th century, Ming court designers added a further prestigious motif around the robe's hem, the *lishui*: waves breaking against rocks depicting a cosmic landscape for the imperial dragon. But this cosmic symbolism was only complete when the garment was worn. The human body then became the world's axis, supporting the visible universe; at the center of that universe was the head of the august personage donning the magnificent robe.

Although the most exquisitely embroidered dragon robes were only worn at the highest levels of the imperial court, less ornate copies were made for the marketplace to be sold to Han [273] and Manchu [274] women, both of whom used them as bridal attire. Some robes were also used as glittering costumes for the opera [275].

SPECIAL COSTUMES

The Confucian-based bureaucracy was a world particularly sensitive to the carefully graded relationships existing between the court's twelve grades of nobles and nine each of civil and military officials. This system was made clearly visible by the insignia badges, or *buzi*. First and foremost, of course, was the emperor's badge [276], a full-facing dragon depicted in a roundel; round shapes were reserved for only the highest of rank. Dragon insignia depicted in various other, less prestigious forms also distinguished lesser members of the imperial clan [see 270]. Other types of animal badges were used to represent the military grades [277], while bird images served to depict the varying ranks of civil officials [278].

276 The emperor's circular badge featuring a front-facing dragon. Ming dynasty, 16th century, slit tapestry weave. Diameter 15³⁄₈ in. (39 cm).

277 The insignia of the military also featured various animals. This leopard denotes a third-rank military officer. 18th century, brocaded silk satin. Length 10³⁄₈ in. (26.6 cm), width 10³⁄₈ in. (26.2 cm).

278 The badges of civil servants featured a variety of birds. Length 12 in. (30.5 cm), width 11¾ in. (29.8 cm).

TRANSITIONAL DRESS

The Manchu's Qing dynasty ruled until 1911 when, under pressures from internal decline and external threat, imperial China's long dynastic cycle was brought to an end. Court attire thus ceased to serve a function, no longer an important part of the Chinese governmental structure. The magnificent imperial robes, however, were far from forgotten. Indeed, copies of those memorable garments were—and still are—worn by fashionable women throughout the Western world [279].

As the Chinese population steadily increased, nothing had been done to meet the farmers' need for land, hence the number of the indentured and landless continued to grow. It was their involvement that brought about the greatest of China's peasant revolts that finally ended nearly 3,000 years of imperial history.

280 (below) During the early stages of the land reform—a primary aim of the 20th-century Chinese Revolution—the landlords were often run down, tried and quickly punished by peasants and soldiers in revolt. Here the enraged masses, all wearing their worn work clothes, have tied up their impeding long trousers at the knee for swifter retaliation.

279 (above) William McGregor Paxton, *The Yellow Jacket*, 1907. Although imperial China's magnificent silk robes were no longer a feature of the governmental structure after the 1911 Revolution, they continued to influence Western attire. Here an aristocratic Boston lady of the early 20th century wears a Chinese-inspired robe whose densely patterned facing trim contrasts with the body of the garment in a manner originating during the Shang dynasty. Her robe closes to the right with a curved overlap, a style introduced to the Qing court by the nomadic Manchu conquerors.

Once the inevitable revolution had started, Chinese cultural traditions dissolved rapidly; Confucianism and the social and legal order fell together. Clearly, there was no going back to the old stable state, but what should the new direction be? Although Western liberalism was under attack because of its association with exploiting foreigners, there was one new ideological force in the West that commanded attention: the Russian Bolshevik revolution became the model for the Chinese Communist Party, formed in 1921.[18]

By 1949, after decades of war and tribulation [280], the Chinese Communists were fully in power under their charismatic leader, the farmer's son Mao Zedong. By 1965, despite the thousands of "liquidations" of the first five years of the People's Republic and the millions of casualties of Mao's second Five Year Plan, the Great Leap Forward, the population had reached 835 million, making China one of the most highly and densely populated countries in the world. Social ferment ran high: from 1966 to 1969 the Cultural Revolution raged. The new emphasis was upon physical labor, self-sacrifice and subordination to the thoughts of Mao. By 1968 the country had been turned upside down by the young "Red Guards" fighting entrenched officialdom [281] as well as battling that most conservative of all Chinese institutions, the family, a battle they did not win [282].

Of all the great revolutions of world history, that of the Chinese has unquestionably been one of the most far reaching. It had to be because in China—as nowhere else—society, government and the economy were enmeshed and integrated into a single system that constituted the most unchanging society on earth.

281 The Revolution of 1911 and the subsequent Cultural Revolution created a class of rabid reformers whose campaign against traditional symbols of the old regime included gleefully cutting off Manchu-style pigtails.

282 The Cultural Revolution did not succeed in dissolving all family ties; here are four generations of healthy peasant women, previously a rare sight in China where starvation and a short life span were too often the mean. The clothing of these women reflects the "Mao jacket"-type of apparel prevalent throughout China following the Revolution.

THE OTHER CHINA

By 1987, the Han Chinese made up about 93% of China's approximately one billion people. The remainder of the approximately 70 million non-Han today consists of 55 officially recognized ethnic minorities. Some of these groups are discussed in "Central Asia" and "The Himalayan Kingdoms." Pertinent to this section are the minorities living in China's tropical south [283].

Over the centuries, the Han relentlessly expanded south, assimilating alien groups or driving a bewildering mix of tribal peoples before the rising Chinese tide. This pattern of southwest infiltration, occupation and domination began more than 2,000 years before the Christian era and continued into the 20th century. As a result, nowhere in China is there such a vibrant racial mixture as in the mountain melting pot of the southwest provinces [Map 16].

Through the jumbled terrain of Guizhou, across the ranges of humid, misty Yunnan and in the pleasant valleys of Guanjxi live a fascinating mix of peoples, an ethnic heritage left behind by history. In Guizhou alone, seven million minority peoples make up more than a quarter of the population, celebrating a hundred major festivities and thousands of minor ones each year, creating the impression of a populace almost continually in ceremonial mode [284]. Most of the festivals of this population, which consists of eighty different ethnic minorities, are held on auspicious lunar dates, such as the third day of the third lunar month or the sixth of the sixth. The magnificent special-purpose clothing worn by these groups is designed to ornament their celebrations, with each minority resplendent in its own distinctive, colorful tribal fashion [285].

283 In mountainous Guanjxi Province live China's largest minority race, the Zhuang, who are among the nation's most skilled farmers. This worker is clad in a comfortably loose top and trousers, as well as protective turban-like headgear—appropriate clothing for arduous tasks.

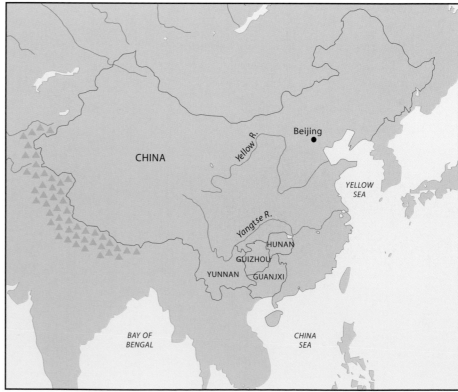

Map 16 Map of China, showing the southern provinces where many of the country's ethnic minorities live.

Of all the imaginative costumes worn in China's southwest, none are more memorable than those worn by the Miao of Guizhou Province. Their most famous garments are those made of "brown shiny cloth,"[19] known in the area since the 7th century [286]. The complete everyday costume consists of a jacket and knife-pleated skirt, with at least five hundred pleats. After the cloth has been finely woven, it is beaten with a large wooden mallet to force the fibers even closer together. The material is then dyed several times in an indigo bath until a deep, rich, brownish purple is obtained, only to be dyed yet again with a mixture of pig's blood and hide. When the cloth has dried, it is rubbed with egg white to give it the shiny appearance, and also to make it waterproof.

The most remarkable and impressive costumes feature metalwork, a craft specialization of one of the many clans of the Miao peoples. Not only do the women of the Metal Weaving Miao produce aprons encrusted with silver, they also fashion magnificent silver crowns, graduated silver torques, earrings and bracelets [287, 288]. Considering this emphasis on silver, it is interesting that no silver mines exist in Guizhou; the metal is obtained from neighboring Hunan Province or imported from other sources. In the absence of silver, the Miao have resorted to cleaning and polishing old metal toothpaste tubes and then cutting them into narrow strips to be inserted into their weavings to form traditional designs.

284 Miao girls of the Small Flower Clan play flutes at the Dancing Hillside Flower Festival in northwest Guizhou Province. From their bulbous, yarn-covered orange headdresses to their intricately appliquéd and cross-stitch embroidered collars, these young women make a distinctive ethnic statement.

285 A group of Miao from the Hundred Bird Clan who live in a high mountain village of Guizhou Province. Here the girls, dressed in their impressive woven and embroidered wool and feathered costumes, greet visitors.

286 A colorfully embroidered Miao jacket made of the famous "brown shiny" cloth, a tightly woven fabric that is first dyed in a series of indigo baths and then dyed again in a mixture of pig's blood and hide. After the cloth has dried, it is rubbed with egg white to create the requisite shine, and also to make the garment waterproof. Length 32⅞ in. (83.5 cm), width 45⅝ in. (116 cm).

The Miao and the other minority peoples are all Chinese citizens, and Beijing appears committed to preserving their special ethnic status. While minority children must regularly attend school and learn Mandarin, as do all Chinese, the minorities' ethnic languages and indigenous customs are nonetheless jealously guarded by the central government. In addition, the ethnic peoples are not held to the Han one-child policy, hence their populations can continue to grow.[20] As a result of these protective measures, China's gloriously arrayed minority groups appear destined to maintain their unique identity for generations to come [289].

287 (above left) Miao women of the Metal Weaving Clan wear aprons decorated with silver threads laboriously interwoven to form traditional embroidery patterns.

288 (above) Two Miao women of the Metal Weaving Clan dressed in their pleated, purpleish, "brown shiny" cloth skirts and blouses and wearing their festival jewelry—crown-type headgear, three graduated torques, multiple bracelets and long earrings. Such elaborate silver hairpieces and heavy jewelry often comprise the wealth of the Miao girls' villages.

289 A festively dressed young celebrant greets visitors with a cup of rice wine at Lange Village, Leishan County, Guizhou Province.

KOREA

290 In this 18th-century genre painting by Hye-won (aka Sin Yun-bok), three entertainers, or *gisaeng*, and their male companions enjoy *gayageum* music beside a lotus pond. Note the bare-headed man's long hair worn in a tied-up topknot. The wide-brimmed, black horsehair hats worn by the other men in the painting create a quintessential Korean scene.

Given the tumultuous nature of human history, it is most unusual for any of the world's remaining folk costumes to have evolved through a steady, unbroken process. Korea provides a dramatic case in point: the country's current "traditional" dress is the result of a conscious decision to reach back across decades of devastating turmoil to reconstruct the clothing of Korea's final royal dynasty, the Joseon (A.D. 1392–1910). Although the word Joseon[1] translates as "land of the morning calm," the country's history belies any claim to "calm." It could hardly have been otherwise, given Korea's vulnerable geographic position.

The 600-mile-long (965 km) Korean peninsula [Map 17] stretches south from the eastern end of the Asian landmass, facing China across the Yellow Sea, which the Koreans call the West Sea, and Japan to the east and south, across the Sea of Japan, the Koreans' East Sea. China and Russia share the northern border.

Given such powerful and aggressive neighbors, it is not surprising that Korea has had to wage repeated wars to repel invaders. Yet, ironically, the Koreans themselves are an ancient amalgam of groups that migrated down the peninsula from elsewhere.

Modern Korean origins probably lie in the assimilation of local aboriginal peoples—who had come from central and northern Asia, arriving ca. 30,000 B.C.—with newcomers of Central Asian origin, who immigrated into the peninsula between about 5000 and 1000 B.C. Korean creation myths reflect these diverse northern origins: life was brought forth by the creation and subsequent union of a heavenly king and a woman who started life as a bear but became human by living on twenty cloves of garlic in a cave for a hundred days. As Robert Storey and Eunkyong Park wryly note, "The Korean obsession with the pungent garlic clove apparently started early."[2] The bear element in this story is shared by Siberian myths, further supporting the hypothesis of central/northern Asian origins.

Korea's topography is uneven: mountains cover approximately 70% of the peninsula, although few are high. Only about 20% of the land is arable and even that is not usable all year round. Korea has four distinct seasons, including a winter that sweeps down out of Siberia. But whereas the land and climate are varied, the Koreans are not. Indeed, this population is remarkably homogenous; the country has almost no ethnic minorities.

Historically, the peninsula's political entities have been forged in response to outside incursions. During China's Han dynasty, ca. 200 B.C.–ca. A.D. 200, Chinese invaders established an outpost near present-day Pyongyang. The resulting wars brought about an early alliance between the besieged tribes of the northern part of the peninsula who, around the first century, formed the earliest Korean kingdom, Goguryeo. The tribes to the south, not subject to the same immediate pressures, were slower to coalesce. By the 3rd century A.D., however, two powerful southern kingdoms— Baekje and Silla—had emerged. The next four centuries, known as the Three Kingdoms period (57 B.C.–A.D. 668), witnessed a remarkable flowering of the arts, architecture, literature and statecraft. Probably the single most formative influence was Buddhism, introduced from China in the 4th century A.D., which in time became the state religion of all three Korean kingdoms.

The Three Kingdoms period was also the era in which cultural developments that first took place in Korea began to be exported to Japan. Korea has sometimes mistakenly been considered only a bridge for Chinese culture to cross and settle in Japan, but much of this cultural transmigration did not originate in China.[3] For example, architects and builders of the Baekje period were primarily responsible for the great burst of temple construction which occurred in Japan during the 6th century. Indeed, there were times in Japan's early history when there were more Koreans involved in influential secular and religious positions than there were Japanese.[4] Korea's influence on Japan

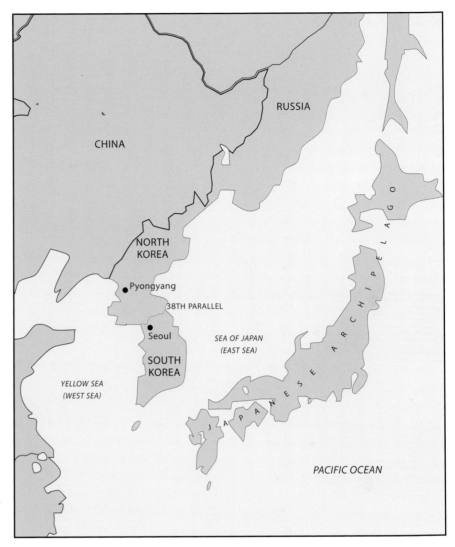

even extends into the sensitive realm of ancestral rulership: in the winter of 2002 the Emperor Akihito actually acknowledged the Japanese royal family's Korean roots.[5]

Depictions of clothing from the Three Kingdoms period provide the earliest clues to Korea's traditional costume, or *hanbok,* thanks to evidence found on tomb murals, clay figurines and illustrations of visiting Koreans found in early Chinese books from the Wei dynasty (A.D. 502–557). All of these garments were, of course, upper-class attire. In each of Korea's three kingdoms, political authority was centered around the king and aristocracy, all of whom wore similar clothing: jackets, pants, and/or skirts [291–293].[6] All of the detailing on these garments, as well as their accessories and hats, varied according to the wearer's social status.

Map 17 The Korean peninsula is located in a vulnerable geographic region, given that it is surrounded by particularly powerful neighbors.

In the subsequent Unified Silla Kingdom (A.D. 668–935), ever more status-based restrictions controlled further aspects of clothing, right down to who was allowed to wear which fabrics. It was during this period that traces of China's Tang dynasty appear in Korean clothing. We are aware of this influence because of the Chinese-style garments depicted on certain figurines excavated from 8th-century tomb sites. These clay figures [294] show women attired in Tang-influenced costumes whose skirts appear to tie up under their arms; 8th-century Korean skirts now began to be worn high at the chest [295]. This is the earliest evidence for the present-day Korean female silhouette which minimizes the upper body while emphasizing the curved line and exaggerated volume of the billowing skirt that conceals the lower torso.

During the Unified Silla period Korean Buddhism also began a glorious era. It is said that in the latter days of the Silla dynasty the capital, Gyeongju, was a city "where the roof lines of Buddhist temples looked like flying geese and pagodas were as thick as the stars."[7] Despite such prosperity, by the beginning of the 10th century the despotic Silla Kingdom had begun to crumble; the Goryeo dynasty (A.D. 918–1392) followed. Although the new government emphasized a Confucian examination system for state officials (see "China," p. 158), the Goryeo regime also lent royal patronage to Buddhism, which now reached the height of its Korean development thanks to considerable secular power obtained through the acquisition of land and money.

The final Korean dynasty, the Joseon, turned away from Buddhism to adopt neo-Confucianism as its official ideology, a system that stressed the hereditary nature of social position, hence the fixed status of each group and gender. As a result, clothing began to reflect a wearer's class even more than before, requiring different garments for different levels. For example, when aristocratic women went on outings they placed a concealing coat, the *jangob*, over their heads so as to shield their faces [296]; in similar circumstances, commoner women simply wore broad-brimmed hats

294 Clay female figurines excavated from an 8th-century tombsite wear Tang Chinese-influenced clothing that includes skirts which appear to tie up under the arms.

295 A reconstruction of a Unified Silla Period woman's outfit based on clay figurines excavated from a tombsite. This apparel reflects cultural interaction with China's 8th-century Tang dynasty.

(Opposite) Reconstructed examples of Three Kingdoms' 7th-century A.D. clothing.

291 Jacket and skirt, Goguryeo.

292 Jacket and pants, Baekje.

293 Jacket, skirt and pants, Silla.

296 The *jangob* coat, a garment with atavistic unused sleeves, was placed over the head of upper-class women when on outings so as to shield their faces from the stares of inferiors. The coat was held in place by grasping it from the inside.

as sunshades [297]. Joseon class distinctions, however, extended far beyond headcoverings, as is evident when considering those most intriguing of Korea's 18th-century women, the entertainers.

Traditionally, most Korean court dances were performed by men but when female dancers were involved [298] they were drawn from the ranks of the highly trained royal entertainers, the *gisaeng* [299]. These were beautiful and charming young women of ostensibly good moral character who were trained from an early age to sing, dance and play a musical instrument [see 290]. Because of the *gisaengs'* contact with scholars, artists and the nation's rulers, they became the most cultured and educated females in the country, playing an important role in the entertaining of distinguished men. Royal patronage of court entertainment, however, ended with Japan's annexation of Korea in 1910.[8]

Through the centuries, Korea had repeatedly experienced painful encounters with her acquisitive neighbors—in the 16th century Japan mounted an unsuccessful invasion, as did the Manchu of China's Qing dynasty in the early 17th century—as well as

tremendous pressure from 19th-century Japan and the Western maritime nations to open her ports to trade. The Japanese and Western powers succeeded in forcing Korea to establish modern relations with them. In response to this open-door policy, Korea faced a variety of problems, including feeling the need to modernize the appearance of Korean males. In 1895 the government ordered the men to cut their long hair—traditionally worn in a tied-up topknot [see 290]—and begin to wear Western-style clothing. As a result of this sweeping edict, the appearance of a great deal of the populus changed almost overnight.

Although these modernizing decisions were considered necessary by the government, they were not enthusiastically accepted by all. In the countryside, many farmers and laborers resisted the new trend, preferring the old ways [300]. Indeed, some Koreans were still wearing traditional *hanbok* in the cities during the 1940s, and some elderly Koreans still prefer *hanbok* today.

Despite repeated problems with aggressive neighbors, only once over the millennia did Korea ever completely lose her sovereignty and independence: the

297 An 18th-century travel scene depicting both upper-class women and commoners. Note that the latter wear simple sunshade hats, whereas the aristocrats use enveloping coats to shield their faces.

298 *Gisaeng* entertainers in graceful dress perform a sword dance before customers in this 18th-century genre painting by Hye-won (aka Sin Yun-bok).

299 Although the *gisaeng* entertainers were young ladies of reputedly good moral character, these attractive young women were not adverse to a secret tryst with an admirer. Note that the young women's dresses completely bypass the waist and instead emphasize and exaggerate the volume of their billowing skirts. Genre painting by Hye-won (aka Sin Yun-bok), 18th century.

300 Four bearers transporting two American ladies in chairs in Seoul, December, 1896. The bearers are all dressed in *hanbok*, traditional daily Korean clothing. The man standing nearest the building wears a mourning outfit—a wide-sleeved, full coat of rough, undyed hemp and an enveloping mourning hat.

period of Japanese annexation, 1910–1945. For Koreans, this 35-year occupation was truly a national trauma, one not yet forgotten or forgiven.

Following the Second World War and pressure from Western powers, the southern half of Korea formally became The Republic of Korea in 1948, setting the stage for the Korean War (1950–52).[9] Following those devastating years, the yearning to honor the country's original heritage began to express itself in efforts to reclaim the arts of the last wholly Korean government. This revival movement included reconstructing traditional Korean clothing based on garments worn during the later decades—i.e. A.D. 1800–1910—of the final royal dynasty, the Joseon.

This is not to say that the Koreans of the new Republic adopted Joseon-type garments for daily wear; by now Korea was firmly a part of the Western-dominated, mid-20th century. From the ashes of war,

South Korea had produced an economic miracle to become a 20th-century industrial superstar, complete with an upscale professional class eager to wear the latest Western fashions. However, on special occasions, *hanbok* was—and still is—worn, serving as an evocation of a rich past and a tangible connection with Korea's old values.

MEN AND WOMEN'S BASIC TRADITIONAL DRESS

The Korean approach to clothing construction differs significantly from that of the West, where a series of garment types are made in standard sizes for a variety of physical types, all of this apparel measured and cut and sewn to fit as closely to the body as possible. In contrast, Korean clothing can be wrapped around any sized body and then adjusted and secured in place with sashes. As a result, the female skirt has neither waist measurement nor specific length; all skirts come in

Components of a woman's *jeogori* (jacket):

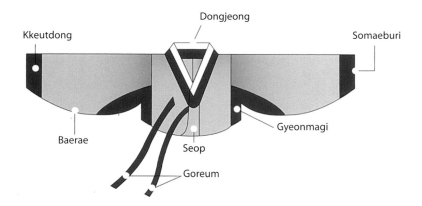

301 A chart illustrating the structure of the basic garments of *hanbok*, the traditional Korean folk costume.

Components of a woman's *chima* (skirt):

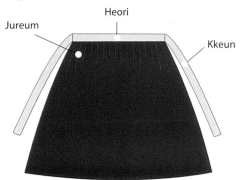

Components of a man's *jeogori* (jacket):   Components of a man's *baji* (pants):

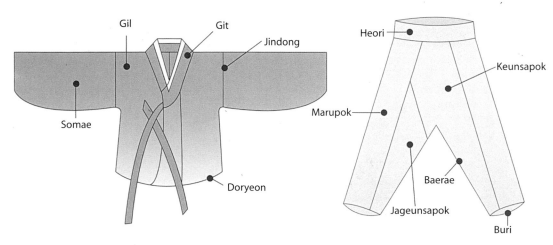

one size and can be adjusted simply by loosening or tightening the sash.

This same unstructured principle governs both men's and women's jackets, *jeogori*: each can be fitted to the body by simply adjusting the attached ribbons that close to form a half bow. The male jacket is worn over pants (*baji*) [301]. Close-fitting, inner pants were replaced by Western-style underwear in the 1920s, but the Korean outer pants are voluminous, which necessitates tying them securely around the ankles. These comfortable and roomy trousers are an ancient legacy from the horsemen of the Asian steppes.

302 (opposite, below) Full, bloomer-like female underwear, *sok-of*, was worn to make the women's traditional outer skirt, the *chima*, appear as voluminous as possible. Some of these inner garments were made of cotton or silk; in the summer, the underwear was often made of ramie or hemp, the fiber used to weave this example. Length 39 in. (99 cm), width 52³/₄ in. (134 cm).

303 (opposite) Korea's traditional female attire consists of:

(above) a short jacket, *jeogori*; note the auspicious designs stamped in gold on this silk garment's blue cuffs and red ties: length 14⁷/₈ in. (38 cm), width 54³/₄ in. (139 cm);

(center, left) the full, high-waisted, silk outer skirt, *chima*, made in a color contrasting to that of the jacket: length 44 in. (111.8 cm), width 77¹/₂ in. (196.8 cm);

(center, right) as many petticoats, *sok-chima*, as possible so as to create a voluminous look for the billowing outer skirt: length 47 in. (119.4 cm), width 38 in. (96.5 cm).

304 A man's summer outer coat, the *durumagi*, made of unlined ramie, a stiff lustrous bast fiber. The garment's subtly patterned white neck band is woven from silk. Length 50⁷/₈ in. (129.2 cm), width 57³/₈ in. (145.7 cm).

305 The white *dapo* coat, belted high across the chest with a tasseled black silk cord, was the streetwear for all classes of 19th-century Korean men. Here the *dapo* is worn with the traditional wide-brimmed *gaht* hat, beneath which appears a horsehair headband to secure the *gaht* in place.

The female jacket—which has become increasingly shorter over the centuries (the present-day garment barely covers the bosom)—is worn over a full skirt, the *chima*. This modest lower-body garment ties above the bust and is worn over many layers of underwear—traditionally a form of bloomers—as well as many petticoats, so as to give volume to the skirt. The resulting silhouette completely ignores the waist; the only break in the torso occurs at the armpits, above the breast. In Korea's Confucian-steeped traditional culture, a woman's modesty and dignity are paramount; the point of female attire is to hide the figure under yards of luxurious brocades, silks and satins [302, 303].

OUTERWEAR

Although men had a choice of outerwear—including the *durumagi* [304]—the coat that appears most frequently in the 18th-century genre paintings is the *dapo* [see 290, 299, 300], which served as streetwear for commoners, scholars, public officials and noblemen, worn either in white for ordinary use [305] or light blue on festive occasions. The *dapo*—with its wide sleeves, narrow cuffs, flared hem and open overflap—was tied at the chest with a long, braided silk cord. For winter the *dapo* was made of silk or cotton; for summer, of ramie or stiffened silk gauze.

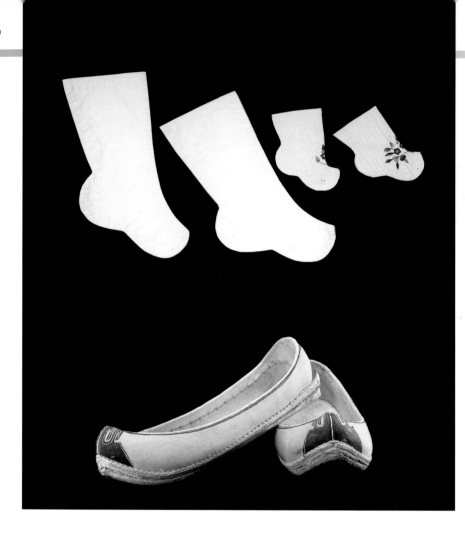

FOOTWEAR

With the *dapo*, as well as with all other attire, men wore a pair of leggings and white cotton socks (*buhsuhn*), unlined in summer, lined in spring and fall, and padded with thin layers of cotton batting in winter [306]. These socks were ubiquitous, used by males and females of all ages and classes.[10] Over the cotton socks were worn low-sided shoes made of straw, felt, leather or silk-covered leather, depending on one's status or gender. Contrasting-colored appliqués were often applied to the toe and heel of a shoe, producing a dapper effect [307; see also 290], but no matter how elegant the shoe, it was always removed when entering a dwelling.

HAIRSTYLES/HEADGEAR

Women entertainers and courtesans arranged their long hair into thick braids that were then secured in fanciful and appealing ways about their heads [308], whereas married women pulled their hair back into

306 (top) The *buhsuhn*, the typical Korean-style cotton socks of mid-calf length with turned-up pointed toes. Adult: length 16 in. (40.6 cm), width 10 in. (25.4 cm). Child: length 5 1/8 in. (13 cm), width 2 5/8 in. (6.7 cm).

307 (above) Outside the home, wide, low-sided shoes known as *woon-hye* were worn over the ubiquitous cotton socks. This pair of women's silk-covered leather shoes have appliqués applied to the heel and toe. Length 10 in. (25.6 cm), width 2 7/8 in. (7.3 cm).

308 In this genre painting by Shi San (aka Yoo Un-hong), 18th-century courtesans can be seen wearing their long, thick braids arranged on top of their heads.

309 The Korean *gaht* is an outdoor hat constructed of horsehair, bamboo and silk.

311 A one-year-old child's ceremonial outfit that displays the same striped sleeves recreated on the adult *o bang jang* coat.

310 The *o bang jang* ceremonial coat, worn only by a man whose parents are still living in order to honor them.

sleek chignons. When an upper-class woman ventured forth, her head was always discreetly covered.

Over the men's traditional topknot, the *santu*, they wore a small, rimless, black horsehair beanie with a bulge at the back that served to hold the topknot in place. This headgear was an inner hat, worn only within the home.

The quintessential Korean outdoor headgear was, and is, the traditional *gaht* [309]. When Confucianism began to dominate Korean society from the end of the 14th century, the *gaht* became an important item of male attire, woven in a loose and airy manner using the long hair from a horse's tail. Above the *gaht*'s wide, straight brim rises a cylindrical, box-like crown made of papier-mâché. To secure the *gaht* on the head, men wore a horsehair band around the forehead [see 290, 305]. For rainy weather, a man might place a rain-hat of pleated and waxed paper over the inner hat that secured his topknot.[11]

SPECIAL COSTUMES

One coat played a particularly special role in Korean culture, the *o bang jang* [310], a familial garment that could only be worn by the adult son of a family where both parents were still living. The purpose of this ceremonial costume was for a man to honor his parents by donning an adult version of the outfit he had worn as a one-year-old baby [311]. The multicolored, striped sleeves of the large and small garments are their connecting symbolism.

312 Present-day wedding attire is based on magnificent robes worn by Joseon Period royalty, with elaborate embroideries of auspicious symbols decorating the front and back.

as early as the 5th century B.C. Even older are carefully worked bone needles found among the personal possessions buried in ancient Chinese tombs dating back to 4000 B.C.[12]

It is believed that Korea's early embroidery skills came from China. By the 1st century, during the Three Kingdoms period, embroidery was well established in Korea, with both men and women practicing the art as an inherited profession. However, traditional embroidery was also carried out within the home, playing an extremely important role in women's lives. From the age of seven, girls were secluded in the female quarters of the house and taught to become seamstresses and embroiderers for the family's everyday wear, as well as for festive apparel. (Embroidery was not restricted to clothing; it also appeared on rank badges, pillow covers, cushions, bedding and even served to enhance folding screens.) Although all embroidery designs served a decorative purpose, some also conveyed traditional birthday wishes as well as featuring honored religious symbols and auspicious motifs such as the ten signs of longevity.[13]

Increasingly in Korean history the upper classes donned elegant attire richly embroidered with gold and silver thread. Although the government repeatedly decreed sumptuary laws prohibiting extravagant clothing, embroidery in varying degrees of opulence continued to prevail among all classes. Indeed, down to the present day the ability to create skillful embroidery continues to be regarded as an admired feminine accomplishment.

For Korean women, no garments were, or are, more important than the ones worn on the day of her marriage [312]. These luxurious and colorful robes are replicas of clothing used by royalty during the final Joseon dynasty: on her wedding day, every Korean bride is literally dressed as a princess.

GARMENT DECORATION

Embroidery has long played an important role in East Asia. In China, the original home of silk thread, embroidered items have been found in ancient burials

ACCESSORIES

Typically, royal Korean women of the Joseon dynasty wore seasonal jewelry: silver and gold in winter, jade in summer. Although the court disapproved of individuals indulging in costly personal adornments inappropriate to their station, luxurious ornaments that originally adorned only the queen and crown princesses—for example, long, dragon-headed crossbars in gold and silver worn in the hair—were often co-opted by wealthy commoners.[14]

TRANSITIONAL DRESS

Traditionally, the color of Korean dress followed a system of use by age: children and young people wore bright hues, culminating in the vivid reds, greens and yellows of the silk wedding robes. The groom donned a hat for the first time on his wedding day; thereafter the couple were dressed in white or other neutrals until they reached old age, the period of life for which white alone had always been the customary color. Indeed, Korea has been called "the land of white people" because of the prevalence of white clothing, a holdover from a former edict to wear white clothing for three years following the death of royalty, but white is also the color of mourning for members of one's own family [see 300].[15]

In addition to a sensitivity concerning age-appropriate color, Koreans still give close attention to the precise arranging of their clothing: the amount of cuff and color revealed, the precise folding of bows and sashes, the exact angle of a hat or hair comb. It is interesting that the colors and patterns now being chosen are in keeping with the older Korean aesthetic, a preference for white and other neutral colors, including subtle pastels, and the continued emphasis on the curved lines of traditional female attire that minimize the upper torso while exaggerating the lower body [313].

313 Korean girls wearing their traditional attire at a fashion show, November, 2003.

JAPAN

314 This two-panel folding screen of the Edo (Tokugawa) period shows "Selection of Silks," a scene from *The Tales of Genji*, a 10th-century novel relating the adventures of fictional Heian court figures. The noble ladies depicted wear the multi-layered silk garments of the period [see 315], as does Prince Genji, who is being shown magnificent silk textiles to be made up into robes.

At one point in their imperial past, the English liked to think of Japan as the Great Britain of the Pacific: both are island kingdoms whose peoples' fortunes have been shaped by the sea, both are located close to neighboring land masses whose influence has been profound, and both, given the size of their populations, have had a disproportionate impact on the world scene.[1] Abetted by Japan's long period of isolation, a complex mythology of uniqueness has grown up around the Japanese, leading them to view themselves as a people apart.

Although this ethnocentric society prefers to believe that it evolved from ancient Ice Age people who were the original occupants of their long string of islands—the Japanese archipelago stretches for nearly 1,500 miles (2,400 km) [Map 18]—modern research demonstrates a diverse heritage, including a major Korean immigration ca. 400 B.C.[2] Such scientific insight is not always welcome; it is difficult to discuss Japan's archaeological evidence dispassionately because Japanese interpretations of the past affect their present behavior. This is particularly true in regard to the Koreans, with whom the Japanese have long had a difficult relationship. Nonetheless, in the winter of 2002, Emperor Akihito publicly acknowledged that the Japanese royal family has Korean roots (see also "Korea," p. 181).[3]

While Japan was still living in the Stone Age, mainland China—her huge and powerful neighbor located some 480 sea miles to the east—had already developed an ancient, sophisticated culture (see "China," p. 155) that was to deeply influence the Japanese. Matters Chinese, be they iron technology, philosophy, religion or clothing styles, entered Japan in the 6th century A.D. through Korea, only 145 sea miles away.

Chinese influence is also reflected in Japan's early political life. Prior to the 7th century A.D., Japan was divided up among a number of clans, presided over by an ill-defined emperor. Then, in A.D. 645, the Fujiwara clan rose to power and proceeded to steer Japan along a new path, the first example of the Japanese ability to redirect their historical trajectory, a pattern that would repeat in subsequent centuries.

Guidance for the new direction was sought from what was then the world's highest example of civilization and power, imperial China. The Japanese result, however, was not a centralized monarchy, as in China, but rather what the English historian J. M. Roberts refers to as "centuries of feudal anarchy:"[4] for almost 900 years it is hard to find a continuous political thread in Japanese history. Japan's social cohesion and aesthetic development, however, are quite a different matter.[5]

The source of the continuity and strength of Japanese society lies in the combination of isolation, family and traditional religion. Just as each clan was an enlarged family, so too was the nation the extended family writ large. The focus of both family and clan was participation in the traditional rites of the only native religion, Shinto—the "way of the gods"[6]—whose essence was communal worship of certain local or personal spirit deities and of the ancestors. When Buddhism entered Japan it was joined to Shintoism.[7] Today most Japanese adhere to both faiths.

Turning to the development of Japanese aesthetics, by the 9th century the powerful chief of the Fujiwara clan had been made regent for the reigning emperor—who was already an adult—to preside over what is known as the Heian era (A.D. 794–1185); the name comes from what was then Japan's capital city, Heian-

Kyō, now known as Kyoto. The Heian period was the apogee of Japan's courtly elegance, when the aristocracy took great interest in their magnificent clothing. The ornate female attire evolved from a Chinese Tang-dynasty prototype—a narrow-sleeved tunic worn over a skirt—into the Japanese noblewoman's *junihitoe*, "12 unlined robes," a costume consisting of a dozen or so unlined garments of different colors—and shades of color—worn one atop the other in such a manner that a narrow band of each robe was visible at the neck, sleeves and hem [315].

The voluminous female costume included an undergarment of unadorned white silk with a small wrist opening, the *kosode* ("small sleeves"), forerunner of modern-day Japan's national costume, the kimono. The noblemen of the Heian court wore the enormous *ōsode* ("large sleeves") robe with its diagnostic wide sleeves with large wrist openings; this garment was worn with long, full trousers [316].

Heian court art can now be seen as the first great peak of Japanese culture. However, as most of Japan's population were peasants who wove and wore only bast fibers, the majority of the people never saw—much less ever touched—the fine silks worn by the lords and ladies of the great Fujiwara court.[8]

Map 18 The Japanese archipelago stretches for nearly 1,500 miles (2,400 km) and encompasses 20 degrees of latitude.

315 (opposite) Japanese noblewomen of the Heian period wore the magnificent multi-layered *junihitoe*, consisting of a series of garments of different colors worn one atop the other. The combination of seasons, specific formal occasions and a woman's sensibilities determined her robe's color scheme [see 314].

316 (above) In A.D. 1192 the powerful ruler Yorimoto, leader of the Minamoto clan, became the lifelong head of all armies, hence the absolute lord of Japan: the shogunate era had begun. Yorimoto wears a high, stiffened hat, the voluminous *ōsode* robe and long, full trousers—all garments that were the sole prerogative of noble rank.

317 A detail from a folding screen depicts samurai warriors—the powerful military retainers of the feudal lords—taking part in the 1615 siege of Osaka Castle. Their protective armor was worn over a simplified undergarment—the *kosode*—inherited from the Heian court.

By the 16th century, magnificently crafted Japanese artifacts began to appear in Western markets and European merchants became increasingly curious about the mysterious islands from whence such beautiful objects came. The Portuguese were the first European wave, arriving in 1543 and bringing new food crops from the Americas—sweet potatoes, maize, sugar cane—as well as muskets, which the Japanese soon learned to duplicate. These new weapons played an important role in bringing the baronial "feudal" wars to an end; a new power emerged, the Tokugawa shogunate (1615–1868), whose capital was moved to Edo, modern-day Tokyo.

During the two and a half centuries of Tokugawa rule, the emperors receded even further into the wings of Japanese politics, firmly kept there by a system that rested on military overlordship. The shoguns by now had become hereditary princes, heads of a stratified social system over which they exercised powers in the name of a series of enfeebled emperors. Below the shoguns, society was strictly and legally separated into hereditary classes: warriors, farmers, craftsmen, merchants.

The Japanese system shared one particular weakness with that of the Chinese: both assumed they were insulated from change, ignoring external stimuli. One obvious threat came from the Europeans, who had already brought imports that were having a profound effect: firearms and Christianity, a religion that preached universal equality in the eyes of God. In the 17th century, when the Japanese realized the subversive potential of the European religion, a savage persecution of Christians began and all Japanese were required to affiliate with a Buddhist temple. Then, in a further dramatic move, Japan withdrew from the outside world: European trade all but came to an end, the Japanese were not allowed to go abroad, and the building of large, sea-going ships was forbidden. The resulting isolation lasted for over two hundred years, a prosperous period but one with later repercussions. Although the "Great Peace" of the Tokugawa shogunate was economically productive, Japan's military skills had so atrophied that when the Westerners returned

During the Heian period, Japan's stratified social order evolved even further. Noblemen who were imperial court officials now began to receive tax-free estates as payment for carrying out their duties. These increasingly powerful clan leaders were feudal barons, *daimyo*, who were sought out by smaller land owners so as to be assured tenure in return for rent and an obligation to provide service.

As was inevitable, the culture of the elite, self-serving Heian court attracted criticism from less privileged provincial clan leaders, who saw in such a rarefied milieu an effete and corrupting influence, sapping both the independence of the court nobles and their loyalty to their own clans. With the fading of the Fujiwara, power passed to the heads of other powerful clans.

Early in this period (A.D. 1185–1333) there appeared the first of a series of military dictators who bore the title shogun [see 316]. Although they ruled in the hereditary emperor's name, they were in fact largely independent. The military retainers of these feudal lords were the samurai, a powerful class of warriors. Both shogun and samurai extolled the Zen Buddhist ideals of frugality and modest conduct: to dress simply became a virtue. As the refined Heian sedentary life gave way to military concerns, the volume of clothing was reduced layer by layer. The samurai class adopted the *kosode*, the simple undergarment of the Heian court, as their principal outer apparel. Their fighting armor, however, was not all that simple [317].⁹

with up-to-date weapons in the 19th century, Japan's military forces were technologically unable to withstand them [318].

The Europeans presented a double threat to the ancient, entrenched Asian civilizations: advanced technology and the pervasive power of European culture. This became clear in China where, for the first time in 2,000 years, Chinese society itself was going to be forced to change rather than the imported culture of the Western "barbarian" conquerors: the Chinese Revolution was approaching.[10]

By the 1840s Japan's rulers had become alarmed by what was happening in China vis-à-vis the Western powers, who were obviously determined to break into Asian trade, and clearly had the strength to do so. What was peculiar to Japan was the urgency that their observation of China's fate lent to their own program of radical change. At the beginning of the 19th century there was little to show a superficial observer that Japan had the ability to adapt more successfully to challenges from the West than did China. Actually, however, Japan was already on its way to modernism.

Despite the strictures of the Tokugawa era, its economic success had led to a diversified society with a money economy that undermined the old feudal system and produced a growing urban population. By the last years of the shogunate, the port of Osaka—the greatest of Japan's mercantile centers—had grown to 300,000–400,000 and Edo had expanded to a million people, a thriving metropolis which included the city's licensed recreational districts where a free-wheeling, creative atmosphere inspired some of Japan's most influential art [319; see also 325–327]. Osaka and Edo were great centers of consumption that "made a mockery of the old notion of the inferiority of the merchant class."[11] Social change was already stirring in Japan, leading to a philosophical change that made the nation more receptive to Western influence, which soon arrived.

Foreign ships increasingly began to challenge Japan's isolation. Finally, in 1853, the U.S. Naval Commander Matthew Perry forced open relations with the Japanese. Soon thereafter the Tokugawa shogunate

318 A samurai helmet with gilded horns, face mask and armor, late Edo period, 19th century: overall height 68 in. (173 cm). These protective warrior suits, characterized by lightness and flexibility, were composed of lacquered iron plates, connecting silk cords and armored sleeve, elbow, hand and shin guards. This type of armor was first developed in the 16th century and remained in use up to and during the Edo period.

came to an end, feudalism was abolished, and power was returned to the imperial court. The Meiji ("enlightened rule") Restoration (1868–1912) had begun under the talented young emperor, Mutsuhito. Four of Japan's greatest clans returned their lands to the emperor, "so that a uniform rule may prevail throughout the empire. Thus the country will be able to rank equally with other nations of the world."[12] This altruistic act was an expression of the patriotic ethic that was to inspire Japan's leaders for the next half-century, a view widely held in a small country with a high degree of literacy. Clearly, Japan aimed for parity with the West and, with typically disciplined determination, set about achieving it.

To attain equality, the new Japanese government soon realized it would have to meet the West on its own terms; under the slogan "rich country, strong military"[13] the economy underwent a crash course in Westernization and industrialization. In the first five years Japan put in place a prefectural system of administration, a postal system, a daily newspaper, a ministry of education, a railroad, religious toleration, the Gregorian calendar and military conscription. The now-outdated samurai warriors went into a modernized army, instructed by the Prussians, or into the navy, advised by the British; once again, the Japanese sought out proven excellence. Young men were also sent abroad to learn at first hand other secrets of the wonderful and threatening power of the West.

Early in the 20th century, the remarkable success of the Japanese in emulating the expansionist policies of their Western counterparts led them into an audacious war. At that time Russia was the leading European power in the Far East. In 1903 the Russians leased the naval base of Port Arthur from the enfeebled Chinese [see Map 18]. It was clear to the Japanese that the longed-for prize of Korea would elude them if they delayed stopping Russia's advance. In 1904 the Japanese struck, and after a year brought about a humiliating defeat of the Russians, an impressive accomplishment for a nation whose warriors, less than forty years before, had still been fighting in medieval armor.

For the first time since the Middle Ages, non-Europeans had defeated a European power in a major war. The reverberations and repercussions were colossal. It was also becoming clear to the Western powers that dealing with Japan was quite a different matter than bullying China. Japan increasingly was recognized as a "civilized" state, not to be treated like other non-European nations.[14] In the end a heavy cost was paid for such success. Japan's growing nationalism led to the last and most destructive wave of assertive imperialism, the desire to enforce rule over the whole of eastern Asia. This expansionist policy ultimately led to the Japanese downfall in World War II. Within four decades, however, the Japanese ability to refocus, retool and move forward lifted their defeated nation from total devastation into the top ranks of the world's economic powers: by the 1980s, Japan had once again established parity with the West.

319 Ando Hiroshige, *People Walking Under Cherry Trees at Night,* ca. 1834–35. Magnificently clad courtesans, who helped set the fashionable styles of the time, walk towards the gateway of the Yoshiwara, one of urban Edo's pleasure quarters.

MEN AND WOMEN'S TRADITIONAL DRESS

The Meiji Restoration resulted in both a political and sartorial revolution. Among the innovations adopted from the more mechanically oriented West was a new kind of clothing—tailor-made attire, worn almost entirely by men.[15] Western-style military uniforms now appeared, as did Western-style business suits. But such apparel was seen only in public; the clothing worn in private was quite a different matter.

Japan is a culture where many activities—sleeping, eating, entertaining—are performed on the floor. Traditional-style architectural buildings are carpeted with *tatami* mats upon which men sit cross-legged and women kneel [320], postures not comfortably sustained in constrictive, Western-style garments. At home the Japanese wore, and often still wear, a loosely sashed version of the modern-day kimono, the word that—in the late 1800s—replaced the centuries-old term *kosode*.

The geometrical, T-shaped *kosode* was composed of two rectangular fabric lengths draped over the shoulders and sewn together with straight seams at the center back and at the edges. An additional piece of fabric was added at each front edge to assure an adequate overlap; the collar and rectangular sleeves were then added. Unlike Western clothes, a *kosode* had to be fitted to the body each time it was put on; as a result, its look changed depending on the skill of the dresser and the current fashionable silhouette.[16]

A consideration of the greatest period of *kosode* elaboration returns us to the latter part of the Edo period, the high point of the Japanese textile arts, when designers and artisans focused on embellishing the monochrome silk *kosode* with intricate, colorful surface designs, thus overshadowing woven patterning. *Kosode* were brought to new heights of elegance and beauty, thanks to advances in such resist-dyeing techniques as *kasuri* (*ikat*), resist-dyeing yarns before weaving [321]; *shibori* (tie-dye), in which areas of cloth are tied off before dyeing [322]; *yūzen*, paste-resist dyed cloth patterned with freehand, brush-applied dyes [323]; and *shiro-age*, a type of *yūzen* dyeing in which the design is reserved entirely in white

by paste-resist dyeing; often embroidered enhancements were subsequently added [324].

EDO PERIOD DRESS

The *kosode* was the primary garment of both men and women in Japan's Edo period (also known as the Tokugawa period), 1615–1868 [325]. The sash that held the *kosode* in place was called an *obi*. Prior to the 1680s, this had been a narrow, flat tie or rope-like braid but in the first decades of the 19th century the woman's *obi* expanded to reach from under the bust to below the abdomen. This gradual widening of the *obi* during the Edo period broke the visual continuity of *kosode* design, resulting in the different patterning of the upper and lower halves of the robe.

Japanese women did not wear the same style *kosode* throughout their lives. Young, unmarried females wore colorful *furisode*, a version of the *kosode* with long, hanging sleeves, whereas for older women there were prescribed changes in sleeve length, patterning and coloration [326].

Kosode-clad women wore their hair in elaborately fashioned coiffures. Headgear was seldom worn so as

320 The *tatami*-mat floors of traditional-style Japanese architecture are the entertainment areas where hosts and guests sit cross-legged or kneel, postures not conducive to Western-style clothing.

321 The *kasuri* (*ikat*) pattern on this Meiji Period handwoven cotton *haori*—an outer coat of varying lengths worn over a *kosode*—was created when sections of unwoven warp thread were tied off and dyed prior to being stretched taut on a loom. Once in place, the fabric's predetermined pattern was visible. Some of the weft threads of this garment were also resist-dyed, resulting in an impressive double-*ikat* pattern. The front edges of *haoris* are tied together by a pair of braided silk cords. Length 33½ in. (85.1 cm), width 49 in. (124.5 cm).

322 This early Shōwa Period (1926–1989) silk *haori* is patterned in *shibori*-created diagonal stripes. Sections of woven cloth are tied off so as to resist color when submerged in a dye vat. A wide variety of *shibori* techniques exist—folding, stitching, binding—that can be used to achieve a variety of effects. The surface pattern on this *haori* coat is an example of a stitched-and-capped *shibori* resist. Length 39½ in. (100.3 cm), width 49 in. (124.5 cm).

323 This Meiji Period *uchikake*, or formal outer robe, has been treated with the *yūzen* technique, whereby brush-applied dyes are used freehand to decorate textiles with extremely fine lines and multiple colors.

Unlike paste-resist-dyed *tsutsugaki* textiles, which are dipped in a dye vat, *yūzen*-decorated textiles are not usually dyed by immersion. This robe has been given a filling of silk batting inside

the red band at the hemline, which serves to weigh the garment down and give it an elegant flow as the wearer moves. Length 61³⁄₈ in. (156 cm), width 50³⁄₄ in. (129 cm).

324 This late Edo Period summer *kosode*, or *katabira*, is made of ramie fiber enhanced with a technique called *shiro-age*, a type of *yūzen* paste-resist dyeing, whereby all the surface patterns are reserved in white. Once dyed, the garment's imaginary landscape design was further enhanced with the addition of colored embroidery and couched, gold-wrapped threads. This *kosode*'s black embroidery threads have disintegrated, exposing the designer's original sketch lines. Such costly robes were the exclusive prerogative of women from the highest levels of the samurai class, to be worn on important court occasions. Length 66⅞ in. (170 cm), width 46¼ in. (117.5 cm).

not to disturb these complex hair-dos. A geisha's hair was often adorned with a variety of pins and bar-shaped ornaments, *kogai*, as well as elaborate combs, *kushi*, made of ivory, tortoiseshell, wood, silver and lacquer. Except for such adornments, and *obi* fasteners, Japanese women wore no jewelry.

Beauty was associated with pale skin, hence women used rice powder to whiten their faces while still accentuating their eyes and mouth. On entering adulthood, a girl's eyebrows were sometimes shaved off and re-drawn higher on her head. Prior to the Meiji Restoration, it was also customary for men to paint their faces with a thick paste of white powder. In ancient times, men of rank had blackened their teeth as a sign of high birth; black, considered the only color that never changes, was regarded as a token of constancy and fidelity.[17]

Men and women wore the same type of footwear, which included white cotton socks, *tabi*, that had padded soles and a separate division for the big toe to hold in place the thongs attached to their hemp sandals or raised wooden shoes, the *geta*, footwear unique to Japan. Both these elevated clogs and the *zori*, the flat, straw-soled sandals worn by men with formal attire, were secured to the foot by thongs.

Turning to fashion as a means of conspicuous consumption, by the 1680s the urban classes were increasingly interested in the elaborate, surface-patterned *kosode*. This is evident in the popular literature of the time which is filled with the realities of everyday life of the *ukiyo-e*, "floating world," the licensed recreational districts with their hedonistic, momentary diversions. Our knowledge of these milieus comes from the paintings and woodblock prints of the pleasure quarters filled with merchants, artisans, military elite, courtesans and *kabuki* actors [327]. The latter often set the current fashion in *obi* and hairstyles, as well as in *kosode* colors and patterns.

Wealthy merchant-class women were relatively free to go out in public, attending a limited range of leisure activities including the lively *kabuki* theater, which incorporated spoken drama, music and dance. The *kabuki* costumes were one of the most striking aspects

325 (opposite) Kitagawa Utamaro, *A Scene on the Bridge and Below It*, late 18th century. Although the repetitious faces of these fashionable young women are interchangeable, the surface patterning on each of their carefully depicted *kosode* is intricately detailed, a reflection of the Japanese appreciation of the textile arts.

326 (below) Kitagawa Utamaro, *The Upper Class*, late 18th century. The standing young geisha in this scene wears an elaborated *kosode* whose long sleeves are in the *furisode* style, indicating she is unmarried. She also wears geisha-style pins and combs in her complex hairdo. The older woman—who is about to play the *koto*, the native stringed instrument—is appropriately clad in a far more muted *kosode* with shorter sleeves.

327 Utagawa Toyokuni, brocade triptych, 1800. The two males who are about to disembark at the house of the courtesans may be famous *kabuki* actors. Their hair is arranged in the samurai warrior style.

of the performances. At these theaters one could see and be seen; even the less affluent wore their best attire. The custom was for wealthier patrons—both male and female—to change clothing several times during the day-long performances. Teahouses adjacent to the theater accommodated this activity.[18] The women of

the aristocracy and upper echelons of the military also ventured forth on such seasonal excursions as the viewing of spring cherry blossoms [see 319] and autumn maple leaves, all opportunities for showing off the current *kosode* fashions, many designed specifically to create an exuberant, dramatic effect.

SPECIAL COSTUMES

A garment category exempt from the Edo period's ever-changing tastes was the Noh costume. Noh theater reflected the Buddhist view of the world and conveyed universal themes through the use of masks, mime, stylized dancing and chanting. Noh was associated with the shogun/samurai class who became patrons in the latter half of the 14th century. The special attributes of Noh performances led to the development of specific forms of stylized costume and ornament featuring classical motifs, often woven or embroidered [328, 329]. From the 17th through the 19th centuries, these costumes continued the theater's lavish tradition and, even as Edo society fell prey to the fashions of the time, Noh costumes continued to uphold the earlier standards.

328 (right) An 18th-century Edo Period *karaori* "Chinese weave" Noh robe. This stiff, brocade-decorated garment of silk twill weave with silk and gold-leaf paper supplementary-weft patterning has a repeating pattern of golden clouds and snow-covered camellias. It was made specifically for the Noh drama and reflects a style derived from the late 16th century when it was, and still is, worn by male performers when playing women's roles. Length 59 in. (150 cm), width 55¹⁄₈ in. (140 cm).

329 (below) In most Noh dramas there are just two main characters and a few minor ones—all very stylized in manner and dress—as well as a chanting chorus. Masks of women, men, spirits and demons are a main feature of Noh theater and are treated with awe and respect by the male actors who wear them.

330 (right) Elihu Vedder, *The Patrician*, 1872. In the 19th century, after Japanese woodblock prints and World Expositions had influenced many European artists, an era of "Japonisme" became fashionable in the upper-class Western world. Here a European woman poses in a kimono worn in quite a different manner to that of her Japanese counterpart: whereas in the West a display of décolletage was considered erotic, the equivalent zone in Japan was the nape of the neck.

331 (far right) An elaborately coiffed geisha wears a kimono that is draped to emphasize the nape of the neck, an area the Japanese consider particularly appealing.

KIMONOS

Liza Dalby, a scholar of the modern-day kimono, suggests that when Western clothing arrived at the turn of the 20th century, and Japanese men were transfigured in starched shirts and business suits, the shock of the contrast with traditional Japanese dress caused some to feel the need to rename the *kosode*, the ubiquitous, historic robe that never before had needed articulation.[19] The term kimono, "object of wear," was thus brought into service to describe an already existing garment with exactly the same characteristic elements: geometric construction, rectangular sleeves, lap-over collar and use of the *obi*.

In the 19th century the Japanese kimono also became fashionable among upper-class Western women [330]. Today it is only geisha who wear the kimono daily, perhaps in part because it is these beautiful silken robes that enable the professional entertainers to present themselves as works of art [331].[20]

TEXTILES UNIQUE TO JAPAN'S OUTER ISLANDS: OKINAWA AND HOKKAIDO

Although the surface patterning of Japanese kimonos was created through the use of a variety of natural dyes, such as indigo, madder and saffron, and woven from a variety of fibers such as cotton, ramie and silk, distinct dyeing techniques and fiber examples were developed on Japan's outermost islands.

Okinawa—the largest island in the Ryūkyū chain—is located to the south of the Japanese archipelago [see Map 18] but is bound to Japan proper by both ancient and modern cultural traits. However, the Okinawan landscape's blazing sunlight and clear colors differ from Japan's diffused light and often subtle palettes in such a way as to create a particularly Okinawan color sensibility that is reflected in Ryūkyūan stencil-dyed cloths. *Bingata* ("scarlet patterns") textiles are the multicolored fabrics formerly associated with the Ryūkyūan court [332]. The *bingata* dyeing technique is a labor-intensive activity involving many stencils, many dyes and many alternate applications of pigments and resists.

Amanda Mayer Stinchecum, an expert on Okinawan textiles, explains that the mineral pigments that gave *bingata* its special palette included vermillion (cinnabar, *shu*), red lead (*tan*), shell white (*gofun*), pigmentized indigo (*airō*) and Chinese ink (*sumi*).[21] One of the most prominent elements of the *bingata* palette was lac (*enji*), a dye derived from an insect, *Coccus lacca*, imported into Ryūkyū through China and used in pigmented form. The warm pink background seen in many examples of old *bingata* may have been obtained from either lac or madder.

A unique textile fiber was also developed on Okinawa, one obtained from the inner portion of the stalk of the banana-fiber tree, which is closely related to the familiar fruit-bearing variety but does not produce edible fruit. The woven banana-fiber cloth is called *bashō-fu* [333] and was worn year-round by the island's commoners [334].[22]

Hokkaido, the Japanese archipelago's northernmost island [see Map 18], is the present home of the Ainu, the aboriginal people who prior to ca. A.D. 600 inhabited the entire island chain but were subsequently

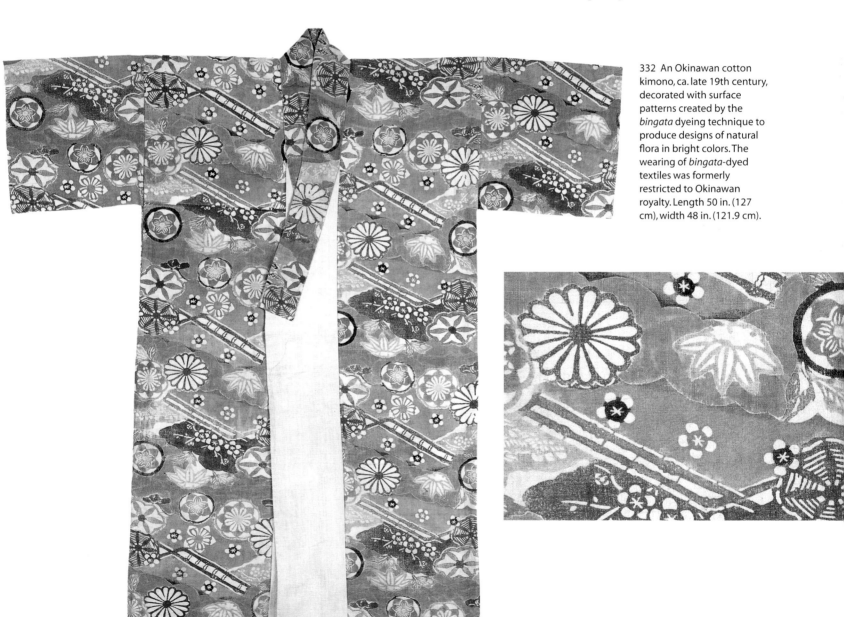

332 An Okinawan cotton kimono, ca. late 19th century, decorated with surface patterns created by the *bingata* dyeing technique to produce designs of natural flora in bright colors. The wearing of *bingata*-dyed textiles was formerly restricted to Okinawan royalty. Length 50 in. (127 cm), width 48 in. (121.9 cm).

pushed north, victims of Japanese expansion. Ainu men—unlike the Japanese—have an unusual profusion of body and facial hair and they often wore long, luxuriant beards which led to their earlier sobriquet, "The Hairy Ainu." Decades ago these people were classified as Caucasoids but recent research suggests that—like their fellow countrymen—the Ainu had ancient Central Asian origins.[23]

Both Ainu men and women wore a unique robe, the *attusi*. The most distinctive form of this garment was woven with a thread called *atsushi*—obtained from the elm tree's inner bark fibers—and then decorated with geometrically shaped surface patterns made from cotton dyed in contrasting colors, usually indigo [335]. The Ainu symmetrical motifs are reminiscent of the geometric designs symmetrically arranged on the

333 A late Edo/Early Meiji Period garment made from hand-loomed *bashō-fu* cloth, a fabric unique to Okinawa. The threads are derived from the inner stalk of the banana-fiber tree. This garment's lighter stripe is the color of the undyed banana fiber; the brown stripe was colored with an indigenous Okinawan dye. The highly labor-intensive processing of banana-fiber thread continued from the 16th to the 19th centuries. Length 46 in. (116.8 cm), width 42 in. (106.7 cm).

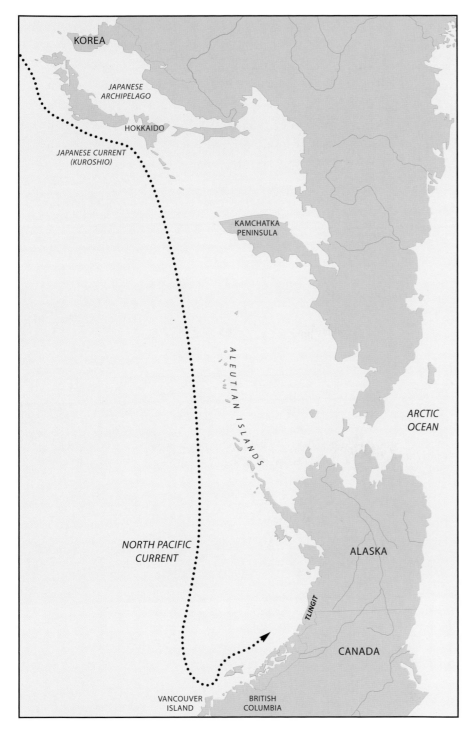

Map 19 The Japanese and Pacific currents flow east past both Hokkaido Island and the Tlingit homeland, located on the northwest coast of North America.

334 (above) Okinawan women, wearing banana-fiber (*bashō-fu*) garments, sun-bleach their ramie-fiber cloths by submerging them in the island's clear coastal waters.

335 (below) On Hokkaido Island Ainu men and women wore garments called *attusi*, woven from thread that was processed from the inner bark of the elm tree. Traditional symmetrical motifs were appliquéd to these robes and then further enhanced with white cotton embroidery thread.

Tlingit Indians' Chilkat blankets from the American Northwest Coast (see pp. 352, 359). There, too, a yarn derived from the inner bark fibers of a tree—the cedar—was used to create clothing (see pp. 347–348). These similarities are particularly interesting in view of the strong Japanese and North Pacific currents that flow east past the island of Hokkaido and then on to skirt the Tlingit homeland located along the coast of British Columbia [Map 19].[24]

5

SOUTH ASIA

SOUTH ASIA is an area of impressive extremes, including the dramatic 5-mile (8 km) contrast in altitude between India's tropical coastal lowlands and the towering, snowy peaks of the Himalayas. This mighty mountain system poses a formidable barrier between the Tibetan plateau to the north and India's alluvial plains to the south, and also acts as a great climatic divide that obstructs the passage of continental winter air into India while forcing the southwest rain-bearing winds, the annual monsoons, to drop their moisture before crossing the mountains. The result is heavy rain and snow on the Indian side of the Himalayas but arid conditions in lofty, cold Tibet. The date of the arrival into South Asia of *Homo erectus*—the ancient hominids who migrated out of Africa—is a matter of debate but it probably occurred some 1,000,000 years ago. Subsequent migrations of anatomically modern *Homo sapiens* brought the ancestors of the area's earliest civilizations. Subsequently, South Asia's ancient cultures were repeatedly influenced by invaders, conquerors, adventurers and traders. The subcontinent is particularly notable for having been the birthplace of several major religions—Hinduism, Jainism, Sikhism and Buddhism, which was eclipsed in the land of its birth by the 7th century A.D. Undaunted elsewhere, Buddhism steadily grew to become the predominant faith throughout Asia, including in a series of small Himalayan kingdoms where archaic Tantric Buddhism has been practiced since the 8th century A.D.[1]

INDIA

336 A group of Hindu worshipers ascend one of the magnificent temples at central India's Kajuraho, a large religious complex built between the 8th and 9th centuries A.D. New attire and ritual ablutions are customary for worship at important sacred celebrations. On such occasions, only the ancient-style, draped garments are appropriate. Note the profusion of the women's festive, brightly colored, wrapped saris and the men's freshly washed hair and bare upper torsos; the traditional *dhoti* is worn around the lower body.

During the past century non-Western peoples around the globe have increasingly exchanged their traditional clothing for Western garb. One striking exception to this worldwide trend is in India where many continue to wear non-stitched, draped garments as they have from the time of India's earliest civilization in the valley of the Indus River some 5,000 years ago.

It is increasingly held that the early population of the Indus Valley included Dravidian peoples, a dark-skinned race usually associated with southern India. The evidence for a Dravidian presence is both archaeological and linguistic (see below) and suggests that the ancient civilization existing in the valley was actually indigenous to the entire subcontinent. Further, a Dravidian linguistic pocket still survives in the mountains north of the Indus Valley, a long way from south India, indicating a far more northerly distribution of Dravidian speakers in early times than was formerly believed.[1]

The 3rd millennium B.C. is known for the rise of the complex cultures that produced the pyramids of Egypt, the ziggurats of Mesopotamia and the large, sophisticated cities located in the Indus Valley of present-day Pakistan: Mohenjodaro to the south, where a sculptural fragment depicts an important male wearing a draped shawl [337], and Harappa in the north, where a figurine was found of a slender young woman clad only in a necklace and numerous bracelets.[2]

Although early India did not create lasting great art or huge monuments on the scale of Egypt or Mesopotamia,[3] her more enduring contributions in the realm of religion and social organization have outlasted the Ancient Near Eastern achievements. These Indian philosophical and social concepts, which differ dramatically from those in the Middle East, were in place a thousand years before the birth of Christ and have continued to the present day.

By 1750 B.C. the Harappan civilization of the Indus Valley was coming to an end, probably devastated both by over-exploitation of the ecosystem and by natural disasters. The winding down of this ancient culture coincided with the arrival into India of the first of several of the subcontinent's outside creative forces, the Aryans. These nomadic Indo-European warriors came out of Central Asia to enter India from the north-west, over the Himalayas. The trouser-clad horsemen from the harsh northern steppes brought a new concept of clothing construction with them: sturdy, tailored garments that follow the lines of the body, a mounted rider's protection against chafing and exposure to the elements (see "Mongolia," p. 130).

The culture that the conquering Aryans initially introduced into India was not nearly so advanced as that of the Harappans.[4] However, as the Aryans slowly evolved from their pastoral ways into agricultural life, influenced by the indigenous Dravidian peoples with whom they interacted during their centuries-long migration south into the subcontinent,[5] they made two fundamental cultural contributions that are still central to Indian life.

The class structure that today is known as the caste system apparently evolved out of the Aryans' post-pastoral social organization. The divisions that earlier had been based on occupation, however, slowly became rigidly hereditary. At the apex of this system were

337 Unstitched, draped garments were worn in the sophisticated urban cities of the Indus Valley some 5,000 years ago, and have remained a preferred form of dress throughout India's history. Our knowledge of the clothing of India's earliest civilization is based on the study of engraved seals and sculpted figures. This small, limestone bust of a male displays a draped shawl with a floral motif that probably represents either block printing or embroidery. Mohenjodaro, Indus Valley, ca. 2500 B.C.

the priestly Brahmins, followed by the land-owning, warrior aristocracy; below were farmers and traders, followed by servants and laborers. To these occupational classifications was soon added a fifth category for non-Aryans, possibly designed to preserve racial integrity—the "untouchables," so-called because contact with them was believed to be defiling.[6]

It was also the Aryans who laid the religious foundation that has ever since been at the heart of Indian civilization. Basic to Aryan religion—which may have been associated with ancient fire worship in Central Asia[7]—was the concept of offerings of simple food stuffs to a sacred fire. It was believed that worshipers could reach their deities through sacrificial gifts such as cereal grains and clarified butter.[8] The Brahmin priests who presided over such ceremonies were given great importance.

Much of our knowledge of both Aryan society and religion comes from an oral Sanskrit text of more than 1,000 accumulated hymns, the Rig-Veda, first written down around 1000 B.C. Three later Vedas written between 1000 and 600 B.C. record the extension of

338 A battle scene from the *Mahabharata* epic, originally compiled ca. A.D. 400 but relating events that took place in India ca. 1400–1000 B.C. This scene was probably drawn in northern India. Note that the clothing depicted is constructed in the tailored, Central Asian manner.

Map 20 Map of India, showing several of the main urban centers.

Hinduism has a philosophical strain of abstruse inquiry and metaphysical quest, hence India's reputation as a "spiritual" land. For most Indians, however, religion is more a matter of the rituals and ceremonies that mark each day, each season and each life passage. But even in India—one of the most conservatively religious of lands—new cross-cultural social currents resulted in new world views.

By the 6th century B.C. several urban centers had arisen in the north [Map 20]. This urbanization, accompanied by widespread trade, led to changes in social stratification that eventually resulted in the emergence of two new religions, Jainism and Buddhism. Jainism, which was founded by Vardhamana Mahavita (540–467 B.C.), stresses respect for all animal life to the point that makes large-scale agriculture or animal husbandry impossible. As a result, many adherents became merchants, and modern Jain communities are among the wealthiest in India.[9]

Buddhism was a particularly heretical faith because it challenged not only Hinduism and its Brahmin dominance but also the caste system. The new belief was based on the teaching of the Buddha, "the

Aryan settlements across the fertile Ganges River Valley. It was in this era that the lengthy *Mahabharata* epic originated, a saga that describes a great war between two powerful clans [338], as well as a remarkable set of Sanskrit writings, the *Upanishads*, which deal with broad philosophical problems and advocate a quest for truth through inquiry.

Religion and ritual have pervaded almost every aspect of Indian life. By the 1st millennium B.C., classical Hinduism had crystallized, a religion that has neither a single Book, God, nor prophet; every community has its own favorite deity, chosen from an ever-expanding pantheon of gods. At one level

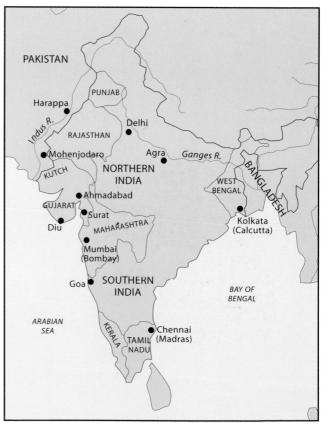

enlightened one," who was born Siddhartha Gautama (566–486 B.C.), a warrior-class prince who found his early life of comfort and affluence unfulfilling. As a result, he left his home and set forth to preach and teach "an austere and ethical doctrine whose aim was liberation from suffering by achieving higher states of consciousness."[10] Buddhism, as the most widespread religion in Asia, has had a particularly far-reaching effect, including establishing a unique style of priestly attire [339]. As India's greatest export, Buddhism has played a potent historical role. Nonetheless, after drastic reforms were made in Hinduism in the 8th and 9th centuries A.D., both Buddhism and most of Jainism were eclipsed on the subcontinent. Although Buddhism was virtually forgotten in India,[11] it moved on into China, Japan and, later, into Tibet, where Vajrayana/Tantric Buddhism particularly thrived (see "The Himalayan Kingdoms," pp. 248–251).

Centuries earlier, India's first empire had been created in 321 B.C. by Chandragupta Maurya, who usurped the throne of a reigning dynasty in central India. On the ruins of that kingdom, the new ruler built an empire that was further extended by his grandson, Asoka (269–232 B.C.), one of India's greatest and most admired rulers.

It was under Asoka that the subcontinent achieved a measure of political unity that would not be matched again for over 2,000 years, when it came under the rule of the British Raj.[12] It is also during this Mauryan period (321–232 B.C.) that the earliest visual evidence is found—aside from that of the ancient Indus sites—for what, to Western eyes, appears to be the sensuous nature of pre-Islamic Indian dress.[13] This scanty attire appears on stone sculptures of folk deities, the male *yaksha* and female *yakshi* [340]. The female is of particular note because she represents the first extant example in a long tradition of sculptures representing the fundamental Indian concept of fertile female beauty: rounded breasts, small waist, broad hips.[14]

After the death of Asoka, the Mauryan Empire rapidly declined and for the next 500 years India returned to a state of political disunity. However, despite the Mauryans' waning power, international trade continued apace throughout India. In the 2nd and 3rd centuries A.D., the strong navies of the competing kingdoms in the far south—Pandyas, Cheras and Chola—played a central role in the commercial transactions that connected India to Rome, Arabia, Southeast Asia and China.[15]

Across the north, local kingdoms rose as a series of mounted warriors—all clad in Central Asian tailored clothing—repeatedly invaded India via the northwest Himalayan routes to establish successive dynasties: Bactrian Indo-Greeks (200–80 B.C.); Indo-Scythian Sakas (80 B.C.); Parthians (1st century A.D.); Kushans (A.D. 50–300). This half-millennium ebb and flow of ruling powers illustrates two great constants in Indian history: the importance of the northwestern frontier as a cultural conduit and the assimilative power of Hindu civilization. Soon the new conquerors were ruling Hindu kingdoms and adopting Indian ways, including wearing certain indigenous, draped garments in response to India's hot and humid climes.

As Kushan rule declined, a new Ganges Valley power—the Gupta dynasty—emerged in north India, and once again a uniting empire came into

339 A Gupta Period (4th century A.D.) red sandstone sculpture of Buddha from northern India. The garment worn by the Buddha gives the impression of a fine, "pleated" fabric, lines that probably indicate the cloth's wrinkling from wear. This style of draped robe is also seen on Chinese and Japanese Buddhist sculptures of the same period. In modern-day India, the garments worn by holy men and monks are still draped in this manner.

340 Mauryan Period (2nd century B.C.) stone sculptures of a pair of folk deities connected with nature and fertility. The *yaksha* (left) wears a loincloth—the decorated ends hang down in front—secured about the waist with a girdle. The upper torsos of such male figures are either bare or draped; their heads are invariably turbaned. The *yakshi* (right) wears a profusion of jewelry, but otherwise only a long, draped loincloth with a bejeweled girdle and waistband.

341 A 12th-century A.D. bronze statue representing the Hindu mother goddess Devi, portrayed with four arms to indicate her multiple and supernatural powers. Note that this deity—like so many Indian goddesses—is clad mainly in her jewelry.

the stage for the flourishing of Dravidian culture and art in the south. Although northern and southern cultural ideals developed together through the intermediary of the Hindu Vedic religion, these concepts did differ in regional ways. For example, the ideal appearance of a southern woman, as described in Dravidian classical poetry, includes a complexion dark as the reddish-brown new leaf of a mango tree; in contrast, a preference for lighter skin was, and is, paramount in the north.[17]

During the cultural climax of Hindu civilization, between Gupta times and the coming of Islam, there appeared an important new religious focus on a mother-goddess, Devi [341], whose worship quickly took hold.[18] Some scholars view Devi as an expression of a new sexual emphasis that characterized not only Hinduism but Buddhism as well. Many of the great works of art that were created between the Mauryan and Gupta periods were inspired by Buddhism, still a major religious presence in India at that time, which now also came to reflect an increasing voluptuousness.

Buddhist stupas were erected all over India, monumental shrine-mounds that were austere and unadorned except for their surrounding gateways and railings. These decorative elements were ornately carved with various figurative sculptures: *yakshas* and *yakshis* [342], as well as a mixture of Hindu Vedic gods, kings, queens, warriors, attendants and events in Buddha's life. These various carved figures are dressed in a variety of stitched and unstitched garments, which suggests that there was a parallel evolution of draped and fitted clothing, the former indigenous to the Indian subcontinent, the latter introduced by the conquering Central Asians.

Like the stupa's fertility deities, the Vedic gods and rulers are all briefly clad in draped garments appropriate to a warm climate. However, the purpose of this sketchy clothing apparently was neither to dress nor hide the body but rather to adorn it, like jewelry, and in so doing accentuate its voluptuous qualities while also communicating the figures' social status. In stark contrast, the attendant servants, soldiers and other menials are invariably dressed in tailored clothing:

being (A.D. 320–500). It was during this Gupta age that a consolidation of India's artistic heritage occurred, resulting in an impressive cultural flowering. Indian civilization now came into its mature, classical stage and—among other outstanding achievements—a great number of impressive stone temples were built, places of worship distinct from the earlier Buddhist cave shrines. These later, magnificently carved Buddhist edifices are among the glories of both Indian art and architecture prior to the Muslim era. Jains, too, built shrines all over India, though their most magnificent temples were constructed later.[16]

In the south, at the end of the 3rd century A.D., the Pallavas—who controlled an area that includes modern-day Chennai [see Map 20]—achieved independence from their Deccan overlords, the Satavahanas, and proceeded to rule triumphant in the south for the next 600 years. Their rise to power set

tunics, coats, trousers and waistbands of varying styles and combinations.[19]

By the Gupta period a matured Hinduism, Buddhism and Jainism had established a philosophical outlook that has marked India ever since—a vision of endless cycles of creation and reabsorption into the divine, a picture of the cosmos that reveals a cyclical rather than a lineal history, as well as a recurring focus on non-violence. Out of this world view have grown social institutions marked by an over-riding concern for the welfare of the group above that of the individual.

Increasing numbers of *bhakti* (devotion) cults across India challenged the Vedic religion—based on orthodox Hindu philosophy—and the upper classes whose authority it legitimated. In response, a south Indian Brahmin, Ramanuja, founded the Shri Vaishnava movement, circa 12th century A.D., by identifying a devotional strain within the Vedic tradition as a result of critical readings of Sanskrit texts, a traditional Brahmanic technique for attaining greater understanding. Thus, in the south, devotional practice was joined to traditional Vedic religion.[20]

Islam first touched India via Arab traders operating along the western coasts; subsequent Central Asian Muslim groups came as conquerors to a land where a constant state of internal warfare rendered it vulnerable to outside attack. These repeated invasions brought new approaches to warfare, clothing, art and architecture, as well as to religion. In the turmoil of political and philosophical conflict with the invaders, the religion of the Sikha was born, founded by Guru Nanak in the 15th century A.D. Sikhism rejects caste hierarchy, preaches the existence of one formless God, and encourages its adherents to remain ready to defend the faith from both Hinduism and Islam. Sikh men are often identifiable by their characteristic turbans [see 348] and uncut beards, the latter sometimes contained within an inconspicuous hairnet attached to each ear.

With Islam came the stricture that Muslim women had to be completely shrouded when in public, with particular emphasis on covering their heads and breasts, in addition to the other areas of the body that all Indian women are accustomed to covering. In the south, however, women continued to keep their heads uncovered and, in some regions, their upper torsos as well. The Islamic conquerors also further reinforced the wearing of male tailored clothing: pants, jackets, shirts, coats, and so on. Although such Central Asian garments were adopted in many parts of the subcontinent by upper-class Hindu men, Indian women continued to wear their traditional draped garment, the sari, discussed below.

The greatest of the Islamic invaders that followed were those who eventually founded the 16th-century Mughul empire ("Mughul" is the Persian word for Mongol). The Mughuls ruled India for over 300 years, although that rule was much more tenuous and intermittent in the southern regions. Under Mughul patronage literature, architecture, and the arts and crafts reached new heights. In addition, the Mughul emperors managed to establish a rich pluralistic culture, blending the best of Islamic and Hindu traditions, which included the continuity of each group's clothing tradition, both the stitched and the draped [343].

342 A *yakshi* fertility figure carved as a bracket element supporting the east gate of a Buddhist shrine, the Great Stupa at Sanchi, located in central India. The seductive fertility goddess presses the base of the tree with her left heel, illustrating the Indian belief that the touch of a beautiful woman's foot will bring a tree into flower. This curvaceous creature is clad in a wrapped, transparent, lower-body garment that reveals her ornate girdle and multiple jewels, adornments that accentuate her sensuous attributes.

343 *The Kiss*, an early 17th-century painting of the Deccani school, depicts a Muslim prince clad in a sleeved and skirted garment of transparent cloth worn over drawstring trousers. Perhaps these trousers are made of gossamer-sheer muslin. The prince is kissing a Hindu woman who wears a traditional Deccani draped sari; her short, fitted blouse, the *choli*, is cut in the Hindu fashion, which reveals a wide expanse of midriff.

Portuguese holdings.[21] These European contacts heralded momentous future events. Yet it was not the coming of the Western traders that ended the great Mughul period. No Indian empire had ever been able to maintain itself for long; the subcontinent was too diverse and each ruling elite too exploitive. By the end of the 17th century, India was once again ripe for yet another set of conquerors.

Initially, European traders were drawn to the subcontinent because the West craved certain exotic spices as well as a type of textile that only India could supply: whereas silk had already been accessed from China, Indian cotton was new to the West. The reputation of India's fine weavers had early spread to the Mediterranean—via overland trade—where the gossamer-fine cotton muslins of Bengal, the *mulmul*, were given such evocative names as "winds," "mist," "woven air" and "night dew."[22] East–West textile trade was also conducted in printed, painted and tie-dyed cotton cloth, as well as *ikats* and other special weaves. The processes of mordanting, dyeing and printing had long been mastered in India and an impressive array of fast vegetable colors were in use. Indigo blue—the dye-stuff whose name identifies its geographic origin—and madder red were particularly popular, not only widespread on the domestic market but also exported abroad.

The Western merchants, in order to set up trading factories in areas where their agents had already settled, began to acquire land, a move that resulted in numerous wars, both against each other and against India's profusion of indigenous princely rulers. The European trading groups—Portuguese, Dutch, French, English—were all organized into companies; by the late 18th century the British had outmaneuvered the others to emerge as the victors [344].[23]

Gaining ascendancy in India was one of the most momentous events in all of British history. By 1857 the British East India Company's control—directly, or by treaty—extended over much of the subcontinent, resulting in vast profits. After the Industrial Revolution, Indian raw materials were sent to mechanized factories in Britain and machine-made goods, particularly

It was during the Mughul period that India's first direct relations with Atlantic Europe began, with the late 15th-century establishment of Portuguese colonies in Goa and Diu on the west coast as well as additional Portuguese settlements up and down both coasts during the 16th century. A hundred years later, the British and Dutch established their first footholds in the Surat-Ahmadabad area, on the west coast, and also on the east coast at Masulipatam. During the 17th century, Danes, Austrians and French added their settlements to India's coasts, while the British and Dutch powers expanded their ports, or took over

British cotton textiles known as "Manchester cloth," were then returned to flood the country. As a result, Indian artisans were impoverished and craft towns and cities declined. Discontent with the alien rulers was growing. Also, unlike all of India's earlier conquerors, the British increasingly maintained a strict social separateness and, from the start, had always retained their own base in their own land. In 1857, a combination of factors led to a major revolution that began as a soldiers' mutiny but soon had gained widespread civilian support.

The foundations of the British Raj were laid after the quelling of the Indian Mutiny of 1857. The East India Company's control ended and its Indian territories became part of the British Empire, to be ruled through a viceroy. During the Raj, the British concern for learning about the communities they ruled and their efforts to uplift groups at the bottom of the social scale were put into practice. Caste-specific styles of draping saris became more numerous as caste groups jockeyed for more favorable positions within the hierarchical British colonial system. Also, Indian women began to adopt full-length slips under their saris and women of the upper-class began to wear Victorian-style British blouses. It was during this period that Indian men began wearing European clothing.

By the end of the Raj in 1947, the abiding legacy of the British was the political unification of the subcontinent achieved through mass Western education, a network of railroads and a centralized administrative system. Paradoxically, these gains contributed to a growing indigenous vision of an independent Indian nation.

344 Francesco Renaldi, *The Palmer Family*, 1786: General William Palmer and his Muslim companion Fyze, their children, a servant and three of Fyze's sisters. Fyze wears a luxurious yet modest Muslim court costume—a long, saffron-colored, gold-trimmed garment and veil over a short bodice, together with diamond earrings, several pearl necklaces and silver anklets. Such Indian companions of British men, known as *bibi*—the Hindi and Urdu word for "wife"—were more acceptable to English society during the period of the East Indian Company than under the subsequent, less tolerant Raj. Discrimination was also increasingly the plight of the mixed-race children of these unions.

345 Mahatma Gandhi, ca. 1930, wearing India's basic loincloth, the draped *dhoti*. He is seen here spinning raw cotton on an Indian spinning wheel, the *charkha*, which became a symbol for India's fight for independence.

appeal and identification with India's poor, the freedom struggle became a mass movement. Gandhi launched a moral crusade of non-violent resistance to British laws and institutions, as well as a heightened concern for the plight of the villages, which manifested itself in his symbolic wearing of the clothing of poor Indian peasants—the plain white, draped garments of Indian tradition—and the spinning and weaving of *khadi* "homespun" cloth [345].

Also working toward the goal of independence were other outstanding Indians, including Pandit Jawaharlal Nehru and Mohammed Ali Jinnah, head of the Muslim League, who was pressing for an independent Muslim state in Pakistan. Finally, at midnight on 14/15 August, 1947, the era of British rule ended and the new independent nations of India and Pakistan were born.

It was during the struggle for independence that the Gandhian-inspired Nationalist urban dress came into being, a modern, non-sectarian Indian ensemble that was neither Hindu nor Muslim.[24] Despite such gestures toward solidarity, traumatic events continued within India. Among other controversial moves, the

The 1885 founding of the Indian National Congress had given Indian politicians a podium from which to demand self-government. This cause was greatly strengthened in 1920 when Mohandas Gandhi, popularly known as Mahatma, or "great soul," took over the party's leadership. Thanks to his charismatic

new government set about incorporating more than 550 princely states into the Indian Union, kingdoms that had been semi-independent under the British and whose rulers served as supportive pillars of the Raj [346]. Much agitation followed. Then, in 1948, Mahatma Gandhi was assassinated. All of the religious factions were so shocked and grieved that peace was finally restored.[25]

As India's first prime minister, Jawaharlal Nehru laid the foundation for the modern nation state; he also popularized a style of Indian urban attire that inspired Nehru jackets in the West [347]. Following Nehru's death in May, 1964, his daughter became prime minister. Indira Gandhi suffered political ups and downs that took her in and out of office. In 1984, when once again back in power, she was assassinated; her son, Rajiv Gandhi, was elected prime minister in a wave of sympathy but then he, too, was assassinated. Following Rajiv Gandhi's death, his Italian-born widow, Sonia, followed him into politics [348]. In present-day India, along with ubiquitous elements of Western dress, a vibrant mix of draped and tailored clothing styles is commonly worn.

347 Jawaharlal Nehru (1889–1964) served as India's first prime minister and is seen here with his daughter Indira Gandhi and grandson Rajiv, both of whom subsequently also served as prime minister. Nehru embodied India's modern-day, upper-class approach to urban attire: the Nationalist cap introduced by Gandhi, a fitted coat with a band collar (the *achkan*) and tight-fitting trousers (the *churidar*). Although the coat reflects influence of Western tailoring, the outfit draws more from the Indian tradition than that of the West, where the "exotic" Nehru jacket became quite popular.

348 The sari-clad Sonia Gandhi and the beturbaned Manmohan Singh, the Sikh economist she chose to be India's prime minister when the Congress Party Gandhi led unexpectedly won the national election in May, 2004. Note that Mr. Singh's turban is wrapped in a manner that accommodates a Sikh's traditional topknot of uncut hair.

346 (opposite) Bourne & Shepherd studio oil painting, presently hanging in the ballroom of the Imperial Hotel, New Delhi. During the height of the Raj, the semi-independent Indian princes played an important and supportive role for the British. This 1912 official portrait features the sumptuously attired Nawab of Malerkotla; to his right is seated Major General Sir Robert Sale, first Commanding Chief of Kandahar. Four of the Nawab's English military cohorts are accompanied by their Victorian-clad wives who, despite India's often hot and humid climate, cling to their encasing, multi-layered style of "proper" dress, and vice versa.

349 (above left) Front and back views of the most popular manner of draping the *dhoti*.

350 (above center) The *veshti-mundu* is worn by men of all castes in India's two southernmost states, Kerala and Tamil Nadu.

351 (above right) For women in the southern state of Kerala and some parts of Tamil Nadu, the *veshti-mundu* is everyday attire. The *mundu* is often draped over the upper body like the decorated end of a sari, the *pallav*.

DRAPED GARMENTS

One of the most impressive aspects of Indian clothing is the historical depth reflected in the subcontinent's wide range of garments. The draped sari, *dhoti* and turban, for example—all created by ingeniously manipulating a long piece of versatile, unstitched cloth around the body—maintain a tradition that reaches back for millennia.

MEN'S AND WOMEN'S *DHOTI*

The world's earliest known examples of cotton come from the Indus Valley sites of some 5,000 years ago,[26] as do the earliest versions of India's most basic draped garments, the male loincloth, the *dhoti*, as well a female *dhoti*, forerunner of the present-day sari. For the male *dhoti*, the costume historian Chantal Boulanger reports seven styles, of which the most common is illustrated [349].[27]

MEN'S AND WOMEN'S *VESHTI* AND *MUNDU*

In the south, in addition to regional *dhotis*, Dravidian wrapped styles are worn, garments which are basically draped in two sections: the *veshti* (from the Sanskrit verb "*vesh:*" to cover, to wrap around, to roll) covers the lower part of the body, wrapped and tucked in at the waist like a bath towel. This is supplemented by a separate shoulder cloth, the lightweight *mundu*. *Veshtis* are usually white, made from 4 yards (12 ft, or 3.5 m) of cotton muslin; the *mundus* are of the same cloth and color. The size of a *mundu* varies, some not much bigger than a handkerchief, others as large as the *veshti* itself, depending on the wearer's likes and needs. *Veshtis* are commonly worn by men in the southern-most part of India [350] and also by women in Kerala State and some areas of the southern state of Tamil Nadu [351].[28]

MEN'S *LUNGI*

An additional draped garment for the lower torso, the *lungi*, is used all across India by Hindus and Muslim men for casual wear or manual labor. The *lungi* is a 6½-foot-long (2 m) cloth sewn into a tube and secured at the waist by one large or several smaller pleat tucks [352].

MEN'S HEADGEAR

Northern India's ubiquitous male headgear is the turban, *pag* (or the smaller *pagri*), a long, narrow cloth—typically 5½ feet by 3 inches (167.5 × 7.5 cm), but some are as long as 20 feet (6 m)—that is wound about the head in a variety of ways. "Turbans" range from a working man's *ad hoc* headcovering on a hot day to religion-associated styles [see 348] and clan-related headcoverings [see 371]. Culturally, a north Indian's turban is often the most important element of his dress. Since Aryan times, a man's lineage, point of origin and status have all been reflected in his turban's cloth, color, patterning and wrapping style [353]. In the south, some kings adopted the wrapped turban headdress, emulating their northern peers, but with the exception of a few local communities most southern men now go bareheaded. On certain special occasions, Hindus, Jains, Sikhs and Muslims all wear some form of headcovering. Indian Muslims are often seen in caps [see 376] or—like most modern, urban Hindu men—go about bareheaded.

352 A young man in southern India wears a simply draped *lungi* as he decorates his cow for the Pongal festival devoted to the veneration of cattle.

353 Lord Edwin Weeks, *Start for the Hunt at Gwalior*, ca. 1887. This painting depicts a group of turbaned men in various relationships to each other—ruler, lieutenant, cavalry, groom, soldiers, onlookers—each wearing a different color and style of turban wrap that reflects his place in society. The turban is essentially a north Indian phenomenon; Gwalior is located south of the northern city of Agra, home of the Taj Mahal.

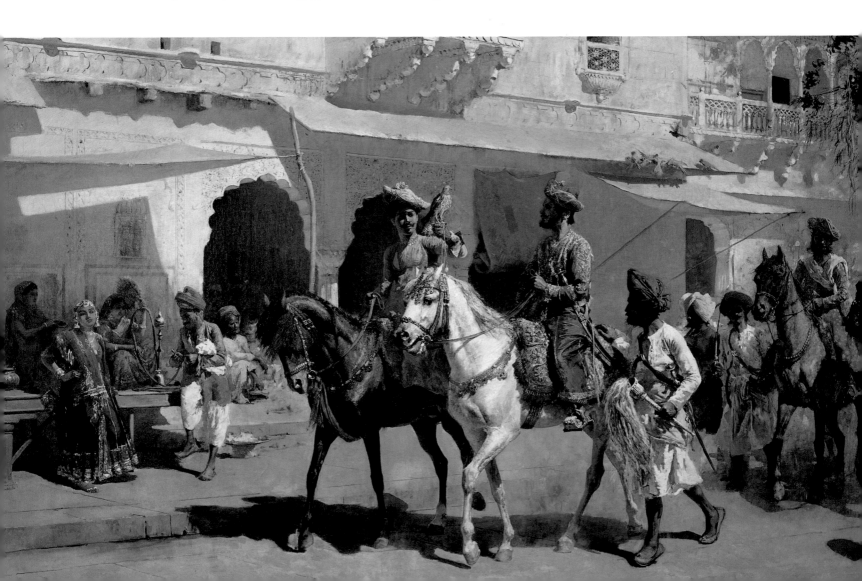

Throughout India, most Hindu men are clean-shaven, although many keep mustaches. The exceptions are the Jain monks who shave everything completely off and Hindu monks who let everything grow unhampered. Upturned mustaches are a sign of high caste status and, in the past, have been forbidden to low-caste and untouchable men. The younger generation in modern-day urban India—and the men of the Indian diaspora as well—are cleanshaven, even some Sikhs.[29]

WOMEN'S SARI

The woman's traditional sari is worn in nearly all regions by females of all classes and religious groups, in both rural and urban areas, and the art of draping it on the body has been developed to a degree that surpasses that of any other people wearing wrapped clothing (see "Southeast Asia," pp. 265–301; "Central Africa," pp. 544–549; "West Africa," pp. 550–557). There are over 100 different ways of wearing the sari,

354 A Kolkata matron models her wedding sari, an inherited garment that has been used by three generations of her family; it is wrapped in the regional style of Bengal. Saris in various shades of red are typically worn for marriage ceremonies. On the woman's forehead is a red dot—the *tikka* or *bindi*— which represents a blessing and is often applied during Hindu religious ceremonies. The red powder marking the part in the woman's hair indicates she is married.

which is a long length of unstitched cloth of varying dimensions that is wrapped around the body to create a woman's main garment, covering both the lower and upper torso, as well as the head [354]. The sari has two dimensions: its length, which varies between 2 to 9 yards (6–27 ft, or 1.8–8.2 m), and its width, from 2 to 4 feet (0.6–1.2 m).[30] Saris are produced in a dazzling array of weaves, colors and metallic threads [see 359–363].[31]

Although modern-day saris are much less likely to signal caste status, their manner of being draped sometimes still reflects geographic origin. For example, in the southern state of Tamil Nadu the traditional wrapping style of the *pinkosu* "back pleats" sari involves creating a fan-effect across the back [355]. In the north-western state of Gujarat [356] the sari is wrapped quite differently from that of the eastern state of West Bengal, where the older-style sari wrap results in only a short length of the cloth available to drape over the shoulder [357].[32] Although the classic Bengali red and white cotton sari is still worn by younger women, they now tend to drape it in the modern, regionless, *nivi* style associated with urban centers all across India [358].[33]

Today almost all Indian sari*s* are worn over two opaque undergarments: the *choli*, which is the short, close-fitting blouse that completely covers the breasts and usually the upper arms and back as well, and a long petticoat that shields the lower torso and legs.

It is interesting to consider the origins of this modest underwear. From the 11th century A.D. forward, Islamic insistence on completely shrouding a Muslim woman when in public resulted in some Hindu females in northern India beginning to cover their heads, and also occasionally their breasts. This modesty was further reinforced by the British [364], who emphasized that only "primitive, uncivilized" women went topless,[34] a rather tactless assertion considering that Hindu females had been scantily clad throughout most of the history of India's high culture [365]. Indeed, in the 13th century the Venetian traveler Marco Polo noted that Indian women "wore hardly anything more than jewels,

355 (right) Back and side views of the fan effect created by the *pinkosu* "back pleats" sari of Tamil Nadu.

356 (far right) The Gujarati-style sari of northwest India. In this manner of draping, the orientation of the front pleats is important, as is the display of the sari's border, the *pallav*, over the torso. Following the custom in Gujarat villages, this young bride holds up a section of her sari to screen her face from her new father-in-law's view. He—and other men of the family senior to her husband—in theory will never behold her full countenance in all the years they will live in the same family compound.

357 (far left) Back and front views of the older-style Bengali sari, which is wrapped in such a way that the section draped over the shoulder is rather short, hence a keyring is tied to the sari's decorative end as a counterweight to hold the desired drape in place.

358 (left) A young Bengali woman in one of Kolkata's flower markets wears the region's classic red and white cotton sari draped in the *nivi* style now seen all over urban India. She has tucked one corner of the sari into her waist in order to protect this decorative *pallav* end while shopping.

359 A resplendently sheer sari from Benares woven in a brocade technique incorporating white silk and gold metallic threads worked in a diamond-grid design, ca. pre-1985. Length 176 in. (4.47 m), width 45 in. (1.14 m).

360 An example of a *patola* silk wedding sari from Gujarat, ca. pre-1981. The complex maroon, blue and beige pattern was produced using the *ikat* tie-and-dye process: the design was dyed on the threads prior to weaving. In this case, a double *ikat* was created; both the warp and the weft threads were pre-dyed. Length 175¹⁄₈ in. (4.45 m), width 38¹⁄₈ in. (0.97 m). India's famous *patola* fabrics had a strong influence on textiles in other parts of Asia (see "Southeast Asia," pp. 286, 298).

361 A Rajasthani sari with a block-printed pattern of red on white silk creates a complex pattern of geometrics, elephants and flowers, ca. pre-1985. Length 214 in. (5.4 m), width 42 in. (1.06 m).

362 A blue silk sari, possibly from Bangladesh, Dhaka or Kolkata, woven in a basic plaid technique with regularly spaced warp and weft threads of contrasting colors and a repeating geometric pattern created using multicolor supplementary wefts, ca. 1920–30. Length 197 in. (5 m), width 43 in. (1.09 m).

363 An unusual example of a south Indian cotton sari that combines a number of techniques—brocade weave, resist-dyed and block-printed patterns, supplementary-weft designs created with gold and silver metallic threads, ca. pre-1985. Length 193 in. (4.9 m), width 44 in. (1.1 m).

366 Cut-and-sewn loose trousers—the *vajani*—worn by two men in northwestern Gujarat. These agriculturalists also wear a long-sleeved, pull-over shirt and have a *chadar* draped over one shoulder for future multipurpose use—shawl, headwrap, carrying cloth, blanket, pillow or seat.

367 (right) A man in northwestern Gujarat wears *churidar* pants with a *kurta* tunic, a Western vest and a regional turban style. On his shoulder rests the folded *chadar*. Note that although this man's *kurta* has Western-style collar and cuffs, the front placket opening still only extends to the middle of the chest in the traditional Indian manner.

368 (far right) The *churidar* pants seen here are worn by a Muslim performer engaged in the presentation of a classical Indian dance called *kathak*.

Today *churidar* pants are worn with the *kameez* tunic everywhere in India as fashion dictates, replacing the traditional *salwar* pants (see below). Aside from this, some Muslim women's tailored ensembles—such as the formal, short-skirted costume of classical *kathak* dancers [368]—have always included *churidar* pants and are worn wherever Muslim communities exist on the subcontinent.

WOMEN'S *SALWAR KAMEEZ* AND *DUPATTA*

The *salwar kameez* is a garment ensemble associated with the Punjab, a vast plain in the northwest of the subcontinent stretching across Pakistan and into that section of India that lies between the Indus River and the drainage of the Ganges.[37] In this area women have long worn the *salwar*, loose-legged trousers that taper down to form a narrow, stitch-embellished cuff at the ankles, and the *kameez*, a tunic whose exact length and degree of fit responds to current fashion. The ensemble's third element, the indispensable

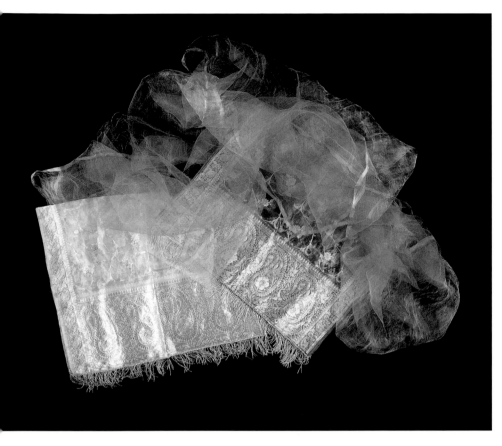

369 Three present-day silk scarves from eastern India. The yellow-and-gold and green-and-gold examples are from Benares. Such scarves are now woven to a size worn in the West, hence in fact are too narrow to be used locally as a *dupatta*. The long, gossamer-thin, orange silk scarf is from Kolkata, West Bengal; this type of very fine weaving is reminiscent of the famously sheer Bengal cotton muslins of earlier times.

dupatta, is a long, flowing veil [369] that is either draped low over the bosom, drawn up over the head, or simply tossed over the shoulders as occasion, activity, companions, age and marital status dictate.[38]

In the 19th and 20th centuries, the *salwar kameez-dupatta* ensemble spread through India as the dress of Punjabi migrants and also as schoolgirls' uniforms, competing with the European style skirt-blouse ensemble. The 1980s "ethnic chic" fashion trend popularized *salwar kameez* dress for college girls and white-collar professional women throughout the four corners of India [370]. In our own time, the *salwar kameez* has become the standard dress for young unmarried adult women of the urban middle and upper class.

370 A sophisticated young Kolkata woman wears a *salwar kameez* and harmonizing *dupatta*. The designer of this ensemble is Anuradha Navlakha of Anuradha's Collection, Kolkata.

WOMEN'S *GHAGHARA*

A woman's ankle-length, gathered skirt—the *ghaghara* [see 381–383]–is worn in northwestern India. These long, full skirts resemble those of the camel-herding nomads of Iran's Zagros mountains (see "The Iranian Plateau," p. 73). As it turns out, at least some of the women living in northwest Gujarat who wear such skirts do have a distant Central Asian connection. The costume historian Judy Frater has traced the ancient migrations of twelve sub-groups of an ethnic people—the Rabari—living in the contiguous northwest states of Gujarat and Rajasthan by combining their oral histories with confirming iconographic clues found in their embroidered clothing and accoutrements. She also states: "Rabaris are traditionally camel herders. This association, and the striking tallness, fairness, and occasional blue or gray eyes of Rabari people suggest that their ancestors were either...camel-herding immigrants...or foreign or indigenous pastoralists who associated intimately with them."[39] Today a number of these Rabari sub-groups live fairly close together in a series of villages concentrated in the region known as Kutch.

REGIONAL DRESS

The range of Indian cloth and clothing that exists among the country's many regional minorities is impressively wide. It may therefore be helpful to focus on one specific area where some of India's most exciting hand-embroidered textiles are being created. Although other ethnic communities wearing similar types of garments are spread thinly across parts of western India and the Himalayan foothills, it is in barren, remote Kutch—home to Hindu and Muslim communities of semi-nomadic herders and agricultural villagers—that a remarkable array of colored, often beautifully embroidered, tailored and draped garments continues to be made and worn.

Men in Kutch wear a variety of tailored garments, many of them white. Although white may seem impractical in such a dusty land, the summer's searing sun and unrelenting heat render this color choice a practical one [371]. One of the most distinctive of Kutch's male fitted garments is the white jacket known as the *kediyun*, worn by Rabari villagers throughout Gujarat and the neighboring state of Rajasthan [372]. Originally the *kediyun* was also worn by other Hindu

371 (right) A goat herder wears the traditional male clothing of the Kachhi Rabari group: the loosely draped white *dhoti*, the Rabari signature white jacket known as a *kediyun*, and a black printed turban.

372 (far right) A Kachhi Rabari man, turban removed within his home, sits comfortably attired in his group's sturdy white jacket, the *kediyun*.

373 (opposite) A Hindu Ahir boy's formal dress from Kutch, ca. 1976. Unlike the region's commonly worn plain long-sleeved cotton shirt, this *kediyun* is richly embroidered, incorporating multiple small mirrors: length 17½ in. (44.5 cm), width 54½ in. (138.4 cm). The voluminous, drawstring cotton pants are decorated with similar embroideries: length 31 in. (78.7 cm), width 41 in. (104.1 cm).

374 A Dhebaria Rabari man's stitched and gathered cotton *kediyun,* ca. pre-1981. Length 48 in. (121.9 cm), width 61½ in. (156.2 cm).

375 Two colorfully dressed young Maldhari (Muslim pastoralist) camel herders wearing *kurta* tunics with matching cut-and-sewn drawstring *salwar* pants and folded *chadars* on their left shoulders. Note the rounded shirttails and high side openings of the *kurtas*.

pastoral and agricultural groups such as the Ahirs [373] and Kambis. The garment is derived from a style brought to India from further west. The prototype "was worn by Mughal and Rajput men at least from the 15th century."[40] This long-sleeved garment is tight-fitting, densely gathered at the underarm level, and secured with ties either to the left side or to the center [374].

The Rabari are but one of several ethnic peoples living in Kutch. The upper-body garment worn today by most of the other Hindu groups, and also by Muslim men both inside and outside Kutch, is the *kurta*, a loose, cut-and-sewn, pull-over tunic that has a buttoned opening at the neck [375, 376; see also 367]. With the *kurta* is usually worn the draped *dhoti*, although other types of lower garment are also seen: loose-legged drawstring pajamas or *salwar* pants. Although only Hindus wear the *dhoti* and its variants, both Hindus and Muslims wear stitched pants.

A traditional male garment worn by all Kutch ethnic groups is the *chadar*, the shoulder cloth that can serve many purposes—a carry-all, a shawl [377], a pillow, or a seat. Among the Rabari, this cloth is usually named for the fabric from which it is made rather than for the function it serves.[41]

In present-day Kutch, as in so many of the world's remaining traditional rural enclaves, men's dress has increasingly shifted to regional, national or global styles. As a result, it is primarily female clothing that distinguishes one ethnic group from another. Many Kutch women wear a three-piece outfit: the backless blouse [378–380], the full *ghaghara* skirt [381–383], and an often tie-dyed veil/headscarf, the *odhani* [384, 385]. This ensemble is favored by various Kutch Hindu groups [386], although in northern rural areas both Hindus and Muslims also wear it. Elsewhere in Kutch, some Muslim groups wear a version of the *salwar kameez*, while the preferred attire of urban Muslim women is a modest, one-piece dress [387].

376 A bearded Muslim *khatri* (dyer), sitting among his recently tie-dyed woolen scarves, wears a white *kurta*, a pair of white drawstring pajama pants and a white Muslim cap, the *topi*.

377 An elderly, white-clad man sits warmly wrapped in his multicolored, multi-purpose shoulder cloth, the *chadar*. His head is wrapped in a turban and his pants are the loose-legged pajama style.

381 A drawstring-gathered red *ghaghara* of *mashru*, a satin weave originally of silk warp and cotton weft, with *ikat* horizontal stripes and a cotton border embroidered with designs that incorporate mirrors. Hindu, Kanbi village, Kutch, ca. pre-1981. Length 32 in. (81.3 cm), width 12¹/₂ in. (31.8 cm).

378 (opposite above) A short, backless *choli* blouse with embroidery that includes elephants and peacocks. The asymmetrically decorated sleeves show geometric patterns on the left arm and florals on the right. Kutch, ca. pre-1981. Length 11 in. (27.9 cm), width 31 in. (78.7 cm).

379 (opposite below left) A cotton *mashru* blouse from the northern Banni region of Kutch, ca. pre-1981. A variety of techniques are incorporated: tie-dye, needle-weaving, embroidery, mirrorwork. Pom-poms decorate the horizontal stripes on the blouse front. A cotton printed fabric is used for the back of the blouse. Length 29 in. (73.7 cm), width 23 in. (58.4 cm).

380 (opposite below right) A backless blouse, the *kanjara*, from the Muslim Matara clan of Kutch's northern Banni district, ca. pre-1982. The carefully executed blouse designs reflect the distinguishing features of Matara embroidery: tiny mirrors and minuscule stitches. Length 26 in. (66 cm), width 20 in. (50.8 cm).

382 A drawstring-gathered green cotton *ghaghara* patterned with regularly spaced embroideries of alternating peacocks and geometric patterns. The contrasting red hem includes elephants among its array of embroidered motifs. Kutch, ca. pre-1981. Length 32 in. (81.3 cm), width 14 in. (35.6 cm).

383 Exceptionally full, drawstring-gathered, purple-brown cotton *ghaghara*, tie-dyed in an overall pattern of yellow and green dots. Mutava (Muslim Maldhari) group, Goriwalli village, Kutch, ca. pre-1981. Length 32 in. (81.3 cm), width 54¹/₂ in. (138.4 cm).

384 (far left) A long, cotton, purple-brown *odhani*, tie-dyed to create yellow, green and blue designs. Kutch, ca. pre-1981. Length 152 in. (386 cm), width 35¹/₂ in. (90.2 cm).

385 (left) A long, red, cotton *odhani*, tie-dyed to create white, blue, green and yellow designs. Kutch, ca. pre-1981. This type of veil is worn by both Hindus and Muslims. Length 129 in. (327.7 cm), width 31 in. (78.7 cm).

386 (right) Kutch women wear various versions of the area's three-piece ensemble—headscarf/veil, blouse, full skirt—as well as the region's one-piece dresses. The attire of the women in this traditional Kachhi Rabari village adds a colorful note to a monochromatic scene of conical, thatched houses—hallmarks of the Kutch landscape.

387 (far right) Garasia Jat women have traditionally worn a long red dress, the *churi*, made of 16–20 feet (5–6 meters) of lightweight cotton gathered at the waist. This mother has added a length of factory-printed cloth to serve as her headcloth, which partially covers her bodice. An example of a Garasia Jat finely embroidered bodice can be seen on the daughter's dress.

For all Kutch communities, the veil is essential, its fabric and decoration an important means of identifying an ethnic group. This is true of the Rabari, for whom historically the two distinguishing features of their veil were its black color and its woolen cloth. Certainly wool is a practical choice of fiber for sheep and goat herders inasmuch as it takes the shearing of two sheep to produce enough wool for either a gathered skirt or an *odhani*.[42] The Rabari black headscarves and full skirts are usually tie-dyed in the

bandhani manner [see 390]: decorative patterns are created with a series of colored dots, the motifs used to express not only a woman's age but also her marital and childbearing status.

Among the Rabari, the most treasured item of the female three-part ensemble is the *kamchali*, the backless blouse, which—for this group—is short, reaching only to the waist and secured across the back with two ties [388]. A woman always tries to cover herself with her headscarf so as never to expose her bare back or head

388 (right) Kachhi Rabari females wear a backless blouse (the *kamchali*)—secured with two strings tied across the back—that is partially shielded from view here by the headscarf. Note that this woman's lower arm is elaborately tattooed, probably in designs that are repeated in the embroidery.

389 (far right) Two Marvada Meghval girls hold up a beautifully decorated blouse (the *kanjara*; see also 380), the type worn with their colorful gathered skirts. This is the attire of the northern Banni region.

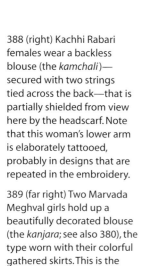

390 Six contemporary scarves from Kutch. These textiles have all been resist-dyed: tiny, individual sections of cloth are tied off to shield them from the dye bath. In India this process is known as *bandhani*, from whence comes the English term "bandana," a type of spotted cotton handkerchief imported from India beginning in the 18th century.

except to close woman-friends. The backless blouses are cut without a pattern, using simple geometric shapes that utilize every bit of cloth. Blouses worn on festive occasions are heavily embroidered: because of this elaborate ornamentation, the Rabari consider these garments to be their most important art form, one that displays a rich panoply of iconographic designs. Other groups also elaborately embroider blouses: the Marvada Meghval are a case in point [389]. However, not all Kutch women who wear the three-piece ensemble today still feature handwork on their clothing [391].

The traditional costume of most Muslim women is a modest, tunic-like dress with matching pants [392, 393] and a veil. Some of these dresses are beautifully elaborated. The bodice portion of the Garasia Jat red *churi* exhibits closely executed cross-stitch embroidery [394]. It sometimes takes as long as two months to a year of a woman's "leisure time" to create a single panel of this exceptional work.[43]

In Kutch, embroidery is highly regarded [395; see also 394, 399] and truly rewarding for the practitioner,

391 A Maru Meghval woman from the village of Sumrasar Sheikh wears a full skirt of factory-printed cloth with matching blouse and harmonizing headcloth, all enhanced by large "ivory" bracelets. This is modern dress, the equivalent of the traditional backless *kamchali* and sleeveless *kurti*, both of which were embroidered.

392 A Muslim woman's magnificently embroidered dark blue cotton tunic (*abho*). The pentagonal front panel (see detail below) has a grid of exceptionally fine interlaced embroidery that incorporates tiny mirrors; this panel is surrounded by well-executed embroidery. There are button fastenings at each side of the neck. The body of the tunic is embroidered with tiny, regularly spaced white, green, red and yellow dots. The red hem is decorated with a horizontal tie-dyed pattern. Length 40½ in. (102.9 cm), width 37 in. (94 cm).

393 The tunic is worn with accompanying dark blue embroidered pants (*ejar*), which appear to be a regional variation of *salwar* pants. These are worn under the tunic and therefore only the cuffs and lower legs which show when worn are embroidered. Length 36 in. (91.4 cm), width 33 in. (83.8 cm).

an activity that provides both satisfaction and companionship. Throughout the area, afternoons find women gathered together with their handwork. Even in families that can afford clothes made from imported cloth, hand-embroidery is still an essential skill for a young girl whose finished work serves to demonstrate her worth when arranging her marriage. Although each ethnic group has its own design corpus, geometric embroidery motifs often serve as ornamental borders, whereas such exotica as stylized elephants, birds, camels and temples are combined to create lively featured designs. Small and large mirrors—square, triangular, diamond-shaped, round—also add to the unique mystique of Kutch textiles [396].

For Kutch herders and agriculturalists, foot coverings range from sandals to sturdy shoes, a desirable solution in a hot and prickly terrain. Traditionally, women wore leather slip-on shoes decorated with an inlay of colored leather strips and thread pompoms. Today females sometimes wear flip-flop rubber sandals but, in the main, women are generally barefoot, the better to display ankle bracelets and toe rings [see 398, 399].

395 An Ahir girl wearing an elaborated traditional version of her three-piece costume, some elements of which convey a social message: the surface pattern of her headcloth and the design of her skirt's tie-dyed cotton fabric and mirror-embroidery all identify her caste.

394 The bodice panels of Garasia Jat dresses are intricately embroidered in one of several traditional designs. Some Jat women prefer to wear tie-dyed headscarves over their red, one-piece dresses. This particular traditional veil, a *chundadi*, has been tie-dyed in the *bandhani* manner.

396 This Muslim child's dress has been lavishly decorated with mirrors, buttons and embroidery. Length 22½ in. (57 cm), width 25 in. (63.5 cm).

397 (below) This little girl displays her many glass bangle bracelets, as well as her rickrack- and lace-trimmed dress.

398 (above right) The colorful clothing of these Meghval females is enhanced by glittering gold and silver jewelry and large "ivory" bracelets.

399 (below right) Dhebaria Rabari females dressed in their best for a wedding. Their black wool, tie-dyed headscarves create a striking background for the profusion of special-event silver jewelry and colorfully embroidered garments that adorn each girl and woman.

In Kutch villages, stylish female hairstyles are not a priority because today the women's long hair is almost always neatly pulled back and covered by a veil. Traditionally, in many ethnic groups the women used elaborate braiding to hold hair ornaments in place and also to keep their hair under control during the arduous nomadic life they formerly led. Men wear their hair short, in the Western manner. Each community traditionally had a unique style of turban, an identity marker. Rabari men, for example, wear a distinctive style of black printed turban [see 371], whereas Muslim men usually wear a cap when out in public.

As is true of women and girls all over India, Kutch women place great emphasis on jewelry [397].[44] There are glass, gold, silver and plastic ornaments for each limb and every digit: arm bracelets, wrist bracelets, ankle bracelets, bangles, necklaces, chokers, earrings, nose studs, nose rings, finger rings, toe rings and a range of jewelry for the hair. Gleaming gold and silver jewelry and, originally, large ivory bracelets further enhance each woman's colorful attire [398; see also 391]. This is also true of the multiple strands of special-event silver jewelry worn at important social events [399]. Much of the jewelry indicates not only community affiliation but also age, marital and childbearing status. In addition, changes in jewelry can indicate the death of a close family member. Jewelry is also sometimes worn by Rabari men, most typically as a part of their wedding finery: necklaces, chains, amulets and earrings.[45]

For added beauty, a woman's hands, arms and neck are often tattooed in traditional designs made up of a series of dots [see 388]. Young girls are sometimes tattooed with a small cross on the cheek or a scorpion on a hand to keep them from being "too beautiful" and thus attracting destructive attention in the form of the Evil Eye. Tattooing is admired and appreciated. As one Rabari bride noted, "Gold may come or go but tattoos are an adornment that stays with you until you die."[46]

TRANSITIONAL DRESS

Since the Indian government outlawed the caste system in 1948, and opportunities for social advancements have opened up for all sections of society, there has been a gradual altering of traditional life, even in remote areas like Kutch. Such change inevitably has had an effect on regional clothing. Today fewer Kutch women, for example, wear hand-embroidered garments. Increasingly, cheaper and more easily accessible mill-woven, roller-patterned fabrics have come to replace the traditional *bandhani*-dyed skirts and headscarves that used to be everyday wear. This is especially true among caste communities at the bottom of society. This change also has to do with economics: women go outside to work, hence are exposed to new influences. Although such women no longer have time to embroider, they now do have money to buy. Nonetheless, an encouraging emphasis on fine handwork continues, and most Indian women—even today, despite the growing influence of foreign fashion trends—continue to dress traditionally. Most men's clothing, on the other hand has incorporated Western elements, even in conservative villages [400], and this, of course, is what is increasingly happening worldwide.

400 As this dramatic scene at a well in western India demonstrates, in 2003 most female villagers were still wearing the draped sari, whereas the men were increasingly dressed in various combinations of Western cut-and-sewn clothing, a growing worldwide trend.

THE HIMALAYAN KINGDOMS

401 In some of the highest valleys of the northeastern Himalayas live the Sherpas, Nepal's famous mountaineering guides and porters. Here early morning finds a group of Sherpanis already busily engaged in transport. Each woman's waist is padded with a sturdy striped textile to protect her lower back, where the carrying basket rests. In the background can be seen a section of the snow-covered Anapurna massif.

Across the northernmost boundary of the Indian subcontinent, a dramatic landscape of towering frozen peaks, high windy plateaux and deep verdant valleys abruptly rises, stretching in an almost unbroken arc from Pakistan, east across inner Asia, to Burma (also known as Myanmar). These enormous, snow-covered mountains comprise the world's loftiest ranges, the mighty Himalayas, a Sanskrit name meaning "Abode of the Snows." These mountain peaks are still regarded by many as sacred. Buddhism in its most archaic Tantric form became

entrenched here in the 8th century A.D., creating a unique civilization that is more than simply the religion that inspired it.

The school of Tantric Buddhism—what most Westerners call Tibetan Buddhism—began in northern India more than 2,500 years ago when a young warrior-caste prince, Siddhartha Gautama, turned away from a life of wealth and privilege to search for liberation from suffering for mankind through the achievement of a higher state of consciousness. By the 12th century A.D., due to pressures from Hinduism and Islam, Buddhism became eclipsed in the land of its birth (see "India," p. 219). Undiminished elsewhere, however, this appealing faith had already slowly seeped northward and taken root firmly in the high plains and cool valleys of the Himalayas. Located along the southern exposure of those mighty ranges were a series of small kingdoms—Ladakh, Mustang, Nepal, Sikkim, Bhutan, Tibet—that exemplified the Tantric Buddhist universe [Map 21].[1] To an observer from the secular West, the almost magical nature of Tantric Buddhism—which links worldly reality with trance, spirits, giant ogres, dream experience and rule by reincarnation—is a sharp contrast to the pragmatic nature of the Occident. This esoteric religion has an intensity and drama that is a match for its spectacular physical environment. Nowhere was this more true than in historic Tibet, the faith's spiritual heartland.

TIBET

Tibet is often referred to as "the roof of the world," because more than half the country is a vast, high-altitude desert, the 15,000-foot (4,570 m) Chang Tang plateau, extending more than 800 miles (1,285 km) from west to east. Tibet is bordered on the north by the Kunlun mountains of Central Asia where, by the 9th century, Tibetan was the language of diplomacy

and Buddhism the culture of the trade routes. The Himalayas, including the world's highest peak, the 29,028 foot-high (8,848 m) Mount Everest, border Tibet on the west and south.

Tibet's lofty altitudes have created a unique climate that combines great aridity with such low humidity that grain can be safely stored for fifty to sixty years, dried raw meat can be saved for more than a year and, in this near-sterile environment, epidemics rarely occur. The country's population has a marked homogeneity: the majority of the 2.5 million Tibetans have the same ethnic origin, practice the same religion and speak the same language.[2] Social divisions existed between the elegantly clad nobility [402] and the less extravagantly dressed peasantry [403], who constituted

Map 21 The small Himalayan kingdoms of Ladakh, Mustang, Nepal, Sikkim, Bhutan and Tibet.

403 An elderly pilgrim, prayer wheel in hand, circumambulates clockwise around a religious shrine in eastern Tibet. The striped shirt worn beneath this nomad's sheepskin-lined *chuba* is visible at cuffs and hem. Around his neck is a white silk scarf, the *kadda*, an essential element of religious attire.

402 A portrait of 19th/20th-century Tibetan royalty. Note that the king's robe, the *chuba*, crosses over the chest to close on the right; his sleeves end in wide cuffs formed by the shirt worn beneath. The two flanking women wear similar but longer robes, which are covered by the quintessential Tibetan female garment, the striped apron. All Tibetans wore the *chuba*; it was the quality of each robe's fabric that denoted its wearer's rank.

404 (right) A Tibetan émigré, now living in the north India foothills near Darjeeling, continues to wear a modest version of his homeland's national robe, the *chuba*.

405 (far right) A Tibetan relocated in Darjeeling continues to wear her homeland's quintessential female garment, the striped apron, over her modest *chuba* robe.

406 Maroon-robed Tibetan monks involved in a lively religious discussion. With dramatic hand gestures, young monks-in-training forcefully present their arguments to a seated partner who serves to rebut their statements.

the overwhelming majority of the population. Economic development, in Western terms, was minimal. Tibet, prior to the 1950s, truly was an entity apart, one that sought isolation from the rest of the world.

The origin of Tibetan theocracy reaches back to the 13th century when the great Mongol ruler Kublai Khan gave a Tibetan lama control over all of Tibet. Beginning in the 16th century, the title of Dalai Lama, "Oceans of Wisdom," was accorded to all subsequent rulers. The outer limit of this Tantric world was, and is, Mongolia, where the few remaining Buddhist shrines surviving the country's Soviet occupation clearly reflect their 13th-century Tibetan origin (see "Mongolia," p. 137). An interesting clothing similarity between the two countries exists as a result of this relationship. In both Mongolia and Tibet, the man's long robe crosses over the chest to fasten on the right, and the garment's long sleeves are usually cuffed.

Buddhism formed the very essence of Tibetan civilization and defined it both as a people and as a nation. For almost six centuries, a succession of Dalai Lamas served as the country's primary religious authorities. In the 17th century, the "Great

Fifth" Dalai Lama formed Tibet's first national government, becoming the secular ruler as well as the spiritual head of the newly unified nation. An unbroken sequence of what Tantric Buddhists believe are reincarnated Dalai Lamas ruled Tibet for the next 300 years,[3] "overseeing a remarkable society in which spiritual development was more valued than material progress and where moral force took precedence over military power."[4]

The relationship between the succession of Tibetan high lamas and their powerful Central and East Asian supporters—both Mongol Khans and Chinese emperors—was that of priest and patron. In the mid-20th century, China invoked that historic connection to strengthen its claim to exercise "sovereignty" over Tibet.

Following the Chinese occupation there was a general diaspora involving a perilous trek across the formidable Himalayas to resettle in such north Indian hill towns as Darjeeling, where typical Tibetan clothing still continues to be worn by émigrés [404, 405]. The Tibetan mass exodus also included the secret flight from Lhasa by the Dalai Lama, who re-established Tibetan Buddhism in Dharamsala, a hill town in northern India, and set up what is, in essence, a Tibetan royal court in exile. This community's abundance of maroon-clad, shaven-headed Buddhist monks [406] recreates the Tibetan monastic world.

NEPAL

Sandwiched between Tibet to the north and the vast plains of India to the south lies the Himalayan country of Nepal [see Map 21], which contains some of the most rugged and difficult mountainous terrain in the world; mountains cover 80% of this country where 80% of the people live off the land. As a result of this geographic challenge, reinforced by self-imposed isolation, Nepal is one of the globe's least developed nations. It is a land roughly the size of Florida containing a population of over 23 million people, which includes some 35 different castes and innumerable ethnic groups who speak as wide a range of languages as are to be found in all of Western Europe. Many of them continue to wear their own traditional dress [407].

In Nepal's southern lowlands live the Gurkhas, the fearless warriors who have faithfully served in the British army for over two centuries [408].

In the high Himalayan valleys of Nepal's northeast trekking area live the Sherpas [see 401], the well-known mountain guides who are practicing Buddhists, in contrast to the majority of Nepal's inhabitants.

The official religion of Nepal is Hinduism and its king is the only ruling Hindu monarch in the world. Some of his more devout subjects consider him the reincarnation of the benevolent Hindu god Lord Vishnu,

407 Homespun garments and multiple necklaces are worn by a young, unmarried tribal girl from Kadagoan, in the district of Humla, located in the northwestern part of Nepal, along the Tibetan border.

408 Gurkha soldiers, carrying their distinctive curved daggers known as *khukris*, are seen here in action with the British Army during World War II.

409 Almost all the men wear the Nepalese national costume in this eastern Nepal hill town, where a market is taking place under the canopy of a pepil tree.

the preserving power of nature. In fact until recently the country harmoniously sustained *two* religions. Indeed, it has been called "a Hindu kingdom with a Buddhist heart."⁵ Within a few miles of Kathmandu City, in the historic and cultural center of Nepal, the Kathmandu valley—rich in fertile soil and advantageously positioned between two trade routes—is the famous Bodhnath Stupa. As a result of the Chinese occupation of Tibet, this has become the world's capital of Tibetan Buddhism.

Nepal has been strongly influenced by India in many ways, an influence reflected not only in its official religion, but also in its costume repertory.

Aside from the traditional clothing and accoutrements of the diverse ethnic groups [see 401, 407, 408], the national dress of Nepalese males clearly relates to similar clothing worn in India: white jodhpur-like pants, a loose white shirt, grey vest and a colorful, jaunty cap, the *topi* [409, 410]. Nepalese urban women are usually clad either in India's quintessential sari or, more frequently, the comfortable *salwar kameez* [411]—known in Nepal as the *kurta surwal*⁶—which includes a handsome shawl [412].

410 The *topi*, the Nepalese man's cap that is typically worn in a jaunty manner. Height 5 in. (12.7 cm), diameter 10 in. (25.4 cm).

411 Two Nepalese women wearing the South Asian *salwar kameez* cross the Kathmandu Durbar Square.

412 A multicolored hand-loomed cotton scarf from the eastern part of Nepal; its distinctive palette and decorative patterns are uniquely Nepalese. Length 70 in. (177.8 cm), width 13 in. (33 cm).

413 A 1904 photograph of Ugyen Wangchuck—who became the first king of Bhutan in 1907—with his entourage. The future ruler is wearing Bhutanese boots and a robe, the *go*, probably made of wild silk, that closely resembles the Tibetan *chuba*. On his head is the "raven crown," a reference to the legendary bird said to have guided the path of the warrior monk credited with unifying Bhutan, Shabdrung Ngawang Namgyel.

BHUTAN

Bhutan is the last of the Himalayas' independent Buddhist kingdoms. Only here—in a tiny, mountainous, forested country southeast of the Tibetan plateau [see Map 21]—is Vajrayana/Tantric Buddhism still practiced as a state religion.

This remote, landlocked kingdom managed to sustain a feudal, medieval existence into the mid-20th century, holding the world at bay while its tempo of life continued much as it had for centuries. Bhutanese traders regularly moved north across the mountain passes into Tibet, carrying cloth, spices, borax, grains and yak tails and returning with salt, wool and sometimes herds of yaks. The takeover of Tibet by the Chinese in the 1950s broke Bhutan's tranquil isolation. Fortunately, aided both by its formidable geography and its leaders' consistent wariness, it has managed to survive with its civic and religious institutions and its national identity still intact.

414 Bhutanese men, women, and children in their best *go* (the men's robe) and *kira* (the women's wrapped dress), as well as monks clad in their maroon robes, are all among the throng at a special festival in the capital, Thimphu. The wearing of the ritual white *knabné*, the men's shoulder cloth, and the *rachu*, the women's shoulder cloth, is imperative on such ceremonial occasions. Note that the children are dressed in miniature versions of adult apparel.

Bhutan's Tibetan Buddhist history reaches back to the 8th century A.D. By the 17th century a theocratic regime ruled the entire country. In 1907 a monarchy was established to replace religious rule: the official robes of this monarch are all but identical to those worn by Tibetan royalty [413; see 402]. Official edict has also decreed that Bhutanese traditional dress be worn by all subjects [414].

Men and boys wear a voluminous robe, the *go*, which is identical in structure to the floor-length Tibetan *chuba* and, like it, is also worn over a long-sleeved shirt that provides the garment's contrasting turned-back cuffs. However, the shortened *go* is worn in a very different manner to the long Tibetan *chuba*. The Bhutanese garment is wrapped around the body in a unique manner and then secured in place [415, 416].

Prior to 1900, a now-archaic type of female garment, the *kushung* tunic [417], was worn in north, central and eastern Bhutan.[7] This tunic not only had a different shape to that of the *kira* (see p. 257), it used objects from daily life as decorative motifs—for example, sacred thunderbolts, charm boxes and elaborately shaped butter offerings.[8]

415 Diagrams illustrating how the Bhutanese *go* is worn. A man puts on the floor-length robe—which, like the Tibetan *chuba*, is quite voluminous—over a loose shirt that will provide the contrasting, turned-back cuffs of the robe. After lining up the seams of the garment on both sides, the man raises the robe to the lower edge of his knees and securely belts it in place. He then blouses the front of the *go* so as to form a pouch—within which personal items can be stored—and pulls the back down over the belt. In recent decades, the *go* has been worn with knee socks and Western shoes.

417 A pre-1900 Bhutanese woman's tunic, the *kushung*, an archaic type of garment no longer woven or worn. These supplementary-weft, patterned tunics are now used only for special rituals and to adorn ancestor figures in local temples. The motifs that decorate the *kushung* often depict actual ceremonial objects. Length 36 in. (91.4 cm), width 53½ in. (136 cm).

416 Examples of the Bhutanese man's robe, the *go,* a 17th-century innovation introduced by Shabdrung Ngawang Namgyel. When the garment is laid out in this flat manner, it resembles the Tibetan *chuba,* but the Bhutanese manner of wearing it—tightly belted and raised to the knees—is decidedly different.

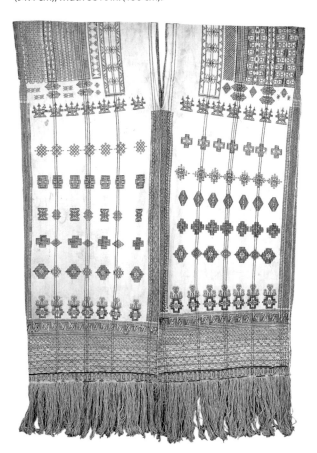

419 (opposite) A diagram showing how the *kira* is worn over a petticoat and long-sleeved blouse. After wrapping the handwoven outer garment under her right arm, a woman secures it with a pin or brooch at the corner of each shoulder. After adjusting and belting the *kira*, she puts on a jacket, usually made of imported Chinese silk brocade, which she then folds back to create contrasting cuffs by using the sleeves of her blouse.

418 Young women are seen here attired in their best ornate dress, the *kira,* which they may put on only once or twice a year. Their fancy jackets are constructed of silk brocade from Hong Kong.

Underneath their handwoven cotton *kiras* they wear bright, long-sleeved cotton or silk blouses which provide the contrasting material for their turned-back cuffs. These girls have casually—somewhat

irreverently—draped their red ceremonial shoulder cloths, the *rachu,* around their necks. Later these ritual scarves will have to be properly placed over the left shoulder.

Women and girls today wear a wraparound dress, the *kira* [418] over a petticoat and a long-sleeved undergarment which provides the contrasting turned-back cuffs worn over the silk brocade jacket that goes on top [419]. The material for these jackets comes from China, but no longer directly. Sometimes the cloth is sent from Hong Kong via Bangkok into Bhutan; other times it comes from Hong Kong via Nepal and then on into Bhutan.

The *kira* is secured at the shoulders with long pins or twin brooches that are attached with ornamental necklaces [420]. Some of these fasteners are made of silver or silver alloys; the most elaborate are of delicately carved gilt with inlays of turquoise or coral.

Handwoven *kiras* represent some of the most beautiful and also technically sophisticated textiles known in South Asia [421]. These intricate weavings are often worn with their pattern bands placed horizontally around the body [see 418]; at other times they are placed vertically. Each of the dresses is composed of three joined panels whose rows of design motifs are deliberately never matched up perfectly.[9]

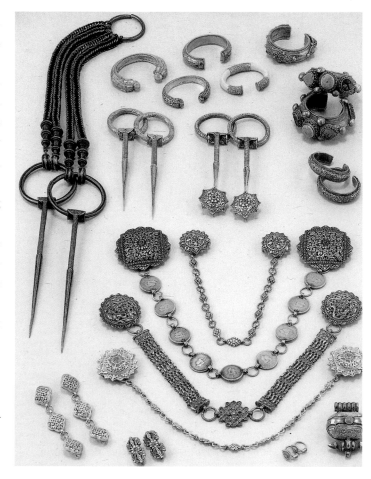

420 (left) The most important items of Bhutanese jewelry are the women's dress fasteners. Originally they were long pins, the simplest made of bamboo. Later, fasteners became more elaborate, with delicate carvings and insets of semi-precious stones. Earrings and finger rings are also favored by Bhutanese women.

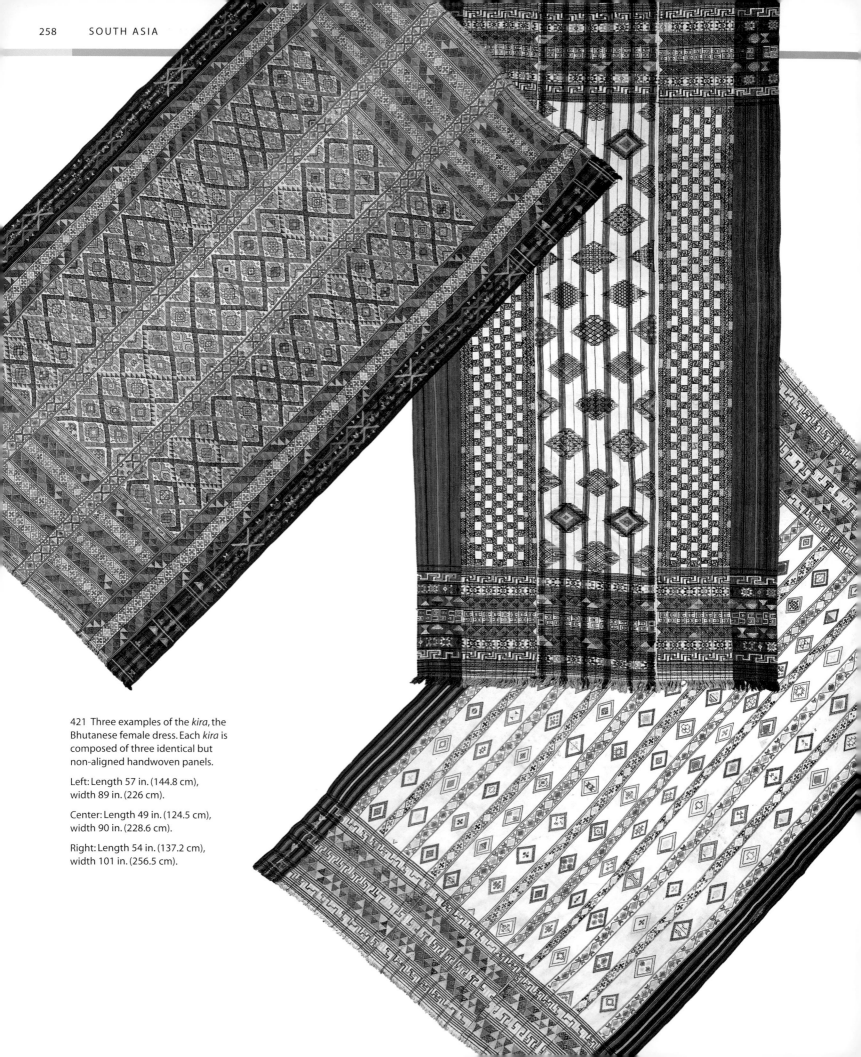

421 Three examples of the *kira*, the
Bhutanese female dress. Each *kira* is
composed of three identical but
non-aligned handwoven panels.

Left: Length 57 in. (144.8 cm),
width 89 in. (226 cm).

Center: Length 49 in. (124.5 cm),
width 90 in. (228.6 cm).

Right: Length 54 in. (137.2 cm),
width 101 in. (256.5 cm).

For inclement weather most Bhutanese today wrap up in plastic sheets or purchased raincoats. Older people, however, are sometimes still seen wearing handwoven, woolen raincloaks [422, 423].

Hats, or headcoverings in general, are not encountered in Bhutanese urban areas. In the country, however, both men and women are often seen wearing a flat, rain-resistant hat of woven bamboo [424; see also 422].

422 A shepherd from the Bumthang valley of eastern Bhutan wears a handwoven, woolen raincloak draped around his shoulders and secured at the front with cloth ties or a pin. On his head rests a flat rain hat made of woven bamboo.

423 A Bhutan man's wool raincloak from the Bumthang area. Such handwoven garments usually combine colorful floral designs with alternate bands of geometric motifs. Length 50$\frac{1}{2}$ in. (128.3 cm), width 48$\frac{1}{2}$ in. (123.2 cm).

424 A Bhutanese rain hat constructed of bamboo. Such flat, handwoven headcoverings are often worn by country people. Height $\frac{1}{2}$ in. (1.27 cm), diameter 13 in. (33 cm).

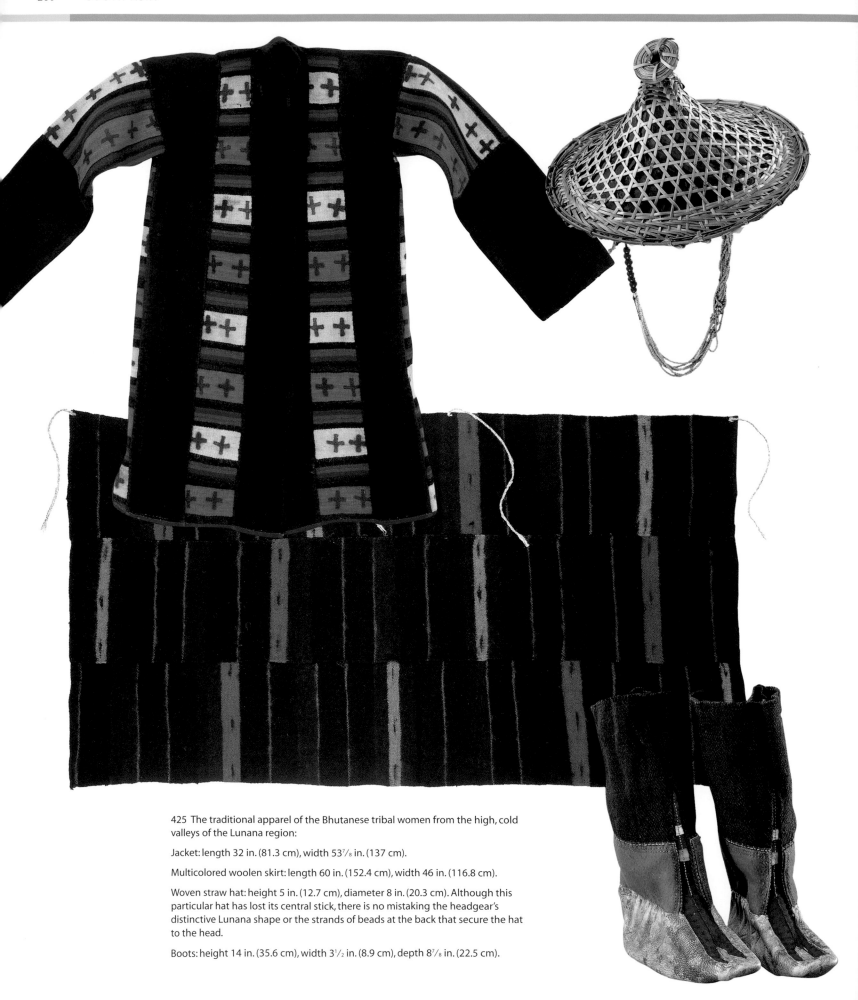

425 The traditional apparel of the Bhutanese tribal women from the high, cold valleys of the Lunana region:

Jacket: length 32 in. (81.3 cm), width 53⁷⁄₈ in. (137 cm).

Multicolored woolen skirt: length 60 in. (152.4 cm), width 46 in. (116.8 cm).

Woven straw hat: height 5 in. (12.7 cm), diameter 8 in. (20.3 cm). Although this particular hat has lost its central stick, there is no mistaking the headgear's distinctive Lunana shape or the strands of beads at the back that secure the hat to the head.

Boots: height 14 in. (35.6 cm), width 3¹⁄₂ in. (8.9 cm), depth 8⁷⁄₈ in. (22.5 cm).

Secular men wear their hair cut short, in the Western manner, whereas monks shave their heads [see 414]. Bhutanese women and girls wear their hair short, the exception being aristocratic women who wear their long hair in a variety of fashionable Western styles.

Bhutanese men and boys wear knee-length stockings and Western shoes with their official *go* robes [see 414]. Women and girls wear either Western-type black shoes, open sandals, or rubber flip-flops [see 418].

The wearing of ceremonial scarves—the *knabné* ritual shoulder cloth for men, the red *rachu* for women—is *de rigueur* on special occasions [see 414]. For males who are not of the aristocracy, the sash is white; for men from the military it is black; only the king and chief abbot are entitled to wear the special, yellow silk shoulder cloth.

Although all Bhutanese are required to wear the nation's traditional dress for public functions (for example, school attendance, official games, work in banks, offices and as tour guides), an exception is made for such tribal groups as the hardy people of the Lunana region who live in the high valley of Laya, far, far up in the Himalayas [425, 426]. Their distinctive woolen clothing is unique to Bhutan.

426 A tribal woman from Bhutan's remote Lunana region, a land of extremely high valleys where—during the brief summer months—the area's hearty herders live in black tents made of yak hair while their herds graze in the mountain meadows. The woman wears her tribe's distinctive woolen clothing and woven straw hat with central stick.

6

SOUTHEAST ASIA

SOUTHEAST ASIA saw the arrival of *Homo erectus* (Java Man) over a million years ago, at the time when the sea level was 655 feet (200 m) lower than it is today. When modern man—*Homo sapiens*— appeared some 100,000 years ago, the post-glacial seas had risen to subdivide the area into mainland and islands, some very large. The principal geographic features of the mainland are vast cultural-highway river systems such as the Irrawaddy, the Red and the Mekong, separated by a series of mountain ranges. In most cases, the lowland flood plains are inhabited by a politically dominant majority and the highlands are home to various minority groups. In the island realm, this lowland/upland cultural divide also exists. Some regional coherence is afforded Southeast Asia by shared weather patterns: all of the area lies in the tropics, resulting in a hot, wet world with— originally—an abundance of evergreen rainforests. By the 4th century B.C. modern man had developed settled, stratified societies of skilled farmers, metalworkers and sailor-traders. Southeast Asia, located pivotally between East Asia and the rest of the world, has long been a magnet for international trade, resulting in external political and economic forces repeatedly crashing their way through the area. From the Age of Discovery's European spice trade, to the Colonial-Industrial Age's demand for tin, rubber and oil, to the Cold War's frontline struggle between the Communist and capitalist worlds, Southeast Asians have repeatedly had to adapt to foreign cultures, technologies and philosophies while still maintaining their own values based on protecting the rights of communities over those of individuals.

MAINLAND

427 A young Akha woman standing at the entrance to her village, located on Burma's borderlands with China, Laos and Thailand. The rural villages of Mainland Southeast Asia often consist of silt houses with broad palm/grass-thatch roofs, woven bamboo walls and wooden pilings that raise the living quarters above the ground. The woman wears her group's striking headdress, which resembles a helmet. It is made of rows of heavy silver baubles, interspersed with beads, sewn on a bamboo cap. The woman's red and black leggings serve to protect her from leeches.

From early times, Mainland Southeast Asia[1] has been a magnet for foreign traders who came in search of exotic goods: rhinoceros horn for dagger handles and aphrodisiacs, rhinoceros skin for armor, deerskin for parchment; elephant tusks, tortoise shells, pearls, rubies, jade, coral, peacock and kingfish feathers for ornamentation; forest dye stuffs for coloring cloth, as well as aromatic sandalwood for creating *objets d'art*. Today international merchants continue to be drawn to the area, now seeking Industrial Age riches: tin, rubber, oil and heroin.

Two fundamental aspects of Mainland Southeast Asia's evolution are of particular note. The first is the important role played by rice. Current evidence indicates that it was initially cultivated some 8,000 years ago in China's Yangtze River Valley.[2] Thanks to the subsequent development of high-yield, wet-rice cropping along Mainland Southeast Asia's swampy riversides and in irrigated banked fields, the area was able to support population densities a hundred times greater than those of the indigenous hunter-gatherers. The result of this early flowering of agriculture, coupled with a growing population, was the early appearance of the Bronze Age; by 1500 B.C. bronze bracelets, spear points and axes were being produced. By 500 B.C. the bronze-working artisans of the Dong-Son culture of northern Vietnam were casting and transporting huge, elaborately decorated bronze drums throughout Island Southeast Asia, evidence of an early, complex trade network.[3]

To some extent, the evolution of prehistoric textile production in Mainland Southeast Asia can also be traced. Various processed fibers have been found in archaeological excavations, although there is no reliable way of relating them to specific groups. However, early indications of weaving—ca. 2500 B.C.—have been found in northern Vietnam and there is linguistic evidence for the word "loom" that goes back 4,000 years in some Southeast Asian cultures. In addition, Thailand mortuary evidence dating to 700–500 B.C.

reveals that silk, hemp, cotton, banana and asbestos fibers were used. There is also clothing information found on early statues and sculptures from Thailand's Davaravati Period, 6th to 9th centuries A.D., which show individuals wearing a long cloth that wrapped around the waist and reached to below the ankles. Neither a blouse nor shirt were worn over the upper body, although women did drape a strip of cloth across their shoulders.[4]

The combined prehistoric evidence suggests that the same style of female dress—with the later addition of cut-and-sewn tailored garments for the upper body, apparel repeatedly introduced by a series of conquerors—has continued on the mainland from early times into the present day [428]. This is a particularly impressive continuity in the light of the area's repeated exposure to outside influences.

Mainland Southeast Asia [Map 22], located between India and China, has always been well positioned for attracting foreign trade as well as for absorbing its powerful crosscurrents. The region's major cultural influences have been threefold: India's Hindu and Buddhist beliefs; China's economic and political clout; and Europe's commercial and colonial domination. A major geographical influence on the contiguous mainland territories[5]—China's Yunnan province, Burma (also known as Myanmar), Thailand, Cambodia, Laos, Vietnam—is the Mekong River, which descends from its headwaters on the windswept plateaux of Himalayan Tibet to flow 3,000 miles (4,800 km) down to culminate in South Vietnam's huge delta, where the river's now-swollen waters merge with the South China Sea.

Along the Mekong live an assortment of peoples speaking a range of Tai languages: the Thai, Lao and other Tai-speaking groups make up a significant portion of the mainland's population. The over-arching Tai-Kadai language family probably originated just south of the Yangtze River (Chiang Jiang) in present-day China. Over the past 2,000 years Tai speakers have migrated south, following along hill ridges and river valleys, paths of least geographic resistance. Today Tai speakers form a majority in the Kingdom of Thailand and the Laos People's

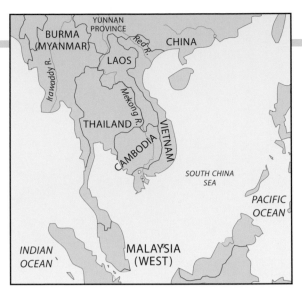

Map 22 Mainland Southeast Asia, divided by a system of vast rivers separated by a series of mountain ranges, is a land of lowland political dominance and highland minority tribes.

Democratic Republic, as well as constituting strategically situated minorities in the Socialist Republic of Vietnam, the Union of Myanmar (Burma) and Yunnan Province of the People's Republic of China, Mekong-adjacent entities all.

Along the course of the Mekong the influence of invaders and intruders is evident. Whether Chinese, British or French—or the Americans who so disastrously followed the French—it has been a foreign presence that has largely underpinned the political course of events in 20th-century Southeast Asia, mostly for the worst. Nowhere is this more pronounced than in Yunnan Province.

Ethnically, geologically and climatically, Yunnan is the most diverse of China's provinces, stretching from the cold southern end of the Tibetan plateau to the humid, torpid tropics of Burma, Laos and Vietnam.

428 In Burma, the least Westernized of Mainland Southeast Asia's countries, national dress is mandated. Both women and men wear a *longyi*, an ancient-style wraparound tubular skirt that reaches to the ankles for women and to mid-calf for men, together with a modest blouse or shirt.

429 A depiction in Shitthaung Pagoda, Mrauk-U, Burma, of 17th-century aristocratic Burmese women wearing ankle-length skirts, breastcloths and shoulder shawls.

Here ancient and secluded non-Chinese kingdoms thrived into the 20th century, as the western reaches of the province were settled by a mixture of Tai-speaking groups who had been forced out of their own homelands due to the northern Han Chinese increasingly moving in to colonize (see "China," p. 176). These Tai speakers moved down from southern China, bringing with them their most basic textile forms: clothing (women's skirts, men's loincloths) as well as utilitarian, decorative and ritual cloths. Evidence indicates that the Tai also brought a weaving technology superior to that existing in the regions to which they moved.

Today most Tai speakers in Thailand, Laos and Burma use a treadle-operated frame loom, a weaving apparatus that originated in China and was adopted in Mainland Southeast Asia perhaps as early as the 13th century A.D.[6] Evidence indicates Tai weavers have used this loom for centuries. However, originally the Tai probably had a far simpler, more transportable weaving device. As Mattiebelle Gittinger and H. Leedom Lefferts, Jr. note: "The core textile forms of the Thai people are all essentially flat, untailored items…that retain the original weft dimensions of the textiles as each was taken from the loom."[7] Evidence from these weft dimensions, as well as patterning techniques found on present-day Tai cloth, suggests the original weaving prototype may have been the far simpler, more easily transportable back-tension loom.[8]

Due to pressure exerted by the arrival of the Han Chinese, and a wish to preserve their ethnic customs and language, a variety of migrating peoples have continued to infiltrate the countries adjoining Yunnan Province. None of these bordering nations has a more diverse population than Burma.

BURMA

Burma has long been a bridge between peoples of the Indian subcontinent and those of East Asia. As a result, multiple traditions exist that document the country's past. This amalgam is apparent in the range of major languages spoken—Burmese, Hindi, Bengali, Chinese and a bit of English, all lingering evidence of Burma's history, conquest and trade. Today it is one of the world's least Western-influenced countries.

There is archaeological documentation for Burma's early cloth in the form of textile fragments from the impressively advanced Pyu kingdoms of the early Christian era, particularly from the Pyu site of Halin, 500–900 A.D. This evidence, together with contemporary Chinese accounts in the *New Tang History*, documents the Pyu people wearing cotton garments that wrapped about the waist, together with silken shawls. The Pyu, devout Buddhists, apparently did not themselves produce silk because of the Buddhist injunction against injury to life. Nonetheless, their court dress did include scarves of gauze silk,[9] probably imported from nearby Hindu India.

Extant 17th-century bas-reliefs show aristocratic Burmese women wearing long, wraparound skirts—known today as *longyi*—which open in front, together with breastcloths that appear to have been tucked in under the arms [429]. In addition, a shawl was worn diagonally over one shoulder.[10]

Today *longyi* are usually woven of cotton, a fiber particularly suited to the tropics. Until the mid-19th century, Burmese women utilized locally grown cotton to produce their family's clothing on the *yakan* treadle loom, a rectangular frame loom with a built-in seat for the weaver.[11] The local cotton (*Gossypium herbaceum*) was readily available to weavers all over the country but, as it turned out, such easy access was doomed.

After Britain annexed Burma as a province of British India, the colonizers determined that the local cotton had a limited commercial return, hence it was more profitable to encourage rice production over most other Burmese crops ("most," but not all; see opium discussed below). As a result, local cotton began to disappear and soon English-manufactured Manchester cotton cloth and Japanese silk and cotton were for sale in shops and bazaars throughout the country. As was the case in India, this availability of cheap, imported fabric put many local weavers out of business.

The British ruled Burma until the Japanese occupied the country in 1942. In 1945, after the English returned briefly, Burma was granted independence and in 1989 it was re-named Myanmar. Since then the country has been ruled by a succession of harsh military dictatorships. The official post-independence Burmese policy of self-sufficiency, limited foreign contact and the wearing of national dress created a renewed demand for locally woven textiles but, as in British times, handwoven textiles still continue to face stiff competition from Western cloth and clothing smuggled in from neighboring countries.

Because of Burma's geographic and political isolation—it was not opened to foreigners until 1982—the costumes of some of the more secluded minorities have changed little in a hundred years [see 427]. These are remote groups that have largely evolved outside the Burmese mainstream. Indeed, often the most obvious characteristics of Burma's hill people—many of whom also spill over into northern Thailand—are their colorful clothing [430] and unusual headgear and jewelry [431]. Each minority group, and subgroup, has its own range of styles and colors [432–434]—clothing that necessitates a great deal of time and effort to create. As a result, ornate new costumes now appear only for ceremonial occasions. The majority of the Burmese population, however, dutifully wear the mandated national dress.

Modern-day Burma abuts China's Yunnan Province to the northeast and is separated from Laos to the east only by the width of the Mekong. It is at this conjunction of Burma, Yunnan and Laos that the infamous Golden Triangle is located, the region that is now one of the world's largest producers of opium

430 The Sqaw Karen, speakers of a Tibeto-Burman language, live in both Burma and northern Thailand. Their distinctive handwoven cotton garments often display the Karens' skill at embroidering with seeds to create repeat patterns of contiguous geometric squares.

431 Burma's elusive Lahta people live in remote, rugged, pine-forested country along the northern Kayah State border with Shan State. Some older Lahta women wear brass coils from wrists to elbow, traditional ornamentation that can make movement of the forearms difficult.

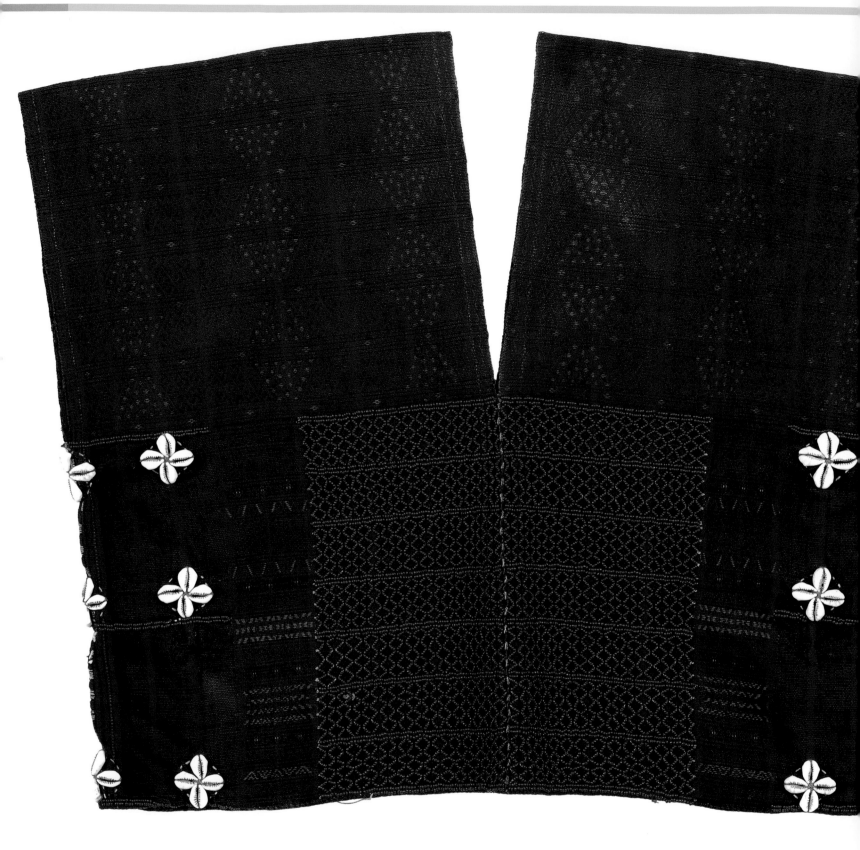

432 A woman's sleeveless blouse made of two pieces of handwoven cloth that incorporates a cotton base with silk supplementary-weft-weave patterning. Laytu peoples (Lemro River area), Chin State, Burma. The top portion of the blouse is covered in geometric designs; the center of the garment's lower portion is decorated with small red beads arranged in bands so as to create diamonds. Eighteen clusters of four cowry shells each complete the decoration. Length 16 1/8 in. (41 cm), width 20 5/8 in. (52.5 cm).

433 A woman's sleeveless tunic made from four pieces of handwoven cotton cloth sewn together vertically. Haka peoples, Chin State, Burma. The upper portion of the tunic is plain black with short bands of supplementary-weft geometric patterning in yellow and red silk thread; the lower section is solidly covered with silk supplementary-weft-weave geometric patterning. Rows of white beads and button clusters serve as added decoration. Length 32³/₈ in. (82.3 cm), width 31³/₈ in. (79.5 cm).

434 A *longyi* made of two joined pieces of silk cloth covered entirely in bands of supplementary-weft-weave geometric patterning. Haka peoples, Chin State, Burma. Length 55⅝ in. (141.3 cm), width 41⅛ in. (104.5 cm).

and its processed product, heroin.[12] Just as Burma is deeply involved in this lucrative trade, so too is neighboring Laos.

LAOS

Laotian farmers have found that opium poppies grow most productively in the alkaline soils of the northern Mekong watershed. The continued emphasis on this profitable crop reflects present-day Laos's long-time ranking as one of the poorest nations on earth. Such was not always the case. Before the arrival of the French in the mid-19th century, Laos was known as Lan Xang—"The Kingdom of a Million Elephants"— whose boundaries stretched into what is now northern Thailand. By the time the French arrived in 1886, however, it had become a land of subsistence farmers, few natural resources, a barter economy and a multiplicity of disaffected, non-Lao hill people.[13] The French always regarded Laos as a lesser adjunct to their most prized possession, Vietnam.

Landlocked Laos is geographically located in a vulnerable position, a pathway through which displaced peoples from India and China have long passed, searching for new areas in which to settle and, in so doing, introducing new religious concepts into a land that previously held mainly animistic beliefs. Today the predominant religion practiced in Laos— as in all of the mainland countries—is Theravada Buddhism, "the Way of the Elders," which emphasizes meditation. In the early mornings, saffron-robed Laotian monks can be seen, alms bowls in hand, patiently queuing up to receive food from devout locals eager to enhance their own karma through such offerings. Many of the monks are young Laos who will only briefly spend time in a *wat*—a Buddhist monastery/temple complex—and will then return to their secular lives [435].

Laos has one of the lowest population densities in Asia, with only 19 people per square kilometer. The majority of its inhabitants are sedentary, wet-rice

farmers who live in compact villages near their fields. These are a largely self-sufficient people. Most of the women are weavers who, until recently, raised their own cotton, tended their own mulberry trees, fed their own silkworms, and—prior to the arrival of synthetic dyes in the early 1970s—obtained their own natural dyes from the surrounding forest.

All Lao groups do resist-dyeing of yarns to create *ikat* patterning as well as supplementary-weft weaving to produce complex brocaded motifs. These intricate designs repeatedly appear on one of the defining aspects of Lao culture: the Tai speakers' tripartite skirts [436]. The motifs on these beautiful garments can indicate not only a person's age but also their marital and social status [437]. As the textile historian Mary F. Connors notes: "The majority of Lao cylindrical skirts are made with a separate waistband and hem piece attached to a narrow, main skirt piece. Human terms are used to describe parts of the skirt. The waist is called 'the head,' the main piece 'the body,' and the hem 'the foot.' This reflects Lao attitudes towards the human body and towards women, in particular their power. The head, especially the top of the head, is

435 A young monk stands beside a Buddhist temple in Luang Prabang. He wears his saffron robe in the customary manner, covering the left shoulder and arm. The garment is wrapped so that one edge, rolled, tucks under the left arm. Novice monks initially shave not only the head but the eyebrows as well.

436 (far left) This 1930s photo of two Lao women clearly shows the three-part structure typical of the skirts of Mainland Southeast Asia's Tai speakers. These garments are made by joining three separately woven pieces of cloth to form a tubular skirt that has a distinctive waistband, a contrasting center section and a differentiated lower border. Only rarely is this tripartite division ever created on a single piece of cloth.

437 (left) Three generations of Lao women attending a religious function. The colors and patterns on their tripartite skirts—the upper-third sections are all covered by the women's blouses—reflect age, marital status and social position.

438 (right) Two Lao women wearing ritual shoulder cloths that are securely wrapped on the body in the manner worn for 19th-century shamanic healing ceremonies. The women also wear traditional double-folded tripartite skirts.

considered the source of personal power. The feet are considered impure and should be avoided. Thus, skirts should clearly indicate top and bottom. No Lao wants to put around the waist material that may have touched the feet. A formal waistband and decorative hem take care of that problem."[14]

The traditional female costume also includes a contrasting shoulder cloth. Only in Vientiane, the capital, is it increasingly common for women to follow the fashionable Western concept of coordinating the colors and designs of a skirt with its bordering hem and accompanying shoulder cloth. These latter garments served a more vital function in the past.

In 19th-century Lao healing practices, shoulder cloths played an important role, wrapped about the torso in such a way that a cloth would not fall off in the course of a ceremony [438, 439]. Other extremely important textiles for such rituals were those worn by the shamans themselves, cloths that set them apart from ordinary people [440].

Returning to the world of the layman, when Lao men are at home they often wear a simple, rectangular

cloth—the *pha* sarong—wrapped around the waist, its color varying with age: the young wear bright plaids, older men wear blue, black or brown plaids [441]. (It is interesting that the Lao do not consider plaids or stripes to be "patterned." It is only women who appear in "patterned" clothes, that is cloth woven with colorful designs, many abstracted from the natural world.) Men also wear the striped *pha khoma*, the indispensable male cloth that originally served as a loincloth but is now used for everything from an arm sling or a headwrap to a baby carrier.

In the past, there was an additional component to the overall Lao male "look;" up to the 1950s heavy tattooing of men's thighs was quite common [442; see also 441]. Indeed, a young man was not considered mature enough to marry until his thighs had been heavily ornamented. Mary F. Connors suggests this painful tattooing may have compensated for the plainness of Lao male attire.[15]

In 1953, concurrent with the cessation of thigh tattooing, Laos gained full independence. Unfortunately, during the "American War"—as the late 1960s–mid-

441 A lowland Lao man wearing a *pha* sarong, together with a striped *pha khoma* (shoulder cloth), here used as a sling. His heavily tattooed thighs were a body decoration commonly seen up to the 1950s.

442 A Lao mural painting from a Chiang Mai temple depicts a young man with his loincloth tied high on the hips, the better to reveal his heavily tattooed thighs.

439 A healing cloth woven with a cotton warp/silk weft and worn by a supplicant seeking aid in shamanic rituals. The complex motifs at either end of the textile relate to spirits that help a shaman in ridding the body of evil forces. Length 98 in. (249 cm), width 18½ in. (47 cm).

440 A cotton warp/silk weft cloth worn by a shaman when engaged in a healing ritual. The textile's dense patterning, which contains a mirror-image repeat, is depicted in a discontinuous supplementary-weft weave. The highly abstracted images encoded in the cloth's design represent mythical creatures upon whom the shaman calls during a trance. This textile consists of two pieces joined together, perhaps indicating that it has been shortened in the course of repair. Length 70⅞ in. (180 cm), width 17⅜ in. (44 cm).

1970s Vietnam conflict is referred to in Southeast Asia—Laos suffered tremendous damage as the result of the United States conducting a covert series of carpet bombings to destroy the Ho Chi Minh trail. This hidden network of mountain paths, named for North Vietnam's Communist leader, ran north through Laos and Cambodia, and was used as a supply line along which the Chinese funneled military equipment to the North Vietnamese guerrilla fighters, the Viet Cong.

The devastation resulting from the continual US assault led to the destabilization of Laos society and the subsequent rise to power of the authoritarian, Communist-sympathizing Pathet Lao government. A similar scenario took place in neighboring Cambodia.

CAMBODIA

The government that controlled Cambodia from 1975 to 1979 carried out what amounted to a nationwide auto-genocide. The soldiers of Pol Pot's army, the Khmer Rouge, had roots deep in the culture of guerrilla warfare as well as a ferocious rural Communist ideology. They symbolized their Khmer heritage by wearing a red and white checked scarf, a *krama* [443]—the only concession made to the menacing severity of the black shirts and trousers.[16] It is interesting that the Viet Cong guerrilla fighters of North Vietnam also wore signature checked scarves, but in black and white [444].

By the end of the Pol Pot regime some two million of the population—as well as a good part of the collective folk and craft knowledge of Cambodian society—had been obliterated.[17] That such an outrage could occur within the same culture that had earlier created one of the world's most beautiful temple complexes makes the tragedy even more devastating.

The brick and stone temples of the Angkor kingdoms that reigned from the 9th to the 14th centuries are the spiritual and historical touchstone of Cambodian civilization, an empire which at one time spread across what is now southern Vietnam, Laos and central Thailand. The ancient Cambodians—who practiced Hinduism before 1300 A.D. and then adopted both

443 (left) The signature red and white checked scarf worn by Cambodia's young Khmer Rouge soldiers during Pol Pot's four-year reign of terror.

444 (right) The signature black and white scarf of North Vietnam's guerrilla fighters, the Viet Cong.

Mahayana and Theravada Buddhism—are depicted on carvings in the temple complex clad in distinctive costume forms, some of which have continued into the present day.[18]

Various styles of draping the ancient Cambodian hipwrapper, the *sampot*, are still worn by both sexes and at all levels of society. These traditional garments are fashioned from flat, rectangular lengths of uncut cloth approximately 19¾ inches (50 cm) wide. Some of the textiles are wrapped in the *sampot chawng kbun* style:[19] the cloth is wound around the lower body by bundling the two end panels together at the front, then pleating or rolling them into a bundle that is passed between the legs and secured at the back [445]. Women, who drape their hipwrappers in this same way [446], also often wear tubular skirts, the *sampot samloy*, or "hipwrappers worn tube-skirt style" [447], which have intricate, lattice-like designs, many with contrasting borders [448]. These richly patterned silk hipcloths are often worn with white lace blouses and the *krama*, the almost ubiquitous Southeast Asian shoulder shawl.

Cambodia's distinctive hipwrapper apparel differs markedly from that of neighboring Vietnam, where today the great majority of the affluent populace wear Western clothing.

445 A team of Cambodian rowers awaiting their turn to compete in the national Water Festival, 1999. All wear the traditional *sampot chawng kbun* hipwrapper style, together with their sponsor's T-shirts. Judging from the company logo, their sponsor may be one of the region's silk cooperatives.

446 (below left) Cambodian girls wearing their silk hipcloths in the *sampot chawng kbun* style. In the ceremony depicted here, the various-colored hipwrappers represent the days of the week; a specific color is required for each as a mark of respect for the deity of that particular day.

447 (below) Cambodian women also drape their traditional hipwrappers in the *sampot samloy* manner—as a tubular skirt—worn here with white lace blouses and patterned shoulder shawls.

448 Three Cambodian silk hipwrappers illustrating characteristic colors and motifs.

Left: length 34¼ in. (87 cm), width 33⅝ in. (85.5 cm).

Center: length 119⅜ in. (303 cm), width 37⅜ in. (95 cm).

Right: length 74⅜ in. (189 cm), width 32½ in. (82.8 cm).

"only now [2002] is such unification finally taking place, though not in the way Ho Chi Minh envisioned. This [amalgamation] has come about as a result of capitalist, not socialist, economics: since the mid-80s, all three of Indochina's countries have become converts to private enterprise."[21]

Unlike Laos and Burma, Vietnam does not have large minority populations. According to some sources 85% of the country's inhabitants are ethnic Vietnamese.[22] However, the country does include a number of small groups whose clothing reflects their own particular history and evolution.

449 A Vietnamese fruit vendor wears the *non la*—the traditional, woven palm-leaf conical hat—with her Chinese-style jacket, wide pajama-like pants and indispensable balance pole.

450 Vietnamese teenagers, all wearing white *ao dai*, bicycle through city streets on their way to school.

451 A group of Flower Hmong women in the Sapa market in northern Vietnam, near the Chinese border. Their impressive traditional clothing combines *batik*-created patterns with embroidery and appliqué.

VIETNAM

The largest nation on the Indochina Peninsula is Vietnam. For over a millennium the mainstream apparel of Vietnam was that of China, long the strongest cultural influence in all of Asia. Today the everyday dress of the non-affluent majority is a combination of Chinese and Western garb, often worn with the *non la*, the woven, palm-leaf conical hat seen throughout the rural areas as well as on city vendors and some students [449]. The other non-Western garment associated with Vietnam is the *ao dai*, the long, tight, vari-colored dress with high slits up each side that is worn over pajama-like pants [450].[20]

Vietnam shares a colonial history with Cambodia and Laos, all having been subjugated by the French in the latter half of the 19th century for purposes of trade and profit. It was to take thirty years of warfare—first against the French, then against the United States—for Vietnam finally to become an independent nation state. The Communist leader Ho Chi Minh also had hoped to liberate and unite the entire Indochina Peninsula but, as travel writer Michael Buckley notes,

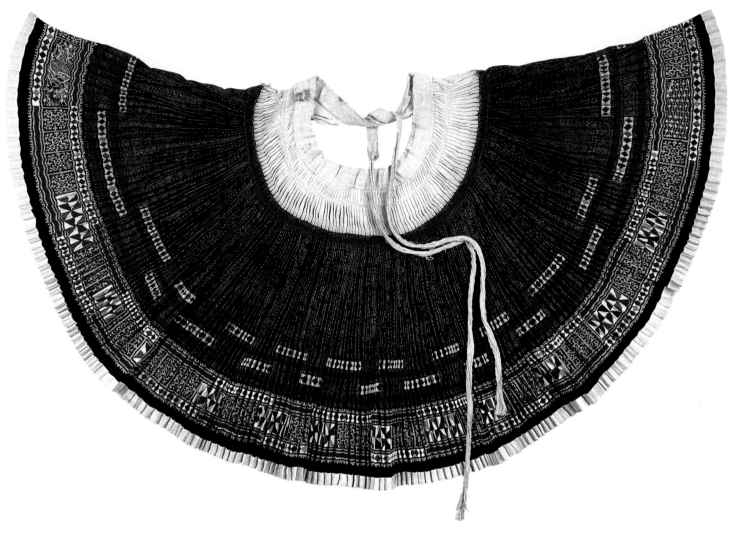

452 A Flower Hmong pleated skirt (see detail, left) that combines an overall repeat pattern of hand-dyed, indigo *batik* with a colorful border of geometric, cross-stitched embroidery augmented by meticulously positioned appliqué.

453 A tripartite skirt woven in a Black Tai community;
the group's name reflects the predominant color of their
clothing. The skirt's waist, or "head," is woven of brown cotton;
the central "body" section is dark blue and brown patterned
with white stripes; the "foot" has silk, supplementary warp
and weft designs in bright pink, green, yellow and white.
Length 34³⁄₈ in. (87.5 cm), width 24 in. (61 cm).

454 A Bahnar skirt constructed in one panel to which a
fringed waist sash (white with brown designs) has been
handstitched. The skirt is indigo with designs in morinda.
Handstitched to the center is a long vertical "pocket" that
has no opening, made from an additional piece of cloth.
Length 35⁵⁄₈ in. (90.5 cm), width 99³⁄₈ in. (252.3 cm).

455 The short blouse of a Bahnar woman
from central Vietnam displays designs created
from a combination of natural cotton thread
together with yarn dyed with plant material—
indigo and morinda. Length 15¹⁄₂ in. (39.5 cm),
width 45⁷⁄₈ in. (116.6 cm).

In the far northwest of the country live over fifty minority groups in the mountainous border areas where Vietnam meets Yunnan Province. Among these diverse peoples live the Flower Hmong [451], a group well known for their beautiful textiles, many of which combine carefully controlled *batik* dyeing together with colorful embroidery and meticulous appliqué work [452]. It must be noted that the geographic distribution of the various Hmong groups[23] is not restricted to the present-day borders of Vietnam: these widely dispersed people are also found in the northern areas of both Laos and Thailand. There are also much larger populations of closely related peoples, such as the Miao, across the border in China, where the true affinities of the Hmong lie (see "China," p. 177).

Other minority groups include Tai speakers. In small, rural communities, Black Tai weavers produce tripartite skirts in patterns distinctive to their own communities [453].

In Vietnam's central highlands live the Bahnar people, whose dialect belongs to the Mon-Khmer language group. The Bahnar are farmers who practice slash-and-burn agriculture. The women weave their cotton into garments whose subdued colors reflect the muted palette often associated with Island Southeast Asian textiles [454, 455]. These blouses and skirts are colored with natural plant dyes.

In contrast to the subtle tonalities of Bahnar textiles is the costume repertory of the Yao people of northern Vietnam who produce shaman garments that are both richly decorated and mystically multifaceted [456]. Shamanic vestments are always of special interest and complexity (see "Mongolia," pp. 128–129). This is particularly evident in Yao robes worn while performing religious ceremonies to guide the souls of the deceased to other realms [457]. These colorful, sleeveless sheaths often display embroidered designs of waves, dragons, a moon, a tiger face and a Chinese character signifying "longevity".

456 A shaman's cotton and silk veil worn over the face while performing a ceremony. The garment's brown and beige raised designs are woven on a dark blue ground. Further ornamentation is provided by short strands of blue beads terminating in brown and white silk tassels. Length 23⅞ in. (60.5 cm), width 16⅝ in. (42.5 cm).

457 (opposite) A Yao shaman's sleeveless tunic or vest embroidered with images that aid in the successful completion of a ritual. Length 37⅛ in. (94.5 cm), width 25⅛ in. (64 cm).

THAILAND

Given Southeast Asia's key strategic location astride the Pacific and Indian oceans, the demise of the European empires left the mainland exposed to the full impact of the larger Cold War, which American involvement in Vietnam turned into a very Hot War indeed. This escalation was particularly true in the greater Indochina area. By 1975 the region was divided along the so-called "Bamboo Curtain:" Vietnam, Laos and Cambodia on the Communist side, Thailand in the capitalist camp.[24]

Prior to 1939, Thailand was known throughout the world as Siam, a nation unique among Southeast Asian states in that it managed to remain uncolonized throughout the 19th and 20th centuries. There was, of course, a price paid for that independence. By the end of the 19th century, Siam had lost over 300,000 square miles (485,000 km²) of territory to the European imperialists, becoming a buffer zone between the British and French spheres of interest, an uncomfortable position to sustain. As was noted at the time, Siam either had "to swim upriver and make friends with the crocodile [the French] or swim out to sea and hang on to the whale [the British]." In swimming with the whale, Siam is said to have skillfully avoided the greater evil of becoming crocodile fodder.[25]

In a similar vein, realistic Thailand accommodated Japan during the Pacific War and the United States in the Cold War. This is not to say that Thailand's rulers aped the West. A constitutional monarchy was retained based on the British model but there was no introduction of similar bicameral parliamentary institutions; it was made clear that although Siam's government was *for* the people, it was not *by* the people. With adept diplomacy, and by playing off one European power against another, Thailand managed to obtain many of the material benefits of colonialism while remaining independent, an anti-Communist oasis in the midst of strife-torn Southeast Asia.[26]

Although Thailand has made remarkable economic, scientific and technological progress in the past fifty years, in its rural villages and hamlets—where the majority of the people live—some handcrafted cloth

458 (opposite above)
A woman's cotton blouse from the Karen people of northern Thailand. The garment is constructed of two cotton panels with carefully embroidered designs in red and yellow applied on a black ground. The blouse is also decorated with white seeds. Length 24³/₈ in. (62 cm), width 34⁵/₈ in. (88 cm).

459 (opposite below) This Tai tripartite cotton skirt has a hem/"foot" section decorated with long floats (not visible here, as they are on the inside of the garment). Sometimes such skirts are worn inside out to protect the floats, and also to demonstrate the complexity of their weaving. Length 34³/₈ in. (87.5 cm), width 26⁷/₈ in. (68.5 cm).

and clothing still continues to be made, as it has been for hundreds of years [458], and the traditional tripartite Tai skirt continues to be woven and worn [459, 460]—even if, incongruously, sometimes with an increasingly prevalent variety of loose, Western-style tailored shirts or jackets [461].

The continuity of traditional textile production has been encouraged by Thailand's constitutional monarchy which, although largely honorary, nonetheless is highly venerated, hence wields a surprising amount of influence. Her Highness Queen Sirikit's successful involvement with village weavers—to the point of having some of her own clothing made from their handiwork—as well as her encouragement for the preservation of historic Thai textiles and the reviving of both sericulture and silk weaving has been highly productive. This royal support has led to the establishment of artisans' cooperatives which permit contemporary handcrafted Thai textiles to reach the international market.[27]

460 Rural Thai women, some with silver offering dishes in hand, wear their traditional tripartite skirts as they pose before a temple.

461 A young Lao woman wears a traditional tripartite Tai skirt together with a modern-day, Western-style tailored shirt and jacket, the latter ornamented with a quintessentially American logo. Laos, January, 2004.

ISLAND

462 A young Balinese girl—resplendent in her Hindu island's sacred, double-*ikat geringsing* cloth and magnificent crown of real and gold flowers—takes part in a swing ceremony. Similar rites occur in Hindu India in connection with the coming of the monsoon season.

Island Southeast Asia is a maritime world surrounded by warm tropical seas whose predictable, moderate winds have long fostered both interregional and international trade. From earliest days, the history of this watery realm has been reflected in the many appellations it has engendered. To neighboring Asian seamen, the area was the *Nanyang,* the Southern Seas. For early Persian, Arab and Indian traders dependent on the monsoons to power their sails, the islands were the Lands Below the Winds. To the initial 16th-century European navigators, their compelling but amorphous destination was the Indies. For the 17th-/20th-century Dutch colonialists, their verdant island chain was the Girdle of Emeralds. To the incipient, mid-20th-century nation-state, the archipelago was Indonesia, a newly coined term with no pre-colonial precedent. But for connoisseurs of traditional weaving, this island world could well be termed "Texlandia," the archipelago from whence comes the greatest range of handcrafted cloth on the globe, textiles unsurpassed in their technical virtuosity and striking variety. This cornucopia of weavings not only reflects the diversity of Indonesia but also Island Southeast Asia's unifying, hands-on commitment to the beautification of cloth and clothing.

For hundreds of years the prize luring many of the world's seafaring merchants to the region was a group of exotic spices that, in earlier times, grew only on a few islands located in remote eastern Indonesia.[1] Europe's 16th-century search for the shortest route to these fabled Spice Islands was to change the course of history.

Apparently it was Hindu-Javanese traders who initially introduced nutmeg and mace to the international market. These aromatic spices first reached Europe about the 6th century A.D.[2] Given the lack of refrigeration in that meat-eating region, it is not surprising that the piquant condiments—the original purveyors of "good taste"—became increasingly popular. Unfortunately, their homelands were frustratingly distant. It was to take almost a thousand years before the West's understanding of oceanic navigation and sailing technology developed to the point where Europe's competitive push to find a shorter passage to the "Indies" touched off the Age of Discovery (in contrast, see "Oceania," p. 307). This period of intense exploration was the beginning of Europe's assault on the globe, the era that fostered the rise of European mercantile endeavors and the subsequent colonial empires that shaped the modern world.

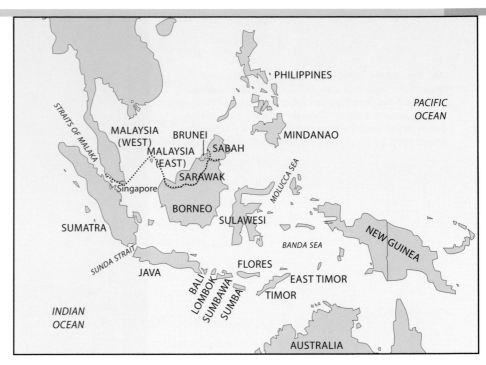

The Spice Islands are but a tiny part of the Indonesian archipelago made up of some 13,677 islands, more than 220 of which are volcanic, a part of the Pacific "Ring of Fire" [Map 23]. This longest of the world's archipelagos arches across the underside of Asia—stretching east from Sumatra almost 3,100 miles (4,990 km) to the coast of New Guinea—and contains a population of some 220 million, divided between some 350 diverse groups. The island chain includes a portion of the country of Malaysia, which is split between Mainland Southeast Asia and the states of Sabah and Sarawak on the island of Borneo.[3]

Throughout Island Southeast Asia the climate is uniformly tropical, resulting in a generally verdant environment providing wood, bamboo and palm but few grasslands; aside from buffalo, pigs and chickens, no livestock are raised. The islanders' diet consists mainly of fish, fruit, coconut and rice, the most important arable crop in both Indonesia and Malaysia. The high-yield, wet-rice production of these countries was, and is, dependent on a combination of extremely rich volcanic soils, an abundance of water, and manure from the water buffalo that fertilize the rice paddies while plowing or clearing the fields.

In the Indonesian archipelago, Java was the long-favored island because it was deemed the most habitable. During the Classical Period (A.D. 500–1500) Java entered its initial phase of economic growth based on the combination of an abundant rice supply and the Javanese ability to attract international shippers to local ports to buy spices. Prior to A.D. 1600, clove and nutmeg trees grew exclusively on the Moluccas Islands, but due to seasonal winds the spice islanders and international merchants were often kept apart. Through providential trans-shipments of the islanders' spices, the Javanese "maintained an effective stranglehold over this ever-expanding trade."[4]

It was also during the Classical Period that Buddhism, Hinduism and Islam spread throughout Southeast Asia. Buddhism became the primary religion of the mainland (see "Mainland Southeast Asia," p. 270), whereas Hinduism ultimately became firmly entrenched only in the Indonesian islands of Bali and Lombok. It was Islam that became the predominant faith of Island Southeast Asia, its ascendancy beginning after A.D. 1400 in the bustling port of Malaka, located on the south coast of the Malay peninsula.

Islam's subsequent diffusion to other parts of the Malay world probably resulted from the increasing presence of Indian traders in the Straits of Malaka. From that strategic location these Muslim merchants were able to monopolize the supply of spices they imported from north Javanese ports. Malaka grew increasingly rich to the point where even its ruler became a Muslim. There were significant gains to be made from royal conversion in a trading enclave such as Malaka: more Muslim merchants were attracted to an Islamic-controlled port. Further, the Muslim faith was accompanied by the Persian notion of kingship, a concept that appealed to Malaka's converted ruler because he now became a sultan, a far higher status than that of the mere rajas of surrounding ports.

Although there had long been merchants from many parts of the world trading in Island Southeast Asia, the Europeans who began to arrive in the 16th century proved to be a completely different breed, and a particularly formidable one. In contrast to traders from China, Persia or India, the Europeans came equipped with faster ships, more powerful weapons and, most importantly, government support for any and all profitable endeavors.

Map 23 Island Southeast Asia, showing the present-day countries of the Philippines: at the top of the map, Malaysia—West and East— situated to the northwest of the map's dotted line, and Indonesia, located to the southeast of the dotted line which reflects the 1824 treaty dividing Island Southeast Asia between Britain's colonies, now Singapore and Malaysia, and those of Holland, now Indonesia.

A clothing revolution took place in Indonesia after the 14th century when Islamic—and later European—traders began to flood the archipelago with elegant Indian weavings. Not that Indian cloths were something new to the islands; they had probably been imported for centuries but only for the nobility, who had the sole right to wear decorated clothing. Now, however, a textile democratization took place as a result of the spice trade which had an unprecedented impact on the range of cloth available to commoners. Traders discovered they could obtain valuable Indonesian spices—worth their weight in gold in some corners of the globe—in exchange for colorful Indian silks and printed cottons. The Indonesians, in turn, discovered they could obtain beautiful cloth in exchange for easily gathered cloves, nutmeg, pepper and fragrant sandalwood.[7]

For Indonesians, fine textiles have long carried a status that transcends that of mere clothing. Indeed, the islanders' weavings are a revered medium that still retains certain old and hallowed associations, reflecting power, protection and status as well as serving as ritual objects, gift-trade items, forms of accumulated wealth, and even as currency. The spinning and dyeing of yarns and the weaving of them into cloth has been regarded as symbolic of the process of creation and is generally an exclusively female function.

Short-staple cotton (i.e. cotton with short-length fibers) is indigenous to the region and closely associated in Indonesia with warp *ikat*, a traditional method of creating designs with warp threads that have been dyed before being woven. To create a desired pattern, certain areas of the thread are tied off with dye-resistant fibers so they cannot absorb the color [465]. All warp *ikats* are distinguished by the grouping of desired motifs into horizontal or vertical bands, a logical outcome of the warp-dyeing process. A simple back-tension loom is used for weaving warp *ikats*, as for all traditional Indonesian cloth [466]. There are two types of these looms depending on the structuring of their warps, some discontinuous, others continuous. In both cases, the tension of the warp is maintained by means of the strap or brace placed around the weaver as she sits on the ground.[8]

To appreciate the impressive diversity of Indonesian cloth it is helpful to consider each of the principal textile-producing islands in turn, starting at the westernmost end of the archipelago.

465 A Flores dyer-weaver carefully ties off sections of warp threads to protect them from absorbing color when immersed in a dye bath. The effect of this warp-*ikat* process is to create a predetermined pattern on the warps, a design that becomes apparent when the weft threads are subsequently woven into cloth. Flores, 1988.

SUMATRA

Sumatra is one of the largest of Indonesia's land masses and the most strategically placed, positioned almost as a guardian of the trade routes that circuitously wind throughout that insular world. Sumatra's advantageous location is reflected in the foreign influences apparent in many of its diverse textiles. Set along the Straits of Malaka, the island's various coastal regions have received Indian, Chinese, Javanese, Arab, Persian, Portuguese and Dutch traders for centuries. The result has been the incorporation of such new materials as silk, metallic thread, beads and mirrored metal as well as new designs, new dye recipes and new techniques.[9]

Songket—a supplementary-weft method of patterning cloth—is a prime example of an adopted foreign technique that reflects Sumatra's trade with Islamic merchants who dealt in Indian cloths woven with gold- and silver-covered threads. The Sumatran gold and silver *songket* cloths from Palembang [467], a prosperous Islamic coastal trading area, are a case in point, as are the shimmering, luxurious textiles made by the Minangkabau peoples of western Sumatra [468]. Coastal Palembang is also well known for its beautiful weft-*ikat* textiles [469].

The Lampung region of Sumatra's far south— a wealthy center of worldwide pepper trade—is known for the local women's *tapis*, beautiful cotton and/or silk sarongs heavily embroidered with metallic, silk or cotton threads [470, 471]; the art of embroidery probably entered Sumatra with early Chinese traders. The elegant Lampung *tapis* are only worn for special commemorative feasts held in conjunction with "life-crisis" rites and elaborate three- and four-day wedding celebrations.

The Lampung area is also famous for its ship cloths [472].[10] However, these textiles—impressive for their technical mastery, iconographic complexity and

466 A Flores weaver creates a *patola*-like textile on her back-tension loom. She controls the tension of the pre-patterned, warp-*ikat* threads by leaning back on the loom's strap or brace, which encircles her waist. Flores, 1991.

Clockwise from above:

467 A man's red and gold silk headcloth from the Palembang area of south Sumatra. The supplementary-weft method used to create this cloth's patterning is *songket*, a weaving technique originating in India and introduced into Sumatra by Muslim traders. Length 83⅝ in. (212.3 cm), width 31¼ in. (79.4 cm).

468 A shoulder cloth (detail, opposite left) from the Minangkabau area of west Sumatra. The shimmering end panel is woven with red-, green- and gold-wrapped threads; the lace trim is constructed of metallic, gold-wrapped thread. Length 113 in. (287 cm), width 20¼ in. (51.5 cm).

469 A woman's red and gold silk tube skirt, patterned using the weft-*ikat* technique for which Palembang is also well known. Length 28⅝ in. (72.5 cm), width 27⅞ in. (71 cm).

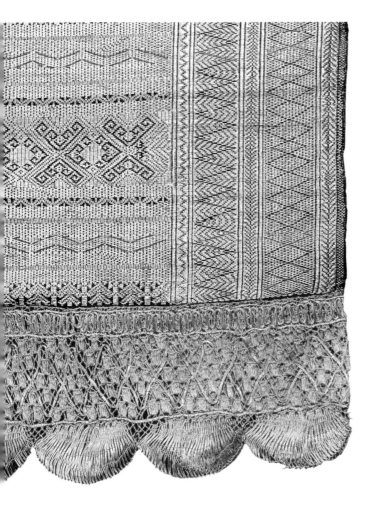

symbolic content—are used solely as ritual hangings and never as clothing.

The Batak, a highland group living in north-central Sumatra, also produce textiles with pronounced symbolism. Each of the Batak sub-groups has its own unique style of traditional cloth, the *ulos*. Perhaps the most famous are the *ulos ragidup*, dark textiles with white-patterned end panels [473, 474]. Though Western-style clothing replaced the *ragidup* in the 20th century, it nonetheless remains indispensable in a variety of ceremonial situations, and is sometimes seen today folded neatly on the shoulder of an individual otherwise dressed in Western clothes.

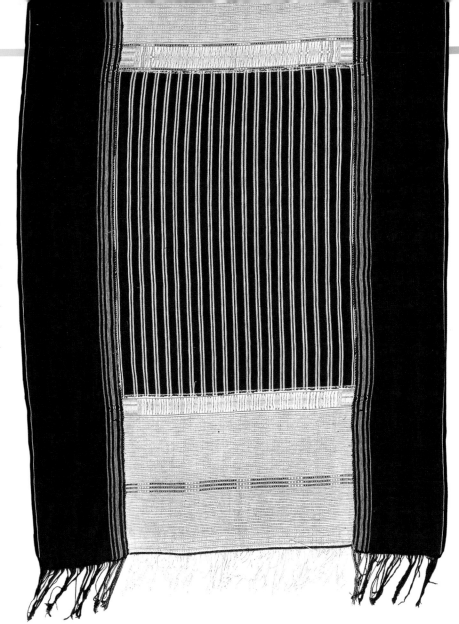

473 (right) A Batak ceremonial *ragidup* textile from highland north Sumatra. The cloth consists of three panels joined at two center seams: the middle, lighter panel is patterned with interlocking warps and with warp striping. Length 71³/₄ in. (182.2 cm), width 41¹/₂ in. (105.4 cm).

474 (below right) The Batak people of highland north-central Sumatra are known for their *ragidup* shawls. These dark textiles with their lighter, patterned end sections were once everyday wear but now appear only on ceremonial occasions or when presented as ritual gifts. Sumatra, 1983.

470 (opposite above) A woman's tube-shaped ceremonial *tapis* from Lampung, southern Sumatra. These garments are unusual in Indonesia because they rely primarily on embroidery for decoration. This garment also displays couching of imported metallic-wrapped yarns and appliquéing of mirror paillettes onto a handwoven base of striped cotton cloth. Length 46³/₄ in. (118.7 cm), width 25¹/₂ in. (64.7 cm).

471 (opposite below left) A Lampung woman from southern Sumatra wearing a *tapis*, or cotton sarong embroidered with metallic thread. This garment—together with an accompanying winged crown—is worn only for ceremonial events.

472 (opposite below right) A *tampan* ship cloth from the Lampung area. Such textiles served various ritual functions, particularly those connected with marriage. The iconography is of interest: nobles in the upper register wear *dodots*, huge cloths that wrap around the hips; large daggers, *kris*, can be seen at their waists. Length 30¹/₄ in. (76.8 cm), width 28 in. (71.1 cm).

475 (right) A woman's cotton *kain panjang* (skirt cloth), patterned with natural dyes applied in the free-hand or *tulis batik* method. North coast of Java, early 20th century. Length 104½ in. (265.5 cm), width 41⅞ in. (106.5 cm).

476 (far right) A woman's *kain panjang*, patterned with the *tulis batik* method. Central Java, mid-20th century. Length 99 in. (251.5 cm), width 40⅞ in. (104 cm).

JAVA

Just east of Sumatra is the island of Java, whose textile story is mainly that of *batik*, the complex patterning process resulting from a wax-resist dyeing procedure which involves first drawing intricate designs on cloth with a "pen," a copper tool known as a *canting* [475–477]. As a result of the intricacy of these hand-drawn designs, Javanese *batik* is considered the finest in the world, reaching its apex at the turn of the 19th/20th century when labor was abundant, demand was high and there was a steady supply of the fine imported cotton cloth necessary to carry out this complex process.[11]

BALI

This small volcanic island, lying barely two miles (3.2 km) off the east coast of Java, is where in the 15th century Islamic forces brought an end to Java's Hindu kingdoms. As a result, a number of Javanese fled to Bali, which ever since has remained a tiny Hindu enclave in a vast Muslim sea.

On the island, the art of dyeing and weaving cotton *ikat* textiles has reached its zenith. It is only on Bali, in all of Indonesia, that the challenging double-*ikat geringsing* cloths are created in the community of Tenganan Pageringsingan [478; see also 462]. This eastern Balinese village is one of only three places in

477 The most prized of Java's *batik* is that which is first carefully drawn by hand, the *tulis* process. All areas of the cloth that are not to be colored in the initial dyeing are outlined in wax to make certain they remain protected. After the first submission in dye, the wax is scraped off and reapplied again and again to subsequent areas of the designs before they, too, are immersed into a series of dye baths. This photograph dates from ca. early 20th century.

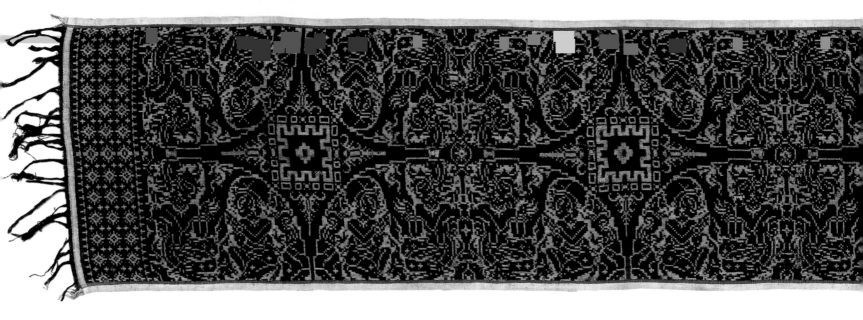

the world—the others being India and Japan—to produce traditionally these labor-intensive textiles on which designs are created using both tie-dyed warp and weft threads to form the pre-determined patterns. The *geringsing* cloths are dyed with indigo and morinda—a dye derived from the morinda or *mengkudu* root—to produce reddish-purple designs on a cream background.

SUMBA

Warp-*ikat* cotton textiles are made mainly in the eastern outer islands, in particular on Sumba, Flores and Timor. Perhaps the most famous of these distinctive weavings are the men's *hinggi* mantles from the east coast of Sumba [479; see also 481]. The cloths are famous for their rich colors, finely defined details and bold, horizontal patterns of stylized human and animal figures. Some *hinggi* also include depictions of "skull trees," reminders that the Sumba islanders were until recently head-hunters. *Hinggi* are usually produced in identical pairs, one to wrap about the body, the other to drape over the shoulders. These appealing textiles have been valuable trade items for centuries and were exported extensively in the 19th century by the Dutch. The Sumbanese woman's garment is a tube skirt, the *lau* [480; see also 482].

478 A handspun double-*ikat* cotton *geringsing* textile with a temple motif featuring two four-pointed stars and repeated pairs of seated shadow puppets, the *wayang*. Length 80½ in. (204.5 cm), width 19½ in. (49.5 cm).

479 (far left) A 1920s photograph taken on Sumba shows Sumbanese men wearing pairs of large mantles called *hinggi*, one wrapped about the hips, the other draped over the shoulders.

480 (left) The Sumba woman's skirt-like *lau* often displays motifs similar to those that appear on the men's *hinggi* but these skirts are patterned using the supplementary-warp process rather than the *ikat* technique.

481 A man's cotton *hinggi*, executed with natural dyes in the warp-*ikat* technique, early 20th century. The rows of symmetrical rampant animals are depicted in a medieval heraldic manner, perhaps borrowed from the Dutch coat of arms. Length 99 in. (251.5 cm), width 49¼ in. (125.1 cm).

482 A woman's *lau*, patterned using the supplementary-warp process. Note that horses—particularly associated with Sumba—are incorporated into the design. Length 51⅝ in. (131.3 cm), width 23⅜ in. (59.2 cm).

483 A shoulder cloth produced by a Lio weaver from the south-central Flores coast. The colors and structuring of this textile's overall pattern are reminiscent of the *patola* trade cloths which have strongly influenced the Lio weavers. Length 89 in. (226 cm), width 48³/₈ in. (123 cm).

484 A man's ceremonial shoulder cloth produced by a Ngadha dyer/weaver from the center-west of Flores. This warp-*ikat lu'e* depicts stylized horses, dogs and humans, all pre-dyed into the warps before the cloth was woven. To execute this *ikat* resist process, palm-leaf fibers are tied around pre-determined bundles of warp yarns to protect them from the dye bath. Length 85³/₄ in. (217.8 cm), width 53³/₈ in. (135.8 cm).

485 (below right) Timor men wear their wide, warp-*ikat* patterned cloths tied about their waists.

486 (right) A ceremonial shawl with alternating red and black rows decorated with animals and birds indigenous to East Timor. The formal, symmetrical arrangement of the roosters and squirrels is reminiscent of medieval European heraldry. Length 75 in. (190.5 cm), width 28½ in. (72.4 cm).

FLORES

The rugged topography of Flores has created formidable barriers to both communication and transport. As a result, the island encompasses several diverse weaving traditions; one in particular is a clear case of textile design reflecting trading history. Some weavings from the Ende region of the south-central coast clearly demonstrate the influence of Indian *patola* imports. There is direct copying of these distinctive trade cloths by the area's Lio weavers [483; see also 463, 466].[12] A further reflection of *patola* influence on Flores is the process of morinda dyeing, a complex technique generally used to create *patola*-like colors and designs, similarities that suggest this dye may have been introduced in tandem with famous Indian trade textiles.[13]

Flores is also home to the Ngadha people who live around Bajawa in the center-west of the island. Among the cloths produced by this group are a distinctive set of warp-*ikat* weavings called *lu'e* that are worn over the shoulder as part of a man's dance costume.[14] These textiles tend to display white motifs of stylized humans and animals on an indigo ground [484].

TIMOR

Timor is another of the outer islands known for its distinctive warp *ikats*. The brightly colored Timor textiles often include bold anthropomorphic images and bird forms. This is particularly true of the cloths of the Atoni people who live in the island's western half. The broad rectangular webs produced by Atoni weavers are often sewn together in the warp direction to create wider garments. Men use these flat, fringed pieces to wrap around the hips [485]; some single-web cloths serve as ceremonial shawls [486]. To the iconographically aware Timorese, each stranger's clothing telegraphs a message of home locale and alliance, often unsettling revelations in earlier, head-hunting times.

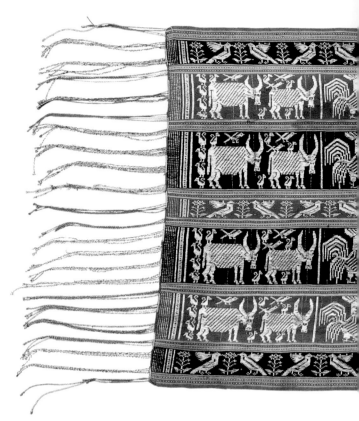

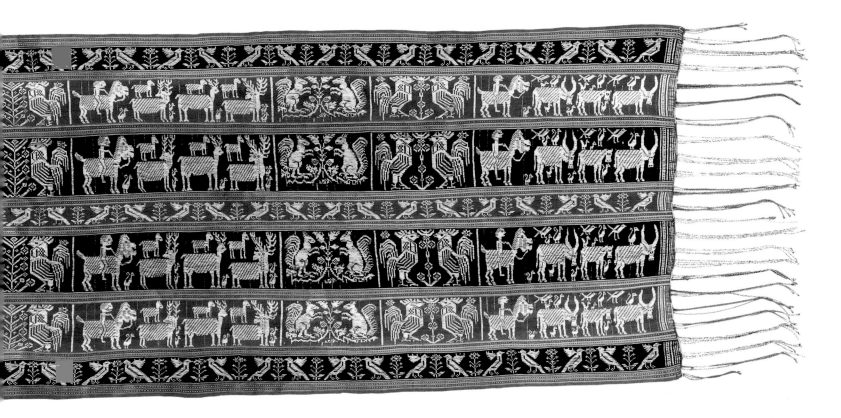

SULAWESI

Sulawesi is an oddly shaped island with a rough, mountainous center and four far-flung peninsulas, each with a different history and textile tradition. None of these diverse areas is more fascinating than Torajaland. The Toraja people of upland central and south Sulawesi have traditionally made particularly fine bark cloth by boiling the inner bark of the pandanus plant and/or paper mulberry tree and then beating the resulting pulp into extremely soft and pliable sheets called *fuya*. This material is then painted or stamped using natural pigments and fashioned into garments, some tailored [see 464]. Today certain of the descendants of these garments—blouses now called *lemba*—are made of indigo-dyed cotton and decorated with designs that sometimes echo those used in the famous Torajan carving [487, 488]. These blouses are traditionally worn with a voluminous skirt and cylindrical head ornaments on great ceremonial occasions.

487 In this 1929 photograph Torajan women wear their elaborately worked *lemba* shirts with full skirts and ceremonial headgear.

488 A Toraja woman's blouse of indigo-dyed cotton decorated with motifs executed in appliqué and beadwork. These *lemba* are worn only for ceremonial occasions. Their historical prototypes were made of bark cloth but commercial cotton fabric is now used. Length 21⁵⁄₈ in. (55 cm), width 34¼ in. (87 cm).

489 An *ikat* textile from Sulawesi illustrates a stylized genealogical repeating motif known as a *sekong*. The repetition of abstracted human figures connected to one another conveys the idea of endless descent and relationship.

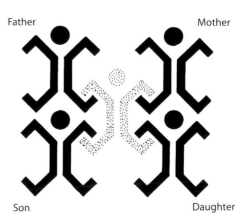

Father   Mother

Son   Daughter

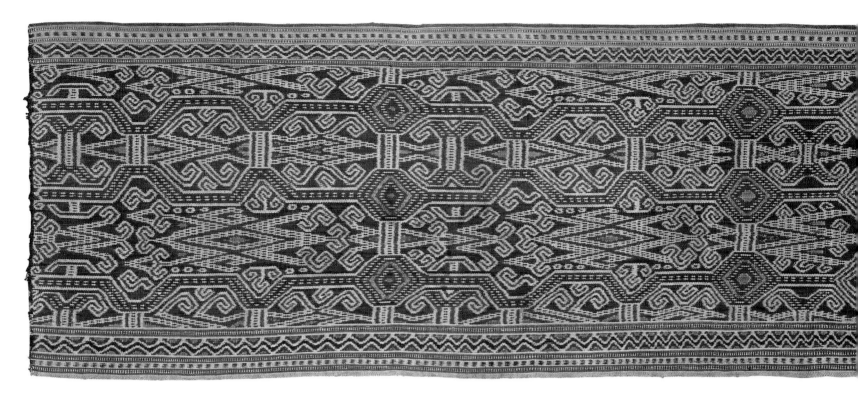

Reflecting their long heritage on Sulawesi, some textiles also show complex genealogical patterns that reflect kinship lineages. These rare and highly valued textiles are called *Pa Poritonoling* (*Pa* design; *Pori ikat*; *tonoling* village where woven) [489].[15]

BORNEO

The people of Borneo have a rich decorative legacy of intricate carving, painted bark cloth, elaborate beadwork and exuberant tattooing. The group known as the Iban—most of whom now live in Sarawak, in eastern Malaysia—also developed a particularly notable weaving tradition, producing finely woven patterned skirts, loincloths, jackets and shoulder cloths as well as large hangings or blankets called *pua*. The *pua*, decorated with complex warp-*ikat* designs, are among the most famous of Iban textiles [490].

The intricate *pua* cloths were the work of extremely talented women dyers; it has been said that "only one in fifty could do such work."[16] These textiles are mythically tied to the practice of headhunting, once the unifying, defining aspect of Iban society. Even into the late 19th century "no man's prowess was confirmed until he had taken the head of an enemy, and no woman was fully recognized until she had woven a *pua*."[17] The woman's lengthy preparation of the necessary yarns by mordanting them before their immersion in a dye bath, and her subsequent laying out of these dyed warps, was equated with the male feat of headhunting, hence female dyeing/weaving was called "the warpath of the women" [491].[18]

490 A *pua* cloth sarong of handspun cotton and warp-*ikat* using natural dyes. The arrangement of the patterned areas is reminiscent of *patola* layouts. Length 103 1/8 in. (262 cm), width 63 3/8 in. (161 cm).

491 Only those Iban women who had demonstrated particular proficiency in dyeing and weaving were allowed tattoos at the base of each thumb, just as only successful Iban headhunters could tattoo the back of their hands. Borneo, 1988.

492 A Bagobo man's jacket of burnished *abaca* fiber ornamented with beadwork and embroidery. Length 21⁵⁄₈ in. (55 cm), width 43³⁄₈ in. (110 cm).

493 A Bagobo man's short trousers of burnished *abaca* fiber decorated with complex, beaded designs. The fabric of these trousers also includes some narrow stripes of *ikat*. The large gusset in the garment's crotch is typical of Middle Eastern tailoring, an example of Islamic influence on Mindanao dress. The trouser's beaded cuffs are made as separate pieces and attached to the bottom of the woven fabric. Length 22⁷⁄₈ in. (58 cm), width 33⁷⁄₈ in. (86 cm).

494 A young Bagobo man wearing a jacket and short trousers of handwoven *abaca* cloth heavily decorated with intricate beadwork. Mindanao, early 20th century.

THE PHILIPPINE ARCHIPELAGO

In addition to the Indonesian archipelago, insular Southeast Asia contains a second major island chain, the Philippines. Three distinctive sets of clothing from the southern island of Mindanao provide an additional dimension to the overall Southeast Asian textile picture. These garments reflect contrasting physical and social environments: isolated highland groups and Westernized coastal people.

The Bagobo of mountainous central and southern Mindanao were known for their beautifully crafted cloth woven from the fiber of the *abaca* plant (*Musa textilis*), a close relative of the banana. Bagobo men once wore highly burnished and intricately decorated jackets and short trousers [492–494]. To the proud Bagobo, the wearing of beautiful clothing was particularly important because personal adornment equated with virtuous character.

An adjacent south-central Mindanao people also produced burnished *abaca* fiber trousers and jackets but their garments were intricately patterned using the *tritik* resist-dye technique [495, 496].

The Islamic Maranao, Maguindanao, Tausug and Yakan people of Mindanao's west coast—the only region in the southern Philippines where textiles made of imported silk thread are found—are known for their colorful attire and appreciation of color symbolism [497–499]. Indeed, in their epic literature reference is made to "capturing the colors of the rainbow,"[19] and this penchant has continued into the present day [500].

495 A south-central Mindanao man's jacket of burnished *abaca* fiber decorated with complex designs created using the *tritik* resist-dye process. Length 21⅝ in. (55 cm), width 43⅜ in. (110 cm).

496 A south-central Mindanao man's trousers of burnished *abaca* fiber decorated with designs created using the *tritik* resist-dye process. Length 23¼ in. (59 cm), width 27¾ in. (70.5 cm).

500 (opposite) A 1997 photograph of Sultan Aksara, a Maranao ruler from the coastal area of Bubong Macadar, on the Philippines' southern island of Mindanao. He wears the type of colorful clothing for which his Islamic coastal people are known.

497 A colorful silk headcloth. Yakan peoples, Basilan Island, Mindanao. Length 35 in. (88.9 cm), width 32⁷/₈ in. (83.6 cm).

498 Fitted jacket of silk and cotton thread, with 18 silver buttons: the garment's cut reflects strong Western influence. Yakan peoples, Basilan Island, Mindanao. Length 31 in. (78.8 cm), width 53⁵/₈ in. (136.2 cm).

499 Colorful striped pants woven of silk and cotton thread. Yakan peoples, Basilan Island, Mindanao. Length 42⁷/₈ in. (108.8 cm), width 19³/₈ in. (49.2 cm).

7

OCEANIA

"THE PACIFIC—rimmed by fire, its first inhabitants born of the Ice Age—proved the staging ground for one of man's most epic achievements:"[1] the initial peopling of Australia/New Guinea and, subsequently, the migration of Austronesian-speaking colonists out into the myriad islands of Oceania, those remote landfalls sprinkled sparsely across Earth's largest body of water. When the Late Pleistocene world was still in the grip of the last glacial epoch, dark-skinned hunter-gatherers from Island Southeast Asia first began penetrating the margins of the Pacific. At that time the Solomon archipelago formed the eastern limit of human habitation. In the middle of the 2nd millennium B.C., a major intrusion of Austronesian speakers moved into the Pacific from the Indonesian archipelago; by around 1100–900 B.C. these highly mobile mariners had made their way to Fiji. The final stage in the exploration of Oceania was carried out by master canoemakers, the Polynesians. The exploration of the Pacific by these intrepid seafarers was one of mankind's final organized, systematic migrations and settlements of unknown, uninhabited parts of the Earth's surface. The voyagers' golden age of colonization was between the 11th and 13th centuries A.D., when they established their way of life as the most geographically dispersed culture on Earth. All of the far-flung islands in the Polynesian Triangle were discovered and colonized while Westerners still feared venturing too far from land, believing that an ocean's far horizon marked the flat Earth's dropping-off point. Indeed, when Europeans finally arrived in Oceania in the 17th/18th centuries they found it hard to accept that the Polynesians' distant voyages could have been carried out without compass, sextant or astrolabe. In Oceania, a navigator's only aid was his ability to read the subtle clues of the vast Pacific and the enormous sky that arched above it.

OCEANIA

501 Mikhail Tikhanov, *Boki and Hekili on the Sloop "Kamchatka,"* 1818. When the Russian sloop *Kamchatka* stopped in Honolulu in 1818, King Kamehameha ordered the governor of Oahu, Boki, and the commander of the Hawaiian navy, Hekili, to welcome the visitors and help re-supply their ship. Boki is depicted wearing a simple *tapa* loincloth and a magnificent, long, feathered cloak and helmet, as is his compatriot. To the left are seated two *tapa*-draped aristocratic women; one wears a carved whale's-tooth pendant and a *lei* of fruit sections as a headband. The early European voyagers often brought with them not only Old World diseases but fermented spirits as well, both to the islanders' detriment.

With the possible exception of the still-controversial question of when the Americas were peopled,[1] the colonization of Oceania may well have been the last major movement into an unknown area, a finale to mankind's long series of demographic adventures. This migration took place across the Pacific Ocean, the globe's largest single geographic feature, covering one-third of the planet [Map 24]. While most of the Pacific's remote islands had not been discovered or settled until after 1200 B.C., by A.D. 1300 all of the remotest habitable outliers had been colonized and the Oceanic way of life had adapted to an impressive range of environments: the infertility of low coral atolls, the rich fertility of high volcanic islands, the phosphoric guano-based soils of upraised limestone isles, the mountainous cloud forests of New Guinea and the dense rainforests of the Solomons.[2]

The first stage in the lengthy migration began some 40,000 to 60,000 years ago, when bands of hunter-gatherers from Island Southeast Asia—perhaps driven out by more aggressive groups—started moving east until they arrived at the end of the Indonesian archipelago, probably the island of Timor. From there they somehow managed the truly impressive feat of reaching the large, then-joined land mass of Australia/New Guinea. Even with so much of the world's ocean water locked into the huge glacial sheets of the last Ice Age, and with the sea some 410 feet (125 m) below its present level, to reach Australia from Timor one still had to accomplish a sea crossing of some 55 miles (88.5 km), most of it out of sight of land.[3] The ancestors of the present-day Australian Aborigines accomplished this 40,000 to 50,000 years ago.[4] Their achievement was likely the first open-ocean crossing by modern humans,[5] presumably carried out in rickety bark canoes like those being used by the coastal Aborigines when first observed by European explorers.

Some scholars refer to these early migrants as Indo-Pacific peoples. They had dark skin, broad noses and frizzy hair, reflecting an origin near the equator where darker skin serves as protection against damage by the sun's ultraviolet rays [502]. We now know these migrants as the early Melanesians.[6]

With the melting of the great ice sheets, the sea level again rose and New Guinea was cut off from Australia. The Melanesian hunter-gatherers who remained in New Guinea are known as the Papuans. Then, in the middle of the 2nd millennium B.C., there appeared a new group of highly mobile colonists and explorers, a taller, heavier, lighter-skinned people from the Indonesian archipelago. These newcomers spoke an Austronesian language[7] and would leave behind evidence of their far-ranging migrations in the form of potshards of an incised and applied-relief type of pottery called Lapita ware, "Lapita" being the name of the archaeological site on the west coast of New Caledonia where fragments of this earthenware were first excavated.

The ceramic-making migrants were something entirely new and intrusive on the cultural landscape of the Pacific island world. Very early traces of the Lapita-culture appear in the Bismarck archipelago by at least 3000 B.C.; by around 1200 B.C. long-distance voyaging and colonization had begun for these people.

The earliest dates for their presence on Fiji are 1100–900 B.C.; from there the colonists moved into western Polynesia, settling in Tonga and Samoa some 3,000 years ago. The sea-borne Austronesians had moved from New Caledonia to Tonga and Samoa in a matter of two or three centuries, having explored almost 3,000 miles (4,850 km) of uncharted ocean during 15 to 25 successive human generations, one of the great sagas of world prehistory.[8]

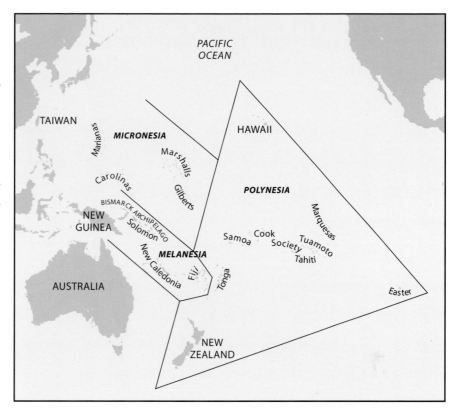

Map 24 Melanesia, Micronesia and the Polynesian Triangle. The archipelagos of Hawaii in the north and New Zealand in the south are separated by 4,400 miles (7,100 km).

502 A Melanesian wearing characteristically dramatic headgear of flowers and fern leaves.

503 The tattoos on the Maori chief's face are typical of the swirling patterns found in New Zealand, the last of the Pacific islands to be colonized by the Polynesians.

What motives compelled these people to keep exploring south and east into the unknown Pacific? Within the small-scale Lapita societies there was tremendous emphasis on sibling ranking: birth order determined access to both resources and privileges. Great importance was placed not only on genealogical order but also on a founding ancestor who, to those first-born males in the line of descent, bestowed both rights of access to land as well as to spiritual power, *mana*. As a result, younger siblings were motivated to set forth on open-ocean exploration to create their own prestigious dynasties.[9] Wherever these Lapita people sailed, they carried along their own food plants, animals and cultural know-how; it was this transplanting of their own landscapes that enabled the voyagers to colonize throughout Oceania. During the period when the Lapita-culture Austronesians were launching themselves out into the vast, uncharted reaches of the Pacific, their full cultural complex developed *in situ* within Polynesia itself; indeed, it was in Polynesia that the Polynesians became the intrepid Vikings of the Pacific [503].

In terms of the design and building of their large, ingenious, sea-going canoes, the Polynesians were in

a class of their own. By the birth of Christ, these far-ranging seafarers had come of age. After establishing a foothold in the Marquesa Islands—2,000 miles (3,220 km) east of Samoa—and then in the Society Islands, they began to colonize the Pacific in all directions. Between A.D. 800 and 1000 they settled Hawaii, Easter Island and New Zealand, the far points of the huge Polynesian Triangle [see Map 24].

Because Oceania's long colonization was episodic, segmented and widely dispersed, it is helpful to consider each of the major landfalls in turn so as to focus on the distinctive designs, body decoration and clothing—or the lack of them—that have continued on into the 21st century. Before proceeding, however, it must be noted that before the last half-century's archaeological, genetic and comparative-ethnology research, a chronology for Oceania's ancient migration history could only be dimly perceived: none of the Austronesians' early seafaring exploits were ever written down prior to European arrival.[10]

AUSTRALIA

Early European settlers reported that the Australian Aborigines wore little or no clothing beyond perhaps a belt of hair or animal fur used to support tools and weapons. Some belts had a flap in front, a modification that may have been added in the name of modesty during European colonization. In winter months or in the cooler temperate zones, the indigenous people wrapped themselves in cloaks made of animal hides such as possum and kangaroo. These skin cloaks were sewn together with sinew from kangaroos' tails and were worn either fur-side out or fur-side in. If the latter, the remarkable designs incised with a sharp mussel shell into the leather side could be displayed.[11] For, despite the paucity in range of indigenous clothing, the Aborigines were not lacking in a rich pictorial corpus.

Australian Aboriginal society in fact has the world's oldest continuous artistic tradition. "Native Australians began painting rock walls some 50,000 years ago: in contrast, early Europeans would not decorate the caves of Lascaux for another 30,000 years."[12] Communal

504 These residents of Fitzroy Crossing, in remote northwestern Australia, sit atop *Ngurrara II*, a 26 x 32 foot (7.9 x 9.75 m) painting created by more than 60 Aboriginal artists, which displays some of the intricate designs that perpetuate motifs used in traditional art and body decoration.

works were made during secret rites to celebrate The Dreamtime, when the wandering "creation ancestors" formed every aspect of the continent's landscape. Details about these epic journeys have been passed down in narratives known as Dreamings. Each Aboriginal inherited a responsibility to honor a particular Dreaming story and the land on which that particular act of creation took place. The distinctive geometric designs, wavy lines, circles, lozenges and zigzags that have come to characterize Aboriginal art were used to decorate the body and the skin cloaks that were worn [504, 505], and it is reported that a particular combination of patterns could help identify the wearer and the identity of his or her clan group[13]— a rich legacy of thousands of years of traditional iconography.

505 The skill of constructing and designing possum-skin cloaks is still a part of the Gunditjmara community today. The designs on the inside of this Lake Condah cloak are representative of the eel aquaculture system that the Gunditjmara have constructed over the past 8,000 years along the lava flow and wetlands of the Budj Bim National Heritage Landscape.

506 A Melanesian from Eipomek village, Irian Jaya, adorned in indigenous highland attire: a fiber-plaited wig, bone nose ornament, shell necklace and pendant, fiber arm and waist bands, and a penis sheath.

507 A selection of Irian Jaya's penis sheaths. The smaller examples in the foreground are worn over the glans.

MELANESIA

NEW GUINEA

New Guinea is one of the world's largest islands, a land whose center is dominated by a chain of high mountains rising to altitudes of over 15,000 feet (4,600 m). Surrounding this spiny backbone are coastal plains, swamps and smaller mountain ranges. This diverse geography has resulted in a rugged, isolating terrain whose human inhabitants arrived over 50,000 years ago. Today some half a million of New Guinea's Melanesian people live in a multitude of small, widely dispersed enclaves and speak over 740 different languages.[14] The island's *lingua franca* is a pidgin made up of a mixture of simplified European and Melanesian languages.

Although prior to the 1970s New Guinea's indigenous people had never joined together to develop an island-wide centralized power, in the realm of horticulture they made an important contribution with the early development of one of the world's important staples, taro (*Colocasia esculenta*), grown for its edible starchy root. When the subsequent Oceanic migrations moved out into the vast Pacific, the great voyaging canoes were carrying not rice, Southeast Asia's staple, but taro, New Guinea's gift.

Although variants of the same culture pervade all of New Guinea, politically the island is divided: the Indonesian province of Irian Jaya covers the western section, the now-independent nation of Papua New Guinea occupies the eastern half. Today, Western clothing has been adopted for everyday dress all over the island. That said, there are still a few isolated groups living in remote areas of the rugged highlands where men daily wear the islanders' traditional apparel: wig, nose ornament, pendant, arm bands, belt and that quintessentially New Guinean accoutrement, the penis sheath [506, 507].

In the highlands, ceremonies known as *singsings* are held regularly. Originally hosted by a local "Big Man" to build up his extra-clan relationships, the dances are now sponsored by the Papua New Guinea government to foster inter-group tranquility. These recurrent events are particularly memorable for the dancers' impressive dress [508] and body decoration [509]. Indeed, highland *singsings* display some of the world's most colorful and impressive indigenous costuming. This is not the case for the island's females. Prior to the advent of Western clothing, women's garments were restricted to a netted bag—the better to tote heavy garden produce, firewood, pigs or babies—and an array of grass and twisted-fiber skirts [510, 511].

509 Some highland dancers, like this Kauil tribesman from the Tambul area, Western Highlands Province, Papua New Guinea, attempt to block out their individuality by disappearing into their costuming, often applying a great deal of charcoal to their faces and bodies so as to meld into an ensemble.

508 The New Guinea highlands are famous for colorful *singsing* ceremonies that involve columns of men arrayed in memorable costumes: vari-colored grass skirts, towering feathered headdresses and colorful body painting, as seen on these Mendi tribesmen parading at Sangre village. Today dancers apply commercial paint to their bodies so as to create as vibrant an effect as possible. The patterns they choose are neither totemic nor magical; the men claim their designs are copied from those of the native birds with which they live so closely.

510 New Guinea women's fiber-plaited carrying bags.

Above: length 18 in. (45.7 cm), width 16³⁄₄ in. (42.5 cm).

Right: length 31¹⁄₂ in. (80 cm), width 34¹⁄₄ in. (87 cm).

511 Examples of Irian Jaya women's grass skirts. Four are "rope skirts," constructed of twisted and knotted fiber dyed in varying colors; two (see overleaf) are constructed of long pieces of grass fiber whose tips have been dyed.

Above: length 13¾ in. (35 cm), width 72 in. (183 cm). Below: length 13 in. (33 cm), width 81⅞ in. (208 cm).

Above: length 40⅛ in. (102 cm), width 11⅜ in. (29 cm). Below: length 118⅞ in. (302 cm), width 14⅝ in. (37 cm).

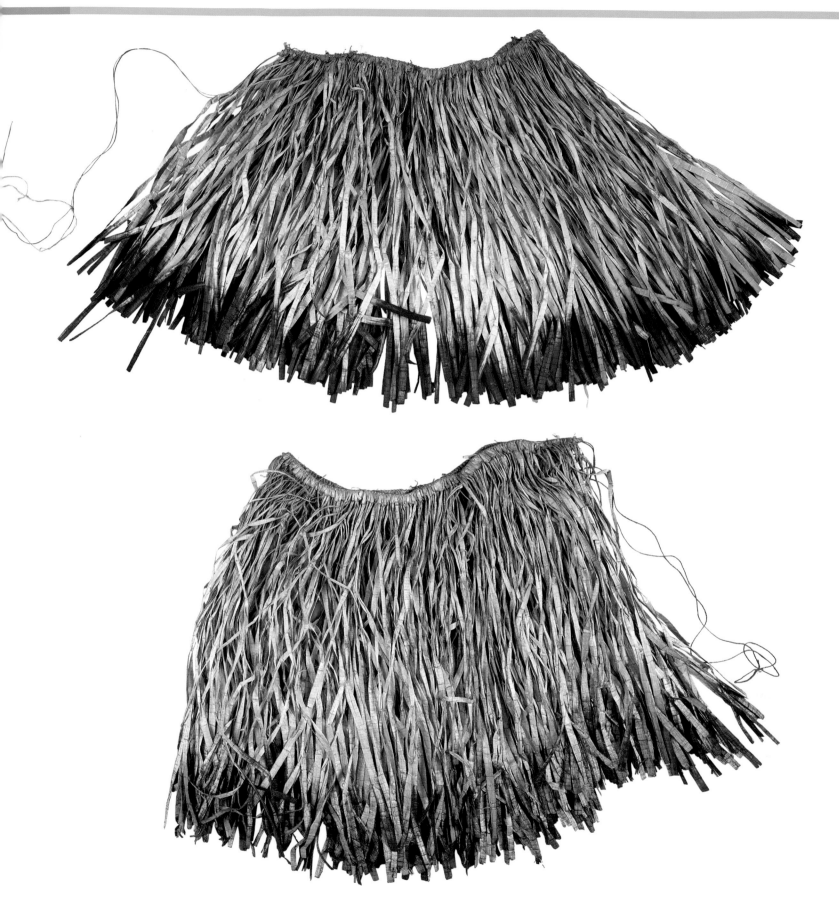

Above: length 18⅞ in. (48 cm), width 33⅜ in. (85 cm). Below: length 41⅜ in. (105 cm), width 18½ in. (47 cm).

SOUTHERN ISLANDS OF MELANESIA

Although the peoples of New Guinea are Melanesians, there is also a large geographic portion of the Pacific that is known as Melanesia [see Map 24]. This is a particularly heterogeneous area where hundreds of languages and dialects are spoken, a diversity that no doubt reflects languages evolving in various micro-environments over a long period of time. A principal Melanesian cultural center is Fiji, located at the southeast end of the long island chain that stretches out from New Guinea some 2,000 miles (3,200 km) into the Pacific. From this vantage point, Fiji played an interactive role with its "nearby" Polynesian neighbors, Tonga and Samoa, located to the northeast across, respectively, 500 and 750 miles (805 and 1,205 km) of open ocean.

Peter Buck, the early 20th-century Oceanic scholar,[15] points out that, among other similarities between Fiji and Tonga/Samoa, all three islands produced fine bark cloth, or *tapa* [512]. Bark cloth is primarily created from the inner bark of the cultivated

paper mulberry tree—a thin, woody-stemmed, tropical plant—that was initially carried into Oceania from Southeast Asia and then transported by voyaging canoes to the Pacific's volcanic islands in whose rich soils it thrived.

To produce *tapa*, the paper mulberry's soft inner bark had to be separated from its stiff outer bark by placing the inner section on a sloping board and scraping it with seashell scrapers, keeping both the board and the bark moist to promote the softening and spreading of the fibers. The bark was then soaked and beaten with a wooden mallet on a wooden anvil. Longitudinal grooves on the surface of the mallet further aided in the spreading of the inner bark's fibers, but for the final beating the smooth side of the mallet was used to create a finished surface.[16] Bamboo stamps were carved with various patterns and then dipped into natural dyes and printed on the *tapa* to create a wide variety of designs. Throughout the Pacific, including northern Australia and New Guinea, the manufacture of *tapa* reflected local innovations.

512 Untailored, wraparound *tapa* cloth garments from Fiji. With the exception of the example at top right, which is worn by men, the other three are women's attire.

Left: length 18 in. (45.7 cm), width 93⁷/₈ in. (238.6 cm).

Top right: length 27¹/₄ in. (69.2 cm), width 109 in. (276.8 cm).

Below left: length 17¹/₄ in. (43.9 cm), width 77 in. (195.6 cm).

Below right: length 58 in. (147.3 cm), width 124 in. (315.2 cm).

513 A young Micronesian collecting coconuts on the island of Yap. The fibers of the plant are knotted together for use as hardwearing garments. The coconut palm is also one of the few Oceanic food plants that will grow in Micronesia.

MICRONESIA

The world of Micronesia appears to have been discovered and colonized by migrating Lapita-culture Austronesians, who moved into this area from the Bismarck archipelago and on to the southeast Solomon Islands before 1500 B.C. Micronesia is made up of a multitude of some 2,100 islands, along with low-lying atolls, scattered across the ocean to the north and northeast of New Guinea; the area includes such island groups as the Marianas, Marshalls, Gilberts and Carolinas. Because of the infertile soil of Micronesia's coral atolls, only a limited number of the migrants' cultivated plants could survive: coarse taro, certain long-stem grasses and the coconut palm [513]. It is these raw materials that have been crafted into Micronesian garments: woven bast-fiber wraparound skirts [514], and bast fibers worked into grass skirts [515, 516] worn by both sexes, as well as coconut-palm fibers skillfully knotted into encasing warrior suits, complete with protective armor [517].

514 Wraparound skirts made of either hibiscus or banana fiber from Ulithi Atoll, Micronesia. These skirts are examples of Oceania's few loom-woven garments.

Left: length 77 in. (195.5 cm), width 19¹/₂ in. (49.5 cm).

Second left: length 67¹/₂ in. (171.5 cm), width 19⁵/₈ in. (50 cm).

Third left: length 79 in. (200.5 cm), width 19 in. (48.5 cm).

Right: length 65 in. (165 cm), width 19 in. (48.5 cm).

515 A Micronesian male dancer's grass skirt from Funafuti, Tuvalu. The skirt's top layer has wide pieces of palm leaf dyed orange and purple. Two of these vertical flaps are covered with a handwritten text in dark ink, perhaps pages from some handwritten journal. Other outside flaps are decorated with geometric patterns. The skirt's bottom layers consist of thinner strips of undyed palm leaf. The ties are made of twisted plant fiber. Length 27⅞ in. (71 cm), width 37⅞ in. (96 cm).

516 Two multicolored grass skirts from Micronesia's Ulithi Atoll.

Left: length 10 in. (25.4 cm), width 14 in. (35.5 cm).

Below: length 22 in. (56 cm), width 27 in. (68.5 cm).

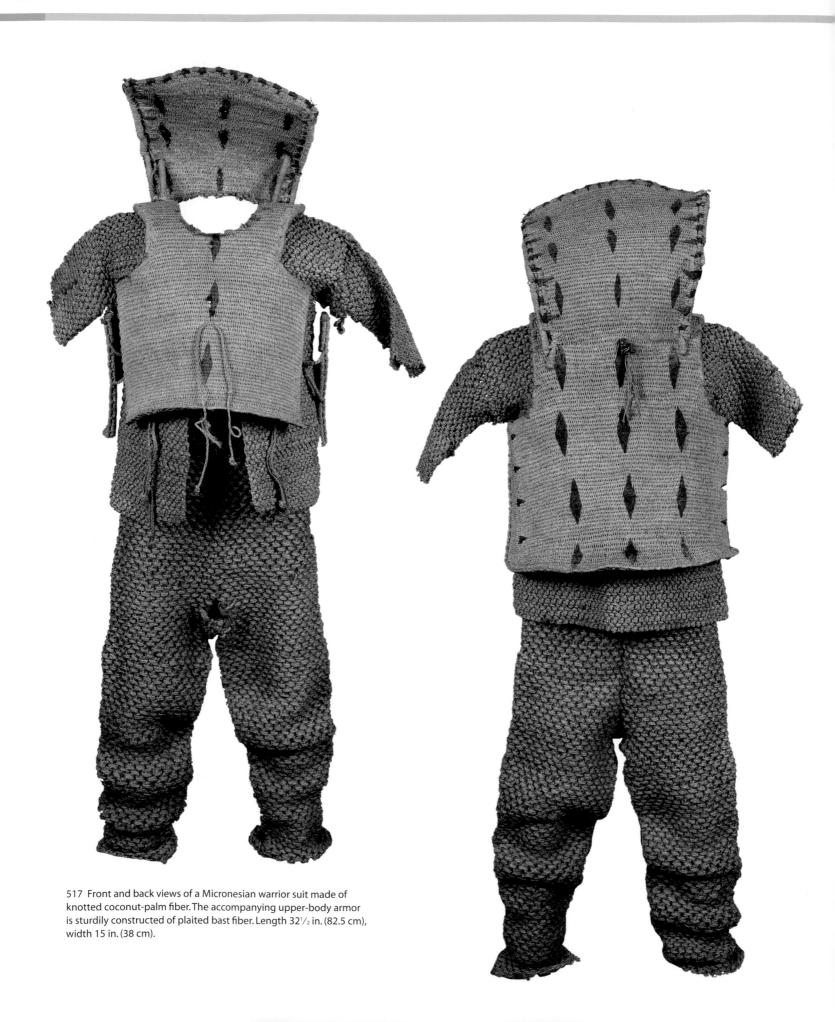

517 Front and back views of a Micronesian warrior suit made of
knotted coconut-palm fiber. The accompanying upper-body armor
is sturdily constructed of plaited bast fiber. Length 32½ in. (82.5 cm),
width 15 in. (38 cm).

POLYNESIA

Polynesia was not discovered or settled by humans until after about 1200 B.C., and some islands as recently as A.D. 1000. The ancestral Polynesian culture emerged out of its Lapita predecessor during the course of the first millennia B.C. in a vast world where the great voyaging canoe stands to ancient Oceanic culture "as the invention of the wheel to ground transportation."[17] The Polynesians' 50- to 150-foot-long (15–45 m), double-hulled canoes—lashed together with cross-beams for stability and strength, with a central platform for living, working and storage—were powered by plaited-leaf sails and human sinew as the voyagers' long, deep-sea paddles cut into the Pacific. The seafarers' instrument of navigation was the navigator himself whose six senses were all employed to respond to the wind's fluctuations, the ocean's currents, swells and wave patterns, the sun's position, the heaven's cloud formations, the birds' flight paths and the star tracks that moved across the night sky.

The initial discoveries of the far-flung archipelagos were later followed by great colonizing expeditions carrying the necessities for establishing a new life on a distant, often not-too-hospitable shore. The Pacific's unoccupied islands were decidedly meager in human food. The cultivated plants that now characterize Oceanic flora—bananas, breadfruit, coconut palms, taro, yams and the sweet potato—had to await human transport. Similarly, the other cultural commonalities that exist throughout homogenous Polynesia—the basic language, myths, traditions, religion—were all introduced during the great colonization period

518 A group of Samoans proudly display traditional ceremonial attire. Note the emphasis on red parrot feathers as decorations for their finely plaited, bast-fiber garments.

519 A Samoan woman's ceremonial outfit. The skirt and sleeveless blouse are finely plaited bast fiber and decorated with red parrot feathers. A headdress and hairpiece are also part of the ensemble.

Clockwise from above:
Blouse: length 20¼ in. (51.4 cm), width 21 in. (53.3 cm).

Headdress: length 23⅝ in. (60 cm), width 5⅞ in. (15 cm).

Hairpiece: length 7 in. (18 cm), width 5⅞ in. (15 cm).

Skirt: length 63 in. (160 cm), width 25½ in. (64.8 cm).

between the 8th and 11th centuries. Peter Buck contends that settlement of the far-flung archipelagos was by individual canoes arriving at different times rather than by single, mass migrations.[18]

While Tonga and Samoa in western Polynesia were colonized by 1000 B.C., the earliest known archaeological assemblage from eastern Polynesia dates around 200 B.C.–A.D. 1. This leaves a "Long Pause" of as much as 1,600 years in the eastern expansion beyond Tonga and Samoa followed by a burst of exploration and discovery that takes the Austronesian speakers into every habitable island and remote archipelago of the Pacific within a mere four centuries (i.e. by A.D. 1000). The causes and duration of the so-called "Long Pause" are still under investigation.[19]

Tonga and Samoa, meanwhile, both benefitted from their relative proximity to the Melanesian trading post of Fiji. Among the range of specialized goods the island offered were red feathers from local parrots. These vibrant decorations were very important to the Polynesian Samoans as embellishments for their ceremonial attire [518, 519]. In contrast, the beautifully twisted, coiled and plaited bast-fiber overskirts—perhaps made of *pandanus* leaf—from neighboring Tonga are all devoid of off-island elements; these imaginatively worked Polynesian skirts are a Tongan innovation [520].

It is, however, in the contrasting worlds of the tropical Hawaiian Islands to the far north[20] and the temperate New Zealand archipelago to the far south that the past and present range of Polynesian clothing can best be understood.

520 Four leaf-fiber—perhaps *pandanus*—overskirts from Polynesian Tonga, each crafted in a unique style.

Length 32⅝ in. (83 cm), width 13⅞ in. (35 cm).

Length 35⅜ in. (90 cm), width 14⅝ in. (37 cm).

Length 38 in. (96.5 cm), width 24⅜ in. (62 cm).

Length 47⅜ in. (120.5 cm), width 19½ in. (49.6 cm).

521 Theodore Wores, *The Lei Maker*, 1901. This young Hawaiian woman wears a *muumuu*, the total cover-up garment imposed by the Christian missionaries who arrived in Hawaii in the early 19th century. The missionaries insisted that native women should radically change their ways, emphasizing more clothing and less dancing. The visiting whalers encouraged exactly the opposite.

THE HAWAIIAN ISLANDS

The discovery and subsequent colonizations of Hawaii resulted in a vibrant, sharply stratified society that had dispersed throughout the island chain by the time of European contact in the late 18th century.[21] The Hawaiians' most common garments were the men's loincloths and the women's skirts—all made of *tapa*, pounded bark cloth [see 501]. Hawaiian *tapa* not only displayed the Pacific's greatest variety of weights— both the thickest and thinnest—but also the greatest range of textures: in place of the usual parallel lines found on Pacific bark-cloth pounders, various patterns were carved into the Hawaiian beaters, resulting in a variety of watermarks being impressed into the finished cloth. In addition, a wide range of colorful designs were printed on the *tapa*, all created with natural dyes: green, yellow, pink, red, blue and blue-grey. Sadly, in the mid-1920s *tapa* ceased to be produced in the Hawaiian Islands. European colonizers and, especially, Christian missionaries effectively wiped out many Polynesian traditions and customs by imposing Western belief systems and cultural ways. These changes included the need for wearing "proper clothing" [521].

In addition to indigenous Hawaiian garments made by beating were those made by plaiting. Such pieces were constructed from fiber obtained from either the outer covering of banana trunks or from *ti* leaves[22] and were plaited around the waist, close to the skin, with long strips of fiber hanging down below. These garments were the prototypes of today's famous Hawaiian grass skirts, worn by the islands' hula dancers [522, 523].

The epitome of Hawaiian dress was the islanders' magnificent feather attire, capes and cloaks that marked the social distinction of high chiefs and ruling kings; feather-covered helmets were also worn [524; see also 501]. The native craftsmen who created these garments exhibited the highest standards of technical skill and color patterning. Captain Cook deemed Hawaiian feather garments to be truly elegant, comparing their surface to the thickest and richest of velvets in both texture and sheen.[23]

Feather garments appear to have developed within Polynesia itself and were confined to Hawaii, Tahiti and New Zealand. In Hawaii, these capes and cloaks were constructed on extremely fine netting—made to the required size with fisherman's knots—to which were attached small bunches of feathers placed in overlapping rows and secured with a separate binding thread. The particularly high value placed on red and yellow feathers induced many a Hawaiian to become a professional bird hunter and led to the extinction of some colorful species.

522 Hawaiian hula dancers wear what the world views as *the* stereotypical Pacific garment: the grass skirt.

523 A Hawaiian grass skirt (see detail, below left). Firmly plaited at the waist, the skirt is made of either *ti* leaves or the outer covering of a banana tree. Length 27⅞ in. (71 cm), width 29⅞ in. (76 cm).

Accompanying ankle adornments are made of the same fiber as the skirt. Length 9 in. (22.8 cm), width 2½ in. (6.4 cm) each.

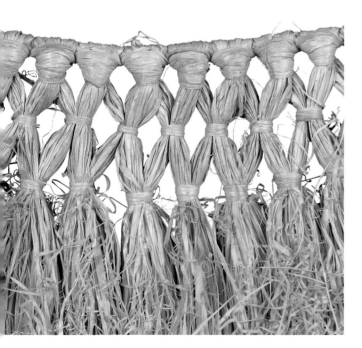

527 A watercolor sketch by C. D. Barraud of the Maori chief Rangihaeata in full regalia: a dogskin cape bordered with geometric *taaniko* designs, a greenstone pendant and large greenstone celt. The chief's face is tattooed with the Maori's swirling patterns; in his earlobes are what may be small pieces of traditional Polynesian bark cloth, a rare commodity in temperate New Zealand. To the chief's left grows a clump of New Zealand flax, the archipelago's indigenous textile plant.

528 A mid-1800s *korowai* cloak of flax, whose alternate light-dark patterning is reminiscent of the earlier, prestigious dogskin capes. Length 43³⁄₈ in. (110 cm), width 52³⁄₄ in. (134 cm).

529 A *kaitaka* cloak made of finely woven flax and bordered with a geometric pattern. Length 48³⁄₈ in. (123 cm), width 72⁷⁄₈ in. (185 cm).

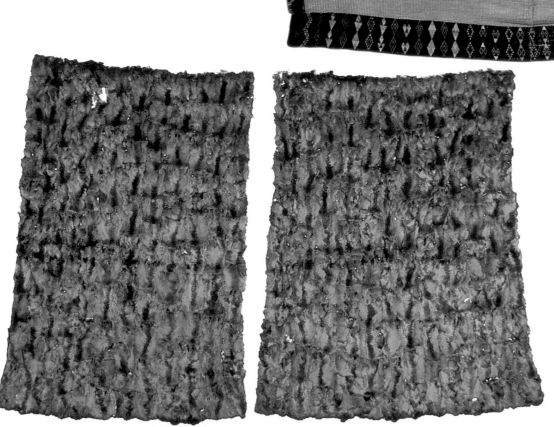

530 A pair of shimmering cloaks of pigeon feathers made to sell to European visitors.

Left: length 36³⁄₈ in. (92.5 cm), width 24 in. (61 cm).

Right: length 36¹⁄₈ in. (92 cm), width 30³⁄₈ in. (77 cm).

531 The type of prestigious feather cape worn by aristocratic Maori men. Length 37⁷⁄₈ in. (96 cm), width 53¹⁄₈ in. (135 cm).

532 (below) An aristocratic Maori woman wearing a prestigious feather cape, ca. early 20th century. Her lips and chin are tattooed with designs appropriate to her noble rank.

533 (below right) The type of prestigious feather cape worn by aristocratic Maori women. Length 38⁷⁄₈ in. (99 cm), width 57³⁄₈ in. (146 cm).

finely woven rectangle of flax on which were sewn strips of dogskin fur placed so closely that the underlying fabric was barely visible. Often these cloaks were bordered with prestigious black, brown/red and white *taaniko* designs, geometric patterns created using the finger-weaving technique.

By the mid-1800s, the dogskin garments had become increasingly rare and were replaced by *korowai* cloaks [528], decorated with contrasting columns of black and white, a patterning reminiscent of the earlier, vertically striped dogskin capes.

Subsequently, *kaitaka* cloaks came into fashion—flax garments with distinctive geometric borders [529]. These silky cloaks have now all but disappeared, as they were greatly favored—hence widely collected—by Europeans, as were the Maori's feathered capes [530].[32]

As early as 1769 European voyagers were favorably commenting on New Zealand's feather apparel, never as popular with the Maori as their dogskin and *kaitaka* cloaks. Subsequently, feather cloaks rose to prominence among the Maori as prestige items [531]. These

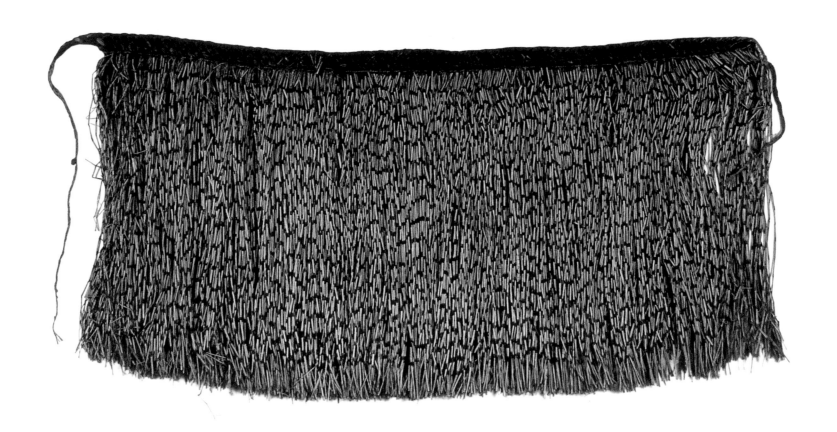

garments were constructed from many types of feathers: duck, kiwi, pigeon, parrot, chicken, pheasant, guinea fowl. It is interesting that Maori women of rank were allowed to wear certain designs of these feather cloaks [532, 533], whereas their Hawaiian counterparts were strictly forbidden such attire.

Just as the Maori continued the Polynesian custom of the ruling class wearing long, elegant cloaks—many of them feathered—so too the Maori retained the custom of using free-swinging, bast-fiber skirts, *piupiu*, as ceremonial attire for both men and women [534].[33] The distinguishing features of these distinctive garments were their encircling, tightly grouped strands of tubular, patterned flax that swung freely from the waistband [535]—temperate New Zealand's creative interpretation of tropical Oceania's ubiquitous grass skirt.

534 A Maori *piupiu*, the ceremonial garment worn by both men and women. The free-swinging overskirt is constructed of tubes of flax fiber decorated with alternating dark and light sections. Length 25⅝ in. (65 cm), width 46⅜ in. (118 cm).

535 The modern-day Maori ceremonial costume for women. This celebrant has tied around her waist a *piupiu* overskirt (men wear a shorter version of this attire). Her headband and bodice both display geometric *taaniko* patterns. She is also adorned with shark-tooth earrings and a carved greenstone pendant.

8

NORTH AMERICA

SOMETIME AROUND 15,000 B.C., while glaciers of the last Ice Age still covered parts of North America, small bands of Stone Age hunters began moving out of Siberia. Archaeological evidence suggests that Central Asia's earliest inhabitants may well have been among North America's first settlers.[1] Possibly there had been one migration or more before this, extending back as early as 30,000 B.C. Here, as in other areas of the New World, the population may have been much larger than previously believed.[2] Some of the newcomers migrated across the land bridge that spanned the Bering Straits, drifting southward following ice-free valleys in pursuit of game. Other groups may have skirted the glacial barrier by water, using seaworthy coastal crafts to explore and settle along the west coasts of North, Central and South America. By whatever means the migrants came, this populating of the Western Hemisphere was to last for thousands of years and involve people who differed in appearance, customs and language. What they all shared was the ability to adapt to their new environment. Some settled in areas that suited them and thrived, bands growing into tribes. Others continued to wander. By the time of the famous 1492 "Discovery of America," the continent was already well-populated with diverse cultures ranging from the rudimentary hunting economies of the Eskimo/Inuit to the great prehispanic high cultures that flourished in that part of Mexico and Central America now known as Mesoamerica.[3]

540 An animal-skin parka from Nome, Alaska, ca. 1922, decorated with mosaic bands of small brown, white and black fur triangles placed at the hem and sleeve tops. The long-haired fur around the hood and hem may be wolf, used because it does not attract frost. Length 39 in. (99 cm), width 24½ in. (62 cm).

541 A caribou-skin parka from Labrador is trimmed in red fox fur around the hood and cuffs. Length 42 in. (106.7 cm).

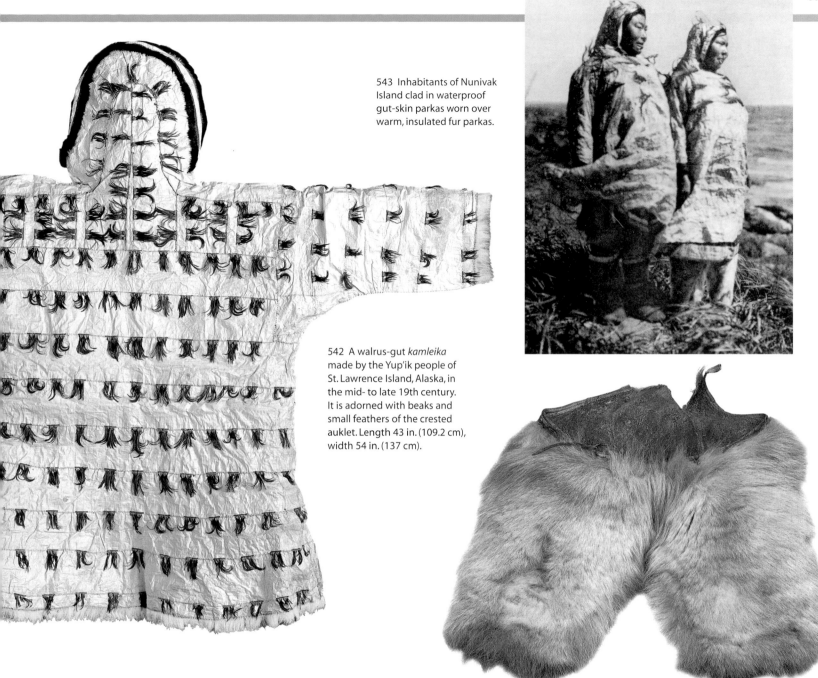

543 Inhabitants of Nunivak Island clad in waterproof gut-skin parkas worn over warm, insulated fur parkas.

542 A walrus-gut *kamleika* made by the Yup'ik people of St. Lawrence Island, Alaska, in the mid- to late 19th century. It is adorned with beaks and small feathers of the crested auklet. Length 43 in. (109.2 cm), width 54 in. (137 cm).

OUTERWEAR

Among the most impressive of all Arctic garments was the *kamleika*, a parka or shirt made of sea-mammal intestines that had been removed intact, turned inside out, scraped clean with a mussel shell, washed in water and urine, blown up with air, hung up to dry and then split open and laid out to bleach. The resulting long white strips were then sewn together, either horizontally or vertically, and adorned for dress wear with tufts of fur or feathers [542, 543]. Undecorated gut-skin garments took approximately one month to make and were usually replaced every four to six months.[7] The lightweight, waterproof outerwear was put on over a fur parka for protection from wind, rain and sea spray. The *kamleika* were especially useful for hunters in kayaks, the Eskimos' lightweight skin boats: the parkas were tightly tied at the neck and wrist and then laced securely into the wooden ring surrounding the hatch of the kayak. A hunter thus encased could stay dry even in turbulent seas. These gut-skin garments had many uses and, after European contact, evolved into diverse forms: by the mid-19th century the Aleuts were fashioning *kamleika* for their own use in the style of Russian officers' capes.

544 A pair of polar-bear fur pants worn by the Polar Eskimos of Greenland. Length 31 1/8 in. (79 cm), width 25 5/8 in. (65 cm), depth 5 7/8 in. (15 cm).

THE NORTHWEST COAST

559 In Charles M. Russell's 1905 painting of Meriwether Lewis and William Clark on the Lower Columbia River, note the contrast between the explorers' protective, limb-encasing, buckskin clothing and the—erroneous—artistic concept of the scanty apparel worn by the American Indians on the damp Northwest Coast. The misty atmosphere in the painting, however, is exactly right.

The dramatic nature of Northwest Coast culture was matched by the grandeur of its setting, a narrow, island-fringed coastal strip stretching from southern Alaska to northern California [Map 26]. To the west, a rugged range of precipitous mountains plunges almost directly into the Pacific where cold Arctic waters mix with the warm Japanese current to produce a mild but damp climate of lingering fogs and abundant rainfall, an environment that has created "a true rainforest with dense stands of fir, hemlock and cedar."[1] From earliest times—perhaps as early as 9000 B.C.—native peoples drew their subsistence from both sea and forest; their worldview, however, was directed more toward the fertile sea than the encroaching forest.

The center of the unique Northwest Coast culture was to the north, in the areas inhabited by the Nuu-chah-nulth (formerly Nootka), the Kwakwaka'wakw (formerly Kwakiutl), Nuxalk (formerly Bella Coola), Tsimshian, Haida and Tlingit. Although these peoples spoke different languages, they shared a common coastal culture—with subtle differences—that was dependent on marine resources. In the winter they lived in permanent villages marked by large, cedar-plank clan houses and towering, heraldic totem poles. The coastal villages were separated from the interior by mountain ranges and dense forests but these barriers did not hinder trade because the Indians traveled widely in large, remarkably carved and painted canoes [see 559], threading their way through the thousands of islands along a network of coastal and riverine waterways. The canoe was to the Northwest Coast what the horse was to the Plains, a leveler of isolation.

In this world of Nature's bounty, there was no agriculture; there was neither room nor need for it. Nor was there pottery or—other than the dog—any domesticated animal. Although wild berries and starchy roots were collected in season, the diet was largely one of animal fats, thanks to abundant supplies of salmon as well as other fish. Some of the Northwest Coast groups were also whale hunters, hence whale as well as fish oil was available. Indeed, so much oil was used that certain of the waterways were known as the "grease trails."[2]

This was primarily a wood culture. Both shelter and clothing came from giant cedar trees, as essential to life as the salmon. The cedar provided most physical and spiritual needs—planks to be crafted into dwellings and trunks to be carved into sea-going canoes, bentwood boxes, lofty totem poles and magnificent ceremonial masks and rattles [560, 561; see also

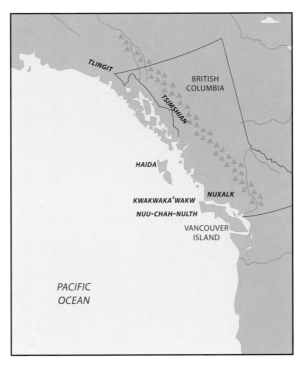

Map 26 Map of the Northwest Coast.

578, 579, 582–588]. Further, the cedar's bark was the basic fiber for garments, apparel well adapted to the Northwest's rainy climate.

The most common textiles were woven from the fibrous inner layer of red or yellow cedar. The inner bark was dried, split and shredded by beating it to separate it into thin strands [562]. These strands were then twisted into string by rubbing them along the thigh with the palm of the hand. This string was woven on a simple two-bar loom using a twining technique to create everyday clothing—tunics for cold weather [563] and conical

560 (below left) A 19th-century Tlingit Raven rattle used in ceremonial dances. The body of this rattle represents the raven, a mischievous and powerful mythological being. Some conjecture that this bird is in the process of performing one of his most admirable acts: stealing the sun from a box where a malevolent creature had hidden it away from humankind. Length 14¼ in. (36.2 cm), height 4½ in. (11.4 cm), depth 5 in. (12.7 cm).

561 (below) A 19th-century Tlingit shaman's oyster-catcher rattle depicting an oyster-catcher bird transporting a frog with a witch on its back; the twisted hair of the tortured witch is bound to the frog's hands. Length 15¼ in. (38.7 cm), height 5 in. (12.7 cm), depth 4 in. (10.2 cm).

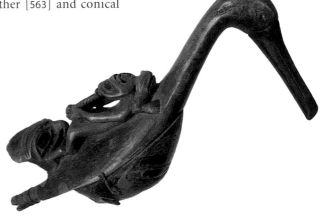

Following the fur trade came the missionaries—Protestant and Catholic—to convert the Indians and attempt to change their culture to that of the whites. Settlers followed, as did the usual conflicts over land. The native inhabitants were soon viewed as second-class citizens but in many cases were able to remain on ancestral lands. Nonetheless, this new life proved a crushing experience, and particularly so when the potlatch was officially outlawed in British Columbia in 1884. Although these ceremonies often continued covertly, during this period many sacred ceremonial objects were destroyed by the government, or impounded, or simply stolen, sometimes by collectors.[5]

MEN'S BASIC DRESS

In summer, many Northwest Coast men used little or no clothing, adding a tunic only as needed, a doubled piece of rectangular woven cedar bark that was worn as a knee-length, belted garment trimmed with rabbit or otter fur [see 563].

WOMEN'S BASIC DRESS

In mild weather, women wore an apron of woven lengths of cedar bark attached to a waistband that tied in the back. In winter, however, a wraparound skirt of woven cedar bark was put on over the apron, or a tunic similar to that of the men was worn.

568 A 19th-century Tlingit Chilkat blanket woven of mountain-goat wool and cedar-bark fiber. These were worn by dancers during ceremonies and also by distinguished men at potlatches. Length 72 in. (182.9 cm), width 35 in. (88.9 cm).

FOOTWEAR

Along the Northwest Coast, almost everyone went barefoot. For these coastal people, who were constantly in and out of canoes, shoes would have been a problem. Only those living upriver found a need for hide moccasins.

OUTERWEAR

During cold and rainy weather, waist-length conical capes made of a double layer of cedar bark [see 564] were worn, as well as cedar-bark blankets or robes made from a variety of furs, and even some of feathers. Sea otter was the most prized fur but full-skin bear robes were also worn, as well as robes made from the skins of ducks or loons. All were held in place by thongs or blanket pins made of wood or bone.

The most famous Northwest Coast weavings were the Chilkat blankets [568; see also 566], named for a sub-group of the Tlingit, although both the Tsimshian and Haida also made these ceremonial garments. It was the women who spun, dyed and wove the yarn, in a twilled-twining technique, for these famous, five-cornered dancing blankets made with warps of mountain-goat wool—wrapped around a core of cedar-bark fiber—and wefts of pure wool. The men provided the wool, made the wooden frame upon which the blankets were woven, prepared the necessary measuring sticks and painted the pattern boards from which the women copied the designs.

In the construction of Chilkat blankets, the warps hung loose, an unusual feature in the weaving process. To avoid entanglement, clumps of warps were loosely tied off in small gut bags. Because the rounded design forms on the blankets are alien to weaving techniques, these segments were woven as separate panels and then sewn in place with sinew, the joinings covered by a kind of false embroidery. The labor-intensive and highly-valued Chilkat blankets took from six months to a year to complete.

HAIRSTYLES

Women wore their hair in one or two braids, whereas men generally wore their hair loose and long, or coiled into a bun secured at the top of the head. It is of interest that Northwest Coast men commonly have facial hair—a rarity among native peoples of the Americas—which allows them to grow full mustaches, goatees or beards.

HEADGEAR

The Northwest Coast is famous for its unique hats. Those of the lower classes were constructed of a basketry of cedar-bark fiber, whereas upper-class

569 A noblewoman wears an ornamented basketry hat made of split spruce roots. She also wears a cedar-bark robe, an iron nose ring, abalone earrings and five prestigious silver bracelets.

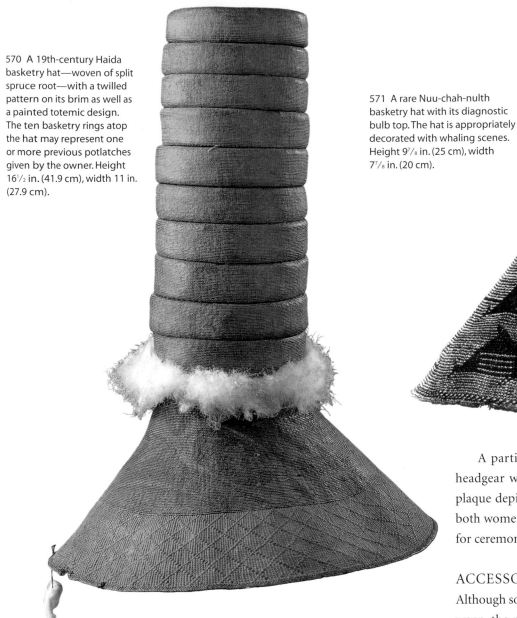

570 A 19th-century Haida basketry hat—woven of split spruce root—with a twilled pattern on its brim as well as a painted totemic design. The ten basketry rings atop the hat may represent one or more previous potlatches given by the owner. Height 16¹⁄₂ in. (41.9 cm), width 11 in. (27.9 cm).

571 A rare Nuu-chah-nulth basketry hat with its diagnostic bulb top. The hat is appropriately decorated with whaling scenes. Height 9⁷⁄₈ in. (25 cm), width 7⁷⁄₈ in. (20 cm).

572 (opposite) A 19th-century Tlingit frontlet of carved wood with abalone-shell insets. Originally this headdress— worn on the forehead— would have been adorned with ermine skins at the sides and back. Sea-lion whiskers would also have protruded from the top of the frontlet, enclosing pieces of eagle down. Height 8 in. (20.3 cm), width 6¹⁄₂ in. (16.5 cm), depth 1¹⁄₄ in. (3.2 cm).

women wore headgear woven of split spruce roots and painted with designs, usually those connected with the owner's totem [569]. During potlatches, high-ranking males wore tall, curved, wooden hats topped with a column of rings [570; see also 566] and/or animal crests that echoed the heraldic imagery displayed on a clan's totem poles. The Nuu-chah-nulth, the Coast's principal whalers, had a distinctive "whaler's" hat with a bulbous extension at its top [571]. But whatever the shape or material of a hat, they all shared a wide brim and were decorated with painted designs of totemic birds, fish or animals. Many had an inside headband of braided cedar fibers and were secured under the chin with ties.

A particularly magnificent form of ceremonial headgear was the frontlet, a carved, inlaid wooden plaque depicting a major crest figure [572]. Worn by both women and men, frontlets continue to be made for ceremonials.

ACCESSORIES

Although some arm bands of fur or braided fiber were worn, the major clothing accessories were pouches. These bags were mainly intended to hold dentallium shells, which served the Northwest Coast as a form of currency. The pouches were made of diagonally plaited cedar bark and attached to a belt—also made of braided cedar bark, or of leather—decorated with shells, animal teeth or claws.

Further down the coast, Far West tribes such as the Hupa, Pomo, Miwok and Chumash became renowned for their basketmaking. The Hupa, in particular, made twined basket "purses" that symbolized wealth and were carried in the lavish Jump Dance performed by Hupa men adorned in shell necklaces and distinctive headdresses decorated with red woodpecker scalps.[6]

573 Wide bracelets made of thin-beaten silver and adorned with totemic imagery. Such bracelets as these, which may be Haida pieces, were among the most prestigious of Northwest Coast jewelry.

Left: height 1 in. (2.5 cm), width 2¹⁄₄ in. (5.7 cm).

Center: height 1 in. (2.5 cm), width 2³⁄₄ in. (7 cm).

Right: height 1¹⁄₂ in. (3.8 cm), width 3 in. (7.6 cm).

JEWELRY

No item of jewelry was more important than the bracelet [573], a principal symbol of rank; indeed, the wealthy wore five or more on each arm [see 569]. Following European contact, these bracelets were hammered from gold and silver coins or from medals. It has been speculated by Lois Sherr Dubin, an authority on North American jewelry, that perhaps Northwest Coast bracelets were intended to replace tattooing, a practice discouraged by the missionaries.[7]

The northernmost of the Coastal peoples wore labrets—elliptical plugs of bone, wood or ivory that were inserted in the lower lip. Among the Tlingit, all women except slaves wore labrets; the largest were reserved for older women of high rank. When a girl reached puberty her lip was perforated. Both males and females also pierced the nasal septum to insert nose rings of iron or pieces of bone, wood, dentallium shell or abalone, the best of which came from California. Impressive abalone earrings were also a status item [see 569].

ARMOR

Protective armor varied by group. The Tsimshian—in their wars to acquire slaves, avenge wrongs, or take plunder—wore protective suits made up of wooden slats or rods, as did the Tlingit who also used a sleeveless tunic composed of double layers of elk hide. Other groups wrapped heavy cord or rope around the torso for protection [574]. With all types of armor, high wooden face and neck protectors were worn; Chinese coins were also often attached, both for protection and decoration. With the introduction of firearms, all types of indigenous armor became obsolete.

574 A Kwakwaka'wakw warrior, adorned with an iron nose ring, wears rope-coiled armor over his cedar-bark tunic.

SPECIAL COSTUMES

It is in the category of special costumes that the clothing of the Northwest Coast is most spectacular. At the flamboyant potlatches, attire was as prestigious and colorful as an individual could afford [575; see also 566]. The guests served as witnesses to validate the host's claim to privilege and rank by observing him deliberately burn vast quantities of oil or cut up and throw into the sea such valuables as Chilkat

575 A Kwakwaka'wakw potlatch costume made of canvas and decorated with profile views of back-to-back wolves. Below the narrow row of fur adorning the neck are pendants of abalone shell. Length 45 in. (114.3 cm).

GARMENT DECORATION

The unique iconography of Northwest Coast art—whether expressed on totem poles, masks, bracelets or blankets—reflects an ancient aesthetic language made up of a vocabulary of formlines: a network of curvilinear, swelling and tapering lines that delineate the major feature of an image—whether an ovoid, U-form and S-form or a squared off, oval "eye"—and relate these disparate design sections in a continuous pattern that fills an entire surface area.[8] Further hallmarks of Northwest Coast art are bilateral symmetry, split images and the repeated use of a narrow range of flat colors, primarily off-white, black, pale blue, pale yellow, red and green.

FACE AND BODY MODIFICATION

Face painting was common for both sexes, applied daily for practical purposes—protection against insects and the elements—but done with special care for ceremonial events, when the application of heraldic crests was deemed particularly appropriate [see 566]. Some tattooing was done. For example, Haida men often had their upper bodies tattooed with crest figures as expressions of beauty, protection against misfortune and identification of status. Most groups, however, confined tattooing to the backs of the hands and to women's forearms.[9]

Among some groups of the Kwakwaka'wakw, reshaping of the head was considered desirable in order to create an aristocratic, tall, sugar-loaf form that came to a high point in the back. This deformation was achieved by tying a padded cedar board around the head of an infant and then continually applying pressure while the baby was still in the cradle board.

582 (opposite) A transformation mask, ca. 1865. At the moment of ceremonial transformation, this bird mask was opened to reveal a human face inside, surrounded by an intricately detailed corona. Height 13 in. (33 cm), width 14⁷⁄₈ in. (38 cm), depth 26⁷⁄₈ in. (68.5 cm).

MASKS

On the Northwest Coast there existed a rich masking tradition—perhaps the highest art form of the carvers—and spectacular pieces were used in presenting the dramatic dances and ceremonies [582–587]. These powerful masks represented spirit helpers, crest animals and mythical creatures. In the dance dramas that re-enacted heroic deeds, the masks' visages of anguish, fright and power served as vehicles for both shamanistic vision quests and an initiate's transformation. They provided heightened intensity to the dances performed at night in the ceremonial houses that were illuminated only by firelight.

583 A Kwakwaka'wakw articulated bird-monster mask, whose beak shudders and snaps with a frightening sound as the dancer performs during a ceremonial drama. Length 23 in. (58.4 cm), height 9 in. (22.9 cm), depth 9 in. (22.9 cm).

584 The mask of the fearsome female giant Dzonokwa who is both monstrous—she sometimes roams the woods kidnapping and eating babies—and also beneficent, for at other times she bestows wealth on those she favors. Her open, red-ringed mouth, almost sucking in victims, gives clear indication of her bloodthirstiness, while her disheveled hair, flying all askew, suggests her wildness. Length 9 in. (22.9 cm), height 12 in. (30.5 cm), depth 9 in. (22.9 cm).

585 A bird-monster mask with an articulated bill. Length 18½ in. (47 cm), height 8 in. (20.3 cm), depth 9½ in. (24.1 cm).

586 A 19th-century Kaigani-Haida mask, with moveable eyes framed by four painted slats of wood that outline a gabled house front. Whales' tails of stuffed black cloth hang from the corners of the mouth. Height 23 in. (58.4 cm), width 26½ in. (67.3 cm), depth 6⅝ in. (17 cm).

587 A Tsimshian wolf forehead-mask, with eyes of abalone shell and teeth of small operculum shells. Height 4⅛ in. (10.5 cm), width 6⅝ in. (17 cm), depth 8⅝ in. (22 cm).

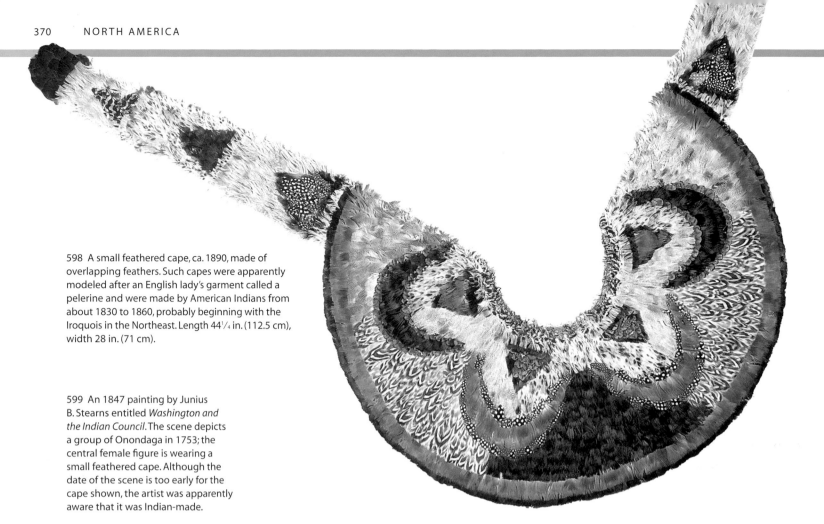

598 A small feathered cape, ca. 1890, made of overlapping feathers. Such capes were apparently modeled after an English lady's garment called a pelerine and were made by American Indians from about 1830 to 1860, probably beginning with the Iroquois in the Northeast. Length 44¼ in. (112.5 cm), width 28 in. (71 cm).

599 An 1847 painting by Junius B. Stearns entitled *Washington and the Indian Council*. The scene depicts a group of Onondaga in 1753; the central female figure is wearing a small feathered cape. Although the date of the scene is too early for the cape shown, the artist was apparently aware that it was Indian-made.

WOMEN'S BASIC DRESS

In the early period, the women of the Northeast wore a simple knee-length deerskin wraparound skirt, held in place by a belt; in winter, a skin poncho was added. By Contact period, women were wearing the strap-and-sleeve dress: two matched skins seamed at the sides, with straps attached at the shoulders. To this basic garment could be added separate sleeves that fastened at the back of the neck and were caught together in front by a strip of buckskin that often continued around the waist. The removable sleeves, which lacked underarm seams, fastened at the wrists. These dresses—their length depending on the height of the wearer or the dimension of the skins—were worn with knee-length leggings fitted to the ankles by ties or lacings. By the 19th century, short feathered capes were also worn by women in the western Great Lakes region [598, 599]. "The technique for making these capes diffused—via the St. Lawrence River—as far west as Iowa."[4]

In the Southeast, women wore wraparound skirts of deerskin, twined mulberry bark or woven buffalo hair, together with an apron or draped piece that extended from waist to knee. An additional garment was a shawl or cape that draped under one arm and fastened on the opposite shoulder. When leggings were worn, they were knee-length and gartered.

FOOTWEAR

Northeastern moccasins—the name derives from an Algonquin term—were of two general types. The first was a one-piece style with a seam up front and back, and a thong attached to tie the moccasin tightly around the ankle. The second type was a three-piece style: the sole was puckered up to fit an oval or U-shaped vamp over the instep; the third piece was used as a cuff. The oval insert and/or cuffs could be embellished with quillwork, embroidery or beading [600, 601].

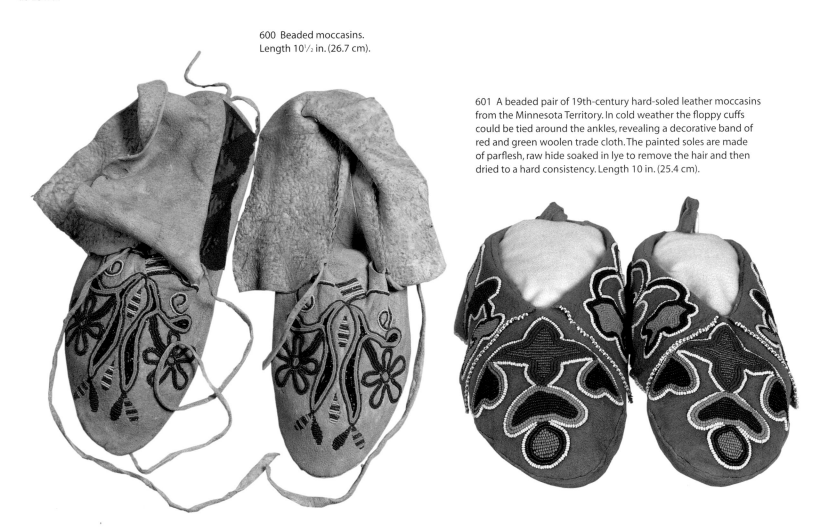

600 Beaded moccasins.
Length 10½ in. (26.7 cm).

601 A beaded pair of 19th-century hard-soled leather moccasins from the Minnesota Territory. In cold weather the floppy cuffs could be tied around the ankles, revealing a decorative band of red and green woolen trade cloth. The painted soles are made of parflesh, raw hide soaked in lye to remove the hair and then dried to a hard consistency. Length 10 in. (25.4 cm).

The 18th-century Cherokee wore a distinctive type of one-piece deerskin moccasin that encased the entire foot to join in a single seam that ran up the center of the top of the foot[5] [see central figure, 594]. In the warmer climate of the southern Southeast, both males and females normally went barefoot around their houses but made use of woven hemp moccasins when traveling.

In such rough or wet terrains as those of the Seminole, "swamp moccasins" were worn. A single piece of skin or hide was laced up the back or at the toes with thongs. These back laces were left long so they could be tied around the ankles for protection. Sometimes an additional piece of hide was sewn on the bottom for a heavier sole. A more fashionable version buttoned up the leg [602].

HAIRSTYLES

Throughout the Woodlands, warrior headdresses—believed to contain spirit guardians—served as powerful amulets. Lois Sherr Dubin, the authority on native American adornment, notes that "an age-old style [was] called the roach…. Warriors plucked, singed or, later, shaved the head except for one long scalp lock." To this length of hair was secured the roach, a hairpiece made of red-dyed deer hair, horse hair, porcupine guard hair and/or moose mane [603; see also 595]. "When attached to the braided scalp lock at the center of the head, the roach resembled the imposing crest of a large, enraged woodpecker, a traditional warrior symbol."[6]

In the Northeast, women sometimes pulled their long, loose hair back from their face, giving it a beaver tail look and decorating it with quillwork; it was then referred to as being "clubbed." Both sexes dressed their hair daily with bear fat to keep it smooth and shining. In the Southeast, most women cut their hair short at times of mourning but otherwise wore it long and loose. In contrast, Seminole women arranged their hair in a tight, flat roll on the top of the head, achieving a sunshade effect [see 614].

602 Charles Bird King's 1835 portrait of the Seminole Chief Tudo-See-Mathla—also known as John Hicks—wearing buttoned "swamp moccasins" and a shirt adorned with the multicolored rickrack that continues to be a hallmark of Seminole garments to this day. From the silver gorget around his neck hangs a United States peace medal, a gift typically given to Indian chiefs when they visited Washington where their portraits were sometimes painted.

603 A Chippewa roach headdress made of fuschia-dyed deer hair and black horse hair. This piece was collected in Minnesota in the 19th century. Length 10 in. (25.4 cm), width 5½ in. (14 cm).

604 Front and back views of a 19th-century Chippewa vest fashioned over a man's standard suit vest by adding black velvet panels richly ornamented with beaded floral designs. Length 22 in. (55.9 cm), width 19 in. (48.3 cm).

OUTERWEAR

The Southeastern Indians made beautiful mantles of feathers, especially turkey feathers that were individually attached to a fiber matting. These prestigious garments were the prerogative of men. In the Great Lakes region, men wore beautifully beaded vests [604]. In these colder climes, winter cloaks were made of a variety of skins: deer, bear, elk and, in the western areas, buffalo.

605 Sequoyah (ca. 1773–1843), son of a Cherokee mother and English father, wears a turban of European fabric. He also wears a United States peace medal hanging from a ribbon around his neck. Sequoyah believed that literacy was the source of the white man's power and is the only person in history known to have singlehandedly created a written language. Here he is shown with his Cherokee syllabary.

HEADGEAR

In the bitter Northeastern winters, women sometimes wore a fur cap or hood but otherwise went bare-headed. However, both men and women occasionally donned woven headbands to which feathers and other ornaments might be added. Hunters, when stalking game, sometimes wore antlers on their heads and animal skins on their bodies. At other times, "the entire skin of a fox or otter would be tied about the head, the tail left flapping."[7]

In the Southeast, headgear was not a particularly featured item. The Indians normally went bareheaded although feathered headdresses made of turkey, crane, heron, eagle or swan were usually a prestigious male prerogative and were worn by men of higher status. Following Contact, turbans of imported European fabric became fashionable [605].

ACCESSORIES

Northeastern men wore pouches or bags—with one strap over the shoulder—made of deerskin and embroidered with quillwork or embroidery. Sashes in bright geometric patterns were used as accessories, as were small bags of basswood or other fibers [606, 607]. Among the Indians of the Southeast accessories were few, with the exception of superbly woven sashes, many of mulberry inner bark executed in a finger-weaving technique and often adorned with beads that were worked into complex designs [608]. Pouches, some made from a deer's paunch or bladder, hung from the belt and often held a pipe, tobacco and fire-making equipment. In the far south, the Seminoles used scarves for pocketbooks which held beads and sacred medicine such as herbs and grasses.

606 (opposite) A small Chippewa "octopus" bag—named for the six fringe pieces—made of deerskin with floral beadwork decoration. Length 5 in. (12.7 cm).

607 The sashes of the Great Lakes region were woven by a loomless method known as "oblique interlace," an ancient technique in eastern North America. By the 18th century braided sashes from L'Assomption, Quebec, were standard wear for French Canadian and Metis Indians involved in the fur trade. Today these textiles of worsted yarn are referred to in the literature as "Assomption" sashes. Length 58 in. (147.3 cm), width 12 in. (30.5 cm).

608 A man's woolen shoulder sash with ten old Iroquois silver brooches attached to it. The glass trade beads on the long fringe were interwoven into each strand. This remarkably fine specimen was once owned and worn by a Seneca chief. Length of sash proper 30 in. (76.2 cm); with fringe 9 ft. 8 in. (3 m).

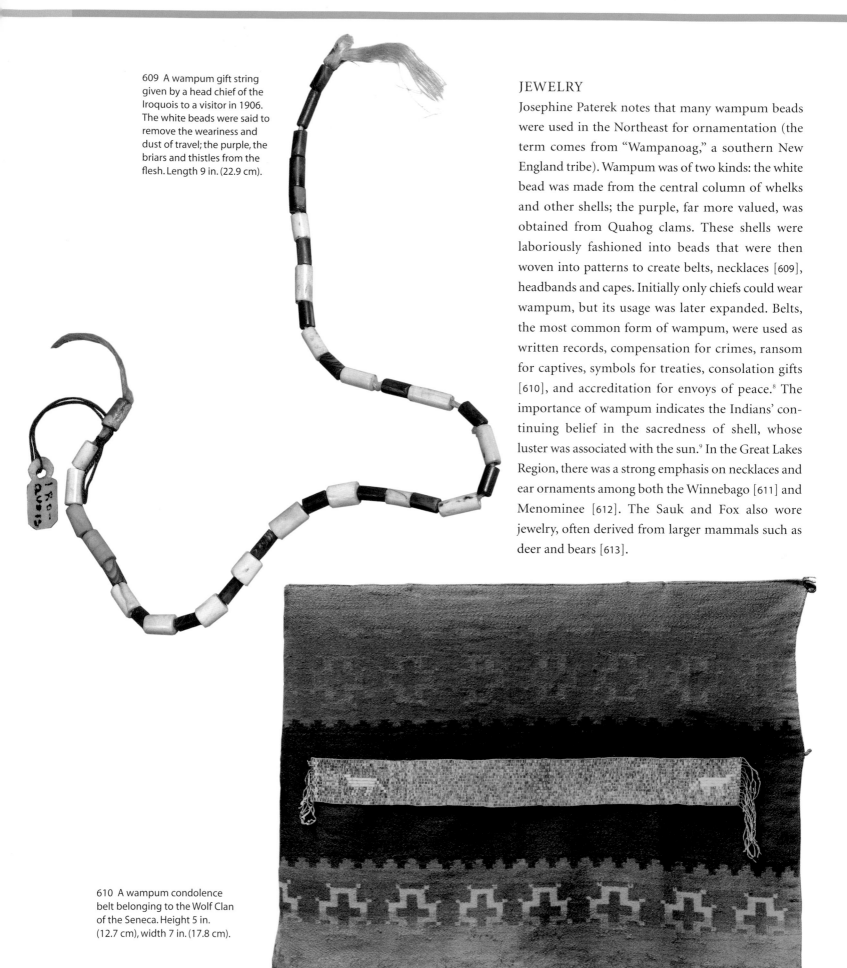

609 A wampum gift string given by a head chief of the Iroquois to a visitor in 1906. The white beads were said to remove the weariness and dust of travel; the purple, the briars and thistles from the flesh. Length 9 in. (22.9 cm).

JEWELRY

Josephine Paterek notes that many wampum beads were used in the Northeast for ornamentation (the term comes from "Wampanoag," a southern New England tribe). Wampum was of two kinds: the white bead was made from the central column of whelks and other shells; the purple, far more valued, was obtained from Quahog clams. These shells were laboriously fashioned into beads that were then woven into patterns to create belts, necklaces [609], headbands and capes. Initially only chiefs could wear wampum, but its usage was later expanded. Belts, the most common form of wampum, were used as written records, compensation for crimes, ransom for captives, symbols for treaties, consolation gifts [610], and accreditation for envoys of peace.[8] The importance of wampum indicates the Indians' continuing belief in the sacredness of shell, whose luster was associated with the sun.[9] In the Great Lakes Region, there was a strong emphasis on necklaces and ear ornaments among both the Winnebago [611] and Menominee [612]. The Sauk and Fox also wore jewelry, often derived from larger mammals such as deer and bears [613].

610 A wampum condolence belt belonging to the Wolf Clan of the Seneca. Height 5 in. (12.7 cm), width 7 in. (17.8 cm).

611 (far left) A 19th-century studio portrait taken in Winnebago, Wisconsin, of a Winnebago woman and boy wearing ornate necklaces with their traditional clothing.

612 (left) A 19th-century Menominee woman and girl adorned with traditional jewelry, scarves and sashes.

613 (below) A Sauk/Fox bear-claw necklace strung on deerskin together with fourteen large blue beads and two long antelope bones. Length 25 in. (63.5 cm).

A variety of jewelry was worn in the Southeast but special attention was paid to adorning the ears. Men slit the ear along the edge, binding the lobe with thongs until it healed. A piece of lead was then added to lengthen the opening which subsequently was bound with copper wire; often eagle plumes were inserted into the opening [see 594]. Women pierced their ears—although not as extensively as men—and inserted strings of pearls in the lobes as well as bird claws, buttons or plugs. Necklaces were also made of pearls or beads of copper; some beads were worn around the ankle or just below the knee. Chest ornaments called gorgets were made of large shells that were often delicately incised with designs; these may have served as emblems of authority, status or religion.[10]

Seminole jewelry is unique. When a girl is quite young she is given a string of beads. Additional strings

614 (above) A 1910 Seminole family attired in traditional clothing. The distinctive Seminole hair roll can be seen on the woman. Note, too, the girls' few beginning strands of beads in contrast to the many necklaces already acquired by their mother.

615 (right) These two squares of black velvet, each intricately beaded in complex floral designs, were probably either end of an apron-style loincloth of the type worn in the Great Lakes region ca. 1885. Height 17 in. (43.2 cm), width 29½ in. (74.9 cm).

are added from time to time until the young woman is wearing necklaces coiled almost to her ears. A Seminole woman would feel immodestly dressed without her impressive jewelry [614].

SPECIAL COSTUMES/MASKS

Aside from shamans or medicine men, whose attire incorporated powerful symbolic items revealed in dreams or revelations, special costuming was not a feature of the Woodlands. The exception is the masking tradition of the Iroquois False Face Society, whose wooden masks depict twisted faces that were used in curing rites. Considered supernatural, these masks—made and worn only by men—were carved from living trees in order to capture their spirit. Also a part of the curing rites were cornhusk masks made by the women, but worn by both sexes.

The Cherokee also had a masking tradition, one not as well known as that of the Iroquois and used in a different context. Cherokee masks were worn in dance dramas to identify disruptive forces that threatened the balance of Cherokee stability and hence had to be cast out to reinforce social solidarity.[11]

GARMENT DECORATION

In the pre-Contact Southeast, the tanned skins used for clothing were often dyed various colors—red, green, blue and black. This propensity for colored garments no doubt influenced the rapid assimilation of colorful European clothing. Finger-woven belts and sashes featured geometric designs including circular motifs such as double curves. These same forms continued to be used in 19th-century beadwork. In the Northeast, some finger-weaving was also done with bast fibers, buffalo wool and opossum hair. Using a twining technique, these fibers were woven into bags, pouches, garters and sashes and were decorated with quillwork and moose-hair embroidery. Black-dyed buckskin was used by many eastern tribes [see 593] and, significantly, black trade cloth and black velvet were popular with the Woodland tribes in the 18th century [615].

European glass beads were valued from earliest post-Contact times, especially those of blue and white. The indigenous tendency to adorn surfaces with repetitive units such as shells was a precedent for embroidered glass beadwork. The French introduced floral designs in about 1639 at their Indian missions in eastern Canada,[12] and floral beaded designs were particularly characteristic of the Woodlands [see 606]. Another decorative garment element was ribbon appliqué made with multi-hued silk ribbons brought in by the traders. A mirror-image design was cut from one ribbon and then sewn onto a ribbon of contrasting color so as to create strips that were applied for a pleasing effect [see 596].

FACE AND BODY MODIFICATION

In the Southeast, head deformation by skull flattening was practiced by some tribes, using a bag of sand or a block of wood wrapped in buckskin to apply pressure to an infant's head. For adults, personal adornment took many forms. Body paint was popular for both war and games. But, throughout the Woodlands, it was tattooing that was ubiquitous [see 594]. In a world where the body was substantially exposed for much of the year, a person adorned with body paint, tattooing

and hair adornment was considered to be richly dressed.[13] Tattooing was usually blue and designs ranged from scrolls to flowers, stars, animals, crescents and esoteric symbols. Although both sexes favored tattooing, it was males who were most ornamented. Their decorations, in most cases, were based on status, and woe to the unqualified usurper: he was forced to remove all of his pretentious tattoos, a painful process.[14]

TRANSITIONAL DRESS

Shortly after Contact, the clothing of the Woodlands became a mixture of Indian and European styles [616]. In some cases cloth replaced skins without a change in the basic patterns—for example, imported woolen stroud cloth was used instead of deerskin for loincloths—but in other instances patterns rather than materials were changed: deerskins were tailored into trousers and shirts [617] instead of being used for leggings and robes. The pre-Contact decorative materials—porcupine quills, moose-hair embroidery, shells—were largely replaced by shiny glass beads. Also, an excess of silk ribbon, no longer fashionable in France following the mandates of "Simplicity in Dress" fostered by the 1789 French Revolution, entered North America through the fur trade.[15]

It is of interest that Woodlands tribes welcomed certain trade goods as a result of their existing aesthetic traditions and indigenous beliefs. For example, the popularity of silk ribbon appliqué may stem from the ribbon's luminous surface, reminiscent of the sheen of aboriginal shell and copper, shimmering substances long revered by native peoples. Similarly, glass beads extended beliefs in the sacred quality of crystal, and no doubt the acceptance of silver was influenced by a reverence for the reflective quality of shell.[16]

Although in pre-Contact times the Indians did hammer implements from metals—principally pure copper—metalwork never progressed past this rudimentary stage, hence metal implements were rare before the Colonial Period. However, once the Indians recognized the superiority of European metal they eagerly began to trade for all kinds, including ornaments of brass, silver, and "German silver," not

616 An 1850 photo of Caroline S. Parker, a Seneca woman shown wearing a mixture of Seneca and Western attire that reflects the hybrid nature of 19th-century Woodlands clothing.

617 (opposite above) This beaded buckskin shirt from the northern Great Lakes region is an example of Western garment styles being fashioned from indigenous materials. Length 33 in. (83.8 cm).

618 (opposite below) The two sides of an 1825 peace medal with the raised profile of the then-president, John Quincy Adams, clearly outlined on the front; on the reverse side are the clasped hands of peace and friendship, together with a crossed pipe and tomahawk. This bronze medal was no doubt originally silver-plated. Length 3 in. (7.6 cm).

silver at all but rather an alloy of copper, zinc and nickel. The French, English and the new United States Government—as well as the independent traders— all used a great deal of metal jewelry for trading purposes in their competition for the Indians as allies and suppliers of furs [see 608]. The earliest trade ornaments of brass and copper were subsequently supplanted by silver jewelry, most of which was made by English silversmiths who lived in Philadelphia, Montreal and London. The Indians themselves began to manufacture metal ornaments around 1800, using coins and tableware as raw materials. Popularly worn, too, were the silver-plated peace medals distributed by the Government [618; see also 593, 602, 605].

Particularly colorful transitional dress occurred among the Seminole. Among their distinct life ways is a propensity for colorful cotton clothing decorated with the traditional red and yellow designs of patchwork and rickrack [619]. It is of interest that a version of the Seminole man's tunic depicted by Charles Bird King in the 1830s [see 602] was still being worn in 1910, when it was known as "the Big Shirt" [620].

619 A modern-day Seminole man's patchwork coat decorated in the traditional manner with multiple patterns created by juxtaposing small pieces of colored cloth. Length 27 in. (68.6 cm).

620 A 1910 photo of a Seminole guide skinning a bird in the south Florida swamps; he wears the Seminoles' traditional "Big Shirt."

THE PLAINS

621 Henry Farney, *In the Foothills of the Rockies*, 1898. In this summer camp, some of the men wear buckskin garments while others are wrapped in commercial trade blankets. All wear indigenous moccasins and hairstyles. Three of the men in the foreground display a single eagle feather in their hair— a protective amulet that symbolized valor.

Long before the plains and prairies of the Midwest were tamed into farmland they were a free, unbroken sea of rolling grass extending across the heartland of the North American continent, reaching from the banks of the Mississippi to the foothills of the Rockies [see 621], from southern Texas north into western Canada [Map 28]. For millennia this enormous grazing land provided a multitude of huge animals with one of earth's most nutritious pastures. By 15,000 years ago, humans had begun migrating into North America in pursuit of this big game. The fluted stone spear and dart points of these Paleo-Indians have been found in caves and at kill sites among the bones of the slaughtered behemoths who defined their way of life.

Following the end of the Paleolithic, climatic changes and overhunting caused several animal species—big-horn bison, mammoth, mastadon, the Pleistocene horse—to become extinct, forcing the Indians to find new food sources. Smaller game and wild plants were sought wherever available. These localized hunters and gatherers are known as the Archaic peoples, in contrast to the earlier Paleo-Indians of the Ice Age. In some parts of North America, their way of life continued until the arrival of the Europeans. Such was the case on the Great Plains, where an inherited world view continued on as well. Spirituality was at the foundation of the Native Americans' lives. Religion intertwined with nearly every aspect of daily life, reflecting a belief system based on a shamanistic cosmology and a ritual system that had roots in the Upper Paleolithic of the Old World.[1]

By the late 16th century, the horse had been re-introduced into North America by the Spaniards and slowly spread northward from their settlements in the Southwest. It was with the nomadic hunting tribes of the Plains that this meeting of horse and man had the greatest impact [622], leading to the legendary horse/buffalo/Indian culture.

For the nomadic peoples of the Plains, the world was one of motion. The undulating grasslands were stirred by the incessant wind and waves of migrating buffalo, followed by the migrating tribes themselves.[2] In such a world, clothing had to be easily transported as well as quickly responsive to dramatic seasonal changes. Like the Indians themselves, their dress was highly individualistic, although throughout the Plains there was also constant trading, gift-giving and inter-communication between the tribes.

Prior to the arrival of white traders, Indian garments were made of animal hides, skins that required skilled processing: flesh was scraped from the inside and, where desirable, hair was also removed from the outer hide. The skin was washed and stretched on a frame where a paste made of deer brains, oil and wood ash was worked into it. The hide was then washed

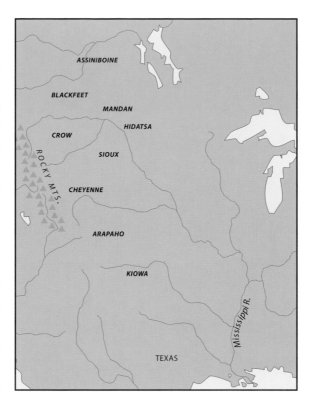

Map 28 The Plains region of North America.

622 Blackfeet riders, led by "Little Plume," parade prior to a Sun Dance ceremony. Note the magnificent eagle-feather war bonnets worn by many among this distinguished group. It was only the exceptional warrior who earned the right to wear this regalia, which reflected his many exploits in battle.

again, twisted dry, and softened by working it between the hands and rubbing it with a stick. Finally, the skin was smoked to increase its durability by inhibiting the growth of mold.

Of all the animals involved in the Plains clothing repertory—which included deer, antelope, elk, moose, big-horn sheep, otter and beaver—it was the buffalo that made the Indians' way of life possible, providing food, clothing, shelter, and even fuel from droppings; the stripped bones themselves were finally utilized for saddles, camping equipment, tools and other transportable articles. This nomadic existence was surprisingly short-lived, lasting little more than a century. By 1890 the buffalo were nearly extinct. Whites had moved into the region—often violently—and the classic Plains Indian culture was gone, leaving behind a popular, all-encompassing stereotype of what the "American Indian" was like, a picture that persists in most quarters to this day.

MEN'S BASIC DRESS

While men's costumes varied considerably from north to south, the most basic of Plains garments was the loincloth, either a piece of hide wrapped around the body or a buckskin apron attached at the waist to a thong belt. This same belt also supported the males' thigh-high leggings usually constructed of untrimmed, tanned skins [623], made by either being folded over and tied down at the sides or sewn with sinew; the leggings' cuffs were usually left tattered. Bands of paint, quillwork or beading also sometimes adorned the outside seams [624]. In the absence of a written language, the decoration on clothing was an important element in Indian communication, conveying many levels of information. Because the Plains Indians highly prized personal bravery, their garments often displayed marks of distinction earned through valor in battle.

The earliest of the men's skin shirts were worn uncut, retaining the shape of the hides from which they were made, perhaps in deference to the spirit of the animal involved. Two skins of either deer, elk, antelope,

623 Mandan Indians— clad only in loincloths and leggings—engaged in a ceremonial dance.

big-horn sheep or small buffalo—matched for size and shape—were laced or tied together in a poncho style [625].[3] Invariably both shirts and leggings were fringed, an important Plains decorative element [626, 627]. It has been suggested that fringes symbolically extended the essence of an individual beyond the confines of the garment being worn.[4]

624 These Northern Plains fringed leggings date from the early 20th century and may be Blackfeet. Length 35 in. (88.9 cm), width 13 in. (33 cm).

625 A Lakota hair-fringed ceremonial shirt, ca. 1865–1875. Length 36 in. (91.4 cm). Among the Sioux bands, one of the most important duties was the appointment of "shirt wearers." Such shirts—whose main distinguishing feature was the hair-lock fringe on the sleeves—symbolized the high status of the wearer and signaled his obligations not only in war but also in tribal leadership. The owner's war record is recorded on his leggings: the number of war pipes smoked, battles fought, enemies slain. The red and blue paint on the shirt and leggings are symbolic references to the earth and sky. The bird-wing headdress and stretched, painted, buffalo-hide shield completed the outfit.

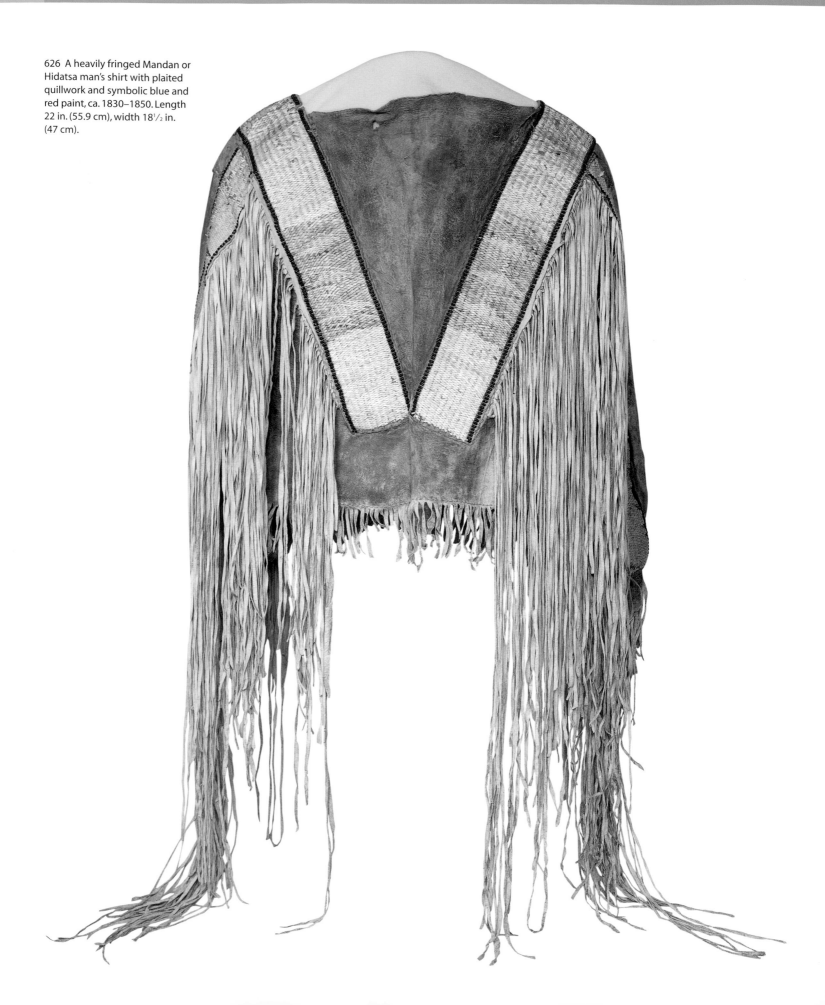

626 A heavily fringed Mandan or Hidatsa man's shirt with plaited quillwork and symbolic blue and red paint, ca. 1830–1850. Length 22 in. (55.9 cm), width 18½ in. (47 cm).

627 A Kiowa boy's shirt with triangular "shield," leggings and moccasins.

Shirt: length 18 in. (45.7 cm).

Leggings: length 17½ in. (44.5 cm), width 8 in. (20.3 cm).

Moccasins: length 7¼ in. (18.4 cm).

628 A Cheyenne girl's two-skin dress, ca. 1870–1880. Over this carefully beaded buckskin dress, which also incorporates large Russian blue glass trade beads, is worn an intricate 45-inch-long (115 cm) dentalia hairpipe necklace that hangs down front and back [see 642]. Dress: length 28½ in. (72.4 cm), width 22 in. (55.9 cm).

629 A Lakota Sioux beaded dress, ca. 1870–1880. Blue, the color of the heavens, held a sacred place in Lakota symbolism. The heavily ornamented yoke on this deerskin dress was called "blue breast beading." Using the lazy-stitch technique, the beads were sewn with sinew in parallel rows ³/₈ of an inch (10 mm) or so wide. The work is so carefully done that little of the stitching can be seen on the skin's back side. Note the extended panels at either side of the hem that preserve the configuration of the animal's front legs. Length 68½ in. (174 cm), width 54³/₈ in. (138 cm).

WOMEN'S BASIC DRESS

The earliest attire for women was a simple wraparound skirt, held in place by a belt, with a poncho/cape added for inclement weather. As the Indians became more mobile, thanks to the horse, skins became more available, hence more complex female garments evolved. There is evidence of an early side-fold dress derived from a folded animal skin. The later "two-skin" dress [628] was made of two full, untrimmed deer or elk hides laced together. The hind legs became the shoulders; ornamentation followed the lines of the original skins. On such dresses, the animal's front legs often hung down on either side of the skirt, creating panel-like extensions at the hem. On the subsequent "three-skin" dress, the top was made of one skin folded over to form a yoke that was sewn to a skirt made of two hides joined together; the side-extension panels continued to appear at the hem [629].

With the arrival of European traders, stroud (trade) cloth was introduced, a heavy woolen fabric made in Stroudwater, England, often dyed scarlet red or navy blue.[5] It was stroud cloth that provided soft material for men's loincloths and also the ground cloth for the prestigious elk-tooth dress [630, 631], a symbol of both long life and wealth (in 1852 a dress

630 The Arapaho woman "Freckled Face" wears a lavishly decorated elk-tooth dress and hairpipe jewelry.

631 A Crow elk-tooth dress. European woolens were an early trade item with the North American Indians; these soft, warm and malleable fabrics quickly began to replace winter garments of skin and fur. From stroud cloth were cut simple two-piece dresses to which were sewn decorative items such as shells, metal tinklers or elks' teeth. This Crow dress is an example of antler or bone being carved to resemble the difficult-to-obtain elks' teeth.

Dress: length 44 in. (111.8 cm), width 18 in. (45.7 cm).

Moccasins: height 10 in. (25.4 cm), width 5¼ in. (13.3 cm).

632 A Cheyenne stroud cloth dress, decorated at the bodice with dentalium shells that came to the Plains from Vancouver Island, British Columbia, via the indigenous trade network. Note the elongated panels on either side of the dress's hem, atavistic survivals of the earlier skin dresses. Length 28 in. (71.1 cm).

ornamented with 300 elk teeth was the equivalent in value to a good horse). Such costly garments were therefore worn by Plains women and girls only on special occasions. Since elk have just two lower incisor milk teeth, imitations were often made from elk antler or bone to complete the requisite ornamentation. It is of interest that some of these trade-cloth dresses also incorporated side panels at the hem, an atavistic survival of the earlier animal-skin garments [632]. But whatever the style of a Plains woman's dress, in winter and at ceremonies she wore leggings with it [633]— gartered above or below the knees with leather thongs or strips of otter fur—and some form of moccasin.

633 A Sioux woman's buckskin leggings beaded in geometric designs resembling the animal-hide tepees that served as the lodges of the Plains Indians. These leggings probably date from the 1890s. Length 15 in. (38.1 cm), width 7½ in. (19 cm).

FOOTWEAR

Plains moccasins were of two general types, either a soft-soled, one-piece foot covering cut from a single section of leather and seamed at the outer edge of the foot and heel or, later, a two-piece style with a hard, rawhide sole and a soft skin upper. This latter type was cut with a tongue, or one was added [634]. When whites were still struggling with the discomfort of both shoes constructed alike, Indians were wearing moccasins designed for the right and left feet.[6]

Winter moccasins were made with the hide's hair left on—usually with cuffs added to turn up and tie around the ankles—and were cut larger to accommodate a warm stuffing of grass or fur. Ceremonial moccasins were often decorated with bands of quill or beadwork, sometimes even on the soles [635]. Such examples were used as status items and were often called "parade" moccasins. The impractical decoration of moccasin soles reflects an Indian tendency toward the incorporation of self-directed, hidden designs.[7] Some high-status moccasins were even fitted with appendages that trailed along behind them. Only a proven warrior could be granted the honor of wearing strips of skunk fur or a wolf tail attached to his moccasins [see 636].

634 Beaded Sioux moccasins, ca. 1890. Length 10½ in. (26.7 cm).

635 Lakota Sioux quillwork moccasins with decorated soles, ca. 1880–1900. Length 8 in. (20.3 cm), width 3¼ in. (8.3 cm).

636 This painting—made between 1832 and 1834 by the German artist Karl Bodmer—depicts two Mandan warriors attired in high-status moccasins and enveloping buffalo robes. The complexities of properly curing these heavy skins were such that they were sometimes cut in half, processed, and then re-assembled with an elegant quill or beaded decorative band ornamenting the join.

OUTERWEAR

The robe was the wrap of the Plains Indians, providing comfort by day, bedding by night [636]. Lightweight robes were made of deer or elk skin but in the winter buffalo robes were worn, with the fur on the inside; these cumbersome garments often weighed up to 90 pounds (40 kg). Men's robes also served as ceremonial garb, with the hide's tanned outer side painted. One of the men's most dramatic motifs appeared on the "exploit robe," a pictographic record of the owner's war deeds, including stylized figures in battle scenes complete with many warriors and horses. When shamans and chiefs sat together wrapped in their buffalo robes it was said to convey the appearance of a group of buffalo, a sight conceived as a symbolic transfer of power from beast to man. The women's buffalo robes featured geometric designs such as the "box and border" [637, 638], thought by some to represent abstract reproductive motifs.[8]

637 A Dakota Sioux woman wears a buffalo robe—painted with a "box and border" design—over her fringed deerskin dress, which is decorated at the hem with tiny metal ornaments called "tinklers." This painting was also made by Karl Bodmer between 1832 and 1834 (an engraver later added the figure of an Assiniboine girl to the scene).

638 A Lakota woman's "box and border" buffalo robe, ca. 1870–1880. Robes such as this were painted by the women themselves. The designs accentuate the shape of the animal's hide; the central "box" is an abstract reference to the animal's internal organs. The entire hide, together with its painted pattern, symbolizes the relationship between the woman and the power of the buffalo. In Plains society there are continuous symbolic links between women and bison. Length 79 1/8 in. (201 cm), width 63 in. (160 cm).

641 (opposite) This flaring headdress is composed of prime eagle feathers from the bird's tail and wings, as well as beadwork, horse-hair strands and the skins of ermine, an animal acknowledged to be a fierce fighter and hence good war medicine. Length 30 in. (76.2 cm).

As the buffalo began to diminish, woven blankets slowly replaced the heavy buffalo robes. Navajo "Chief blankets" (see "The Southwest," pp. 411–412) were highly valued, as were Hudson Bay commercial blankets, often made in white with "candy-striped" colored bands at either end and marked with short parallel stripes on one side. These lines, or "points," indicated the size of a blanket and hence, by extension, had a relationship to its cost, thus serving as a kind of price tag to indicate the "point value" or number of beaver pelts required in trade.[9]

HAIRSTYLES

Women generally wore their hair in two braids; unmarried women wore them hanging down their back, married women wore the braids forward, over the shoulder. For men, however, hair styling was more complex. In the north, men's hair was usually sectioned into several parts, sometimes braided and wrapped in otter fur [639]. In the south, the hair was worn loose.

Many men displayed a scalp lock, a long thin section of hair, usually unbraided, to which ornaments could be attached. This scalp lock was maintained even when men affected the dramatic roach hairstyle, whereby the head was shaved except for a brush standing up at the top. To this clump of hair was attached a roach spreader that supported an arrangement of dyed porcupine hair that stood erect at the top of the head, creating an unbroken span from front to back (see "The Woodlands," pp. 369 and 372). Today we know this hairstyle as the Mohawk, a tribal term from the northeastern Woodlands.

HEADGEAR

In their daily life, the Indians went bareheaded all year round except for occasional fur capes in the winter. Ceremonial headgear, however, was a hallmark of Plains attire, particularly the famous eagle-feather war bonnet [640, 641], regarded as a "feathered sun" that spiritually transformed the

639 (right) This portrait of Sitting Bull, whose long braids are wrapped in otter fur and who wears a single eagle feather in his hair, was taken in Bismarck, Dakota, in 1885. He was a medicine man for the Hunkpapa Sioux and became the guiding spirit of the combined Indian forces at the Battle of the Little Big Horn, also known as Custer's Last Stand or—by the Indians —the Battle of Greasy Grass.

640 (far right) "Two Guns," a Blackfeet warrior, wearing the prestigious feathered warrior headdress. This style is referred to as a "flared" bonnet.

wearer into an eagle, soaring toward the Sky World and the sun's rays.[10] For American Indians, feathers served as a metaphor for birds and the powers of the sky. And of all birds, the eagle was considered the most spiritual. Eagle-feather war bonnets were worn by exceptional warriors, men who had accomplished four honors during battle: leading a war party, horse-raiding, removing a gun from an enemy, and counting coup.[11]

The act of counting coup was at the foundation of the warriors' honor system; it included the taking of a life or a scalp, touching the badge of an enemy, or stealing a bow, gun or dart. Each feather in the "halo" of a war bonnet, and in the feathered trailer behind [see 622], represented a battle incident or other distinguished honor. Each feather stood for an enemy; the tip of the hair fastened to the feathers and dyed red represented the foe's scalp lock. Before the feather could be fastened on the warrior's bonnet, he had to recount the war honor which entitled him to wear that feather. If ermine was fastened to the bonnet it was said to represent the desired characteristics of the animal itself—alertness and skill in evading pursuit.

JEWELRY

For the Plains Indians, jewelry was an intricate part of attire, worn about the neck, on the wrist or suspended from the ears. Indeed, ear ornaments that combined beads, shells and hairpipes could total as much as half a pound (0.25 kg) in weight. Necklaces of grizzly-bear claws were considered to contain great power. Chokers were made of fur strips and dentalium shells, obtained in trade from the Pacific. Rolls of otter skin, stuffed and decorated with quillwork and hairpipe beads, sometimes supported shell gorgets or pectorals. Peace medals were treasured by the chiefs. These official government gifts measured 3 to 6 inches (7.5–15 cm) in diameter and carried the image of the current president on one side and, sometimes, a crossed peacepipe and tomahawk on the other (see "The Woodlands," p. 380).

642 A Lakota Sioux hairpipe necklace, ca. 1870–1880. This would have been worn over a beaded animal-hide dress [see 629].

ACCESSORIES

Women wore leather belts, often painted and ornamented with quill- or beadwork, to which were attached important items such as awl cases and bags of paint. Men, however, wore two belts, an inner thong that held the loincloth and leggings in place [see 623] and a dress belt of rawhide put on over the thong but under the skirt. Because indigenous clothing had no pockets, it was from a man's outer belt that his accessories were hung: pouches, tools, weapons and the all-important "medicine" bag, the most sacred item an individual could possess. This spiritual aid contained herbs and artifacts that often had been revealed to its owner in a vision or dream.

After 1850 some Indian men wore breastplates fashioned from tubular ornaments of white shell known as hairpipe beads, so named by the traders. These beads measured from 2 to 5 in. long (5–12.7 cm) and were originally made in the eastern United States from the lip of a West Indian conch shell (*Strombus gigas*). By 1860, hairpipes began to be made from bone as shell had become too expensive. The long, cylindrical beads were strung in two to four sections and were also worn by women [642; see also 628, 630].

ARMOR

The Plains Indians did not wear armor as such but did carry circular shields made of heavy rawhide taken from the neck of the buffalo, laced on a hoop and painted. Sometimes they were further embellished with feathers and the claws of birds and other animals for greater power [see 625]. Although one of the shield's primary purposes was defense in battle, like so much of Plains attire it also had a spiritual aspect. Shield designs were often received in visions and hence were believed to provide an individual with supernatural power or protection. The triangular neck section on a Plains shirt [see 627] was also known as a "shield". This was held to be a protective device similar in intent to the symbolic designs painted on the warrior's actual shields.[12]

SPECIAL COSTUMES

Among the Plains Indians there were no costumes specifically for chiefs, although during battles they carried special wooden staffs or lances and wore prestigious warrior dress, including the flamboyant war bonnet. Distinctive headdresses were also worn in tribal dances by members of the various warrior societies, groups that helped to foster courage and a spirit of daring, important qualities for the warlike people of the Plains [643]. Most tribes had several men's organizations bearing such names as Crazy Dogs, Lunyswood and Bulls. Each society had its own distinctive regalia and ceremonies; some were primarily religious and were believed to contribute to general tribal welfare.

Shaman/medicine men often dressed differently to others. This was particularly true during curing ceremonies. For example, a shaman might don a bearskin to further empower a healing, since the bear was an important source of protective medicine. Since Paleolithic times bears have been sacred. It was believed that, of all animals, the bear had the most dangerous soul, hence the medicine man often sought this powerful animal as a spirit helper.[13] The shaman—clad in a bear skin complete with the head that created a mask—would rattle loudly, grunting and snarling like a bear while leaping wildly around his patient in an attempt to infuse the life force of the powerful animal into the waning spirit of the human patient.

643 Captured Sioux warriors, ca. 1890. These prisoners are dressed in a combination of buckskin and commercial-cloth garments. Many are also wrapped in trade blankets. The woman warrior #3, at lower left, wears a Hudson Bay blanket with multiple bands indicating its cost in beaver pelts.

The prisoners are named as follows: 1. Crow Kane, 2. Medicine Horse, 3. Call Her Name, 4. Kicking Bear—Chief, 5. Short Bull, 6. Come and Grunt, 7. High Eagle, 8. Horn Eagle, 9. Sorrell Horse, 10. Scatter, 11. Standing Bear, 12. Lone Bull, 13. Standing Bear, 14. Close to House, 15. One Star, 16. Know His Voice, 17. Own The White Horse, 18. Take The Shield Away, 19. Brave.

GARMENT DECORATION

Porcupine quillwork was an important element in Plains culture, not only as material for ornamentation but also as a source of great spiritual power, at times almost constituting a prayer to a supernatural being. Because the porcupine climbs high into trees, it was associated with the sun and its quills with the sun's rays.[14] Some sixteen different quillworking methods were used by Plains Indians, including sewing, warping, plaiting and weaving. But whatever techniques were used, the quills first had to be laboriously prepared—soaked to soften, split open, flattened and only then dyed and used for ornamentation. Quillwork was one of the paramount decorative elements until beadwork began to develop in the late 18th century and for a time the two techniques occurred together, sometimes on the same piece. Indeed, in the early stages beadwork continued to emulate the geometric designs of quillwork. Later, however, beadwork became the predominant expression.

By about 1780, European fur traders had begun bartering for pelts with large opaque bead necklaces and pony beads, so named for the traders' pony pack trains. By the 1860s the smaller, highly desirable seed beads had become available, tiny beads of varied hues that could be used to form complex, curvilinear designs. Several methods were used to attach these beads—for example, the overlay stitch where many beads on one thread were fastened down at frequent intervals by a second thread; or the "lazy" stitch in which five or more beads were strung on a thread before being fastened in place, a good technique for filling large areas.

A great many of the beautiful Indian objects that we treasure today were made between the 1880s and the 1920s when the Indians were forced off their lands by the government to live in restricted areas, the reservations. It was during this Reservation Period that there occurred a vast outpouring of impressive decorative pieces that have come to be regarded as the quintessential art of the Plains people. Through those years this corpus of work lost neither its indigenous character nor its integrity, a reality ignored by many earlier ethnologists. Instead, beadwork became the major form of artistic tradition, but now the narrative shifted from warrior scenes to reminders of the old life-ways and social activities [644]. Also, beadwork became more complex, particularly on children's clothing [645] and amulets [646].

FACE AND BODY MODIFICATION

Face and body painting were an important element of Plains culture, not only for ornamentation but also for the evoking of great spiritual power. Each individual made his or her own decision as to what decorations were to be used. Painting had several social and religious purposes: to indicate membership in a military society, to commemorate participation in certain ceremonies, as protection in battle, and also to signify mourning.

TRANSITIONAL DRESS

Because of the elaborate pre-Contact trade network that existed throughout North America, European products early found their way onto the Plains. It is particularly striking that the foreign-goods replacement followed long-established patterns. For example, American Indians considered the shiny surfaces of shells and polished stones to be reflections of spiritual power, hence the traders' gleaming glass beads found a ready market. Stroud and American-produced flannel cloth replaced leather loincloths, leggings and dresses but the favored colors remained red, as well as the combination of a dark ground and red trim, reminiscent of indigenous tanned skins with red ochre ornamentation. Metal quickly replaced not only stone tools but also certain indigenous decorations. However, such new items as "tinklers"—the small metal cones used to ornament dresses, leggings, shirts and moccasins—served the same purpose as the jangling deer dewclaws of earlier days.

The Western market also made use of traded indigenous goods. During the 1820s and 1830s, for example, the demand for beaver pelts reached its peak,

644 Reservation Period beaded bags depicting aspects of the "Old Days."

Left: A courting scene: length 26 in. (66 cm), width 8½ in. (21.6 cm).

Below: Three Indian couples dancing: length 18 in. (45.7 cm), width 12¾ in. (32.4 cm).

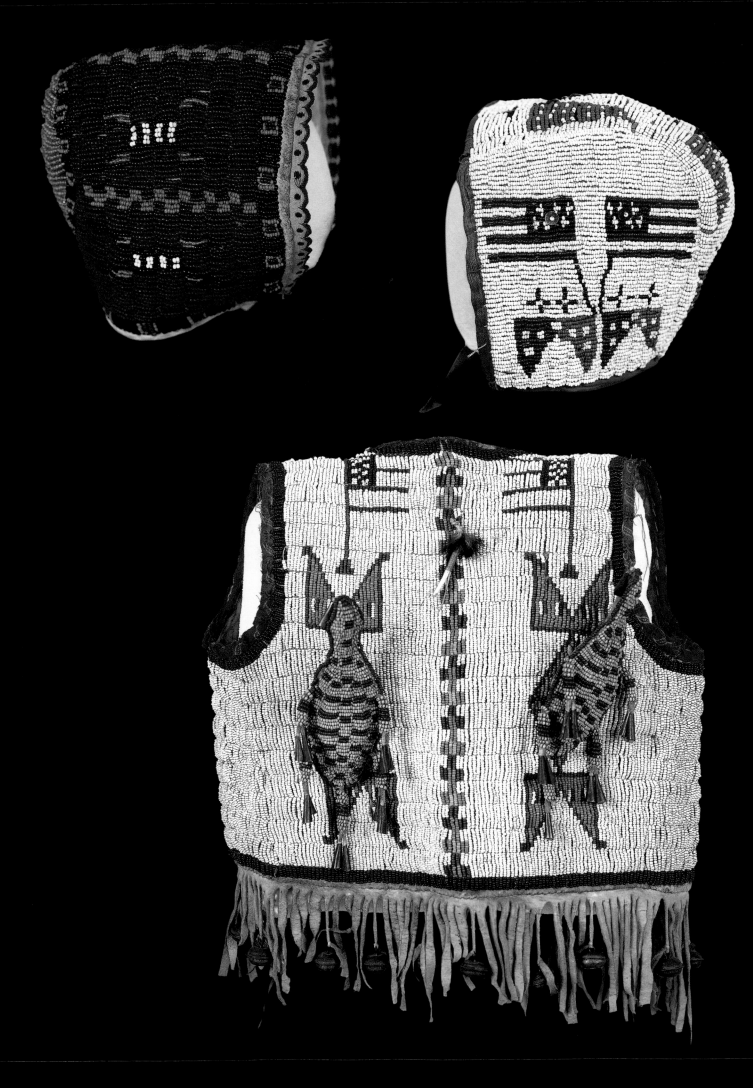

with beaver-felt hats in fashion as far away as the Mandarin courts of China [647]. The lucrative trade in beaver fur helped open up the largely uncharted territories from the Mississippi River to the Pacific Ocean. Trappers would bring their catches to St. Louis in bundles of 10 to 20 skins pressed into 100-pound bales. The price—bringing from $4 to $6 per pound for prime, adult male fur—depended on the English and eastern United States markets for beaver-felt hats.[15] Beaver-fur felt was created through the action of heat, moisture, chemicals and pressure. The first step was to remove the beaver's thick hair from the pelt and then soak the hair in noxious chemicals. Mercury was sometimes used, with often adverse effects for the workmen.[16]

Although Western dress became increasingly seductive [648], with all of the conversions the Plains Indians made, what was never fully replaced was the underlying native aesthetic with its roots reaching far back into an ancient, shamanic world.

647 A beaver-felt hat, the height of fashion in the early 19th century.

645 (opposite above) Two baby bonnets from the Reservation Period.

Left: length 6 in. (15.2 cm), width 5½ in. (14 cm).

Right: length 6 in. (15.2 cm), width 5 in. (12.7 cm).

646 (opposite below) A Lakota child's beaded vest with attached navel amulets in the form of lizards, a propitious animal because it is hard to catch and hence to kill. Such amulets contained a baby's umbilical cord and, through the sympathetic magic inherent in the charm, served to protect the child during its formative years. Length 13 in. (33 cm).

648 An Assiniboine warrior—The Pigeon's Egg Head—before and after his visit to Washington in the winter of 1832. His fashionable suit of "regimentals" is worn with a stylish beaver-felt hat.

THE SOUTHWEST

649 Edgar Payne (1883–1947), *Navajo Riders*. Three Navajo men are dressed in typical attire: long-sleeved, hip-length shirts of colorful commercial cloth, girded by a leather belt decorated with silver medallions called "conchas." Their long hair is tied back in the typical Southwestern style, the *chongo*, and a cotton kerchief is tied across the forehead.

The Southwest is a land of dramatic contrasts where mountains reach to 12,000 feet (3,650 m) and deserts lie barely above sea level, or even below [Map 29]. In this arid world of huge overhanging cliffs, towering table-top mesas and improbable rock formations, water is at a premium. There are few permanent rivers; only after violent thunderstorms do raging torrents briefly surge down dry, rocky washes.[1] Further, the Southwest lacks grass-rich plains and attendant big game.

People have inhabited the Southwest since at least 12,000 B.C. The Anasazi, thought by some to be forerunners of the Pueblo peoples, were established in the region by about 400 B.C., centered in the Four Corners' region. The Hohokam Culture of the Gila and Salt rivers experienced a parallel development. Both cultures collapsed after A.D. 1400. Eventually the early Indians settled along the dependable rivers where they could farm the rich soil. Cultivation of Mesoamerica's

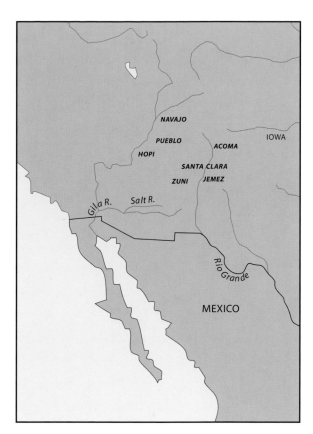

Map 29 The Southwest region.

missionaries and settlers who subsequently began arriving in 1598 attempted to replace the indigenous "pagan" religion with Catholicism. Although the Indians superficially accepted the Spaniards' faith, they quietly continued with their own beliefs and ceremonies. In 1821 Mexico achieved independence from Spain and the Southwest briefly became part of the Mexican Republic, but when the United States won the Mexican War in 1848 the region once again became the victor's spoils.

Despite exposure to the devastating effects of European diseases and superior weapons, as well as the forceful relocation of some groups, until recently the Indians have maintained much of their culture intact. Their distinctive clothing has reflected this. North of Mexico, it was only in the Southwest that pre-Contact woven cotton garments were worn. Also—with the exception of the Arctic—this is one of the few North American regions where examples of true native dress continued into the 20th century.

The first serious studies of Southwestern peoples took place between 1880 and 1930. It is during this 50-year period that many of the most informative photographs were taken of the region's native inhabitants, before the impact of mass media and mass tourism.

sacred triad—corn, beans and squash—provided a stable food supply; populations and villages grew. Trade with the Mexican civilizations to the south further enriched the lives of these sedentary farmers. By A.D. 1000, the people of the Pueblos had reached a "Golden Age."

In the mid-14th century the Pueblo domain was entered, and altered, by the ancestors of the Athabascan-speaking Navajo and Apache. Their constant raiding forced the settled farmers to fortify their towns, or abandon them entirely. When the Spaniards arrived in the 16th century the Puebloan population was concentrated in the Western villages of Acoma, Hopi and Zuni as well as along the Rio Grande Valley. The Navajo, who eventually metamorphosed into pastoral herders, and the Apache, who maintained their raiding pursuits, held sway over the intervening areas.

The Indians of the Southwest have survived a series of intrusive overlords. The Spanish under Coronado invaded the region in 1539–1540, bringing the horse, the sword and the cross. The Spanish

MEN'S BASIC DRESS

Prior to the introduction of cotton from the south around A.D. 500, the clothing of the peoples living in the prehistoric Southwest was made of tanned deerskin or some form of fabric constructed by twining, braiding or other finger-weaving techniques, using such indigenous plants as yucca or Indian hemp. The simple loom—one without shed-manipulation devices—was present prior to A.D. 700. These vertical frames were used to produce twined fur and feather robes. The true heddle loom appeared in the Southwest about A.D. 700 and with it came loom-woven fabrics. By A.D. 700–900, cotton was sufficiently common to be the sole fiber represented in the majority of archaeological textile assemblages.[2] Puebloan garments of particular significance were woven of white cotton, perhaps because the raw fibers—

650 (below) Armed
Chiricahua Apache, led by
Geronimo, wear traditional
clothing, including large
white cotton loincloths and
headbands.

651 (right) Three Hopi elders
photographed on the Hopi
Reservation in 1901. Note
their loosely fitting cotton
trousers and long-sleeved
fitted shirts.

when fluffed-up for spinning—resemble rain clouds.
Woven cotton clothing was prized both for its symbolic
contribution to ceremonials and its white ground that
provided a base for the colorful, intricate embroideries
that conveyed spiritually important designs.

The white cotton loincloth was the fundamental
item of male attire. Some of these garments were fitted,
passing through the crotch and secured under a belt,
while others were of the apron type, hanging in front
and back and tied at the waist. The loincloths of the
Chiricahua Apache of Geronimo fame were the latter,
unusually wide as well as long, reaching to the knees
[650]. As for the Puebloans, the ends of their white
loincloths were enhanced with twill-pattern bands.
Following Spanish contact and the subsequent introduction of sheep, these garments were made of dark blue
or black wool woven in float weaves in a diagonal twill,
sometimes embellished with diamond twill borders.

Among the Hopi it was mainly men who wove but
in other communities that role was filled by women,

652 A Jemez man's shirt,
1920–1930. Body: length 23 in.
(58.5 cm), width 21¼ in. (54 cm).
Sleeves: length 18½ in. (47 cm),
width 13½ in. (34.5 cm).

who also did the embroidery. Over the loincloth, Southwest men sometimes wore a wraparound kilt that reached from waist to knee. This garment still appears today in many Pueblo, Navajo and Apache ceremonials [see 661 (fourth from left), 676].

Leggings were often necessary for protection in the desert. These garments were essentially snug-fitting, footless stockings—looped, knitted or made of buckskin—that reached to the calf and were held in place by a garter at the knee and a strap beneath the foot. In the 19th century, however, many men adopted the Mexicans' white cotton pants, worn loose and baggy in the early days, closer fitting in the 20th century [651].

Throughout the Southwest, archaic skin ponchos gave way to shirts of plain-weave cotton constructed in a square-cut style, with or without sleeves: one piece for the front, another for the back, a folded piece for each sleeve. These simple garments were loosely stitched part-way up the sides and lower arms [652, 653]. In many areas, shirts were worn outside the trousers and belted.

653 A Hopi man's
shirt. Length 53⅜ in.
(135.5 cm), width 22 in.
(56 cm).

The availability of colorful commercial cloth in the 19th century changed Navajo attire. With the advent of the trading posts between the 1860s and the 1880s, the typical Navajo man's costume came into being [see 649]: long-sleeved, hip-length shirts of colorful velveteen or corduroy worn with white or dark pants and girded at the waist with the signature Southwest belt, the concha. This name comes from the silver medallions—the conchas—that are attached to these leather belts.

WOMEN'S BASIC DRESS

Among Pueblo women, the rectangular *manta*, or mantle, served as both shawl and knee-length dress, wrapping around the body with the open edge on the right, fastening on the right shoulder, and passing under the left arm [654–656]. The dress was sewn part-way down the side and held in place by a long, woven belt of red and green wool. But fashion, like time, moves on, even in non-Western enclaves. Today at Hopi, as in most New Mexican pueblos, the black wool *mantas*—seen now only occasionally at ceremonials or on other special occasions—have been exchanged for cotton dresses constructed in the same style but with commercial fabric. To these modern-day garments have been added flowered, sometimes lace-trimmed blouses and printed aprons.

Navajo women's clothing has quite a different history. By at least A.D. 1700 Navajo women had begun to weave on Pueblo-style upright looms, perhaps learning their techniques through observation of the impressive Pueblo weaving technology.[3] However, in contrast to the Pueblos' emphasis on cotton for special ceremonial garments, the sheep-herding Navajos based their weaving on wool.

From at least 1750 through 1868 Navajo women were wearing the *biil*, a wool dress made of a single rectangular panel or two panels joined at the sides [657, 658]. After the Navajos' devastating internment at Bosque Redondo between 1864 and 1868, they underwent a dress change that came about in response to the cheap commercial cloth newly available in the trading posts. It was during this period that the women began to wear Anglo-style dresses: long, full, cotton skirts and distinctive long-sleeved, hip-length, velveteen blouses. They received sewing instructions for the making of such garments from military and traders' wives, as well as from the missionaries.

By 1868 Apache women had also adopted an Anglo-style garment. In place of their previous hide dresses, they began wearing what became their characteristic attire, the camp dress: a long, full-sleeved, hip-length, cotton blouse and full skirt of decorative bands with a flounce at the bottom [see 679].

654 A 1901 photograph, taken at the Hopi pueblo of Shungapovi, showing two young women dressed in *mantas*. They are at the final stage of creating the "butterfly" hairstyle worn by Hopi girls.

655 An Acoma embroidered brown wool *manta* dress, 1860–1875. Length 42⅛ in. (107 cm), width 54 in. (137.3 cm).

656 A Santa Clara embroidered black wool *manta* dress, 1920–1930. Length 42⅞ in. (109 cm), width 24⅝ in. (62.5 cm).

657 A Navajo woman's two-piece dress, the *biil*, 1885–1900. Length 50 in. (127 cm), width 34¼ in. (87 cm).

658 A Navajo woman's pictorial *biil*, or *beeldéi*, 1880–1900. Length 38½ in. (98 cm), width 57 in. (145 cm).

FOOTWEAR

Few articles of American Indian footwear surpassed the prehistoric craftsmen's beautiful sandals made of various fibers, but especially yucca and Indian hemp. They were of two general types: square-toed or round-toed, both held in place by thongs. Following Spanish contact, Puebloan men began to wear knee-high boots of tanned leather with painted rawhide soles. The women wore ankle-high boots, also with painted soles, and wrapped their legs with strips of leather, whitened with clay, in a "puttee" manner; the bulkier the effect, the better [659]. By the mid-19th century the Navajo were wearing knee-high, rust-colored, cowhide moccasins that tied at the side. From early days the Apache wore simple two-piece, soft-soled moccasins with separate skin leggings; this archaic footwear evolved into the distinctive Apache legging/moccasin with turned-up toes [660; see also 679].

659 An Acoma woman wearing wrapped boots, a traditional dark *manta*, and silver and turquoise jewelry.

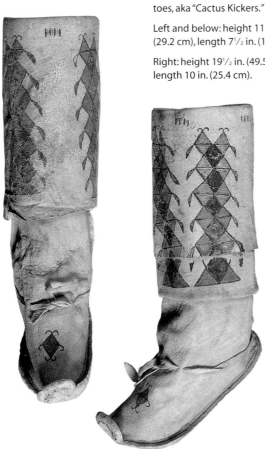

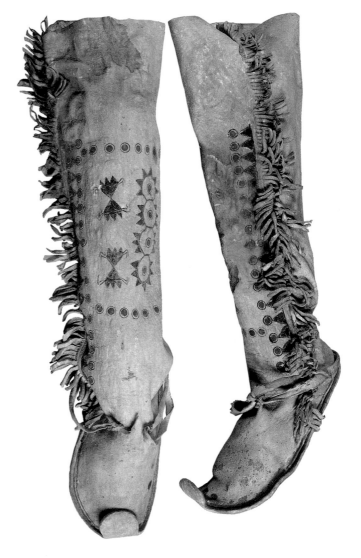

660 Apache leggings/moccasins with their distinctive turned-up toes, aka "Cactus Kickers."

Left and below: height 11½ in. (29.2 cm), length 7½ in. (19 cm).

Right: height 19½ in. (49.5 cm), length 10 in. (25.4 cm).

661 Seven types of Pueblo textiles. From left:
Bachelor's blanket: length 46⅝ in. (118.5 cm), width 61⅜ in. (156 cm).
Girl's shawl: length 32½ in. (82.5 cm), width 29 in. (74 cm).
Sampler: length 41½ in. (105.4 cm), width 14¼ in. (36.2 cm).
Kilt: length 53⅛ in. (135 cm), width 19⅜ in. (49 cm).
Blanket: length 62¼ in. (158.1 cm), width 60⅞ in. (154.5 cm).
Hopi *manta*: length 44 in. (112 cm), width 56⅝ in. (144 cm).
Blanket: length 70 in. (178 cm), width 49⅛ in. (125 cm).

OUTERWEAR

As might seem in phase for militant marauders [see 650], the Apaches' early upper-body hide garments were replaced by military-like shirts replete with martial-looking silver buttons.

In the Pueblos, rabbit-skin shoulder blankets made of strips of rabbit pelt cut in a spiral and then twined on yucca cords were utilized, as were twill and plain-weave cotton blankets [661]. Commercial shawls in checks and plaids from Pendleton mills became popular with Pueblo women by the 1880s when the influential traders began introducing them into the area.

Once Navajo women began to weave [662], they consistently produced distinctive blankets with striking geometric patterns [663]. Red was especially favored; the weavers sometimes obtained their brilliant scarlet/crimson yarns by raveling trade cloth. From the time they began weaving, the Navajo were making blankets

662 A Navajo woman spinning wool beside her loom.

for trade; from there it was but a step to producing the larger, heavier rugs requested by the traders [664]. For outerwear, the Navajo themselves began to adopt commercial Pendleton blankets, particularly those with banded or horizontal elements, designs they had also preferred in their earlier handwoven shoulder wraps.

The Navajo also specialized in "Chief blankets"— a term that refers to the design on the garment rather than to the wearer [665-667]. These men's shoulder blankets were woven on an upright heddle loom. The Navajo also created strikingly patterned ponchos [668] and wearing blankets for women [669].

663 Models of blanket-clad Navajo men, ca. 1840–1880.

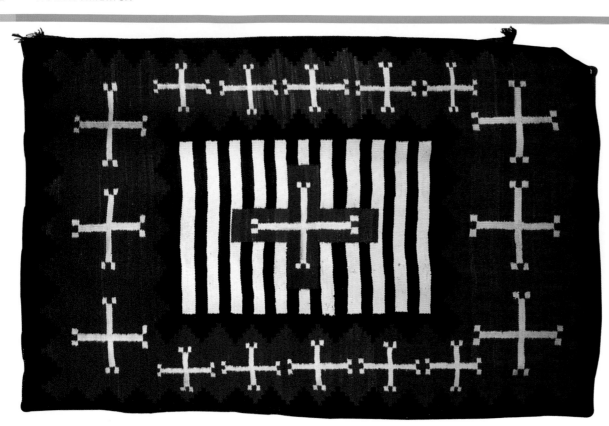

664 (left) A Navajo early Crystal-style rug, 1900–1911. Length 76 in. (193 cm), width 43 in. (109.2 cm).

665 (below left) A Navajo First-Phase Chief-style blanket, 1800–1850. Length 48¹/₂ in. (123.2 cm), width 82 in. (208.3 cm).

666 (below center) A Navajo Second-Phase Chief-style blanket, 1850–1865. Length 48 in. (121.9 cm), width 68 in. (172.7 cm).

667 (below) A Navajo Third-Phase Chief-style blanket, 1865–1875. Length 53 in. (134.6 cm), width 60 in. (152.4 cm).

668 A Navajo man's early Classic-style poncho, 1840–1860. Length 84³⁄₈ in. (214.5 cm), width 56 in. (142.2 cm).

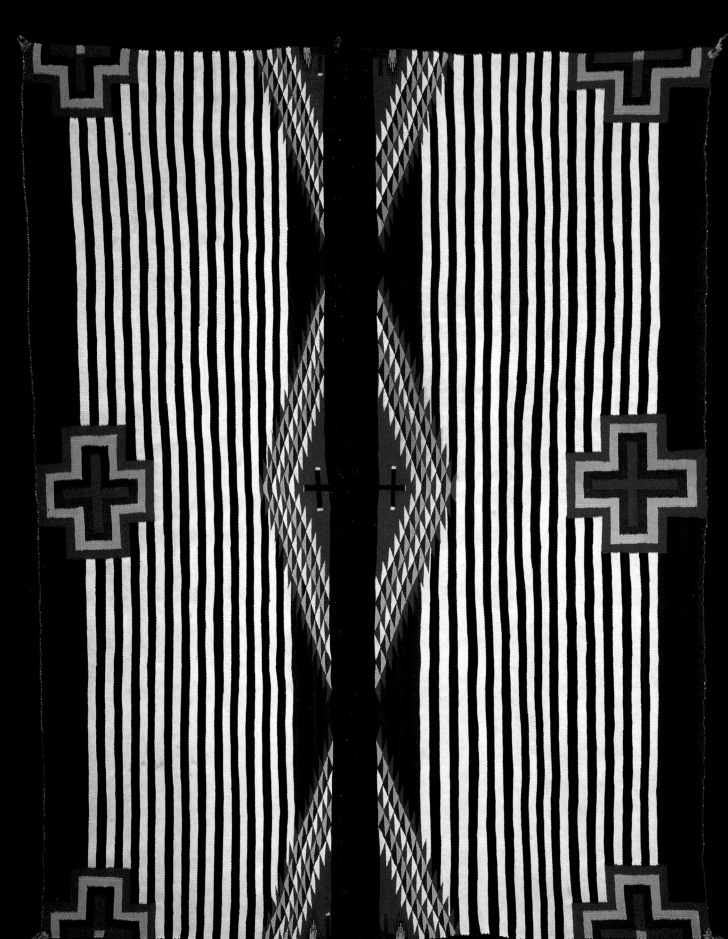

HAIRSTYLES

The early characteristic hairstyle of the Southwest was the *chongo*: the long hair was coiled at the back and bound with ties, a style the Navajo adopted from the Pueblos [see 649, 663]. Navajo women tied the *chongo* with strands of handspun cotton, wool or commercial twine; Navajo men preferred a colored cotton kerchief tied about the head. As a typical style, the *chongo* lasted into the mid-20th century but then both Navajo and Puebloan men began to cut their hair at the jaw or shoulder line and hold it in place with a cloth band [670]. Many of the older Navajo women, however, still continue to favor the *chongo* style.

At Hopi Pueblo, young girls wore the characteristic "butterfly" hairstyle: the hair was parted in the middle and each side was wound around a wooden, U-shaped "hair bow" in a figure of eight, tied with a thong, and then spread out in a whorl shape or disk about 8 inches (20 cm) in diameter [see 654]. Following marriage, a bride's hair was worn hanging down, wrapped into long twists or braids.

HEADGEAR

With the exception of ceremonial headgear, Puebloan men and women went bareheaded most of the time. With the advent of trade cloth, men sometimes wrapped their heads with a wide band of material, tying it in the front or on the side to keep their hair in place. Whereas Navajo women have always gone bareheaded, in the late 20th century many Navajo men adopted the light-colored Western hat of felt or straw with a curved brim, or the straight-sided, flat-brimmed hat [see 675]. Early on, Apache men wore a cloth headband [see 650], but by the 20th century they, too, had often adopted Anglo or Mexican hats.

ACCESSORIES

The Puebloans are known for producing beautiful sashes [671], examples of which are still worn during their ceremonials. These warp-faced belts, as well as garters and headbands, were woven by women on narrow belt looms using red, green and black wool

670 A Navajo silversmith and boy wearing cloth hair bands, Grand Canyon, 1927.

671 A woven sash (main section and fringed end shown), an embroidered sash, and a rain sash, all Hopi.

Woven sash: length 132⅝ in. (337 cm), width 4⅜ in. (11 cm).

Embroidered sash: length 99⅛ in. (252 cm), width 3¾ in. (9.5 cm).

Rain sash: length 68 in. (172.7 cm), width 4½ in. (11.4 cm).

669 (opposite) A Navajo Chief-style variant woman's wearing blanket, 1875–1885. Length 51⅞ in. (132 cm), width 70 in. (178 cm).

672 Examples of Navajo silverwork: concha belts and variations on the squash-blossom necklace.

in a floating-warp technique. By the late 1800s concha belts were also being worn. Originally they were obtained in trade from the Navajo, who learned the art of silvermaking from their Mexican neighbors in the mid-19th century. Subsequently, Pueblo silversmiths also began to make the typically Southwestern concha belts [see 651]. For the Navajo, concha belts were always important. Among the Apache, a cloth neckerchief, often fastened with a concha, was a popular male accessory. Both sexes wore amulets of unpainted wood, items of personal spiritual significance.

JEWELRY

In earliest times, stone and shell beads were in great abundance. After A.D. 500, there was an increasing use among the Puebloan people of turquoise; some necklaces were made of thousands of beautifully handcrafted beads. The combining of silver and turquoise has produced popular jewelry particularly associated with the Navajo, who have a worldwide reputation for their craftsmanship [see 670]. To them turquoise is of paramount importance, transcending even its value as jewelry to serve almost as an agent for prayer.

Turquoise and silver jewelry was worked first for personal use and subsequently for the tourist trade. By 1889, the Navajo were filling orders for the Fred Harvey Company. However, jewelry was, and still is, worn in great abundance by the Navajo themselves: belts, necklaces, bracelets, rings, hatbands, buttons and earrings [672].

ARMOR

Early Southwestern warriors used basketry for armor and wore close-fitting medicine caps of tanned skin, often ventilated with numerous holes and decorated with feathers. They sometimes went into battle with their torsos wrapped in several layers of deerskin. Many of the men of the Rio Grande Pueblos, as well as the Apache, also carried shields: two thick pieces of leather stitched together and painted or otherwise adorned with significant symbols.

GARMENT DECORATION

In the early pre-Contact period, Pueblo clothing items such as belts, straps and sandals were decorated with painted fiber strands arranged in simple geometric designs. Subsequently, when working in either cotton or wool, textiles were woven in plain weave, diamond-twill or diagonal-twill patterns. Following Spanish contact, kilts, loincloths, shirts and sashes were decorated with bands of wool embroidery [see 652, 661, 671], a technique learned from the Spaniards. Subsequently, the women's woolen *mantas* and cotton dresses had embroidered bands attached that also featured geometric designs—often in red, blue, green and yellow—which conveyed specific symbolic messages [673, 674].

Decorations on Navajo woolen textiles were carried out by way of the weaving structures themselves—in both float, twill and plain weaves—as well as through the incorporation of colored bands and geometric designs [see 662]. Decorations on Navajo blouses and dresses consist of silver coins, and buttons made from melted-down coins, placed in rows down front openings, around collars, and on both sleeves and cuffs [675].

673 Joseph Henry Sharp (1958–1953), *The Pottery Decorators.* Pueblo women in a stone-and-adobe dwelling, wearing woolen *mantas* with embroidered bands and geometric designs.

674 A Pueblo woman's carefully embroidered white cotton dress. Length 42⁷⁄₈ in. (109 cm), width 24⁵⁄₈ in. (62.5 cm).

675 R. Brownell McGrew, *Off to the Trading Post*, ca. 1965–1975. Coin and button decoration can be seen on the shirt of the Navajo girl in the foreground. She also wears a concha belt. The seated rider has adopted a flat-brimmed Western hat.

SPECIAL COSTUMES

Best known of the Puebloan special costumes are those associated with ceremonies involving the *katsina*, symbolic human effigies of the many ancestral messengers in their pantheon. For example, among the Hopi there are about 30 major messengers and over 400 lesser ones. Masks and headdresses are the distinctive aspect of *katsina* costumes. Only men take part in these ceremonies.

At most Pueblo ceremonies, men wear white cotton kilts—their ends embroidered in black, green and red—together with a "rain sash," a long, white cotton sash with fringes representing falling rain [676; see also 671]. At summer solstice ceremonies, women wear their traditional black *mantas* and "maiden shawls," white with blue and red borders [677]. *Tablitas*, flat upright painted plaques of wood, tower above the women dancers' heads.

676 An 1888 photograph of a Pueblo Corn (or Tablita) Dance, a non-*katsina* ceremony performed to ensure fertility. The faces of the dancers are painted. The men wear wraparound kilts and rain sashes, and the women wear the *tablita* headdress.

677 A Hopi blue- and red-bordered white wool "maiden shawl" worn over a dark wool *manta*, 1890–1920.

Shawl: length 32½ in. (82.5 cm), width 29 in. (73.7 cm).

Manta: length 29 in. (74 cm), width 34 in. (86.5 cm).

The major ceremonials of the Navajo are their curing rites, performed by medicine men to restore the balance of nature, during which they sing chants or "ways." Accompanying these chants are the dances of the *yeibichai*, the holy beings who embody natural forces such as wind and thunder. The male dancers wear kilts [678]. Although only men take part in these ceremonies, both sexes are portrayed; all are masked.

At the Chiricahua Apache puberty ceremony, girls wear a special version of the traditional camp-dress style. Some of these dresses are colored yellow, rubbed with sacred pollen and decorated with beaded or painted designs. The accompanying male "Gan" dancers, their torsos bare, wear kilts of tanned leather painted yellow and the turned-up-toe Apache footwear. On the Gans' heads are headdresses made of wooden slats or agave stalks, symbolic of Apache belief; dancers' faces are covered with simple black leather or cloth masks with holes for eyes and mouth.

678 A Navajo Yeibichai tapestry featuring four Yeibichai dancers, three wearing kilts, ca. 1930–1936. Length 56 in. (142.2 cm), width 116 in. (294.6 cm).

FACE AND BODY MODIFICATION

In the Southwest, face and body paint were used with ceremonial costumes; the paints were derived from earth ochres and plant stains. Also, there was some inadvertent flattening of the skull caused by binding infants onto hard cradle boards.

MASKS

The different tribal traditions of masked dances in the Southwest suggest a common origin to which each tribe has applied its own distinctive elaboration. The *katsina* dances of the Pueblos are the most ancient and best known of the ceremonial dramas where masks are used. An historical thread appears to connect the ancient Pueblo masking tradition to that of the Navajo masked participants of the Night Way ceremonies and the Apache's Gan dancers and Mountain Spirits performers [679].

TRANSITIONAL DRESS

The Pueblo weavers' creativity was connected to a communal thought process and dictated by strict social controls, rites of passage, class status, ritual and technical efficiency. Textiles were made for individuals who had special family or clan relationships to the weaver. Such garments identified the wearer's age and gender, marked initiations into social groups and signified one's social station.[4] However, by the early 20th century, most Pueblo women in New Mexico had exchanged their scratchy wool *mantas* for cotton dresses of the same style, plus cotton aprons with lace edgings. Men adopted the Anglo dark vest, worn with belted cotton shirts that hung out over either dark pants or the white cotton pants many wear today. Some men still retain the shoulder-length hairstyle held in place with a cotton headband. Sneakers or tennis shoes and other store-bought footwear are commonplace, although most men like to wear cowboy boots and favor the Western look with cowboy hats and Levis.

In contrast to their Pueblo counterparts, Navajo weavers of the past were experimental and showed a taste for the visually flamboyant,[5] producing a range of distinctive textiles prized not only throughout the Southwest and Great Plains but by Mexicans and Anglos alike. Today, most Navajo men, like the Pueblo, favor Western-looking clothing, including jeans, boots and cowboy hats. While many Navajo women have also adopted Western clothing, among the older community the velveteen blouse and calico skirt can still be seen, often worn with the traditional squash-blossom necklace and other items of silver and turquoise jewelry.

The Chiricahua Apache men changed in the late 19th century from Mexican-style dress to Western garb, including cowboy hats, Levis, plaid shirts and cowboy boots. Women still wore the camp dress of the 19th century with its full, ruffled cotton skirt and fitted blouse, but today they intermingle Anglo fashions via purchased clothing. However, older Apache women and many other attendants at the ceremonials—spectators and participants alike—can still be seen wearing items of traditional clothing.

679 Apache dancers performing the Mountain Spirit Ceremony. The women wear the camp dress. The men wear turned-up-toe leggings/moccasins.

MESOAMERICA

680 William de Leftwich Dodge, *The Last Days of Tenochtitlan: Conquest of Mexico by Cortés*, 1899 (detail). In ca. A.D. 1325 the Aztecs founded their capital, Tenochtitlan, on an island in central Mexico's Lake Texcoco. The city flourished for nearly 200 years until the Spaniard Hernan Cortés and his companions conquered and destroyed it. Recent archaeological excavations have uncovered a rare prehispanic textile in the Templo Mayor (Main Temple), the building depicted here in an imaginatively dramatic scene.

The country we know today as Mexico suffered a traumatic birth. In 1521, at the time of the Spanish Conquest, the Aztec capital of Tenochtitlan was a thriving metropolis of some 200,000 inhabitants; the overall population of central Mexico alone stood at between 10 and 20 million. By the end of the 16th century—as the result of European diseases, Spanish exploitation and the breakdown of prehispanic society—"New Spain" could count but a million souls, the largest population drop in recorded history [see 680]. And this level of human devastation extended throughout Mesoamerica, one of the world's six primary hearths of ancient civilization (see "The Ancient Near East," p. 14).

The term Mesoamerica[1] encompasses that portion of present-day Mexico and Central America where a succession of great high cultures flourished before Spanish contact [Map 30]. This florescence began in 1000 B.C. with the Olmec and continued on through the Maya, Zapotec, Teotihuacanos, Toltec and Aztec. Because decades of investigations have been carried out on these early complex societies, far more is known about Mesoamerica's pre-European clothing[2] than that of the other five North American regions.

In 1519, when Hernan Cortés arrived prior to the Spanish Conquest, Mesoamerica was a thriving and culturally sophisticated world where a dense population was supported by an intensive agricultural system featuring corn, beans and squash. Throughout the entire region, an abundant variety of fresh foods, raw materials and manufactured items was moved back and forth between the hot fertile lowlands and the high arid central plateau. All of these goods were transported on the backs of human porters; Mesoamerica lacked large domesticated animals. The combination of a network of well-organized merchant groups and a highly developed market system made a variety of fibers available for processing into the region's clothing, attire that reflected Mesoamerica's sharply stratified society.

The Mesoamerican population was divided into nobles, artisans, commoners and slaves, and all classes were deeply influenced by one of history's most pervasive and complex religious-ritual systems. In the service of this all-encompassing ideology was a great elaboration of art and architecture—lofty pyramids, fine ceramics, colorful murals, monumental sculpture, magnificent textiles—as well as a complex calendrical system that served both divinatory-religious needs and, more practically, secular ends. The Mesoamericans also developed a hieroglyphic writing system that enabled them to record matters of importance in a series of bark-paper and skin screenfold books. Some 15 of these Late Postclassic (A.D. 1250–1519) manuscripts still exist,[3] plus a number of early-colonial documents done in the indigenous style. All of these pictorials contain drawings of people in appropriate attire. There are also clothing depictions found on pre-Contact murals, pottery, clay figurines and stone sculpture.

The earliest extant Mesoamerican fabrics were found at the pre-ceramic cave site of Guila Naquitz in Oaxaca. The fragments, produced by methods that did not require looms, include coiled basketry, cordage and knotted netting. These techniques may have been brought into the Americas across the Bering Strait by early hunter-gatherer migrants.[4] All of the ancient pieces were made of non-cotton plant fiber dating around 8000 B.C. Similar fragments from the Great Basin and Peru have comparable dates. The first evidence in Mesoamerica of unspun cotton was found in Coxcatlan Cave in the Tehuacan Valley of southern Puebla and dates to before 5000 B.C. From that same area comes the earliest indication of weaving in the form of a plain-weave impressed sherd dating from between 1500 and 900 B.C.[5]

The earliest depictions of Mesoamerican clothing date to the Middle Preclassic Period (1150–400 B.C.) and can be seen on small clay figurines found on Mexico's high central plateau. The females are shown in short skirts, the males in loin covers. By the Classic Period (A.D. 250–900), males throughout Mesoamerica were wearing some combination of a wraparound loincloth and a tie-on cape.[6]

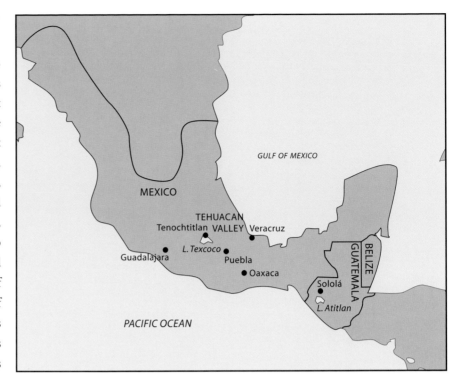

Map 30 Some of the main sites of Mesoamerica.

Because of our extensive knowledge of the Aztecs, Mesoamerica's ruling power at the time of European arrival, we can speak with particular authority regarding early 16th-century, pre-Contact clothing. Of all the newly discovered people in the Age of Discovery, it was the Contact-period Aztecs of central Mexico who were most fully documented. As a result, it is Aztec garments, as well as those of their contemporary neighbors and immediate antecedents, about which we know most. As is true the world over, their dress reflected their circumstance.

The fabric, shape and construction of a people's clothing depend on the materials and techniques available to them. Unlike the inhabitants of the other New World high civilization, the Andeans, the Mesoamericans had no domesticated, wool-producing animals, hence all of their textiles had to be made from plant fibers. Some of these were far more difficult to process than others. In the production of the thread from which cloth is woven, what is desired are long, strong, flexible strands. Unfortunately, natural products in their raw state seldom are long, strong and flexible enough, hence some degree of processing is necessary. When working with cotton (*Gossypium hirsutum*)—Mesoamerica's high-status fiber—that processing involves removing the seeds from the boll,

681 (above) An Aztec woman twirls her spindle to draw out thread from a fillet of cleaned, fluffed-up cotton fibers.

682 (above right) An Aztec mother teaches her fourteen-year-old daughter (allowed only two corn tortillas with each meal) how to weave on the backstrap loom.

cleaning the freed fibers, beating them into a froth and then drawing out the fluffed cotton and, through spinning, joining short fibers to create long thread [681]. However, the majority of the Mesoamerican populace were not allowed to wear cotton clothing. Their garments were made of strong, woody bast fibers from the phloem of such long-leafed plants as maguey (agave), yucca or palm. The metamorphosis of these tough, rigid plants into long, supple thread involved tremendous labor: roasting, soaking, rotting, retting, scraping, washing, combing, fluffing and, only then, spinning.

Once thread is spun, the next step is weaving. The Mesoamerican women's ubiquitous backstrap loom [682] produced webs of woven cloth that had all four sides—the selvedges—completely finished.[7] As a result, a long narrow piece of cloth could be taken directly from the loom and worn as a loincloth without any further processing, or two wider webs could be joined at the selvedges to create a man's ample cape or a woman's wraparound skirt.

PREHISPANIC MEN'S BASIC DRESS

From as early as A.D. 250, the basic Mesoamerican male garment was a long loincloth that encircled the waist, passed between the legs and tied in such a manner that the ends hung down in front and back of the body.

In the case of the Aztecs, the garment's two ends were brought to the front of the waist and tied in the distinctive "Aztec Knot" [683].[8] The accompanying garment was the cape, the culture's principal status marker. Although all Mesoamerican males wore these same two simple garments, class distinctions were made quite apparent via differing types of fiber, surface decoration and accompanying accoutrements, if any. The beautifully clad nobles were always visually obvious [684]. The Aztec sumptuary laws are reported to have dictated the fiber, length and degree of ornamentation of all male cloaks.[9]

PREHISPANIC WOMEN'S BASIC DRESS

The women's indispensable garment, the equivalent of the male loincloth, was the wraparound skirt. Whether made of cotton or bast fiber, consisting of two or more joined webs of cloth, pleated in the front, back or side, the ubiquitous skirt was—and remains—the essential female garment worn throughout Mesoamerica. It is held in place by a handsome, distinctive and colorful belt.

There were two basic upper-body female garments worn at the time of the Spanish Conquest [685]. One was the huipil (from the Nahuatl: [h]uipilli "blouse"),[10] a loose, sleeveless tunic made of two or three joined webs of cloth sewn together lengthwise and then

683 (far left) An Aztec priest wears a loincloth—tied in the "Aztec Knot"— and a simple cape, as he ritually sweeps in a temple. (The bloody stain in front of his ear is the result of repeated autosacrifice to provide offerings to the gods.)

684 (left) A richly attired Aztec king, carrying two flower bouquets, wears the prestigious *plangi* (tie-dyed) cotton cape—the official imperial cloak—together with jade and gold jewelry, a jade lip-plug and a quetzal-feather hair ornament.

completed with a cut-out neck opening and sewn-up sides to create either very tiny arm openings or very large ones, depending on the geographic area [686]. The second female upper-body garment was the *quechquemitl* (from the Nahuatl: *quechtli* "neck" and *quemi* "to put on a manta or cape"),[11] a garment composed of two rectangles of cloth joined in such a way that a triangle is formed when pulled on over the neck.

Strangely, these two were—and still are—mutually exclusive geographically. If one draws an imaginary line from Veracruz to Puebla and then northwest to Guadalajara and on further west to the Pacific Coast, the *quechquemitl* occurs only north of that division, and has since A.D. 200.[12] In contrast, the *huipil* is, and has been, worn only south of the aforementioned line. Aztec females wore *huipils* and never used the *quechquemitl* as daily wear, utilizing it instead only as a special-purpose ritual costume to adorn effigies of fertility goddesses and deity impersonators.[13]

SPANISH-IMPOSED TRANSITIONAL DRESS

Shortly after the 1521 Spanish Conquest, the European treadle loom [687] was introduced into Mexico.[14] This weaving device was necessary for the production of the broad lengths of cloth needed to implement a concept

685 The two upper-body Mesoamerican female garments worn at the time of Spanish Contact: the *quechquemitl* on the left, the *huipil* on the right.

686 Eight upper-class Aztec females wearing richly patterned, wide, sleeveless *huipils*. The unmarried girls wear their hair long; the married women are shown wearing the two-tufted hairstyle.

687 A 13th-century drawing of a European treadle loom.

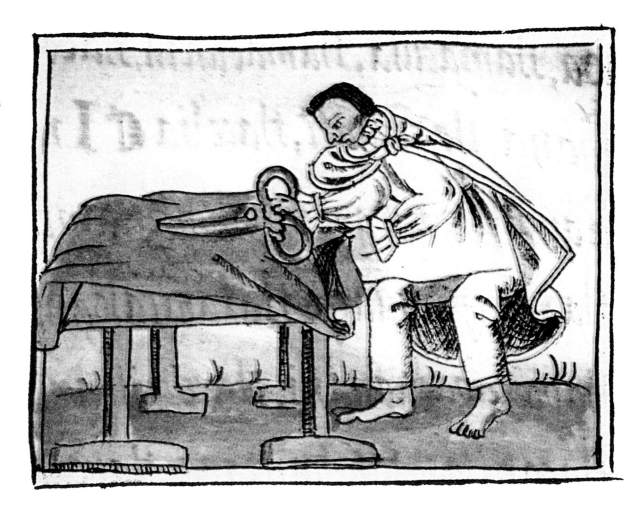

688 A post-Conquest drawing of an Indian man who—although clothed in the new, European-style clothing—still wears the prehispanic cape as he cuts into a wide piece of cloth produced on the treadle loom.

689 Indian men—still wearing prehispanic capes over their mandated European clothes—showing obsequious respect to their Spanish overlords.

690 In certain conservative regions, such as the Sierra Norte de Puebla in central Mexico, Indian men often continue to wear undecorated white pants.

of clothing construction completely foreign to Mesoamerica: tailoring, the cutting out [688] and sewing together of small pieces of cloth to create limb-encasing garments that followed the lines of the body.

Because the early Spanish priests regarded the men's indigenous attire as "immodest" [see 683, 684], the Indians were forced to don cover-up pantaloons (*calzones*) and shirts (*camisas*). Decades later old men bitterly recalled that they were all made to dress in white; nonetheless, the conquered natives had little choice but to comply. However, the old ways apparently died hard because early colonial-period pictorials often show the prehispanic cape still being worn over the newly mandated European attire [689]. Slowly this practice disappeared but the simple, straight, cotton pants—introduced almost half a millennium ago—continue to be worn in conservative Indian areas [690] and vestiges of European tailoring practices are still evident in the construction of some of these.[15] In the area around Cuetzalan, Puebla, the seat of the men's white cotton pants is formed with the insertion of two gusset panels, resulting in three distinctive seams identical to those visible on similar garments depicted in 16th-century paintings.[16] Today, however, *calzones* are sometimes decorated in imaginative ways [691].

691 Decorated white cotton pants form part of a Huichol man's costume, northwestern Mexico.

Hat: height 3$\frac{1}{2}$ in. (9 cm), diameter 15$\frac{1}{2}$ in. (39.5 cm).

Cape: length 36 in. (91.6 cm), width 33$\frac{7}{8}$ in. (86.2 cm).

Shirt: length 42$\frac{1}{8}$ in. (107 cm), width 56$\frac{3}{8}$ in. (143 cm).

Belt: height 4$\frac{7}{8}$ in. (12.5 cm), length 32$\frac{3}{8}$ in. (82 cm).

Pants: length 36$\frac{1}{8}$ in. (92 cm), width 13$\frac{7}{8}$ in. (35.5 cm).

692 A Nahuatl-speaking woman in Cuetzalan, central Mexico, wears a colonial-style blouse beneath her hand-woven gauze *quechquemitl*. Her prehispanic-style turban coiffure—created by interwinding woolen cords into her hair—is crowned by a second *quechquemitl*. Still another of these ancient "shoulder shawls" is partially finished on the woman's loom at lower right.

693 Throughout the *quechquemitl*-wearing regions of the Sierra Norte de Puebla, central Mexico, many women still appear in prehispanic-style traditional clothing. Today the ancient *quechquemitl* is decorated in many ways; for example, with cross-stitch in San Francisco, with supplementary brocade in Pantepec, with gauze in Cuetzalan, and with embroidery in San Pablito.

Because the proselytizing missionaries considered the Indian women's dress modest, the *quechquemitl* [692, 693] and the *huipil* [694–697] were allowed to continue unaltered into the present day, with one addition.

694 As can be seen on the little girls at center and right, from Santa Catarina Polopó in the highlands of Guatemala, the lower section of the *huipil* is covered by the wraparound skirt, creating a waist that is accentuated with a tightly wrapped, decorative belt.

695 (opposite) In southern Mexico the *huipil* is usually worn over the wraparound skirt. Here a Chinantec woman of Usila, Oaxaca, is painting areas of a handwoven *huipil* with *fuchina* dye, 1964.

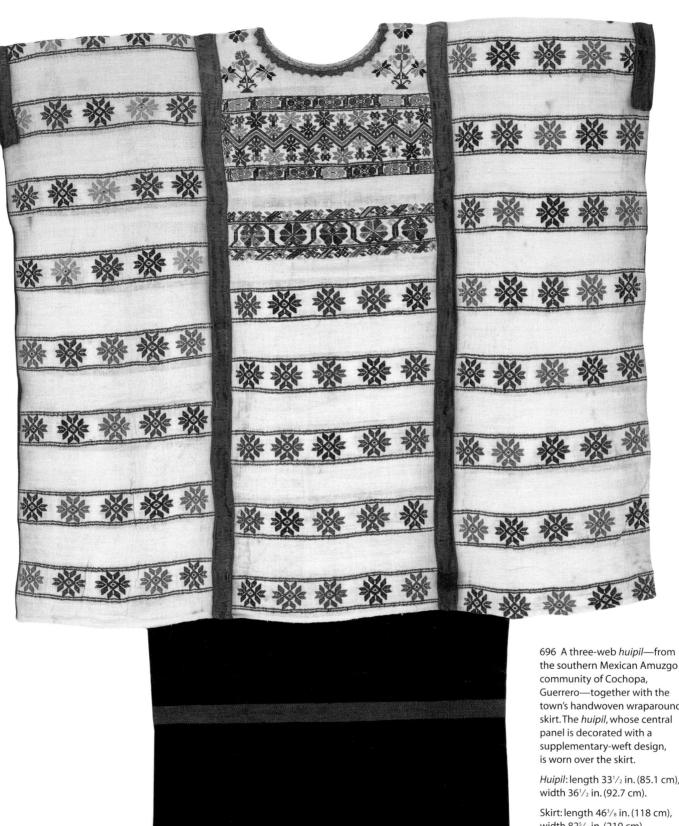

696 A three-web *huipil*—from the southern Mexican Amuzgo community of Cochopa, Guerrero—together with the town's handwoven wraparound skirt. The *huipil*, whose central panel is decorated with a supplementary-weft design, is worn over the skirt.

Huipil: length 33¹/₂ in. (85.1 cm), width 36¹/₂ in. (92.7 cm).

Skirt: length 46³/₈ in. (118 cm), width 82⁵/₈ in. (210 cm).

697 A two-web *huipil* from Chajul, highland Guatemala. This *huipil* is worn inside the skirt and is accentuated with a colorful belt woven in a supplementary-weft design. The town's typical hair ribbon and *tzute/*headcloth are also illustrated.

Huipil: length 24 in. (61 cm), width 32³⁄₈ in. (82 cm).

Headcloth: length 84 in. (213.5 cm), width 39³⁄₈ in. (100 cm).

Hair ribbon: length 184¼ in. (468 cm), width 2 in. (5 cm).

Belt: length 144 in. (365.8 cm), width 8 in. (20.3 cm).

Skirt: length 164³⁄₈ in. (417.5 cm), width 42¹⁄₂ in. (108 cm).

698 Beneath the *quechquemitl* are worn colonial-style blouses that combine commercial cloth with hand-embroidered yokes and sleeves. These blouse examples come from San Pablito, Coacuila and Chachahuantla, Sierran communities all.

San Pablito: length 24 in. (61 cm), width 31½ in. (80 cm).

Coacuila: length 19½ in. (49.5 cm), width 38 in. (96.5 cm).

Chachahuantla: length 28 in. (71.1 cm), width 27 in. (68.6 cm).

699 Otomí Indian women embroidering panels to be incorporated into the yoke and sleeves of colonial-style blouses.

In many of the *quechquemitl*-wearing regions, these shoulder shawls were woven in transparent, "immodest" gauze patterns [see 692, 693 (right)]: as a result, during the colonial period, a Spanish-type blouse [698] was introduced, to be worn under the *quechquemitl*. This cover-up garment was apparently modeled on the 16th-century European chemise. Today the neckline and sleeves of these blouses are richly embroidered with European-style floral and animal designs [699].

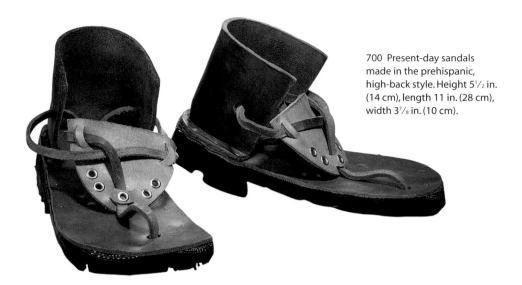

700 Present-day sandals made in the prehispanic, high-back style. Height 5¹⁄₂ in. (14 cm), length 11 in. (28 cm), width 3⁷⁄₈ in. (10 cm).

FOOTWEAR

Throughout both the prehispanic and colonial pictorials, sandals with high-backed heel guards are depicted, but only on deities, the ruling elite, high-status warriors or such important individuals as the emperor's emissaries traveling to distant regions. Men in conservative Indian communities still wear sandals; a few are constructed in the prehispanic style [700]. Today most sandals have soles made from old automobile tires. The majority of Indian women still go barefoot, although now some are seen in the large weekly markets wearing flimsy, inexpensive, plastic shoes.

OUTERWEAR

On Mexico's high central plateau, and throughout the mountainous highlands of Guatemala, *tierra fria* elevations necessitate warm outer garments. One of these is the *cotorina*, a sleeveless woolen jacket with a decorative hem fringe [701]. The *cotorina* is a very ancient garment style, one that had particular importance to the Aztecs, whose name for it was *xicolli*, the "Godly Jacket." The *xicolli* was worn by deity effigies [702] and priests.[17] Because Aztec priests donned the *xicolli* when performing human sacrifice,[18] it is surprising that this particular garment style escaped the scrutiny of the proselytizing Spanish missionaries. The jacket's survival into the modern era is probably due to the garment metamorphosing early on from "heathen" deity attire into innocuous utility wear [see 701].

701 On a chilly day, a man in a highland town wears a wool *cotorina*.

702 A stone sculpture of an Aztec deity, now known as the Churubusco Idol, wearing the ritual *xicolli*, the sleeveless jacket with a diagnostic fringe at the hem, the ancient garment that was the forerunner of the present-day *cotorina*.

703 The men of the market town of Sololá, located above Lake Atitlan in highland Guatemala, are easily recognizable in their tailored grey and white wool jackets trimmed in decorative black braid. They also wear hand-woven striped shirts, pants, belts, bags and black and white checked *rodilleras* wrapped around their hips.

Jacket: length 26⁷⁄₈ in. (68 cm), width 51⁷⁄₈ in. (132 cm).

Camisa: length 36³⁄₈ in. (92.4 cm), width 55⁷⁄₈ in. (142 cm).

Pants: length 34³⁄₈ in. (87.5 cm), width 25 in. (63.5 cm).

Rodillera: length 49 in. (124.5 cm), width 22 in. (56 cm).

Belt: length 74 in. (188 cm), width 7³⁄₄ in. (19.8 cm).

Bag: length 57 in. (144.8 cm), width 33 in. (83.8 cm).

704 A sweater-clad Indian man chatting with a woman wearing a colonial-style blouse.

Today, in highland winter weather, Indian men also wear simple tailored jackets [703], wool ponchos or inexpensive, machine-made sweaters [704]. Women wrap themselves in *rebozos*, long, multi-purpose shawls used for warmth as well as for carrying children, handiwork and market purchases.

ACCESSORIES

In prehispanic Mesoamerica, almost every accessory conveyed a message concerning status and role [see 684]. Among the Aztecs, imperial messengers carried a staff of office, and sometimes also a fan. As for the warriors, the most desirable of the magnificent towering back-devices and shimmering feathered warrior suits [see 706]—as well as the accompanying shell necklaces, bracelets, nose and lip ornaments—were not for sale in the marketplace: such prestigious items were bestowed only as rewards for prowess in battle. Clearly, this most coveted of flamboyant attire served as a powerful inducement to aggressive battleground behavior, further evidence of the overwhelming martial thrust of Aztec culture.

Today, in conservative Indian villages the men wear hats made of straw, or an imitation thereof. Many carry a shoulder bag [see 690, 703] because their traditional pants have no pockets. Although women sometimes also have carrying bags, the *rebozo* usually serves for most transport purposes.

Belts are often intricate and colorful. The characteristic Huichol belt has from seven to nine tiny bags—woven of cotton and trimmed in wool—joined together in a single string [see 691]. Middle American belts also have a particular charm [705].

HAIRSTYLES

Most prehispanic men wore their hair cut to a little below the ears. Among the Aztecs, the priests pulled their long hair away from the face and tied it back with a cloth band [see 683]. Small boys were completely shorn until age ten when a tuft of hair was allowed to grow at the back of the head. By age fifteen this lock was quite long, but the young man was not allowed to cut it off until he had taken a captive in battle,[19] yet another indication of the social pressure placed on Aztec youths to become effective warriors. Today Indian men cut their hair in a conservative, Western-style manner.

The hair of unmarried Aztec girls hung loosely down to their shoulders. Married women, however, wore their hair in two hornlike tufts created by dividing the hair in the middle, binding it with a cord and then folding it up in such a way as to leave the bulk of the hair resting on the nape of the neck

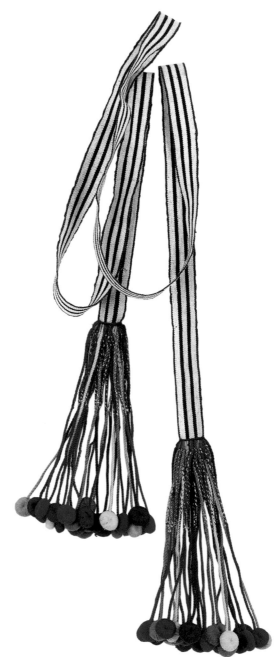

705 Belt from Santiago Sacatepéquez, Guatemala. Length 105⅛ in. (267 cm), width 1⅛ in. (3 cm).

706 A valiant Aztec warrior of the Otomí grade (i.e. five prisoners taken in battle) wears the prestigious Pillar-of-Stone hairstyle, a warrior suit made of resplendent green feathers, a "Claw" back-device topped with quetzal feathers and a bone labret. His captive—who wears a boar's-tusk labret—has been stripped of his feathered finery and is clad only in quilted cotton armor, Mesoamerica's basic martial garment.

while the two ends were secured at the top of the head [see 686]. Today women generally wear their long hair pulled back from the face, usually arranged in braids.

HEADGEAR

The most dramatic examples of prehispanic headgear were the towering feathered headpieces worn by the rulers depicted on Classic Period Maya stelae. These magnificent constructions contained many long, shimmering, green and gold quetzal feathers, one of the most precious of Mesoamerican treasures. The Aztec rulers also had impressive ceremonial headgear. The great quetzal-feather headdress worn by Motecuhzoma, the last Aztec emperor, still exists in Vienna's Museum für Völkerkunde.

Aside from the comparatively simple head-gear of the Aztec goddess effigies, females are not depicted in any specific head ornamentation in the pictorials. However, prehispanic figurines clearly indicate that in some Mesoamerican regions women worked cords into their hair to create a turban-like effect; this custom still exists in certain conservative Indian communities [see 692]. In some villages, long, ornamental hair ribbons—often in part beaded—are interwoven into braids and allowed to hang down the back. Also, throughout the Indian market-places of Middle America women balance folded *rebozos* atop their heads as sunshades.

ARMOR

The quilted cotton armor worn by the Indians at the time of Spanish contact [706] was so effective against Mesoamerica's martial weapons—stones, arrows, obsidian-implanted clubs and lances—that the Spaniards quickly adopted it. All too soon, however, the Indians learned that no matter how thick their protective body-encasing garments, they were no match for the Spaniards' swords and lances of Toledo steel. Following the Conquest, the indigenous armor fell into disuse.

JEWELRY

Blue-green stones, including turquoise, were the most highly prized of all jewelry. Indeed, the diamonds and sables of Mesoamerica were jade and quetzal feathers [see 684]. Soft metals—gold, silver and copper—were certainly valued but not to the same degree. Quartz crystal also served as an elite accoutrement, notably for lip plugs. Further important elite adornments were flowers, arranged as long-handled nosegays to be carried for ceremonial occasions, and also to be enjoyed in private.

GARMENT DECORATION

In addition to the rich variety of complex weaves that existed in Mesoamerica's textiles,[20] decorative embroidery threads were applied with a needle to already-woven fabric to enhance cloth. One highly prized embroidery yarn, *tochomitl*, incorporated the soft underbelly fur of rabbits.[21] Filaments of a wild silk were also used in small quantities for decorative purposes, as was the brightly colored plumage of tropical birds. These costly feathers were either interwoven or carefully sewn onto high-status tex-tiles. Additional decorative materials applied to cloth included sea and snail shells, stones of different qualities and colors, and thin plaques of copper, gold or silver.

Prehispanic textiles were also enhanced through painting or dyeing. Three methods of dyeing were employed: either the fiber was dyed before spinning, the thread was soaked in dye after spinning, or the cloth was dyed after weaving. The range of resist-dye techniques known included *ikat, plangi*, bound-resist and *batik. Ikat* involved tying off ("reserving") portions of the thread and dyeing it before the cloth was woven; *plangi* entailed the creation of small, round or square patterns on an already-woven textile by tying off sections of the cloth and then dyeing it [see 684]; bound-resist involved rolling and binding cloth prior to dyeing to create a series of dyed and undyed stripes; *batik* utilized a waxy substance applied to specific areas of woven cloth to shield those sections from the dye bath (see "Island Southeast Asia," p. 294).

Dyeing materials were of vegetable, animal and mineral origin. Mordants such as alum and copperas (ferrous sulphate) were used to fix or modify the dye colors. Vegetable dyes came from flowers, leaves, stems, roots, wood bark and fruit. Colors of animal origin included the famous *caracol*, a light purple shellfish dye (*Purpura patula pansa*), and the carmine red *grana* or cochineal made from crushed, dried bodies of the tiny female insect *Dactylopius* (*coccus*) that lives on the nopal cactus (*Opuntic* or prickly pear). Mineral dyes from certain earths and oxides were also utilized.[22]

The archaeological record indicates that Meso-american textile crafts were probably older than pottery and agriculture; ethnographic analogs suggest that the making of cloth might have consumed more hours of labor per year than ceramics and food production combined. As Elizabeth W. Barber notes, it was the late 18th-century Industrial Revolution—with its cotton gins, spinning jennys, power looms and great cloth mills—that freed the modern Western world from dependence on handmade fabric.[23] We have forgotten the tremendous effort involved in such an enterprise, but not so long ago textile production was humankind's single most time-consuming labor. This certainly was true throughout Mesoamerica, a civilization that produced magnificent cloth and clothing.

MODERN TRANSITIONAL DRESS

Immediately following the Conquest, both the Spanish overlords and upper-class mestizos—those of mixed Spanish/Indian parentage—wore fashionable European-style clothes. This pattern of the elite wearing high-style Western fashion continued through the colonial period and into the modern day. Such was not the case among the indigenous population. Indeed, certain prehispanic and early colonial dress customs still survive in some areas [see 690–701]. However, Western influences—Levis, T-shirts, athletic shoes—are creating as dramatic a transformation in Indian attire as did the Spaniards almost half a millennium ago [707].

707 New clothes, old clothes worn in a highland market: clothing change inevitably moves on.

9

SOUTH AMERICA

SOUTH AMERICA is a continent of superlatives: the world's longest mountain range, largest rainforest, most extensive river system and some of the globe's highest peaks and driest deserts. Marching down the western flanks of the Andean cordillera are a succession of ancient habitation sites that culminate in the southernmost point of the Americas, Tierra del Fuego. Whether South America's first arrivals came from Asia/Siberia/North America via sea in sturdy coastal craft, or over land by foot, all were lured by the hope of more abundant food. After extinction of the large, glacial-age mammals about 8000 B.C., a greater variety of small animals were hunted and wild plants gathered. In certain areas, farming eventually became an important supplement to gathering and fishing, and the subsequent Andean high civilizations were based on a combination of agricultural communities that could support large permanent settlements and social institutions that could channel labor to public goals. East of the Andes lie the vast tropical lowlands of Amazonia. About 12,000 to 6,000 years ago, some of the region's nomadic hunting-and-gathering peoples began to settle near major waterways. Certain of those living along the Amazon River developed sophisticated chiefdoms. By the time of European contact, many of those groups had climaxed and declined, others were still flourishing.

THE ANCIENT ANDES

708 An Andean Central Coast slit-tapestry fragment—possibly used as a coca bag—woven of cotton and camelid-hair yarns. Length 9³/₈ in. (24 cm), width 5¹/₂ in. (14 cm).

The Andean world is a stark domain where towering mountain ranges plunge steeply to narrow coastal deserts, a geographically diverse realm where there early developed one of history's most extraordinary weaving traditions [Map 31]. For thousands of years textiles marked important political, social and religious distinctions to a degree not exceeded elsewhere in the world. Indeed, cloth served as the foundation of the entire aesthetic system.[1] This abiding fascination with fine textiles was a hallmark of the ancient Andean world, one of the six primary hearths of ancient civilization (see "The Ancient Near East," p. 14). Many surviving weavings are artistic masterpieces; all reflect a tradition of fiberwork that preceded pottery by several millennia. The earliest preserved plant-fiber fabrics have been dated between 8600 and 8000 B.C. These basketry fragments were discovered in the dry Guitarrero cave of the Callejón de Huaylas in modern Peru's central highlands; the oldest pieces display finger-manipulated weft-twining and looping.[2]

At lower altitudes, along Peru's north coast, non-loomed fabric was being made ca. 3000 B.C. from newly domesticated cotton fibers. Among the best known of these ancient fragments are those from the pre-ceramic village site of Huaca Prieta. In these elaborately twined textiles, some of the animal, human and geometric motifs already existed that would be combined in Andean weavings over the next 4,000 years—images that would be repeated, inverted, interlocked and arranged as mirror images when they appeared and reappeared in sequential Andean cultures. Despite such early coastal activity, it was in the highlands that a series of revolutionary weaving breakthroughs took place, inventions that were to have a profound effect on subsequent textile traditions.

The first far-reaching Peruvian culture had its beginnings in the central Andean highlands, following the gradual, local development of the heddle-operated loom, ca. 2000 B.C. to 1400 B.C.[3] Chavín culture—named for an ancient site near the present-day village of Chavín

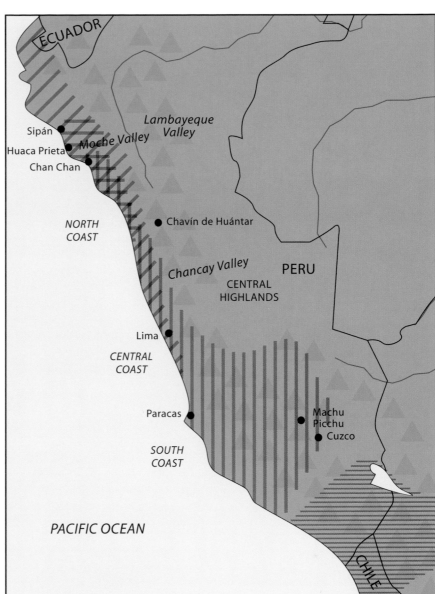

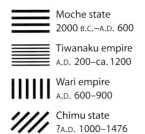

709 A Chavín-style textile fragment from the central Andes. Length 29¹/₈ in. (74 cm), width 12¹/₈ in. (31 cm). Although this piece was found in a South Coast burial, it was probably woven in the central Peruvian highlands, ca. 1000 B.C. Neither this textile, nor any related Chavín-style pieces, can be identified as garments. Such fragments serve as examples of the embryonic Peruvian textile technology.

de Huántar—dominated Peru from ca. 1200 B.C. to 600 B.C. This early period produced not only a remarkable religious art style involving complex imagery [709] but influential technological advances as well. These innovations incorporated new weaving techniques that included the first use of supplementary, discontinuous elements and the initial use of cloth as a surface for painted designs. A wave of all of these advanced technologies accompanied the Chavín art style as it spread throughout the Andes.[4] There is also evidence for relatively early dyed camelid hair textiles, but they appear to have been in a local rather than Chavín style.[5]

Since it is the nature of cloth to be fugitive, one might well ask how we can know so much about early Andean weaving. The answer lies in a combination

Map 31 Map of the Ancient Andes region.

Moche state
2000 B.C.–A.D. 600

Tiwanaku empire
A.D. 200–ca. 1200

Wari empire
A.D. 600–900

Chimu state
?A.D. 1000–1476

710 An Inka high-altitude burial discovered on the 22,109-foot-high (6,740 m) peak of Cerro Llullaillaco. This sacrificed boy wears a richly colored camelid-fiber mantle over a tunic woven of red camelid yarn. Buried with the child were additional highly valued offerings to the mountain gods—for example, small silver figurines and a spondylus-shell necklace.

of ancient burial practices and extreme climatic conditions. Early coastal people inhabiting northern Chile and southernmost Peru were preparing mummies and depositing them in the dry and desiccating sands of the coastal desert more than 7,800 years ago. Some of these mummies may have been regularly unearthed and displayed—as was the practice millennia later, in Inka (formerly Inca) times—or else permanently buried in bulky, fabric-swathed bundles like those found on the arid, desolate Paracas Peninsula, one of the richest of Andean burial grounds.

We also have gained knowledge of early Andean weaving from a number of high-altitude frozen burials discovered in recent decades, burials that date back five centuries [710]. Inka children were sacrificed to the mountain gods who controlled the weather and hence gave or withheld life. Each sacrificial offering was interred completely attired in clothing made from warm, soft, beautifully colored, camelid-hair yarn, the highland product whose dyed strands imbue such radiance to Andean textiles. In addition, such weavings reflect an ancient tradition of economic exchange between regions of markedly different elevation. Many Andean textiles combined ecologically distinct cotton and camelid-hair yarns.

The Andean peoples lived in a unique topography of ecological "islands" that formed a vertical archipelago, ranging down from the 14,000-foot-high (4,265 m) grasslands of the camelid pastures to the cultivated lands of the high-mountain plots, the lower-intermountain terraced valleys, the steep western foothills and, finally, the Pacific's dry coast. It was along the narrow coast that, thanks to rivers descending from the mountain heights, irrigated desert valleys produced the basic food staples of corn, beans and squash, as well as one of the basic textile fibers, cotton.[6] Indeed, Andean civilization was based on four great technological breakthroughs: irrigation, terracing, long-term storage of dried and frozen foods, and weaving on heddle-operated looms. The creating of two-dimensional fabric structures from one-dimensional thread was a fundamental human invention, one carried by the Andeans to a level seldom rivaled in the pre-Industrial world.

In ancient Andean culture there were several types of looms upon which cloth was woven: an A-frame, an X-frame, an upright frame [711], a body-tension backstrap [712] and a ground-staked horizontal loom.[7] Andean garments were constructed of webs of uncut cloth generally used just as they came from a loom; little further processing was necessary because all clothing was unfitted. Tailoring—the cutting out and sewing together of pieces of cloth to follow the lines of the body—did not exist in the Andes prior to European contact. Indeed, the Inkas considered the cutting of cloth a sacrilegious act when the Spanish instituted the practice in the early Colonial years.[8]

We have an understanding of prehispanic Andean clothing from several sources. One has already been mentioned, ancient archaeological cloth which includes miniature garments that were probably fashioned as religious offerings. Further sources are the detailed colonial descriptions of a 17th-century Jesuit priest, Bernabé Cobo, as well as a series of colonial drawings, based on conversations with older Andeans, that illustrate a lengthy letter written to the Spanish court sometime between 1567 and 1615. The letter's author was a native Andean, Guaman Poma de Ayala ("Falcon Puma"), a courageous and compassionate spokesman against Spanish injustice. His more than 150 illustrations reveal particularities of Inka customs, religion and dress [see 711–713, 717, 720].

The combination of archaeological, descriptive and pictorial data—plus the area's persistent absence of tailoring, which kept garment shapes much the same even as weaving techniques evolved—makes it possible to extrapolate cautiously back to a millennia-old pattern of Andean dress. Although the surface details of each epoch's clothing reflected regional and temporal differences, the basic construction principles and general shape of the limited number of garment types remained essentially the same. Because our most detailed knowledge comes from the Spanish Conquest period, those data are particularly insightful. The Andean power at that time was the Inka Empire; the ruler himself, the ultimate authority, was known as "the Inka."

711 (right) An ethnically non-Inka man—note his provincial moccasins, a style worn in the southern Andes—weaving a tapestry textile on a vertical upright frame loom; various colored wefts await use at his feet. Although this depiction is from the Colonial Period, earlier Inka tapestry looms were probably similar but no doubt wider and not so high.

712 (far right) An Inka woman weaving on the body-tension backstrap loom, a heddle-operated mechanism that produced webs of cloth with all four sides—the selvedges—completely finished, hence ready for use directly from the loom.

713 (right) An Inka emperor wearing an elaborate version of Andean men's basic apparel: a tunic, mantle, sandals and, in this case, royal headgear. The fringed ligatures at the ruler's knees and ankles were high-status accoutrements worn only by emperors and military men.

MEN'S BASIC DRESS

Andean men wore a loincloth, a pull-over tunic, a rectangular mantle and some form of headgear [713]. In contrast to women's clothing, which had horizontal apertures for both head and arms, men's tunics had vertical neck and arm slits. Male apparel also differed by elevation. In the central highlands, Inka males' sleeveless tunics were longer than wide, reaching to the knee. The Wari (formerly Huari) and Tiwanaku (formerly Tiahuanaco) tunics of an earlier period—ca A.D. 650–850—were more or less square. All of these highland garments were usually densely woven in warm, camelid-hair yarn [714[9], 715[10], 716[11]]. Along the coast, men's wider, shorter tunics reached only to the waist, exposing decorated loincloths, and sometimes had sleeves [see 722]; characteristically, extremely large mantles were worn over them.

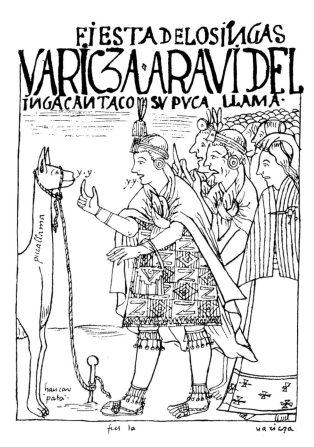

714 Highland Inka, A.D. 1440–1540. Cotton and camelid-hair yarn. Height 35⅞ in. (91 cm), width 29⅞ in. (76 cm). This outstanding geometric textile is the only known example of an Inka tunic of royal quality, one exceptionally well woven in the tapestry technique, with interlocked and dovetailed weft joins. The technique was reserved for textiles of the highest status, generally official state tunics. The overall pattern on the tunic is composed of a series of small rectangles called *t'oqapu*. In Guaman Poma illustrations, the only males wearing tunics decorated with any of these units—much less a garment completely covered by them—were high-ranking nobles. Guaman Poma states that the eighth-listed of Inka rulers was Viracocha, "an ingenious inventor of fancy textile patterns." This tunic may well be an example of a *"Viracocha t'oqapu."* (Viracocha was most likely mythical.)

The tunic displays a total of 312 *t'oqapu* arranged in regular rows. Within these units are 22 or 23 basic patterns. Only two of these designs are recognizable depictions: Inka tunics, woven in the standard black and white checkerboard pattern, so detailed that even their vertical neck slits are visible, and the "key" design—a diagonal line with a square in the opposing corners—that appears on other Inka tunics. The remaining design units are unique, appearing nowhere else in the corpus of Inka textile design motifs.

Interlocked tapestry weave.

One type of dovetailed tapestry weave.

715 Wari, possibly highland. Camelid-hair yarn. Height 34 in. (86.5 cm), width 48 in. (122 cm). The remarkable multi-staged process used to create a complex multicolored Wari textile such as the one illustrated here is unique in world fiber history and underscores how important it was to the Andeans not to cut fabric.

The Wari technique is based on the use of both discontinuous warps and wefts, threads that do not go from edge to edge on the cloth, but serve purely for design purposes. Scaffolds of weft yarns were stretched horizontally across the loom before the warp yarns were ever set up in a series of differently shaped, stair-stepped combinations of large-scale rectangles, frets or step-block forms. These geometric units were probably woven in strips—perhaps with more than one strip on the loom at once—of undyed alpaca-hair yarns with the warps dovetailed around the various levels of the weft yarns' scaffolds. After the weaving was complete and the scaffolds removed, the freed geometric units were tie-dyed in different colors and then reassembled with undyed alpaca yarns running through the warp yarns' loops, where the scaffolds of weft yarns had originally been. Finally, the slits between the strips—and between the weft yarns' edges on the geometric motifs— were closed by sewing, creating a textile that intermixed regular and irregular patterning. This complex technique may be highland in origin. There are also Wari-style ceramics that depict these kinds of tunics.

Dovetailed warp yarns.

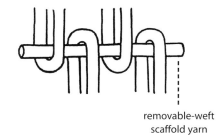

removable-weft
scaffold yarn

716 Highland Wari style, coast of Peru, ca. A.D. 500–800. Camelid-hair yarn weft and cotton warp. Height 41⅝ in. (106 cm), width 37⅜ in. (95 cm). Wari-style textiles such as this repetitive, geometric tunic present a degree of abstraction that makes them difficult to read, a characteristic of the Wari style in general and of Wari tunics in particular. That does not mean, however, that such designs were not fully understood at the time of the Wari Empire.

It has been pointed out that just as artists of the European Renaissance developed perspective—a vanishing-*point* format in Western painting—so the weavers of the southern highlands developed a vanishing-*line* format. The point of the "vanishing line" is that the motifs toward the center of the tunic are wider than those at the side. In the case of this interlocked tapestry (see diagram on p. 447), there are profile faces in the triangular spaces next to the stepped frets.

QVINTA CALLE
CIPAS·COIA

717 An Inka woman, busily spinning yarn, displays basic central Andean female attire: an ankle-length wraparound dress secured at the shoulders with pins and at the waist with a wide belt; her enveloping shawl is held in place with a simple pin.

WOMEN'S BASIC DRESS

Inka women's neck-to-ankle dresses were wrapped under the arms, the cloth pulled up over each shoulder and secured with pins and a belt; an enveloping shawl was pinned over the chest, covering the bare arms [717]. In contrast, coastal tunic-like dresses [see 724] were sewn up the sides, over the shoulders and usually were not belted.[12] The varying surface patterning and weaving techniques of highland and coastal attire are discussed in the regional sections below.

FOOTWEAR

Perhaps in response to the rough vertical terrain, the Inka wore sandals. Cobo describes their footwear as being made of untanned leather taken from the neck of camelid hides; the soles were of leather or braided plant fiber. Nobles' sandals had colorful woolen ties.[13] The moccasins on the sacrificed boy in the high-altitude burial [see 710] are an indication that he was ethnically non-Inka and from a conquered southern province; the burial took place in an Aymara-speaking area. Guaman Poma depicts similar footwear in some of his illustrations of individuals who were ethnically non-Inka [see 711].

OUTERWEAR

Rectangular mantles/shawls were worn by both sexes for warmth, each garment of a weight and degree of decoration appropriate to the individual's gender, physical environment, rank or status. For the Inka, mantles sometimes also served a social purpose: at times of grief or penitence a cloak was draped loosely over the head.[14] Inka men's mantles were made of two joined pieces of undecorated cloth tied on the shoulder or over the chest and worn loosely [see 713]. Inka women's shawls were pinned at the neck [see 717].

HAIRSTYLES

Inka men wore their hair trimmed as close to the head as possible. Several of the Inka sacrifices, both men and women, wore their hair in multiple small braids, a style that is still current in some very conservative highland areas. Although Guaman Poma depicts Inka women with long, flowing tresses that were bound about the forehead with a woven headband, contemporary figurines show the women's hair fastened with some other sort of device.

HEADGEAR

In the Andes, headgear varied by region and hence served as an identifying marker, a factor regularly put to use within the Inka Empire—where conquered peoples were often relocated—to indicate ethnic or geographic origin. Apparently headgear was considered so individualistic that it was not included in either the taxation or redistribution systems. Cobo describes the most prevalent male Inka headbands as being made of a braided, camelid-fiber band the thickness of half a finger and the width of a finger, wound many times around the head to the width of a hand [see 710].[15]

The surviving ceremonial headdresses of the coastal Chimu culture—far more of these examples have survived than Inka ones—were resplendent with magnificent Amazonian tropical feathers such as those of the blue and yellow macaw, the scarlet macaw, the mealy parrot, the paradise tanager and even the tiny, iridescent feathers of the hummingbird.[16] Inka nobles regularly wore a metal plaque tied over the forehead [see 713]. The ruling Inka's royal headband incorporated a red fringe that was suspended from small gold tubes; this fringe served as the ruler's symbol of office, analogous to a European crown.

ACCESSORIES

For highland women, the primary accessories were the pins and belts that held their wraparound dresses together and their shawls in place. Cobo reports that these pins ranged in length from 4 to 11 in. (10–28 cm) and were made of gold, silver and copper.[17] Then, as now, a desirable feature of Inka belts was their double-woven construction—usually warp-faced and warp-patterned—making them thicker, stiffer and stronger, hence an aid for abdominal support as well.[18] In as much as all Andean clothing lacked pockets, a variety of woven bags were carried by both men and women. The primary purpose of most of these bags—which were common diplomatic gifts—was to hold coca leaves [see 708] which, when chewed with lime, served as the Andes' widespread mild stimulant.

JEWELRY

The artifacts discovered in Andean site excavations include many types of beads, necklaces, anklets, rings, collars, plumes, metal or shell pincers for beard plucking, and bracelets.[19] Inka and provincial nobles often wore a wide gold or silver bracelet, usually on the right forearm.[20] Necklaces made of spondylus shells were particularly valued; indeed, more highly prized than gold [see 710].

Nose ornaments were also sometimes worn ceremonially, as were ear plugs [718, 719]. Ear spools—some inlaid with gold and semi-precious stones, others

718 A mannequin dressed in the attire of the Lord of Sipán. This costume was reproduced with replicas of objects found in Tomb 1 at Sipán, North Coast, Peru.

with feathers—were developed to a state of high refinement in the Andes. Large earplugs—some 1½ in. wide, 2½ in. thick (4 x 6.5 cm)—were the most distinguishing mark of Inka men; indeed, they were nicknamed "Earplug Men," a term the Spaniards translated as *orejón* ("big ear").

ARMOR

In Andean warfare, obsidian-pointed lances, clubs, bolas, spear throwers, axes and halberds were employed, as was the hurling of stones; fabric slings augmented the effectiveness of these missiles. Inka protective martial clothing included leather helmets and shields. A disk pendant was worn by the commander [720].

720 To the left, Inka noblemen wear leather military headgear; a disk pendant is worn by the commander. Such pendants were bestowed by the emperor as diplomatic gifts. The hapless provincials seem to have no armor at all.

FACE AND BODY MODIFICATION

The re-forming of infants' heads into artificial shapes had a long history in the Andes. During the 1925 South Coast Paracas excavations by the Peruvian archaeologist Julio C. Tello, very elongated skulls that dated ca. 600 to 150 B.C. were repeatedly discovered. Along the Central Coast, in Max Uhle's excavation at Pachacamac, a variety of cranial modifications were found among the graves of the sacrificed women who date from the period of the Inka Empire. These females had originally come from several different highland Inka provinces.[21]

GARMENT DECORATION

Over many millennia, Andean weavers produced some of the ancient world's most outstanding cloth, textiles incorporating an amazing array of techniques: painted, tie-dyed, embroidered and brocaded plain weave; interlocked and slit tapestry; double cloth; triple cloth; shaped weaving; sprang; twill; and gauze, among others. In addition, these textiles exhibit some of the highest thread counts per inch ever achieved in the pre-Industrial world. Most of the decoration that appears on ancient Andean garments was woven into the fabric itself, although a variety of supplemental materials—feathers, fringes of bells and tassels, as well as gold and silver plaques—were sometimes added.

Among the Inka, there were two qualities of cloth: the finest, *qompi*—the Spaniards wrote it *cumbi*—was made from the best young camelid-fiber yarn and worn only by the elite. Cobo states that *qompi*—which was finished on both sides—was woven on a vertical upright loom [see 711], ideal for creating the colorful, interlocked-tapestry cloth preferred in the highlands. Along the coast, the region's beautiful slit-tapestry fabrics were probably woven on A- or X-frame looms. But highlands or coast, common people wore only coarse cloth, woven on whatever type of loom was common to any given area.

The truly impressive range of Andean weaving techniques was perhaps matched by the important variation in the size and proportion of garment types, distinctions as important as decoration styles in

719 (opposite) A magnificently detailed Moche ear ornament of hammered sheet gold features a warrior clad in a turquoise tunic and adorned with several detachable accoutrements: a removable shield held in one hand, a removable war club in the other. The warrior's crescent-shaped nose ornament swings freely and his chest is covered with a removable owl-head necklace. This ear ornament—whose figure is about the size of a thumb—is part of the treasure from the Royal Tombs of Sipán, located near Lambayeque on Peru's North Coast. Diameter 3⅝ in. (9.4 cm).

721 A fragment of a Lambayeque-style slit tapestry textile from the North Coast archaeological site of Pacatnamu, Peru, ca. A.D. 1000. Cotton and camelid-hair yarn. 9 in. (23 cm) square, excluding tassels. The complex iconography on this unusual piece (see also drawing opposite) shows ceremonial activities that may once have been part of the social and religious life of the inhabitants.

distinguishing one area from another. Given the absence of tailoring, variations in regional textiles are identifiable by their shape, size, structural weaves and decorative patterns. Each of the ancient Andean cultures had its own distinctive weaving focus, its own textile personality.

NORTH COAST

The Moche of Peru's North Coast—ca. A.D. 1 to 850—produced some of the most elaborate ceremonial costuming of the ancient Andean world. Nowhere was this more evident than in the wealth of accoutrements from the site of Sipán, the richest set of tombs ever excavated in the Western hemisphere [see 718, 719].

Following the end of Moche dominance, the Lambayeque textile tradition flowered in the North Coast's neighboring Jequetepeque Valley, ca. A.D. 1000–1350.[22] As in the preceding Moche art style, exceptional Lambayeque-style textiles sometimes include narrative scenes incorporating architecture, animals and human figures performing a variety of activities [721], recalling Moche paintings on both murals and pottery.[23]

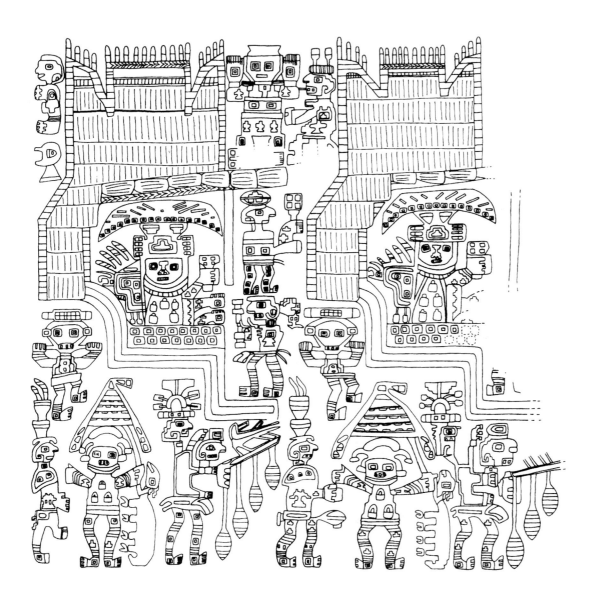

The subsequent kingdom of Chimor was centered in the Moche Valley. The Chimu also had a highly stratified society with much of the valley's population living in crowded, irregular housing at their capital city of Chan Chan. The elite, however, may have occupied the large compounds whose adobe walls were often decorated with distinctive motifs that also appear in Chimu weavings, such as the austerely beautiful white gauze garments that often display stylized sea-bird motifs identical to those on the Chan Chan adobe friezes [722].

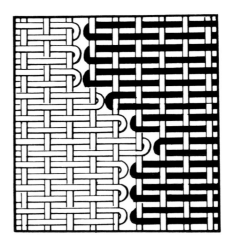

Slit tapestry weave.

One type of gauze weave.

One type of brocaded plain weave.

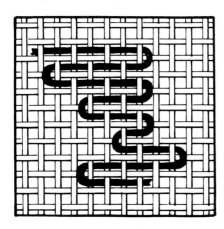

722 North Coast Chimu, cotton, ca. A.D. 1000. This related group of white garments reflects one of the characteristics of the Chimu textile corpus: a propensity for men's matched clothing sets that included a tunic, loincloth, rectangular mantle and various kinds of headgear. Most of the ensemble illustrated here is woven in the prevalent Pelican Style: finely spun, undyed cotton thread creates designs carried out in white-on-white gauze and brocaded plain-weave construction.

Tunic: length 23^1/$_8$ in. (59 cm), width 45^5/$_8$ in. (116 cm).

Hat: height 13^7/$_8$ in. (35.5 cm), width 10^5/$_8$ in. (27 cm); ties 34^5/$_8$ in. (88 cm), width 2^1/$_2$ in. (6.5 cm).

Mantle: 110^1/$_4$ in. (280 cm), width 69^3/$_8$ in. (176 cm).

Loincloth, not originally part of this ensemble: length 95^5/$_8$ in. (243 cm), width including ties 175^7/$_8$ in. (447 cm). Height of each tie 7 in. (18 cm).

Band with tassels: length 123^1/$_8$ in. (313 cm), width 2^1/$_8$ in. (5.5 cm).

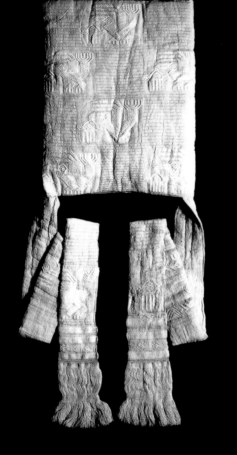

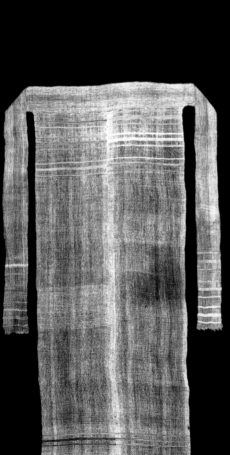

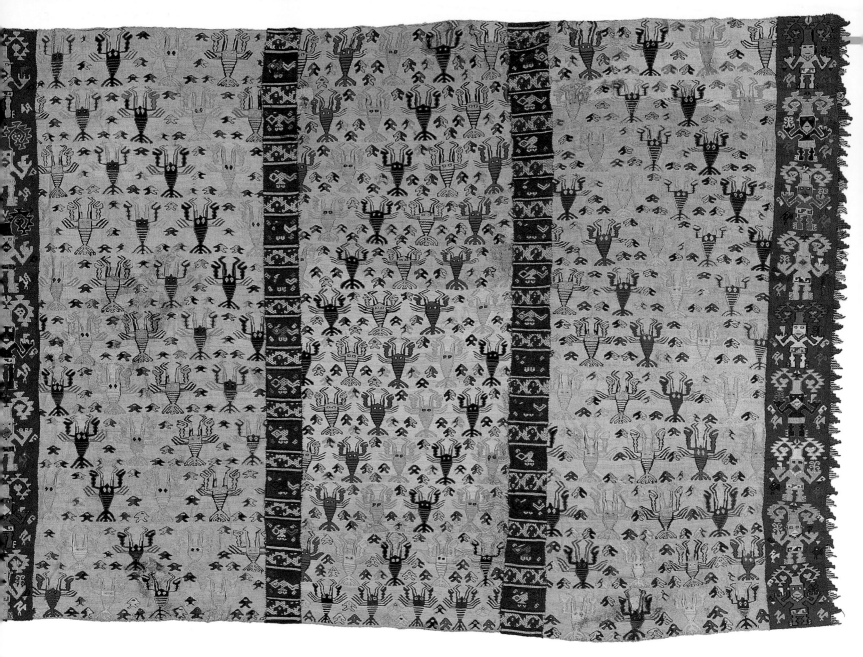

723 Central Coast, cotton and camelid-hair yarn, A.D. 1000. Length 63³⁄₈ in. (161 cm), width 44 in. (112 cm). This textile depicts sea birds, fish, crayfish and, in the matching vertical outer borders, ceremonially attired males holding what appears to be a plant in one hand and some kind of implement in the other. The textile is woven in the slit tapestry technique (see diagram on p. 455), a hallmark of coastal weaving; in the highlands there was a preference for the sturdier interlocked tapestry. The advantage of both interlocked and slit tapestry is their ability to combine many diverse colors closely; the disadvantages of slit tapestry— in a cloth with many varied-color motifs in its field patterning—are the repeated, color-change slits that weaken a textile's construction. This luxurious, colorful, intricately woven piece—a triumph of art over practicality—may have been worn as a mantle by an important man on an important occasion, or perhaps it served as a hanging. The truncated textile is not complete: the upper edge has been cut and the two horizontal borders are missing. Such losses are not uncommon in extant ancient Peruvian textiles.

CENTRAL COAST

The best-preserved textiles from the Central Coast come from the Chancay Valley and date from the 300-year period prior to the Spanish Conquest, although this region had an ancient weaving history. Late Central Coast textiles often featured fauna of the local environment. Since the sea played a major role in Andean myth and legend, it is not surprising that fish, crustaceans and sea bird motifs are emphasized in coastal textiles [723].[24]

Figural sculptures constructed of reeds, yarn and cloth [724] are a unique source of information on the use of Chancay textiles. Such figures—often called "mummy dolls," although their exact meaning remains unknown—were often found in association with Chancay burial bundles. These small, fragile sculptures were created with great care and skill, their faces usually woven in tapestry technique and their miniature garments made specifically for each piece. Crude copies of these figures—often made with ancient cloth—are sold as mummy dolls in large numbers in present-day Peru.

SOUTH COAST

The best-known textiles from the South Coast come from the ancient Paracas culture, 600–175 B.C. The often large, decorated Paracas mantles are constructed of plain-weave cloth embroidered with brightly colored images. The majority of these elaborately worked pieces may have been made as ceremonial burial offerings, although some show signs of having been used in life [725].[25] During Julio C. Tello's Paracas excavation—probably the most spectacular discovery of Peruvian textiles ever made—more than 400 mummies were unearthed. Most of these were adult men buried at least 2,000 years ago, their burial bundles wrapped in as many as sixty layers of both huge, plain-weave, undecorated cotton cloth and finely worked camelid-fiber textiles, some intricately embroidered.

724 Effigy figures such as this fiber sculpture have been referred to as *muñecas*, "dolls," but there is no evidence that they were ever used as playthings; instead, they were apparently highly symbolic, often appearing in ritual scenes that were placed in burials. This figure represents a female with stepped facial decoration, wearing a Chancay-style patterned dress with a horizontal neck slit, a head scarf, two belts and a trophy-head pendant. Height 13 in. (33 cm), width 5 in. (12.7 cm), depth 1 in. (2.54 cm).

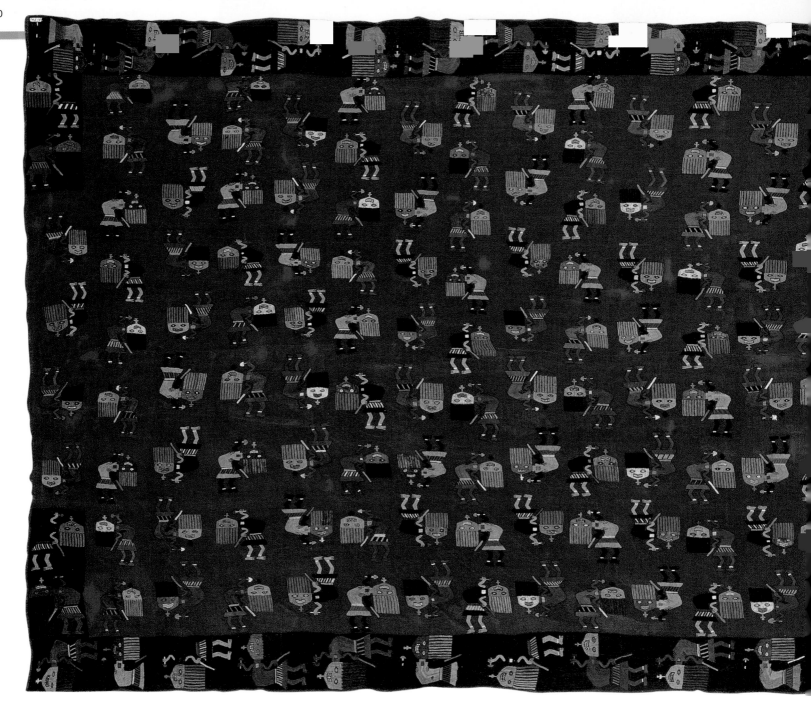

725 South Coast Paracas mantle, ca. 200 B.C. Camelid-hair yarn, plain weave with stem-stitch embroidery. Height 55⅞ in. (142 cm), width 94⅞ in. (241 cm). Much of the cloth found in the bulky Paracas mummy bundles was ceremonial attire. Many of these magnificent pieces were mantles that in life are presumed to have been worn draped lengthwise around the neck and over the shoulders and arms, like a cloak. The images on the mantles were created with camelid-hair yarn, used in stem-stitch embroidery—the addition, with a needle and thread, of individual stitches to a plain-weave ground fabric. When forward-moving stitches overlap one another—as in stem-stitch—solidly covered areas can be created.

Paracas weavers devised a remarkable solution to the age-old problem of threading the needle: a needle was permanently threaded with a circular loop of thread closed by the weaver with a tiny splice. Embroidery yarns were then subsequently threaded through the loop rather than through the needle itself.

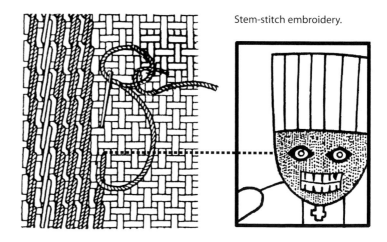

Stem-stitch embroidery.

For the highland Wari, the ancient prototype was Chavín, whose religious symbols featured a variety of deity motifs [see 709]. Abstracted forms of these figures appear and reappear on many subsequent Andean textiles as a series of cultures adopted the Chavín cult; the widespread sharing of these religious-political images reflected a broadened sense of social identity. Slowly an Andean tradition emerged that—under the Wari and Inka empires—politically united previously unrelated cultures of highlands and coast.

Some of the most complex imagery of the ancient Andes is found on Wari and Inka garments [see 714–716]. Sometimes Wari tunics were worn with four-pointed hats, fabricated in geometric designs and made in a knotting technique that utilized an armature consisting of a knotted or looped network. The combination of a geometric hat, a geometric tunic and textile-inspired geometric face-paint

726 The combination of a Wari-style geometric four-cornered hat, geometric tunic and geometric face-paint—a textile-derived pattern—transforms the wearer into a dynamic geometric presence.

HIGHLANDS

The Andean cordillera was homeland to the most dominant of ancient Peruvian cultures, among them two groups widely separated in time, the Wari and Inka. The textiles of these cultures are better known than other highland styles because of their more extensive ties to the coast between A.D. 600–850 and 1460–1532. Coastal mummy bundles sometimes included Inka textiles that had been granted to the lowland elite. There is ample documentation for such gifts in the Inka Empire, and it would not be surprising if the Wari had a similar system.

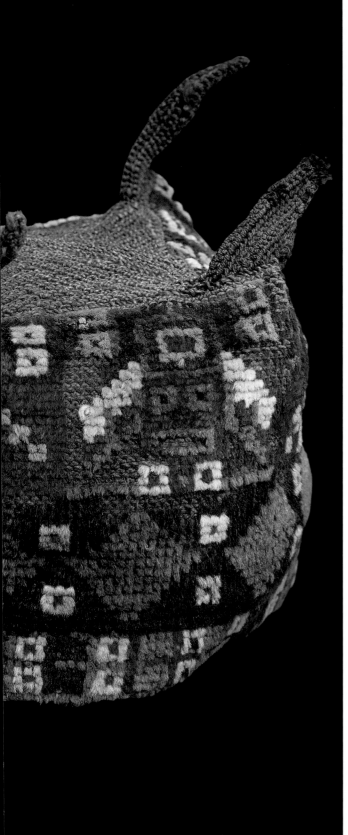

produces an effect that is almost a celebration of geometry itself [726, 727].

TRANSITIONAL DRESS

By the 16th century, the aggressive, powerful Inka ruled over a vast realm, reaching from the border of modern-day northern Ecuador down to central Chile. Each of the geographical divisions under their domination included diverse, sometimes relocated, ethnic peoples, and a road network of 14,300 miles (23,000 km) connected the divisions to the Inka capital, Cuzco. But, on November 15, 1532, the realm of the Inka was invaded by the Spanish. This confrontation occurred at the city of Cajamarca in the central Andes. The ruling Inka, Atahualpa—recent victor in a dispute over rulership with his half-brother—was taken hostage. A few months later, despite desperate delivery of one of the richest ransoms in history, the Inka and many of his nobles were killed by the conquerors. The Spanish then incorporated the indigenous elite into their administration. It was not until Peru became independent of Spain that this upper class disappeared from view. As for the lower strata of Andean society, in isolated places many of their everyday cultural practices survived, but not most of their indigenous attire.

Following the Conquest, the use of traditional dress was particularly prohibited in the central and southern Andes, heartland of the Inka Empire. This edict was in the interest of repressing Indian identities and deculturalizing the common population; focus was placed on the male tunic and mantle, both emblematic of ancient Andean culture. During this epoch much of the native male population was compelled to adopt the provincial dress of Spanish peasants: pants, jackets and vests. It was during this period that the poncho became the common garment of the Indian.[26] As for women's dress, judging from many present-day Peruvian female garments, here too Spanish peasant costume was mandated.

727 Two four-cornered hats decorated with colorful geometric designs, A.D. 500–800. The hats' tops and points were constructed separately from the sides. The points may represent animal ears; the raised, knotted thread on the upper, pile hat may be an imitation of fur. These rather small, adult men's hats were placed high on the head and were sometimes worn together with a geometric tunic. Similar hats are available in Peruvian markets today.

Left: height 5¹/₂ in. (14 cm), diameter 5⁵/₈ in. (14.5 cm).

Right: height 5¹/₂ in. (14 cm), diameter 6¹/₈ in. (15.5 cm).

THE PRESENT ANDES

728 A Quechua woman from Pitu Marca, Cusco, Peru, weaving a warp-faced textile on her backstrap loom. She wears a finished example of such work as a shawl.

Following the traumatic conquest of the Andes in the mid-16th century, the Spanish presence was increasingly concentrated along the coast where the native population had been decimated both through warfare and disease. It was in these coastal areas that the decline of weaving occurred earliest and was most complete. In contrast, the indigenous culture—including prehispanic dress—persisted in the mountainous highlands; indeed, too prominently for the comfort of the new overlords. This continuity of traditional life was particularly evident in the heartland of the Inka Empire where the natives' identification with their imperial past was a constant source of vexation to the Spanish [Map 32].

In 1572, some forty years after the Conquest, Viceroy Francisco de Toledo prohibited the wearing of "native dress" in an effort to eliminate all memory of the Inka. The plan was to replace indigenous dress—region by region—with Spanish peasant clothing. Subsequently, in response to a series of indigenous rebellions, a stronger decree was issued in 1780 to insist that the Indians wear the foreign clothes. The result was a melding of the two forms, with the natives adopting aspects of Spanish dress that suited them. Men changed from the indigenous tunic—a knee-length shirt without collar or sleeves—to a short jacket, knee-length trousers and Spanish-style hats; in place of the female wraparound dress, most women began to wear a skirt, blouse and sometimes also a short jacket. The natives, however, continued weaving and wearing their indigenous accessories, and these prehispanic-style items are still in evidence today—women's shawls and carrying cloths, bags used for carrying personal items, and belts and sashes worn by all [729–732].

The result of this Spanish-Indian fusion is the popular dress we see today. It has changed over the years to accommodate new dyes, materials, inventions and forms, but in certain conservative areas Andean clothing has remained relatively true to the 18th-century model.[1] Inasmuch as each community has its own distinctive style, there is marked variation in dress throughout the Andes, making for a fascinating mosaic of regional clothing.

The vast expanse of the Inka Empire (see p. 463) encompassed a multitude of ethnic groups, each with its own prehispanic attire and weaving tradition. Into these ancient traditions the Spanish introduced a new means of creating cloth, the European treadle loom, which operates under principles quite different from those of the heddle-rod and shed-rod mechanisms of the indigenous looms.[2] The concept of using foot treadles to operate the shed-changing mechanisms of the European loom probably originated in China and spread first to the Middle East and then to Europe, around the 11th or 12th centuries.[3] In the Americas, as in Europe, the treadle loom was introduced as a commercial venture and the work was done by men, whether or not weaving traditionally had been done by males in an area. Indeed, weaving in the infamous Spanish *obrajes*—colonial workshops—was done by native men on treadle looms.

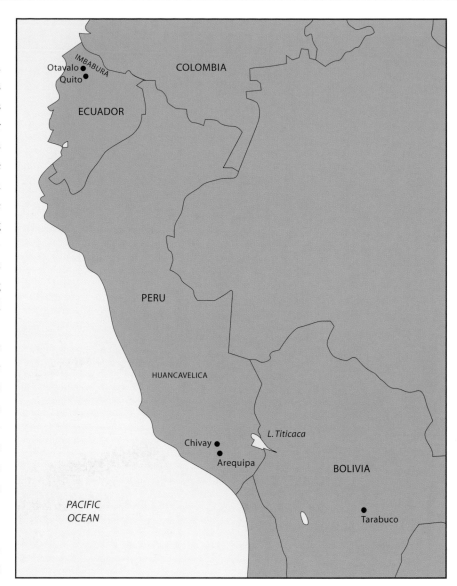

Today a mix of fibers is represented in Andean clothing; cotton (*Gossypium barbadense*) and camelid hair—mainly alpaca—continue to be used, as does wool. The Spanish introduced sheep into the Andes almost immediately after the Conquest. Sheep's wool differs from other animal hairs in being covered with tiny scales that make wool feel much rougher than the indigenous Andean camelid hair, which has few scales. The scales of sheep's wool, however, lend the fiber to felting, a technique for creating cloth through the action of moisture, agitation, heat and chemicals. Felting is used in making many of the European-style hats worn in the Andes today.[4] In addition to the ancient indigenous fibers, some synthetic, man-made yarns and factory-produced cloth have now been adopted.[5]

Map 32 Map showing sites in the present-day Andean region.

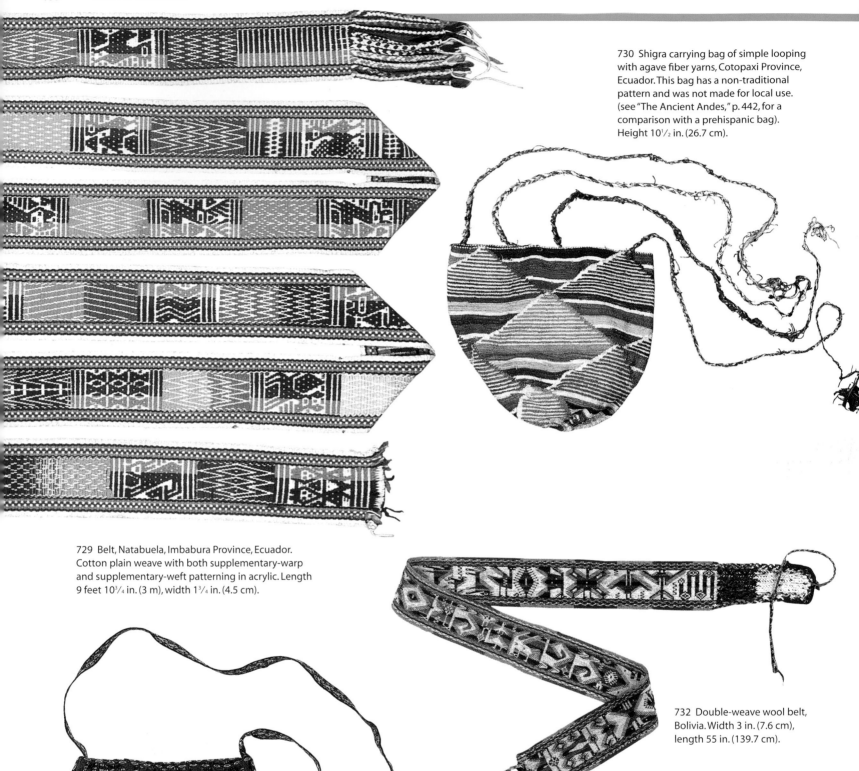

730 Shigra carrying bag of simple looping with agave fiber yarns, Cotopaxi Province, Ecuador. This bag has a non-traditional pattern and was not made for local use. (see "The Ancient Andes," p. 442, for a comparison with a prehispanic bag). Height 10¹⁄₂ in. (26.7 cm).

729 Belt, Natabuela, Imbabura Province, Ecuador. Cotton plain weave with both supplementary-warp and supplementary-weft patterning in acrylic. Length 9 feet 10³⁄₄ in. (3 m), width 1³⁄₄ in. (4.5 cm).

732 Double-weave wool belt, Bolivia. Width 3 in. (7.6 cm), length 55 in. (139.7 cm).

731 Coca bag, Avaroa Province, Department of Oruro, Bolivia. Alpaca, 19th century. Warp-faced plain weave with bands of complementary-warp weave, crossed-warp borders, and wrapped tassels. Long warp threads were used for the three small pockets that open from the side of the bag. The many tassels are neatly wrapped and sewn with tiny stitches. Bag warp 7³⁄₈ in. (19 cm), weft 8¹⁄₄ in. (21 cm). Strap warp 42¹⁄₈ in. (107 cm), weft ³⁄₈ in. (1 cm)

MEN'S BASIC DRESS

The substitution of 18th-century Spanish peasant dress for Inka-style clothing—particularly the tunic—is evident throughout the Andes in the men's shirts and headcoverings as well as in their close-fitting pants, today far more apt to reach to the ankle than the knee. Although variants of these same garment types are worn throughout the highlands, each area has evolved its own forms and combinations.

In the northern Andes, the best known man's costume is that of Otavalo, a famous market town located 65 miles (105 km) north of Quito, at an elevation of 9,300 feet (2,835 m). The area's 60,000–70,000 Quechua-speaking population is certainly the best known indigenous group in all of Ecuador—and perhaps in all of Latin America—because of their monopoly on the region's cottage-industry textile trade and associated tourism. The traditional dress of the Otavalo men for the past hundred years has been white cotton pants, a white cotton shirt, white sandals (*alpargatas*), a felt hat and a distinctive red or blue striped wool poncho [733]. Until as recently as the 1960s, the Otavalo white pants were made from handspun and handwoven cotton cloth in a style with wide, calf-length legs. Now only older men wear this style [734].[6]

In sharp contrast to the white cotton clothing of Ecuadorian Otavalo is the wool attire of the men of the Quechua-speaking island of Taquile, located near the western (Peruvian) shore of Lake Titicaca. On this small, high-altitude island—3.4 miles (5.5 km) long, 0.9 miles (1.5 km) wide, 12,507 feet

733 The men celebrating this wedding at the church of San Luís in Otavalo, Imbabura Province, Ecuador, in November 1993, wear machine-made white pants of a modern cut, together with large ponchos. The bride wears two white wraparound skirts and a blouse with white embroidery. One of her *padrinas* (supporters) wears a headcloth intricately folded into a hat-like shape.

734 An Ecuadorian couple and grandson from the community of Natabuela, Imbabura Province, wear clothing that is a sub-style of the Otavalo costume. The two males wear white cotton shirts and wide pants, *alpargatas*, enveloping ponchos and dark brown fedoras. The grandmother wears the old-style white felt hat, an embroidered blouse, a woven belt, a single wraparound skirt, a wool mantle and multi-strands of shimmering glass beads.

(3,810 m) high—the men wear warm handmade clothes: a cream-colored, coarsely woven wool shirt with full sleeves attached to a dropped shoulder line, black/navy full-length wool trousers, and a woolen sleeveless white vest with black front and side panels. To this basic ensemble is often added a wide, cummerbund-like belt in red or maroon with horizontal bands of white figurative designs. Some men also tie a flat, squarish bag with two tiny pockets to their waist. Taquile men wear large knitted caps, usually with tasseled ends. It is the men

who knit these caps and they also weave—on a treadle loom—the rough woolen fabric, *bayeta*, used to make their shirts, vests, trousers and mantles [735, 736–740].[7] In turn, the women perpetuate the indigenous fabric tradition using their four-stake ground looms to produce carrying cloths, coca bags and belts [see 729–731]. Yarn-spinning tasks are shared but in general the finest spinning is done by women, with men helping to produce the coarser-spun yarns.[8]

735 The daily dress of Taquile Island, Peru. The men, in their distinctive attire, are usually the more colorful. Under their dark trousers they often wear an extra, white pair for warmth; an additional shirt is also worn beneath the full, cream-colored outer garment. As for the women, only married ladies wear a red top. Beneath the wife's outer skirt she wears two to four additional, colored underskirts, all protective attire in a cold clime.

736 Man's wool shirt, Taquile Island, Peru. Height 28³⁄₄ in. (73 cm), width 59 in. (1.5 m), including sleeves.

737 Man's mantle, treadle-loom woven, with crocheted ends, Taquile Island, Peru.

738 Man's wool pants, Taquile Island, Peru. Treadle-loom woven cloth, 2/2 twill. Height 35 in. (89 cm), width 28³⁄₈ in. (72 cm).

739 Man's knitted wool hat, Taquile Island, Peru. Height 20⁷⁄₈ in. (53 cm), width 9⁵⁄₈ in. (24.5 cm).

740 Belt, Taquile Island, Peru. Length 75 in. (1.9 m), width 6³⁄₈ in. (16 cm), excluding tie.

741 Two 16th-century drawings from Guaman Poma de Ayala's chronicle depicting Colla (Aymara) men wearing tunics with wide vertical stripes. Note the distinct difference between the Inka and Aymara clothing in the grisly first drawing.

On the eastern (Bolivian) side of Lake Titicaca live Aymara speakers who have continued an ancient textile tradition up to the present day. Evidence for the time depth of this continuity is documented in 16th-century illustrations found in Guaman Poma de Ayala's *El Primer Nueva Corónica y Buen Gobierno* wherein are clearly depicted two prehispanic Aymara tunics [741]. These garments, with their broad vertical stripes, are almost identical to venerable ceremonial tunics still worn today by Aymara dignitaries on important occasions. In daily life, many Aymara men don sturdy, commercially manufactured dark pants, European-style jackets and distinctive ponchos, as well as the conical knitted cap of the cold altiplano, now often worn beneath dark brown fedoras [742].

742 The man standing at center of this Aymara group from Calamarca, Bolivia, wears a fedora over his knitted conical cap. This type of cap can be clearly seen on the man seated on the ground. The chieftain's wife, at left, in the ceremonial handwoven skirt that is a symbol of her important position, wears a straw and cloth hat; the woman to the right wears a felt bowler.

743 A 1950s woman from Tupe, in the Peruvian province of Yauyos. Her dress preserves obvious prehispanic characteristics. The basic garment is a full-length, broad rectangle woven of black alpaca hair and bordered with red and black edgings. As in Inka times, the dress is wrapped around the body below the arms with the cloth pulled over the shoulders and secured with pins, forming a kind of tunic that reaches down to the ankles. Originally the garment was worn over the naked body; Spanish morality obliged women to wear a long black woolen smock beneath. This Tupe wraparound dress is belted with two sashes and the shoulders are covered with a woolen shawl decorated with stripes and secured with a large silver pin, the *tupu*. The woman's head is covered with an industrially manufactured red cotton kerchief; her slippers are made of untanned leather and edged with colored wool fiber, a style that dates back to prehispanic times.

WOMEN'S BASIC DRESS

The Inka full-length, wraparound dress revealed a woman's leg when she walked, a feature deemed highly immodest by the Spanish authorities so the garment was all but eliminated.[9] Although some examples of this dress style continued into the 20th century [743],[10] they were worn over a long, enveloping tunic, hence full modesty was attained. Some indigenous forms, notably wraparound dresses and skirts, survived longer in Ecuador than in most of Peru.

The women's attire in Otavalo, Ecuador [see 733 and 734] consists of a blouse-and-slip combination—probably introduced sometime in the 19th century—over which are worn two waist-to-ankle straight, wrapped skirts, one navy blue/black, the other white. The ends of the darker skirt meet over one side, revealing the white one beneath. Each skirt is wrapped so as to include a single pleat; these overlapping garments are held in place with two belts—a "mother" and a "baby" belt—one worn atop the other.[11]

In many areas of highland Bolivia, women wear a one-piece flared dress. In the small town of Tarabuco, these dresses are embroidered in a distinctive manner featuring designs that also appear on the men's shirts. The women of the Tarabuco region also wear an overskirt—a garment of prehispanic origin—made from two four-selvedge pieces sewn together and worn with the warp horizontal [744].[12]

744 The women of Tarabuco, Bolivia, wear a distinctive one-piece flared dress plus an overskirt pinned over one shoulder, usually with safety pins sold in the local market.

The main focus of the 18th-century female costume change was the skirt; a common Andean example is full, bell-shaped and pleated [745, 746; see also 735, 742, 753]. These descendants of earlier Spanish peasant skirts occur in a variety of lengths and are worn in a varying number of layers, giving many Andean women a stout and bulky appearance. As the American textile scholar Mary Weismantel has noted of the women's clothing in Zumbagua, Ecuador: "It is often a surprise to encounter a woman washing her hair in her own patio on a sunny day, wearing only her innermost slip, and discover a slim, muscular person instead of the familiar rotund figure. The roundness of the female form is enhanced by the fact that women carry everything from babies to food, tools, money, or gifts for friends tucked into the voluminous folds of their shawls and skirts, garments that provide women protection, privacy, and warmth, enabling them to carry on their many, arduous tasks out in the fields and pasturelands. Many women do heavy agricultural work on a daily basis, enduring burning sun, cold rain, sleet, hail and strong winds, and their clothing is designed to fit their needs."[13]

745 The traditional dress of the women of Chivay, Province of Cailloma, Department of Arequipa, Peru, ca. 1970s.

746 Woman's black wool overskirt from Taquile Island, Peru, woven on a four-stake loom. Length 2 ft (63 cm), width 10 ft (3 m). The garment actually comprises 20 ft (6 m) of gathered fabric.

FOOTWEAR

As in other aspects of Andean dress, footwear varies by region; climate is not the determining factor. Women and children living in the high altitudes of the bitterly cold Lake Titicaca Basin often go about barefoot, whereas even the poorest of Ecuadorian women—living at lower, warmer altitudes—wear inexpensive plastic shoes when away from home. Today, throughout the Andes, the most common footwear is either tire-tread sandals or inexpensive athletic shoes. There are exceptions. The men of Otavalo have worn their distinctive *alpargatas* since colonial times [747]. These attractive white sandals are composed of a plaited white cotton string toe-piece and heel-strap with fiber soles of braided and coiled *furcraea*, a sturdy leaf fiber that was also used for prehispanic sandal soles.

747 Otavalo men's *alpargatas*, one from each of three pairs, purchased in the Otavalo market, Imbabura Province, Ecuador.

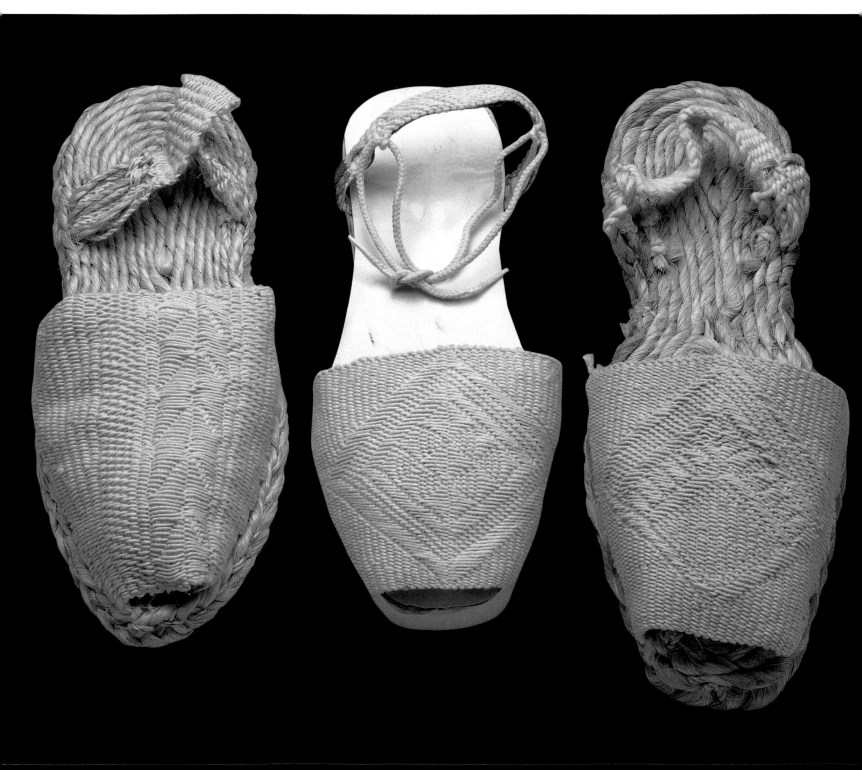

OUTERWEAR

In the 20th century, the poncho—which replaced the prehispanic mantle, not the tunic—has been *the* indigenous Andean garment. Ponchos usually cover the entire torso and are typically made of joined squares or rectangles of cloth handwoven on indigenous looms. There is speculation that the poncho may have been adapted from a prehispanic-style tunic with the side seams opened to facilitate use on horseback.[14]

During the Wars of Independence against Spain in the early 19th century, the poncho was popularized among both the *criollo* (New World-born Spanish) and Indian populations. The garment was perfect for use by cavalry regiments and all of the *criollo* generals—including José de San Martín and Simón Bolívar—wore large ponchos that had bands running down the center of the garment and around its border, decorative embellishments that featured coats of arms and Spanish floral designs. The auxiliary Indian troops were quick to adopt this large poncho style, using indigenous rather than European designs.[15]

Andean women's outerwear consists of a headcloth and/or shawl. These garments are usually made of two rectangular pieces of cloth sewn together. Aymara women, in addition to their principal shawls, have accessory pieces for adornment, ceremonies, or to be used as carrying cloths [see 742].[16] For daily wear, Otavalo women use both a headcloth and shawl, each now made of either factory-produced fine wool or commercially manufactured acrylic or velour.[17] Taquilean women use their shawls both as head-coverings [see 735] and baby-carrying cloths.

HAIRSTYLES

In Otavalo, a child's hair is considered sacred, not to be cut before three or four years of age for fear of causing physical harm to the little one. Both men and women wear their hair long and the condition of one's health is judged by the thickness and sheen of one's hair. Women and girls almost never cut their hair, pulling it back and wrapping it in a single long band that is woven either on a treadle or backstrap loom. Otavalo men also pull their hair back from the face, wearing it in one long, single braid.

Taquilean women often plait their hair into multiple braids, starting in a straight line almost at the base of the hairline above the neck. Up until about two generations ago, men also braided their hair in this same fashion. Today men's hair is cut short but for certain festival dances they wear wigs consisting of at least twenty-five braids, all 15 inches (38 cm) long, or more [748].[18]

748 A man from Taquile Island, Peru, wearing a wig consisting of some 25 braids, a style surviving from two generations ago.

749 The height and ornamentation of Andean knitted caps are creative expressions that seldom fail to delight the viewer. These two examples are worn by the Mamani brothers from Northern Potosí, Bolivia (1988).

HEADGEAR

Hats are a hallmark of Andean attire, some woven of straw, some made of straw and cloth [see 742], others knitted [749], many made from felted sheep's wool and fashioned on European-style models [750, 751]. The making of hats has been important in the Andes since the 16th century when hatmakers arrived from Spain and taught the natives how to create felt. Andean felt hats range in shape from the fedora, a soft felt with the crown creased lengthwise, to a stiff hat with a dome-shaped crown and narrow brim, the bowler, named for a 19th-century family of English hatters. Increasingly, it is the fedora—a modern style—that is most popular [see 742]. Fedoras and bowlers are usually machine- made.

It has been suggested that Aymara men began to wear European-style headcoverings in response to the 1572 edict by Viceroy Francisco Toledo forbidding the practice of reshaping the head, a prehispanic tradition among this group.[19] More recently, men in southern Peru and Bolivia have been wearing a knitted conical cap, with designs copied from the local weaving. This headgear may or may not be prehispanic. The current name for it in Aymara is *chucu*; in Quechua the term is *ch'ullu*, a word that appears in no early Inka dictionary. As for the cap's modern construction, knitting did not exist in the Andes until the Spanish introduced it, although the prehispanic looping technique produces a somewhat similar effect.[20] Whatever the antiquity of these caps, they continue to be worn, now often under fedoras [see 742].

Otavalo men's handmade felt hats used to be identical to those of the women but during the 1940s some men began to wear broad-brimmed fedoras; by the 1960s most men were wearing this style [see 734], whereas today most Otavalo women no longer wear hats. In the 1970s and 1980s, young men wore their hats backwards to indicate they were out looking for— or at—girls, a common occurrence on Friday nights. In recent years this custom seems to have disappeared but—as ethnographer Lynn Meisch aptly notes—not the flirting.[21]

750 The originality of modern-day Andean headcoverings is an endlessly impressive aspect of the area's regional dress, as is evident in this photograph of a young family from northern Potosí, Bolivia, 1988.

751 The variation in size and decoration of these six felt hats is evidence of the influence European-based headgear continues to play in the Andes.

752 The distinctive Sunday outfit of young bachelors in the Peruvian province of Huancavelica, ca. 1970s.

ACCESSORIES

The major Andean accessories are the ubiquitous, prehispanic-style carrying bags and belts [see 729–732]. In some areas, additional accessories are added. For example, in the Peruvian province of Huancavelica, on Sundays and holidays, young unmarried men wear a remarkably original outfit [752]. To their everyday suit of bluish-black baize—a course woolen fabric woven on a treadle loom—they make unique adjustments and add colorful accessories. Their jackets are turned inside out, displaying the seams as a sign of bachelorhood. Hanging from the jacket's pockets are brightly colored kerchiefs, and over the vest is worn a red belt that ends in long, fringed strings which fall down the back of the jacket and stick out below. Essential and characteristic additions to this unusual ensemble are knitted over-sleeves and stockings of colored wool worked in geometric designs and animal figures. The crowning glory of this eyecatching array is the flower-bedecked felt hat, made of bluish-black sheep's wool and worn with the brim raised over the forehead.[22]

JEWELRY

For whatever reason, jewelry seems less important in Peru and Bolivia than in Ecuador. Multiple strands of gilded glass beads, some the size of grapes, are particularly popular in the Ecuadorian province of Imbabura [see 734]. Another style, worn in Saraguro, consists of smaller beads joined to form linear patterns. Evangelical missionaries in certain converted towns of southern Ecuador have forbidden the wearing of necklaces that incorporate coins and crosses, but other prominent items of Andean jewelry are earrings—some up to 4½ in. (11.5 cm) in length—often made from old Peruvian silver coins, as are certain of the silver *tupus*, the women's shawl pins [see 743].

753 Taquile Island fiesta dress. A woman's prestige increases according to the number of full, gathered skirts she wears. On a daily basis, women wear two to four skirts; on Sundays six or eight; to dance at a fiesta a woman may put on as many as fifteen or eighteen skirts, one atop the other, forming colorful layers.

SPECIAL COSTUMES

In many Andean villages, clothing worn for fiestas is more ornate than that of daily wear [753].²³ In certain Ecuadorian communities, at such ceremonies as weddings or baptisms, Western clothing is *de rigueur*, even among traditional families, whereas for holidays such as Easter, Corpus Christi and All Souls' Day only newly handwoven indigenous clothing is appropriate.²⁴ Among the Quechua-speakers of Peru's Taquile Island, clothing is specially woven for weddings [754].²⁵ The inventory of these nuptial garments may or may not include the so-called "calendar belt," whose wide center stripe combines "traditional" and invented images.²⁶

754 A Taquile couple in their wedding attire. When a couple marry they set aside their old clothes to make room for a new set of garments specially woven by both the man and woman for the wedding. To acknowledge that they are married, the bride will change the color of her shirt from white to red; the groom will exchange his knitted cap with a white tip to one completely covered with designs on a red and blue background.

755 A Chivay woman's hat.

GARMENT DECORATION

Embroidery, whether done by hand or machine, is a major form of Andean garment decoration. In the southern Peruvian town of Chivay, located north of Arequipa, women dress in highly ornate clothing [755–759]. Their full-length skirts are bordered by rows of multicolored embroidery of birds, fish and flowers. Indeed, all their garments have some form of decoration or lace. It is of interest that both women and men embroider these female garments on pedal sewing machines.[27]

756 A Chivay woman's blouse.

757 A Chivay woman's jacket.

758 A Chivay woman's red overskirt (see detail, right).

TRANSITIONAL DRESS

As in many other ways, even traditional Otavalo is in the vanguard of costume change, with male attire changing faster than female dress. That said, it must be noted that when young girls leave southern Imbabura Province to work elsewhere, they become increasingly aware of the value of wearing an elaborated version of their regional costume, the better to advertise their ethnicity. Not so their male counterparts. As Lynn Meisch has noted, when young Otavalan men go abroad during their travels as musicians or merchants they bring back Western-style clothing and accessories bought in Europe and the United States.[28] Nonetheless, the long braid or ponytail remains the *sine qua non* of Otavalo male identity.

Elsewhere in the Andes, where there is no tradition of international travel, it is nevertheless common for men to wear fewer vestiges of indigenous dress. Schooling has also taken a toll on traditional clothing: when children spend a significant amount of time in class they often lack the opportunity to learn to weave. In addition, forcing Indian students to wear the same clothing as their mestizo schoolmates—a common, though not universal, practice—further breaks down the tradition of native dress. Despite these changes, native clothing continues to be worn in certain conservative Andean communities. Ironically, tourism can reinforce this tradition. On Peru's Taquile Island, the inhabitants have learned that their distinctive attire—a reinforcement of community solidarity—serves as an attraction to the outside world and thus also benefits the Taquilean economically.

759 A Chivay woman's green underskirt.

Indian tribes. During those five centuries of European contact, the number of Amazonian Indians dropped precipitously, from estimates of 6,000,000 in A.D. 1500 to some 250,000 today. Slave raids, epidemic diseases, colonization, the ravages of the rubber boom and ever-encroaching deforestation have all taken their toll. Most of the Indians who did not lose their lives lost their indigenous culture. It is in tribute to the original tropical-forest inhabitants that their colorful, exotic world is documented here.

MEN'S AND WOMEN'S BASIC DRESS
Despite the vast extent of Amazonia, much cultural similarity existed among its tribes, hence it is possible to discern many shared patterns. Although the majority of the lowland Indians wore almost no clothing, most tropical-forest tribes had a tradition of producing some form of fabric, if only cordage made from wild plants. For example, palm fibers were spun into cord that was either twined, netted, looped or woven via finger manipulation into such essentials as bags, nets and ropes, as well as into Amazonia's contribution to tropical comfort, the hammock.[5] Other tribes used small, simple looms to produce such minimal articles as arm bands, belts and abbreviated pubic covers [762, 763]. The principal fiber for these items was cultivated tree cotton (*Gossypium barbadense*), planted and tended by women near their huts.

Cotton trees commonly grow to heights ranging from 6 to 12 feet (1.5–3.5 m). The white cotton bolls were collected in July/August and stored in leaf-lined baskets that were hung from rafters; subsequently these bolls were ginned by hand and spun into yarn as needed. A few groups limited their weaving to only narrow strips because larger fabrics had little use in the lowlands' hot, humid climate. There were, however, western Amazonian tribes living in the Montaña region—1,000 to 2,000 feet (300–600 m) above sea level—who indeed did weave and wear body-encompassing garments.

The Montaña is an ecological corridor that runs north-south along the eastern slopes of the Andes from the Oriente of Ecuador to the Yungas of Bolivia. Although located at an elevation of over 1,300 feet (400 m), the area has a tropical-forest environment. In this region of high jungle, located just below the Andean cloudforests, clothing had adaptive value as the usually hot climate occasionally turns cold, windy and rainy from December to March, with clouds of mosquitoes and sand flies haunting such northward flowing rivers as the Ucayali.[6]

762 An E'ñepa man's pubic apron of cotton dyed with the red plant pigment *Bixa orellana*. The women spun, wove and dyed these men's garments. At the outset of puberty, boys were solemnly presented with their first loincloth in a ritual lasting several days.

763 A Ye'kuana woman's beaded apron of cotton thread with glass beads. These traditional trapezoid garments were woven on a simple frame shaped like a bow. When making their beaded aprons, the Ye'kuana used mainly red, blue and white beads, together with diverse materials for pendants.

764 This especially fine ca. 1940 Shipibo/Conibo storage-fermentation jar is an example of the most complex painted polychrome terracotta tradition in Amazonia.

765 This 1950s Conibo man is clad in a *cushma*, a long, wide, poncho-like cotton tunic that has been worn in the area since prehispanic times. The brown to black dye used in decorating these garments is obtained by boiling mahogany bark.

The Montaña craft tradition was influenced by long contact with the prehispanic Andean high cultures [764]. As a result, some of the region's tribes wore such enveloping clothing as poncho/tunics—commonly called *cushmas*—[765] and wraparound dresses, skirts and kilts, all woven on the pre-Columbian backstrap loom, which originated in the highlands. The majority of these Montaña textiles shared a common feature with ancient Andean weavings: each piece was individually woven to shape; there was no tradition of cutting down or altering the original size of a loomed rectangle of cloth. In the case of the *cushma*, two large rectangular pieces were stitched together. The garment's geometric linear decorations were then painted in dark tones of brown, ochre or black over a light background.[7] Other geometric designs—obviously inherited from an ancient decorative tradition—were said to represent serpents, the alignment of certain stars and other concepts related to the Shipibo people's beliefs [766].[8]

766 A Shipibo/Conibo man's tunic, or *tari*, ca. 1940, that was woven, hand-embroidered, dyed and appliquéd by Shipibo women.

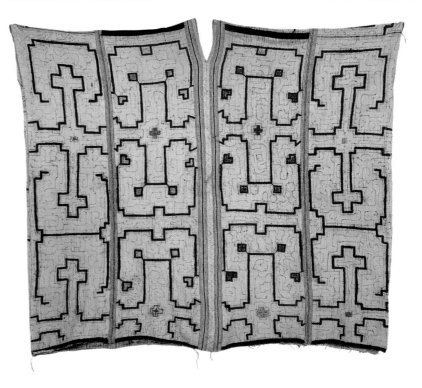

771 (below) The jaguar played an important role in Amazonia, as is evident in this photo of the animal's skin being passed over a patient in a Héta curing ceremony. The attendant shaman wears a cylindrical jaguar-skin hat. The jaguar, the forest's strongest animal, serves as a fitting symbol of shamanic authority. Among some tribes, like those of the Upper Xingú, a piece of jaguar pelt was placed over a basketry crown headdress as a symbol of high office.

772 (below right) A young Amahuaca woman wearing a crown headdress made from a shaved-down piece of the inner bark of split bamboo. She is adorned with black body paint and a nose ring, and wears multiple necklaces and arm bands made of monkey teeth and beads.

OUTERWEAR

In the terrain of the lowlands of Amazonia, no outerwear was needed. In the slightly higher elevations of the Montaña, encompassing cotton *cushmas* [see 765] and wraparound garments served as both inner and outerwear.

HAIRSTYLES

Among the Yanomami—one of the most numerous of the ethnic groups of the northern Amazon lowlands, numbering some 20,000—men wore their hair shaped in a round style, whereas women wore their hair long.[15] Other Amazonian women usually wore their hair shoulder-length and cut in bangs over the forehead. Indian men tended to cut their hair in a variety of ways.

HEADGEAR

During such ceremonies as initiations, funerary rites, planting ceremonies and shamanistic practices, a variety of headgear was used. Among the Héta, a cylindrical jaguar-skin hat was donned by shamans as they performed curing rituals [771]. The Amahuaca women's traditional bamboo headdress was worn on most occasions, including the planting of maize [772].

Among the most flamboyant of the Amazonian men's adornments—together with their war clubs, masks and carved wooden stools—were their feathered headdresses [773, 774]. Like peacocks, it was the males who were the most beautifully bedecked. The rich and variegated plumage of the region's tropical birds provided decorative feathers of the most varied hues. The armature for headdresses was traditionally a basketry frame that provided the supporting base for the addition of the feathers [775].

773 A Rikbaktsá man's radial feather crown headdress with a nape.

774 A cylindrical cane crown headdress with filmy white egret feather projections and scarlet macaw plumes, made by the Waiwai tribe. A variant of this headdress utilizes harpy eagle breast feathers instead of egret plumes.

Indeed, of all the living creatures encountered by the European explorers of South America and the West Indies, it was the birds—especially the parrots, macaws and toucans—that they felt best epitomized the brilliance and beauty of nature in the New World. Columbus brought parrots back from his first voyage, and Brazil became known as The Land of the Parrots. Most of these colorful birds still exist in Amazonia and magnificent feathered pieces are still being created for rituals and ceremonies linked to initiations, funerary rites, shamanic practices and social visiting.

775 Kayapó girls carrying U-shaped headdresses at a naming ceremony marking autumn. This occasion involved a typical role-reversal ceremony when the women and girls were permitted to wear the elaborate dorsal headdresses of the men. At this stage of the ceremony, the females had briefly taken over the center of the men's normally prohibited hut. Then, without warning, celebrants wearing conical anteater masks danced into the village from the forest to restore the normal social order.

776 (above) A model of a Rikbaktsá man—wearing a bast-fiber pubic apron, ceremonial feather ornaments, and bead-and-tooth necklaces. He is playing a panpipe made of eagle quills.

777 (above right) A Héta woman carrying her baby in a narrow sling and her family's possessions in a large carrying basket; the steel ax was a recent acquisition.

ACCESSORIES

Woven cotton arm and leg bands, belts and loin coverings were widely worn, as were varying forms of bast-fiber pubic aprons, some fabricated in non-loom techniques such as finger-manipulated twining, looping and netting [776; see also 762, 767, 768]. Males' belts were often adorned with such materials as jaguar skin and monkey hair; female belts were decorated with seed pods and sometimes with land-snail shells, ornaments that jingled as the women moved in their ritual dances.

Another female accoutrement for some tribes was the narrow baby-carrying sling that was worn diagonally across the body [777]. These slings—made of bark strips or bark cloth rather than cotton—were usually undecorated. Some baby carriers, however, displayed dyed bast-fiber weft threads that formed a subtle pattern. Occasionally additional objects were added to these slings, such as bone tinklers [778].

778 A Campa baby-carrying sling decorated both with linear motifs created by dyed weft threads and a row of 45 attached tinkling bones, each etched with a unique design.

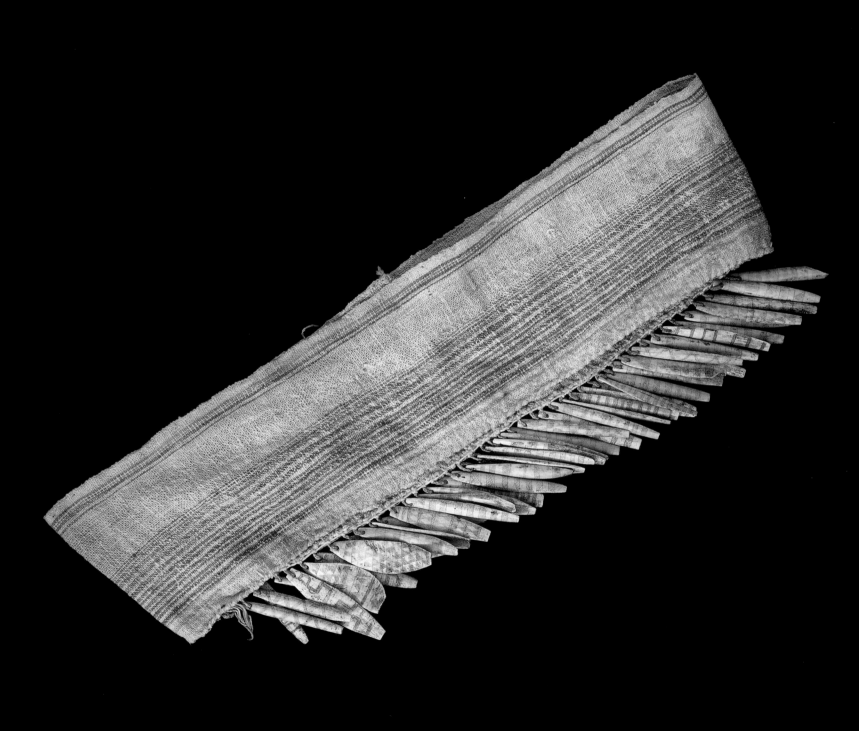

780 A Ye'kuana man's necklace made of peccary teeth, cotton string and plant pigment. The sharp canines of the peccary are used for necklaces and amulets. The number of teeth gives information on the wearer's prowess in hunting.

779 This upper-arm, radial-feather projection "wing" assemblage is from the Mashco Amarakaeri tribe of the Peruvian Montaña.

JEWELRY

Men wore ceremonial feather ornaments on their arms, ears and nose [779-783]. Intricate ensembles of macaw plumes, parrot feathers, fiber, monkey teeth, snail shells and bird pelts displayed the complexity of Amazonian sartorial decoration.[16]

Men also wore multiple necklaces made of beads and seeds combined with monkey and peccary teeth. Other ornate necklaces—also worn by women—were created by combining vivid, colorful feathers—turquoise tanager, yellow toucan, purple cotinga, scarlet and varicolored macaw, and tiny blue hummingbird feathers—with seed beads as well as various animal and insect parts, such as armadillo and jaguar claws, the teeth of the peccary, coati and monkey as well as inlaid shell disks fringed with green beetle-wing covers.

To Western eyes, one of the most distinctive articles of Amazonian adornment was the commonly worn lip plug, which could take two forms: long pendants that hung from a hole in the lower lip or circular disks that fit into an opening that was periodically expanded by inserting an ever-larger plug [see 770]. These accoutrements were made from an

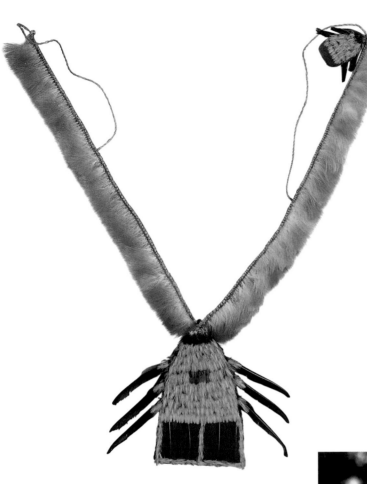

782 A pair of three-strand, iridescent green beetle-wing-casing ear ornaments with toucan-feather danglers, made by the Aguaruna tribe.

783 A Héta man wearing a lip plug consisting of a cross-piece of wood—worn horizontally inside the mouth—and a piece of resin projecting through the lower lip. His necklace is made of a 14 in. (35.5 cm) semi-flexible rod decorated with animal teeth. His ear pendants are fully plumed bird skins.

781 An Urubú-Kaapor necklace with a centerpiece composed of iridescent blue hummingbird breast and black wing feathers. This necklace was actually worn by a woman.

assortment of materials including wood and resin. Among the Héta, lip plugs were made of a wooden cross-bar, worn horizontally inside the mouth, attached to an oval piece of polished, translucent resin that protruded down through a perforation in the lower lip [see 783].

Ear ornaments could take the form of pendants, hanging from a hole in the earlobe, or could be worn as a series of progressively larger wooden plugs. Insects' wing casings were also made up into impressive ear ornaments, as well as necklaces. These stiff casings, in addition to their iridescent properties, functioned as rattles, clattering as their wearer danced, or even turned his head [see 782].[17]

784 Two Kamayurá men decorating one of the wooden posts used in the Kuarup ceremony. Each log is painted with characteristic designs, wrapped with textiles and given a headdress that is adorned with colorful feathers, in order to represent the spirit of a high-ranking deceased village ancestor. Note how the conical shape of the Kamayurá house in the background is echoed in the local dance costume [see 785, below].

SPECIAL COSTUMES

Special costumes are worn either by celebrants or by representations of celebrants [784].[18] Ceremonial dance costumes are made by combining bark cloth or wooden crowns with long, shredded inner-bark fringe or palm leaflets from the burití palm, *Mauritia flexuosa*: these are the only completely body-encasing garments worn in Amazonia [785–787]. Each guest invited to a ceremony made a costume which disguised identity by covering the body, although the wearer could see through eye holes in the thin bark cloth. Such costumes—which were generally standardized within a tribe—may well have impersonated the spirits and hence had some religious significance, but they are nonetheless said by some to have been ephemeral, constructed only for the purpose of the ceremony and then discarded and allowed to disintegrate.[19] However, this is not always the case. Sometimes the costumes are kept till next time, although they are prone to suffer from wear and tear and are subject to insect infestation, which shortens their lives.[20]

785 A huge wooden dance-costume mask with feather projections, twill-weave horizontal tube arms and a massive, stepped palm-fiber crinoline. Made by the Kamayurá, the mask evokes a lake spirit in a healing ceremony.

786 A Tikuna bark-cloth dance costume painted with a fish motif. The mask represents the thunder demon and is worn by men during women's initiation ceremonies.

787 Among the most impressive of the tropical lowlands' artifacts were the full body-mask dance costumes worn by men in ceremonies that had to do with maintaining social control. Illlustrated are two of the masks/body costumes worn by the De'aruwa people for their Warime ritual—a magical entreaty to the animal world to prosper, as well as to further consolidate the initiated De'aruwa men's societal standing. The costumes are made of a skirt and cape-like covering, over which dangle the frills from the masks: a peccary on the left, a Capuchin monkey on the right.

FACE AND BODY MODIFICATION

Many tribes practiced tattooing, but in a modest way. The Amazonians punctured the skin with a sharp instrument such as a palm spine or agouti tooth and then rubbed soot or carbonized latex into the wound. The final color of the tattoo, however, was always blue. Usually tattoo marks were limited to a couple of chevrons on the cheeks, or a few lines on the wrist, and served mainly to beautify the person rather than as a tribal emblem. The most delicate details of body decoration were usually reserved for the face.

The Indians, besides decorating themselves with painting and tattooing, sometimes practiced scarification: Karajá Indian women displayed a circular scar on each cheek, a mark burned on with the glowing end of a man's wooden pipe [see 760]. Many Amazonian Indians also assiduously removed all body hair. For example, the Ye'kuana—boatmen of the Upper Orinoco—plucked out or shaved, with a bamboo knife, their eyebrows, eyelashes, and the hair of the armpits and genitals as well as all facial hair.[21]

MASKS

In sections of the northwest Amazon, men pounded the soft inner bark of the *Olmedia aspera* tree into a coarse, felted bark cloth. Although rough and stiff—and therefore uncomfortable to wear as everyday clothing—this fabric provided an excellent base for adding painted decorations to the hooded, body-covering conical masks and the dance-costume masks with huge palm-fiber crinolines [see 785–787].[22]

There were also dramatic painted bark-cloth frontal masks such as those worn by the Tikuna men to frighten initiate girls [788]. Among the Tapirapé,

788 The bold white lines highlighting the features of this fearsome circular Tikuna bark-cloth mask replicate the face paint applied by humans.

trophy-head masks consisted of a flat board to which lots of small feathers had been affixed [789]. Originally, these masks represented the trophy heads of defeated enemy warriors, but in the present pacified times they now are said to honor the spirits of those Tapirapé who have died in the past year.[23]

TRANSITIONAL DRESS

Ironically, what made an Amazonian feel appropriately dressed—his flamboyant body paint, protective decorative ligatures and plethora of feathers—were precisely what made him look savage to his European oppressors, whose concept of "proper clothing" differed dramatically.[24] Over the centuries, these contrasting sartorial views have reached accommodation.

Today, as they go about their hunting and agricultural activities, Amazonian men are most apt to be wearing Brazilian soccer shorts, a T-shirt, with or without logo, and inexpensive rubber flip-flops. The women, depending on degree of acculturation, wear straight, sleeveless dresses or a simple skirt and T-shirt, the better for nursing. However, for ceremonies, sporting events, and sometimes also for social occasions, such groups as the Kayapó, Shavante and Upper Xingú River tribes still adorn themselves with body paint and feather ornaments [790].

Despite the dramatic changes in the 500 years since European contact, and despite the declining numbers of Amazon Indians (with the exception of a few protected—and self-protecting—tribes such as the Kayapó[25]), there are encouraging signs that indigenous groups continue to remember the old tribal ways of their ancient forest home.

789 (opposite) A Tapirapé *upé* trophy-head mask commemorating the death of an important member of the tribe. Also known as a *cara grande* ("big face") in local Portuguese, these special masks were cared for in the men's central hut.

790 A magnificently attired Tikiri, father of Paiakán, Kayapó Indian leader, A-ukre village, Xingú Region, S. Pará State.

PATAGONIA

791 "Inhabitants of Tierra del Fuego" by Alexander Buchan, who accompanied Captain Cook on his 1769 voyage. As well as the baskets on the inside of the hut, note the skins being stretched and dried on frames on the roof and by the right side of the structure: these will become all-encompassing cloaks.

The human urge to explore the unknown is exemplified by the hunters who, as the last Ice Age relaxed its grip, worked their way south to the very tip of the Americas, the rugged wastes of Patagonia.

The topography of southern Patagonia and Tierra del Fuego is dominated on the west and south by the imposing Andean mountain chain and to the east by desiccated plateaux giving way to low plains. It is a harsh land, a huge, roughly triangular territory of more than 560,000 square miles (900,000 km²) located at the far end of South America between latitudes 39º and 55º south.[1] Much of the year Patagonia's climate is cold, with weather marked by snow, hail, sleet and chilling rain, as well as by the frequent bluster of violent winds. The young Englishman Charles Darwin, who arrived in Tierra del Fuego in the month of December, South America's summer (temperatures then ranged between 38º and 45º Fahrenheit) deemed the region's climate "singularly uncongenial."[2]

At the termination of the last Ice Age, some 10 to 14,000 years ago, bands of intrepid hunters and gatherers began to settle this inhospitable terrain. It was not to be until 1519 that the first European— Fernando de Magellan (1480–1521)—navigated through the strait that now bears his name. This strait separates Patagonia from Isla Grande de Tierra del Fuego, while the Beagle Channel cuts Tierra del Fuego off from the outer islands [Map 34]. The Portuguese navigator noted that the natives lit a series of large fires upon sighting his ship, hence the name, Tierra del Fuego ("Land of Fire").[3] Darwin, in 1832, also observed such fires being lit on every point of land as the H.M.S. Beagle moved among the bays, islands and inlets of Tierra del Fuego.[4]

Fernando de Magellan is also connected with the naming of Patagonia. Before actually seeing any of the inhabitants themselves, members of Magellan's crew noticed huge footprints left by the Indians' guanaco-

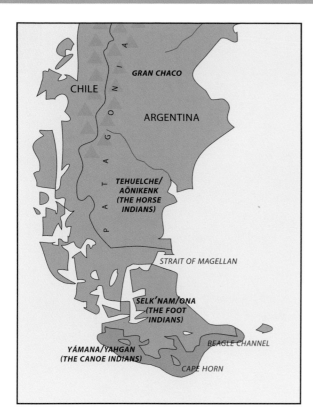

Map 34 Map of Patagonia.

entirely on wild foods. The coastal inhabitants of the many small islands and rocky inlets of Tierra del Fuego—the southernmost native people on earth—relied on fish, shellfish and sea mammals. Such groups as the Yámana/Yahgan are known as the Canoe Indians because, after exhausting the edible fauna near their camps, they would pack up their meager belongings to move on to the next inlet in their canoes, made from the bark of the southern beech (*Nothofagus betuloides*). In these vessels, small fires were often kept burning. The meagerness of the area's resources forced the Canoe Indians to live in small groups, often as few as six to eight persons.

Patagonia's inland peoples were dependent on land animals, mainly the guanaco. This wild relative of the llama was described by a visiting 19th-century Englishman, Captain G. C. Musters, as combining "the neigh of a horse, the wool of a sheep, the neck of a camel, the feet of a deer and the swiftness of the devil."[6] The marked territorial behavior of these creatures, however, made them easy prey because they grazed in the same general areas all year long. Guanaco were the mainstay of the Foot Indians, who hunted their prey on foot, using bows and arrows [792, 793]. Such groups as the Selk'nam/Ona occupied the flat, northeastern part of Tierra del Fuego, living in the open country in groups of up to forty or fifty.

fur moccasins. Some believe that it was these sailors who named the people Patagones, "Big Feet," hence the name Patagonia. An alternate explanation also plays on the idea of "giants," growing out of the Europeans' anticipations for America, the mysterious new land where they expected to see something that was literally "larger than life." In prior annals of European explorers there had been references to an occasional giant; only in South America was a whole race proposed. It was Magellan himself who gave these "giants" the name *Pataghoni*, a term that appears to have come from one of the fantastical characters in the Spanish chivalric tale *Primalón*, a story that tells of an island where there lived not only a giant named Patagón but a whole population of wild men, savages who dressed in the skins of the animals they killed.[5]

Subsequent to Magellan, other famous navigators, explorers and scientists voyaged to Patagonia, among them Sir Francis Drake in 1578 (for whom the infamous, southernmost passage was named), James Cook in 1769 [see 791] and Robert FitzRoy in 1832, carrying aboard the then-promising 23-year-old naturalist, Charles Darwin.

Because Patagonia's climate is unsuitable for agriculture, the indigenous population subsisted

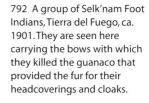

792 A group of Selk'nam Foot Indians, Tierra del Fuego, ca. 1901. They are seen here carrying the bows with which they killed the guanaco that provided the fur for their headcoverings and cloaks.

793 Two Selk'nam women wearing guanaco cloaks.

The most mobile of the Patagonian tribes—indeed, of all the South American peoples—were the Horse Indians, the southern Tehuelche, also known as the Aönikenk. About 1770, these resourceful Indians learned to break, tame and ride the wild horses descended from Spanish runaways. As with the Plains Indians of North America, the horse completely transformed Tehuelche/Aönikenk culture. Groups originally numbering a few dozen people coalesced into units of 500 or more. These large mounted bands might easily cover more than 1,000 miles (1,600 km) a year, skillfully using their bolas to hunt guanacos and rheas as man, beast and bird roamed over the vast, bleak and windy steppes of eastern Patagonia [794].

794 A camp scene of Tehuelche Horse Indians, ca. 1837–1840. The group are all wearing guanaco cloaks secured around the body.

MEN AND WOMEN'S BASIC DRESS

Just as woven tunics were worn by the Andean peoples from Colombia south to central Chile, so fur robes were standard attire for the semi-nomadic groups living from Cape Horn north to the Gran Chaco of south-central South America. Throughout this area there was variation in materials, manufacturing methods and manner of use of these garments, all reflecting the various groups' environmental adaptations. For example, the fur, cape-like robes of the Canoe Indians were made from seal or otter skins, worn fur side out and secured by thongs that tied across the shoulder. These garments were characteristically small—35 × 50 in. (90 × 125 cm)—covering only the upper part of the body [795].[7] Given that the Canoe Indians were in and out of the water constantly, a mantle reaching only to the waist was practical attire for their island world.

In contrast to the short robes of the Canoe Indians, the enveloping, five-foot-square (1.5 m²) guanaco robes of the neighboring Foot Indians reached from neck to ankle; they too were worn with the fur turned out [see 792]. Women's mantles were tied on with thongs at the neck. It is reported that the men simply held their fur robes together, or let them hang loose.[8] When pursuing game on foot, it was apparently advantageous to wear such an unencumbering garment, one that could be shed easily so as to achieve maximum speed and mobility quickly. Darwin commented on this: "The only garment [worn] was a large guanaco skin [cloak] with hair on the outside. This was merely thrown over their shoulders, one arm and leg being bare; for any exercise they must be absolutely naked...."[9]

It was the Tehuelche/Aönikenk Horse Indians who displayed the most ornate of Patagonia's mantles, wearing their large square guanaco wraps, known as *quillangos*, with the fur turned in; the outer, skin side was richly decorated with geometric motifs [796–802]. When in camp these robes were held in place around the body [see 794]. On horseback, the fur mantles were secured by a belt; the arms slipped free as needed. The women's robes were secured both

795 A Yámana Canoe Indian from the Tekenika tribe, Isla Hoste, Tierra del Fuego. His waist-length mantle is made from sea-mammal skin.

796 A mulatto and two Aönikenk men wearing the guanaco skin cloaks known as *quillangos*. Note the geometric decorations painted on the outer, skin side of the robes. This photograph was taken at the beginning of the 20th century.

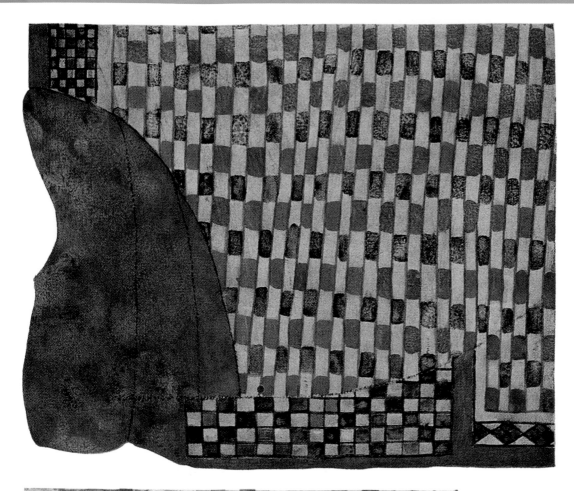

797 The corner of a Tehuelche guanaco *quillango* with painted design motifs.

798 The corner of a Tehuelche guanaco *quillango* with painted design motifs.

799 A section of Aönikenk guanaco *quillango* showing characteristic painted decoration.

800 A section of Aönikenk guanaco *quillango* showing characteristic painted decoration.

801 An Aönikenk guanaco *quillango* decorated with geometric motifs in red and blue.

802 An Aönikenk guanaco *quillango* decorated with motifs that reproduce brands from the different ranches south of Santa Cruz, Chile. This cloak is the work of the mestiza Ana Yebes, begun in the 1930s.

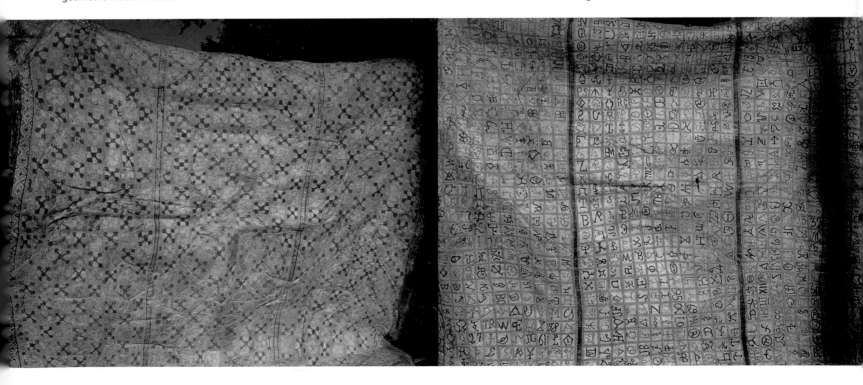

with a belt and a pin at the throat. Under the cape, the women wore a small apron that reached to the knees; the men wore a loincloth of hide or woven material. Following contact with the Mapuche of Chile and the Argentines, the Tehuelche/Aönikenk adopted loom-weaving and started wearing woven blankets decorated with geometric designs for robes as the guanaco herds began to diminish; over half a million hides were shipped out of Patagonia in 1924 alone.[10]

FOOTWEAR

The Yámana/Yahgan Canoe Indians usually went barefoot, but when traveling or hunting on land they wore crudely made, sealskin moccasins stuffed with grass and lined with fur. The Selk'nam/Ona Foot Indians also stuffed grass in their fur-lined moccasins, made from guanaco foreleg skins. Leggings of guanaco fur were used in heavy snow; clumps of twigs were attached to the soles to create a crude type of snow shoe. The mounted Tehuelche wore tall boots with spurs—the *bota de potro*—made of horse hide or from the leg pelt of a large puma. Guanaco-skin overshoes were also sometimes worn in wet weather.[11]

HAIRSTYLES

Among the Canoe and Foot Indians, the hair was worn loose and sometimes cut in bangs with sharp-edged mussel shells. For combing the hair, the jawbone of an otter or porpoise was used or a toothed comb made of whalebone; sometimes a brush comb was constructed out of a bundle of roots.[12] The Tehuelche/Aönikenk held their hair in place with a narrow cord that tied across the forehead [see 794, 796].

HEADGEAR

Among the Yámana/Yahgan Canoe Indians, feather diadems and birdskin, feathers, or down-ornamented fillets and forehead capes were worn. The Selk'nam/Ona hunters wore a triangular peak or head band made of guanaco fur over the forehead [see 792].[13]

ACCESSORIES/JEWELRY

The personal adornments of both the Canoe and Foot Indians were quite simple: necklaces made of bird-leg bones, punched shells strung on braided sinew with shell pendants and wristlets or anklets made of sinew and hide. In addition, the Selk'nam/Ona displayed feathered armlets during foot races. The more affluent Tehuelche, once they had acquired the horse—which led to wider travel and hence greater cultural exposure—wore a far wider range of jewelry: earrings of silver and brass as well as brooches, bracelets and finger rings of hammered silver.

GARMENT DECORATION

The only intricately decorated Patagonian garments were the *quillangos*, the Tehuelche/Aönikenk cloaks made of newborn guanaco skins intricately cut and sewn and then painted on the skin side with geometric designs [see 797–802]. The Chilean archaeologist Alfredo Prieto views the *quillangos*' complex polychrome motifs as an ancient style that appears in different media throughout Tehuelche art. In reference to such work as that of Charles Schuster on genealogical motifs,[14] Prieto suggests that "…perhaps [the designs] embodied a deep sense of bonds of kinship connecting succeeding generations. On the other hand, they [the cloaks] can be admired simply for their mastery of materials."[15]

Among the favorite *quillango* patterns were those with a red ground decorated with black crosses and blue/yellow longitudinal lines or a zigzag of white, blue and red.[16] It is interesting to note that similar motifs also appear on Patagonian rock art and archaeological portable objects.[17] There undoubtedly existed an ancient tradition among the hunters and gatherers of Patagonia—and among the Aönikenk in particular—that was rooted in an understanding and appraisal of pictorial art.[18] In later times, after the introduction of the horse and subsequent inter-ethnic relations, this inherent sensitivity was further enriched with reciprocal knowledge of other stylistic forms.

803 A suit of armor made from seven layers of horse hide. This garment is said to have been acquired, ca. 1827, by a Captain Parker King, from soldiers who had been sent to suppress an Indian rebellion. Length 50 in. (127 cm), width 63³/₄ in. (162 cm).

ARMOR

The principal fighting weapons of the mounted Tehuelche were long lances and bolas. Helmets of bullhide were worn in battle, as well as a thick armor made from as many as seven layers of horse hide [803, 804].[19]

SPECIAL COSTUMES

Among the most intriguing of Patagonian costumes were those connected with initiation rites. The Canoe and Foot Indians had similar coming-of-age ceremonies but only the Yámana Canoe Indians included adolescent girls. Perhaps this inclusion reflected the fact that females played such an indispensable role in the group's subsistence. The work of the women was arduous and highly specialized; reportedly only they paddled and moored the bark canoes and then swam ashore—often with a baby on their back—to set up camp. Although it was the men who manufactured the canoes, they mainly devoted themselves to killing seals and dolphins from these small craft, hence

804 The Aönikenk Chief Kongre wearing a leather helmet and hide armor. At the time of this drawing, the Aönikenk were also known as the Araucanos.

805 Participants in the 1920 Yámana initiation ceremony, the Chiexaus. All of the group wear special feathered headbands of kelp goose skin. The initiates also hold pointed wands.

806 During the Hain, the Selk'nams' all-male initiation ceremony, a shaman presented an initiate as a "newborn baby" to the supposedly credulous female audience.

neither learned to swim nor often assisted with the rowing.[20] Throughout the Yámanas' lengthy ceremony, known as the Chiexaus, a distinctive feathered headband was worn by all participants [805].

The Selk'nam coming-of-age ceremony, the Hain, was restricted only to males. Nonetheless, females were required to act as a credulous audience when an elaborately decorated initiate [806] was presented to them as having just emerged from his coming-of-age ceremony a "newly delivered baby."

The semi-nomadic Fuegans' periodic gatherings for initiation ceremonies could continue anywhere from a week to a month, depending on when the food ran out. A beached whale was a much sought-after source for the abundant feasting that accompanied these memorable rituals.

FACE AND BODY MODIFICATION

Depilation was practiced by all of the Patagonian groups: face and body hair was removed using mussel shells as tweezers. These natives also practiced scarification as a mourning observance and tattooing as an initiation rite; neither practice served a purely decorative purpose. All the groups smeared the body with grease or oil, as much for practical as decorative purposes. Face and body painting was common: a small spatula was used to apply the red, black and white paint in simple designs of lines, dots and—less commonly—circles. Body paint was used by the foot hunters as camouflage in the chase. The mounted Tehuelche painted their faces with various colors but particularly with black so as to protect the skin on cold days when on the march.[21]

TRANSITIONAL DRESS

In 1843 it was estimated that Patagonia contained between 10,000 to 11,000 Indians. As the eminent Patagonian scholar Mateo Martinic B has noted, by 1910 fewer than 1,500 were left.[22] In scarcely six decades, colonization had succeeded in profoundly altering and eventually destroying an ancient culture at the very tip of South America. Following European contact, navigators, explorers, colonists, mercantile traders, miners, missionaries and the military all contributed to the natives' demise, wiping them out with alcohol, diseases, displacement and forced confinement. By the end of the 19th century, the remnants of several tribes were moved into the Salesian Mission of San Rafael in an attempt to "adapt" these Indians to the dictates of Western culture—a move that only served to accelerate their demise [807].[23] By the 1950s, the last vestiges of the indigenous way of life had virtually disappeared.

Over a century earlier Charles Darwin had commented on the impressive physical traits of the Patagonians: "…their voices are wonderfully powerful…[they] could make themselves heard at treble the distance of an Englishman. All of the organs of sense are highly perfected; sailors are well known for their good eye-sight and yet the Fuegans were as superior as another almost would be with a glass."[24] The young scientist added further evidence of the Fuegans' physiological adaptation to their cold clime, one that allowed them to go about all but naked in their often frigid world. He tells of the English visitors and a group of natives gathered about a blazing fire, "…although naked they streamed with perspiration at sitting so near the fire, which we found only comfortable."[25]

In sum, though at first glance Patagonian clothing might appear utterly inadequate for the area's harsh weather, given the native peoples' relatively good health prior to contact it would seem they had evolved a way of life and manner of dressing well-suited to their extreme environment, the true measure of any group's successful adaptation. Darwin stated the case succinctly: "Nature, by making habit omnipotent, has fitted the Fuegian to the climate and productions of his country."[26]

807 The Salesian Mission of San Rafael, Isla Dawson, where remnants of several Patagonian tribes were moved at the end of the 19th century in an attempt to "adapt" them to the dictates of Western culture.

10

AFRICA

AFRICA'S HUGE LANDMASS stretches for some 5,000 miles (8,000 km) from north to south, spanning the world's largest desert, the Sahara, along whose southern rim extends the Sahel—a semi-arid band of grazing land subject to cyclical droughts—which reaches from modern-day Senegal on the west to Sudan on the east. To the south of the Sahel lie the productive agricultural lands of West Africa, the deep rainforests of the Congo River Basin, the unbroken grasslands of the Serengeti, and the rich volcanic soils and fertile croplands of the Great Rift Valley, birthplace of our species. Africa is the continent where some seven million years ago the evolutionary lines of apes and protohumans diverged, and where our ancestors lived until around two million years ago when *Homo erectus* expanded out of Africa into Europe and Asia. Over the next 1.5 million years the populations of those three continents each followed different evolutionary paths that produced different species: Europe's hominids became Neanderthals, Asia's remained *Homo erectus*, and Africa's evolved into our own *Homo sapiens*. Then, sometime around 100,000 to 50,000 years ago, our ancestors underwent a further profound change that transformed them into modern people like ourselves, who once again expanded into Europe and Asia, replacing the Neanderthals and Asia's hominids to become the dominant human species throughout the world.[1] While the history of Africa's indigenous peoples is unique because of its time depth and its extraordinary human diversity, it has also been uniquely savaged, in more recent times, by the transatlantic slave trade and almost-total European colonization.

EAST AFRICA

808 Among the Southeastern Nuba of Sudan's Kordofan Province there has evolved an unusual and exacting tradition of practicing art on the person, an artistic form where the medium truly is the message. This is an aesthetic expression whose purpose is to celebrate and enhance a strong and healthy body through the application of highly stylized, non-representational designs. That said, only a young man who is a successful knife-bracelet fighter may shave off two wedge-shaped patches of hair to create a design that tapers from the temples to the back of the head.

While East Africa's strongest textile-producing culture is located in the cotton-growing areas of Ethiopia, where weavers produce cloth for their distinctive shawls and other garments, sometimes richly embroidered,[1] the region is most famous for another, very different "clothing" tradition. In present-day Sudan, Kenya and Tanzania, the agriculturalists and pastoralists of the Serengeti plateau [Map 35] boast a tradition of body adornment that ranges from remarkable beadwork to face and body adornment.

THE AGRICULTURALISTS

The ancient domain of the desert kingdom of Nubia—located in the central part of the Nile basin—is the present territory of the Democratic Republic of Sudan [see Map 35]. In the remote, semi-arid mountains of Sudan's Kordofan Province live a tall, slender, Nilo-Saharan people called the Nuba—Niger-Kordofanian speakers—who divide into a hundred or more small sub-groups. Of these, it is the Southeastern Nuba who have perfected the practice of producing their art on their person: body and face painting [see 808].[2]

These agriculturalists live in three neighboring mountainside villages, none with a population of more than 2,500. The villagers' fields are located at some distance from their homes; the principal crop is sorghum, a particularly nutritious grain. The farmers also grow groundnuts from which they extract the oil that makes it possible for colored pigments to adhere to the body, the foundation of Nuba art.

The Southeastern Nuba are a relatively isolated and classless people whose social world is organized according to age-grade. Indeed, East African societies have a highly developed age-set system: a series of clearly defined stages through which every member of the group passes, each period specifying an expected role and behavior. For Nuba males, each of these stages is defined by the wearing of certain prescribed

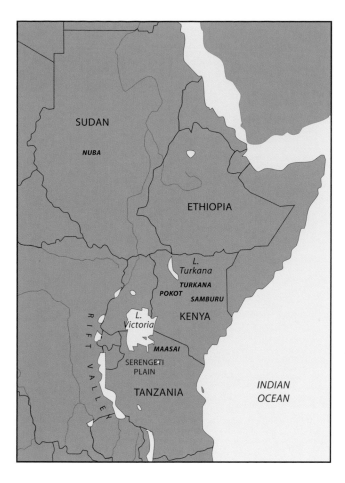

With advancement to the final, elder, *kadonga* grade a man retires from knife-bracelet wrestling; the practice of secular body painting usually also stops. The attitude of the Southeastern Nuba is that when one becomes *kadonga,* the body is no longer pleasing to view, no longer youthful and firm, so why would anyone want to call attention to it through decoration? However, at this stage there is a greater use of ritual painting because these older men are now in positions of leadership and decision-making in the group's ceremonial societies and clan priesthoods.

The Southeastern Nuba are an unusually tall and handsome people who admire young, healthy, athletic bodies, and only those exhibiting such qualities are encouraged to go about nude. The decorating of the body is not a cosmological expression but rather a personal aesthetic whose prime purpose is to celebrate and enhance a strong physique. Although the styles of decoration follow precise social rules and commonly serve as status indicators,[3] whatever the source of a chosen design the central factor is that the body must

Map 35 Map of East Africa, showing places and peoples mentioned in the text.

809 Two Southeastern Nubans briefly rest while observing a knife-bracelet wrestling match. In addition to the young men's hairstyles, body paint, jewelry and ornamented belts, note their dangerous knife-bracelets.

hairstyles and body paints as well as by the type of sports and competitive athletics allowed. The transition from one age-set to the next is marked by ritual and ceremony.

The *loer* grade stage lasts from ages 8 through 16. The activities involve implementing a series of hair decorations and body ornamentations. A boy's initial hairstyle is a small, skull-cap-like coiffure that features a tuft of hair on the crown; as the youth grows his skull-cap expands in circumference. In addition to grey-white body paint, the use of red is permitted. This grade's sport is wrestling.

The ages of 17 to approximately 30 mark the *kadundor* stage and are the prime years of a Southeastern Nuba man's life. Entry into this much-anticipated grade involves a change of hairstyle and the use of additional colors for body decoration, including the right to use certain ritual hues for various functions. It is during this period that the bloody knife-bracelet wrestling matches take place against men from the nearby villages [809].

810 The use of a rich, deep-black body paint made from charcoal is normally reserved for knife-bracelet fights so as to make a contender appear larger to his opponent. This formidable-looking wrestler carries both his knife-bracelet and jousting stave. He also wears a pair of protective fiber sandals as well as the Southeastern Nubas' indispensable belt.

be emphasized, complemented and enhanced. The oiling of the body is always a prerequisite to applying the colored ochres for which these people are famous. Before putting on the groundnut oil, one must first wash and remove all body hair. It is only after the oil has been applied that the designs can be crafted. The various ochre colors are extracted from the hard clays and rocks found throughout the region: reds come from iron ores, yellows and oranges from nearby clays, and black—the most highly valued of all colors [810]—comes from charcoal.

The Nuba's carefully attended coiffures are produced by first shaving certain sections of the head and then waxing and coloring the hair [see 808].

Among the Nuba, jewelry is common but apparently carries no particular social significance. Younger women often display brass ankle and waist bracelets, and both young men and women wear small brass buckles strung on leather straps on their wrists [see 809]. Both sexes are sometimes seen in earrings and young women often also add nose rings or plugs. Both sexes appear in beads, usually a single strand for men and a variety of different types for women. But whatever jewelry one does or does not choose to wear,

811 From the age of four onward, Southeastern Nuba girls apply oil and ochre daily to their scarified bodies. In public, an un-oiled girl would feel naked, just as she would if seen without her belt.

there is one item of apparel that is *de rigueur* for both sexes and all ages: the belt. Although a belt can be made of almost any material, it is always considered essential to proper appearance; to be seen without a belt is to be considered naked and shameful.[4]

Just as young men make a genuine cult of their bodies, so too do young girls for whom the oiling of the body, application of colored ochre and careful arranging of the hair is a daily occurrence; particular care is taken if a dance is scheduled. For a girl to be seen in public without body color is not only to be improperly attired but also to be ritually removed from normal interactions. The practice of daily oiling and applying colored ochre continues until the beginning of the first pregnancy and thereafter is discontinued; clothing is henceforth worn.

The patterned scars on a girl's body are also an indispensable part of her allure [811]. Although females do not have the males' formalized rites of passage, they do undergo a series of scarifications—also known as cicatrization[5]—related to their stage

of physical and social development. The initial set of scars is applied prior to puberty, the second during adolescence, the third following motherhood. These sessions, particularly the third, are extremely painful but are undergone stoically. All scarring takes place out on the mountainside above each village to insure privacy.[6]

Although the scarified, glisteningly oiled young girls might appear to Western eyes as nude, they are always seen wearing a narrow belt, usually some jewelry, and—on special occasions—carrying whip-like switches as they take part in the dances that often follow the tense and bloody knife-bracelet wrestling matches [812]. The Nuba girls' ornamentation clearly demonstrates that definitions of "dress" are culturally specific.

Although the young men's multicolored body decorations are noteworthy, it is the Southeastern Nubas' face painting that is particularly impressive [see 808]. While many of the world's people wear face paint (see "Oceania," p. 313), none has brought this form of personal embellishment to such a high pitch of artistic refinement as the Southeastern Nuba. Once freed from the responsibility of tending the fields, the demanding art of face painting takes place on a regular basis. In fact, in a single day some young men will wash off one creation and reappear in another. Needless to say, some males are more skilled at this art form than others; anyone senior to the artist is free to criticize, and apparently often does. The meticulous art of face painting is a challenging practice, and it is also one that a man who has passed his physical prime ceases to perform.

The agricultural life of the Sudan's Southeastern Nuba is entirely distinct from that of the nomadic peoples living to the south. Because the rainfall needed for even minimal crop cultivation is often barely adequate in the northern sections of present-day Kenya and Tanzania, the most feasible land use is for the grazing of animals.

812 When taking part in the sensuous dances that follow knife-bracelet fights, supple switches are carried by Southeastern Nuba girls. Their long, slender limbs are enhanced by the daily application of oil and ochre. Depending on a girl's sub-clan affiliation, she is supposed to use a designated color. However, if that particular shade does not enhance her skin, a girl may choose another pigment; aesthetic considerations outrank ritual precepts.

THE NOMADIC PASTURALISTS

To the east of Africa's Great Rift Valley extends a vast landscape marked by open grasslands and relatively few trees, homeland to a proliferation of wild herds that roam over the extensive Serengeti plains. These spectacular assemblages of big-game animals have survived into the modern day largely because of their immunity to the tsetse fly—an advantage not shared with domestic cattle or humans—hence the sparsely populated grasslands can support both the wild herbivores and the nomads' herds, each tending its own preferred habitat.

THE MAASAI

Of necessity, pastoralists are a migratory people dependent on the grazing of their herds for survival; cattle are the predominant and favored animal, although their flocks also include sheep, goats and a few donkeys. Among these groups are the Maasai, who have become one of the most celebrated peoples in all of Africa. These aggressive nomads, who are particularly renowned for their strength and fighting spirit, probably moved from the north into what is now central Kenya in the mid-18th century. Because the Maasai were oriented toward warfare, great power was placed in the hands of their young warriors, the *moran*. Although the Maasai were not particularly numerous, they were able to dominate a considerable region and terrorize their neighbors. Their chief victims were Bantu agriculturalists, who could offer little effective resistance against the unexpected raids of the Maasai, who were organized into effective raiding parties.[7]

The Maasai are a cattle people *par excellence*: cattle are their source of wealth, their currency, their dowry and above all, their religion. The Maasai believe that they are the sole custodians of the earth's cattle. Since all cattle belong to them, they are justified in going on raids to retrieve other groups' herds, which they believe must have been stolen from them long ago.[8] Even today, these warriors of the Serengeti still see themselves as lords of creation, moving their cattle when and where they choose. Further, they view their agriculturalist neighbors as degraded by cultivation: in a land of little and unpredictable rain, animals can be moved to water in dry years, crops cannot.

A nomadic way of life limits the accumulation of goods and chattels—energy and ownership are invested in animals rather than in land—but socially the pastoralists' world is as stringently ordered by age-grade as is that of East Africa's agriculturalists. As chroniclers of the Maasai have succinctly noted: "The life of a Maasai male is a well-ordered progression through a series of life-stages, which are determined by age, initiated by ceremonies, and marked by specific duties and privileges."[9]

In childhood Maasai boys learn to tend the herds and do menial chores around the camp. This initial stage ends at puberty with an impressive initiation ceremony that carries an adolescent through to his next stage, the longed-for period of warriorhood. When a young man at last becomes a *moran*, the golden years of his life begin. For a Maasai warrior, this is a time of personal aggrandizement and indulgence in beautification, including the regular application of red ochre and animal fat to his hair and body and the adorning of his face and legs with non-symbolic designs [813].

A warrior's glorious, self-indulgent life ends when he moves into the third and final stage of his life, elderhood. This is a serious and subdued time that involves a traumatic rite of passage: the *moran*'s beloved, carefully tended long hair is cut off. His head is shaved and ochred, and the newly confirmed junior elder—who henceforth will be wrapped in a simple, factory-made blanket—is now expected to seek out a wife, raise a family and take on serious tribal responsibility.

Just as Maasai boys pass through a series of life-stages so too do girls, but their maturation is un-accompanied by the public ceremonies attending male rites of passage. When a girl reaches puberty, between the ages of 9 and 12, she is eligible to become a girlfriend of one of the warriors, which includes visiting his encampment. However, as a girl moves closer to marriageable age her freedom ends and she undergoes a circumcision ceremony, an operation in which the clitoris and labia minora are removed.

Following her six-week recovery period, the girl is soon married.[10]

In the Maasai world, it is the young men who grow their hair long and the young women who cut their hair short, or indeed shave it all off [814]. The females' bald heads highlight their jewelry: layers of flat, multicolored-bead collars and beads that extend from the neck to below the breasts [815–819]. There are some forty different types and designs of Maasai beadwork made by women and girls for themselves, and also for the glamorous warriors.[11] The women and girls also wear beaded necklaces and ear ornaments [820, 821].

813 (opposite) A Maasai warrior in full regalia, including his buffalo-hide shield; he carries a fragrant bunch of *lelehwa* leaves beneath his arm as a deodorant. Note this *moran*'s carefully arranged red-ochre-dyed hair and the non-symbolic designs that adorn his face and legs.

814 (below) Whereas young Maasai men grow their hair long, young Maasai women shave their hair off, the better to display their multiple, flat, beaded collars and dramatic head jewelry. When the women dance, their collars take on a life of their own.

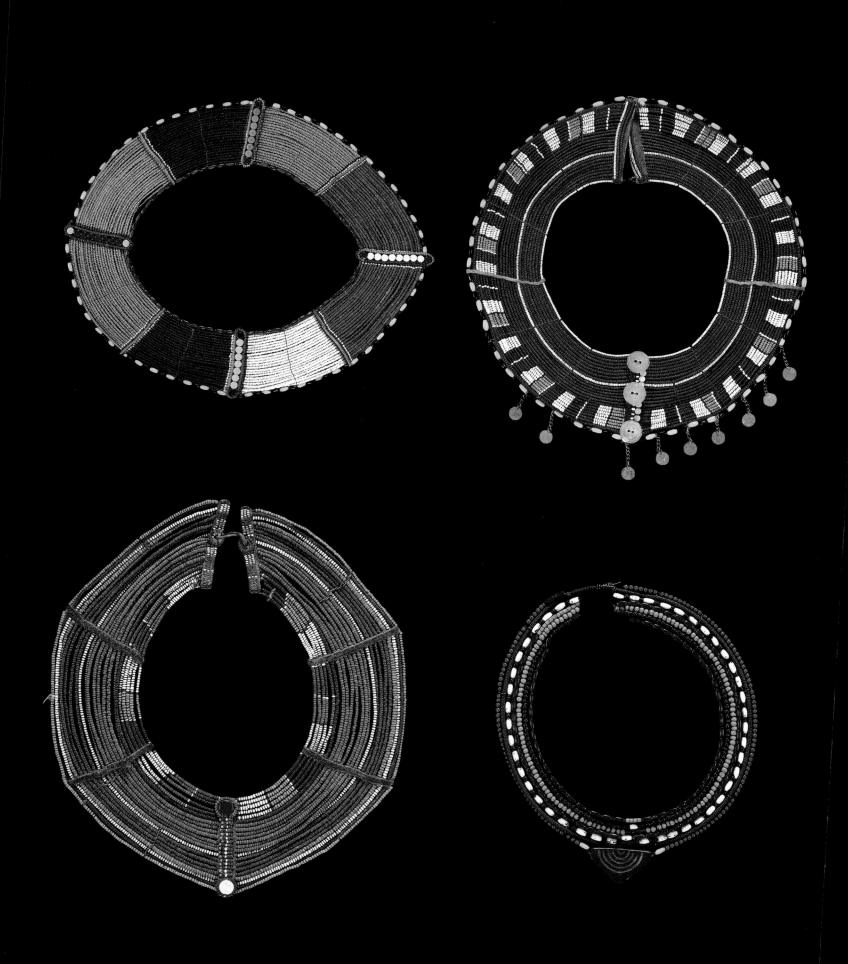

Maasai females wear a series of flat, collar-like necklaces of multicolored beads strung on stiff wire thread and spaced with strips of cowhide. Often as many as four or five collars are worn at the same time, all designed to call attention to a girl's every movement and to enhance her natural grace.

815 (opposite above left) Diameter 12½ in. (32 cm).

816 (opposite above right) Diameter 11⅜ in. (29.1 cm).

817 (opposite below left) Diameter 9⅜ in. (24 cm).

818 (opposite below right) Diameter 8⅝ in. (22 cm).

819 (left) Diameter 11⅜ in. (29 cm).

820 (far left) Maasai married women sometimes wear an elongated beaded necklace that ends in coiled metal medallions. Length 28¾ in. (73 cm), width 1½ in. (4 cm).

821 (left) One symbol of female marital status is elongated leather earrings decorated with multicolored beads; some terminate in coiled metal medallions. Length 8¼ in. (21 cm), width 3⅛ in. (8 cm).

In addition to their impressive jewelry, Maasai females wear wraparound skirts and cloaks made of factory-produced cloth that is often printed in checked patterns in shades of red, pink or orange [822]. The men's wraparound kilts and cloaks are made of this same type of fabric and in the same color range [823]. In some instances, white factory cloth is purchased from traders and dyed a reddish hue with the red mineral pigment regularly used for body decoration. These reddish tones may well have a particular appeal for the Maasai because they are reminiscent of their body paint and facial make-up.

The Maasai are not the only East African herders who move across the plains in search of fresh grazing land. In the fluid, semi-arid world of northern Kenya there exist a number of additional pastoral peoples, each using their own unique body decoration, jewelry, and clothing to define their ethnic and social boundaries/identities.

THE SAMBURU, TURKANA AND POKOT

The Samburu, Turkana and Pokot are all Nilo-Saharan peoples who inhabit the marginal grasslands to the west and south of Lake Turkana (formerly known

822 Maasai females now wear skirts and cloaks of factory-produced cloth, many patterned in checks or stripes in hues reminiscent of the reddish color of their body paint. The married women at the rear of this procession wear long beaded earrings, markers of marital status.

823 These Maasai men wear orange kilts made of factory-produced cloth. They have all applied red ochre to their hair and bodies, and decorated their legs with non-representational designs. Several carry sharpened spears. Those warriors who have not yet killed a lion wear high, ostrich-plumed headdresses.

824 This Samburu warrior has lengthened his hair by entwining it with sisal string and then coated it with animal fat and red ochre. To make his hair stand out like a visor, he has supported it with a piece of cloth, also dyed with red ochre. The Samburu, besides having more elaborate hairstyles than the Maasai, are further distinguished by the ivory rings in their ears and more elaborate facial make-up.

as Lake Rudolf). The diverse styles and personal adornment of these nomadic people all reflect the age-grade system that prevails throughout East Africa. In some areas these groups live quite close together—as is indicated by their shared conventions in personal arts—but each is culturally and linguistically distinct.

Among these pastoralists are the Samburu, who are closely related to the Maasai in language, custom and dress. (Samburu means butterfly, an apt name for these colorful, nomadic warriors.) A Samburu *moran*, like his Maasai counterpart, lets his hair grow long [824] and regularly applies fat and red pigment to his face and body. He can while away hours decorating his body, discussing his looks and, whenever possible,

admiring himself in the wing mirrors of the cars that occasionally pass by.[12]

In none of the three cultures is the dress or decoration ceremonial. Most is worn continually, day and night, until a change of status calls for a parallel, partial or complete change in personal embellishment. A further shared trait is the decorative emphasis placed on the upper body: head, neck and shoulders. Among females, the impulse is to extend the apparent length of the neck by building up multiple circles of beads, in some cases from mid-chest to chin [825].[13] Samburu girls wear many strands of beads rather than the flat collars favored by their neighbors, the Maasai [see 822].

825 Samburu girls wear many strands of loose beads, gifts from admirers. The ideal amount of beads is said to be enough to support a girl's chin. It is believed that by the age of 15 or 16 a girl should have collected enough of these circlets to invite a proposal of marriage. This girl's beaded headband features a stylized bird made of aluminium.

826 (above) A small leather apron that was worn by a six- or seven-year-old. This apron is decorated at the bottom by three small pieces of heavily beaded leather that have been attached by a stitching of raw hide. Length 9⁷/₈ in. (25 cm), width 9 in. (23 cm).

827 (above right) A type of leather cape that is worn slung over one shoulder by uncircumcised girls. The garment is made by the wearer or an older sister, or by the girl's mother. The skin, after having been dried out in the sun, is scraped with an iron tool, rubbed in the hands to soften it and then oiled. Girls' capes are always made of kidskin and have a fringe of hair left on around all the edges. Length 17⁵/₈ in. (45 cm), width 23⁵/₈ in. (60 cm).

The northern Kenyan female clothing below the shoulders consists of leather front- and/or back-skirts, belts, pubic aprons and longer shawls that tie around the neck [826, 827]. When animal skins are to be used for clothing, the hides have to be stretched, softened and colored with animal fat and ochre. Most skin garments are then decorated either with commercial or handmade beads, according to each group's tradition. The beads are secured to the leather using a thin wire thread. Samburu women change their hide skirts and beaded pubic aprons once they marry. As is true in all of East Africa's age-grade societies, garment styles and beaded decorations indicate whether or not a girl has undergone a circumcision or a woman has married.

Throughout the region there are also certain unifying features in body decoration. Although the specific designs may differ in detail, the basic forms and functions are shared cross-culturally. An example is the oiling and coloring of upper body parts, which is especially prevalent among younger women. Samburu and Turkana females, and uninitiated Pokot girls, prefer to use red camwood; married Pokot women favor a sooty black substance. These pigments, mixed with oil or grease, are applied to heads and upper bodies and sometimes, among the Pokot, even to beadwork, apparently to nullify the contrasts in bead

Opposite: 828 (top left) A pair of earrings that is worn in the lobe of older uncircumcised girls, beginning at the age of 12. On the top of the helix—the incurved rim of the ear—the girls wear bead earrings; they also wear tiny sticks inserted in holes in the lower helix. Length 11⁷/₈ in. (30 cm), width ³/₄ in. (2 cm) each.

829 (top right) A headband that is typical of those worn by married women, circumcised girls and also uncircumcised girls about 12–13 years of age (older women, particularly those past childbearing age, no longer wear them). The two beaded loops hold up the heavy brass earrings that are worn in the lobe of the ear. Women flick their earrings at the men while dancing and the men, in turn, flick their headdress feathers back. Length 26⁷/₈ in. (68 cm), width 2³/₈ in. (6 cm).

830 (center left) A large, wide necklace/collar of ostrich eggshell beads that is stained with the black pigment and fat with which Pokot women cover themselves. This type of collar is worn by elderly women and is probably a prototype of present-day trade-bead necklaces. Diameter 12¹/₈ in. (31 cm).

831 (center right) A type of flat-collar necklace that is constructed of alternating red and green beads with leather spacers. Such necklaces are made during the circumcision seclusion and worn thereafter. The money for the beads is given a girl by her father, or obtained from passing men. As with most Pokot necklaces, this one has been stained with fat and black pigment. Diameter 13³/₈ in. (34 cm).

832 (below) A necklace-like "bandolier" that is made of four strands of beads twisted together and worn across the chest by uncircumcised girls, circumcised girls and men, but never by married women. Diameter 16⁷/₈ in. (43 cm).

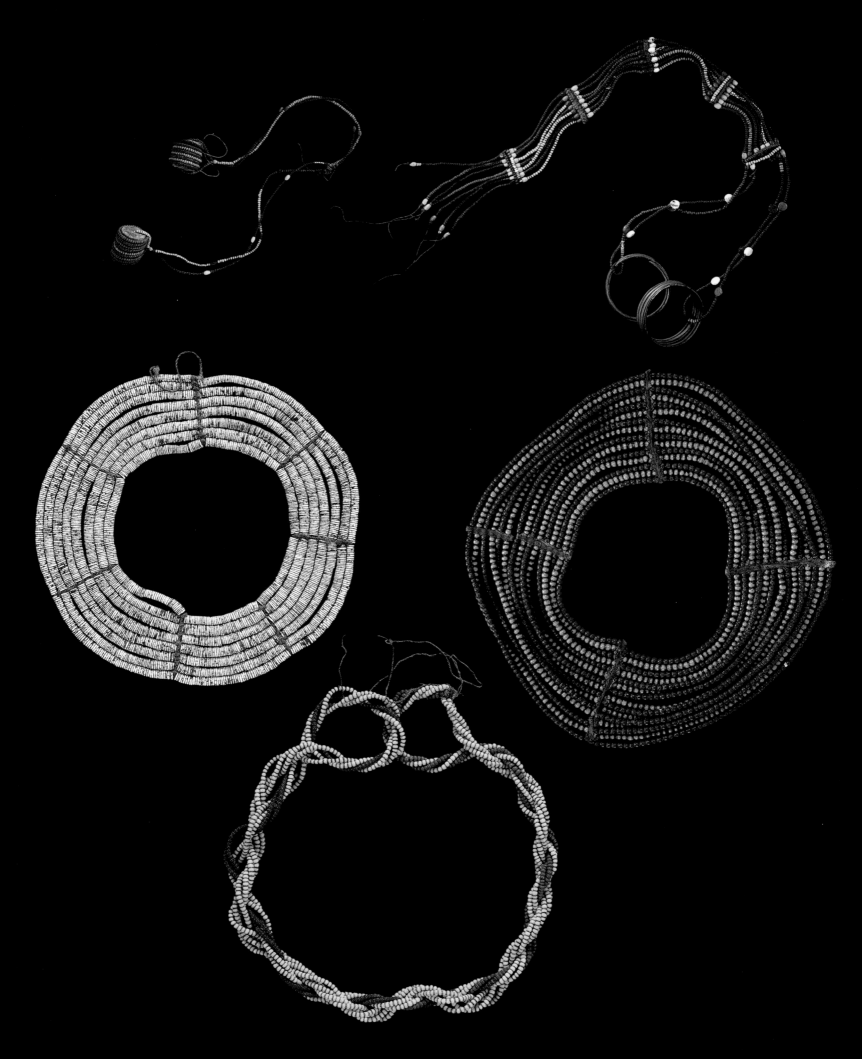

833 (top) A type of long, coiled, copper armlet that is worn by both sexes, although multi-coiled bracelets are more commonly seen on women. Similar coiled bracelets are also made of brass wire acquired through trade, from telephone lines and also out of cartridge cases. Height 3¹⁄₈ in. (8 cm), length 7³⁄₈ in. (19 cm).

834 (above) A nine-strand bead armlet, strung on wire with leather ends, that is worn purely for ornament, either above or below the elbow, by circumcised girls, older uncircumcised girls and married women. Diameter 3¹⁄₈ in. (8 cm).

colors. The desired result is a massed, overall coloration.[14] As for the jewelry itself, much of it seems to have been designed to dramatize and reinforce the sounds and motions of dancing [828–834].

While the female aesthetic among these groups favors overall effects in color and mass, the male preference runs to accents and small units [835; see also 838–844]. Males decorate themselves more sparsely, highlighting different parts of the body so as to draw attention to the naturally sculpted body surface. However, it is hairstyles that are the basic keys to male status. Masculine pride centers on the hair and men give a great deal of attention to hairdressing, which is particularly associated with warfare and warriors. The Samburu feature twisted or braided styles [see 824], whereas the Turkana [836] and Pokot [837] dress their hair using mudpacks in a variety of ways. The hairstyles of Turkana men remain the same throughout their lives. Changes of status are indicated by inserting new sets of ostrich feathers into holders of cow gut or macramé, which were initially placed in the hair while the mudpack was still wet. Such a hairstyle may take up to three days to perfect and is meticulously remade every three months.

In all cases, men spend a great deal of time arranging their hair and, as pastoralists, they have the leisure to indulge themselves. Their uncluttered life releases them from time-consuming agricultural pursuits. In the heat of the day, each gender carries on separately with their beautification activities, each under its "own tree," sometimes for hours on end.[15] The primary motivation is to display taste and style and thus attract the opposite sex.

In addition to body paint, hairstyles and jewelry, Pokot men wear relatively short, wraparound garments in dark colors while the Samburu and Turkana normally wear bright shades, particularly red. Factory-made fabrics have come to replace the stiff leather capes and leopard skins which were *de rigueur* in earlier times, and may still be seen on ceremonial occasions. What is consistent among all of these nomadic peoples is their regular use of colorful beads to enhance their appearance.

Throughout East Africa's pastoralist world, beads have played a prominent role in all forms of enhancement. Until the end of the 19th century, ornaments were made from natural substances gleaned from nature: bones, teeth, clay, skins, stones, roots and shells [see 825]. Ostrich eggshell beads are made by the women themselves. They collect the eggshells from ostrich nests and break them into roughly the size of the finished beads. The holes in the beads are then bored through with an awl, smoothed with a stone and, over time and through repeated wearing, further smoothed by contact with the skin. The process of making eggshell beads has been known in Kenya since at least 7000 B.C.[16] In the 20th century, imported beads became increasingly available. An authority on African decoration briefly reviews the history of these adornments: "Glass beads, originally brought from Persia and China by Arab traders and later from Europe by the Portuguese had been widely used as a form of barter. By the turn of the century, mass-produced beads from Europe were being traded by the millions along the East African coast. These were known as 'trade-wind beads' in Kenya, and as 'pound beads' (sold by the pound) in Sudan; small, regular and brightly colored, they were easy to work with and appealed to the nomads. They soon replaced many of the natural elements, although shells and skins of sacrificial animals continue to be used as are sweet-smelling roots which perfume the wearer's body."[17]

A further shared trait among East Africa's pastoralists is the special stress placed on personal adornment at a particular period of life: adolescence through the prime years of adulthood. The practice of polygamy accounts for this emphasis on beautification, which is aimed at attracting the opposite sex: women tend to marry young, men later. The result is a large number of marriageable females who, because of the early age in which they begin to take an active part in society, become socially older than males of the same chronological age. Also, men are often proscribed from marrying until their twenties or, as among the Samburu, even until their early thirties.[18]

Whatever the cultural tradition of each group, whether pastoralist or agriculturalist, in East Africa the decoration of the body has always been the main outlet for artistic expression.

835 A Pokot father wears a leaf-shaped aluminium nose ornament to announce his daughter's engagement. Note the man's many-feathered, mudpack hairstyle.

836 A Turkana man, wearing an ivory ball attached with a pin through a hole below his lip, has a mudpack hairstyle that is adorned with dyed ostrich feathers. When these elaborate hairstyles are being constructed, the hair is twisted into small plaits which are then covered with clay and shaped into a bun on top of the head.

837 Young Pokot men remodel their elaborate clay-bun coiffures when they are initiated into adulthood. This recent initiate has a feathered, blue mudcap; his ochred front hair reflects his lowly status. Note that an old zipper has been imbedded spirally into the separate front piece of his mudpack hairdo.

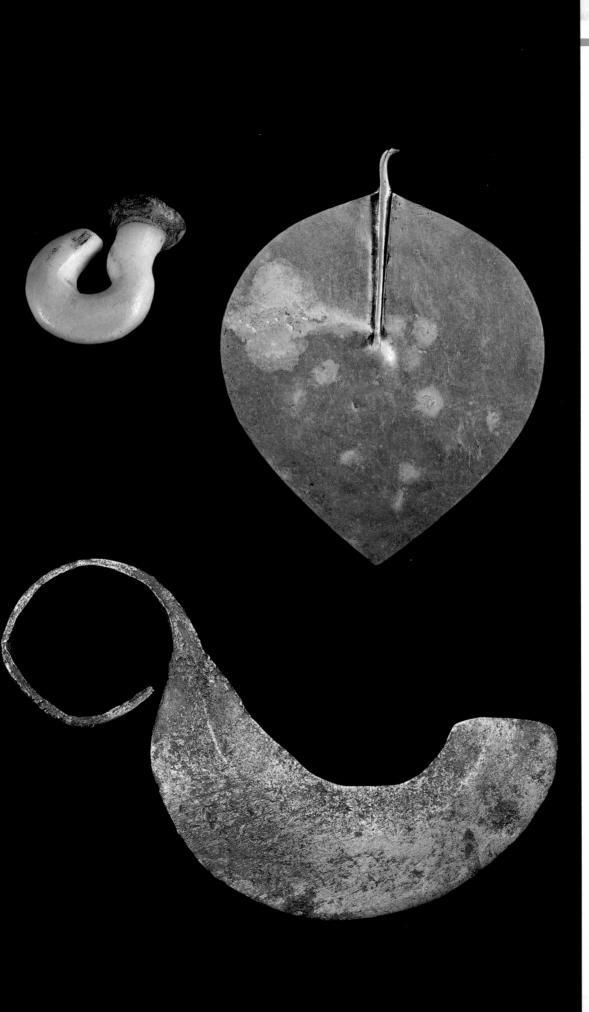

Clockwise from top left:

838 A beaded forehead band that is made of six strands of beads separated by leather spacers that extend down into bead-covered leather circles. These bands are made by the wearers, or their wives or girlfriends, and are worn high on the forehead, just below the separate front piece of the mud-pack hairdo [see 837]. Length 18$\frac{1}{2}$ in. (47 cm), width 1$\frac{7}{8}$ in. (5 cm).

839 A hook-shaped lip ornament— said to be ivory but actually plastic—worn by both sexes, set downward. In the past, the wearing of such an adornment was fashionable. Length 1$\frac{1}{8}$ in. (3 cm), width $\frac{3}{4}$ in. (2 cm).

840 A nose ornament worn by an older, initiated man to announce his daughter's engagement [see 835]. This example was made from an old aluminium cooking pot, cut and then beaten to shape with a stone. A craftsman usually makes these adornments, not a blacksmith; in the past these leaf-shaped ornaments are said to have been made of very thin iron. Length 5$\frac{1}{8}$ in. (13 cm), width 3$\frac{7}{8}$ in. (10 cm).

841 A general-purpose ring-knife used for cutting string, hide, meat, and so on. Such a ring was made by men from a large nail bought in a shop and cold-forged on any nearby hard stone using another stone as a hammer. Each man usually made his own. Only men wear these rings and they are very skilled in their use. Length 2$\frac{7}{8}$ in. (7.5 cm), width $\frac{3}{4}$ in. (2 cm).

842 A small neck choker of beads that has rubber spacers and raffia string ties. This adornment was made and worn by a young, uninitiated boy. Diameter 3$\frac{1}{8}$ in. (8 cm).

843 A thick necklace that has a cowhide core with beads coiled around it. Although typically a man's necklace, this particular adornment was worn by a Pokot woman, hence has been coated with oil and black pigment. Diameter 7$\frac{3}{8}$ in. (18.5 cm).

844 An eight-strand necklace that is composed of small barrel-shaped beads. This is a man's or a boy's necklace of typical coloring. The strands are held together by four small beaded rings; from one ring hangs a shell. Such necklaces almost always have a pendant shell that the maker has either found or purchased. Diameter 8 in. (20.5 cm).

SOUTH AFRICA

845 An Ndebele matron wearing a beaded apron decorated with geometric designs similar to those of the colorful mural painted on the wall of her house. Such murals are a characteristic of the small villages of the southern Ndebele people.

The subsequent history of South Africa has been one of culture collisions and displacements of native groups. The heavy-handed supplanting or subjugation of the indigenous peoples began with the arrival of European colonists.

The Dutch East India Company established the first European settlement in South Africa at the Cape of Good Hope in 1652. South Africa's geographic location—almost entirely south of the Tropic of Capricorn and hence within temperate climatic zones analogous to those of western Europe [Map 36]—contributed to rapid European settlement on a scale unknown elsewhere in Africa. The first white settlers, who came from the pre-industrialized Netherlands, were mostly farmers who developed a close-knit community with their own dialect, Afrikaans, and Calvinist religion, the Dutch Reformed Church.

Southern Africa is a semi-arid land and the Boers—the Dutch-Afrikaaner farmers—soon found that most of the area they occupied was unsuitable for cultivation. This realization forced the colonists to disperse and become a self-sufficient, semi-nomadic, pastoral people mainly dependent on their cattle. Prior to 1870, as the Boers expanded into new grazing lands, they were unhampered by any law behind or enemy ahead. However, as the Boers slowly spread east they began to come into violent contact with Bantu pastoral groups moving down from the north.

Although their expansion was temporarily halted by the Bantu, the Boers' further eastward movement was hastened after the English annexed the Cape in 1806. These new European colonists, who came from industrialized Britain and tended to be urban dwellers, viewed the world in quite a different manner. The British abolition of slavery in 1834 was regarded by the intransigent Boers as an intolerable interference in their affairs and led to their migration across the Orange River two years later. This move, made to free themselves from British rule, became known as the Great Trek.

So far as is known, the first modern humans in southern Africa were the Khoisan-speaking San and their closely related kin, the Khoikhoi, known in the colonial period respectively as Bushmen and Hottentots. In the 11th century Bantu speakers arrived in the area and settled in the region's northeast and along the east coast. By the 15th century the Bantu had occupied most of the eastern half of southern Africa, pushing the Khoisan speakers into peripheral areas. These Bantu pastoralists—for whom cattle and care of the herds was of overriding importance—were an Iron Age people whose advanced smelting techniques were reflected in their effective metal weapons.

Pressure on the Bantu from both the Boers and the British caused political and social changes in the indigenous areas of coastal Natal,[1] resulting in the rise of the powerful Zulu king Shaka in the early 19th century [846]. This ruler's policy of total war on neighboring groups caused immense suffering and mass migrations. It was into this chaos that the Boers moved in their search for new lands, and the British were not far behind. The formidable Zulu were eventually defeated, but relations between the Boers and the British remained tense—particularly after the Boers formed the Republic of the Free State and Transvaal. The resulting tensions led to the 1899–1902 Anglo-Boer War in which the Boers lost and the British imposed their rule over the entire country.

In 1910 the Union of South Africa was created, giving complete political control to the whites. Inevitably this prompted black resistance in the form of strikes and the formation of political organizations. Despite the moderate tone of these early resistance groups, the government reacted by intensifying repressive segregation policies, forerunners of later apartheid policies which were increasingly harsh.

South Africa's black population is composed of four Bantu linguistic groups: the largest is the Nguni, who include various Zulu, Ndebele, Xhosa and Swazi peoples, together constituting more than half of South Africa's total black population.[2] The Zulu are by far the best known of the Nguni Bantu, probably because of the worldwide attention attracted by their mid-19th-century wars against both the Boers and the British.

In spite of the upheavals of the centuries, much of this indigenous population has maintained a remarkable continuity of cultural tradition. Beads and beadwork have been an important part of South African culture for hundreds of years, perhaps for millennia. Particularly striking is the use of multicolored trade beads [847] as jewelry for personal adornment; indeed, in southern Africa elaborately beaded pieces often virtually take the form of costume.

Since South African beadwork serves to link the living to their ancestors, it is a spiritual art whose many colors, patterns and motifs convey symbolic messages.

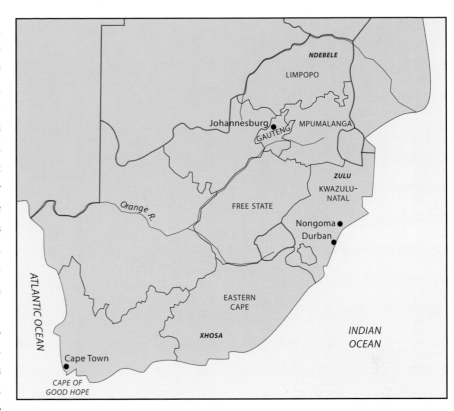

846 G. F. Angas, *Utimuni, Nephew of* [Zulu king] *Shaka*, 1849. A contemporary European observer noted that Zulu chiefs and principals wore a profusion of beads, as well as brass bracelets from wrist to elbow.

Map 36 Present-day South Africa. Prior to 1994 the provinces of Gauteng, Limpopo and Mpumalanga constituted the Transvaal. In the same year Natal Province became Kwazulu-Natal Province, and Orange Free State became known as Free State.

847 A page from a European bead catalog for potential traders, ca. 1890–1926.

Like flags or languages, beaded pieces convey a sense of belonging to a particular people, place, and chain of traditions. Beadwork ensembles also serve to reveal social identities: gender, age-grade, marital status, and sometimes social rank and role, and even one's spiritual state. Further, the abstract elements in beadwork play a key role in denoting affiliations within the society, similar to the role tartan plaids play in the kilts of the Scottish clans.[3]

XHOSA BEADWORK

Beadwork is the prime sacred art form among the Xhosa people, cattle herders who live along the southeast coast of South Africa [848]. The Xhosa are Africa's southernmost Bantu language group, living primarily in Eastern Cape Province.

When the flowering of Xhosa beadwork traditions peaked in the 1950s and '60s, its appearance at ceremonial occasions became an essential aspect of both identity and tradition. The Xhosa believed that beautiful ethnic dress, beadwork, songs and dances

848 An older Xhosa couple dressed in the beaded attire of the 1960s.

were the proper media to be employed in ancestor worship, and the traditionalists among them still hold to that belief.[4] They regarded white as the primary color of purity and meditation; only white beads were used as offerings to the spirits. It is probable that beadwork containing reflective beads, shells and brass buttons was particularly effective because they "were possessed of divine shine."[5] Mother-of-pearl buttons were particularly desirable.[6]

For ordinary Xhosa, contact with the ancestors was closest on ceremonial occasions, when animal sacrifices were made or beer was drunk, since both summoned the ancestors and were closely associated with them. On these occasions, a profusion of beads was worn; the heaviness of the glass probably impressed upon the wearer the weight of symbolism contained in the beads.

ZULU BEADWORK

Zulu beadwork, acknowledged to be among the finest in all of Africa, has been recognized by anthropologists as an important social regulator as well as an index of status within the society. Older pieces of Zulu beadwork were made from indigenous stone, ostrich shell, seed and wood, as well as from cowrie shells and glass beads imported by Arab traders from India, Persia, Arabia and the Far East. The Arabs monopolized the trade routes to East Africa until exploration by the Portuguese in the early 16th century opened up the area to European exploitation. Modern beads, brought by the Portuguese and English [see 847], are smaller and mass-produced, hence regular in size and shape—an advantage for a beadworker— and generally indistinguishable one from the other. Whereas older beads were used to indicate one's wealth and status, the modern beads were available in plentiful quantities and colors to everyone because they were used as currency by traders, settlers and missionaries.[7]

Among modern-day Zulu, beadwork is not usually part of everyday wear but rather typically appears on such occasions as coming-of-age ceremonies, weddings, visits to relatives, and family gatherings of all

849 A Zulu baby girl wears beads before she wears clothes. South Africa's Muden area, ca. 1975.

kinds. Beadwork is of particular importance if dancing is involved.

The Zulu wear varying styles of beadwork and bead-adorned garments as they move from babyhood to childhood to adolescence and on into maturity. When a child begins to crawl, a medicinal amulet—a single berry acting as a charm for good health—is replaced by a single string of beads. In fact, babies wear beads before they wear clothing [849]. As children grow older, they wear increasingly ornate attire for special occasions, including varying sizes of neck and waist hoops [850; see also 852–855]. A young girl's beadwork becomes ever more elaborate until, at puberty, she adorns herself with multicolored loin aprons [see 856–858] or, for special dances, a short red or blue cloth skirt that extends from waist to mid-thigh and is richly decorated with beads [851].

850 Zulu children of the Cele clan adorned in some of their older sister's ceremonial finery: beaded headbands, necklaces, loin aprons and various sizes of beaded hoops worn about the neck and waist.

851 Ornately beaded frontal aprons and matching bands of beadwork are standard features of young adolescent girls' dance uniforms; so, too, are their short red or blue skirts. The designs and colors of an apron's beadwork are the wearer's personal choice. Photographed in 1989 at the July Festival, held in Ebuhleni, a holy place that is the center of a religious pilgrimage.

This page: Beaded hoops—tubes made of bundles of grass fiber or twisted cotton, covered with coils of beadwork that form geometric designs. These decorative hoops are made by Zulu and Ndebele women to be worn on the hands, wrists, arms, neck, shoulders and around the waist. Different styles of beaded hoop indicate the various stages in a woman's life.

852 Diameter 13³⁄₈ in. (34 cm).

853 Diameter 10⁵⁄₈ in. (27 cm).

854 Diameter 5³⁄₄ in. (14.6 cm).

855 Diameter 11³⁄₈ in. (29 cm).

Opposite: Loin aprons worn by young Zulu girls. The beaded patterns are sometimes symbolic of a clan or specific locale. On 856, note the lace-like quality of the four rows of white beadwork, perhaps a reflection of the lace worn by the Victorians in the 19th century.

856 Height 5¹⁄₂ in. (14 cm), width 39 in. (99 cm).

857 Height 3 in. (8 cm), width 44 in. (112 cm).

858 Height 13³⁄₈ in. (34 cm), width 36¹⁄₈ in. (92 cm).

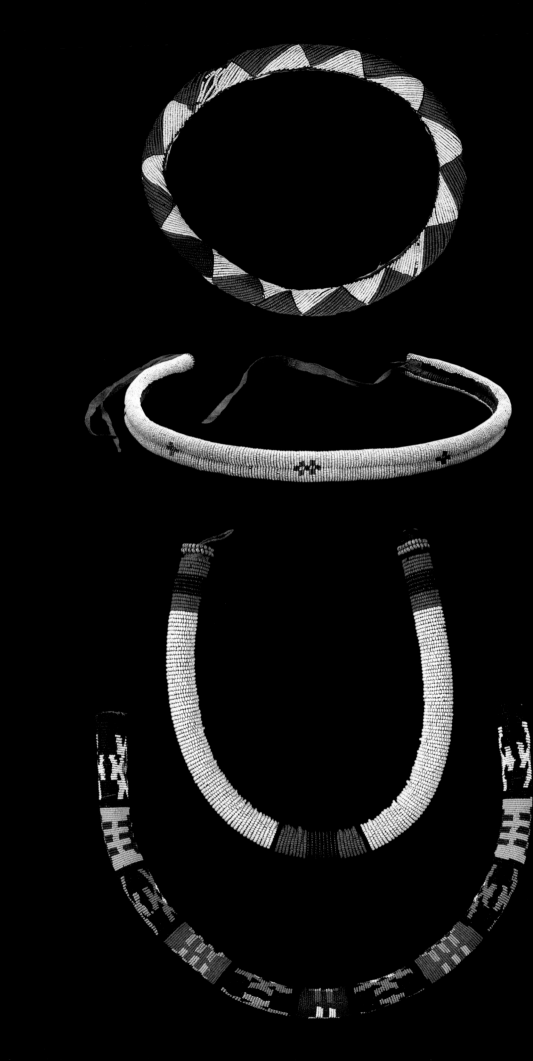

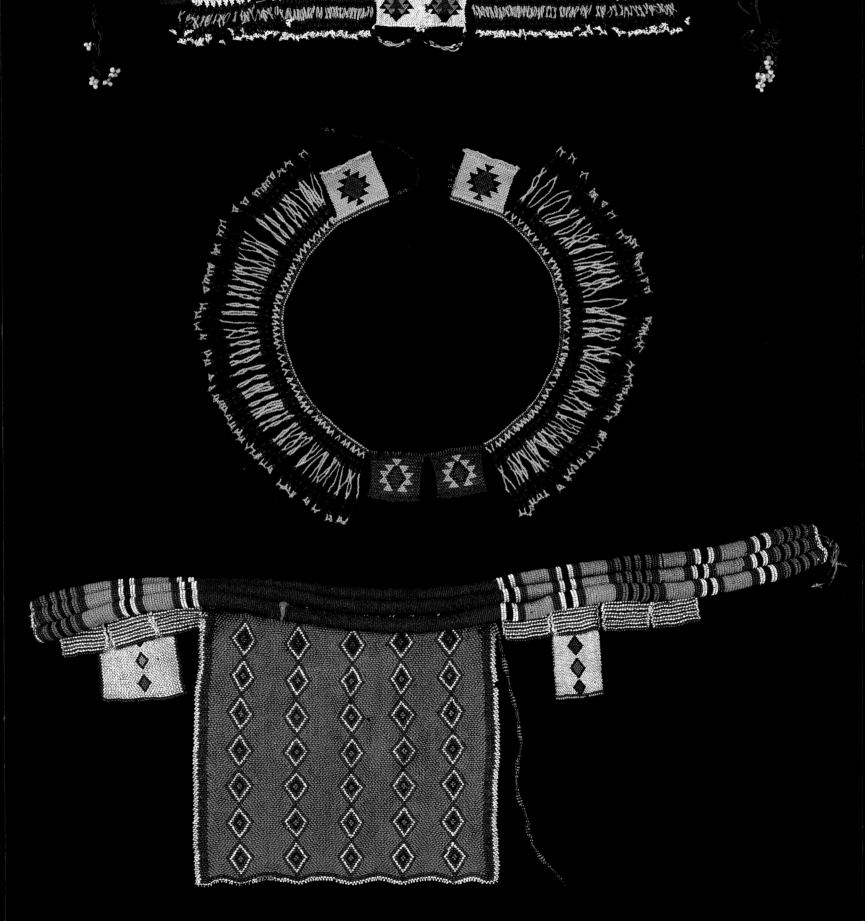

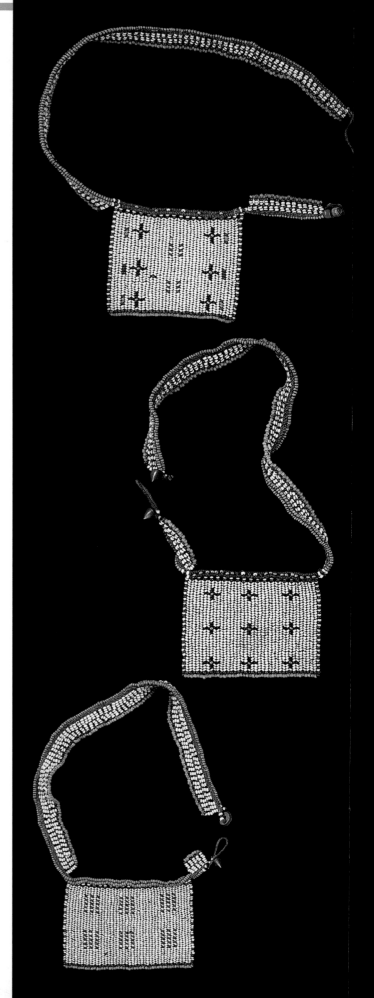

Beadwork plays a particularly important role in courtship and preparation for marriage. In various ways, beads mark one's emotional progression from adolescent love to flirtatious courtship to serious marriage. The most symbolic of Zulu beadwork communicates the state of one's love life, both publicly and privately. The famous Zulu "love letters"—called in Zulu *ubala abuyisse* or "one writes in order that the other reply"[8]—are given to men by their girlfriends. These tokens of affection are highly prized by Zulu men, who wear them around their necks, heads and chests [859, 860–866]. The greater the number of love letters a man displays, the more sweethearts or wives he is shown to have, each addition reflecting on his wealth and status.

859 South African black men usually wear Western clothing, probably a reflection of the country's migrant labor system. However, when workers return to visit their villages their attire can reflect the Zulu bead tradition. Judging from this young man's adornments, he has a devoted, industrious girlfriend. In addition to the "love letters" around his neck, he wears a "strengthener of love," the lozenge-shaped ornament lodged centrally in his hatband. Ca. late 1960s.

Color-coded beaded messages are said to be contained in the tabs of these necklaces, known as *ubala abuyisse*, or "love letters," which are made by young girls and are much prized by the young men to whom they are given. The three examples on this page all pre-date 1965.

860 (above) Length 9 in. (23 cm), width 3³/₈ in (8.5 cm).

861 (center) Length 9 in. (23 cm), width 3¹/₂ in. (9 cm).

862 (below) Length 9¹/₂ in. (24 cm), width 4 in. (10 cm).

The four beaded necklaces from the mid-1970s on the opposite page were made for sale to tourists and are copies of the older, authentic "love letters."

863 (above left) Length 7⁷/₈ in. (20 cm), width 2 in. (5.5 cm).

864 (above right) Length 8⁵/₈ in. (22 cm), width 6 in. (15 cm).

865 (below left) Length 15⁷/₈ in. (40 cm), width 2³/₈ in. (6 cm).

866 (below right) Length 17³/₈ in. (44 cm), width 4¹/₂ in. (11.5 cm).

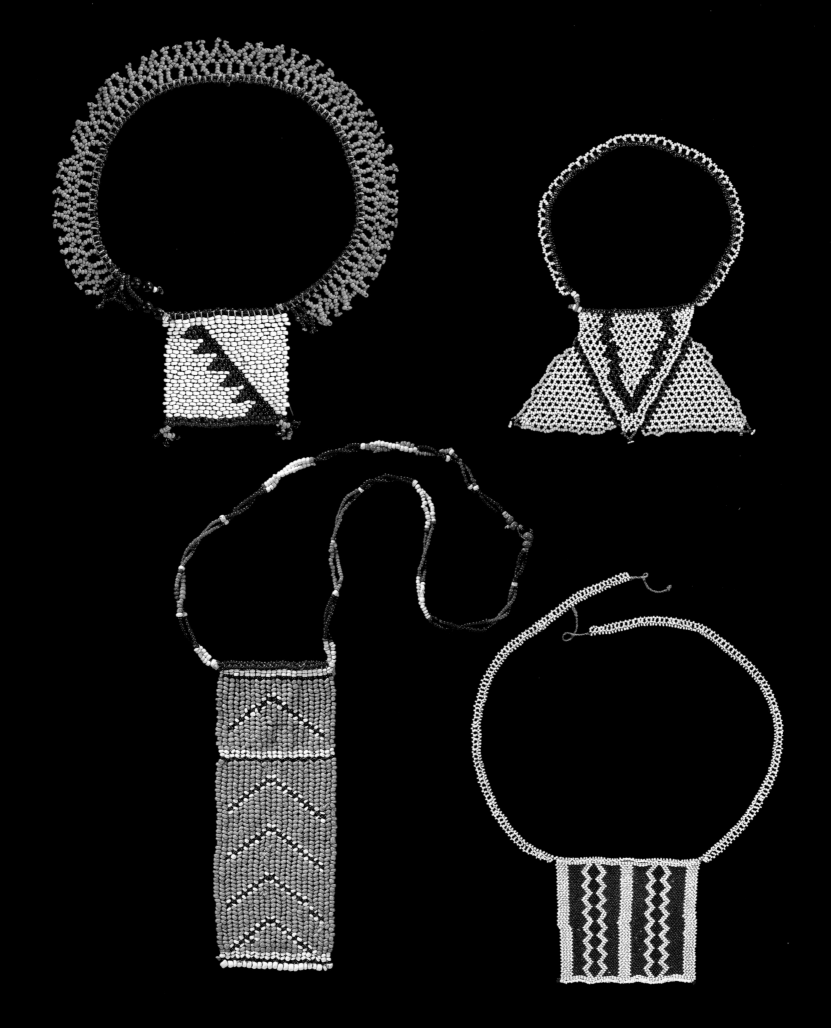

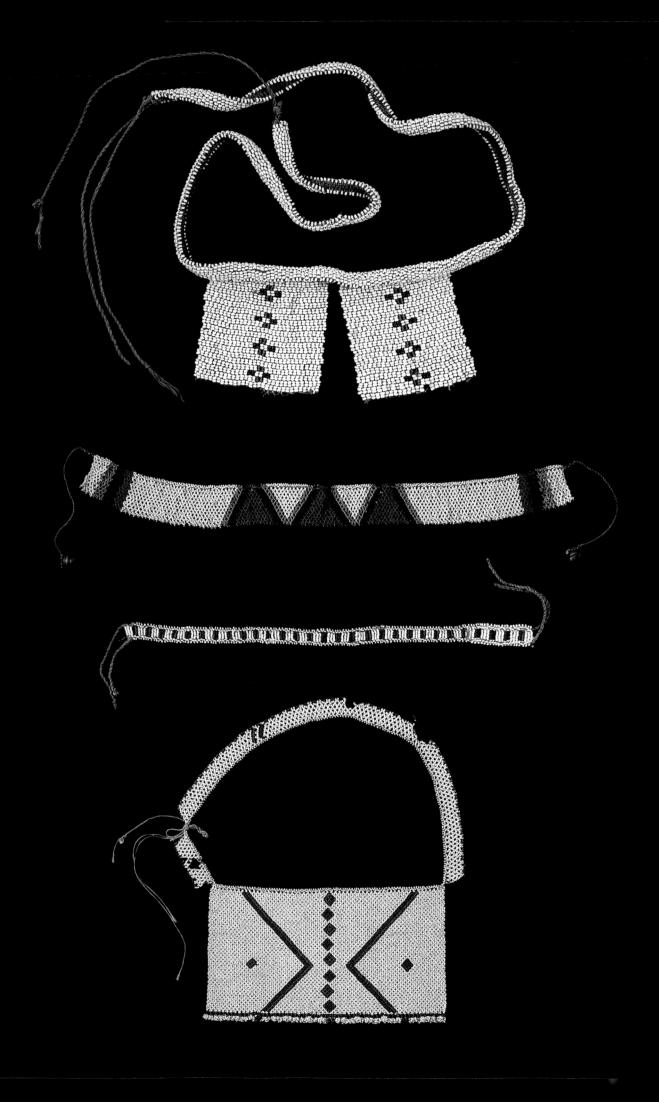

Apropos of the love letters, certain colors seem to have retained general meanings that are shared by all Zulus: opaque white beads stand for the purity of love; pink symbolizes poverty; yellow signifies wealth; blue refers to a dove. Thus a string of beads incorporating these colors could be interpreted in this manner: "My heart is pure and white in the long weary days (white beads); if I were a dove I would fly to your home and pick up food at your door (blue beads); darkness prevents my coming to you (black beads)."[9]

As the scholar Gary van Wyk has pointed out, "Red, white, and black are the main sacred colors in Zulu symbolism."[10] For men, the wearing of beadwork is now usually associated with special ceremonies and their beaded articles often incorporate designs specific to certain locales. These same regional motifs also appear on a range of other beaded objects [867–870, 871]. Probably the most ebullient of Zulu beadwork is seen in such recreational areas as the Durban boardwalk, where the ornate attire of the rickshaw pullers is truly a memorable sight [872–874].

Four beaded garments (opposite) reflecting the white, red, black and "sap green" regional style of Nongoma, the Zulu capital located in northern Natal Province.

867 A beaded skirt: length 5¹/₂ in. (14 cm), width 33 in. (83 cm).

868 A beaded belt: height 1⁷/₈ in. (5 cm), length 35⁷/₈ in. (91 cm).

869 A beaded headband: height ³/₈ in. (1 cm), length 20 in. (51 cm).

870 A beaded loin covering: height 10 in. (25 cm), width 15 in. (38 cm).

871 Zulu men in ceremonial attire at the 1992 Umhlanga, "Reed Dance," festival celebrated annually in northern Natal Province at the royal capital near Nongoma. It is usually only at such important ceremonies that modern-day Zulu men appear in traditional dress. The beadwork panels worn by the central figure are in the unmistakable Nongoma style: beads of white, red, black and "sap green" (named for the grass that sustains the cattle) fashioned in triangular "shield" patterns.

872 (above) Rickshaw pullers on the Durban beachfront in the early 1980s. The men's ornate garments reflect the Nongoma and Mahlabatini regional styles of beadwork. The central figure wears a medal awarded for best costume.

873 (top right) A rickshaw puller's towering headpiece: height 59 in. (150 cm), width 28⅞ in. (73 cm).

874 (right) The body costume of a Durban rickshaw puller: length 81½ in. (207 cm), width 57 in. (145 cm).

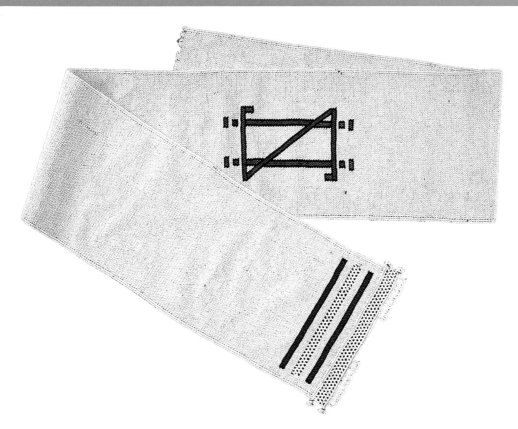

875 An Ndebele beaded wedding train, the *nyoga*, whose snake-like qualities are reflected in its long and sinuous dimensions. Length 66½ in. (169 cm), width 8 in. (20 cm).

NDEBELE BEADWORK

Among the Ndebele, traditional beadwork plays an important role in the marriage ceremony. A long, train-like beaded piece, the *nyoga*, forms part of the bridal costume [875]. The Africanist scholars Suzanne Priebatsch and Natalie Knight note that "these extraordinary beaded objects, which are often up to 1.5 meters [5 ft] in length, hang from the shoulders and trail on the ground, making snake-like motions on the earth as the bride dances. The word *nyoga* in fact means 'snake.'"[11]

Once married, women and men wear little beadwork. Among the Ndebele, beaded ceremonial clothing is almost exclusively the realm of women; men wear Western dress except on such rare occasions as an initiation. One important Ndebele female garment is the ceremonial beaded blanket, often worn with a huge neckband [876]. After an Ndebele woman marries, the initial symbol of her marital status is a five-paneled ceremonial apron called a *jocolo* [877]. This garment is often made by the bride's mother-in-law, whereas subsequent beaded aprons, the *mapoto*, are made by the young matron herself [878; see also 845].

876 One of the Ndebele females' most impressive ceremonial garments is a very heavy beaded blanket that is often worn with a wide neck ring—decorated either with beads or studded with carpet tacks—that lends a further regal dimension to a woman's elongated neck.

TRANSITIONAL DRESS

Traditional Xhosa, Zulu and Ndebele beadwork can be appreciated at several levels. Certainly these beautifully crafted pieces are an aesthetic delight, but it is also intriguing to consider what role beadwork originally may have served in the older, traditional societies. The Africanist Frank Jolles, who studied styles of Zulu beadwork in Natal Province's Msinga district, makes an interesting point: "In Msinga four main color schemes…exist side by side throughout a region inhabited by a number of different clans…the function of these color schemes may originally have been to signify the clan affiliation of the wearer…this hypothesis is supported by the fact that at least two of the names of the color schemes derive from districts or clans. [This] would account for their surprising continuity, and the coexistence of distinct color schemes in a pure form. It would also explain the resistance to the introduction of new or replacement colors reported by some traders."[12]

Among the modern-day Xhosa, Zulu and Ndebele, specific color combinations and patterns are often still characteristic of particular areas and hence continue to indicate a person's origin and sometimes his/her class. Such regional and social indicators are particularly important in a culture that practices exogamy [879].[13]

The important role that beadwork has played in South Africa cannot be overstated. Between 1932 and 1955, the world's major bead manufacturer, who then had a virtual monopoly, exported to South Africa about half of all beads sold on the continent, which consumed more beads than any other part of the world. As Gary van Wyk notes: "In that era, South Africa was most certainly the globe's greatest producer of beadwork."[14] Today it remains a remarkably democratic vehicle for aesthetic expression, available not just to leaders but to everyone and continuing to adapt to ever-changing personal styles, allowing traditionalists to adorn themselves in the latest, up-to-the-moment attire [880].

879 This Zulu girl's elaborately beaded necklaces, arm bands, chest bands and loin apron indicate that she is of the Thembu clan, located in the Tugela Ferry area of former central Natal Province.

880 A ca. 1960s Xhosa bride and groom resplendent in contemporary beaded attire. The young man's black collar was made from seals for industrial piping systems from the gold mines of Johannesburg, where young men go for stints of work before circumcision. His spectacles and plastic armbands are further indicators of his "modernity." The young girl wears a charm necklace, or "necklace of promise."

877 (opposite above) An Ndebele five-pointed marital apron, the *jocolo*. Length 21½ in. (54.7 cm), width 14 in. (36 cm).

878 (opposite below) The Ndebeles' less formal marital apron, the *mapoto*, is rectangular with knotted and beaded fringes separating the two rectangular panels on either side. Length 20½ in. (52.2 cm), width 18⅞ in. (47.8 cm).

CENTRAL AFRICA

881 A Kuba official of the Bushoong ethnic group wearing formal attire: feathered conical cap, goat-hair collar, beaded necklace, red-black-white raffia-cloth skirt with bobble fringe, beaded ornaments and flywhisk. Democratic Republic of the Congo, ca. 1970s.

Geographically, the defining feature of Central Africa is its huge rainforest, characterized by year-round warmth and high rainfall; the Congo River Basin annually receives over 48 in. (120 cm) of rain. Through the forest winds the mighty Congo River, second only to the Amazon in the volume of water it carries and the extent of its drainage area. The

Congo basin is isolated from the coastal plain to the west by the granite Massif du Chaillu, to the northwest by the volcanoes and ranges of the Cameroon Ridge, and to the east by the high mountains that fall steeply to the lakes of the Great Rift Valley. Politically, Central Africa is home to Gabon, Congo, Cameroon, sections of the Central African Republic, Angola and Chad, as well as the largest of the Congo Basin's nations, the Democratic Republic of the Congo, formerly known as Zaire.[1]

This massive rainforest is home to pygmy tribes, such as the Imbuti, who fashion loincloths from the inner bark of the tropical fig trees that grow in their environment. The bark is made pliable by being soaked in water or left to absorb moisture from the atmosphere and is then beaten over a hardwood log until it expands widthways. This treated bark cloth is decorated with asymmetrical linear designs made either with charcoal that is applied by stick and fixed with vegetable juice, or, if color is wanted, mud is daubed onto the cloth with a finger.[2]

Cotton is also used to create textiles in the region. Both northern Cameroon and southern Chad have cotton-growing areas. In Cameroon the cotton is woven on double-heddle horizontal looms and used to create garments that include impressive gowns, often heavily decorated. The most famous regional cotton textile is the resist-stitched, indigo-dyed *ndop*, which originated in the grasslands of Cameroon. Raffia fiber is used to stitch geometric designs into the base fabric, which is then soaked in indigo dye-pits; when the stitches are removed, the leftover pattern shows up white against the vivid blue background.[3]

There is, however, an additional rich textile heritage in Central Africa that is far more celebrated than either its bark-cloth or cotton fabrics. This involves the use of raffia not just to create resist-stitchwork but rather to create entire garments—and there is one area in Central Africa where this decorative tradition is particularly remarkable.

Although much of sub-Saharan Africa's population is organized into small village polities and fiefdoms, the continent once contained a number of large and independent kingdoms. These royal courts were replete with aristocratic courtiers, ceremonial pomp and retinues of expert artisans; authority rested in the person of a divine king who was invested with particular powers that linked the physical, political and symbolic worlds. One such kingdom still exists within Central Africa, despite the violence that has occurred in the region in recent decades. Even today the eastern section of the Congo Basin remains a dangerous, ongoing battlefield where rebels and government forces struggle for control,[4] but outside that military zone can be found the multi-ethnic kingdom of Kuba, organized in the early 17th century by Bantu speakers. The Kuba realm is located approximately 700 miles (1,120 km) east of the Atlantic Ocean in the fertile area between the Kasai and Sankuru rivers in the south-central section of the Democratic Republic of the Congo [Map 37].[5]

The various peoples who live within Kubaland have long been known for the production of spectacular regalia [882], as well as velvet-like cut-pile textiles, all of which play a role in various court ceremonies and funerals. These impressive activities take place throughout the realm but particularly in the king's court in Mushenge, the capital of the Bushoong, one of whose clans is viewed as royalty. The wealth of a Kuba king is regarded as proportional to his power, whether measured by the dimensions of his home, the number of his wives or the expanse of his fields. In the

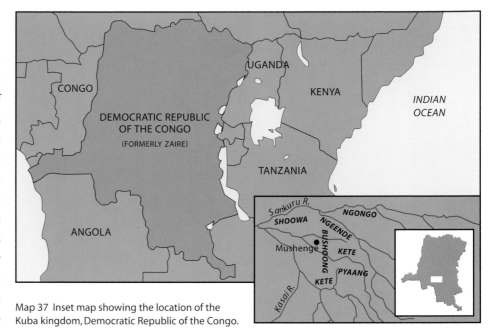

Map 37 Inset map showing the location of the Kuba kingdom, Democratic Republic of the Congo.

882 The *nyim*, the Kuba king a-Mbeeky III, covered in ornate regalia at the time of a 1970 *itul* festival held in Nshyeeng, Democratic Republic of the Congo. At these particular ceremonies, every participant had to wear precisely what ancient custom dictated. Note the sovereign's skirt, belts, necklaces, bracelets, anklets, footwear—all covered in beads and shells—as well as his multicolored feathered headdress and bead-and-cowrie-shell adorned staff, all indicators of wealth in the traditional attire expected of a ruler at an *itul* event.

883 A Shoowa man at his obliquely angled single-heddle loom, ca. 1970s. This loom utilizes untwisted single lengths of raffia fiber for both warp and weft. The loose ends of the individual strips of raffia have been inserted as wefts to produce the Kuba's plain-weave cloth.

1950s, the treasury of the Bushoong *nyim*, Kuba's sacred sovereign, included a household of some 600 wives as well as more than five storehouses stacked with baskets, knives, pottery, elephant tusks, leopard skins, masks, precious sculptures and magnificently embroidered cloth and clothing.[6]

The yarn used to produce all Kuba cloth is obtained from the leaves of the raffia palm, *Raphia vinifera*.[7] Throughout the Kuba area, the cultivation of raffia palms at the edge of villages or in special garden plots—as well as the weaving of the raffia cloth—is exclusively a male activity. Young boys strip the fibrous palm leaves and then split them. The fibers are made more pliant by rubbing them repeatedly by hand, after which they are bound into skeins, ready for the weavers. The Africanist Monni Adams points out that in comparison with comparable single-heddle looms from other regions of the world, those of the southern Congo are set up at an unusually oblique angle [883].[8] Although most men are weavers, some are specialists who produce particularly fine cloths. The size of each piece is determined by the natural length of the palm leaves.

The raffia leaf itself varies from white to light brown; the basic added tones are ecru or beige, red, black and brown. Additional colors come in a wider range of shades: pale rose to wine red, bright to dark blue, yellow to orange, green. Color tones vary somewhat within the various ethnic groups that make up the Kuba kingdom; almost all of the dyes are obtained from regional plant sources.[9]

When cut from the loom, the woven raffia cloths are stiff, coarsely textured and have no selvedge. If the cloth is to be used for a woman's skirt, it has to be pounded in a mortar and undergo other softening processes, all laborious activities that are carried out by women before the cloth is hemmed, dyed and decorated. As the Africanist Patricia Darish has noted: "These treatments change the stiff raffia cloth into a flexible and supple cloth approaching the quality of fine linen."[10]

Darish also makes the point that "the social dimensions of Kuba textiles can best be understood in terms of the dynamics of their production and use, as well as the interdependent contributions of both men and women. This shared mode of production is linked to Kuba ideas regarding social responsibility, ethnic identity and religious beliefs."[11] The Kuba trace descent through the female line and their villages are composed of clan sections made up of matrilineages. As this social system applies to textiles, most decorated raffia skirts are neither fabricated nor owned by a single individual but rather result from the cooperative efforts of men and women of each clan section, defined by a matrilineage. The chart of social relationships reflected in communal artistry challenges Western notions of "artisanship" or "ownership." Even textiles made by a single person are never considered the property of that individual; they always belong to the clan section of the matrilineage.[12] Thus the construction of a woman's skirt, for example, might be the work of half a dozen women of various ages, some located at a distance but all belonging to the same clan. Initially the female head of one of the clan sections directs the production of the skirt, which would be made up of small and large sections of cloth embroidered by several women [see 888]. Assembling these various pieces into a completed skirt could continue over several years; the completion of a man's skirt could take even longer.[13]

The geometric designs of the raffia embroideries are part of a decorative system that extends beyond the textiles themselves. These motifs are part of a larger visual tradition that appears throughout the Kuba universe, not only in female body scarification but also on rugs, carved boxes, house poles, cups, drums, screens [see 887], and so on. In fact, historically *all* Kuba manufactured objects were decorated with geometric designs. Some scholars see tremendous time depth—going as far back as the Upper Paleolithic period—in such schematic symbols.[14]

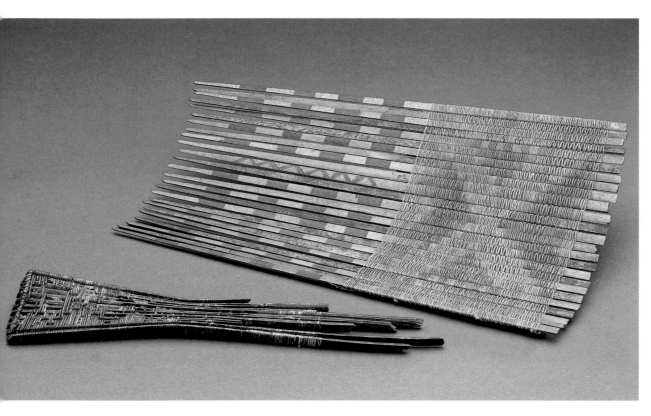

884 Raffia-rib combs made of cane strips bound together with string are accessories worn by novices at initiation.

INITIATES' COSTUMES

Although in daily life Kuba men and women now wear Western clothing or contemporary pan-African dress, on certain ritual occasions traditional attire must be worn. This is especially important during the boys' coming-of-age initiations because their distinctive novice costumes are a critical element of the ceremony [884].

When the uninitiated boys leave their village for a secret forest camp, they are no longer permitted to wear their former clothing. Only short pants are allowed, over which will be worn the dance costume that each boy now must make from raffia leaves gathered not from the cultivated palms close to home, but rather from the uncultivated raffia palms that grow wild in the forest near lakes and streams, the abode of nature spirits. The boys' dance skirts are put together using rudimentary hand-tying techniques. The completed costume consists of a short overskirt resembling a ruff worn over a full, knee-length skirt. Both pieces are secured by tying the stripped raffia leaflets onto a raffia cord approximately 15 feet (4.5 m) long.

Once the novices' costumes have been completed—and the boys have attained the initiates' secret knowledge—they return to dance in the village [885] and then are accorded adult male status; henceforth these young men will move in a world where woven raffia textiles are *de rigueur* for ritual occasions.[15]

885 Northern Kete novices performing dances in the village of Kambash, 1981. The initiates wear unwoven raffia skirts constructed of wild raffia-palm leaflets collected in the forest. Note that the women and uninitiated onlookers must stay at a safe distance from the initiates' powerful—and dangerous—forest paraphernalia.

886 A Kuba man's raffia-cloth skirt: the central section is bordered by narrower pieces completed with raffia bobble fringe made by binding a hank of raffia fibers at regular intervals. All of the small panels that make up the skirt's borders are made of black raffia cloth and are embroidered with undyed raffia thread. Length 32⅝ in. (83 cm), width 294½ in. (748 cm).

887 A Kubaland Dekese chief in formal attire. His checkered skirt has cut-pile borders of varying designs. Note the mat at the chief's back; its patterning is an example of the recurring geometric decorative theme that runs throughout Kuba culture. Democratic Republic of the Congo, 1976.

CEREMONIAL REGALIA

The Kuba are famous for the regalia worn by royal men and women on important occasions, such as the installation of a king. The historian Jan Vansina describes a ceremony in the 1950s involving a Bushoong king's entry into the palace plaza with his officials to attend an *itul* festival:[16] "It was a magnificent spectacle; there were more than a hundred of them in full costume. One saw only baldrics and collars, covered with beads and shells, veloured and embroidered cloths, ornaments of metal glittering in the sun, headdresses surmounted with bundles of multicolored feathers, a meter in height, and waving in the breeze. Each held in his hand his insignia of office."[17]

The skirts worn by the privileged Bushoong nobility are remarkable in terms of their elaboration, the complexity of their designs and their producers' division of labor. As Patricia Darish explains: "The fabrication of skirts for the most part was gender specific: men assembled and decorated men's skirts,

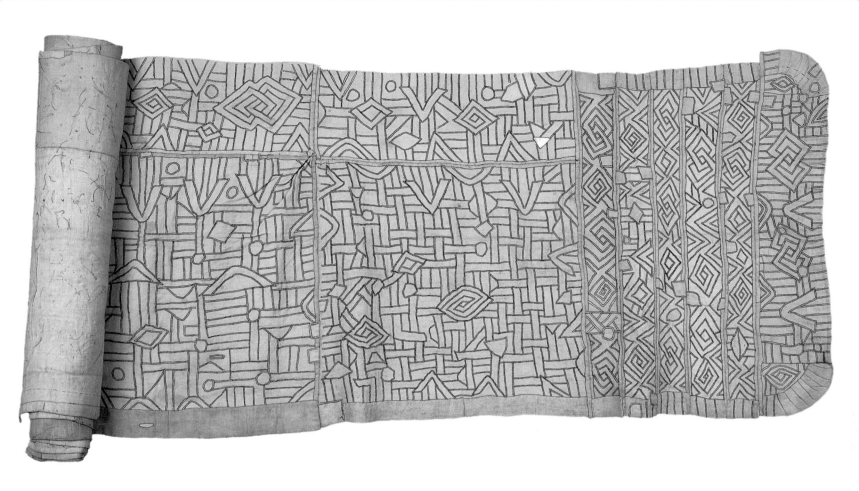

women assembled and decorated women's skirts. Several kinds of decorative techniques were utilized by both genders: various embroidery stitches, appliqué and reverse appliqué, patchwork, dyeing, stitch-dyeing, and tie-dyeing."[18]

Darish further notes that each gender's garments are differentiated by their length, the configuration of their skirt panels, and the style of their borders. Men's raffia skirts are usually almost twice as long as women's and are assembled with central sections framed by narrower borders completed with raffia bobble fringe [886]. Men wear these skirts with the length fully gathered around the waist and hips and the top border folded down over or under a belt [see 881]. On some men's skirts, the lower edge hangs down below the knees, with special border ornamentation consisting of embroidered designs, fringes and tassels. These garments—together with additional special accoutrements such as caps, feathers, belts, pendants and hand-held objects—publicly indicate the special titles and ranks held by individual officers and chiefs [887].

888 A Bushoong woman's raffia-fiber skirt composed of eight central panels sewn side by side and hemmed along one edge by nine smaller, horizontal panels (the last is visible at center top). All of the embroidered and appliquéd shapes were sewn with black raffia thread in a dense buttonhole stitch on an undyed background. Each of the panels was patterned with abstract, geometric motifs, a decorative theme that recurs throughout items of Kuba material culture. Length 36 in. (91.5 cm), width 230³/₈ in. (585 cm).

889 At an *itul* ceremony, dancers from the king's household carry horns decorated with buffalo tails and cowries. As their bulky, raffia-fiber skirts are 6 to 9 yards in length, they have to be wrapped about the body three or four times.

890 A Kuba royal wife (left) in ceremonial costume. The front section of her skirt was formerly a length of cut-pile embroidery but later that panel was replaced by red trade cloth.
A Kuba royal woman (right), wearing a long, sparsely appliquéd and embroidered wraparound skirt under a flounce-edged overskirt of linear-patterned embroidery.

891 The Queen Mother embroidering a panel for a Bushoong overskirt composed entirely of embroidered lines. Mushenge, Democratic Republic of the Congo, 1976.

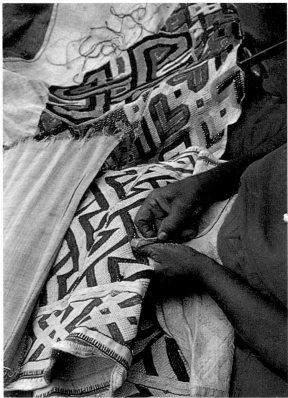

892 (opposite above) Shoowa cut-pile panel: length 19 in. (48.4 cm), width 23¼ in. (59.1 cm).

893 (opposite center) Shoowa cut-pile panel: length 26 in. (66 cm), width 17 in. (43.5 cm).

894 (opposite below) Shoowa cut-pile panel: length 25½ in. (65 cm), width 28⅜ in. (72 cm).

The women's long ceremonial skirts are sometimes 6 to 9 yards (18–27 ft, or 5.5–8 m) in length and are often unbordered. These raffia-fiber garments are worn wrapped around the body and secured with a belt, the lower edges of the skirt reaching below mid-calf [888, 889]. Bushoong women's skirts are covered with geometric designs in black embroidery stitching and sometimes have other types of fabric added to them [890, left]. Also, some Bushoong women add a smaller skirt—approximately 1½ yards (4½ ft, or 1.4 m) in length—over their wraparound skirt. These "over-skirts" consist of a central panel of embroidered black designs on raffia cloth with an edging that is curled in a unique manner, adding an element of motion to the bulky, sculptural costume [890, right].[19]

Kuba decorated skirts [891] are "highly prized … [and often] used as gifts in establishing relations of reciprocity.… [A]t a betrothal a youth's female relatives embroider a skirt that he has woven for the bride-to-be and later the in-laws will benefit from the work performed by the wife. Men's or women's decorated skirts [also] serve as compensation in legal settlements, as in adultery or divorce cases."[20]

FUNERAL ATTIRE

In terms of surface decoration, the most famous of the Kuba textiles are the rectangular or square panels of woven palm-leaf fiber enhanced by geometric designs executed in linear embroidery and other stitches. The loops of these embroidery threads are cut to form pile surfaces resembling velvet; indeed, the panels are sometimes known as "Kasai velvets" or "plush cloths" [892–896].[21] These panels had a large number of uses. The Shoowa regarded them as status symbols, as dowry payments, and as chair and floor coverings. They also sewed them together for use as funeral shrouds.[22]

It is at funerals that Kuba textiles are most typically displayed, both by mourners [897] and by the deceased, who is adorned with the prerequisite amount of cloths, belts, anklets, bracelets and hats. After the body is properly attired, it is presented to the mourners. The majority of the textiles and accessories on display belong to the clan section of the deceased, and it is the clan that

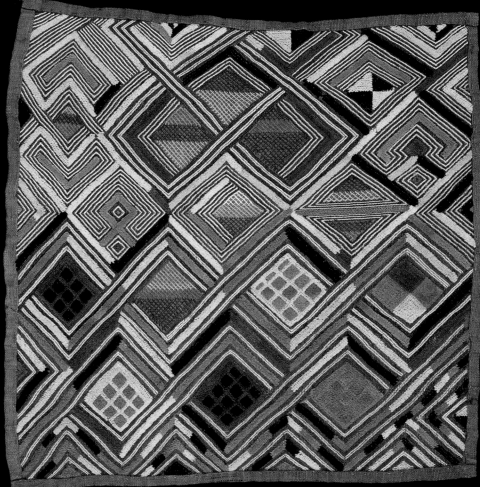

decides which textiles are chosen to be placed on the corpse, and subsequently buried with it. The excellence of each cloth counts because it reflects on the prestige of the clan. One of the primary activities at funerals is gossiping about the quality of certain of the displayed goods.[23]

Because the Kuba believe there is a "Land of the Dead" where the deceased goes until he or she is reborn after several generations, it is important that the body be properly dressed at burial. Only raffia textiles are appropriate because otherwise the deceased will not be recognized by relatives who have passed on before. Indeed, if a Kuba were to be buried in attire that was non-traditional, it would be akin to being buried naked.[24]

The raffia textiles and the raffia-palm material from which they are made are powerful symbols of abundance and wealth, hence the display of raffia cloth at funerals is a potent symbol of security and continuity, actively linking the living to one another as well as to the clan of the recently deceased. Further, the internment of raffia cloths with the deceased is a reflection of the Kuba belief that the actual process of making textiles is as important as the cloths themselves, and their public display reaffirms the enduring social relationship between men and women. The process of transferring the textiles from the living to the dead is also an affirmation of Kuba beliefs in the afterlife.[25]

One can only imagine the number of beautifully decorated Kuba cut-pile panels formerly produced and now buried. However, despite Central Africa's long years of turmoil and disruption, the production of cut-pile raffia textiles goes on; indeed, they have become lucrative tourist items.[26] And just as the weaving and embroidery of these cloths continues, so too does the cultivation of the source of it all, the *Raphia vinifera*. As the Bushoong proverb states, "You can take from a raffia palm, but you can never deplete its supply."[27]

895 (opposite above) Shoowa cut-pile panel: length 21⅝ in. (55 cm), width 25⅞ in. (66 cm).

896 (opposite below) Shoowa cut-pile panel: length 20⅝ in. (52.6 cm), width 20 in. (51 cm).

897 Kuba men dancing in ceremonial attire at a funeral. Bansueba, Democratic Republic of the Congo, 1989.

WEST AFRICA

898 Voluminous robes, protective turbans, impressively attired retainers and richly caparisoned horses are part of the aristocratic Hausa tradition of northern Nigeria. When this personal messenger for the emir of Kano State is on official business, his important mission is made known by the lowering of his robe's enormous sleeves to completely cover his hands.

the north [Map 38]. Over the centuries, the continuous movement of peoples throughout the area has led to a complicated linguistic pattern. It is now believed that most West Africans speak variants of the Niger-Congo language family but there are also Afro-Asiatic speakers in the north and Nilo-Saharan speakers in the east.[1]

In the period from about A.D. 500 to 1470, the semi-arid Sudanic zone was characterized by the rise and fall of a series of states and empires. The first was ancient Ghana—an early, powerful kingdom of the Western Sudan that is not to be confused with the modern state of that name—situated on the edge of the desert between the Senegal and Niger rivers. The Ghanaians controlled the gold fields drained by the Upper Senegal River. Their empire (A.D. 750–1240) fell under attacks from the militant missionary orders of the Muslim Almoravid who, as a religious duty, set forth on a *jihad* to convert nonbelievers in a holy war waged on behalf of Islam.

From the 11th to 16th centuries, a series of kingdoms in the Sudan and southern Sahara grew, coalesced, divided and diminished. It was during this period that what were to become longer-lasting nations began to come into being as regional alliances of local interests emerged, fused into centers of power, acquired geographical identity and thus developed into highly organized political entities such as the famed empires of the Hausa states of northern Nigeria's savannah, the Yoruba kingdoms of western Nigeria's forest belt and the Asante Confederacy of Ghana's Gold Coast.[2]

Toward the end of the 15th century, trading contacts with Western powers began to flourish as European sailors learned to navigate around Africa's western bulge and thus gain lucrative access to the Gulf of Guinea's coast. Trade in valuable commodities has long been a defining feature of West Africa. During the 15th and 16th centuries, gold was the principal attraction for the European powers but in the 17th century this focus gave way to the slave

West Africa is a land of immense geographic, climatic and linguistic diversity. The region lies entirely in the tropics but, because it is sandwiched between the western section of the Sahara to the north and the equatorial Atlantic to the south, it displays a gradual climatic change as one moves inland from the Guinea Coast's hot, lowland, tropical rainforests and humid mangrove swamps, to the extensive, fertile grasslands of the savannah, to the very hot, dry, arid deserts of

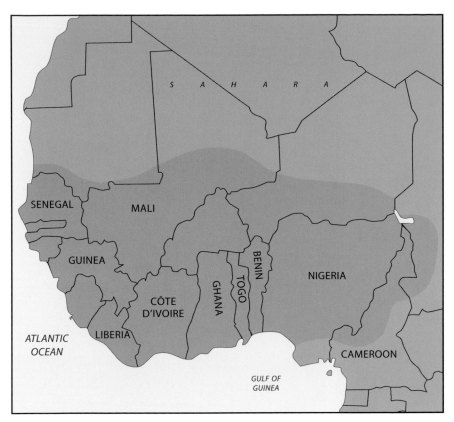

trade, which grew to dominate the area's commerce by the 18th century.³ The importance of trade in West Africa is reflected in the historic designations still attached to successive sections of the Guinea Coast: the shore bordering modern-day Liberia is referred to as the Grain Coast, the country of Côte d'Ivoire as the Ivory Coast, Ghana's shore as the Gold Coast, the shoreline bordering Togo and Benin as the Slave Coast.⁴ Considering West Africa's impressive range of unusual and magnificent cloth and clothing, the Gulf of Guinea's entire shore might well be termed the Textile Coast.

Because West Africa's production of cloth and clothing is so rich and diverse, choices have to be made as to which of the many weaving, dyeing and handcraft traditions can be included here. Initially, however, the region's unique technique of narrowband weaving (also known as strip-weaving) must be acknowledged. Men and boys weave on horizontal narrow-strip portable looms with double heddles and foot pedals to produce 1- to 5-inch (2.5–12.5 cm) strips of cloth of indefinite length [899, 900]. This technique is limited to West Africa south of the Sahara, from Senegal in the west to

Map 38 West Africa is a region rich in unique cloth and clothing traditions. The shading indicates the zone where narrowband weaving takes place.

899 An urban Fulani weaver working on a narrow-strip loom in Mali. These horizontal looms are portable despite their complex double heddles and foot pedals.

900 As male artisans in Mali weave in individual shaded sheds, each slowly pulls his long, weighted warp forward as the work proceeds. The drag stones secure the warp and provide the necessary tension as the weaver winds the completed fabric onto his cloth bar.

Cameroon in the east [see Map 38]. The long narrowband strips—of cotton, or cotton and silk, or cotton and rayon—are joined selvedge to selvedge to create large, vibrantly colored, geometrically patterned cloths. Principally associated with the Asante of Ghana and the Ewe of southern Ghana, Togo and Benin, *kente* cloths are among Africa's most iconic textiles [901–905].

901 A Ghanaian chief adorned in his official gold regalia and ceremonial *kente* cloth composed of joined cotton and silk narrowband strips, which create a large and impressive wrapper.

GHANA

The now famous and widely available *kente* cloths were originally the royal, highly restricted wrappers of the ruling Asante, the best known and most populous of the Akan peoples of Ghana who occupy the south-central portion of the country. The naming of the modern-day state of Ghana—formerly the British colony known as the Gold Coast—after the

902 *Kente* cloth has been adopted as an emblem of African identity in other parts of the world. Here, the Reverend Cecil L. Murray of the First A.M.E. Church wears *kente* cloth-adorned robes, Los Angeles, 1998.

903 An Asante man's *kente* cloth. This type of prestigious wrapper is characterized by its gold-colored warp. Length 116¹/₂ in. (296 cm), width 70⁷/₈ in. (180 cm).

904 An Ewe multi-strip *kente* cloth featuring four different warp stripes with an embellishment of figurative weft designs. Length 130³/₈ in. (331 cm), width 76³/₈ in. (194 cm).

905 An Asante man's *kente* cloth woven of rayon yarns. Length 125¹/₈ in. (318 cm), width 81⁷/₈ in. (208 cm).

medieval kingdom of that same name may reflect an early migration from the north by the present-day Ghanaian people.

At its height, the basis of the social organization of the Asante Confederacy was the rule of matrilineal descent. Political organization was decentralized and all offices, from the kingship on down, were hereditary within the lineage of the community where the office was held. The permanent sacred king, the Asantehene, was not an absolute ruler but rather was controlled to a certain extent by a council made up of the queen mother, the chiefs of the most important provinces [see 901], and the general of the army. The symbol of national unity was and is the famous Golden Stool, which came into being in the 18th century.[5]

The Asante Confederacy is made up of three states, each controlled by a chief who has his own important ceremonial regalia including a royal stool, palanquin, fans, jewelry, and particular, unique patterns of cotton and silk strip-weave *kente* cloth.

It appears that the development of *kente* was stimulated by and under the control of royal patronage. A significant percentage of the *kente* cloth patterns—the warp-strip configurations—were once solely the prerogative of the noble chiefs.[6] Further, the Asante traded local gold and imported salt to the Europeans for colorful China silks, which were then unraveled so the thread might be rewoven into shimmering narrowband-patterned strips to create the royal *kente* cloths.[7]

Today the finest examples of *kente* are still the high-status wrappers worn on special occasions and hence most frequently seen during the spectacular array of public festivals that periodically illuminate most of southern Ghana and neighboring Togo. The Ghanaian festivals and the attendant donning of *kente* are not solely adult prerogatives; *kente*-clad boys and girls often play key roles in these proceedings. *Kente*-patterned cloth is now readily for sale to everyone in Ghanaian markets. Although this commercial, roller-printed fabric is not of the same high quality as the rulers' elegant strip-woven attire, these colorful, affordable wrappers are still regularly purchased to wear on special occasions.

It must be noted that *kente* continues to serve an important social role even after death. As with the Kuba's cut-pile textiles (see "Central Africa," pp. 546–549), displays of *kente* appear at funerals, used to decorate rooms and beds where important personages lie in state, adorning temporary funeral tents, draped over coffins, and sometimes even buried within.[8]

With the exception of *kente* cloth, all of the textiles included in this survey come from further to the east, largely from what is probably Africa's most populous country, present-day Nigeria, justly famous for its diverse clothing, weaving and dyeing traditions. Many aspects of Nigerian dress can best be understood by considering the country's geography and climate, and its great diversity of language speakers and ethnic groups. The Y-shape formed by the confluence of the Niger and Benue rivers geographically divides Nigeria into three main zones: western, northern, and eastern [Map 39].[9]

Map 39 The populous and diverse West African country of Nigeria. The Niger and Benue rivers form a Y-shape that creates three major geographic areas that are markedly different from one another, resulting in climatic contrasts that influence the type of clothing worn by the inhabitants of western, northern and eastern Nigeria.

WESTERN NIGERIA

The coastal forest zone of southwest Nigeria is the heartland of the homogeneous Yoruba empire where urbanism is ancient, probably dating to A.D. 800–1000. The nation was and is made up of a series of complex city-states or kingdoms, each headed by an Oba, a divine ruler—either male or female—together with councils of elders and chiefs. Some of the ruling families of these Yoruba kingdoms, such as the dynasty of kings at Ife, remain unbroken up to the present day.

The Yoruba of the Ijebu kingdom of the coastal plain (A.D. 1400–1900) early became master traders along the region's lagoons, creeks and rivers. These entrepreneurs were the first of the coastal peoples to establish trading ties with Europeans in the late 15th century. Over the next four centuries the Yoruba kingdoms prospered but then declined as the devastating effects of the slave trade and internecine warfare of the 19th century took their toll.[10] The stage was thus set for the ascendancy of the British and the advent of colonial rule at the end of the 19th century.

Yorubaland, a rich agricultural region, is characterized by numerous densely populated urban centers surrounded by fields growing cash crops, including cotton. In West Africa's gentler climes, dress for women and non-Muslim men has long been a wrapper, an untailored cloth wrapped or draped around the body. In Yorubaland women wear their wrappers and matching head ties with particular style and flair [906]. The Yoruba have a propensity for the color blue, reflecting their skillful use of indigo, one of the world's most important dyes.[11]

Prominent among the Yoruba arts has been the production of outstanding textiles, including the famous blue *adire* cloth [907], a product of dyeing with indigo (*Indigofera tinctoria*), a craft that often goes hand in hand with extensive cotton production. Fortunately, in places where the humid climate and growing conditions are ideal, such as Yorubaland, excellent dye can also be produced from wild indigo plants.[12]

906 Yoruba women sometimes belong to social groups where members dress almost identically for certain public occasions. Here all three women wear voluminous wrappers with matching head-ties, all constructed of joined narrowband strips. Although two of the three sets of wrapper/head-ties are indigo-dyed to a dark blue-black, textiles in a range of other colors are also worn in Yorubaland.

907 A Yoruba cloth market in the 1960s presents a magnificent display of blue indigo-dyed *adire* textiles richly decorated with designs created using tie-dye resist, machine-stitched resist and starch-resist dyeing techniques, all methods for creating patterns on cloth.

909 (opposite above left) An *adire* cloth patterned using the tie-dye technique: sections of undyed cloth were tied up with raffia string; when the fabric was immersed in indigo these tied-off portions resisted the dye. Used as a woman's wrapper. Length 57 in. (145 cm), width 70 in. (178 cm).

910 (opposite above right) An *adire* cloth displaying a pattern named "threepences are scattered throughout the house." This design was achieved by pleating the cloth in sections of three thicknesses each, which were then machine-sewn in looped lines to form the threepenny bits. Used as a woman's wrapper. Length 68½ in. (174 cm), width 68½ in. (174 cm).

911 (opposite below left) An *adire* cloth patterned by the free-hand painting of starch to create designs on undyed cloth, then dyeing the fabric in indigo and, finally, washing out the starch. Used as a woman's wrapper. Length 64⅛ in. (163 cm), width 72 in. (183 cm).

912 (opposite below right) A commemorative, jubilee *adire* cloth patterned by applying starch to the fabric through a metal stencil, followed by immersing the prepared cloth in indigo and then washing out the starch. Used as a woman's wrapper. Length 65¾ in. (167 cm), width 69⅝ in. (177 cm).

908 Yoruba women prepare indigo dye in tiered ceramic containers. They create the lye needed to process the indigo by filtering water through oak wood-ash balls placed in the upper clay pots. The resulting alkaline liquid is then cooled in bowls inserted through holes in the lower pots. Nigeria, 1960s.

In Yorubaland, the women dyers carry out the preparation of their dye in sets of ceramic pots [908]. The process takes a long time: like leavening bread or making beer, indigo production is based on bacterial fermentation, hence is "alive" and cannot be hurried as the microbes need time to do their work. In the case of indigo, this involves converting the dye into a soluble, reduced state.

Once the liquid indigo dye has been processed, it is ready for application. Yoruba dyers are deservedly famous for their skill with a variety of decorative techniques. Although handwoven cloth was originally used for Yoruba indigo dyeing, mill-woven cotton yardage—either domestic or imported—has been increasingly available since the early 20th century. *Adire* cloth is patterned using several resist-dye techniques: tie-dye resist, machine-stitch resist, hand-painted starch resist and stenciled starch resist.[13] All these techniques keep dye from penetrating certain reserved sections of a cloth [909–912].

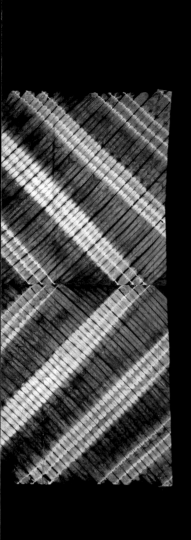
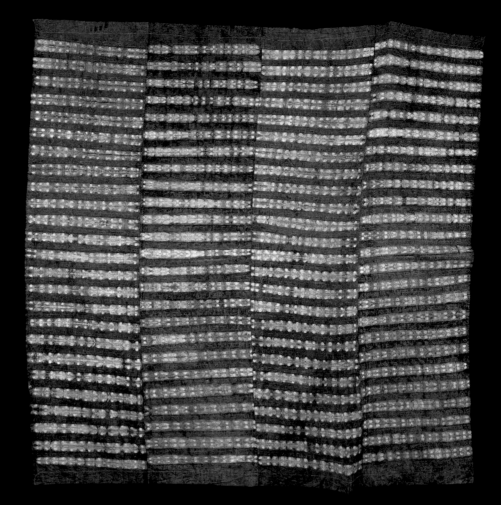

NORTHERN NIGERIA

Nigeria's northern zone is a semi-arid region that also includes fertile, rolling grasslands. This savannah region lies at the heart of the caravan trade routes that link North and West Africa, resulting in a constant exchange of ideas and artifacts between the traveling merchants and local people.[14] The inhabitants' loose, flowing clothing reflects these long contacts with Islamic North Africa and the Middle East, plus the need for protection against northern Nigeria's intense sun and often drying winds and duststorms.

This region is the realm of the historic Hausa,[15] which was made up of a series of non-homogeneous city states whose emergence appears to have been closely associated with capital cities that became centers of political power. These urban settlements were often situated in fertile areas where long-distance trade routes converged; they were also locations that could be fortified against attack. The centers, seats of

a new type of political power, resulted in a hierarchy of specialized officials with a king who reigned over all the surrounding territory.

The power of the ruler depended on the degree to which he could command the service of supporters. The establishment of this new form of government by a king and fief-holding officials entailed a substantial reorganization of the society. In addition to new territorial groupings—the seven great Hausa states[16]—there also emerged new social classes with little mobility between them. No one state of the competing Hausa states ever possessed enough power to effectively impose its control over all of the others.

Although northern Nigeria had felt the influence of internationalist Islam since the 15th century, it was the establishment of the Sokoto Caliphate (1810–1908), founded by a *jihad* led by the Fulani (see p. 560), that firmly established Islam in Hausaland. As a result, the conflicting Hausa states finally found the political order and stability needed for their integration.[17] The region's male clothing continues to reflect both the pervasive Islamic religion and the Hausa empire's class divisions.

The tall and impressive Hausa, Muslims all, are famous for producing men's voluminous robes, often referred to as gowns. The most famous of these impressive garments are those worn by the ruling elite. At the top of the Hausa political hierarchy are the various states' emirs selected from the ruling lineages by a council of clerics. Aristocrats of the Kano emirate are well aware of the value of projecting public images that reflect wealth, high social status, religious piety and political authority. Nowhere is this message more clearly conveyed than through the Hausas' magnificently embroidered great robe, called a *babban riga* [913–915], part of the "big gown" ensemble consisting of a *riga* (the outer garment; a second, less voluminous gown is worn beneath), a special turban and handcrafted, embellished leather slippers or boots. While big gowns may be worn by any man, they particularly tend to be the province of the aristocracy, as well as of their special retainers [see 898]. Layering these *riga*—i.e. wearing several at a time—adds further to the

913 A Hausa aristocrat wears an embroidered cloak over a gown made of imported white cloth decorated—according to Islamic doctrine—with asymmetrical, non-representational motifs created with green embroidery. The noble's turban is tied with projecting "ears" and a long flowing loop down the back to symbolize the word "Allah" in Arabic script. Kano City, northern Nigeria, 1981.

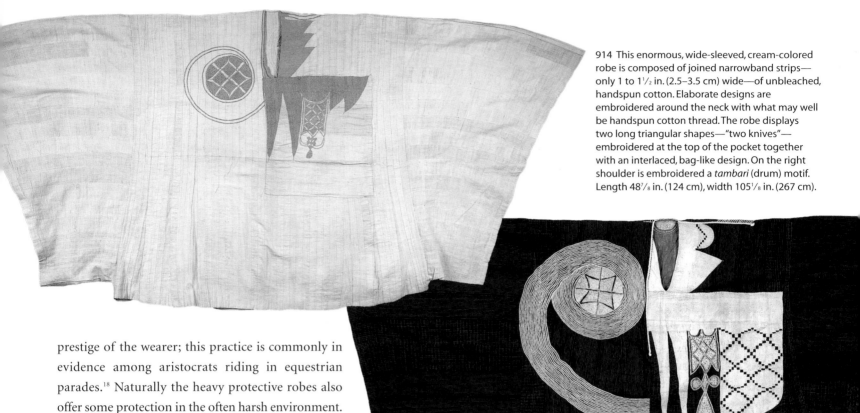

914 This enormous, wide-sleeved, cream-colored robe is composed of joined narrowband strips— only 1 to 1 1/2 in. (2.5–3.5 cm) wide—of unbleached, handspun cotton. Elaborate designs are embroidered around the neck with what may well be handspun cotton thread. The robe displays two long triangular shapes—"two knives"— embroidered at the top of the pocket together with an interlaced, bag-like design. On the right shoulder is embroidered a *tambari* (drum) motif. Length 48 7/8 in. (124 cm), width 105 1/8 in. (267 cm).

prestige of the wearer; this practice is commonly in evidence among aristocrats riding in equestrian parades.[18] Naturally the heavy protective robes also offer some protection in the often harsh environment.

The *riga* are prestige textiles, constructed of either finely spun cotton or silk woven on narrowband looms and decorated with intricate embroidery. Hanging from shoulder to ground, these huge garments are worn over embroidered trousers and long-sleeved shirts. In Africa, as the writers John Picton and John Mack have noted, "embroidery is an art generally associated with the Islamic culture of West Africa."[19] Traditionally, the elaborate designs that appear on Hausa men's robes, trousers and caps are all done by male embroiderers using dense stitches to create motifs that are asymmetrical and non-representational, in accordance with Islamic doctrine. The embroiderers employ a relatively small number of geometric elements, which they put together in various ways. Three types of stitching are primarily used: chain stitch, buttonhole stitch and couching. The work is usually done either with imported or indigenous thread on either imported or handwoven narrowband strip cloth.

By the mid-1970s, machine-embroidery had become increasingly popular all over Nigeria and in other parts of West Africa as well. Traditional Hausa designs were copied and new adaptations developed. Machine-embroidered clothing—for men, women and children—is still being made in both traditional and Western styles.[20]

Like the Yoruba, the Hausa are indigo dyers but in a markedly different way. Whereas in Yorubaland it is women who dye in ceramic vessels [see 908], among the Hausa it is men who do the dyeing, and in circular earthen pits. Further, Yoruba dyeing occurs in almost every village, whereas Hausa dyeing takes place in specific locales, one of which is the city of Kano.[21] Kano dyers specialized mainly in dyeing plain, undecorated, strip-woven white cloth in order to produce extraordinarily polished indigo fabric for turbans. After the cloth has been heavily overloaded with dye it is beaten to produce a shiny, burnished finish. According to Picton and Mack, "These elegant turbans are highly prized, not only among the Hausa but throughout the northern fringes of the Sahara (see "North Africa," p. 572).[22]

915 This huge robe, once worn by a Yoruba Muslim man, is composed of indigo-dyed narrowband strips with elaborate embroidery around the neck composed of "two knives" and adjacent designs. On the right shoulder is a *tambari* (drum) design intricately worked in light blue thread. Length 47 1/4 in. (120 cm), width 99 5/8 in. (253 cm).

916 (right) A settled Fulani dressed in colorful clothing that protects him from the harsh elements of semi-arid northern Nigeria. The town-dwelling Fulani are ardent Muslims; the amulet this man wears no doubt contains verses from the Koran.

917 (far right) Fully adorned, the young Fulani men dance to display their enhanced beauty, hoping to enthrall the young women attending a Gerewol festival, Niger, ca. 1980.

Additional inhabitants of northern Nigeria are two contrasting groups of the Fulani who, although speaking a common Niger-Congo language, Fulfulde, lead dramatically different lives.[23] One group consists of settled Muslim townspeople [916], who are found not only in northern Nigeria but also in Mali and Niger. The other Fulani group—also known as Fellata, Fula, Penu or Wodaabe—are nomadic pastoralists who sustain themselves in the harsh environment of central Niger's semi-arid grazing land, the Sahel.

The Sahel is the inhospitable world, subject to cyclical droughts, through which the nomadic Fulani move with the seasons over hundreds of miles in search of water and grazing land for their long-horned cattle, sheep, goats, donkeys and camels. For these intrepid nomads, the climax of the year comes at the end of the rainy season when Gerewol festivals—"Gerewol" is the term for both the celebration and its principal dance—are held by kin groups in various watered areas. A Gerewol brings together two Fulani lineages, who meet at an appointed place so that the young men can compete in a display of their beauty, which they carefully augment. The dancers lighten their skin with a pale yellow pigment and blacken their eyes and lips with kohl so as to emphasize the milky whiteness of their eyes and dazzling teeth [917].

As many as 1,000 people may be camped together to attend the lengthy dances, which take place each afternoon and evening for seven days. The host lineage provides all of the food for the guest lineage, who customarily eat very little: these dances are contests of both beauty and endurance. The most handsome young men of each lineage compete against each other, presenting themselves to the women of the other lineage to be judged: these encounters can result in spontaneous liaisons or even second or third marriages. While the women's embroidered, handwoven, dark blue wrappers are purchased at weekly markets [918, 919], the men dance in leather skirts covered by diaphanous, finely embroidered tunics that the women of their lineage have worked on for months [920].[24]

918 A woman's blue, indigo-dyed wrapper composed of two joined cloths produced on a vertical loom with four supplementary-weft squares woven into the cloth, which was subsequently decorated with multicolored chainstitch embroidery on one side of the wrapper and across a section of the hem. Length 65¼ in. (165.7 cm), width 41⅛ in. (104.4 cm).

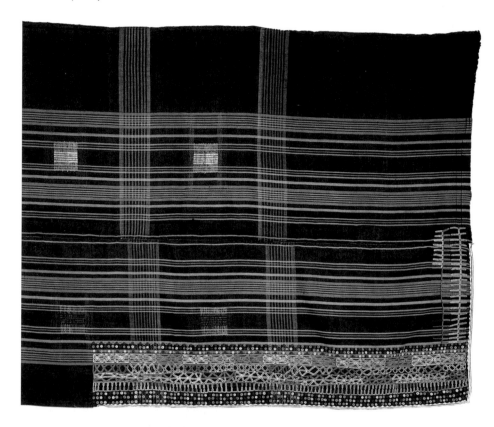

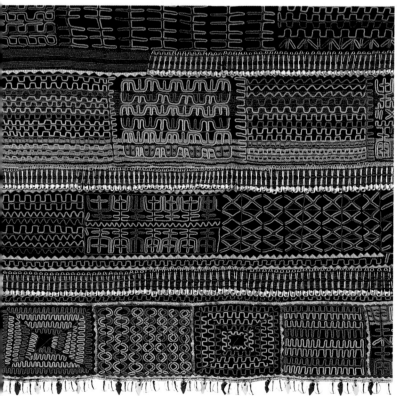

919 A woman's wrapper composed of joined, black, indigo-dyed narrowband strips ½ inch to 3 inches (1.5–7.5 cm) in width and then decorated with multicolored chainstitch embroidery in patterned, non-repeating rectangles, as well as a series of uniformly placed safety pins and a hem decoration of alternating cowrie shells and red and yellow plastic beads. Length 68⅛ in. (173 cm), width 27½ in. (70 cm).

920 A man's tunic composed of joined, indigo-dyed, narrowband strips of ½ to 1½ inches (1.5–3 cm) in width. The chainstitch embroidery is applied in series of rectangular sections whose distinctive, varicolored patterns do not repeat. Length 50⅞ in. (129 cm), width 31⅝ in. (80.5 cm).

921 An Igbo woman displays examples of cloth woven on vertical looms in the eastern Nigeria town of Akwete. Note the complex inlaid designs created using the supplementary-weft process.

922 (opposite above left) A light-colored Akwete cloth patterned in a stylized "tortoise" motif: length 44 in. (112 cm), width 78¾ in. (200 cm).

923 (opposite above right) This red, grey and green Akwete cloth displays a pattern called "money in the palm," a variation on the traditional tortoise motif: length 45 in. (114.3 cm), width 64½ in. (163.8 cm).

924 (opposite below left) This burgundy Akwete cloth is woven with discontinuous supplementary-weft floats created in a meander design called "good people's knees," a motif alleged to have come into existence around the time Christianity was introduced in Akwete. The pattern takes its name from the acute angle formed by the legs of those kneeling in prayer. Length 64½ in. (164 cm), width 45³/₈ in. (115.5 cm).

925 (opposite below right) This red, blue and green textile is a sampler of patterns attributed to the legendary woman weaver, Dada Nwakwata. The cloth displays examples of designs developed by Akwete weavers since they first adopted weft-float motifs in the 19th century. The cloth includes rows of the following designs: grains of corn; bands of triangles called "rocket" or "scissors;" a linear pattern known as "friend's fingers;" and a checked pattern that is referred to as a mat. Length 71 in. (180.3 cm), width 46 in. (116.8 cm).

SOUTHEASTERN NIGERIA

The country of Nigeria takes its name from its principal watercourse, the meandering Niger, which is the main river of western Africa and the continent's third longest. The Niger flows some 2,600 miles (4,200 km) along such a far-flung course that early European explorers at first thought they were dealing with not one but two distinct rivers. When the Niger finally reaches its delta in southeastern Nigeria, it breaks into an intricate network of channels. In this riverine environment, now officially known as the Federal Republic of Nigeria's Rivers State, there was formerly no centralized administration because the political organizations of the region's inhabitants had never developed beyond the chiefdom level. It is in this area that two very different types of textiles are still produced by two distinct peoples, both living in the locale where Igboland meets the delta. The first type of cloth to be considered is woven in Akwete, an Igbo village in the southern section of Rivers State.

Although the vertical, single-heddle broadloom is used by several Igbo groups, it is the women weavers of Akwete who, contrary to the general pattern of Nigerian craftswomen, are full-time weavers. The cloth they produce is unique in that its length is set before it is ever woven: the warp threads of these textiles are placed on the loom in one continuous circle, causing the length of the finished cloth to be pre-determined at the time the loom is warped. The average dimensions of an Akwete cloth are approximately 46 inches wide by 60 inches long (1.17 × 1.5 m). This is considerably longer than that of other Nigerian groups, which are more commonly 12–24 in. (30–60 cm) long.

Akwete textiles [921–925] are patterned with geometric and stylized designs created using the supplementary-weft method, also known as weft-float patterning: a weaver envisions a motif and then creates her design with an extra yarn—the supplementary weft—placed on top of the cloth's basic weft. The inlaid yarn is either machine-spun cotton or lustrous rayon.[25] The beauty of Akwete cloth has made it so successful that the Akwete designs have been widely copied by other Nigerian weavers, who also work on vertical broadlooms.[26] However, since Akwete cloths are the broadest fabrics produced on this type of loom, the breadth of a woven textile has now become the distinguishing feature of genuine Akwete cloth.

There has long been a profitable patron-weaver relationship between the neighboring Ijo people—traveling merchants dealing in palm oil—and the Akwete Igbo craftswomen. Many of the geometric and stylized patterns that the Akwete weave can be traced to earlier, specific, Ijo cloth designs. The Ijo, in turn, are dealers who can sell the popular Akwete cloth far outside the Akwete area, either to Europeans or to rich Nigerian women living in Lagos or Kano. It should also be noted that the women who make Akwete textiles are unusual in their control over their own economic lives, selling all of their output directly to the Ijo rather than going through a middleman. Further, unlike West African male weavers who belong to guilds, Akwete women work independently, and protect the secrets of their weaving skills.[27]

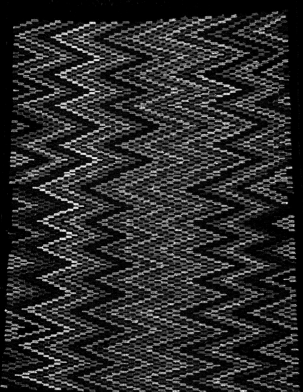

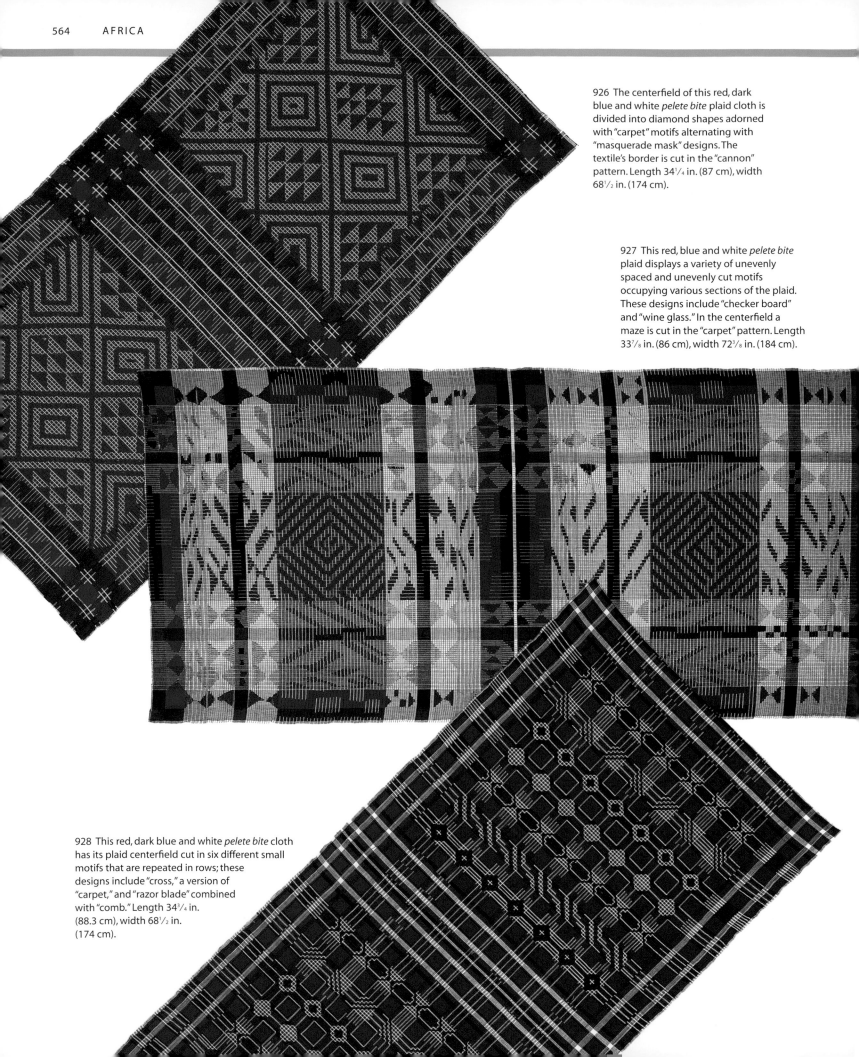

926 The centerfield of this red, dark blue and white *pelete bite* plaid cloth is divided into diamond shapes adorned with "carpet" motifs alternating with "masquerade mask" designs. The textile's border is cut in the "cannon" pattern. Length 34¼ in. (87 cm), width 68½ in. (174 cm).

927 This red, blue and white *pelete bite* plaid displays a variety of unevenly spaced and unevenly cut motifs occupying various sections of the plaid. These designs include "checker board" and "wine glass." In the centerfield a maze is cut in the "carpet" pattern. Length 33⅞ in. (86 cm), width 72⅜ in. (184 cm).

928 This red, dark blue and white *pelete bite* cloth has its plaid centerfield cut in six different small motifs that are repeated in rows; these designs include "cross," a version of "carpet," and "razor blade" combined with "comb." Length 34¾ in. (88.3 cm), width 68½ in. (174 cm).

The second unique cloth produced in Rivers State is made by the Kalabari Ijo who live at the southernmost tip of the Niger Delta. They create a completely transformed type of fabric from an already existing textile: commercially woven cloth is structurally altered and renamed *pelete bite* (cut-thread cloth) and *fimate bite* (drawn-thread cloth) [926–928].[28] The original, geometrically patterned textiles—either plaid, striped or checked fabrics such as gingham and madras—are traditionally imported from India and England. These commercial cotton fabrics are readily available to the Kalabari, who purchase them in the market or from itinerant cloth sellers to wear as wrappers [929].

Pelete bite and *fimate bite* are created by a hand technique which involves women skillfully taking a razor or penknife blade to cut certain threads, and then carefully removing them. A new design thus emerges, making the reconstructed textile lacy and supple in contrast to the original fabric which was compact and firm. The difference between *pelete bite* and *fimate bite* is that the former's motifs have both warp and weft threads cut and removed, whereas *fimate bite* designs result in stripes because it is only the weft threads that are cut and removed. *Pelete bite* have the most intricately created designs.

The cutting of Kalabari cloth is a woman's art—some girls start to learn as young as six—and is used for both men's and women's wrappers. The effect of the cutting is extremely subtle. Only knowledgeable "insiders"—the Kalabari themselves—can generally discern the transformation of an original cloth whose geometric designs have been removed to create such ingenious patterns as millipede, python or tiger paws, as well as many others [930].[29] In addition to wearing their cut-thread cloths as skirt-like wrappers, the Kalabari use these textiles to adorn funeral beds, a practice also shared by the Ghanaian Asante and Central African Kuba, a custom reflecting the importance placed by all three groups on their own distinctive type of cloth.

West Africa's diverse array of textiles continues to exert its appeal despite the increasing influx of inexpensive Western clothing into African marketplaces. Although different techniques are sometimes tried to hasten time-honored methods of cloth production, it is almost always traditional dress that appears on festive occasions, a tribute to the impressive longevity and vibrancy of West Africa's array of handcrafted cloth and clothing.

929 A Kalabari Ijo woman from the island town of Buguma in eastern Nigeria's Niger Delta wears a drawnwork *pelete bite* wrapper created by subtracting threads from a piece of imported gingham woven in an English textile mill. This restructured textile has been converted into a lacy fabric with openwork motifs located at regular intervals.

930 A *pelete bite* motif glossary.

A Selection

sibi dalaye – comb

alu – masquerade mask

cross

wine glass tail – glass tail

abili – checker board

etere – mat, carpet

sangolo – fish gill

ikoli – chain

NORTH AFRICA

931 Sahrawi nomads, descendants of Arab-Berber Bedouin, crossing the dunes of the western Sahara with their camels. Their all-enveloping robes and headscarves protect the tribesmen from the heat and sand of the desert environment.

The region that lies west of Egypt has long been known as the Maghreb, the Arab word for "west," which encompasses the modern-day countries of Morocco, Tunisia, Algeria and the western portion of Libya. The Maghreb reflects the influence of many invaders, both European and—most importantly—Arab, which has given the region an almost universal Islamic flavor and common Arabic language.[2]

In North Africa the main sources of good farmland are in the sheltered valleys of the Atlas Mountains, the Nile Valley and Delta, and along the Mediterranean coast. In these fertile areas a wide variety of crops are grown, including wheat, barley, rice and cotton. But not all of the inhabitants of Africa's far north are agriculturalists; some are pastoralists raising descendants of the sheep and goats that originally spread into northeast Africa from Asia around 7000 B.C.

THE MOUNTAIN BERBER

Among the original inhabitants of the Maghreb were the Berber peoples, many of whom now live high on the slopes of the Atlas Mountains or along the arid fringes of the Sahara Desert. Although the Berber are practicing Muslims, their women have never covered their faces [932]. By comparison with heavily veiled Arab women (see "The Arabian Peninsula," pp. 46–48), Berber females enjoy a far greater freedom; some who live in the High Atlas are even allowed to choose their own marriage partners.

The economy of many Berber groups in the Atlas Mountains is based primarily on raising sheep, hence wool is their most important fiber.[3] Aside from an occasional festivity, there is a harsh monotony to daily life in this mountain fastness. For half the year, many live snowbound behind village walls on the rugged slopes, but when spring comes the sheep are moved up to high pastures by the shepherds and their families who then spend the summer in tents.

North Africa, when seen from space via satellite, is dominated by the Sahara Desert, which in fact covers nearly one-third of the African continent. This vast, desolate expanse—the largest equatorial desert on Earth—is characterized by a combination of sand seas composed of immense dunes, numerous mountains and vast rocky plains, as well as occasional oases and dry river beds. To the northeast, the course of Egypt's Nile River is clearly visible thanks to its green river banks that culminate in the Nile Delta to the north. Further east lies the rocky desert of the Sinai. To the northwest rise the Atlas Mountains, green with vegetation on both their seaward slopes and coastal plains. Beyond the mountains can be seen the Mediterranean bordering Africa's northern coast [Map 40].[1]

Wool production is largely a family matter. After the sheep are sheared in May, the fleeces are broken up, soaked in cold river water, beaten to emulsify the fats in the wool, and then combed prior to being spun. The warp yarns come from a fleece's harder, longer fibers; weft yarns are spun from the softer, shorter strands.

The Berber women of the eastern High Atlas have long used a vertically mounted, single-heddle loom to weave their unique cloaks [see 932]. Men's garments are usually the color of the wool used, often plain white. As recently as the late 20th century men were still wearing long, hooded tunics and large, semi-circular, hooded cloaks [933]. These garments are not cut from a rectangular piece of cloth—a waste of

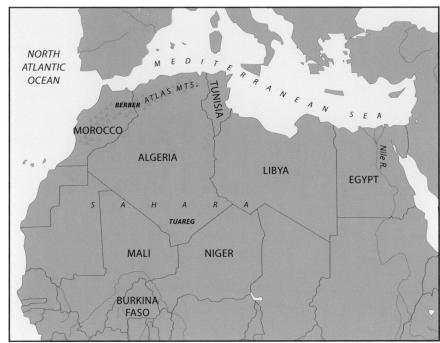

Map 40 Map of North Africa, showing places and peoples mentioned in the text.

laboriously produced wool—but rather are woven in one single, semi-circular piece that includes the hood. The men then decorate their capes, fashioning the garments' tassels and the small decorative sections at the throat. Berber men also knit or crochet their own wool trousers, leggings and hats.

The traditional costume of a mountain woman consists of a long woolen tunic draped horizontally around the body and fastened by pulling the cloth at the back across the shoulders and pinning it in front with two brooches; a woolen belt is secured about the waist. Over her tunic, a woman wears the rectangular cloak patterned with weft stripes. Among the various High Atlas peoples there are many of these weft-stripe patterns, each particular to a certain group so the affiliation of the wearer is immediately apparent [934].[4]

Berber women take pleasure in wearing a great deal of jewelry [see 932]. Despite the teachings of Islam that forbid the representations of human and animal forms, the Berber often depict creatures in their decorative designs that they believe have magical

932 A Berber woman from an Aît Hadiddu village high in Morocco's Atlas Mountains wears the traditional weft-striped hooded cloak that identifies her group. Around her neck is a necklace composed of large amber and coral beads and embossed silver amulets.

933 (right) A semi-circular hooded cape of felted wool (see detail, above) woven by Berber women for a Berber bridegroom of the high Atlas Mountains, Tunisia, pre-1970. Length 67³/₈ in. (171.2 cm), width 83⁷/₈ in. (213 cm).

934 (opposite) An unmarried woman's fringed cloak (see details, above) from a Berber community in the Atlas Mountains, Tunisia, pre-1970. This felted wool garment is decorated along the hem and sides with supplementary-weft patterning; the shoulder and neck section displays hand-embroidered designs as well as 18 small, multicolored tassels. Length 44⁷/₈ in. (114.2 cm), width 46¹/₂ in. (118.1 cm).

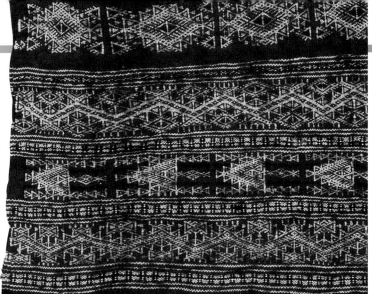

attributes. Faith in the power of such animal depictions—the head of a snake or ram, a jackal's paw, a dove's foot—stems from ancient Berber beliefs. Of particular importance are those representations that offer protection against the evil eye, feared throughout the Mediterranean world—symbols that have continued to exert their power and that still provide inspiration for many jewelry pieces made today.

Although the Berber often wear large amber and coral necklaces [see 932], they particularly value jewelry executed in silver which, to them, symbolizes purity and honesty. Despite the high standard of craftsmanship of Maghreb silver jewelry, its market price is not much more than the value of the metal alone.

935 Seated astride his prestigious white camel, this Tuareg nomad proudly wears the distinctive *tagulmust,* the traditional Tuareg turban/veil made of shimmering blue, indigo-dyed, *aleshu* cloth. Talak region, Niger, 2001.

Unless silver pieces are taken by traders to the larger towns for sale to Europeans, jewelry will be sold back to a silversmith who will then melt it down to be refashioned for the next customer. A Berber woman considers secondhand or antique jewelry inferior, always preferring pieces which have been crafted especially for her, as she views her jewelry as embodying her personal aesthetic and cultural ideals.

The Berber love of naturally formed elements, together with the more refined techniques of silverworking, combines the primitive and sophisticated, the essence of traditional Berber jewelry.[5] A different aesthetic exists to the south among a related Berber group, the nomadic Tuareg, who live across a vast area—the present-day countries of Niger, Mali and Burkina Faso, as well as parts of Algeria and Libya—and have long been esteemed for their ability to prosper in the Sahara Desert's harsh expanse.

THE SAHARAN TUAREG

The Tuareg way of life evolved sometime between the 1st millennium B.C. and A.D. 300 as the result of two life-altering events. First, the humped Arabian camel (*Camelus dromedarius*) was introduced into North Africa around the 1st century A.D. from the Near East, where the animal had initially been domesticated between the 13th and 11th centuries B.C. (see "The Arabian Peninsula," p. 42). Berber groups, who previously had been raising a few hardy sheep and goats along the desert fringes, suddenly gained a new large domestic animal capable of producing greater supplies of meat and milk. Even more important, these camels were already adapted to an arid climate, enabling the formerly marginalized Berber to penetrate and crisscross the desert for trading purposes. Indeed, during the first three centuries of the current era, the Berber of the western desert, most notably the ancestral Tuareg, passed through a dual transition, from transhumanism (living between temporary and permanent camps) to true nomadism (always living in impermanent structures) as they became camel breeders capable of sustaining a fully pastoral livelihood [935].[6]

In conjunction with this nomadic way of life, a second major change came about. By the 4th century A.D. a new commercial sphere opened when the trans-Saharan trade began to link the indigenous African world of the western and central Sudan with the Mediterranean region, Europe and the Middle East. In response, the desert-dwelling Tuareg became shrewd traders as well as formidable warriors, fully capable of defending the Sahara's major caravan routes as well as themselves.

By the time the colonizing French appeared on the scene in the 18th century, Tuareg society was already sharply stratified, dividing into five social classes: 1) nobles, descendants of the camel breeders who had dominated, 2) vassal groups of goat herders as well as, 3) Islamic teachers, 4) the *inadan*, jewelry smiths and artists, and 5) groups of war captives, the enslaved.

The Tuareg's unique form of dress, refined aesthetic sense, and pride and skill in negotiating the desert landscape have long attracted attention. They call themselves "men who wear the veil,"[7] referring to their most distinctive garment, the 16½ foot-long (5-meter) *tagulmust*—a white or shimmering-blue cloth that serves simultaneously as both turban and veil—that each male receives at initiation. Scholars have long pondered the origin of the Tuareg male veil because, in Islamic cultures, it is usually women whose faces are hidden. Whatever the *tagulmust*'s source, it serves several functions: the wrapped head-and-face covering helps men keep a social distance from in-laws and strangers it assures that evil spirits cannot enter the body through the mouth and it protects the wearer from the Sahara's heat and duststorms. Although in larger towns, some younger men today wear red, purple or green veils—or have even given up the veil altogether—many rural Tuareg men continue to dress in long blue or white cotton gowns, together with a white or dark blue *tagulmust* [936].

936 This male Tuareg figure wears pants and a shirt under a voluminous pale blue cotton gown, and his head is wrapped in the characteristic *tagulmust*. He wears sandals and holds a knife encased in a sheath [see 937, below left].

Turban: length 78³/₈ in. (198.9 cm), width 8⁷/₈ in. (22.4 cm).

Gown: length 53⁷/₈ in. (137 cm), width 69⁷/₈ in. (177.5 cm).

Shirt: length 39 in. (99 cm), width 60⁷/₈ in. (154.2 cm).

Pants: length 39⁷/₈ in. (101.5 cm), width 41³/₈ in. (105 cm).

937 Man's knife and sheath.
Knife: length 8¹/₂ in. (21.6 cm), width 1³/₈ in. (3.7 cm).
Sheath: length 15¹/₈ in. (38.5 cm), width 3⁷/₈ in. (10 cm).

938 Early 20th-century Tuareg nobles attired in their finest array. Each wears enveloping multiple robes as well as an indigo-dyed *tagulmust* turban/veil with additional bands of cloth wrapped over it.

Among the nobles, dress conveys honor and dignity. In the precolonial social order, the wearing and use of voluminous robes, men's face veils, and such accessories as a sword, silver jewelry and amulets, as well as the use of the white camel, were governed by sumptuary laws that restricted certain attire to nobles [938]. For Tuareg men, and particularly for the nobles, dress styles emphasize the head, height and vertical lines, reflecting the positive value of endurance and the toughness of the old warriors who dominated the society. Rural men are still generally lean and muscular from a life spent roaming the desert.

Equally important to the total effect of male dress are gait, posture and gestures, all intended to express degrees of elegance, refinement and strength. Indeed, there are specific gestures associated with the man's veil relating to the warrior code of honor. Traditionally, the wearing of the *tagulmust* was primarily restricted to the nobles but now has become a pervasive symbol for nearly all Tuareg men, albeit in different styles according to region, age, social stratum and situation [939].

Tuareg women also receive a headscarf at the time of their initiation and it also serves to show adult status. A woman, however, only covers her nose and mouth on certain social occasions. Since the Tuareg have no weaving tradition, their headcovers are obtained from other groups, often from the Nigerian Hausa (see "West Africa," p. 559) who produce a distinctive cloth known as *aleshu*, made of many joined narrowband cotton strips, over-dyed with indigo and then beaten until a shimmering effect is achieved [940]. Because the indigo dye on these heavily saturated textiles tends to rub off on the skin, the Tuareg are sometimes referred to as the "Blue People of the Sahara."[8]

939 A Tuareg man wearing a *tagulmust* in a manner that demonstrates reserve and hence politeness. Ayourou, Niger, 1980.

940 This female Tuareg figure wears a headwrap but it does not cover her face; although the Tuareg are Muslims, only the men are routinely veiled. The woman's wrapper skirt is a blue, commercially patterned cloth that is machine-embroidered on the body of the garment and along its side seam. She wears an embroidered blouse under an over-blouse of *aleshu* cloth. The woman also wears leather sandals and a silver and plastic necklace, and has a small, decorated leather wallet hanging on a cord around her neck [see 941, right].

Headwrap: length 93³/₈ in. (237 cm), width 28³/₈ in. (72 cm).

Over-blouse: length 17⁵/₈ in. (45 cm), width 47¹/₄ in. (120 cm).

Blouse: length 23⁷/₈ in. (60.5 cm), width 54³/₈ in. (138 cm).

Wrapper/skirt: length 143¹/₈ in. (363.5 cm), width 48³/₈ in. (123 cm).

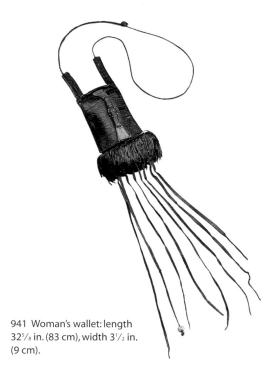

941 Woman's wallet: length 32⁵/₈ in. (83 cm), width 3¹/₂ in. (9 cm).

942 Two contrasting styles of Tuareg female apparel. The woman holding a child wears a typical embroidered blouse but uses a commercial "Dutch wax" print cloth for her skirt wrapper. Her friend is enshrouded in dark garments more typical of the rural Tuareg. Azel, Niger, 1988.

Tuareg female dress consists of a voluminous, somewhat cumbersome robe that resembles a Greek toga or a Hindu sari. This garment has several sections to it, all named, and each needs to be draped in a specific manner in response to a given social context. Many rural women still wear this long, dark clothing but their headcover is usually draped in a

more relaxed manner than the men's veil [942]. More recently, Tuareg cloths have been industrially manufactured. Although many women continue to wear a typical embroidered blouse [943], some wear a modern, industrially printed cloth as a hip wrapper. Urban Tuareg women particularly favor wrappers of printed "Dutch waxes."[9]

943 A young Tuareg woman wearing an embroidered blouse, along with a headscarf, loop earrings and a *tcherot* amulet. Agadez, Niger, 1980.

In contrast to the male aesthetic, Tuareg women's styles used to emphasize layering and bulk, reflecting the long-held positive value of fatness as a sign of feminine beauty. If a woman had the economic means, she would attempt to avoid physical exertion and consume large quantities of milk and meat in order to fatten herself. Increasingly, however, this aesthetic is changing [944]. As the Africanist Kristyne Loughran has pointed out, "Corpulence is no longer a sign of beauty among the younger generation because the models and actresses they see in foreign fashion magazines all have slender bodies."[10]

Many Tuareg, however, still find voluminous clothing not only to be more protective, given the Sahara's harsh climate, but also more beautiful. They value the billowing, flowing sleeves and robes that freely sway or fall over the shoulder since these motions are considered aesthetically appealing. The movement of the garments is also considered flirtatious; some contend that the more layers a woman drapes herself in the more men want to unveil.[11]

Tuareg men and women both wear open sandals [945, 946]. They also both wear jewelry. Unlike some northern Berber groups, Tuareg jewelry does not include large amber or coral beads [see 932]. Indeed,

944 Two fashionably slender young Tuareg women attired in their finest clothing and jewelry while attending a wedding dance. Agadez, Niger, 1988.

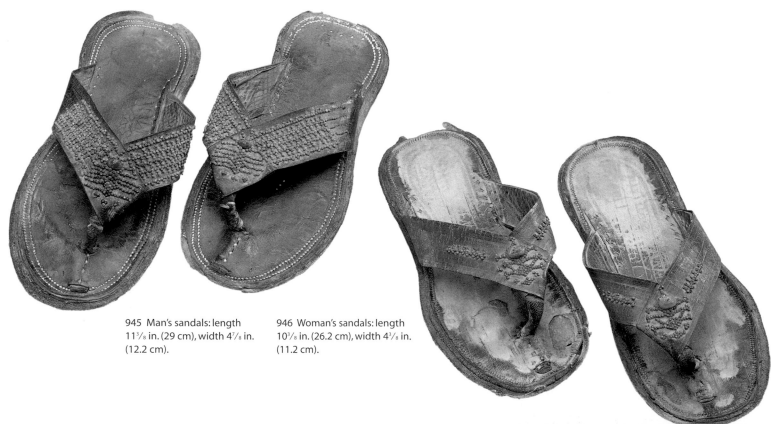

945 Man's sandals: length 11³/₈ in. (29 cm), width 4⁷/₈ in. (12.2 cm).

946 Woman's sandals: length 10³/₈ in. (26.2 cm), width 4³/₈ in. (11.2 cm).

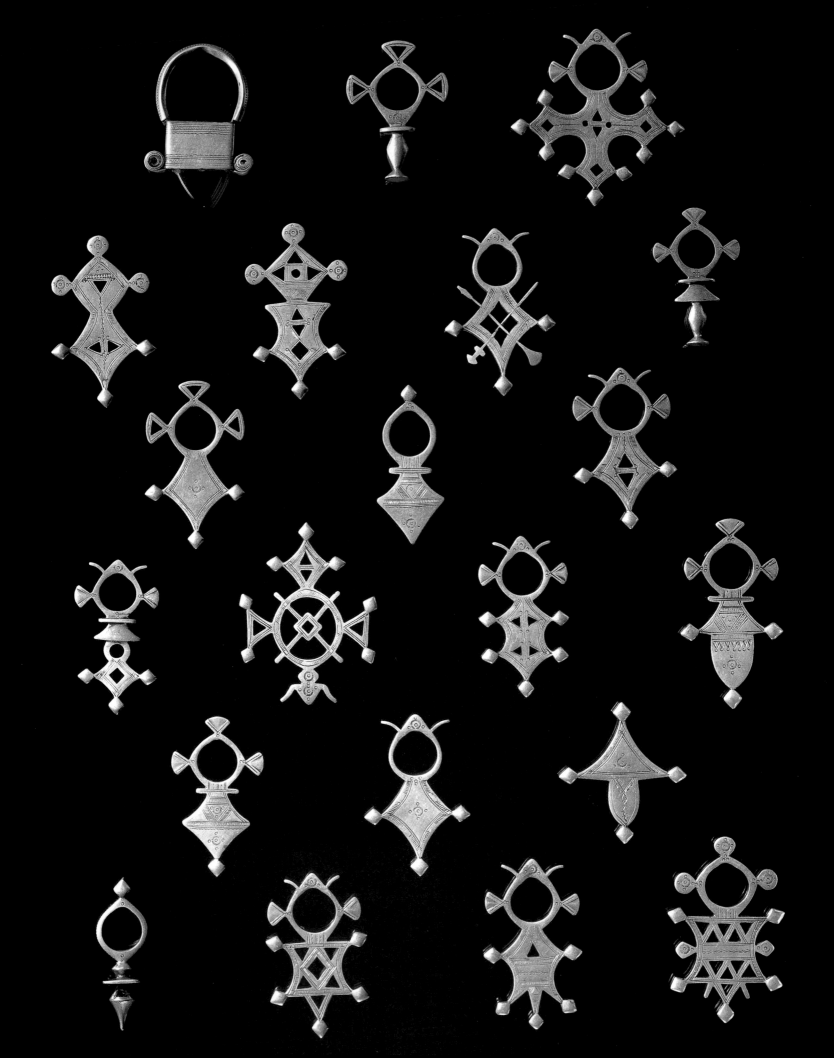

by comparison, Tuareg pieces are relatively sober and somewhat repetitive, with similar shapes and designs reappearing on a range of pieces [947]. Jewelry forms are forged or cast using the lost-wax process, then polished with sand and engraved, incised, or decorated with geometric motifs in repoussé. Producing jewelry is the work of the *inadan*. These silversmith artists are now to be found living and working in urban centers, but for centuries they lived among the Tuareg groups, passing their skills down the generations, and produced all Tuareg jewelry.

The classical Tuareg repertory [948–960] has remained remarkably stable over time, although alterations do occur to satisfy the demands of a younger clientele. Silver has long been preferred to gold, although this preference is beginning to change in the larger towns. The older jewelry was often made of coins, either Maria Theresa thalers or French francs, hence these earlier pieces are heavier than the jewelry made today. The Tuareg prefer silver jewelry crafted from the thaler coins, believing these pieces to be warmer and to reflect more light. Silver is appreciated for its luminosity as well as its ability to acquire a tactile quality and texture through the process of gaining a patina.

Men wear bracelets (often in pairs), rings (similar in form to the women's and worn daily) and amulets (hung about the neck or attached to the turban). Some Tuareg believe that their amulets—which display power and prestige as well as the desire to be protected—must be beautiful to be most effective.

Kristyne Loughran notes that women place silver ornaments "at the back of the head, at the temple, attached to the hair or braids, or sometimes in the middle of the forehead."[12] Female earrings are round loops, often so heavy they are worn around the ear, stabilized by the hair. These earrings not only emphasize the women's elegant hairstyles but some also sway when the women walk; like clothing, jewelry should move in order to adorn properly. In today's world, women are usually able to earn their own money and thus can buy their own jewelry which is then theirs to keep, or to dispose of at will. For Tuareg women, jewelry empowers.[13]

As the Tuareg expert Tom Seligman has pointed out, over the last half-century the combination of thirty years of drought plus the introduction of a cash economy have brought about drastic changes in Tuareg life. Many nobles have lost their herds and must now work

947 (opposite) Examples of each of the twenty-one "regional" Tuareg crosses, a display that demonstrates the Tuareg principle of rearranging a repertory of similar shapes in the creation of their jewelry.

948 Woman's necklace: length 8⅞ in. (22.5 cm), width 1⅛ in. (3 cm).

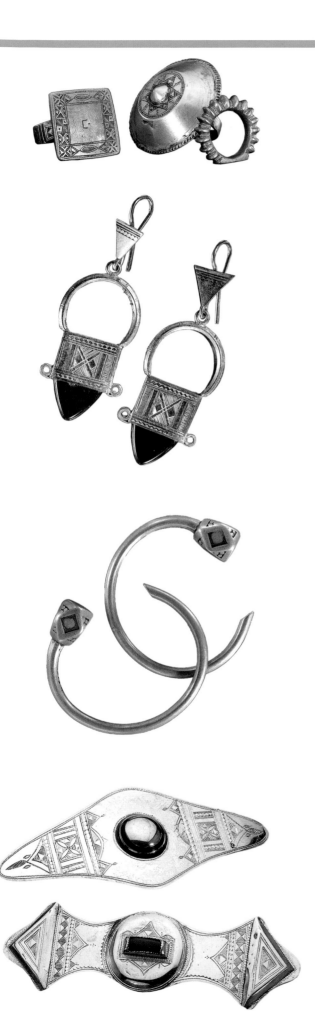

as security guards for wealthy Africans and Europeans. The former Tuareg vassals and enslaved peoples—theoretically freed by the French and, subsequently, North Africa's independent countries—have attained some formal education and now work in cities and large towns, as do the *inadan* who have continued making jewelry in urban areas, but now for both Tuareg and non-Tuareg alike. Teachers of the Koran are now running Islamic schools and producing protective amulets.[14]

Despite the changes wrought by modern times, however, the Tuareg ideal of freedom—to move across the Sahara at will, to master the desert, whether alone on a camel using only the stars as a guide or in a 4x4 vehicle with a global positioning system for navigation—is still to maintain independence in an increasingly interdependent world.

WITH NORTH AFRICA's Saharan Tuareg, this survey of the world's non-Western clothing has come full circle, concluding with a people whose culture is essentially that of the Near East, the area where both this book and Western civilization began.

Opposite, clockwise from top left:

949 A silver amulet, with a raised, engraved pattern, suspended from a fiber cord. Some amulets contain a Koranic inscription prepared by an Islamic religious leader. Niger, pre-1988. Length 20 in. (51 cm), width 3³/₈ in. (8.8 cm).

950 A silver amulet suspended on a plastic cord that is embellished with three rings and a plastic emblem. This beautifully crafted piece has attained a soft patina as a result of long being worn against the skin. Mali, pre-1988. Length 9⁵/₈ in. (24.7 cm), width 3¹/₂ in. (8.9 cm).

951 A woman's lightweight silver bracelet made from sheet silver and engraved with geometric designs. Niger, pre-1988. Diameter 3 in. (7.7 cm).

952 A silver bracelet consisting of a flat, circular band that closes with a hinge and is decorated with repoussé bosses and engraved lines. Niger, pre-1988. Diameter 2¹/₈ in. (5.5 cm).

953 Tuareg bracelets are often worn in pairs. These heavy, solid silver bracelets for women have end knobs pointed toward the side of the wrist. Niger, pre-1988. Length 2³/₈ in. (6 cm), width 2¹/₂ in. (6.5 cm), diameter ³/₄ in. (2 cm).

This page from top:

954 (top left) Silver ring. Mali, pre-1988. Height 1¹/₈ in. (3 cm), width 1 in. (2.7 cm), diameter ³/₄ in. (2 cm).

955 (top center) During weddings and festivals, women sometimes wear domed rings that rattle due to the little seeds set inside. Niger, pre-1988. Diameter 1⁷/₈ in. (4.5 cm).

956 (top right) Silver ring. Mali, pre-1988. Length ⁷/₈ in. (2.5 cm), width 1¹/₈ in. (3 cm).

957 A pair of women's earrings for pierced ears. These pieces have been hammered and then engraved; the stones may be agate. Niger, pre-1997. Length 2¹/₈ in. (5.5 cm), width ³/₄ in. (2 cm).

958 A pair of heavy silver earrings that can be worn through the earlobes but often have additional support from a string attached to the hair. This type of earring also can be worn wrapped around the back of the ear. Niger, pre-1988. Length 2³/₄ in. (7 cm), width 2⁵/₈ in. (6.8 cm).

959 A silver and ebony hair clip. Niger pre-1997. Height 1³/₈ in. (3.5 cm), width 4¹/₈ in. (10.7 cm).

960 A silver and glass hair clip. Niger, pre-1997. Height 1³/₈ in. (3.5 cm), width 4¹/₈ in. (10.7 cm).

NOTES

THE MIDDLE EAST

THE ANCIENT NEAR EAST

1. Balter 2000: 205–206.
2. Klein 1989: 170–171.
3. The Bible: Genesis 12: 4–5.
4. Roberts 1998, Vol. 1: 84.
5. Ibid.: 120.
6. Baines and Málek 1980: 30–49; Roberts 1998, Vol. 1: 104.
7. Barber 1994: 42–45.
8. Barber 1991: 12.
9. Ibid.: 33.
10. Barber 1994: 129.
11. Personal communication: Elizabeth Barber, May, 2001.
12. Barber 1994: 78–79, 83.
13. Barber 1991: 27.
14. Although there is Mesopotamian linguistic evidence in the form of terms for various items of clothing worn by commoners, e.g. belts, girdles, headbands, caps, headdresses, scarves, wigs, sandals, leggings, cloaks and burial shrouds (personal communication: Kathryn Keith, April, 2001), such garments were seldom recorded pictorially.
15. There is disagreement in the literature as to the material from which these shaggy garments were made. Roberts (1998, Vol. 1: 86) and Barber (1994: 133–134) refer to them as sheepskin skirts; Barber, however, also allows that the garments might have been made of a shaggy-weave textile. Hansen (1998: 46, 59) refers to the garment as a flounced or fleecy skirt or an apron with tassels. The Louvre Museum's label copy reads "fur skirt."
16. Boucher 1987: 34–36.
17. See Boucher 1987: 48–51 for several additional examples of medieval *kaunakés* cloth.
18. See Curtis and Reade 1995: 45, 46, 48, 67, 70, 72, 73, 76, 77, 79, 80 for depictions of Assyrian soldiers clad in short kilts.
19. Personal communication: Kathryn Keith, April, 2001.
20. Hall 1986: 9, 10. It is now evident that there was much more wool used both in domestic and funerary contexts than was previously realized. Wool was probably always worn for much-needed warm clothing, especially for cloaks.

21. Barber 1994: 135–136.
22. *The New Encyclopedia Britannica* 1992, Vol. 17: 479.
23. See Vogelsang-Eastwood 1993 for a detailed discussion of Egyptian clothing that has survived; she also discusses the range of garments worn on a daily basis.
24. *The New Encyclopedia Britannica* 1992, Vol. 17: 479–480; Hall 1986: 10.
25. Curtis and Reade 1995: 55.
26. *The New Encyclopedia Britannica* 1992, Vol. 17: 481.
27. Ibid.: 480.
28. Roberts 1998, Vol. 1: 87.
29. Vogelsang-Eastwood 1993: 169–178.
30. Personal communication: Elizabeth Barber, January, 2001.
31. Zettler and Horne 1998: 89–92.
32. Carter and Mace 1977: Plate LXXIX.
33. *The New Encyclopedia Britannica* 1992, Vol. 17: 508.
34. Curtis and Reade 1995: 171.
35. Lawler 2001: 42–43.
36. Boucher 1987: 98.
37. Barber 1991: 166.
38. Personal communication: Elizabeth Barber, May, 2001.
39. *The New Encyclopedia Britannica* 1992, Vol. 17: 524.
40. There is evidence that 2nd-millennium B.C. Assyrian women were already veiled. The practice goes as far back as the Assyrian law code enacted under Tiglath-Pileser I in the 1100s B.C. It reads in part: "The daughters of a lord whether it is with a shawl or a robe or a mantle must veil themselves…slaves, servants and harlots…must not [be veiled]" (Pritchard 1955: 183).

THE ARABIAN PENINSULA

1. On maps originating in Arab lands this body of water is listed as the Arabian Gulf. Henceforth the neutral term, "the Gulf," will appear.
2. The word "Arab" will be used throughout to refer to all people whose main language is Arabic.
3. Pritchard 1955: 279. In the 9th century B.C., Assyrians refer to camel troops from Arabia.
4. Early caravan trade also included textiles. Those from Yemen were particularly valued. Yemen was

involved in the Indian Ocean trade, an interaction that was reflected in the region's weavings. In the late Middle Ages it was famous for its *ikat* textiles.
5. The Five Pillars of Islam are: 1) Testimony (i.e. there is no god but God [Allah] and Muhammad is His Prophet); 2) Prayers; 3) Fasting; 4) Alms; 5) Pilgrimage to Mecca.
6. See Nicholas Clapp 2001 for a lively discussion of Yemen's ancient agriculture and the famous Marib Dam (its dramatic rupture brought havoc to the area) in a region that may have been the fabled land of the Queen of Sheba.
7. Abercrombie 1988: 648.
8. Ross 1994: 35.
9. Alireza 1987: 423.
10. Mauger 1993: 39–51.
11. The practice of veiling goes at least as far back as the Assyrian law code enacted under Tiglath-Pileser I in the 1100s B.C. It reads in part: "The daughters of a lord whether it is with a shawl or a robe or a mantle must veil themselves…slaves, servants and harlots…must not [be veiled]" (Pritchard 1955: 183). See also "The Ancient Near East," p. 41, note 40.
12. Mackey 1987: 154.
13. Campbell 1999: 85.
14. Keohane 1999: 149–150.
15. Mackey 1987: 225.
16. Ibid.: 154.

THE EASTERN MEDITERRANEAN

1. Abercrombie 1972: 37.
2. *The New Encyclopedia Britannica* 1992, Vol. 25: 407.
3. Stillman 1979: 11.
4. Ibid.: 45.
5. Weir 1989: 105.
6. Ibid.: 58.
7. Stillman 1979: 22.
8. Ibid.: 23–25.
9. Ibid.: 37.
10. Weir 1989: 54.
11. Stillman 1979: 38.
12. Weir 1989: 61.
13. Ibid.
14. Ibid.: 193–194.
15. Ibid.: 61, 63.
16. Seger 1981: 156.
17. Weir 1989: 272.

THE IRANIAN PLATEAU

1. The 1935 change of Persia's name to Iran was instigated by Reza Shah Pahlavi (1878–1944), the strong-willed army officer who rose through the ranks to become Shah of Iran from 1925 to 1941. Originally named Reza Khan, the Shah was from a family of the Pahlevan clan (*The New Encyclopedia Britannica* 1992, Vol. 10: 15). Pahlevi is also the name of the ancient Persian language spoken by the 3rd-century A.D. Sassanians (*Webster's Dictionary* 1990: 846). There were clearly several motives behind Reza Shah's choice of the term Pahlavi for his newly established dynasty.
2. The area of Pars is also referred to as Fars from whence comes the term Farsi, the name of the principal Indo-European language spoken in Iran today.
3. The Shiite constitute the smaller of the two major branches of Islam, the larger being the Sunni. In early Islamic history, the Shiah were a political faction that supported the authority of Ali—the son-in-law of the Prophet Muhammad—and his descendants to lead the Muslim world. Except for the two periods of the Fatimid (A.D. 909–1171) and Safavid (A.D. 1502–1736) imperial dynasties, Shiite communities were almost everywhere a minority until they gained ascendancy in Persia at the start of the 16th century.
4. The word *chador* defines both the outer wrap and the nomad's black, goat-hair tent. It has been suggested that this double meaning reflects women being at the central core of family honor (Allgrove 1976: 26).
5. Scarce 1981: 32.
6. When Reza Shah Pahlavi deposed and banished the Qashqai-friendly governor of Shiraz, the tribe lined the exiled governor's passage into the desert with hundreds of their magnificent rugs—a tradition said to have led to the English phrase "red carpet treatment" (Farmanian and Farmanian 1997: 142).
7. Yassavoli 2001: 180.

8. Scarce 1981: 36.
9. Allgrove 1976: 35–36.
10. Scarce 1981: 32–33.
11. Allgrove 1976: 36–37.
12. Ibid.: 36.
13. Ibid.
14. Allgrove 1976: 36.
15. Scarce 1981: 38.
16. Graves 1975: 7.
17. The rounded top of the Pahlavi crown and its distinctive side "flaps" also bear an interesting resemblance to the Qashqai felt hat, a similarity no doubt unrecognized by Reza Shah Pahlavi (personal communication: Irene Bierman, January, 2002).

EUROPE

1. Roberts 1996: 3, 7, 9.

PREHISTORIC EUROPE

1. Culotta et al 2001; Shute 2001; Morris 2000: 3–4.
2. It is still hotly debated whether some degree of interbreeding of *Homo neanderthalensis* and *Homo sapiens sapiens* occurred or if *H. neanderthalensis* was replaced by modern man.
3. Soffer et al 2000: 522–523.
4. Schuster and Carpenter 1986: 47.
5. The world's oldest known cave paintings—some date to more than 32,000 years ago—were discovered in 1994 on the walls of France's Grotte Chauvet. These impressive scenes display such sophisticated graphic techniques as shading and perspective. A more recent discovery—in September of 2000—is that of Cussac Cave in southern France's Dordogne Valley. Cussac contains human remains that date to between 22,000 and 28,000 years ago. "The engravings on the cave walls include fantasy animals with deformed heads and gaping mouths and a voluptuous nude female profile" (Balter 2001: 31).
6. Balter 1999: 922.
7. The same Upper Paleolithic cultural period—dating from 27,000 to 20,000 years ago—is referred to in the archaeological literature by two names: Pavlov, the Russian's term derived from an Eastern European site, and

Gravettian, the Western name drawn from a French site.

8. Adovasio 1996: 527.

9. Angier 1999: D2.

10. Soffer et al 2000: 528.

11. Ibid.: 514.

12. Ibid.: 517–518.

13. Ibid.: 518.

14. Barber 1999: 29–30.

15. Soffer et al 2000: 518.

16. Hald 1980: 59.

17. Soffer et al 2000: 519.

18. Angier 1999: D2.

19. Soffer et al 2000: 523.

20. Personal communication: Elizabeth Barber, July, 2002. Barber's subsequent work on the repeated association of string skirts with fertility in much later European cultures supports her position on the fundamental purpose of the prototypical Venus garments. (See also "The European Folk Tradition," pp. 114–116.)

21. Roberts 1998, Vol. 1: 44.

22. *The New Encyclopedia Britannica* 1992, Vol. 17: 478.

CLASSICAL EUROPE

1. Roberts 1998, Vol. 2: 84–85.

2. Diamond 1997: 93–103, 157–175, 176–191.

3. The invention of agriculture took place in the Near East at least 11,000 years ago, perhaps in northern Syria. The mainstays of European agriculture—wheat, barley, sheep and goats, as well as the earliest textile fiber, flax— all have wild ancestors in the Near East, but not in Europe. Subsequently, agriculture was also invented independently in China and Mexico (Kunzig 2002: 52–54).

4. Barber 1994: 110.

5. Ibid.: 113–114.

6. Tailored clothing initially appeared in the Upper Paleolithic when protective, cut-and-sewn fur garments were created so as to follow the lines of the body, totally encasing trunk and limbs.

7. Barber 1994: 110–113, 141–142.

8. The Myceneans' T-shaped garment had a silhouette similar to that of Old Kingdom Egypt's sleeved tunic but was conceived and constructed differently, perhaps originating in Semitic Syria.

9. The Mycenean clothing styles that later reappeared in southeastern Europe also included the Mycenean-type leather shoes with turned-up toes, still the traditional footwear in much of the Balkans (see Barber 1994: 144–145).

10. Barber 1994: 137.

11. Barber 1991: 197.

12. Goldman 1994: 213.

13. Bonfante 1975: 56–57.

14. Ridgway 1977: 56.

15. Tortora and Eubank 1994: 49.

16. Barber 1991: 372.

17. Ibid.: 31–33.

18. *The New Encyclopedia Britannica* 1992, Vol. 17: 511.

19. Bonfante 1975: 55.

20. Ibid.: 57.

21. Roberts 1998, Vol. 3: 6.

22. Ibid., Vol. 2: 178.

23. Goldman 1994: 217.

24. Ibid.: 233.

25. Ibid.

26. Ibid.: 235.

27. La Follette 1994: 55.

28. Barber 1994: 113, 115.

29. La Follette 1994: 55–56.

30. Stone 1994: 17.

31. Ibid.: 16.

32. Ibid.: 21.

33. Tortora and Eubank 1994: 68.

34. Gergel 1994: 191.

35. The 1350 B.C. slip-on prototype (see Barber 1991: 160–162) is richly decorated with embroidery—a Syrian rather than Egyptian technique— employed to create Syrian motifs, suggesting that the garment may well have originated in Syria. To this day, the country continues to be a thriving center for the production of cloth and clothing, with manufactured textiles regularly exported to many areas of the Middle East (see "The Eastern Mediterranean," pp. 55–57).

36. Tortora and Eubank 1994: 80–83.

37. Boucher 1987: 166.

38. See Barber 1999: 13–31.

THE EUROPEAN FOLK TRADITION

1. This discussion is restricted to the clothing of Europe's rural peoples; the attire of the urban affluent has already been extensively covered in other sources. For example, see François Boucher's 1967/1987 *20,000 Years of Western Fashion: The History of Costume and Personal Adornment* for a historical survey of upper-class European clothing.

2. See Snowden's 1979 *The Folk Dress of Europe* for detailed descriptions of a wide range of regional clothing.

3. Ibid.: 7.

4. Stack 1990: 5.

5. Paine 1990: 131.

6. The appearance of handprints on Upper Paleolithic cave walls demonstrates that images of hands were a part of the prehistoric iconographic corpus (see "Prehistoric Europe," p. 81).

7. Paine 1990: 148.

8. Ibid.

9. Ibid.: 151–152.

10. Schuster and Carpenter 1986, Vol. I: 1, 16, 47, 62.

11. Paine 1990: 80.

12. Kelly 1996: 31, 41.

13. Gimbutas 2001.

14. Paine 1990: 67.

15. Ibid.: 60.

16. Snowden (1979: 102–103) notes that although the end of the 18th century saw the development of regional styles almost everywhere throughout Europe, there apparently was little influence of the Romantic Age in Belgium, nor was there a strong folk-art tradition there. Certainly there was class distinction in dress but—as in England—there existed almost no distinction between geographic localities. What did exist was occupational dress mainly for urban workers.

17. The chemise was already in the Balkans by 1900 B.C.; the sleeve apparently is a Eurasian addition (personal communication: Elizabeth Barber, January, 2003).

18. Snowden 1979: 12.

19. Barber 1999: 13–20.

20. Ibid. Barber, following Russian scholars, suggests the hooked lozenge design may represent the female vulva. Paine (1999: 70) suggests the "sown field" design may represent the human act of giving birth, but Barber (1999: 16) shows that the oldest examples of the design (on Neolithic clay figurines of the Tripolye culture in Ukraine) are quite literally "sown fields," since the dots were formed by pressing grains of wheat into the clay between the "furrows." Presumably the symbolism is that the woman, like the field, has been sown with seed and now ensures the outcome.

21. Barber 1994: 139–141.

22. Drawing on both archaeological and linguistic data, Elizabeth Barber equates two distinct phases of early textile evolution with, first, the invention of the string skirt and, much later, the woven back-apron. Around 25,000 B.C., string itself had just been invented and hence was newly available for social as well as practical practices: the string skirt emerged. Late in the Neolithic, around 4000 B.C., weaving and woolen yarns had just been developed: the *panjóva* back-apron appeared.

23. Barber 1999: 21–27.

24. Personal communication: Elizabeth Barber, July, 2002.

25. Morgan 1992: 79–81.

26. I am grateful to Dr. John Pohl for his knowledgeable assistance in telescoping the evolution of the Scottish kilt into a succinct overview.

27. Anderson 1920: 16.

28. Trevor-Roper 1983: 19.

29. Saliklis 1999: 221.

CENTRAL ASIA

MONGOLIA

1. See Narantuya 2002: 23 for a detailed description of Mongolian felt-making, to which the picture caption on p. 126 is indebted. This illustration is a detail from a much larger work, which depicts all of the activities that might take place in the country within a single day. This huge painting hangs in the Zanabazar Museum of Fine Arts in the Mongolian capital, Ulaanbaatar.

2. The Russian word for the Central Asian felt tent is *yurt*; the Mongolians, understandably, prefer to use their own term, *ger*.

3. One notable exception to the predominance of felt in Mongolia is in the far north, where the nomadic Tsataan, the "reindeer people," rely on their reindeer herds to provide skins for clothing.

4. Burkett 1979: 20–21.

5. Mayhew 2001: 13–15, 16.

6. Genghis Khan left more than just bloodshed in his wake. A recent team of 23 international scientists have found a striking genetic similarity in the Y chromosome of 8% of the males throughout a large part of Asia. In other words, it is possible that some 16 million men living between Afghanistan and northeastern China— almost one in every 200 men now alive—belong to a single patrilineal lineage. According to Chris Tyler-Smith—a biochemist at Oxford University who published online a study of this research in the *American Journal of Human Genetics*, February, 2003—neither natural selection nor chance can account for the chromosome's high frequency. The researchers suggest that this particular version of the Y chromosome can be traced to a single man living in Central Asia about 1,000 years ago. Genghis Khan not only had numerous wives but also had access to other females; during his conquests the most beautiful women were reserved for the "Universal

Ruler." This may be a dramatic example of social history affecting genetic diversity (*Science*, Vol. 299, 2003: 1179).

7. Mayhew 2001: 17.

8. The USSR controlled Mongolia from 1924 to 1991. During that time, the Communists did their utmost to convert a nomadic society into an industrial one. Following the Soviet collapse, the age-old pattern of nomadic pastoralism increasingly has returned to the fore in newly independent Mongolia.

9. "Country Overview of Mongolia," The American Museum of Natural History, ca. 2002.

10. Harner and Harner 2000: 20.

11. The practice of shamanism is not entrusted solely to males; women can also serve as practitioners. Nor are shaman costumes always worn, although it is believed that dramatic attire aids in the healing process. Harner and Harner (op. cit.) also note: "Until the present century, shamanism was practiced on all inhabited continents by indigenous peoples, including by such widely separated peoples as the Sami (Lapps) of northernmost Europe, the aboriginal peoples of Australia, the Kung Bushmen of southern Africa and the Native North and South Americans."

12. Hansen 1994: 156.

13. Note that the 3,000-year-old mummy, Cherchen Man, who lived in Central Asia, was already wearing trousers ca. 1000–2000 B.C. (see "The Silk Road," p. 139 and Barber 1999: Plate I).

14. Vollmer (1977: 22–24) explains the rationale behind the herdsman's upper-body garment: "Whether long or short, the horseman's coat was designed for movement and a life outdoors. Closely fitting the upper body with long, tight sleeves and usually belted at the waist, the coat helped conserve body heat, while giving free arm movement for riding or for conducting military operations from horseback. The lower part of the coat was slashed or vented to prevent it from bunching at the waist when the rider was seated in the saddle. Long, tight sleeves prevented the wind from blowing up the arm and were often cut generously long so they could be pulled down to cover the hand. Flaring sleeve extensions, such as the characteristic Manchu

as a result of the tendency of families to send at least one son into a monastery, an effective form of birth control.

3. Farber 2003: 55. "It is possible for any family, regardless of social status, to become the home for a realized being and Dali [sic] Lamas have been born into both noble and peasant families. The traditional way of discovering a Dali Lama involves many complex factors. Dali Lamas and Panchen Lamas—the second highest-ranking Tibetan spiritual figure—have recognized each other's successors since the 17th century…once found, a [Dali Lama] candidate, [a tulka,] is extensively tested and expected to identify ritual objects belonging to his former incarnation."

4. Ibid.: 53.

5. Crossette 1995: xiii.

6. Personal communication: Sanjib Raj Mishra, Kathmandu, Nepal, October, 2004.

7. Wall text, Bhutan National Textile Museum.

8. Myers and Bean 1994: 106–112.

9. "The designs on the three panels of the dress should never match perfectly when the panels are stitched together. If they do, the weaver will die." Namgay Dema, a weaver from Phimsong, Tashigam Dzong Khag (Bhutan National Textile Museum).

SOUTHEAST ASIA
MAINLAND

1. In the 19th century, the various regions of Southeast Asia were known by the names of their European colonial masters (e.g. British Burma; French Indochina; Dutch Indonesia). It was not until the end of World War II and the emergence of the area's independent states that the term "Southeast Asia" came into common usage (Connors 1996: 6). A series of scholarly studies were subsequently undertaken of the diverse minority groups who have produced the handcrafted textiles depicted in this book (see Bibliography, p. 591).

2. Bray 2003: 425.

3. Barwise and White 2002: 23–28.

4. Gittinger and Lefferts, Jr. 1992: 18–19. "Shoulder cloths continue to be among the most valuable elements of [Mainland Southeast Asian] culture. They serve to cover the shoulders during wat or other ceremonies or as head cloths, carrying cloths, baby hammocks, bathing

cloths or as decorative textiles" (ibid.: 223).

5. Mainland West Malaysia is not included in this section because that geographically divided country is more closely allied to Indonesia—East Malaysia occupies a portion of the island of Borneo—hence is discussed in "Island Southeast Asia."

6. Gittinger and Lefferts 1992: 41.

7. Ibid.: 29–30.

8. Ibid.: 29–30, 34. It is interesting to note that in present-day Central and South America the equivalent of Southeast Asia's back-tension loom is known as a back-strap loom. Textile historian Mary Elizabeth King (1979: 365–373) has suggested that this simple New World weaving device may have originated in Southeast Asia and subsequently diffused to the Americas in prehispanic times, together with certain intriguingly similar resist-dyeing techniques.

9. Fraser-Lu 1994: 8–16, 252.

10. Ibid.: 254.

11. Ibid.: 257.

12. The rural poverty of Burma—as well as that of neighboring Laos—continues to spur the cultivation of poppies, as do the appetites of Western addicts. In retrospect it is clear that it was not the Burmese farmers on their own initiative who suddenly began to grow opium in commercial quantities; they received rigorous encouragement from the colonizing British. By the late 20th century Burma had become firmly woven into the fabric of the international drug trade, as one of the world's biggest exporters of illicit raw opium, producing over 2,000 tons each year (Gargan 2002: 139–140).

13. The present Laos government recognizes "47 [non-Laotian] ethnic groups but scholars insist that [within the country's borders] roughly 200 languages are spoken by roughly an equal number of ethnic peoples" (Gargan 2002: 124).

14. Connors 1996: 54.

15. Ibid.: 66–67.

16. The producing of the red and white krama was the only officially sanctioned weaving activity permitted during the repressive Pol Pot regime (Green 2004: 204).

17. Gargan 2002: 210; Green 2003: 193.

18. Green 2003: 186; Green 2004: 10.

19. "The phrase sampot chawng

kbun derives from sampot meaning a length of cloth for covering, chawng meaning to bind and kbun meaning a cover for the private parts" (Green 2004: 24).

20. The Vietnamese ao dai is similar to India's salwar kameez: both combine a tunic worn over pajama-like pants. In Vietnam the tunic is longer, and often tighter, and incorporates high slits up each side. Also, the ao dai is not accompanied by a harmonizing scarf, as is invariably the case with the salwar kameez as worn on the subcontinent (see "India," pp. 234–235).

21. Buckley 2002: 5.

22. The Peoples and Cultures of Cambodia, Laos and Vietnam 1981: 61.

23. The names of various Hmong groups—e.g. Flower Hmong, Black Hmong, White Hmong—have been differentiated according to various aspects of their traditional dress.

24. Barwise and White 2002: 211.

25. Ibid.: 156.

26. Ibid.: 156, 208, 210.

27. Gittinger and Lefferts, Jr. 1992: 9.

ISLAND

1. There were several groups of Spice Islands. In the 16th/17th centuries, cinnamon and pepper were produced primarily on Ceylon (present-day Sri Lanka) and Sumatra but also in India and Java. Cloves were grown on certain of the eastern Moluccas (Maluku) Islands—tiny volcanic specks of land that dot the sea just north of the equator, between Timor and New Guinea. Some 400 miles (645 km) to the south are a cluster of even smaller volcanic "specks," the five tiny Banda islands which at that time produced the world's supply of prime nutmeg and mace, two parts of the same fruit. After the arrival of the colonizing Dutch in 1621, the Bandanese, who had freely sold their spices to all visiting European and Asian merchants, suffered a brutal conquest as the Dutch determinedly set about monopolizing the spice trade. Thereafter these islands became a rigidly regulated Dutch horticultural preserve. Eventually nutmeg seedlings were smuggled out by the French and English; by the 18th century nutmeg exports from the Banda islands had dwindled to a trickle (Oey 1989: 261, 267).

2. Ibid.: 267.

3. The northern section of Borneo includes the Sultanate of Brunei, one of the world's last princely states.

4. Barwise and White 2002: 67.

5. Ibid.: 146.

6. Ibid.: 211, 251.

7. Oey 1989: 313–314.

8. Gittinger 1991: 13–49.

9. Ibid.: 79.

10. See Gittinger 1991: 84, 88–97 for information on ship cloths, which she regards as perhaps the most remarkable weavings ever created in the Indonesian archipelago.

11. "Java's great batiks were only possible when the textiles to be worked with the wax resist had a tight, smooth surface. Because locally woven textiles did not possess these properties, imported cottons had to be available before the development of the more intricate forms [of batik] could occur" (Gittinger 1991: 115).

12. For a detailed discussion and illustration of patola-Flores similarities, see Hamilton 1994: 32.

13. Gittinger 1991: 169.

14. Hamilton 1994: 100–103, 110.

15. Personal communication: Dr. Anne Summerfield, February 28, 2002.

16. Gittinger 1991: 214.

17. Ibid.: 218, 219.

18. Gavin 1996: 13.

19. Hamilton 1998: 15–17.

OCEANIA

1. Holmes 1993: 3.

OCEANIA

1. Until the 1990s it was believed that the Americas were originally peopled around 15,000 B.C., based on the dating of Clovis Points, early North American flint projectiles. Recently much earlier (but still controversial) dates of around 40,000 B.C. have come from the site of Meadowcroft, located in present-day Maryland, as well as dates of around 30,000+ B.C. from the Mesa Verde site located on the south coast of Chile.

2. Herter 1993: 18.

3. Bellwood 1997: 22.

4. Kirch 2002: 67–68.

5. Dates from two sites on the Indonesian island of Flores indicate that the early hominid Homo erectus was able to navigate open waters between 800,000 and 900,000 years ago. Flores could only be reached from the nearest island by crossing a strait that was 11.4

miles (18.3 km) wide, even at times of lowest sea level. Previously, the modern humans who colonized Australia were credited with the earliest sea crossing, 40,000 to 60,000 years ago (Rose 1998: 22).

6. In 1832 the French voyager Dumont d'Urville classified the Pacific islands into three geographic groups, their terms derived from the Greek: Melanesia, "dark islands;" Micronesia, "little islands;" and Polynesia, "many islands" (Kirch 2002: 4–5).

7. Kirch 2002: 87–98. The term Austronesian applies to the language family that developed in Taiwan—from original roots in southern China—about 5,500 B.C. and then spread into the Indonesian archipelago.

A short article that appeared in PLOS Biology 2005 3 (8): e281, a peer-reviewed journal of the Public Library of Science, further confirms an ancient connection between Taiwan and Polynesia. According to this study, the original settlers of the Polynesian islands were longtime residents of Taiwan, not migrants from China who used Taiwan as a staging point before traveling deeper into the Pacific Ocean. Researchers arrived at this conclusion as a result of studying the DNA of nine indigenous Taiwanese tribes and found they shared three specific genetic mutations with today's Polynesians. Those mutations, not seen in mainland Chinese, suggest the Taiwanese left China roughly 10,000 to 20,000 years before embarking for the Polynesian islands. The Han Chinese who dominate Taiwan today came to the island a mere 400 years ago.

8. Kirch 2002: 96.

9. Ibid.: 97–98. Whereas early 21st-century Oceanic research is based on environmental, demographic and economic data, together with the advantage of DNA evidence, scholars of 70 years ago approached such problems as the root cause of migration from the standpoint of accumulated folklore and myth, resulting in quite different and far more romantic explanations. Buck (1943: 212) is a case in point: "The primary motive for migration was defeat in war. After battle, the vanquished were hunted like game and consumed by the victorious warriors. A chance for life on the open sea

was preferable to almost certain death on shore. Although conquered people were sometimes spared through the influence of powerful relatives on the victorious side they remained in disgrace and servitude. No family with any pride could submit to such disgrace. In the course of time, it became established that honor was saved by migrating."

10. England's Captain James Cook (1728–1779), perhaps the greatest explorer in Europe's second age of global exploration, was the first to realize and document that a vast region of the Pacific was occupied by a single people sharing a common culture. As for accepting the idea of a Polynesian origin in Island Southeast Asia, Cook saw an obstacle: the proposed migration trail led through tropical latitudes and in the tropics easterly trade wings normally prevail. However, Cook learned from his Tahitian informant Tupaia that during the months of November–January the trades frequently die down to be replaced by spells of westerly winds. Drawing on his seaman's expertise, Cook concluded that the early voyagers had worked their way eastward from the Asian side of the Pacific by exploiting seasonal westerly-wind reversals to move from island to island, eventually settling all of Polynesia. Ironically, Cook died in the Polynesia he had so accurately mapped and deciphered. In his years of Pacific exploration, "he had peacefully changed the map of the world more than any other single man in history" (*The New Encyclopedia Britannica* 1992, Vol. 3: 595).

11. Fabri Blacklock, "Aboriginal Skin Cloaks," in *Essays about Quilts* [n.d.], http://amol.org.au/nqr/fabri.htm.

12. Brooks 2003: 62.

13. Blacklock, op. cit. See also *Traditional Aboriginal Art Symbols* [n.d.], www.aboriginalartonline.com: "Through the use of ancestrally inherited designs, artists continue their connections to country and The Dreaming…. In central Australia inherited designs are painted onto the face and body using ochres ground to a paste with water and applied in stripes or circles. The modern paintings of the Central and Western Desert are based on these designs."

14. Herter (1993: 23) suggests that in New Guinea each steep valley between each high mountain ridge provided a more formidable barrier to communication than did the stretches of empty ocean that lay between Polynesia's widely dispersed but culturally homogenous islands where everyone spoke closely related dialects of Austronesian.

The Austronesian language family is the most widely dispersed in the world (Kirch 2002: 91).

15. Buck 1943. Sir Peter H. Buck (Te Rangi Hiroa: 1880–1951) was the son of a New Zealand Maori mother and an Irish father. For the last 15 years of his distinguished medical and anthropological career, he served as director of the Bernice Pauahi Bishop Museum in Honolulu, a treasure house of Oceanic art, artifacts, original contact documents and scholarly tomes relating to the Pacific.

16. Sowell 2000: 19.

17. Holmes 1993: 4.

18. Buck 1943: 95–96.

19. Kirch 2002: 232–233.

20. Buck (1943: 59, 250–252) contends that the Polynesians were not the first to discover the Hawaiian Islands: the Menehuene—the legendary "Little People"—arrived before them. Buck identifies these supposedly mythical "dwarfs" as real flesh-and-blood people, the smaller-boned, darker-skinned Micronesians [see 513] who could have sailed from the Gilbert Islands [see Map 24] to make a new home in the Hawaiian archipelago. Tales of these magical little people, the Menehuene, are also found in Samoa and the Society Islands.

21. Among the natural aids assisting early Polynesian navigators was what is called a "star compass:" points on the horizon marked by the rising and setting of certain stars. When the early group of voyagers sailed north from the Marquesas they found that, after crossing the equator, the Southern Cross—the constellation which marked several southerly points for a navigator—became increasingly less visible. In steering north the navigator had not only left his world behind, he sailed out of his *universe*, outstripping all accumulated references.

Herter (1993: 33) relates the traditional tale of how that initial long, exhausting voyage into the all-but-empty North Pacific was saved by a sea bird that stopped briefly on the canoe's mast and then flew away northward. The Marquesans quickly trimmed their sails and followed. Soon an enormous, island-marking cumulus cloud appeared on the horizon. Beyond there slowly rose the tallest island in the Pacific, the Earth's largest shield volcano—the 14,000-foot-high (4,265 m) Mauna Kea—located on the Big Island of Hawaii. The intrepid southern voyagers had discovered the world's most remote archipelago, located some 2,400 miles (3,860 km) north of the Marquesas, one of the greatest feats in the history of exploration.

22. Any of several Asian and Pacific trees or shrubs (genus *coryline*) of the lily family with leaves in terminal tufts (*Webster's Dictionary* 1990: 1232).

23. Buck 1957: 215.

24. Ibid.: 215–217, 230.

25. Ibid.: 230.

26. The time of year to sail southwest from Tahiti to New Zealand was in the lunar month of November/December; the Polynesians' sailing instructions: a little to the left of the setting sun (Buck 1943: 269).

27. The European "discoverer" of New Zealand was the Dutchman Abel Tasman in 1642. Because the Maori were very warlike, and the landscape did not seem all that enticing, the Dutch did not land. New Zealand was subsequently named in 1648 by Joan Blaeu, the official cartographer for the Dutch chartered East India Company (McEvedy 1998: 48–49).

28. The sweet potato plant *Ipomoea batatas* was known to the Polynesians before they ever began their round of discoveries; they were also familiar with the plant's original South American Andean name, *kumara* (McEvedy 1998: 17n; Kirch 2002: 241).

The tuberous root was "pre-adapted" to a temperate climate because of its Andean derivation. In those areas of New Zealand where horticulture was feasible, the sweet potato became the principal basis for the Maori economy (Kirch 2002: 273, 280).

29. Lacking much of their familiar food, the Maori initially

subsisted in part on New Zealand's indigenous creatures, animals with no sense of predation. Flightless birds were particularly vulnerable, resulting in many extinctions, including the moa, *Dinornis giganteus*, New Zealand's equivalent of the ostrich (McEvedy 1998: 24; Kirch 2002: 278).

30. Buck 1943: 276. Finger weaving—or downward weaving, as it is sometimes called—is the process by which the change of the weaving shed occurs with each individual crossing of a weft thread over a warp thread (Mead 1968: 9).

31. *Maori Textiles in the Collection of the UCLA Fowler Museum of Cultural History* [n.d.].

32. Ibid.

33. The *piupiu* skirt emerged as a distinctive class of apparel in New Zealand as European clothes replaced Maori everyday dress and an emphasis was placed on developing unique costumes for Maori ceremonies. *Piupiu* are made of cylindrical strands of dried flax, each scraped and dyed at intervals so that the whole forms an overall pattern (Mead 1968: 11).

NORTH AMERICA

1. Even today there are certain superficial similarities between Mongolians and Native Americans—facial features; the teepees of the Tsataan reindeer herders of the far north; the practice of shamanism (Bradley Mayhew, *Mongolia*, Melbourne, Oakland, London and Paris, 2001: 13).

2. Mann 2005: 151–192.

3. The schematic map of western North America on p. 333 and accompanying text are based on Tom Bahti's *Southwestern Indian Tribes*, Flagstaff, K. C. Publications, 1968: 30. The text is also indebted to Donald R. Morris, "The Peopling of the New World," in Newsletter Vol. X, No. 50, Houston, Trident Syndicate, 1998, and Mann 2005: 151–192.

THE ARCTIC

1. Today there are more Eskimos living in Anchorage than in the rural areas. Their total population has grown to over 100,000 and their way of life has changed dramatically as they have become increasingly involved in modern Western culture (personal communication: Molly Lee,

University of Alaska Museum, November, 1999).

2. Graburn and Lee 1990: 23.

3. Schweitzer and Lee 1997: 31.

4. Weyer 1962: 3; Schweitzer and Lee 1997: 39.

5. Dubin 1999: 63; Fitzhugh and Crowell 1988: 13.

6. Dubin 1999: 87.

7. Kahlenberg 1998: 240.

8. In 1778 Captain Cook dubbed these sunshades "snouted" visors (Maxwell 1978: 389).

9. Paterek 1994: 388.

10. Ibid.: 387, 409, 419.

11. Maxwell 1978: 363.

12. Paterek 1994: 385.

13. Ibid.: 405.

14. Fitzhugh and Crowell 1988: 227.

15. Schweitzer and Lee 1997: 44.

16. Weyer 1962: 307.

17. Paterek 1994: 386.

18. Fitzhugh and Crowell 1988: 224.

19. Paterek 1994: 429.

THE NORTHWEST COAST

1. Paterek 1994: 293.

2. Dubin 1999: 383.

3. Ibid.: 403.

4. Paterek 1994: 294.

5. Joseph 1998: 26–27.

6. Penney 2004: 134.

7. Dubin 1999: 410.

8. Ibid.: 398, 409.

9. Ibid.: 410.

10. Joseph 1998: 29–30; personal communication: Aldona Jonaitis, December, 1999.

THE WOODLANDS

1. Longfellow 1911: 9.

2. The term "Iroquois" apparently grew out of the French interpretation of the Algonquin word *Irinakhoiw*, "real adders" (*Webster's Dictionary* 1980: 606).

3. Personal communication: Dr. John Pohl, Consultant, Cherokee Homelands Museum, June, 1999.

4. Lurie and Anderson 1998: 6.

5. Personal communication: Dr. Duane King, December, 1999.

6. Dubin 1999: 164.

7. Paterek 1994: 44.

8. Ibid.

9. Dubin 1999: 151.

10. Paterek 1994: 7.

11. Personal communication: Dr. Duane King, December, 1999.

12. Johnson and Hook 1990: 43.

13. Dubin 1999: 164.

14. Paterek 1994: 8.

15. Dubin 1999: 227.

16. Ibid.: 164.

THE PLAINS

1. Chang 1986: 421.

2. Dubin 1999: 238.

3. Ibid.: 278.

4. Ibid.: 246.

5. Paterek 1994: 469.

fiber to the same length as the end on the other side of the weft element. This results in an even tuft of fibers held in the middle without a knot by the tightness of the weave. Work on one high-quality velvet may last a year or more. One part of the work produced by the Shoowa has polychromy in its continuous embroidery and cut-pile surfaces. The embroidered line, usually with lines on either side of it (the number of these lines may fluctuate).... [The fiber] may be colored: there are ranges of reds, yellows, blues, violets and, more rarely, greens. Vegetable dyes are used, except in the case of green (copper oxide) and colors of European origin from the 1920s onward.... Areas of the dyed base left uncovered by cut-pile may enter into the composition as a tonality within the relationships of values and colors..." (Meurant 1986: 137).

22. Gillow 2003: 196.
23. Darish 1989: 130–131, 136.
24. Ibid.: 135.
25. Ibid.: 135–138.
26. The 1980s were a critical period in the production of Kuba textiles. It was then that the focus shifted from cloth made primarily for internal consumption to one aimed solely at export. This change had several dramatic effects: at some funerals, textiles were taken from the body and returned to the family storehouse in lieu of being buried with the deceased; in other cases, graves were robbed in order to sell the funerary textiles to the West. Also, this new market orientation resulted not only in a change from an exclusively woman's craft to one that now included boys and young men—embroidering textiles for the first time—but also a shift from a part-time activity to a full-time occupation (Darish 1996: 65). As a result of these changes, the Kuba kingdom is no longer the sole source of the famous, and increasingly lucrative, cut-pile raffia panels. These cloths are now also being produced—in a somewhat different "Kuba manner"—from adjacent areas, as well as from as far away as Johannesburg in South Africa (personal communication: Dr. Patricia Darish, February, 2006).
27. Darish 1989: 137.

WEST AFRICA

1. As a heritage of West Africa's European colonization, French is the official language of communication in most nations to the north and west—Senegal, Guinea, Côte d'Ivoire, Mali, Niger—whereas English is officially spoken further to the southeast, in such countries as Ghana and Nigeria. In everyday life, however, the Yoruba speak Yoruba, the Hausa speak Hausa, etc.
2. Mabogunje 1976: 15.
3. When trade in human beings proved more profitable than other cargos, traders began to export the more lucrative product. Most of the enslaved Africans sent to the Americas were captured in and shipped out of West Africa.
4. Heritage 1999: 122.
5. During the reign of the Asante king Osei Tutu (A.D. 1700–1730), a priest delivered a solid gold stool from the heavens that landed gently on the king's knees. This stool was said to house the soul and spirit of the Asante nation. The golden stool was never used as a seat; to this day it rests on its own chair (Ross 1998: 31).
6. Mabogunje 1976: 24–25; Ross 1998: 20, 31–33.
7. Ross 1998: 78, 152.
8. Ibid.: 46–47.
9. Eicher 1976: 1.
10. Mabogunje 1976: 23; Drewel 1989: 13. One of the effects of the 18th- and 19th-century slave trade was the dispersal of millions of Yoruba peoples over the globe, primarily to the Americas—Haiti, Cuba, Trinidad, Brazil—where their late arrival and enormous numbers infused a strong Yoruba character into the artistic, religious, and social lives of Africans in the New World.
11. Jenny Balfour-Paul, an authority on indigo, provides a summary of the dye's worldwide importance. "It is only during the twentieth century that synthetic dyestuffs, invented in the second half of the previous century, became widely available. Before that, for well over four millennia, all dyestuffs were made from natural ingredients found mostly in the plant kingdom, with the exception of the important red insect dyes (kermes, cochineal, and lac), some metallic oxides, and the renowned shellfish purple dye.... Indigo and its close relation shellfish purple

are chemically in a class apart. They form the extraordinary 'indigoid' group, whose production methods are so intriguing that they still tantalize today's organic chemists. The word indigo refers to the blue coloring matter extracted from the leaves of various plants including woad.... The reason for distinguishing between indigo and woad is that traditional processing of woad leaves produces a low indigo yield suitable for dyeing absorbent wool fibers, whereas the foreign indigo plants yield much higher concentrations which are ideal for dyeing the less absorbent vegetable fibers such as cotton and flax. But chemically speaking all produce the same indigo blue. No other dyestuff has been valued by mankind so widely and for so long. One of the world's oldest dyes, it remains the last natural dye used in places that have embraced synthetic dyes for every other color.... Finding that nature could produce a colorfast blue dyestuff [that did not need a mordant] by a process akin to alchemy must have been an extraordinary revelation, whose impact is hard to imagine in today's multi-colored world" (Balfour-Paul 1998: 2, 4).
12. As well as *Indigofera tinctoria*, the varieties of wild indigo that grow throughout Nigeria include *Indigofera arrecta, Indigofera sufficotosa* and *Lonchocarpus cyanescens* (Eicher 1976: 27–28).
13. Eicher 1976: 65. For *adire* pattern names, see Borgatti 1983: 31, 32, 33, 59–60.
14. Northern Nigeria's long tradition of an exchange of beliefs, news and trade goods is in marked contrast to the isolation of the East African nomads who, until recently, wandered with their cattle relatively undisturbed by the outside world (see "East Africa," pp. 514–525).
15. Today the word Hausa is mainly of linguistic significance, denoting all those peoples of the Western and Central Sudan who speak the Hausa language as their mother tongue (Mabogunje 1976: 20).
16. The seven Hausa states were Kano, Katsina (the core of 14th-century Hausaland [Adeleye 1976: 556–559]), Rano, Zaria, Gobir, Daura and Biram.
17. Adeleye 1976: 578–579, 601.

18. Perani and Wolff 1992: 70–71.
19. Picton and Mack 1979: 189.
20. Eicher 1976: 83–85, 87.
21. In the mid-19th century the Hausa city of Kano was famous for its large number of dye-pits, estimated at some 2,000. The Hausa dug their round holes directly into the earth and then lined these pits with the type of cement traditionally used in building (Picton and Mack 1979: 40, 147).
22. Picton and Mack 1979: 147. No Hausa man may wear a turban until he has made a pilgrimage to Mecca, a journey all Muslims are expected to make in their lifetime (Perani and Wolff 1992: 76).
23. Beckwith and van Offelen 1983: 17.
24. Ibid.: 180–223.
25. Eicher 1976: 47.
26. For Akwete pattern names, see Borgatti 1983: 54.
27. The anthropologist Lisa Aronson, who lived among the Akwete for a year and a half in the mid-1970s, discovered—after returning home—that her careful study and recording of the Akwete weaving tradition was misunderstood by the weavers, who assumed she was trying to steal their secrets. As Aronson plaintively notes, she could just barely lift the heavy beater stick and insert it into the shed let alone hope to actually learn to weave a complex Akwete cloth (Aronson 1982: 66).
28. For *pelete bite* pattern names, see Borgatti 1983: 56–57.
29. Eicher, Erekosima and Thieme 1982: 4.

NORTH AFRICA

1. Heritage 1999: 130; Seligman 2006: 28.
2. Heritage 1999: 128.
3. Picton and Mack 1979: 23–27, 62–67.
4. Ibid.: 65.
5. Fisher 1984: 229–231.
6. Ehret 2002: 226.
7. Seligman 2006: 22.
8. Ibid.: 25–27.
9. Rasmussen 2006: 144, 148.
10. Loughran 2006: 188; Rasmussen 2006: 149.
11. Rasmussen 2006: 148.
12. Loughran 2006: 169, 175, 184–185, 189–190.
13. Ibid.: 189–190.
14. Seligman 2006: 27.

BIBLIOGRAPHY

GENERAL REFERENCE

Barber, Elizabeth W. *Women's Work: The First 20,000 Years; Women, Cloth and Society in Early Times.* New York and London: W. W. Norton, 1994.

Boucher, François. *20,000 Years of Fashion: The History of Costume and Personal Adornment.* New York: Harry N. Abrams, 1987.

Bruhn, Wolfgang, and Max Tilke. *A Pictorial History of Costume: A Survey of Costume of all Periods and Peoples from Antiquity to Modern Times including National Costume in Europe and Non-European Countries.* New York: Frederick A. Praeger, 1955.

The New Encyclopedia Britannica. Chicago: University of Chicago, 1992, 2005.

Heritage, Andrew, editor-in-chief, *World Atlas Millennium Edition.* London: Dorling Kindersley, 1999.

Racinet, Albert. *The Historical Encyclopedia of Costumes.* New York: Facts on File, 1997.

Roberts, J. M. *The Illustrated History of the World,* 10 volumes. Alexandria, Va.: Time-Life Books, 1998.

Tortora, Phyllis, and Keith Eubank. *Survey of Historic Costume.* New York: Fairchild, 1994.

Webster's New Collegiate Dictionary. Springfield, Mass.: Merriam-Webster, 1973, 1980, 1983, 1990.

THE MIDDLE EAST

THE ANCIENT NEAR EAST

Baines, John, and Jaromír Málek. *Atlas of Ancient Egypt.* New York: Facts on File, 1980.

Balter, Michael. "Dredging at Israeli Site Prompts Mudslinging." In *Science,* Vol. 287, 2000: 205–206.

Barber, Elizabeth J. W. *Prehistoric Textiles: The Development of Cloth in the Neolithic and Bronze Ages with Special Reference to the Aegean.* Princeton: Princeton University Press, 1991.

Carter, Howard, and A. C. Mace. *The Discovery of the Tomb of Tutankhamen.* New York: Dover Publications, 1977.

Curtis, J. E., and J. E. Reade, eds. *Art and Empire: Treasures from Assyria in the British Museum.* New York: Metropolitan Museum of Art, 1995.

Flaherty, Thomas H., editor-in-chief. *Time Frame: The Enterprise of War.* Alexandria, Va.: Time-Life Books, 1991.

Freed, Rita E., and Yvonne J. Markowitz. *Pharaohs of the Sun: Akhenaten, Nefertiti, Tutankhamen.* Boston: Museum of Fine Arts and New York: Bulfinch Press/Little, Brown and Co., 1999.

Hall, Rosalind. *Egyptian Textiles.* Aylesbury: Shire Publications, 1986.

Hansen, Donald P. "Art of the Royal Tombs of Ur: A Brief Interpretation." In Zettler and Horne, eds., op. cit., 43–72.

James, T. G. H. *Tutankhamen.* Milan: Friedman/Fairfax, 2000.

Klein, Richard G. *The Human Career: Human Biological and Cultural Origins.* Chicago: University of Chicago Press, 1989.

Lawler, Andrew. "Banished Assyrian Gold to Reemerge from Vault." In *Science,* Vol. 293, No. 5527, 2001: 42–43.

Pittman, Holly. "Cylinder Seals." In Zettler and Horne, eds., op. cit., 75–84.

Pritchard, James B., ed. *Ancient Near Eastern Texts Relating the Old Testament.* Princeton: Princeton University Press, 1955.

Vogelsang-Eastwood, G. M. *Tutankhamun's Wardrobe.* Rotterdam: Barjesteh van Waalwijk van Doorn & Co's. Uitgeversmaatschappij, 1999.

Vogelsang-Eastwood, Gillian. *Pharaonic Egyptian Clothing.* Leiden, New York and Cologne: E. J. Brill, 1993.

Zettler, Richard L., and Lee Horne, eds. *Treasures from the Royal Tombs of Ur.* Philadelphia: University of Pennsylvania Museum of Archaeology and Anthropology, 1998.

THE ARABIAN PENINSULA

Abercrombie, Thomas J. "Beyond the Veil of Troubled Yemen." In *National Geographic* 125 (3) (1964): 402–445.

———. "Arabia's Frankincense Trail." In *National Geographic* 168 (4) (1985): 474–513.

———. "The Persian Gulf: Living in Harm's Way." In *National*

Geographic 173 (5) (1988): 648–671.

Alireza, Marianne. "Women of Saudi Arabia." In *National Geographic* 172 (4) (1987): 423–453.

Aramco World, Vol. 50, No. 1. Dhahran: Saudi Arabian Oil Company, Jan/Feb 1999.

Brooks, Geraldine. *Nine Parts of Desire: The Hidden World of Islamic Women.* New York: Anchor Books, Doubleday, 1995.

Campbell, Kay Hardy. "Days of Song and Dance." In *Aramco World,* Saudi Arabia, Jan/Feb 1999: 78–87.

Clapp, Nicholas. *Sheba: Through the Desert in Search of the Legendary Queen.* Boston and New York: Houghton Mifflin Co., 2001.

Hill, Ann, Daryl Hill and Norma Ashworth. *The Sultanate of Oman: A Heritage.* London and New York: Longman, 1977.

Housman, Laurence. *Stories from The Arabian Nights.* New York: Charles Scribner's Sons, 1907.

Keohane, Alan. *Bedouin: Nomads of the Desert.* London: Kyle Cathie, 1999.

Mackey, Sandra. *The Saudis: Inside the Desert Kingdom.* Boston: Houghton Mifflin Co., 1987 (paperback London: Signet, Penguin Group, 1990).

———. *Passion and Politics: The Turbulent World of the Arabs.* New York: Plume, Penguin Books, USA, 1992.

The March of Islam: Timeframe A.D. *600–800.* Alexandria, Va.: Time-Life Books, 1988.

Mauger, Thierry. *Undiscovered Asir.* London: Stacey International, 1993.

Peyton, W. D. *Old Oman.* London: Stacey International, 1983.

Pritchard, James B., ed. *Ancient Near Eastern Texts Relating the Old Testament.* Princeton: Princeton University Press, 1955.

Ross, Heather Colyear. *The Art of Arabian Costume: A Saudi Arabian Profile.* Studio City, Calif.: Empire Publishing Service/Players Press, 1994.

Saudi Gazette. *Janadriya: 16th National Heritage and Folk Culture Festival,* Al Watania Consolidation Distribution Company, January 17, 2001.

Trench, Richard. *Arabian Travellers.* Topsfield, Mass.: Salem House, 1986.

THE EASTERN MEDITERRANEAN

Abercrombie, Thomas J. "The Sword and the Sermon." In *National Geographic,* July, 1972: 3–43.

Atil, Esin. *The Age of Sultan Süleyman the Magnificent.* New York: Harry N. Abrams, 1987.

Chico, Beverly. "Gender Headwear Tradition in Judaism and Islam." In *Dress: The Annual Journal of the Costume Society of America,* Vol. 27 (2000): 18–36.

Ettinghausen, Richard. *Treasures of Asia: Arab Painting.* Cleveland: Editions d'Art Albert Skira, The World Publishing Co., 1962.

Landau, Jacob M. *Abdul-Hamid's Palestine.* London: André Deutsch, 1979.

Seger, Karen, ed. *Portrait of a Palestinian Village: The Photographs of Hilma Granqvist.* London: The Third World Center for Research and Publishing, 1981.

Siver-Brody, Vivienne. *Documentors of the Dream: Pioneer Jewish Photographers in the Land of Israel 1890–1933.* Jerusalem: Magnes Press, Hebrew University, 1998.

Stillman, Yedida Kafon. *Palestinian Costume and Jewelry.* Albuquerque: University of New Mexico Press, 1979.

Tuglaci, Pars. *The Ottoman Palace Women.* Istanbul: Cem Yayinevi, 1985.

Weir, Shelagh. *Palestinian Costume.* Austin: University of Texas Press, 1989.

THE IRANIAN PLATEAU

Allgrove, Joan. *The Qashqai of Iran.* World of Islam Festival, 1976. Manchester: Whitworth Art Gallery, University of Manchester, 1976.

Beck, Lois. *The Qashqai of Iran.* New Haven and London: Yale University Press, 1986.

Farmanian, Manucher, and Roxanne Farmanian. *Blood and Oil: Inside the Shah's Iran.* New York: World Library, 1997.

Graves, William. "Iran: Desert Miracle." In *National Geographic* 147 (1): 2–47.

Guide for Treasury of National Jewels. Tehran: Central Bank of the Islamic Republic of Iran, 1999.

O'Donnell, Terence. "Twenty-Five Centuries of Persia." In *Horizon,* Vol. 5, No. 3 (1963): 40–72.

Scarce, Jennifer M. *Middle Eastern Costume from Tribes and Cities of Iran and Turkey.* Edinburgh: Royal Scottish Museum, 1981.

Yassavoli, Javad. *The Fabulous Land of Iran: Colorful and Vigorous Folklore.* Tehran: Yassavoli Productions, 2001.

EUROPE

PREHISTORIC EUROPE

Adovasio, J. M., O. Soffer, and B. Klima. "Paleolithic Fiber Technology: Data from Pavlov I, ca. 26,000 B. P.," in *Antiquity,* 70, 1996: 526–34.

Angier, Natalie. "Furs for Evening but Cloth was the Stone Age Standby." In *The New York Times,* December 14, 1999: D1–D2.

Balter, Michael. "New Light on the Oldest Art." In *Science,* Vol. 283, 1999: 920–922.

———. "Stone Age Artists—or Art Lovers—Unmasked?" In *Science,* Vol. 294, 2001: 31.

Barber, Elizabeth J. W. *Prehistoric Textiles: The Development of Cloth in the Neolithic and Bronze Ages with Special Reference to the Aegean.* Princeton: Princeton University Press, 1991.

———. "On the Antiquity of East European Bridal Clothing." In *Folk Dress in Europe and Anatolia: Beliefs About Protection and Fertility,* ed. Linda Welters, 13–32. Oxford and New York: Berg, 1999.

Culotta, Elizabeth, Andrew Sugden, Brooks Hanson, S. H. Ambrose, Michael Balter, R. L. Cann, Ann Gibbons, Elliot Marshal, M. P. H. Stumpf and D. B. Goldstein. "Human Evolution: Migrations." In *Science,* Vol. 291, 2001: 1721–1753.

Hald, Margrethe, "Ancient Danish Textiles from Bogs and Burials: A Comparative Study of Costume and Iron Age Textiles" (trans. Jean Olsen). Archaeological-historical series; Vol. 21. National

96–110. London: Journal of the Costume Society, 1991.

Prochaska, Rita. *Taquile: Weavers of a Magic World*. Lima: Arius S. A., 1988.

Rowe, Ann Pollard, ed. *Costume and Identity in Highland Ecuador*. Washington, D.C.: The Textile Museum and Seattle and London: University of Washington Press, 1998.

——. "Conclusions." In Rowe., ed., op. cit., 280–281.

Rowe, Ann Pollard and Lynn A. Meisch. "Ecuadorian Textile Technology." In Rowe., ed., op. cit., 16–38.

Weismantel, Mary J. "Cotopaxi Province." In Rowe., ed., op. cit., 110–116.

Zorn, Elayne. "Encircling Meaning: Economics and Aesthetics in Taquile, Peru." In *Andean Aesthetics: Textiles of Peru and Bolivia*, ed. Blenda Femenias, 67–79. Madison: Elvehjem Museum of Art, University of Wisconsin, 1987.

AMAZONIA

Braun, Barbara, ed. *Arts of the Amazon*. New York: Thames & Hudson, 1995.

Carneiro, Robert L. "Indians of the Amazonian Forest." In *People of the Tropical Rain Forest*, ed. Julie Sloan Denslow and Christine Padoch, 73–86. Berkeley and Los Angeles: University of California Press, 1988.

Castañeda León, Luisa. *Vestido Tradicional del Peru: Traditional Dress of Peru*. Lima: Museo Nacional de la Cultura Peruana, 1981.

Delgado, Lelia, and Gabriele Herzog-Schröder, eds. *Orinoco-Parima: Indian Societies in Venezuela, The Cisneros Collection*. Fundación Cisneros – Kunst und Ausstellungshalle der Bundesrepublik Deutschland, Hatje Cantz, Ostfildern-Ruit, 1999.

Kozák, Vladimír, and David Baxter, Laila Williamson, Robert L. Carneiro. "The Héta Indians: Fish in a Dry Pond." Vol. 55: Part 6. *Anthropological Papers of the American Museum of Natural History*, New York, 1979.

Meggers, Betty. *Amazonia: Man and Culture in a Counterfeit Paradise*. Atherton, Chicago and New York: Aldine, 1971.

O'Neal, Lila. "Weaving." In *Handbook of South American Indians*, ed. Julian H. Steward, and prepared in cooperation with the U.S. Department of State as a project of the Interdepartmental Committee on Cultural and Scientific

Cooperation. 7 vols. Washington, D.C.: U.S. Government Printing Office, 1946–63, Vol. 5, 1963: 97–138.

Owen, Ruth. "Peruvian Peasant Dress." In *Costume*, The Journal of the Costume Society, No. 25, 96–110, London, 1991.

Roosevelt, Anna Curtenius. *Moundbuilders of the Amazon: Geophysical Archaeology on Marajo Island, Brazil*. San Diego, New York and Boston: Academic Press, 1991.

PATAGONIA

Chapman, Anne. "The Great Ceremonies of the Selk'nam and the Yámana: A Comparative Analysis." In McEwan et al, eds., op. cit., 82–109.

Cooper, John M. "The Yahgan." In *Bulletin No. 143 of the Bureau of American Ethnology, Handbook of the South American Indians. Volume I, Marginal Tribes*, ed. Julian H. Steward, 81–106. Washington, D.C.: U.S. Government Printing Office, 1946a.

——. "The Ona." In Steward, ed., op. cit., 107–125, 1946b.

——. "The Patagonian and Pampean Hunters." In Steward, ed., op. cit., 127–168, 1946c.

Darwin, Charles. *Charles Darwin's Diary of the Voyage of H.M.S. Beagle*. Ed. from the MS by Nora Barlow. Cambridge: Cambridge University Press, 1933.

Duviols, Jean-Paul. "The Patagonia 'Giants.'" In McEwan, Borrero and Prieto, eds., op. cit., 127–139.

Kipling, Rudyard. *Rudyard Kipling Complete Verse: Definitive Edition*. New York: Anchor, Doubleday, 1940.

Lothrop, S. K. "Polychrome Guanaco Cloaks of Patagonia." In *Contributions from the Museum of the American Indian, Heye Foundation*, Vol. VII, No. 6. New York: Museum of the American Indian, Heye Foundation, 1929.

Mateo Martinic B. *Los Aónikenk. Historia y Cultura*. Punta Arenas: Ediciones de la Universidad de Magallanes, 1995.

——. "The Meeting of Two Cultures: Indians and Colonists in the Magellan Region." In McEwan, Borrero and Prieto, eds., op. cit., 110–126.

McCulloch, Robert D., Chalmers M. Clapperton, Jorge Rabassa and Andrew P. Currant. "The Natural Setting: The Glacial and Post-Glacial Environmental History of Fuego-Patagonia." In McEwan, Borrero and Prieto, eds., op. cit., 12–31.

McEwan, Colin, Luis A. Borrero and Alfredo Prieto, eds. *Patagonia: Natural History, Prehistory and Ethnography at the Uttermost End of the Earth*. Published for the Trustees of the British Museum by British Museum Press, 1997.

Mena, Francisco. "Middle to Late Holocene Adaptations in Patagonia." In McEwan, Borrero and Prieto, eds., op. cit., 46–59.

Musters, G. C. *At Home with the Patagonians*. London: John Murray, 1871.

Prieto, Alfredo. "Patagonian Painted Cloaks: An Ancient Puzzle." In McEwan, Borrero and Prieto, eds., op. cit., 172–185.

Schuster, Charles. "Observations on the Painted Designs of Patagonian Skin Robes." In *Essays in Pre-Columbian Art and Archaeology*, ed. Samuel K. Lothrop, 421–483. Cambridge, Mass.: Harvard University Press, 1961.

AFRICA

EAST AFRICA

Cole, Herbert M. "Vital Arts in Northern Kenya." In *African Arts*, Winter, Vol. VII, No. 2, 1974: 12–24.

Faris, James C. *Nuba Personal Art*. Art and Society Series. London: Gerald Duckworth & Co., 1972.

Fisher, Angela, *Africa Adorned*. New York: Harry N. Abrams, 1984.

Gillow, John, *African Textiles*. London: Thames & Hudson, 2003.

Holden, Constance. "Kenyan Edict Threatens Famed Park." In *Science*, Vol. 310, No. 5749, 2005: 215.

Riefenstahl, Leni. *The Last of the Nuba*. New York: Harper & Row, 1973.

——. *The People of Kau*. New York: Harper & Row, 1976.

——. "The Masai, Samburu and Nomads." In *Africa*. Cologne: Taschen, 2005: 236–299.

Saitoti, Tepilit Ole, and Carol Beckwith. *Maasai*. New York: Harry N. Abrams, 1980.

SOUTH AFRICA

Broster, Joan A. *Red Blanket Valley*. Denver and Johannesburg: Hugh Keartland, 1967.

Brottem, Bronwyn V., and Ann Lang. "Zulu Beadwork." In *African Arts*, Vol. VI, No. 3, 1973: 8–14.

Elliot, Aubrey. *The Zulu: Traditions and Culture*. Cape Town: Struik, 1990.

Jolles, Frank. "Traditional Zulu Beadwork of the Msinga Area." In *African Arts*, Vol. XXVI, No. 1, 1993: 42–53.

Morris, Jean, and Eleanor Preston-Whyte. *Speaking with Beads: Zulu Arts from Southern Africa*. London and New York: Thames & Hudson, 1994.

Priebatsch, Suzanne, and Natalie Knight. "Traditional Ndebele Beadwork." In *African Arts*, Vol. XI, No. 2, 1978: 24–27.

Tyrrell, Barbara. *Tribal Peoples of Southern Africa*. 2nd edition. Cape Town: Books of Africa, 1971a.

——. *Suspicion is My Name*. Cape Town: T. V. Bulpin, 1971b.

van Wyk, Gary. "Illuminated Signs: Style and Meaning in the Beadwork of the Xhosa and Zulu-Speaking Peoples." In *African Arts*, Vol. XXXVI, No. 3, 2003: 12–33.

Webb, Virginia-Lee. "Fact and Fiction: Nineteenth-Century Photographs of the Zulu." In *African Arts*, Vol. XXV, No. 1, 1992: 50–59.

CENTRAL AFRICA

Adams, Monni. "Kuba Embroidered Cloth." In *African Arts*, Vol. XII, No. 1, 1978: 24–39.

Coquet, Michele. *African Royal Court Art* (trans. Jane Marie Todd). Chicago and London: University of Chicago Press, 1998.

Cornet, Joseph. "The *Itul* Celebration of the Kuba." In *African Arts*, Vol. XIII, No. 3, 1980: 29–32.

Darish, Patricia. "Dressing for the Next Life." In *Cloth and Human Experience*, ed. Annette B. Weiner and Jane Schneider, 117–140. Washington and London: Smithsonian Institution Press, 1989.

——. "Dressing for Success: Ritual Occasions for Ceremonial Raffia Dress Among the Kuba of South-Central Zaire." In *Iowa Studies in African Art*, Vol. III, 1990: 179–191.

——. "This is Our Wealth: Towards an Understanding of a Shoowa Textile Aesthetic." In *Elvehjem Museum of Art*, 1996: 57–68.

Gillow, John, *African Textiles*. London: Thames & Hudson, 2003.

Meurant, Georges. *Shoowa Design: African Textiles from the Kingdom of Kuba*. London and New York: Thames & Hudson, 1986.

Picton, John, and John Mack. *African Textiles*. London: British Museum Press, 1979.

Schuster, Carl, and Edmund Carpenter. *Materials for the Study of Social Symbolism in Ancient and Tribal Art: A Record of Tradition and Continuity*. 12 vols. New York: Rock Foundation, 1986.

Vansina, Jan. *Le Royaume Kuba*. Brussels: *Annales Science Humaines*, ser. 80, 49: 1964.

WEST AFRICA

Adeleye, R. A. "Hausaland and Borno, 1600–1800." In Ajayi and Crowden, eds., op. cit., Vol. I: 556–601.

Ajayi, J. F. A., and Michael Crowden, eds., *History of West Africa*. New York: Columbia University Press, 1976.

Arkilla Kerka: Tekstileja Lansi-Afrikasta. Finland: Pyynikinlinna, 1992.

Aronson, Lisa Louise. *Akwete Weaving: A Study of Change in Response to the Palm Oil Trade in the Nineteenth Century*. Ann Arbor, Mich.: University Microfilms International, 1982.

Balfour-Paul, Jenny. *Indigo*. London: British Museum Press, 1998.

Beckwith, Carol, and Marion van Offelen. *Nomads of Niger*. New York: Harry N. Abrams, 1983.

Borgatti, Jean. *Cloth as Metaphor: Nigerian Textiles from the Museum of Cultural History*. Monograph Series, No. 20. Los Angeles: UCLA Fowler Museum of Cultural History, 1983.

Drewel, Henry John. *Yoruba: Nine Centuries of African Art and Thought*. New York: Center for African Art in Association with Harry N. Abrams, 1989.

Eicher, Joanne Bubolz. *Nigerian Handcrafted Textiles*. Ile-Ife: University of Ife Press, 1976.

——, and Tonye Victor Erekosima. Technical Analysis by Otto Charles Thieme. *Pelete Bite: Kalabari Cut-Thread Cloth*. St Paul, Minn.: Goldstein Gallery, University of Minnesota, 1982.

Fisher, Angela. *Africa Adorned*. New York: Harry N. Abrams, 1984.

Gilfoy, Peggy Stoltz. *Patterns of Life: West Africa's Strip-Weaving Tradition*. Washington, D.C. and London: National Museum of African Art by the Smithsonian Institution Press, 1987.

Greenberg, Joseph H. *The Languages of Africa*. Bloomington: Indiana University Press, 1970.

Kriger, Colleen. "Robes of the Sokoto Caliphate." In *African Arts*, Vol. XXI, No. 3. Los Angeles: University of California, 1988: 52–86.

——. "Textile Production in the Lower Niger Basin: New Evidence from the 1841 Niger Expedition Collection." In *Textile History*, 21 (1). Edington, England, 1990: 31–56.

GLOSSARY

——. "Textile Production and Gender in the Sokoto Caliphate." In *Journal of African History*, Cambridge University Press, 34, 1993: 361–401.

Mabogunje, Akin. "The Land and Peoples of West Africa." In Ajayi and Crowden, eds., op. cit., Vol. I: 1–32.

Perani, Judith, and Norma Wolff. "Embroidered Gown and Equestrian Ensembles of the Kano Aristocracy." In *African Arts*, Vol. XXV, No. 3, 1992: 70–81.

Picton, John, and John Mack. *African Textiles*. London: British Museum Press, 1979.

Ross, Doran. *Wrapped in Pride: Ghanaian Kente and African American Identity*. Los Angeles: UCLA Fowler Museum of Cultural History, 1998.

NORTH AFRICA

Ehret, Christopher. *The Civilizations of Africa: A History to 1800*. Charlottesville: University of Virginia Press, 2002.

Fisher, Angela. *Africa Adorned*. New York: Harry N. Abrams, 1984.

Loughran, Kristyne. "Tuareg Women and their Jewelry." In Seligman and Loughran, eds., op. cit., 167–193.

Picton, John, and John Mack. *African Textiles*. London: British Museum Press, 1979.

Rasmussen, Susan. "Dress, Identity, and Gender in Tuareg Culture and Society." In Seligman and Loughran, eds., op. cit., 139–157.

Seligman, Thomas K. "An Introduction to the Tuareg." In Seligman and Loughran, eds., op. cit.

Seligman, Thomas K., and Kristyne Loughran, eds. *Art of Being Tuareg: Sahara Nomads in a Modern World*. Los Angeles: UCLA Fowler Museum of Cultural History, 2006.

Abaya (*abayah*): Floor-length black all-encompassing cotton, rayon or silk garment, worn in public by northern Arabian women either over the head or around the shoulders, and held closed with a hand. Under the *abaya*, the face is concealed by a black veil in the case of urban women or a colorful, decorated, mask-like veil in the case of Bedouin tribeswomen.

Abayeh: Simple unisex Eastern Mediterranean mantle that could serve as a cape, coat, shoulder cover or, when pulled over the head, giant veil.

Abho: Embroidered cotton tunic worn with pants by Muslim women in the Kutch area of northwestern Gujarat. *See also ejar.*

Achkan: Urban Indian man's knee-length, fitted coat with buttons down to the waist.

Agal (*'agal, iqal, igaal*): Double rings of black rope or cord that hold an Arabian man's headcloth in place.

Aleshu: Cotton textile made by the Hausa of Nigeria and composed of joined narrowband strips that have been over-dyed with indigo and beaten until the fabric achieves a shimmering blue appearance.

Alpargatas (Spanish): Ecuadorian sandals, usually made with braided *furcraea* fiber soles or rubber soles and cloth uppers; also found in Colombia and Spain. The adopted English equivalent term is *espadrilles*.

Anorak: Another name for a parka, especially in eastern Canada and Greenland. The *anorak* was made of hide, bird skins or, later, of cloth.

Ao dai: Vietnamese long, tight dress with high slits up each side worn over pajama-like pants.

Appliqué: Cutout decoration that is fastened to a larger piece of material in order to create a motif.

Atsushi: Thread made from elm bark that the Ainu of Japan use to weave their distinctive robes.

Attusi: Elm-bark fiber robes worn by the Ainu of Japan.

Baby belt: The *wawa chumbi* (Quechua) is a long, narrow belt worn over the mother belt (*Mama chumbi*). *See also* mother belt.

Baby harness: Strap of leather or braided thongs—later of braided yarn—around the back of an Eskimo woman's parka, fastened in front with a toggle, to help carry and distribute the weight of a baby in the hood.

Backstrap loom: Weaving device in which the tension is maintained by a strap around the weaver's back or hips. The Mesoamerican backstrap loom was a true loom with the ability to open and close the alternating sheds (sets of warp threads that can be opened to allow the weft to pass through).

Baghmal: Tadjik and Uzbek *ikat*-dyed silk velvet.

Baji: Korean male pants. The fitted, inner pants were replaced by Western underwear in the 1920s. The roomy, comfortable outer pants are so voluminous they must be tied securely at the ankles (Yang 1997: 127–128).

Bandhani: Indian tie-dyeing technique whereby cloth is patterned with small dots; the word also refers to textiles decorated in this manner.

Bark cloth: Coarse, felted fabric made by pounding the soft inner bark of the *Olmedia aspera* tree (probably the tree also known locally as *llanchama*) and used for the frontal masks and conical headpieces that are part of Amazonian full-body dance costumes.

Bashofu: Thread made from the banana-fiber plant that is unique to Okinawa.

Bast fiber: Stem structure of a dicotyledonous plant—notably flax, also apocynum, jute, hemp, nettle, ramie, etc. The term "inner bark" refers to bast (not bark) fiber—either to the extracted fibers or to sections of the interlaced networks of fibers that lie under the bark of certain trees and shrubs and can be utilized for beaten bark cloth (Emery 1966: 5).

Batik: Resist-dye technique whereby textiles are patterned using wax, or an equivalent, to coat sections of cloth to protect them in the dye bath.

Batting: Sheets of fibre, e.g. cotton or silk, used for padding, as in quilting.

Bayeta (Spanish): Coarse treadle-loom woven wool fabric. The equivalent English fabric name is baize.

Biil: Wool dress made of one or two rectangular panels joined at the sides, worn by Navajo women.

Bindi: *See tikka.*

Bingata: Paste-resist technique used on Okinawa to create the island's distinctively colorful textiles.

Bisht: Large, square-cut, floor-length cloak made of finely woven camel hair or wool and trimmed with black cord or gold braid. Worn over the shoulders, like a cape, by upper-class men on the Arabian Peninsula, the *bisht* encloses the arms but is open in front; small slits in the side seams allow the hands to extend when desired.

Bixa orellana: Shrub that produces pods filled with seeds which are covered in a pasty red substance used as body paint throughout South America, known as *urucú* or *achiote* in Brazil, *annotto* and *onoto* in Venezuela, and *annatto* in Guyana.

Blanket strip: Beaded or quilled strip, often embellished with rosettes, placed over the center seam of a Plains robe of hide or stroud cloth.

Bobble fringe: A Central African type of raffia-fiber trim at a cloth's edges; the bobbles are made by tying together the ends of warp/weft threads.

Bola: South American weapon consisting of two or more stones or iron balls attached to the ends of a cord for hurling at and entangling an animal; the weapon of choice of the Tehuelche/Aönikenk Horse Indians of Patagonia.

Bota de potro: Tall, spurred boot made of horse hide or puma pelt, worn by Patagonia's Tehuelche Indians.

Brocade: Patterned fabric produced by the addition of non-essential, supplementary thread when the ground material is woven.

Brocaded plain weave: Textile structure with a plain weave ground augmented by discontinuous supplementary-weft yarns (*see also* brocade), which pass back and forth within their own pattern areas but are not carried from one pattern area to another.

Bufu: Literally, "coat with a patch." A front-opening surcoat worn at the Chinese court by those other than members of the imperial family. Insignia badges (*see buzi*) were attached at the chest and back. For Manchu men, the *bufu* was three-quarter-length; for women it was full-length.

Buhsuhn: Korean cotton socks of mid-calf length with upturned toes, worn unlined in summer but padded with cotton batting in winter (Yang 1997: 91).

Buriti (*Mauritia flexuosa*): Palm whose leaves were used to construct the body-encasing dance masks used in many Amazonian ceremonials.

Burqa: Face-covering of varying design that becomes the public visage of the woman who wears it. Some half-veils, which begin below the level of the eyes, are combined with a hair-covering that continues over the back of the head and down the back. The women of southern Arabian tribes tend to wear face-masks of cotton stiffened with a support that runs the length of the mask along the line of the nose, and often elaborated with small chains, coins and beads.

Butterfly: Hairstyle worn by Hopi girls of Southwest America, in which the hair at each side is wound onto a large whorl. Also sometimes called the "squash blossom" style.

Button blanket: Ceremonial blanket/robe of the American Northwest Coast area made of heavy fabric, typically a Hudson Bay trade blanket, on which was appliquéd a red cloth family crest pattern that was then outlined with white pearl buttons.

Buzi: Insignia badge worn at the Chinese imperial court to designate ranking. *Buzi* for the emperor and members of his clan were round in shape; other nobles, civil officials and

reaches to below the knees. The combination of *kurta* and *dhoti* is India's traditional male attire; regional variations include a Western-style collar and cuffs.

Kurta surwal: Nepalese term for the *salwar kameez*.

Kurti: Sleeveless vest sometimes worn by women in the Kutch area of northwestern Gujarat.

Kushi: Elaborate combs worn in geisha coiffures in Japan.

Kushung: Woman's decorated tunic worn prior to 1900 in north, central and eastern Bhutan.

Kutiyah: Small, white, brimless skullcap worn beneath the Saudi headcloth to help position the supporting cords. In informal situations, younger boys and men often wear only the skullcap. Many Muslim men also wear their skullcaps when at prayer.

Labret: Carved piece of wood, bone, ivory or stone worn in a perforation in the lower lip or cheek and held in place by a flared retainer. Worn by Eskimo men and women; also worn in Amazonia.

Last: Form—made of wood, metal or plastic—which is shaped like a human foot and over which a shoe is shaped or repaired.

Lau: Sumbanese woman's tubular garment that is sometimes decorated by supplementary warp, other times by shells and beads.

Leggings: Leg-covering—a separate one for each leg—commonly made of buckskin, though after European contact frequently of woolen stroud cloth, worn especially in the Woodlands and Plains areas of North America. Men's leggings were tied with thongs to a belt at the waist and were ankle-length, occasionally gartered at the knee. Women's leggings reached from knee to ankle and were always gartered at the knee. In some regions, leggings connected with moccasins.

Lemba: Torajan women's modern-day, commercial-cotton blouse that is a descendant of a bark-cloth garment.

Lingzhi: Chinese hat ornament made of peacock tail feathers, signifying distinguished service to the throne. The plume was inserted into a tubular fitting attached under the finials of court hats and worn at the back.

Lishui: Literally, "standing water." The pattern of parallel sets of wave bands at the hem of Chinese robes and insignia badges symbolized the universal ocean surrounding the earth.

Long: Five-clawed Chinese dragon. See *mang*.

Longpao: Full-length Chinese court robe featuring a high round neck, front overlap to the right fastened at the neck, clavicle and right side with loops and toggles, and decorated with five-clawed dragons. Worn as part of *jifu*, or semi-formal court attire. *Longpao* may also refer to dragon robes used in quasi-official contexts, such as weddings, and for garments presented to deities to be displayed on statues in temples. The earliest surviving dragon robes date from the time of the Liao imperial dynasty, which occupied the Dragon Throne from A.D. 907 to 1125.

Longyi: Wraparound skirt made from a single rectangle of flat cloth that serves as the lower-body component of Burmese national dress and is worn by both sexes.

Loom: Construction for weaving. Simple looms involve only uprights and crosspieces. *See also* **backstrap loom**, **heddle loom**, **strip loom** and **treadle loom**.

Loop and toggle: System of fastening or holding a garment closed, whereby a fabric loop is attached to one edge of the garment while, on the corresponding edge, a second fabric loop with a knotted fabric or metal toggle button is engaged in the loop.

Lu'e: Shoulder cloth worn as part of a man's dance costume by the Ngadha people of West Flores.

Lungi: Lower-body wrapped garment used all over India by both Hindu and Muslim men for casual wear or manual labor.

Mang: Four-clawed Chinese dragon. See *long*.

Manta: Woolen shawl/dress of the North American Pueblo women, embellished with embroidery and fastened on the right shoulder, leaving the left shoulder bare.

Mapoto: Ndebele marital apron, less formal than the *jocolo*.

Matixiu: Literally, "horsehoof cuffs." Flaring Manchu sleeve extensions that provided protection for the back of the hand in the absence of gloves or mittens.

Maxie: Literally, "horse boots." Boots worn by Manchu men with court attire.

Medicine bag: Small pouch containing items of sacred significance to the wearer; worn especially on the North American Plains.

Mitten: Hand-covering; in the Arctic of leather or fur, sometimes with two thumb stalls so the mitten could be turned when the palm became wet.

Moccasin: North American foot-covering, usually of buckskin, sometimes with a hard sole of rawhide, and at times with attached cuffs. Moccasins were often elaborately decorated with quillwork, embroidery or beadwork. *See also* **swamp moccasin**.

Mordant: Urine or chemical applied when dyeing cloth to cause the dye to become more permanent.

Mother belt: The *mama chumbi* (Quechua) is a wide underbelt. Those worn in Ecuadorian Otavalo and central Chimborazo are red with green borders, have four selvedges and are woven with a heavy *furcraea* or cotton weft. *See also* **baby belt**.

Mukluk: Eskimo boot of sealskin that had a large sole puckered into a vamp. The term *mukluk* was used only in Alaska; in the eastern Arctic the term was *kamik*.

Mulmul: Gossamer-fine cotton muslin woven in Bengal and traded to Europe as early as Roman times.

Mundu: See *veshti-mundu*.

Muumuu: Cover-up garment imposed on Hawaiian women by early 19th-century Christian missionaries.

Navajo blanket: Wool blanket made by Navajo women, characterized by stripes, diamonds and zigzag patterns and woven on a true loom, one that can form a "shed," or passage, for the shuttle to pass through.

New Zealand flax: *Phormium tenax* is native to New Zealand and provided the fiber for traditional Maori clothing. Genus *Phormium* is not a true flax (genus *Linum*) but rather an unrelated plant in the lily family (personal communication: Roy Hamilton, September, 2005). *See also* **flax**.

Nivi: Modern, regionless style of sari drape increasingly worn all over India by women in urban centers.

Non la: Traditional Vietnamese conical hat of woven palm leaf.

Nose ornaments: Decorations including iron rings, bone pins, wooden skewers or dentalia, abalone or other types of shell worn in the pierced nasal septum of many North American Indians.

Nyoga: Ndebele long, serpent-like, beaded wedding train.

O bang jang: Multicolored, stripe-sleeved, Korean ceremonial coat worn in honor by the adult son of a family where both parents are still living; the infant version of the coat is worn by the boy when he is a year old.

Obi: Wide Japanese sash holding the *kosode*/kimono in place.

Obrajes (Spanish): Colonial workshop for the production of textiles through the use of indigenous labor.

Odhani: See **dupatta**. The root of the word *odhani* refers to the act of covering oneself.

Osode: Voluminous robe worn by Japanese nobles of the Heian court, ca. A.D. 794–1185.

Pag: Northern Indian turban consisting of a long, narrow cloth that is wound around the head in a variety of ways. The turban's color, pattern and wrapping style all convey a specific social message.

Pagri: Smaller version of the wrapped turban, the *pag*.

Palla, pallium: Warm, wraparound Roman mantle made of elliptical, rectangular, circular or half-circular woolen cloth of varying sizes. The female wrap was the *palla* and the male wrap the *pallium*.

Pallav: Wide, decorated border of an Indian sari.

Panjóva: Back-apron/skirt, originally an uncut, unsewn rectangle of cloth patterned into small squares and belted on at the waist, which probably evolved in the Neolithic era but is still found in Russia and the Ukraine, and is sometimes elaborately embellished.

Pao: Full-length Chinese robe. Men's and women's styles of *chaopao*, the full-length robe worn as part of formal court dress, differ in cut, but both have asymmetrical front overlaps fastened with loops and toggles.

Paranja: All-encompassing, floor-length garment with mock sleeves hanging down the back, worn over the head by Turkistani women.

Parka: Outer pullover made of sea-mammal skin, fur, birdskin, bleached sea-mammal intestines or cloth, usually with an attached hood, worn in the northern regions of the Arctic.

Patola: Double-*ikat* textile, with no reverse side, originating in the northern Gujarat region of India. The cloth was traded in Southeast Asia at the peak of the

spice trade in the 16th and 17th centuries (Gittinger 1991: 234).

Peace medal: Decorated silver or brass disk given by the United States government to an Indian chief or other native person of distinction and usually hung around the neck by means of a ribbon or thong.

Pectoral: Ornament worn on the breast/chest.

Pelete bite: "Cut-thread cloth," often with intricate motifs, created by the Kalabari Ijo of the Niger Delta by cutting and removing selected warp and weft threads from an already existing textile. *See also* **fimate bite**.

Peplos: Female outer garment worn by some Classical Greek women. This rather heavy rectangle of woolen cloth was folded vertically and then wrapped around the body, with an overfold at the top that allowed the length to be adjusted to fit the wearer. A soft linen chemise was worn underneath.

Pha sarong: Laos man's hipwrapper, usually woven in a plaid pattern.

Pile: Plush or shaggy surface on a textile resulting from loops or the ends of yarn projecting from the plane of the textile. In Andean pile hats, supplementary yarns are caught in the knotted foundation to form the pile.

Pinkosu: Voluminous eight-yard (24 ft/7.3 m) sari worn in the southern India Tamil area and folded in such a way that pleats form a fan shape across the lower back.

Piupiu: Ceremonial kilts and skirts for Maori men and women, consisting of free-swinging, tightly grouped strands of patterned, tubular New Zealand flax hanging down from a waistband.

Plain weave: The simplest possible interlacing of warp and weft yarns, in which each weft yarn passes alternately over and under successive warp yarns.

Plaiting: One set of element structures in which the elements interlink with adjacent ones (Emery 1966: 61).

Plush: Fabric with an even pile longer and less dense than velvet pile (*Webster's* 1973: 878).

Poncho (Spanish): Square or rectangular overgarment worn by men, usually consisting of two pieces of handwoven cloth sewn together with a slit in the center for the head.

Pony beads: Large glass beads, so called because they were brought into North American

Indian areas by the traders on ponies. *See also* **seed beads**.

Pua: Ceremonial blanket, or hanging, of the Iban people of highland Borneo.

Pubic apron: Long strip of woven cloth or non-loomed bast-fiber fabric, which is worn around the waist or hips to shield the genitals, and is held in place by either tying the length of the material or securing it with a belt.

Qiuxiangse: Literally, "tawny incense." A color, ranging from brown to plum tones, used by members of the Chinese imperial clan other than the emperor and empress and their sons and highest-ranking consorts. Imperial consorts and some ranks of imperial princesses wore *xiangse*, a greenish-yellow color. *See also* **huang**.

Qixie: Literally, "banner shoes." Manchu women's shoes set on a wooden sole or platform.

Quechquemitl: Woman's prehispanic-style upper garment, worn in central and northwestern Mexico, that is constructed of two rectangular webs of cloth joined in such a way that a triangle is formed when the "points" are worn in front and back. These garments vary in size and decoration by community, depending on the dimension of the webs of cloth and the degree of their ornamentation.

Quillango: Large guanaco cape worn with the fur side turned in by the Tehuelche/Aönikenk Horse Indians of Patagonia. The outer skin sides were decorated with painted geometric motifs.

Quillwork: North American decorative technique using dyed porcupine or bird quills to create distinctive patterns on garments.

Qumbaz: Unisex Eastern Mediterranean outer garment reaching to the calf or ankle and opening all the way down the front with the right side brought over the left, under the arm, and then fastened in place. This manner of draping upper-body garments was introduced into the region by early Turkic conquerors.

Qun: Paired aprons worn over leggings or trousers by Han Chinese women.

Rachu: Bhutanese women's ceremonial red shoulder cloth.

Raffia cloth: Textile woven from yarn extracted from the leaves of the cultivated raffia palm, *Raphia vinifera*. The wild forest palms provide the raw material

for Central African boys' unwoven initiation costumes.

Ragidup: Prestige textile with white end panels made and worn by the Batak of highland Sumatra.

Ramie: Asian perennial plant (*Boehmeria nivea*) of the nettle family; also the stiff lustrous bast fiber of this plant (*Webster's* 1980: 947).

Resist-dyeing: Wide-ranging technique of textile patterning whereby dye absorption of designated areas of a cloth is prevented by tying, knotting, binding, folding, sewing, tightly wrapping or coating the sections so that, when the fabric is immersed in a dye solution, the dye cannot penetrate the prepared areas. Both *batik* and *ikat* are examples of resist-dye techniques.

Riga: Hausa word for "gown" and, combined with the word *babba*, also used for the voluminous and often richly embroidered robes (*babban riga*) that are worn by the Hausa men of Nigeria.

Roach: A Woodlands and Plains Indian manner of wearing the hair in which the head was plucked, singed or shaved except for a crest in the middle. Later roaches were sometimes made artificially of deer hair, horse hair, porcupine guard hair, moose mane or skunk hair, and were often painted red. Roaches were fastened to a scalp lock and the hairs separated with a "roach spreader." Modern Indian dancers wear a roach, but it has to be tied under the chin because they lack a scalp lock. *See also* **scalp lock**.

Rodillera (from the Spanish *rodilla*, "knee"): Small woolen blanket wrapped around the hips from waist to knees, often woven in a black and white check pattern and worn around Lake Atitlan and Sololá, with one end lapping over at the side front.

Roundel: Decorative arrangement of consolidated ornament that contrasts with the rest of the garment fabric.

Salwar kameez: Woman's sleeved tunic (the *kameez*), whose exact length and degree of fit vary according to fashion, worn with wide-legged trousers that taper down to stitched cuffs with designs at the ankles (the *salwar*). Long worn in the Punjab region of northern India and adjacent areas, the *salwar kameez* has, since the 1980s, also been worn by fashionable young urban women. *See also* **kurta surwal**.

Sampot: Cambodian hipwrapper made from a rectangular length of flat uncut cloth, worn by both men and women.

Sarafan: Long, sleeveless dress held up by two straps and hanging from under the arms straight down to the ankles. Best known in Russia but also historically in parts of Western Europe.

Sari: Length of unstitched cotton or silk fabric that is draped around an Indian woman's body to serve as her principal garment, both skirt and headcover.

Sash: Long band of material, finger-woven in diamond, zigzag or similar geometric patterns, and worn around the waist or over the shoulder by North American Indians.

Satin stitch: Series of stitches laid side by side for decoration or to affix one piece of fabric to another.

Scalp lock: Hair at crown of head, left to grow long and braided. A roach headdress could be attached to the scalp lock. *See also* **roach**.

Scarification: Method of creating patterns on the skin by inducing a raised scar as a result of making small cuts on the body. This practice is also known as cicatrization.

Seed beads: Tiny beads of many hues replacing the larger pony beads of the early 19th century. *See also* **pony beads**.

Selvedge: The edge of a cloth where the weft yarns reverse direction around the outside warp yarns. Most woven textiles have weft (side) selvedges parallel to the warp direction; many Peruvian textiles have warp (end) selvedges as well.

Sheath: Unbelted, body-skimming garment worn in the Ancient Near East.

Shente: Ancient Egyptian triangular loincloth made of a long, narrow piece of woven linen worn by placing the cloth between the legs, wrapping it around the body and folding the end into a protective tab above the waist, thus enabling the wearer to tighten the garment. Sometimes the ends of the loincloth were fastened with cord ties. Pharaohs were occasionally depicted wearing only the *shente* (Boucher 1987: 434).

Shibori: Japanese resist-dye technique whereby sections of a cloth are tied off before dyeing.

Shield cover: Plains and Southwestern Indian deerskin, canvas or other cloth cover, which was often decorated and

was sometimes removed prior to conflict to expose the spiritual power of the shield.

Shigra (Quechua): Carrying bag made of looped agave or *furcraea* fiber that is commonly used to carry food.

Shiro-age: Japanese resist-dye technique whereby designs on a cloth are reserved in white through the application of a paste resist prior to the fabric being placed in a dye vat.

Side-fold dress: Early buckskin dress, made of a large piece of skin folded over and fastened at the side, with a fold-over yoke and shoulder straps, worn on the northern Plains and in Northeast America. Early hide dresses included three other major types: strap-and-sleeve, two-skin and three-skin.

Sinew: Tendons stripped from along the backbone of caribou, deer or moose, for use as thread in sewing by North American Indians.

Sirwaal: Long underpants, with a cord or elastic at the waistband to pull the garment in, worn by both men and women. The spacious so-called "Arabian drawers" are the female version of the *sirwaal*. The only sections that ever show beneath a dress or *abaya* are the cuffs, which accordingly are richly embroidered. Today decorative cuffs can be purchased in local markets.

Sok-chima: Slip or petticoat worn in multiple layers to provide as voluminous a look as possible to the Korean outer-skirt, the *chima* (Yang 1997: 60).

Sok-of: Full, bloomer-like underwear—made in cotton, silk, ramie or hemp—worn by Korean women to create the desired added volume to the outer-skirt, the *chima* (Yang 1997: 130)

Songket: Sumatran term for a supplementary-weft weaving technique, usually using metallic threads.

Spinning: The process of twisting together and drawing out massed short fibers into a continuous strand of yarn.

Sprang: "'Plaiting with stretched threads' and…closely related to the string game known…as 'cat's cradle.' Threads are stretched between two parallel beams, much like a warp on a two-beam loom, but the fabric is made by twisting neighboring threads around each other (as in cat's cradle) and not by introducing a weft. The twists are pushed symmetrically to both ends and held by a rod until the next twist

can be put in to secure it. The work progresses in this fashion until the two groups of twists meet in the middle, where a cord is darned in (or some other special step taken) to keep everything from unraveling. The resulting fabric—not a true "textile," in the narrow sense, but a cloth-like object nonetheless—is very elastic in nature, unlike most woven cloth, and seems to have been much used for hairnets, stockings and sleeves, which had to go around great lumps like hair buns or awkward corners like knees and elbows" (Elizabeth J. W. Barber, *Prehistoric Textiles: The Development of Cloth in the Neolithic and Bronze Ages with Special Reference to the Aegean*. Princeton: Princeton University Press, 1991: 122).

"Squash blossom:" Necklace of cast silver beads and items in a squash blossom shape, made by Navajo craftsmen and widely traded. Many featured inlaid pieces of turquoise, and sometimes coral.

Stem stitch: Linear embroidery stitch in which the thread is carried forward in a long stitch on the front surface, and then back in a shorter stitch directly underneath, usually for half the length of the stitch on the surface. Further, the thread is carried to the left of (or above) the needle, forming a Z-slant. In Ancient Andean Paracas embroidery, the yarn is commonly carried forward over four threads of the ground and back under two. Rows of such stitches abut each other to cover the ground fabric completely.

Strap-and-sleeve dress: Belted deerskin dress, held in place with shoulder straps and worn by Woodlands Indian women; separate sleeves could be tied on when needed. *See also* **side-fold dress**.

Strike-a-light bag: Arctic pouch in which were carried such materials as flint and tinder for starting a fire.

Strip loom: West African portable loom with double heddles and foot pedals that can produce narrow strips of cloth of indefinite length.

Stroud: Also 'strouding'. A heavy woolen cloth made in Stroudwater, England, usually scarlet red or dark navy blue, sometimes green. Originally it was a 'blotter cloth', a cheap textile used to soak up excess dyes when making finer

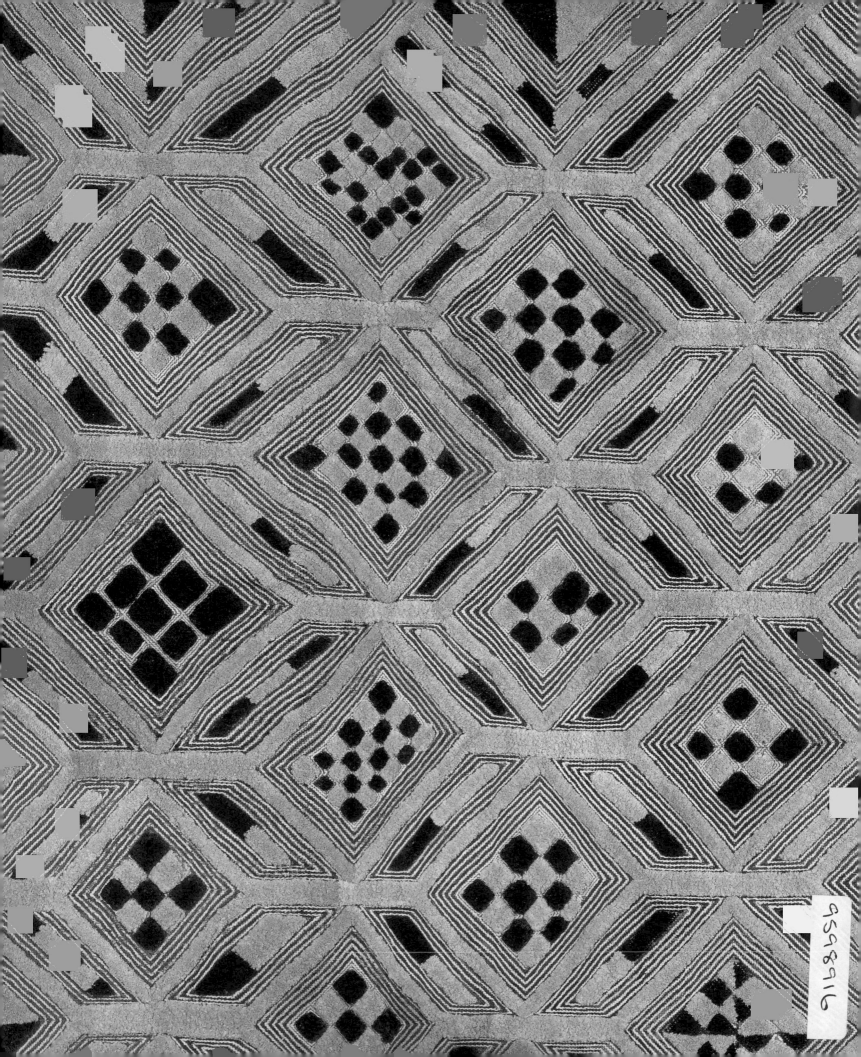

916858P